"THE THUNDERER"
IN THE MAKING

THOMAS BARNES
Editor of *The Times*
1817-1841

THE HISTORY OF
THE TIMES

"THE THUNDERER"
IN THE MAKING

1785 - 1841

LONDON
WRITTEN, PRINTED AND PUBLISHED AT
THE OFFICE OF *THE TIMES*
PRINTING HOUSE SQUARE
1935

PRINTED IN GREAT BRITAIN
BY
JARROLD AND SONS LIMITED NORWICH
BY PHOTO LITHOGRAPHY
1950

INTRODUCTION

T HE occasion of this book is the hundred and fiftieth anniversary of the first publication of *The Times*, or, as it was called for the first three years of its existence, the *Daily Universal Register*. The full project is to complete the story down to recent years in three volumes, to be issued in succession, for which a large part of the material has already been collected and prepared. Apart from convenience in handling it, there happens to be good reason for this division in the record itself, which falls naturally into three parts. The present volume covers the period from the foundation of the paper by the first JOHN WALTER, through the great changes wrought by his successor, not only in the influence of *The Times* but in the whole standing of British journalism, down to the death of THOMAS BARNES in 1841.

BARNES, of whom too little has hitherto been known, was the first man to become a responsible editor in the sense familiar to later generations. He it was who turned to full account the weapon placed in his hands by the sturdy independence and business acumen of JOHN WALTER THE SECOND. It was under his direction that *The Times* became known as " The Thunderer," that it achieved its position as a recognized national institution, and that it led the way by which every great newspaper passed from its old eighteenth century character of a marketable means of publicity to that of an independent organ of public opinion. The death of BARNES, therefore, following hard on some of his most signal political triumphs, may fairly be regarded as the end of an epoch in the history of *The Times*. The next volume will take the story through the better known period of the editorship of J. T. DELANE, and the third will deal approximately with the last half century.

The scope of the book is precisely what its title professes, no more and no less. It is the history of *The Times*, not of contemporary politics as seen from Printing House Square. It devotes no greater space to public affairs than is essential to explaining the growth and development of the newspaper. Nevertheless it may fairly claim to be a contribution to English history in the true sense of the word, for (as the list of sources printed at the end of this volume testifies) it has involved much original research, which has brought to light a number of hitherto unpublished documents with an important bearing on the evolution of British journalism. Full use has been made of the papers preserved in the WALTER family. Many others have been found in the national archives, never previously searched for this purpose. Apart from these two sources there are comparatively few personal records relating to the earlier period of the narrative. An undertaking given by JOHN WALTER II that the public men of his day were safe with *The Times* suggests that their correspondence was destroyed almost as a matter of principle. The public men of the present generation will find no new revelations or scandals or sensations about their predecessors. Such readjustment of values as may follow will affect only those who were directly concerned with the production of *The Times*. But the work and character of these men have been revealed to the utmost extent that research has rendered possible. Nothing has been omitted, however unpalatable, which could contribute to a complete understanding of the truth. It is perhaps the first occasion on which any private business has exposed the whole of its past without the slightest attempt at concealment or palliation. The fact that the fruits of laborious research have been treated with absolute candour is a second reason why the book may fairly claim to be a contribution to history.

Candour of this kind, however, naturally presupposes in the reader a certain historical background and perspective. During the eighteenth century there had been three recognized methods of directing the politics of a newspaper. It might support an Administration in return for payment either directly from the Treasury, or in news or advertisements ; it might support an Opposition in return for cash contributions from party funds ; or it might support an individual statesman in return for a subsidy paid by himself or by his friends. There was no secret about these methods, and no shame on the part of those who employed them, except, indeed, that journalism was everywhere regarded and despised as a hireling trade. They were universal throughout the period of JOHN WALTER I and persisted well into the lifetime of JOHN WALTER II, who was the first newspaper proprietor to make a stand against them. As the following pages will show, *The Times* was fulminating as late as 1834 against the management of the Press by the Whig Government which had just fallen—" a committee regularly organized, an inquisition, a secret tribunal, used to hold daily sittings in a Government Office and contrive things for the reward of the servile and the damage of the untractable." There was nothing unusual, therefore, and certainly nothing to shock opinion in these enlightened days, in the fact that forty years earlier JOHN WALTER I, to whom his newspaper was a mere appendage of his printing business, should be accepting payment for " inserting such paragraphs as were sent me " by PITT's Press managers, should be taking what were called " contradiction and suppression fees," and should even be in the enjoyment of a small regular salary " to support the Measures of Government." He was only following the common practice of his contemporaries, well understood and condoned by public opinion, and a tradition which was as old as newspapers themselves.

The present volume, then, traces the development of *The Times* from its foundation under these old conditions into a medium of news and comment free from all control by Government or party. It is the story, broadly speaking, of the work of three men. JOHN WALTER I, having been ruined as an underwriter by the American War, sought to retrieve his position by securing the appointment of King's Printer, for which the possession of a printing patent might seem to recommend him. In pursuance of this object he took the old " King's Printing House," and on January 1, 1785, established there a newspaper, designed, in the first instance, to advertise his patent and himself. Only the delays which followed drove him to concentrate his attentions upon the newspaper itself and to supplement his income by the prevalent methods already described. In 1788 he changed a cumbersome title to *The Times*, did a good deal to modernize the text and arrangement, and may thus be held responsible not only for the foundation of the paper but for many of its early improvements ; but his purpose in making them was primarily to qualify himself for the financial favours which were available in those days to any journal of sufficient standing to be of political service. The years that followed were full of vicissitudes for *The Times* and for its founder. Thanks to the " paragraphs which were sent me " JOHN WALTER was twice sentenced (in 1789 and again in 1790) to a year's imprisonment for libel. A measure of subsequent compensation from the real authors of his misfortune did something to maintain the paper in existence, but it was again in serious difficulties by the beginning of the century, and there was talk of dropping it altogether and reverting solely to the old printing business.

At this point JOHN WALTER II came on the scene. He had been associated with the family enterprises since he came of age in 1797, and during the next six years he steadily superseded his father and a brother, both of whom had lost interest in that side of their work, in the conduct of *The Times*. From 1803 onwards (in spite of an endlessly complicated arrangement for the division of the WALTER interests) his control was virtually unchallenged. He had interposed when the abandonment of the paper was in contemplation, and its revival during the next decade was his work alone. A sound business man, he contributed for the first time something like expert business management in a newspaper office. He was responsible, ten years later, for supporting and making use of the steam printing press, an invention which was to revolutionize newspaper production. More important still, he recognized from the outset that the success and power of the newspaper of the future would depend upon the independence of its judgment and its freedom from control. He waged long and successful war with the Post Office for the prompt delivery of communications from the correspondents of *The Times* abroad ; and thus secured, at a moment when foreign affairs were of absorbing interest, a reputation for early and accurate news. Above all, he enlisted the services of a type of writer which had been unknown in journalism before and was not too anxious at first to enter so dubious a profession. Among them, slowly forging his way to the highest place through a number of eminent candidates, was THOMAS BARNES.

BARNES was not only the nominee but the true successor of JOHN WALTER II, who, having once secured his services as responsible editor, tended more and more to disinterest himself in the daily conduct of *The Times* and to devote his energies, and his increasing income, to establishing himself as a country gentleman in Berkshire in preparation for a Parliamentary career. The formal transfer of authority to the new editor dates from 1819, but it was not for another twelve years that BARNES's control of *The Times*, its contents, and its policy became complete. From 1831 to his death in 1841 his authority was supreme, and from this critical decade may be dated the beginning of independent editorial responsibility as it is understood in modern days.

He started with several rare conditions in his favour. Thanks to the prudence and courage of JOHN WALTER II *The Times* need no longer depend on any extraneous source for financial subsidies. The simultaneous rise of a great industrial community was just giving new meaning and importance to public opinion. BARNES himself, carefully selected as editor after a long period of trial and experiment, was allowed a free hand to make what he chose of an unprecedented position, and with this equipment he set himself to win for *The Times* the same independence for its opinions that had already been won for its news. From the politicians and the parties he appealed to the public, spreading a network of correspondents through the country to keep himself informed of its tendencies. To both parties in turn he made *The Times* anathema. He was already " thundering for Reform " in 1831 ; played a leading part in the passage of the great Reform Bill, of which, as Peel told the House of Commons, *The Times* was " the great, principal, and powerful advocate " ; threw over the Whigs when they seemed to him to be clinging impotently to office ; emerged victorious from their " war " upon the paper ; and committed *The Times* to Conservatism when Conservatism under Wellington, and more conspicuously under Peel, took the form which he believed that the interests of the country demanded. In all this BARNES was not merely following the gusts of popular opinion. He was often far ahead of his public, as was shown when the paper suffered serious losses in the early days of its conversion to Conservatism. But the twenty years which followed the Tamworth Manifesto, in which Barnes himself had a hand, brought sufficient proof that he had been right in his judgment. Before he died he had made himself, in LYNDHURST'S view, " the most powerful man in the country," and had turned an efficient newspaper into a great political instrument.

The book is anonymous—not from any desire in the part of its authors to appear either modest or mysterious. It is the work of a number of past and present members of the staff of *The Times*, of some more than of others, but in general of a body of men whose tradition and training have predisposed them to anonymity. That tradition, as readers of the present volume will note, derives from BARNES himself, who set great store by it and was at pains to explain it when correspondents denounced the protection afforded by nameless articles. Thus

> The impunity [said *The Times* in 1835] is purely nominal ; for though the writer in a newspaper is obliged by a bond of honourable confidence not to claim even the honour due to his own writings, he is sufficiently known to be subject to all the usual responsibilities and penalties for any violation of social decorum. The public is a gainer because it obtains a full and free discussion without any mixture of that egotism and self-intrusion which are almost inseparable from the compositions of any individual writer in his own personal character.

To this quotation should be added another from a country clergyman who became a writer of leading articles for *The Times* in the generation following BARNES, and is said to have been the author of some two thousand of them. Among his papers at his death was found the following estimate of the journalist's anonymous but now established calling :

> He must [he wrote] be content to be counted as nothing in the future, as in the present, to be unknown or set aside, and never to take rank among the real influences of his time. His labours will be rewarded, but not as men ordinarily count reward. He will have a real power—his work will be deep and lasting, but his name will be obscure or evanescent. He will affect the tone of the nation for which he writes, and will thus be the indirect cause of its most noble after-growth. The pillar will not be of his raising, and will certainly not bear his name inscribed upon it, but he will be the foundation of the whole, the first necessary condition of the state of public sentiment from which it has been raised to seeming independence. To those who are dissatisfied with such a position among the unrecognized forces of the world we will say only that they must try some other line, for they have not the temper of journalists.

No words could express more completely the spirit in which their profession was regarded and handed down by THOMAS BARNES and the men who worked with him. It was something new in their day, but the tradition goes on.

ACKNOWLEDGMENT

THE present volume has been exceptionally fortunate in attracting generous assistance in more than one country. It has been able to draw upon records, in public and private ownership, that are of peculiar importance for a period of journalism of which relatively little has been known with accuracy hitherto.

The Statistical Department of the Inland Revenue, Somerset House, has made transcripts from its registers. The Post Office has permitted access to documents not hitherto published. The French Ministry of Foreign Affairs has opened its archives freely and has given permission for the publication of the Osmond-Richelieu paper on the London Press which is printed as an appendix. The Director of the Department of Manuscripts, Bibliothèque Nationale, has allowed examination of the Decazes papers usually reserved.

Lord Durham has lent for transcription letters to the first Earl from Barnes, Parkes, Ellice and others. Mr. John Walter has placed the papers in his possession at the complete disposal of the History, and Mr. Ralph Walter has put it in touch with valuable sources. Sir Herbert Le Marchant, Bt., and Mr. H. C. Le Marchant have allowed quotations from the unpublished Le Marchant papers. Major Coningsby Disraeli has lent the letters which Barnes and Lord Lyndhurst wrote to Benjamin Disraeli. The Manchester Co-operative Society has provided copies of the letters which passed between Barnes and Robert Owen. Mr. Aubrey Attwater, Fellow of Pembroke College, Cambridge, has furnished information about Barnes from the books of the College. The Master and Fellows of Christ's College, Cambridge, have lent the portrait of Peter Fraser which hangs in the College Library. Professor Randolph G. Adams, of Ann Arbor University, Michigan, has sent copies of the correspondence between John Walter II and Croker, the originals of which are in the William

ACKNOWLEDGMENT

L. Clements Library. Mrs. Caroline Hastings gave permission to make extracts from the unpublished diary of Thomas Thornton.

Messrs. Koenig and Bauer, besides providing transcripts of the letters written by Friedrich Koenig to John Walter, have contributed a photograph of their printing machine of 1814, and the Master and Fellows of Christ's College, Cambridge, have granted permission for the reproduction of the portrait of Peter Fraser which hangs in the College.

Professor M. F. Brightfield, of the University of California, who is now engaged upon a Life of Croker, has read the chapters in which Croker appears.

Professor Temperley and Dr. Keith Feiling have read all the proofs and have offered invaluable suggestions. While many passages in the text reflect the benefit of their help, the responsibility for any shortcomings that it may present remains, undivided, with *The Times*.

To them and to all who have contributed so readily to the preparation of the volume this more than formal expression of thanks is offered.

CONTENTS

CONTENTS

ILLUSTRATIONS

ILLUSTRATIONS

I

JOHN WALTER I

THE founder of *The Times* was John Walter, who was born in 1738 and died in 1812. His father, Richard Walter, was Clerk of the Parish of St James, Duke's Place, London, adjoining Queenhithe. John began his business career at an early age, entering the City immediately after the death of his father. For a dozen years he traded as a coal merchant, with a satisfactory reward before a period of excessive competition brought down profits to a minimum. His industry and enterprise secured for him the position of manager of the Coal Market, and, in accordance with the custom of the trade, he shared in the underwriting of vessels engaged in coal shipment. An early indication of his professional eminence is to be found in his letter, written at the solicitation of many colleagues to the elder Pitt, drawing attention to the amount of French insurance placed in London. The letter is dated " Clapham Rise," March 17, 1778. When he found himself losing as a merchant he increased his interest in underwriting, and in 1781 finally left the Coal Exchange for Lloyd's Rooms. His resignation from the body of coal buyers was regretted by his colleagues in the following terms :

> Coal Exchange,
> February 28, 1781.

Sir,

Your favour of the 3rd instant, directed to the body of coal buyers, I read to them at a general meeting held on that day. The gentlemen expressed their sorrow at your determination to quit their Chair, which you have filled so ably and so honourably ; they were unanimous in giving their testimony of the high opinion entertained of your conduct, by their passing a vote of thanks which I am desired to communicate ; and assure you I think the most pleasing part of my office.

> I am, Sir,
> Your most obedient, humble servant,
> JAMES RANDALL.

John Walter, Esq.

Even if he could have foreseen the inroads which American privateers and French men-of-war would make upon commerce,

John Walter might still have engaged in the hazardous business of underwriting ; he never lacked courage. In the result he lost much money. Finally, a hurricane which drove many ships on shore at Jamaica dealt the last blow at his underwriting prospects.

In view of his losses on the Coal Exchange, John Walter had already in 1780 felt " obliged to make a sacrifice of [his] desirable habitation at Battersea Rise, where [he] had resided ten years, and expended a considerable sum of money, the fruits of many years' industry." After the Jamaican blow he looked into his affairs and found that he was possessed of a balance of only £9,000, from which had to be deducted a fourth owing by brokers themselves driven bankrupt. " I therefore, without attempting to borrow a shilling from any friends, resorting to false credit, or using any subterfuge whatever, after depositing what money remained in my hands, the property of others, laid the state of my affairs before my creditors." He went to live in Queen Square, Blooms-bury. The creditors, seeing him straightforward, acted with liberality. " No messenger was put in my house, as usual under the Bankruptcy laws. They made me a present of all my household furniture, plate and effects which it contained, gave me my certificate the very day of the third meeting, appointed me to collect in above £20,000 due to my estate, without taking any security, with a percentage for collecting it, made me a present of a freehold share of the Coal Exchange which had been raised under my directions."[1] Some years later his estate was cleared up. The following paragraph is from *The Times* of April 17, 1790 :

JOHN WALTER'S COMMISSION

The unsatisfied creditors (if any) of John Walter, formerly of Exchange Alley, London, Merchant and Insurer, may receive the whole of their demands on him, (except arising from Policies of Insurance) on sending in their Accounts to the Office of *The Times*, in Printing House Square, Blackfriars.

The collapse of John Walter's fortunes, leaving him without capital for the restarting of a commercial career, drove him to seek advice from his friends. A number of eminent City men petitioned the Treasury to find him " some respectable post under Government " ; and after a kind reception from Lord John Cavendish, Chancellor of the Exchequer in the Fox and North Coalition, he confidently expected such an appointment. He was

[1] John Walter to Lord Kenyon, July 6, 1799.

2

JOHN WALTER I
From a portrait in oils painted 1783-4, now in the
possession of John Walter, Esq.

introduced to the third Duke of Portland, Prime Minister of the Coalition, by Dent the banker, but the dismissal of the Administration in December, 1783, spoilt his chances. Failing to secure the interest of William Pitt, who succeeded the friendly Minister as Chancellor of the Exchequer, John Walter turned his thoughts " to a matter which appeared capable of being a most essential improvement in the conduct of the press." The reference is to a method of typographical composition which, " by great attention and assiduity for a year past, is now reduced from a very voluminous state, and great incorrectness, to a system which I hope will meet the public approbation and countenance." And he resolved to engage in the commercial exploitation of the patent rights of this essential improvement.

The novelty was not Walter's invention, but that of Henry Johnson, a London printer. It was a " method of printing with types or figures so connected as to prevent the possibility of error in all business where figures are used, particularly in taking down the numbers of blanks and prizes in the lottery numerically arranged." The patent was registered No. 1201 and dated November 9, 1778, and the means patented were " types or figures cast on a body, so as at one impression to form any number or numbers." Johnson had invented his method in and for the circumstances attending the composition of lottery blanks. Walter's attention having been directed to Johnson's patent in 1782, he planned an extension of the system to general letterpress. After Walter had purchased the patent, Johnson for some time shared in the effort to establish the invention on a business basis. *An Introduction to Logography: Or the Art of Arranging and Composing with words Intire, their Radices and Terminations, instead of Single Letters*, by Henry Johnson, was published in 1783. Walter, in the same year, introduced logography to Benjamin Franklin, then at Passy. As Franklin himself had experimented to similar purpose, he was able to enter into the details, and he gave Walter considerable encouragement.

With the financial support of Thomas Holl, a merchant in Fenchurch Street, and Samuel Brown,[1] a solicitor of Norfolk Street in the Strand, Walter sought a printing house in which to put logography to commercial practice. He came upon the modern building in Blackfriars erected after the burning of the house of Mark Baskett, the last member of a famous family of Royal printers, whose patent had expired. Mark was probably

---

[1] Samuel Brown became the godfather of John Walter II.

the son of Thomas Baskett and the grandson of John Baskett, owner of the Scottish patent of King's Printer from 1709, and Master of the Stationers' Company in 1714 and 1715. In 1770, the patent of King's Printer reverted to Charles Eyre, who, not a practical printer but a capitalist, entered into an agreement with William Strahan by which, for the sum of £5,000, he was to have a third share of the patent and manage the King's Printing House. By this transaction the King's Printing House after sixty years was removed from Blackfriars to a new home in the ward of Farringdon Within, where statutes and the like were " printed by Charles Eyre and William Strahan." Mark Baskett's office in Blackfriars appears to have been unoccupied for a number of years when early in 1784 John Walter, as patentee of the Logographic Press, purchased, with the assistance of Samuel Brown,

all that Capital Messuage or Tenement and Premises formerly called or known by the name of the King's Printing House and all the rooms warehouses outhouses yards gardens premises and appurtenances whatsoever thereto belonging situate lying and being in the parish of St Anne Blackfriars in the City of London which said premises were heretofore in the tenure or occupation of the Printers of Her late Majesty Queen Anne their Farmers or Partners and have since been used as a Printing house & late were with tenure or occupation of [Mark] Baskett & since of ———— Cornish And also all that piece or parcel of ground lying and being in the West end or side of the said printing house . . . which said capital messuage or tenement ground hereditaments and premises were by certain Indentures of Lease and Release bearing date respectively on or about the 24th and 25th day of March in the year 1784 made between Samuel Sandys Esquire of the one part and the said John Walter the Elder of the other part . . . conveyed and assured unto and to the use of the said John Walter the elder his heirs and assigns And also all that piece or parcel of ground situate lying and being in or adjoining to the said Printing House Yard or Court in the Parish of St Anne Blackfriars aforesaid in the tenure or occupation of Mark Baskett Esquire abutting on the said Printing House Court or Yard towards the West . . . towards the North upon the houses standing backwards or behind the piece or parcel of ground from the said Printing House Yard or Court and fronting towards Jackson's Court or some other court there towards the East.

The first mention of John Walter's typographical innovation occurs in the summary of his affairs related in a folio pamphlet entitled *The Case of Mr John Walter of London, Merchant*, undated, but probably published a few months before he acquired

THE OFFICE OF *THE TIMES*
1811

THE OFFICE
from a Water-colour

THE TIMES
S. Shepherd, 1811

the lease of the Baskett printing house. " Such is the brief state of a case," concludes John Walter, " which I trust humanity will consider deserving a better fate. Judge what must be my sensations on this trying occasion ; 26 years in the prime of life passed away, all the fortune I had acquired by a studious attention to business sunk by hasty strides, and the world to begin afresh, with the daily introduction to my view of a wife and six children, unprovided for and depending on me for support—feeling hearts may sympathise at the relation, none but parents can conceive the anxiety of my mind in a state of uncertainty and suspence."

With such responsibilities John Walter faced the task of making a career for himself as a printer. It is unlikely that the new owners of the Royal Patent removed all the equipment from Blackfriars. William Strahan had been engaged in business on his own account and had his office in New Street, where he had long printed for the best known publishers and booksellers, such as Longman, Knapton and Rivington. In all probability, therefore, when John Walter took possession of the old King's Printing House, he found it furnished with somewhat dilapidated equipment. A prominent feature of the exterior, as shown in the accompanying water-colour, is the Royal coat-of-arms carved in stone placed in the spandrel over the entrance. This coat-of-arms carries the old bearings, quartering the lilies of France which were suppressed in the year 1802. The rebuilding of the premises by John Walter III in 1874, while sparing the private house built for the accommodation of the Baskett family, and subsequently tenanted by John Walter I and his successors, left no trace of the original exterior except the Royal arms, which were preserved and placed over the entrance to what are now the composing, machining and foundry departments on the north side of Printing House Square. Part of the original name, " The King's Printing House " (replaced with a new set of capitals reading " The Times Office "), was preserved in the designation of the square and the street leading to the office of the bookseller-printer, " John Walter, Printing-House-Square, Black-Friars."

Walter's programme was at first limited to books and pamphlets. The labour-saving economy of his printing speciality would, it was hoped, enable him to make a manufacturer's plus a retailer's profit. In the spring of 1784, on the suggestion of a friend, he decided upon the foundation of a daily newspaper as a means of drawing public attention to his logographic patent. A long letter from John Walter to Benjamin Franklin dated May, 1784, describes the patent and the difficulties of working it, the eccentricity and extravagance of Mr. Johnson, the inventor, the encouraging commendations of the Duke of Richmond and other noblemen, and his plans to offer a logographic fount to the Courts of France and Russia. The letter concludes by informing Franklin : " I am going to publish a newspaper by my Plan, & intend very shortly bringing forward a new Edition of the classics."[1]

So the *Daily Universal Register* made its appearance on January 1, 1785, though bookselling remained the primary consideration until 1790. The 940th number of the newspaper on January 1, 1788, was published under a new title, *The Times or Daily Universal Register* ; and, while the secondary branch was thus progressing, Walter's difficulties with the logographic method, and with bookselling conventions, were giving him an additional motive to relinquish the attempt to make money out of the patent.

The patent had been expected to expedite the composition of leaflets, tracts, pamphlets and books. The Logographic Press was designed as a book-printing office, performing the same functions and enjoying the same status as the printing offices of Rivington or Strahan. John Walter gave his best attention to the task he had undertaken. With high typographical ambitions he issued numerous volumes. The first, a piece of propaganda, was *Miscellanies in Prose and Verse intended as a specimen of the Types at the Logographic Printing Office.* The imprint of this duodecimo is " London, Printed and Sold by J. Walter, Printing House Square, Blackfryars, and at No. 45 Lombard Street." The date printed is " M DCC LXXXV," but the likelihood is that the book was ready before the end of the previous year, for no mention of an office in the City occurs in the advertisements published in the *Daily Universal Register.* The *Miscellanies,* a disorderly piece of work, prints a querulous Introduction complaining of the criticism of " my Logographic-press " from " those who understood not what they condemned, or who sickened at its superior merits and success." For the better proof of the value of the method " books for which I have been favoured with subscriptions shall be published without the least unnecessary delay ; and the work shall be executed in the most elegant letter-press." The " first publication after this specimen " was to be an octavo edition of Dr.

1 Eddy, George Simpson : *Correspondence between Dr. Benjamin Franklin and John Walter* in the " Proceedings " of the American Antiquarian Society, Worcester, Mass., October, 1928.

THE

IMPROVEMENT

OF THE

M I N D:

CONTAINING A VARIETY OF

REMARKS AND RULES

FOR THE

ATTAINMENT AND COMMUNICATION

OF USEFUL

KNOWLEDGE IN RELIGION, IN THE
SCIENCES, AND IN COMMON LIFE.

———◆———

BY I. WATTS, D. D.

———◆———

LONDON.

PRINTED AT THE

LOGOGRAPHIC PRESS,

AND SOLD BY

J. WALTER, PRINTING HOUSE SQUARE,
BLACK - FRIARS.

MDCCLXXXV.

The Title-page of the First Logographic Publication

Watts's *Improvement of the Mind*, to be followed " by others of the highest reputation in the republic of letters." The Press made arrangements to print for the Literary Society, founded by the Rev. Dr. John Trusler, a well-known literary adventurer, whose three-volume novel entitled *Modern Times or the Adventures of Gabriel Outcast*, published in 1785, ended with a page addressed " TO LITERARY MEN " :

It having long been lamented, that in the present enlightened age, so little encouragement should have been given to Literature, and that Authors should be obliged to accept a price for their works very inadequate to their worth, from an unwillingness, or inability, to risk the printing of them themselves ; by which means, not only they, but their families after them, have been deprived of the fruits of their labour : The Rev. Dr. Trusler, who, about twenty years since, stood forward in an Association, called THE LITERARY SOCIETY, (whose object was to print works of reputation, giving authors all profits arising from the same, and leaving them in full and free possession of their copy-right) proposes, as this public scheme was dropped, to revive it now, and for this purpose has connected himself with several Literary Men, who will print and publish, at their own risk, all such new and original works, as shall be submitted to their perusal, and shall be thought by them worth printing, on the terms to be had (gratis) of J. WALTER, Printing-House Square, Black Friars.

Among the works which came to the Logographic Press as the result of John Walter's connexion with the Literary Society was the *Apology for the Life of George Anne Bellamy*. Mrs. Bellamy had eloped from boarding school with Lord Tyrawley and subsequently been mistress to half the aristocracy of London ; her memoirs—six duodecimo volumes—were a rich prize for any bookseller or printer of that age. When she took to authorship as a way of repairing her finances she announced from her address in York Street, Piccadilly, that she was writing a book in which would be mentioned the names and characters of every well-known man about town. The Rev. Dr. Trusler offered the assistance of his Literary Society, and the work duly came to Printing House Square to be set up by the Logographic Press. The final page of the concluding volume printed the notice " To Literary Men " quoted above, but with a new paragraph following the name of J. Walter :

This undertaking being set on foot solely for the benefit of literary Men, the Gentlemen concerned hope it may meet with that encouragement they persuade themselves it is entitled to, and that men of reading will do them the honour to apply as above for such books as they shall then publish. The great object here being the advancement of literature, whenever the booksellers shall adopt this plan generally, Dr Trusler and those with whom he is associated will discontinue it.

Here is an echo of controversy with the booksellers, not then concluded. Copyright vitally concerned the booksellers, as John Walter discovered. The most energetic, as well as the most fashionable bookseller of the day, John Bell, persuaded Mrs. Bellamy to allow him to sell the general edition. Bell was not an orthodox bookseller, being himself at loggerheads with the trade over his own reprinted classics. Moreover, he was the most exacting publisher in London ; he wished to rank as the finest typographer of his time under the imprint of " The Apollo Press." *Bellamy* was published under the clumsy imprint " Printed for the author by the Literary Society at the Logographic Press and sold by J. Bell at the British Library in the Strand, 1785." When the printer delivered the books to Bell he refused payment on account of alleged errors and wrote to the *Morning Post*, of which he was a proprietor, saying that his reputation required him to set up a new edition under his own eye. The logographic reply was as follows :

To the Editor of the *Morning Post*

Sir, A letter appeared in your paper of Tuesday the 15th inst. and was copied into the *Morning Herald* the day following, signed by one John Bell, which is evidently intended to injure my character, my property and an infant art ; I shall not enter into an animadversion with the assertion it contains, but will bring the matter before a jury to whose justice I consider it my duty to appeal.

JOHN WALTER

Printing House Square, Blackfryars, February 22, 1785.

Walter had the satisfaction of getting his verdict and his money. His connexion with Trusler continued until 1790. The Logographic Press counted among its productions the *Clerical and Universal Almanack* edited by Dr. Trusler and brought out annually from 1785. *The Times* of October 23, 1790, prepared readers for a change of editor of the Almanack for 1791 :

Great complaints having been made last year of its being very incorrect, has induced the Proprietor to separate from the person who had hitherto compiled it, and the greatest pains has been taken to prevent such complaints in future.—Many new articles are this year added, which renders it the completest and most useful Almanack published.

The Logographic Press was the object of criticism from others besides booksellers. Its proprietor, or patentee as he chose to call himself, produced in 1785 a four-page folio reply to trade attacks, in which he championed the logographic principle as saving time and therefore labour. His claim to undersell his rivals necessarily exposed him to envy and calumny from typefounders and printers as well as from booksellers. Walter concluded his pronouncement with no fewer than forty titles of works set up and printed at the Logographic Press by the middle of 1785, and a list of names and addresses of " noblemen and gentlemen who are subscribers to a series of works printing by subscription." Among the interesting names in this list are Dr. Benjamin Franklin, America ; Rt. Hon. Marquess of Lansdowne ; Rt. Hon. Earl Mansfield ; Mr. Palmer, General Post Office ; His Grace the Duke of Richmond ; the Hon. Horace Walpole, Berkeley Square. These and other noblemen and gentlemen to a number of 153 subscribed five guineas each, with the exception of six, who subscribed ten guineas—indeed a noble list for a newcomer.

John Walter spared no effort to demonstrate his practical ability and capacity for official employment. He desired appointment as a Printer to His Majesty's Government, directly under the King or his Ministers. The death in 1785 of William Strahan, owner of the patent, may have given him the mistaken idea that he could secure the position of King's Printer. His efforts to obtain the office were vain ; but he persevered in working for recognition as a printer and bookseller. His determination led h¹m to open a shop in the West End. On January 1, 1789, " Mr. Walter begs leave to acquaint the Nobility, Gentry, and the Public in general, that," he has acquired the premises lately occupied by Mr. Debrett, " where the several elegant and useful Books already printed by him, as well as all other literary Productions, may be had on the most reasonable Terms." A letter to Lord Hawkesbury is explicit. Walter had already and vainly endeavoured to secure consideration from Thomas Steele, of the Treasury :

Piccadilly, May 29, 1789

My Lord,

Not receiving your Lordship's Letter in Time will apologize for my not attendg & be an Excuse for my Son waiting on your Lordship.

I have again written to Mr Steele on the Subject & shall wait his Reply before I trouble your Lordship again.

I confess my Feelings are hurt at the Contrariety of his Demeaner to Me during the short Time we have communicated together. A few Months back when he observ'd the firmness & Fervour of my Attachment in the conduct of the *Times*, & that at my own Hazard I likewise brought forward an Evening Paper[1] to support the Measures of Administration I was receiv'd with Smiles & complacence—at that Time the *World* & *Morning Chronicle* gave evident Symptoms of changing their Politics, but the recovery of the King & that no Change is likely to happen, I find him a different Man & if by Chance in the hasty production of a Newspaper any Paragraph happens to slip in without my observation which he construes adverse or problematical, I am sure to be told of it, & in a Manner I by no Means approve of.

Though my present Situation in Life introduces Me to many bitter Pills, I have feelings and sentiments which would not dishonour Rank & Fortune—I have seen better Days & was in Hopes the many Intimations I have receiv'd from Treasury Promises within these 5 Years past would have been realiz'd by the Appointment of Printer to the Stationery Office which I long entertain'd Hopes of. I flatter myself the Stability I have shewn, & will remain unshaken cannot be a bad recommendation—If my Mind was to have been alter'd I was not without Temptation. I wish to arrogate no Merit to myself further than the Information you may derive from it.

I some Months since establish'd a Booksellers & Stationers Shop opposite Old Bond Street in Piccadilly, which I was in hopes would be better countenanc'd by the Friends of Administration after the active and decided part I had taken, but except in the Sale of some popular Pamphlets I brought forward from my own Press, I cannot boast of much Patronage.

I write this not from a Desire of Complaint, but for your Lordship's Information which indeed I should not have troubled you with knowing the Weight of Business you have under your Lordship's Care, but was encourag'd to do it by Lord Bateman's Advice, who at the same Time paid that Eulogium to your Character which the Public are truly sensible of in the conduct of national Business. I have the Honor to be,

My Lord, with great Respect
Your Lordship's Most Obedt & Devoted Servt
JOHN WALTER

Walter published immediately from this address a new propagandist pamphlet, an octavo of ninety-six pages, entitled

[1] The *Evening Mail*, thrice weekly on the evenings of mail days from March, 1789.

A N

ADDRESS to the PUBLIC,

B Y

J. W A L T E R,

S H E W I N G

THE GREAT IMPROVEMENT

HE HAS MADE IN THE

ART of PRINTING,

B Y

LOGOGRAPHIC ARRANGEMENTS;

S T A T I N G   A L S O

The various Difficulties and Oppofitions he has encountered
during its Progrefs, to the prefent State of Perfection.

———————

L O N D O N:

PRINTED AT THE 𝕷𝔬𝔤𝔬𝔤𝔯𝔞𝔭𝔥𝔦𝔠 𝔓𝔯𝔢𝔰𝔰, PRINTING-
HOUSE-SQUARE, BLACK FRIARS, AND SOLD BY
J. WALTER, NO. 169, FACING BOND-STREET,
PICCADILLY.

MDCCLXXXIX.

The Title-page of one of the Prospectuses of John Walter's
Logographic Patent

An Address to the Public by John Walter shewing the Great Improvement he has made in the Art of Printing by Logographic Arrangements Stating also the Various Difficulties and Oppositions he has encountered during its Progress etc. This pamphlet vigorously champions his virtues and grievances ; it asserts his determination to challenge criticism and resolutely undertakes to defeat opposition to Logography :

In order to make this invention as notorious as I can, and that the encouragement of Arts and Sciences may more conveniently see the work that is done by the Logographic Press, I have opened a shop in Piccadilly, No 179[1], opposite the end of Bond Street, for the purpose of vending all printed books done at the Logographic office :—and that this house may be as convenient to all lovers of Literature as possible, I have appropriated a room for Noblemen and Gentlemen to sit in, to read the newspapers of the day, and whatever new publication may appear in the political world.[2]

The *Address* collects the letters in which Sir Joseph Banks, Benjamin Franklin and others had acknowledged the previously issued logographic pamphlets. In addition there were printed, with somewhat less justification, polite but insubstantial letters from the Duke of Portland and Mr. Barnard, the King's Librarian. An account is given of John Walter's petition to the King asking to be honoured with the " printing of various articles, that in the principal offices of the State are occasionally sent to the press." The petition, accompanied by a fount of the logographic letter, lay in vain at Buckingham Palace. The *Address* tells the public that His Majesty declined to receive it, that the Logographer declined to receive it back, but requested it to be presented to the British Museum, and that the Trustees consigned it to their lumber-room.

Walter attributed the Royal coolness to displeasure with the inclusion of Dr. Franklin's name in the list of subscribers. Writing to Franklin, the logographic printer said :

Now you will be astonish'd when I relate that from some authority I understand you were a Stumbling Block, from the Name of whom *Majesty Shrunk*—certain it is the King was pleas'd with the Plea that his Librarian appear'd to forward it . . . and after I had sent him a List of the Subscribers he shrunk back. . . .

[1] This is a misprint. The number was 169 and is so printed on the title-page of the *Address*.
[2] An *Address*, p. xi.

Thus rebuffed, the logographic patentee, reminded by Benjamin Franklin of the *Nouveau Système typographique, ou moyen de diminuer de moitié . . . le travail et les frais de composition et correction et de distribution ; découvert en* 1774 *par Madame de* ———— (Paris, 1764) and the consequent interest taken in the subject by French experimenters, addressed himself to Monsieur Anisson-Dupéron, Director of the Imprimerie Royale, himself an inventor.

In May, 1785, Monsieur Anisson-Dupéron himself visited Printing House Square, but it is not known that he found himself able to do more than inspect the logographic cases, the five presses, and add his name for the Logographic Series of Classics. " I did not choose to be very particular with Mr. Anisson, as I should flatter myself a thorough Investigation of this Improvement might produce some Gratuity from the Court of France for the expence I have been at." Thus wrote John Walter to Benjamin Franklin, whose help he again asked in May, 1785.[1] In the subscription list his name is duly printed.

The following, addressed to Deton, Anisson's assistant, is the only letter that has been preserved :

Print^g. H^o. Square, March 15th /86

Sir,

I sincerely thank you for the polite offer you made of interesting yourself in the Disposal of my printing Fount now at the Library of Buckingham House to the French Monarch, which though compos'd in the English Language, will be a sufficient Guide to introduce it as a very material Improvement to the Art of Printing in France. After the many Experiments I have set on Foot to mature it for Business a very easy Process will render it equally useful in any Language whatever. Please inform Monsr. Anisson that it is deem'd impracticable as a Matter of Business to cast Words exceeding 3 or 4 Letters, the more so when it is consider'd that every Word must have a separate Matrix, which would make it an enormous Expence & I do not doubt but Mr. Caslon's were cemented (not cast) by which means Words of any Number of Letters might be put together. I shall thank You for any Opportunity which may offer of recommending my Newspaper and press which I flatter myself will be in future much more correct than hitherto, as I confided too much to my Overseer who was very deficient in Care of correction. When any Thing of Moment comes

---

[1] Eddy, *Correspondence*, p. 14.

from my Press in future, I propose revising it myself. I recommend myself to my Lord Bute's[1] Countenance & protection & am with great Respect,

                              Sir,
                    Your Most Obed. Servt.
                              JOHN WALTER[2]

Monsr Deton

The most elaborate work[3] undertaken by John Walter in his capacity of printer and bookseller was a revised and extended edition of Anderson's *History of Commerce*. A prospectus, issued in October, 1786, announced the issue of the work in weekly numbers on a superfine medium paper at one shilling, of which the first " will be published on Saturday, March 3rd, 1787." The edition was dedicated, by permission, to the Right Honourable William Pitt. It.was edited by William Combe (1741-1823), later famous as the author of *Dr. Syntax*, and in these earlier years a salaried Press agent of Pitt's. The work ran to nearly 3,000 pages, took two years to go through the press, and, when finally issued in four quarto volumes, was completed with an engraving by Orme, after a painting by Stothard, representing Commerce pouring riches into a huge cornucopia, supported by Britannia with trident. The book is undeniably handsome ; its production was costly, and it·was probably unremunerative. A letter to Lord Hawkesbury mentions a high figure :

                Printing House Square, Blackfriars, March 7th, 1792
My Lord,

    I return your Lordship my sincere Thanks for the very handsome Manner in which you mention'd Anderson on Commerce in the Debate on Tuesday last, as it may extend the Sale of that valuable Work which cost Me near £3000 Printing, though I observe none of the other prints have notic'd it in their Relation of the Debate.

            I am, with great Respect
            Your Lordship's Most faithful and obedient Servant
                              JOHN WALTER

The single logographic work of permanent value was John Meares's *Voyages to the North West Coast of America*, in two volumes, also edited by Combe and published in 1790. It was the last logographic book of any size, and was seen through the press

---

[1] The 3rd Earl (1713-1792), Prime Minister (1762-3), who finally settled abroad. He subscribed to the Logographic classics.
[2] B.N. Fonds Français 22260.
[3] For a select list of the Logographic classics see Appendix, *Sources*, John Walter I.

by William Walter, John's son, who persuaded Lord Hawkesbury to accept the honour of dedication.

Combe was also the author of the *Devil on Two Sticks in England, Being a Continuation of Le Diable Boiteux* (2 Vols., 1790) and several political pamphlets. None of these works printed at the Logographic Press was signed.[1] Although little is heard of logography after 1792, the business of printing continued at Printing House Square. The Custom House work accounted for a good deal of general jobbing. At peace with the booksellers, with the journeymen and typefounders, the office of John Walter, printer, may be rated, from 1790, an efficient organization with a growing reputation for steadiness and correctness. The death of Benjamin Franklin on April 17, 1790, gave *The Times* an opportunity of testifying to his interest in logography. A long obituary, which does not allude to Franklin's correspondence with John Walter, says :

It is well known that he (Benjamin Franklin) was bred a printer but it is not, perhaps, of general communication that he actually *worked in the Printing House of this Paper* previous to his departure for America where he followed the trade of printing and was himself the Printer of a Newspaper.

Pleasant as it would be to know that Franklin worked in the office of *The Times*, the hypothesis is difficult to entertain. Franklin first arrived in London at Christmas, 1724, returning to Philadelphia in 1726. During this period he worked for John Watts and Samuel Palmer, whose offices were in the neighbourhood of St Bartholomew the Great. Franklin was in London again from 1757 to 1762, and in Paris from 1776 to 1785. This was his last period of service in Europe. He was 79 when he left Havre on July 22 for Southampton, from which port he sailed on the 28th for America.

The struggle to establish the Logographic Press as a centre for the printing and publication of works of literary and political importance occupied seven years. In all probability the profit was too slight, if it existed at all, to justify anything like the energy which the proprietor had put forth. In 1791 the Piccadilly office was given up, and the novels printed at the Logographic Press were remaindered to Mr. William Lane, of the celebrated Minerva Press. The word " Logographic " disappeared from the

[1] Combe's authorship of these and other works was first revealed in the publication by the *Gentleman's Magazine* of a list of his works made for Ackermann, the publisher of *Syntax*.

heading of *The Times* at the beginning of 1792, and the whole experiment thus came to an end. Thenceforward the one publication of the Logographic Press which John Walter relied upon to sustain his fortune was *The Times*, the history of which, during the eighteenth century, falls into two sections : first, 1785-1790, when the paper was scarcely more than a piece of daily publicity, designed to promote the publications of the Logographic Press and the claims the publisher made for them ; and, secondly, 1790-1802, during which it was taken seriously by John Walter and William Walter as the mainstay of their establishment.

II

THE BEGINNINGS OF *THE TIMES*

WHEN John Walter founded the Logographic Press he possessed no knowledge of the art of printing. Nor, in starting his *Daily Universal Register*, could he have known the economic, political, and other conditions of newspaper production, conduct and management. He was willing to work hard and to learn by experience how to manage the daily paper which he had thought of mainly as a convenient advertisement of the facilities at his disposal for printing books and pamphlets, and for general jobbing. His *Register* was first sold at twopence-halfpenny, one-halfpenny below the ruling price of morning journals ; it was inferior in the literary aspect and as a medium of news, but much better printed than the others, and calculated, at any rate, to satisfy those who required a record of market prices and the movements of shipping. If Walter had known, or been warned, of the economic and legal hazards, if he had appreciated the low professional standards of journalism at the time, he might have restricted his paper to the elementary commercial service it provided during the first twelve months or so. However, the poor success of the bookselling department and the small prospect it offered of any substantial increase in profit determined him to subordinate that branch of his business to the other. Accordingly he was launched upon the career of a working conductor of a daily newspaper with all its consequences. The hard-working and enterprising bookseller was slowly educated by experience into a shrewd and not over-scrupulous practising journalist.

The implications of the word " journalist " in the eighteenth century were not pleasant. A journalist, by common conception, was a writer of paragraphs written in, or against, the interest of a political party or personage. In the middle of the century Johnson affirmed in the prospectus of the *London Chronicle* that

Of those Writers who have taken upon themselves the Task of Intelligence, some have given, and others have sold their Abilities, whether small or great, to one or other of the Parties that divide us ; and without a Wish for Truth, or Thought of Decency, without Care of any other Reputation than that of a stubborn Adherence to their Abettors, carry on the same Tenor of Representation through all the Vicissitudes of Right and Wrong, neither depressed by Detection, nor abashed by Confutation ; proud of the hourly Encrease of Infamy, and ready to boast of all the Contumelies that Falsehood and Slander may bring upon them, as new Proofs of their Zeal and Fidelity.

Common opinion was little better a generation later while Walter was considering the establishment of a newspaper. The venality of journalism had gone too far and too deep to be cured within Johnson's lifetime, which ended in the year when books were first composed and printed in Printing House Square. His description of journalists was published January 1, 1757. Not a generation, but nearly a century, of effort was necessary before journalism could win public esteem. The Press of the eighteenth century was the victim, in most instances only too willing, of a conviction, shared by both political parties, that its power must be controlled. All Administrations were jealously afraid of the Press ; they taxed the journals, and taxed the advertisements in the journals. A self-supporting circulation was rendered impossible by the increasing duties. As the advertisements were increasingly taxed, the space cost more than it was worth, more than commerce could afford. The bare sale of copies would not afford more than enough to pay the compositors and printers at thirty shillings a week each. The literary staff demanded more. Freedom of the Press consisted only in the power to sell a paper's columns to better advantage than trade and commerce could yield. No independent, responsible criticism of contemporary political programmes, or their sponsors, existed or could exist so long as paragraphs were inserted because they supported or attacked the Whig or the Tory party, and simply in accordance with a bargain made by the conductor. The tradition of journalists selling their consciences to politicians was old when Walter established his daily newspaper, and its age deprived it of infamy. That a statesman should acquire a newspaper for furthering his personal ambitions was regarded with equanimity, but for an ephemeral writer to entertain convictions of his own savoured of presumption. Not until Thomas Barnes was appointed to the editorial chair of *The Times* in the first quarter of the new century was the modern doctrine of complete editorial independence from political parties and persons within

17

c

prospect of formulation ; it was only after a severe struggle made concrete by example.

The history of the intercourse between the daily Press and the Government is but a footnote to the history of the emergence of public opinion as a social and political force. *The Times* led journalism to rely upon itself ; but although it was alone amongst dailies in its independence, it was not unaided. Emancipation of the daily journals from political dictation, and from the necessity to accept doles from the Treasury or from party funds in return for political support, waited upon the development of commercial advertising. The economic value of the columns set aside for advertising depended upon the abolition of the tax on advertisements and the rise of the middle class, itself dependent upon the expansion of industrialism. The development of English industry, the stimulation of the public appetite for news, first by the French Revolution and secondly by the French wars that followed, finally made *The Times*, under the singularly able business management of John Walter II, a self-supporting news-paper. Acceptance by the Press of payments from the Treasury, or of funds supplied by subscriptions to the Opposition party chest, knew one great exception from 1803, *The Times*. The deter-mination of its later editor, Thomas Barnes, to " thunder for Reform " and to ignore parties and politicians in the service of public opinion, brought the paper in 1821-1841 an unprecedented influence. John Walter I accepted subsidies ; John Walter II ignored them ; Thomas Barnes took it upon himself to destroy the system.

The Ministerial corruption of the Press was proverbial before Johnson wrote in the *London Chronicle*, before John Walter founded the *Daily Universal Register*. It is notorious that Sir Robert Walpole spent large sums on pamphleteers and journalists, but hiring of the Press was a practice before his time. That the sums of money so spent reached a considerable total fifty years before John Walter entered upon the Logographic Press may be seen from the entries in the *Calendar of Treasury Books and Papers for the Years* 1735-1738. It is worth looking at a few entries if the Press activities of the younger Pitt, under whom Walter suffered, are to be rightly appreciated. Walter considered himself poorly paid. On the other hand, William Arnall, *alias* " Francis Walsingham Esq," one of a group of political writers brought together by Walpole, and responsible for the *Free Briton*, founded in 1730 or 1731, was well remunerated, even if the sums mentioned include arrears of pay. On February 13, 1735, the Treasury minute book orders " William Arnall to be paid £950 out of the King's money in Mr Lowther's hands for writing and printing *Free Britons* etc." On May 9, 1735, Mr. Lowther is authorized " to pay out of the King's money in his hands £600 to William Arnall for writing and printing *Free Britons.*" On February 6, 1736, Mr. Lowther is to pay Mr. Arnall £400 " as royal bounty." " Bold Arnall . . . no crab more active in the dirty dance " was even able to claim that he got for *Free Britons* and other writings within the space of four years no less than £10,997 6s. 8d. out of the Treasury. At the same period W. Wilkins, printer of the *London Journal,* was the subject of a paragraph in the Treasury minute book. Mr. Lowther was authorized to pay Wilkins the sum of £1,486 5s. out of the King's money in his hands for *London Journals* delivered to the Post Office 1734 to 1735, March 16 to June 28 following, including £266 13s. 4d. for writing. When it is recollected that Matthew Concanen (who also got a Judgeship) and a host of other hacks received similar sums, it will be realized that the Press disbursements under Walpole reached an enormous sum.

As a matter of course Walpole's political opponents were driven to sustain rival journals and with them rival journalists and rival pamphleteers. The business, indeed, was so vast that Walpole found it advisable to organize a single distributive centre, the office of the *Daily Gazetteer.* The secret Commons Committee on Walpole found that, in the ten years from 1731-1741, he had spent more than £50,000 of the country's money upon authors and printers of the newspapers, &c., known in the trade as " pension papers."[1]

In these circumstances the existence of a free Press was difficult, if not impossible. While the dependence of ambitious statesmen upon the Press was only slightly lessened in the half century after Walpole, the economic importance of the periodical Press improved. The continued existence of that community of political journalists known since the days of the "Mercuries" as Grub Street still tempted political place-seekers to attack rivals by paragraph and pamphlet. But the gradual development of

[1] Budgell's *Letter to the Craftsman*, 1730, instructs the reader that " It is no secret that the *St James's Evening Post* is what the printers call a *pension paper,* that is, it is obliged for its existence to a certain great man, who I am credibly informed, allows £200 per an. for the support of it ; and takes care to have it sent gratis to all the cities and great towns in England."

an independent Press was rendered possible by the expansion of English commerce after the final extinction of Stuart ambitions in the '45.

The circulation of the new " Advertisers," founded after the year 1730, was limited by their design ; they were advertising sheets and nothing more. Their use for political propaganda was impossible as long as they dealt not with politics but with market conditions and ship movements. The discovery of advertising was bound ultimately to revolutionize the Press by changing the balance of power from the directly political to the directly commercial. *The Times* of the next century was enabled only by its superior advertising revenue to maintain its singular independence against party and Administration. It was, however, no more free than any other journal from political subsidy until it had established its circulation and reputation sufficiently to attract advertisers willing to pay its space rates. The objection to the taxation of newspaper advertising is that it tends to take economic power from the business man and give it to the political boss. The commercial interest lies at the root of Press independence in daily journalism. Weekly journalism is less dependent upon advertising. If editors could readily find authors to work for small fees, as Leigh Hunt found them for his *Examiner*, they could, like Leigh Hunt, refuse advertisements—and only then. Such periodicals are exceptional. In the main, the commercial body is essential to journalism, and such freedom as the Press enjoys is dependent upon commercial advertising. The " Advertisers," *i.e.*, the *Daily Advertiser* (1730), the *Public Advertiser*, the *Gazetteer* and the *Public Ledger*, circulated mainly in the City. The country read the " Journals " published at the week-end, and the " Posts," published three times weekly, Tuesdays, Thursdays and Saturdays, in conjunction with the dispatch of the mails from the General Post Office, London. The absence of anything like sufficient advertising in the mid-century " Journals " and " Posts " is evidence enough that the papers were dependent upon a " certain great man " (the phrase is Budgell's) or " the King's money " in the phrase of the Treasury minute books. The change, therefore, was a significant one, when, during the 1770's—a generation after the South Sea Bubble and the Jacobite trouble had been liquidated —the increasing volume of English commerce, with resultant advertising, rendered some measure of independence possible to the " Advertisers " which, then finding it convenient to print news, brought that feature up to the level of any strictly political journal without accepting subventions from political sources. The period witnesses a distinct and beneficial change in the status of London journalism. It was in 1769 that " Junius " began his series of communications, which lasted over three years, to the columns of the *Public Advertiser*.

From the time of " Junius " London daily journalism enters upon a new phase which closed with the activities of John Bell and the unexampled enterprise shown by John Walter II, after his appointment in 1803 as sole manager of *The Times*. The importance of the " Letters of Junius " was both political and journalistic. For the first time in English journalism the influence of an independent writer was exerted upon discriminating readers, and the regularity of the articles, as much as their ability, was responsible for developing the factor in political society now known as " public opinion." An immediate effect of the Letters was to increase the " Advertisers' " area of independence. The proprietor of the *Public Advertiser*, Henry Sampson Woodfall, was the first of a family of London journalists whose eminence is alone comparable with that of the Walters ; he was a relative of George Woodfall, son of William Woodfall, to whom John Walter II was indebted for assistance in the installation of the Koenig Press.[1]

It by no means follows that other newspapers in London were enabled to participate in the new-found independence of the *Public Advertiser* ; nevertheless, the increased public interest in the party system and the processes of government, stimulated by the " Letters of Junius," contributed to the successful outcome of the struggle for freedom of reporting which John Almon and others fought between 1760 and 1785. William Woodfall challenged the power of the Commons to suppress reports of debates. This service of news, which was provided by London booksellers in the last half of the seventeenth century, required the attendance of note-takers in the lobby of the House of Commons, much as reporters represent newspapers to-day. The news-letter, subscribed for by squires and other prominent persons in a constituency, gave, among other details, information of a member's activities. In the eighteenth century, when the written letters were superseded by printed daily newspapers, the friendly relations between shorthand writers and the legislators and politicians underwent a change. The increased circulation of the printed, as against the manuscript, news-sheets, and their more public character, extended by coffee-house reading, provoked

[1] Chapter VIII

suspicion. Moreover, while the authors of the humble manuscript news-letters were easily amenable to correction, it became clear to the authorities that the newspapers, growing in number and strength, were becoming more and more intractable. The risk of discontent among powerful constituents, always an anxiety to members, was increased by the circulation in the country of what had *not* been said in the House of Commons. Upon a Minister the effect of a garbled report might be even more serious ; and in a matter of foreign policy provocation to another country might be calamitous.

The contest between the Press and the Commons was prolonged and bitter, chiefly because members stood out for their "privileges." When the *Flying Post* uttered a critical opinion on the speculation in exchequer bills, the House immediately scented a power able, if unregulated, to stultify the debates in Parliament—so the House considered—by transferring them to the pages of newspapers. Possession by the journals of capital, intelligence and responsibility was accidental and ephemeral, by their very constitution ; hence the attempt to mould political opinion, to wield political influence merely as a business speculation, affronted the sentiment of the House. There was some justice in this view, but to prohibit newspapers from reporting speeches was another matter. Nevertheless, it became

a high indignity to, and a notorious breach of the privileges of this House, for any news writer in letters or other papers, as minutes or under any other denomination, or for any printer, or publisher of any printed newspaper of any denomination in Great Britain, or Ireland, or any other part of His Majesty's Dominions, to presume to insert in the said letters or papers, or to give therein any account of the debates or other proceedings of this House or any committee thereof, as well during the Recess as the sitting of Parliament.

So the House of Commons moved in 1762, and announced that it would "proceed with the utmost severity against such offenders." Yet in 1771, two years after " Junius " began his Letters, several newspapers, at the instigation of John Wilkes, printed reports of speeches in the House, with the names of the speakers, in flat defiance of the orders. The details of the ensuing conflict are not required here, but it records the coming-of-age, so to speak, of the London Press. Wilkes's victory over the House of Commons affirmed two principles : that constituents had a right to be informed of the proceedings of Parliament, and that members could be called to account by their constituents. Nevertheless the Commons were slow in accepting the implication of Wilkes's successful defiance of their authority ; the publication of debates was still declared a breach of privilege, but in practice the offence was committed without action being taken.

An increased public interest in politics resulted from the virtual defeat of the Commons on the issue of reporting the debates, and the growing economic importance of advertising stimulated the foundation of new journals—daily, weekly and thrice a week— during the period of " Junius." The acquittal of H. S. Woodfall on a libel charge of publishing " Junius's " Letter to the King mitigated the fear of printers and booksellers that the issue of the debate-reporting conflict might be sterner laws against libel. In 1769 the *Morning Chronicle* was founded by William Woodfall. It was an able journal, and after getting into its stride took the lead from the *Public Advertiser* in the Parliamentary and theatrical departments. The *Morning Post* was established in November, 1772.

The *Aurora*, organ of the licensed victualling trade, founded in 1781, failed. Vincent Trehearn's *Noon Gazette*, containing summaries of all the news of the other papers, also failed. The morning papers published in London in 1784 reached the handsome total of eight, as follows :

The Daily Advertiser - - - - -	founded 1730
The London Gazetteer - - - -	1748
The Public Advertiser - - - -	1752
The Public Ledger - - - - -	1760
The Morning Chronicle - - - -	1769
The Morning Post - - - - -	1772
The General Advertiser - - - -	1778
The Morning Herald - - - -	1780

In addition, there were published on Tuesday, Thursday and Saturday evenings :

The London Evening Post - - - -	founded 1727
The General Evening Post - - -	1733
The Whitehall Evening Post - - -	1746
The Lloyd's Evening Post - - -	1757
The London Chronicle - - - -	1757
The St. James's Chronicle - - -	1761
The London Packet - - - - -	1769
The Middlesex Journal - - - -	1769
The English Chronicle - - - -	1779

23

The *Public Ledger, or The Daily Register of Commerce and Intelligence*, partook, as its name implies, of the nature of the time-honoured *Advertiser*, made popular by the *Daily* and the *Public Advertiser*. The *Gazetteer* also belonged to the same class of journal. The *Morning Chronicle*, representing the most serious political thought, was directed by William, younger brother of Henry Woodfall, of the *Public Advertiser*. The *Chronicle* was the most successful of the general newspapers. It served as a model for the *Morning Post* when that journal emerged from its first infancy as a cheap daily Advertiser ; and it became a fashionable West End sheet from 1775, when Henry Bate, cleric, beau and boxer, was editor. After five years Bate left to found the *Morning Herald*, another daily in the general style of the *Chronicle*. These were all four-page folios composed with four columns to the page, which had been the make-up for a generation. The *London Evening Post* was the most important of the thrice-weeklies ; it was edited by John Almon, who with William Woodfall bore the brunt of prosecution for reporting Parliamentary proceedings. The *Daily Universal Register*, when it made its first appearance in 1785, was the ninth London morning daily newspaper.

This, then, was the general trade situation in the London Press which confronted John Walter I on adding to the output of the Logographic Press a daily newspaper as " a register of the times." He had in view, naturally, the conventional single sheet, measuring $24\frac{1}{2}$ in. $\times 18\frac{3}{4}$ in., which, folded once, produced a four-page paper in folio $12\frac{1}{4}$ in. $\times 18\frac{3}{4}$ in. The page was " made up " in four-column arrangement. Normal features of the existing journals consisted of the reprint of the *London Gazette*, other foreign intelligence copied from the Continental journals, Parliamentary intelligence (summaries of House of Commons business rendered with great brevity and hesitation in view of the existing state of the laws), Court intelligence, paragraphs on personages of fashion, epigrams at the expense of writers, actors, artists, &c., notices of arrivals and departures of ambassadors, statesmen, and officials. Law and police court decisions were summarily recorded ; space was given in some journals to the names of visitors to fashionable watering-places such as Bath and Tunbridge Wells. The common prices of the public funds as they ruled on the Stock Exchange, notices of meetings of creditors and an extract from the *London Gazette* formed the very meagre commercial intelligence. This John Walter determined to extend. The existing journals generally printed verses. In the political journals the important feature was a letter then addressed " To the printer." Neither the leading article nor the editor yet existed. A literary person was employed by the responsible printer to look over the proofs, and " letters " were supplied by journalists for a fee. The custom of accepting such letters from reporters, and paying for them, obtained until the first quarter of the nineteenth century.

It was the ambition of newspaper proprietors then, as now, to fill the paper with advertisements. When John Walter went into journalism the newspaper gave the theatres first position on the front page, the royal theatres being given preference at the head of the first column. " Capital fire-work entertainments, grand general displays of manly activity, on foot, on horseback or on the solid ground," was the advertisement of Astley's Amphitheatre, and other circus announcements followed. Booksellers', shipping, commercial, and official announcements of the Post Office, Ordnance Office and other departments made up the first page. As a rule the news would occupy less than half the whole disposable space. On exceptional occasions, as, for example, an important trial or a particularly scandalous inquiry, advertisements would be very considerably reduced. But in general it was the desire of the proprietor to cover his first and fourth pages completely with advertising, and to sprinkle the inside pages with paragraphs, or to group them in the first two columns of the second page. The back page generally consisted of notices of auction sales, of real estate, horses, carriages and so forth. There was often a deficiency of " ads," as they were called even in the eighteenth century. On these occasions the proprietor took the situation philosophically and stated in a conspicuous portion of the paper that, owing to the arrival of an important foreign mail, he was under the necessity of disappointing his numerous advertisement customers, whose announcements, they could be assured, would be printed as soon as the pressure of foreign intelligence was relieved. Another device (certainly not unknown to-day), resorted to for the sake of appearance, and to induce business by example, was to copy the advertising in a prosperous contemporary. It was better to give advertisements free than to give none. In an emergency, the official announcements of the Victualling Office could be inserted without authority and the Minister afterwards brought by political pressure to pay for their insertion. But even in the eighteenth century, under such conditions, the foundation of a newspaper was no easy matter.

John Walter's friends, in encouraging him to undertake a daily journal, probably knew the fund of business enterprise upon which he could draw. It is singular that a man new to the trade of printing, having no connexion with the companion trade of bookselling, should have determined to set out on the career of a newspaper proprietor with a daily paper. There were three Sunday papers in existence, but the risk of founding a new weekly, or even an evening paper published thrice a week on post nights, would have been less serious than that involved by a daily. The foreign correspondence, for instance, could be more readily copied without observation from the dailies. John Walter's decision was doubtless due in the first place to a conviction that he could make a success of a daily ; but he must also have known that a daily would best suit the commercial world with whose conditions he had first-hand familiarity, and that only a daily would possess enough significance to impress the authorities. He admitted in his first number that " to bring out a new Paper at the present day, when so many others are already established and confirmed in the public opinion, is certainly an arduous under-taking ; no one can be more fully aware of its difficulties than I am."

January 1, 1785, was a Saturday, not so good a day as Monday for subscriptions. One copy only of the first issue has survived : from the library of the Rev. Dr. Burney, an energetic collector and one " curious in newspapers," for whom, perhaps, a copy, price twopence-halfpenny, of Number 1 of the *Daily Universal Register*, Printed Logographically by His Majesty's Patent, had been ordered in advance. As the Burney copy (now in the British Museum) does not bear a revenue stamp, it was probably part of the gratis issue of a first number commonly made for publicity purposes during the eighteenth century. The prospectus, addressed " To the Public," is signed " J. Walter " :

A News-Paper . . . ought to be the Register of the times and faithful recorder of every species of intelligence ; it ought not to be engrossed by any particular object ; but, like a well covered table, it should contain something suited to every palate ; observations on the dispositions of our own and of foreign Courts should be provided for the political reader ; debates should be reported for the amusement or information of those who may be particularly fond of them ; and a due attention should be paid to the interests of the trade, which are so greatly promoted by advertisements. A Paper that should blend all these advantages, and, by steering clear of extremes, hit the happy

THE Universal DAILY Register,

Printed Logographically — DIEU ET MON DROIT — By His Majesty's Patent

NUMB. 1.] SATURDAY, JANUARY 1, 1785. [Price Two-pence Halfpenny.

The SIXTH NIGHT.
By His MAJESTY's Company
AT the THEATRE ROYAL in DRURY-LANE, this present SATURDAY, will be performed
A New COMEDY, called
The NATURAL SON.
The characters by Mr. King, Mr. Parsons, Mr. Bensley, Mr. Moody, Mr. Baddeley, Mr. Wrighten, and Mr. Palmer. Miss Pope, Miss Tidswell, and Miss Farren.
With new Scenes and Dresses.
The Prologue to be spoken by Mr. Bannister, jun.
And the Epilogue by Miss Farren.
After which will be performed the last New Pantomime Entertainment, in two Parts, called
HARLEQUIN JUNIOR;
Or, The MAGIC CESTUS.
The Characters of the Pantomime, by
Mr. Wright, Mr. Williamson, Mr. Burton, Mr. Staunton, Mr. Williames, Mr. Palmer, Mr. Waldron, Mr. Fawcett, Mr. Chapin, Mr. Phillimore, Mr. Wilson, Mr. Alfred, Mr. Spencer, Mr. Chapman, and Mr. Grimaldi. Mrs. Burnet, Miss Burnett, Miss Tidswell, Miss Barnes, Miss Cranford, and Miss Stageldoir.
To conclude with the Repulse of the Spaniards before
The ROCK of GIBRALTAR.

To-morrow, by particular desire, (for the 4th time) the revived Comedy of the DOUBLE DEALER, with the favorite Masque of ARTHUR and EMMELINE.
On Tuesday the Tragedy of VENICE PRESERVED: Jaffier by Mr. Brereton, Pierre by Mr. Bensley, and Belvidera, by Mrs. Siddons: And on Friday the Carmelite. Massinger's Play of the MAID of HONOUR, (with alterations and Additions) is in Rehearsal and will soon be produced.

NINTH NIGHT. FOR THE AUTHOR.
AT the THEATRE-ROYAL, COVENT-GARDEN, this present SATURDAY, January 1, 1785, will be performed, a New Comedy, called
The FOLLIES of a DAY,
Or, The Marriage of Figaro.
With new Dresses, Decorations, &c.
The principal characters by Mr. Lewis, Mr. Quick, Mr. Edwin, Mr. Wilson, Mr. Wewitzer, Mr. Bonnor, Mr. Thompson, and Mrs. Martyr; Mrs. Bates, Mrs. Webb, Miss Wewitzer, and Miss Younge.
With a new Prologue, to be spoken by Mr. Davies.
To which will be added, for the the sixth time,
A new Pantomime, called,
The MAGIC CAVERN,
Or, VIRTUE's TRIUMPH.
With new Scenery, Machinery, Music, Dresses, and Decorations.
The Scenes chiefly designed by Mr. Richards, and executed by him, Mr. Carver, Mr. Hodgins, and Assistants.
The Overture, Songs, Chorusses, and the Music of the new Pantomime, and composed by Mr. Shield.
Nothing under full Price will be taken.
The Words of the Songs, &c. to be had at the Theatre.

MR. WALTER returns his thanks to his Friends and the Public for the great encouragement and generous support he has already received from them to his new improvement in Printing, by the readiness with which they have subscribed to his intended publication of the works of some eminent Authors: and whilst he solicits a continuance of their favours, begs leave to acquaint them that by
The middle of January will be published,
In One Volume 12mo,
MISCELLANIES IN VERSE AND PROSE,
Intended as a Specimen of his Printing Types at the Logographic Office, Printing-House Square, Blackfriars.— And by the beginning of February, his first volume, containing Watts's Improvement of the Mind, with an Introduction written on the occasion, will be ready to be delivered to the subscribers.

This Day is published, Price 6d.
PLAN of the CHAMBER of COMMERCE, King's-Arms Buildings, Cornhill, London; which is open every day, for Consultation, Opinion, and Advice (verbal or in Writing) Mediation, Assistance, Arbitration, &c. in all *Commercial*, *Maritime*, and *Insurance* Affairs, and matters of *Trade* in general; and the *Laws* and *Usages* relating thereto.——The Address is, To the Director of the Chamber of Commerce, as above.
To be had of Richardson and Urquhart, Royal Exchange; J. Sewell, Cornhill; T. Whieldon, Fleet-street; W. Flexney, Holborn; and at the aforesaid Chamber.
Where may also be had, in one Volume Folio,
Mr. Weskett's COMPLETE DIGEST of the THEORY, LAWS and PRACTICE of INSURANCE; an entire new and comprehensive work, including all the adjudged Cases extant, with several never before printed; Extracts from the Statutes, foreign Ordinances, and marine Treaties; accounts of all the Insurance Companies the Maritime Courts, the commercial and maritime Laws, the Law of Nations, &c. the whole forming (alphabetically) a new *Lex Mercatoria*.
☞ "This Work has been compiled with great Care and Industry, by one who is evidently a Master of the Subject. It abounds with Proofs of extensive Reading, as well as mature Reflection, and judicious Remarks; and if the completest System of Insurance that has hitherto been composed be entitled to Praise, the present useful Digest must meet with the Approbation of the commercial World." Crit. Rev. Vol. 52, p. 443.—All the other Literary Journals speak in similar Terms of this Book; which had already been translated abroad.

This Day is published, in 3 Vols. Price 9s. sewed.
By the LITERARY SOCIETY,
MODERN TIMES: or The ADVENTURES of GABRIEL OUTCAST. A Novel, in Imitation of Gil Blas.
"Qui capit ille facit."
Printed for the Author, and sold by J. Walter, Printing-house Square, Black-friars; where may be had, gratis, the Plan of this Society, associated for the Encouragement of Literature, who propose to print and publish at their own Risk and Expence such original Works as they may approve of, and give their Authors all Profits arising from the same.

MRS. KING begs leave to acquaint her Friends she opens her SCHOOL at CHIGWELL in ESSEX, on Monday, the 10th of January, for the EDUCATION of YOUNG LADIES: as she has always been accustomed to watch and improve the opening mind, hopes to give satisfaction to those who trust her with so important a charge.
Till the 10th of January Mrs. King may be spoke with at Mr. Kerr's, Bitt-maker to his Majesty, in the Mews, Charing-cross.
N. B. Wanted an Apprentice and Half-boarder.

SHIP-PING ADVER-TISEMENTS

For NICE, GENOA, and LEGHORN,
(With Liberty to touch at One Port in the Channel,)
The NANCY.
THOMAS WHITE, Commander,
BURTHEN 160 Tons; Guns and Men answerable. Lying off the Tower, and will absolutely depart on Saturday the 8th instant.
The said Commander to be spoken with every morning at Sam's Coffee-house, near the Custom-house; at Will's Coffee-house, in Cornhill; and at Exchange hours on the French and Italian Walk, or
WILLIAM ELYARD, for the said Commander,
No. 16, Savage-Gardens.

Direct for LISBON,
The NANCY.
JOHN RACKHAM, Commander,
BURTHEN 300 Tons, Men answerable. Lying off Horslydown Chain; Seven-eighths of her Cargo absolutely engaged, and is obliged by Charter-party to depart on Saturday the 8th instant.
The said Commander to be spoken with every morning at Sam's Coffee-house, near the Custom-house; at Will's Coffee-house, in Cornhill; and in Exchange hours in the French and Italian Walk; or
WILLIAM ELYARD, for the said Commander,
No. 16, Savage-Gardens.

For NICE, GENOA, and LEGHORN.
(With Liberty to Touch at One Port in the Channel.)
The LIVELY,
ROBERT BRINE, Commander,
BURTHEN 209 Tons, Guns and Men answerable. Lying off Iron Gate.
The said Commander to be spoke with every Morning at Sam's Coffee-house, near the Custom-house; at Will's Coffee-house in Cornhill; and in Exchange Hours in the French and Italian Walk; or
WILLIAM ELYARD, for the said Commander,
No. 16, Savage-Gardens.

For CONSTANTINOPLE and SMYRNA, or SMYRNA and CONSTANTINOPLE,
(With Liberty to Touch at One Port in the Channel,)
The BETSEY,
ROBERT LANCASTER, Commander,
BURTHEN 200 Tons, Men answerable. Lying at Iron-Gate. Two-thirds of her Cargo engaged, and is obliged to depart by Charterparty, in all the present Month of January.
The said Commander to be spoke with every Morning at Sam's Coffee-house, near the Custom-house; at Will's Coffee-house in Cornhill; and in Exchange Hours in the French and Italian Walk; or
WILLIAM ELYARD, for the said Commender,
No. 16, Savage-Gardens.
N. B. No Goods to be taken on Board the Vessel without an Order from the Broker.

NEW NOVELS.
This Day are published, (in two Volumes, price 5s. sewed,)
THE YOUNG WIDOW; or, the HISTORY of Mrs. LEDWICH.
The HISTORY of Lord BELFORD and Miss SOPHIA WOODLEY, 3 vol. 9s. bound.
Printed for the Editor, and sold by F. Noble, in Holborn; Where may be had lately published,
St. Ruthin's Abbey, a Novel, 3 vols. 9s. bound.
The Woman of Letters; or, History of Fanny Belton, 2 vol. 7s. bound.
A Lesson for Lovers; or, History of Col. Melville and Lady Richly, 2 vols. 7s. bound.
Literary Amusements; or, Evening Entertainer, 2 vol. 7s. bound.
Adventures of a Cavalier, by Daniel Defoe, 3 vols. 9s bound.

T. RICKABY, PRINTER,
No. 15, Duke's Court, Drury Lane;
RESPECTFULLY informs his Friends and the Public in general, that the Partnership between him and Mr. Moore being entirely dissolved, he now intends to carry on every branch of the PRINTING BUSINESS upon his own account;—and having purchased a complete assortment of the neatest and best materials, is determined to pursue a Mode of Printing which he hopes will meet with the approbation of his employers.
N.B. Cards, Hand-Bills, Circular Letters, and all articles of the kind, accurately printed at a few hours notice. in a manner particularly neat, and at the lowest prices.
⁂ An Apprentice wanted.

To the Readers of the London Medical Journal.
This day is first published, price 1s.
SYMPATHY DEFENDED; or, the State MEDICAL CRITICISM in London; written to improve the Principles and Manners of the Editor of the London Medical Journal: To which are added the Contents of the Treatise on Medical Sympathy, and a Postscript, on account of a premature Review in a late Number of the London Medical Journal.
By a Society of Faculties;
Friends to the Public and Enemies to Imposition.
"Cum tua non edas, carpis mea carmina, Laeli,
"Carpere vel noli nostra, vel ede tua."
MART. Epig.
This pamphlet has been hitherto distributed gratuitously. The repeated applications for them, particularly from the country, have become so numerous, that the Society feel themselves under the necessity of putting them into the hands of a publisher.
Sold by J. Murray, Bookseller, Fleet-street.

Nondum lingua suum dextra peregit opus.
MART.
SHORT-HAND, on the latest and most approved Principles taught by J. LARKHAM, No 11, Rose Alley, Bishopsgate Street.
It would exceed the limits of an advertisement merely to mention the various errors either in the *plan* or the *execution* of the different schemes of Short-hand hitherto made public, or to point out the peculiarities and excellencies of the present. Mr. L. therefore only begs leave to observe, that the approbation of many gentlemen well known in the literary world, and well versed in the *Theory* and *Practice* of Short-hand, expressed in stronger terms than delicacy will permit him to repeat, warrants him in saying his will be found a system of short and swift writing, more *easy* to acquire and retain, more *expeditious* more *legible* and more *regular* than any ever yet offered to the Public.
The terms of teaching *one* Guinea, the *usual* time of learning *seven* lessons.

To the Public.

TO bring out a New Paper at the present day, when so many others are already established and confirmed in the public opinion, is certainly an arduous undertaking; and no one can be more fully aware of its difficulties than I am: I, nevertheless, entertain very sanguine hopes, that the nature of the plan on which this paper will be conducted, will ensure it a moderate share at least of public favour; but my pretensions to encouragement, however strong they may appear in my own eyes, must be tried before a tribunal not liable to be blinded by *self-opinion*: to that tribunal I shall now, as I am bound to do, submit these pretensions with deference, and the public will judge whether they are well or ill founded.

It is very far from my intention to detract from the acknowledged merit of the Daily Papers now in existence; it is sufficient that they please the class of readers whose approbation their conductors are ambitious to deserve; nevertheless it is certain some of the best, some of the most respectable, and some of the most useful members of the community, have frequently complained (and the causes of their complaints still exist) that by radical defects in the plans of the present established papers, they were deprived of many advantages, which ought naturally to result from daily publications. Of these some build their fame on the length and accuracy of parliamentary reports, which unquestionably are given with great ability, and with a laudable zeal to please those, who can spare time to read ten or twelve columns of debates. Others are principally attentive to the politics of the day, and make it their study to give satisfaction to the numerous class of politicians, who, blessed with easy circumstances, have nothing better to do, than to amuse themselves with watching the motions of ministers both at home and abroad; and endeavouring to find out the secret springs that set in motion the great machine of government in every state and empire in the world. There is one paper which in no degree interferes with the pursuits of its cotemporaries; it looks upon parliamentary debates as sacred mysteries, that cannot be submitted to vulgar eyes without profanation; political investigations it apprehends to be little short of treason, and therefore *loyally* abstains from them; it deals almost solely in advertisements; and consequently, though a very useful, it is by no means an entertaining paper. Thus it would seem that every News-Paper published in London is calculated for a particular set of readers only; so that if each set were to change its favourite publication for another, the commutation would produce disgust, and dissatisfaction to all; the politician would then find nothing to amuse him but long accounts of petty squabbles about trifles in Parliament, or panegyrics on the men and measures that he most disliked; or libels on those whom he most revered. The person to whom parliamentary debates afford unspeakable delight, would find himself bored with political speculations about the measures that the different courts in Europe might probably adopt; or disgusted with whole pages of advertisements, in which he felt no concern;—whilst the plain shop-keeper who wanted to find a convenient house for his business, and the servant who purchased his paper in hopes of seeing in it an advertisement directing where he might find a place to suit him, would have their labour for their pains, in perusing publications, filled with senatorial debates, or political essays and remarks, which would direct them to nothing less than the house or place they wanted.—A News-Paper, conducted on the true and natural principles of such a publication, ought to be the Register of the times, and faithful recorder of every species of intelligence; it ought not to be engrossed by any particular object; but, like a well covered table, it should contain something suited to every palate: observations on the dispositions of our own and of foreign courts should be provided for the political reader; debates should be reported for the amusement or information of those who may be particularly fond of them; and a due attention should be paid to the interests of trade, which are so greatly promoted by advertisements.—A paper that should blend all these advantages, and by steering clear of extremes, hit the happy medium, has long been expected by the public.—Such, it is intended, shall be the UNIVERSAL REGISTER, the great objects of which will be to facilitate the *commercial* intercourse between the different parts of the community, through the channel of *Advertisements*; to record the principal occurrences of the times; and to abridge the account of debates during the sitting of Parliament.

It is no less the interest of the proprietors of News-Papers, than of the public, that every encouragement should be given to advertising correspondents; yet this private interest of the proprietors is frequently sacrificed to the rage for parliamentary debates, to the great injury of trade; for the extreme length of these debates so greatly retards the publication of the News-Papers which are noted for detailed accounts of them, that the advantages arising from this species of intelligence, though highly acceptable in itself, are frequently over-balanced by the inconveniences occasioned to people in business by the delay. These inconveniences are great and many; it generally happens, that when either House of Parliament has been engaged in the discussion of an important question till after midnight, the papers in which the speeches of the Members are reported at large, cannot be published before noon; nay, they sometimes are not even sent to press so soon; consequently parties interested in *sales* are essentially injured, as the advertisements, inviting the public to attend them at *ten* or *twelve* o'clock, do not appear, on account of a late publication, till some hours after.—From the same source flows another inconvenience; it is sometimes found necessary to *defer* sales, after they have been advertised for a particular day; but the notice of putting them off not appearing early enough, on account of the late hour at which the papers containing it are published, numbers of people, acting under the impression of former advertisements, are unnecessarily put to the trouble of attending.—It will be the object of the *Universal Register* to guard against these great inconveniences, without depriving its readers of the pleasure of learning what passes in Parliament.—It is intended, then, that the debates shall be regularly reported in it; but on the other hand, that the publication may not be delayed to the prejudice of people in trade, the speeches will not be given on a large scale; the *substance* shall be faithfully preserved; but all the uninteresting parts will be omitted. I shall thus be enabled to publish this paper at an early hour; and I propose to bring it out *regularly* every morning at *six* o'clock. The *Universal Register* will therefore have this advantage over the *Daily Advertiser*, that, though published as early, it will contain a substantial account of the proceedings in Parliament the preceding night, which is never to be found in that paper; and compared with the other morning papers it will be found to have the merit of containing in substance, what they give in long detail (which men in business cannot well spare time to read) and, nevertheless, of being published much sooner. These circumstances, it is hoped, will give the *Universal Register* at least an *equal* claim to public favour with the parliamentary papers, and the *trading* part of the metropolis, it is presumed, will find it their advantage to give it the preference.

An essential part of the plan of this new paper is, that, for the convenience of advertising correspondents, their favours shall, *to a certainty*, be inserted on the very day that they shall direct; provided they deliver them at the office in due time. For the *strict* observance of this rule, the credit of the paper shall stand pledged; and its pretensions to public countenance will be renounced, if this fundamental principle in its institution shall ever be violated, except in cases of absolute necessity, which human prudence cannot prevent.—And here I beg it may be understood that I do not make use of the word *necessity* as a reserve, under colour of which, I may, whenever I think fit, be released from my engagements; I mean by that word a necessity arising from accidents that sometimes happen in the printing business, and from which, the most careful man cannot, at all times, be secure. But so far from wishing to shrink from my engagements, I intend, whenever the length of the Gazette, Parliamentary Debates, &c. shall render it impossible for me to insert all the advertisements promised for the day, in *one* sheet, to print an additional half sheet, and publish it with the ordinary paper without any additional charge to my customers.—From the difficulty that people experience in procuring the insertion of their advertisements even in the *Daily Advertiser*; and particularly from the impossibility of obtaining an *early* insertion at some periods of the year, it may be presumed that this regulation will greatly recommend the UNIVERSAL REGISTER to public notice, and procure it support.

These, though in my opinion good, are not the *only* grounds on which I build my hopes of success. I flatter myself, I have some claim to public encouragement, on account of a great improvement which I have made in the art of printing. The inconveniences attending the old and tedious mode of composing with letters taken up *singly*, first suggested the idea of devising some more expeditious method. The cementing of several letters together, so as that the type of a *whole word* might be taken up in as short a time as that of a *single letter*, was the result of much reflection on that subject. But the bare idea of cementing was merely the opening, not the accomplishment or perfection of the improvement. The fount consisting of types of words, and not of letters, was to be so arranged, as that a compositor should be able to find the former with as much facility as he can the latter. This was a work of inconceivable difficulty. I undertook it however, and was fortunate enough, after an infinite number of experiments, and great labour, to bring it to a happy conclusion. The whole English language is now methodically and systematically arranged at my fount: so that printing can now be performed with greater dispatch, and at less expence, than according to the mode hitherto in use.

In bringing this work to perfection, I had not my own advantage solely in view; I wished to be useful to the community; and it is with pleasure I see that the public will derive considerable benefit from my industry; for I have resolved to sell the REGISTER *One halfpenny* UNDER the price paid for seven out of eight of the morning

Front page of the first issue of the *Daily Universal Register*, January 1, 1785

medium, has long been expected by the Public—Such, it is intended, shall be the *Universal Register*.

The writer insisted that the great objects of the paper would be to " facilitate the *commercial* intercourse between the different parts of the community through the channel of *advertisements* ; to record occurrences and to abridge parliamentary debates." The issue of the first number was attended with difficulties usual and unusual. The logographic principle was no doubt responsible for its quota of mechanical troubles. They were the more unfortunate since Walter made a point in his prospectus that publication would take place every morning at six o'clock. But the defects in the logographic organization resulted in the publication of the first number at so late an hour that the hawkers, already on the streets with the other journals, would not wait for their quires of the *Daily Universal Register*. The explanation was given of " an unfortunate accident having prevented the publication of the first number of this paper at as early an hour as the proprietor intended, and the hawkers having taken away so many papers, that he was not able to supply his numerous friends and others according to promise." John Walter, therefore, thought it proper in the second number to repeat his long manifesto, printed, according to the custom of the time, solidly without cross-heads.

The promise that the *Universal Register* should contain nothing that would wound the " ear of delicacy or corrupt the heart,' that there would be " no concealing the native deformity of vice," was honoured for many months. The paper was a businesslike sheet, written for City men. There was no leading article, no political communication. A column of foreign intelligence in the first number was preceded by ten lines of Court News and an Ode for the New Year by Thomas Whitehead, Poet Laureate, which " will be sung in the great Council Chamber." There followed a paragraph on new " Protecting Duties " on Irish imports from Britain. A Guildhall examination of a bankrupt was given almost a column. The issue devoted exactly three of its columns to news and three to the prospectus. There were ten columns of advertisements, including a back page puff of the *Register* signed " Gregory Gazette." The advertisements were inserted for the bare cost of the stamp duty, and the bulk of the issue was doubtless given free. A column and a half in the number for February 8, 1785, was filled by a dialogue between an author and a place-monger, extracted from *Modern Times*. Articles under the heading of " Reflector " bear traces of Dr. Trusler's pen, and it may well be that collaboration between Trusler and Walter was not limited to these contributions. This structure was not greatly varied. The imprint (with the names and addresses of agents for the greater convenience of those residing in the distant parts of the town) read :

LONDON : printed by James Fleming, Printing House Square, Blackfriars ; where Advertisements, Essays, Letters and articles of intelligence will be taken in ; also at *Mr Searle's* No 55 Oxford Street ; *Mr Thrale's* opposite the Admiralty ; *Mrs Wilson's* No 45 Lombard Street ; *Mr Pratt's* No 84 Wapping ; and *Mr Sterney's* No 156 opposite St. George's Church, Southwark.

James Fleming's name was suppressed in Number 10 in favour of " George Brown." Political intelligence increased at the expense of commercial in the course of 1785. The column headed " Poet's Corner " was often filled with an Epilogue from a contemporary play, an insertion calculated to please the theatre manager.[1] The advertisements became fewer. On March 2 Parliament enacted fresh taxes on newspaper advertisements. If the profit from the sales and advertisement revenue of the *Universal Register* balanced the expenses of printing and writing it, the Proprietor had cause for congratulation. But the publicity which the paper gave to the productions of the Logographic Press was of some service to John Walter's further ambition. That ambition remained commercial, for there is no sign that the Proprietor of the Logographic Press entertained hopes of making a serious reputation as an editor, journalist, or newspaper proprietor. The logographic newspaper was designed primarily as an advertisement of the logographic method and of the logographic productions.

During 1786 the *Daily Universal Register*, though maintaining its commercial nature, printing City news, commercial cases and shipping arrivals and departures, market reports and export advertisements, gave more space to literary matter. Parliamentary news did not increase in the same proportion. Long advertisements of logographic books, equally long advertisements of those

---

[1] Not always. The issue of January 2, 1790, contained an *Ode for the New Year ; By T. Warton, Esq Poet Laureat*. The issue for the following Monday contained a correction : " We are sorry to have been imposed upon by the insertion of the Ode in our paper of Saturday said to be written by the Poet Laureat, on the occasion of the New Year. It was sent to the paper at a late hour the preceding evening unknown to the Editor, and turns out to be fictitious." But by this date the paper had become *The Times*, and it will be noticed there was an Editor.

of Dr. Trusler, are frequent in 1786, and, in the text, essays and squibs on social tendencies. There is a clearly observable tendency towards the secular and frivolous rather than the commercial and serious in the body of the paper. Entertainment was offered in place of news. The trend becomes more marked in 1787. Theatrical advertising and intelligence are given more prominence. The logographic paper was evidently not succeeding as an advertiser in the City and was directing its attention to the West End, thereby giving sharper competition to the existing journals. The situation suffered a sudden and permanent change by the starting of the *World and Fashionable Advertiser*, the first number of which was published on Monday, January 1, 1787. This new daily was conducted by Captain Edward Topham and John Bell ; it exercised an immediate influence upon the rest of the daily Press with the exception of the *Advertisers*. The *Daily Universal Register*, like the *Morning Post*, the *Morning Chronicle* and the rest, found itself faced with an intelligent, active and witty rival.

The *World* was something new in journalism ; it was light, and, in accordance with its sub-title, determined to seek the favour of men and women of fashion. Two consequences of the foundation of this stylish paper were, first, the alteration of the name of John Walter's newspaper, and, secondly, its typographical and literary reconstruction in accordance with the appearance and contents of Topham's paper. Furious attacks were exchanged between the *Daily Universal Register* and the *World* during the whole of 1787. Columns of attacks on the *World*, upon Topham and his favourite Mrs. Wells, and upon Bell, were printed by Walter in the course of the year. It was denounced as " upstart," " propagator of falsehood," " vehicle of lies." Meanwhile the *Daily Universal Register*, in common with other dailies, approximated to its style and make-up. At the end of the year Walter notified his readers that their journal would henceforth be entitled *The Times or Daily Universal Register*. On January 1, 1788, No. 940 of the series was so entitled. The final issue of the paper under the title of the *Daily Universal Register* contained the following " Answer to Correspondents " :

The anticipatory eulogium on *The Times* is politely flattering— *We hope to confirm the author's good opinions* ; But it would savour too much of the vanity of The World to *publish a panegyric on ourselves*.

The new form was not identical with that of the *World*, but its typographical consequences were extended in the following March, when the heading was reconstructed. For the cumbrous roman headpiece was substituted the mock-gothic titling invented for Topham's paper. *The Times* did not again use a roman heading until 1932. The issue of Tuesday, March 18, 1788, employs the gothic heading for the first time, but without any notification to the reader. Another typographical innovation of the *World*, the abolition of the long ∫ and its combinations, was not followed by the logographers, who had, in this respect, been given a very practical example of lightening the burden of composition.

Walter's reasons for changing the name of the paper are given in page 3 of No. 940 of the *Universal Register*, now *The Times*, following a short personal notice. The patentee of the Logographic Press, having thanked his friends for their support, promised his enemies an exposure of their "mean and inviduous (*sic*) practices," attacked the *Daily Advertiser*, "generally read by the lower orders of the people," whither he had sent an advertisement for several apprentices, "which Mr Jenour, the printer, refused to insert, though he had received payment several days preceding." The notice concerning the new title, occupying a column and a half, was set out in open style, florid with the capitals, small capitals and italics that Bell had invented for the *World*. The argument was that the word "Register" was too ambiguous and had confused everybody ; some thought it identical with the *Annual Register*, or Harris's *Register of Ladies*. But "Times," "being a *monosyllable*, bids defiance to *corrupters* and *mutilaters* of the language." The new prospectus occupying a column and a half began thus :

THE TIMES

Why change the head ?

This question will naturally come from the Public—and *we*, the TIMES, being the PUBLIC's most humble and most obedient Servants, think ourselves bound to answer.

All things have *heads*,—and all *heads* are liable to *change*—

Every sentence and opinion, advanced and supported by Mr. *Shandy*, on the influence and utility of a well chosen sirname, may be properly applied, in shewing the recommendations and advantages which result from placing a striking title page before a book, or an inviting HEAD on the front page of a NEWS-PAPER—

A HEAD so placed, like those *heads* which once ornamented *Temple-Bar*, or those of the *great Attorney*, or *great Contractor*, which, not long since, were conspicuously elevated, for their *great actions*, and

THE TIMES

OR DAILY UNIVERSAL REGISTER

PRINTED LOGOGRAPHICALLY

NUMB. 940.   TUESDAY, JANUARY 1, 1788.   (Price Three-pence.)

were exhibited in *wooden frames*, at the *East* and *West*-ends of this metropolis, never fails of attracting the eyes of passengers—though indeed we do not expect to experience the enmity shewn to these *great exhibitors* ; for, probably, THE TIMES will be pelted without mercy.

It was promised that " discussion, description, dissection and illustration will employ the press of the most celebrated among the *Literati*," and that the matter of the paper would now comprise literary, political, commercial, philosophical, critical, theatrical, fashionable, humorous and witty departments, the commercial being given third place. Politically, *The Times* was to be " like *Janus*, the Roman Deity, double-faced ; with one countenance it will smile continually on the *friends* of *Old England* and with the other will frown incessantly on her enemies." Finally, the conductor wrote :

The alteration we have made in our *head* is not without precedents. *The World*[1] has parted with half its *Caput Mortuum*, and a moiety of its brains. *The Herald*[2] has cut off half of its head and has lost its original humour. *The Post*, it is true, retains its whole head and its old features ; and as to the other public prints, they appear as having neither *heads* nor *tails*.

The new direction taken by the logographic journal is sufficiently indicated by the first answer addressed " To Correspondents " :

Though much has been said of Lord George Gordon's beard, yet as the subject encreases every day, *The Times* will not let it pass unnoticed. The Shandean *Jeu d'Esprit* will of course be attended to, though perhaps with a little clipping.

It is plain that the paper was being written by a new hand, and that the new head was accompanied by other changes. It is hardly open to doubt that the proprietor himself put together the matter in the *Universal Register* for some time after its foundation, availing himself of such help as he found necessary and at hand. The long advertisements of Dr. Trusler's books imply a *contra* arrangement of some kind, probably for editorial assistance. It is known that Trusler contributed articles to the *Universal Register* and was the author of several logographic publications in addition to assisting the Press with his Literary Society. His experience as a founder with John Bell and others of the *Morning Post* could not fail to be useful to John Walter, who, so far as is known, was

---

[1] The *World* dropped its sub-title *Fashionable Advertiser*.
[2] The *Morning Herald* had dropped its sub-title.

not acquainted with booksellers or journalists and never joined any trade societies. Doubtless, too, William Combe, who edited Anderson's *Commerce* and Meares's *Voyages* for John Walter, contributed to the columns of the *Register*.

In all probability the appointment of a permanent literary conductor dates from the alteration in the title. The name of the editor of *The Times* in 1789 is known as a consequence of the prosecution of John Walter in that year. Certain words[1] reflecting on the Duke of York appeared in *The Times* of February 21, 1789. On November 26, 1789, the paper printed the following letter :

To the Conductor

Sir,

Being informed by many of my friends, that I am considered as the Author of that paragraph in *The Times*, reflecting on the Duke of York, for the publication of which Mr. Walter received judgment on Monday last, I hold it necessary to declare, that it was not written, or caused to be written by me ; and that I never saw it—or even heard of it—until it was published in the paper.

Mr. Walter, I am confident, will do me the justice to acknowledge, that I never did write, or cause to be inserted, any matter in *The Times* which has occasioned the Proprietor, Editor, Printer, or Publisher of that Paper, to be prosecuted.

WILLIAM FINEY

An editorial note is added :
> *Our publication of the above is an acknowledgement of the truth it contains.*

It is known from the Memoirs of Mrs. Wells[2] that Finey continued to act until 1797 as a writer on the staff of *The Times*. The position given him in Mrs. Wells's narrative is that of " Editor," a title probably borne by him within the office as early as the date of the foregoing letter. It is addressed " To the Conductor " as the responsible authority, yet it is clearly the expression of a writer intimately concerned with the production of the paper. There can be little doubt that the Editor of *The Times* from 1788-1797 was William Finey.

---

[1] The paragraphs and the resulting prosecution are separately treated in Chapter IV.
[2] *Cf. Memoirs of Mrs. Sumbel, late Wells* (London, 1811).

III

THE NEWSPAPER TRADE, 1785—1799

THE position of *The Times* during the period immediately following the French Revolution was perhaps fairly satisfactory from the commercial standpoint. The paper claimed a superiority in circulation, in accuracy, and in priority of foreign intelligence. It appears to have spent freely in order to serve its readers. The years 1789-95 rank as the most successful of its youth. There had been changes in the trade since the foundation of the *Daily Universal Register*. The combination which had made the *World* a brilliant success split in 1789 : Bell went off to found a new morning paper, the *Oracle*, and, although Topham continued the *World*, the old paper lost its position and the new one did not replace it. The *Public Advertiser* was slowly weakening ; the *Morning Post* found the struggle for existence almost impossible, with a circulation of under 500 a day ; the *Morning Herald* prospered at the expense of the *Post*. The first regular evening newspaper, the *Star*, was transformed into the *Morning Star* in 1789 after a quarrel of the founder, Peter Stuart, with his partners. In the same year a profoundly important change occurred in the *Morning Chronicle*. Long the most trustworthy reporter of Commons debates, William Woodfall's paper was acquired by James Perry, active some years before in a similar sphere on the *Gazetteer*. Perry was only 33 when he secured control of the *Morning Chronicle* ; at once he paid great attention to the organization of Parliamentary reporting and to the securing of political news. He was a writer himself, an able editor, a wholehearted journalist ; he made the *Morning Chronicle* the most influential journal for thirty years.

In the history of English journalism Perry occupies a position of the greatest distinction. Although, thanks to John Walter, *The Times* surpassed the *Chronicle* in priority of news, Perry's paper outstripped Walter's in political consequence. In influence upon political thought it became the leading journal. Perry died in 1821

D

just as Barnes, with whom he deserves to be compared, was settling into the editorial chair and preparing to strengthen *The Times* on the political side. Barnes accomplished the defeat of the *Chronicle*, then directed, it must be admitted, by far less able men than Perry. The two papers were rivals for nearly three-quarters of a century.

From 1789 to 1795 *The Times* learnt much from the example of the *Chronicle*. The break-up of the Topham and Bell combination, and the grave issues raised by the French Revolution, gave a positive turn to the interest of readers. News being in demand, entertainment was subordinated to it. The change was reflected in the public patronage of the more serious journals. *The Times*, dropping some of Topham's tricks, drew nearer in spirit to the *Chronicle*, and more than maintained circulation in a time of mounting costs and increasing newspaper taxation. Such details of the management as have survived are disappointingly few and vague, and do not present more than a dim outline of the business problem facing a newspaper proprietor in the late eighteenth century. It was a struggle to balance costs and sales *plus* advertising revenue. The net sales of *The Times* were a boast in 1792. A certificate was printed on December 11 :

As some artful and insidious reports have been lately circulated, tending to deprecate the character and sale of the Paper, the Proprietors have thought it prudent to contradict them in the most plain and direct terms.

Accordingly, the following affidavit was yesterday sworn before the Lord Mayor :

Monday, Dec. 3, 1792	2810
4	2824
5	2901
6	2941
7	2901
8	2927
Total	17,304

Thomas Thirlwind	Publisher
Thomas Beveridge	
Simmons Beveridge	
John Fishbourn	Pressmen
Richard Humphreys	

The statement was repeated on December 17 with supplementary figures :

Monday	2923
Tuesday	2910
Wednesday	2966
Thursday	2988
Friday	2975
Saturday	3131
	17,893

As many applications were made for papers during last week, which could not be supplied, it is particularly requested that papers may be applied for before eleven o'clock in the forenoon, that disappointments may not again occur.

In the following year, on November 27, 1793, *The Times* stated its regular sale as " now near 4000 daily, a number which was never before attained by any Morning Paper under any circumstances." This claim is of added importance, for previous publicity had always excepted by name the *Daily Advertiser*, known to be favoured by seekers for jobs or servants, and then admitted to sell " about 100 more." There were constant complaints of late delivery of *The Times*. The reply was in two parts :

Notwithstanding the arrangements we have made to obtain an early publication, by printing the Paper at three Presses instead of two, we still find that complaints are made of the lateness of its delivery in some parts of the Town. This arises from the sale of the Paper having continued to increase daily, in proportion as the delivery has been more early than it was formerly.

The impossibility of obtaining an accurate copy of the Play-Bills of the day, at an early hour in the preceding evening, has frequently delayed the outside Pages of the Paper from being sent to Press ; in future, therefore, the Play-Bills will be inserted immediately preceding the London News. (March 31, 1794.)

Distribution was mainly through the booksellers and hawkers. That the latter could make a fair living is clear from such a notice as the following, which appeared on April 15, 1792 :

NEWS WALK.

An old established NEWS WALK to be disposed of that brings in £1 12s. per week clear profit ; situate in the best part of London, and capable, with care and assiduity, of great improvement: such an opportunity seldom offers for an industrious person.

Enquire tomorrow at No. 14, Portugal Street, Lincoln's-Inn-Fields.

The time of publication to the newsmen varied. News-hawkers in 1794 were divided into Country and Town, the former being served first in accordance with a notice of January 28, 1794, that

those papers which go into the country by the early coaches, may be had whenever they are called for ;—that the Country News Hawkers are supplied at Seven, and the general publication begins at Eight o'Clock, till the whole number is worked off.—But when the Debates are late in the Houses of Parliament, the publication must be regulated by the hour they adjourn.

The hawkers, it seems, were responsible for the delivery of the papers to the coffee-houses. There the town as a whole read *The Times*, and the custom was, no doubt, followed in the country. The papers passed from hand to hand after they had served their turn in the coffee-houses. Regular ordering of a copy by households or individuals other than officials and politicians did not become general for more than fifty years after the foundation of the *Daily Universal Register*. An eighteenth-century person anxious to see *The Times* drank his coffee at his favourite house and took his turn for reading. That there was sometimes disappointment is revealed by a notice " To Correspondents " in the issue of October 30, 1788. One gathers that customers of the Chapter Coffee-House, on calling for their favourite paper, were fobbed off by the waiter with the " stale " excuse, " In hand, sir," that another customer was reading it.

Newspapers delivered in bulk from the printing offices were found to incommode the officials, first by arriving at the General Post Office so late as to retard the making up of the mails, and secondly by frequently coming " in so wet a state as to deface the directions of many of the letters which went in the same bags." So reads a report of the Postmaster-General. Hence a separate office to receive and sort all newspapers, made up in bundles according to the several districts for which they were destined, was established in November, 1787, and known as The Newspaper Office. The bundles were distributed to the postmasters by the Clerks of the Roads for the postal divisions of the country. Subscribers purchased their copies at the local post office.

Single copies were also sent through the General Post Office, Lombard Street. If without covers, in covers open at the ends and signed on the outside by a Member of Parliament, or directed to a Member of Parliament, they were exempt from postage. The system of franking newspapers and letters was abused to a wholesale extent. Probably only a few persons paid any postage at this period. The postal officials, themselves dependent upon fees and perquisites, endeavoured to charge where they could. *The Times* received complaints that subscribers through booksellers had been charged with postage although their agent had used a franked cover. Subscribers were " obliged to pay postage for [their] paper though under cover from a Member of Parliament, because that cover is *printed*[1] on the inside." The paper advised that, " as it is well known, those covers have been given to the Hawkers for the especial purpose of recommending other papers—and the Postmasters have in many places charged postage for them by weight—we recommend our Readers, whenever this happens, to charge the postage against the bill when they pay it, as the only means to prevent it in future." (Nov. 19, 1789.) The Post Office was then going through a crisis, and new rules for newspapers were in preparation. The revenue lost by the gradual decrease in ordinary unfranked newspapers and the increase of franked papers was bound to cause discussion. In 1796 a Bill was presented to the Commons " for regulating the conveyance of newspapers." This measure had the effect of depriving the hawkers and handing over the monopoly to the already entrenched Clerks of the Roads, who, at the office in Lombard Street, had been responsible since the sixteenth century for sorting and taxing, with appropriate postage, all letters going from London to the six roads into which the country was divided for such purposes. Thus the Clerks occupied the position of wholesale newsagents to the country postmasters, and the Post Office became the national distributing agency, with the exception of the town hawkers and booksellers in London. The hawkers and booksellers protested without avail. From 1796 the newspapers were carried post free.

The distribution of *The Times*, therefore, at the end of the eighteenth century was carried out almost exclusively by the Post Office. The Clerks of the Roads, in their dual capacity of dealers in newspapers and overseers of the post, made a considerable

---

[1] There was an advertisement printed on the inside of the wrapper and this novelty was made the excuse for ignoring the right to a frank.

income. An article of March 30, 1798, indicates that supervision was still necessary :

The new Postmaster General, Lord Auckland, has begun very extensive reforms in that department. On Saturday night all the Newspapers were examined, to see that no writing was put upon the stamped sheets, so as to defraud the Revenue of postage. This is assuredly proper. No person has a right to abuse the privilege of free carriage which the Newspapers enjoy for the encouragement of the stamp duties, by smuggling under the cover any private correspondence.

The support given by the newspapers to the new postal arrangements was natural. Increased taxes on printing paper, with a higher cost of living involving demands for increases from compositors and pressmen, raised the selling price of the paper and consequently restricted the number of its readers. The *Daily Universal Register* was 2½d. in January, 1785 ; 3d. from April, 1785. In 1789 the stamp was increased from 1½d. to 2d. and the price of *The Times* to the public became 4d. At this time, August, 1789, the hawkers were first allowed " 13 papers for every 12 they pay for." Certain journals raised their prices to 3½d. In 1794 the wage increases, &c., were responsible for advancing the price to 4½d. In 1797 the stamp was raised to 3½d. and the paper to 6d. a copy.

The economics of editing, printing and publishing *The Times*, or any other eighteenth-century daily newspaper, can only be sketched. The cost of labour in the printing trade in 1793 is available from trade circulars and surviving ledgers. The important item of " overheads " is not accounted for in the ledgers, and the blank description *Sundries* prevents any comprehensive understanding. Hawkers were supplied with the 4½d. paper (as it was in 1794) for 3½d. and allowed two papers in every quire—26 as 24. The circulation system does not seem to have allowed returns ; neither did the Stamp Act allow for spoiled papers. Printing paper, with new duties imposed in 1789, cost the printer £2 2s. for 500 sheets, yielding 1,000 copies. The old tax on double demy, the size used for newspapers, was 8s. 4d. a bundle weighing 106lb., which was less than 1d. a lb. The new duty was 2½d. a lb., which for the bundle of 106lb. is 22s. 1d., being an increase of 13s. 9d. Before 1792 the average net sale of *The Times* may be taken as ranging between 1,250 and 1,650 in accordance with seasonal demands. The 4,000 claimed in 1793 was a winter figure, and exceptional at that. Low summer bills for presswork prove that fewer papers were required from May to September. *The Times* in the eighteenth century was doing fairly well if its daily average of sales was over 1,500 copies. The net average circulation claimed by John Walter in 1794 was 2,000. The cost of production of the paper, including materials, labour and overheads, may be roughly estimated. Take, first, the paper :

4 reams at £1 1s., duty included	-	-	-	-	£4	4	0
2000 duty stamps at 2d. £16 13s. 4d. less 4%		-	-	£16	0	0

The minimum wage for newspaper compositors agreed to by the masters in 1785 was £1 11s. 6d. for full hands, 15s. for supernumeraries. An increase in 1793 brought the full hands to £1 16s. and supernumeraries to 17s. The wages paid by Charles Bell, the printer of *The Times*, differed slightly, as appears from a list for the week ending January 7, 1797, which has been preserved. Mr. Topping, the overseer, received £2 2s. a week. His best men were :

Mr. Ritch
Crowe
Mott
Martin
Jolly who received £1 14s. a week
Bayes took £1 5s. 6d.

and the supernumeraries Young and

Sears received 17s.
Pardon received 19s. 10d.
Coy received 17s. and another 17s. for
work on *The Mail*

The cost of labour for composition that week totalled £15 8s. 4d. There were fly-boys whose wages came to £2 1s., and pressmen who accounted for £14 12s. 8d. Mr. Bell, as printer, received £3 3s. weekly. The labour expenses of composing and printing thus came to £35 5s. The wages of the press readers[1] was an additional £4 14s. 6d. During the summer the wages of pressmen, like the figures of circulation, suffered reduction. The weekly average cost of composing, printing, and reading during 1797 may be taken as :

Composition	Reading	Presswork	
£15 8 4	£4 14 6	£15 0 0	=a total of £35 2 10

[1] An advertisement in the issue of March 14, 1793, reads : " Wanted immediately the services of a Person who is a good scholar, and has been accustomed to correct for the Press. An attendance in the Evening only will be required. Also a good pressman to work this Paper. Apply at the Office of *The Times*."

In addition, the publishing department accounted for three guineas, as follows :

	£	s.	d.
Mr. C. Bell, the printer, also took charge of publishing and received for this duty the sum of	£1	11	6
His assistant, C. Davies, received	1	1	0
And the boy (Battie)		10	6
	£3	3	0

The weekly figures (with an average sale of 2,000) are thus resumed :

PRODUCTION

	£	s.	d.
Six days' paper at £4 4s.	25	4	0
Stamps at £16	96	0	0
Wages of compositors, readers and pressmen	35	2	10
	£156	6	10

SALES

	£	s.	d.
If all 12,000 were sold at 3½d. each to hawkers	175	0	0
Less publishing charges	3	3	0
	£171	17	0

Comparison of the production costs and the sales revenue leaves a credit balance of £15 10s. 2d. with which to pay the overhead charges on the premises and plant. These comprised rent, taxes (nearly half the rent), coals (summer of 1786, 33s. a chaldron), candles (dipped tallow candles, 8s. 4d. a dozen), interest on capital invested in plant, type, ink, &c. Type prices were raised in August, 1793, with pica at 1s. 1½d. and small pica at 1s. 3½d. a lb. Two-line letters cost 1s. 1d., leads (6 to pica) 1s. 6d. If these averaged £4 4s. a week the net surplus, after meeting costs of materials, production and plant overheads, was £11 6s. 2d.

This surplus, however, was not by any means a profit. Other staffs were needed, clerks, messengers, even bookkeepers. *The Times* of January 20, 1792, advertised for "An experienced book-keeper who can bear confinement : security will be required." The writing staff, editors, reporters, translators, foreign corre-spondents and outside contributors must have required a sum in excess of £25. John Walter refers to the "immense" cost of maintaining foreign correspondence at a high standard. That the Parliamentary reporting was an important department, and taken seriously, is shown by the following (from the paper of December 18, 1799) :

Any Gentleman who is competent to take the Parliamentary Reports for this Paper during the ensuing Sessions may meet with an Engagement. Three Gentlemen are already engaged, but a fourth is wanted. Apply at the Office of *The Times*.

The competence of the reporting staff was more than once advertised to readers. On the occasion of the Birmingham Riot of 1791, which caused a sensation throughout the country, *The Times* of August 20 printed a statement that :

We have thought proper, in order to meet the wishes and expectation of the public, to send down to Warwick the gentleman who takes the Law Reports for this paper, to write down the trials in short hand.

The staff was not always sufficient to meet the demands made by special events. The report of the trial of Thomas Hardy, secretary of the London Corresponding Society, was introduced with the following note :

In consequence of the excessive fatigue, which the gentleman who is the principal reporter of this Paper has daily undergone since the commencement of Mr. Hardy's trial, he is unable to proceed further in giving the charge of the Lord Chief Justice yesterday to the Jury which it was his intention to have done almost word for word. The remaining part must, therefore, be deferred till tomorrow ; and the whole will then form a very interesting and valuable paper.

The conditions of employment of an assistant in the Foreign Department are indicated in the following from the issue of September 30, 1793 :

Wanted immediately the assistance of a Person who can translate the Dutch language into English. If he also understands German, it will be the more agreeable. His assistance will be only required two days in the week. Apply this day at the office of *The Times*, Printing House Square, Blackfriars.

Another advertisement for assistance in the Foreign Department is also worth reproduction :

Wanted immediately, A Gentleman who is capable of translating the French Language. In order to prevent trouble, he must be a perfect

Master of the English Language, have some knowledge of the Political State of Europe and be thoroughly capable of the situation he undertakes. His employment will be permanent and take up a considerable share of his attention ; for which a handsome salary will be allowed.

Apply at the office of this Paper between the hours of Five and Six this Evening, or Tomorrow morning, between Eleven and Twelve o'clock. (August 27, 1792.)

The provision of Continental news was expensive and full of difficulty. It was necessary to establish at ports on both sides of the Channel agents responsible for the transmission of the Continental newspapers, besides correspondents in the capitals. John Walter, recognizing that " Continental affairs are so engrossing," made new arrangements in 1792. The paper for May 21 of that year reports that

we have established a new correspondence both at Brussels and Paris, which we trust will furnish us with the most regular and early intelligence that can possibly be obtained. Our communications will not be confined to the ordinary conveyance by the foreign Mails only, as we have taken such measures as will enable us to receive Letters from abroad on those days when the Foreign Mails do not become due. Our new Correspondence commences this day. The foreign Gazettes which chiefly guide the other Morning Prints are become so extremely partial, that they aggravate or suppress almost every material fact, as suits the purpose of their several parties.

The arrangement worked well for a time.

We have some reason to be proud of our Foreign Correspondence in this Day's paper. . . . The Brussels Gazette has been stopped from being printed since the French troops entered Flanders. From this disappointment we are led to believe that none of the other Morning Papers of this Day will have any news from Flanders. (June 26, 1792.)

Notwithstanding interruptions of the service, *The Times* succeeded in anticipating competitors : notably in the matter of the anti-revolutionary declaration of the Duke of Brunswick, which it published exclusively on August 3, 1792. Difficulties increased, however, and in the following month readers were taken into confidence on the subject :

It is a matter of great vexation to us, that the plans we had laid for obtaining the most early correspondence from Paris and Bruxelles should have been so frequently obstructed, by the interruption of letters

42

in the Post-offices abroad. We had taken the most certain measures to procure a Daily Correspondence from both these places, by having Agents at the Out-ports to forward our letters ; but from the circuitous channels which they must now pass through, and from the frequent stoppage of all kind (*sic*) of correspondence from France, which is not tinctured with the spirit of rebellion, we have been subject to daily disappointments.

The Declaration of the Duke of Brunswick which first appeared in this paper, should have reached us a week sooner than it did ;—The Manifesto of the Confederate Powers we now learn, was sent to us four days after its first publication, but has never yet been received. . . . (September 3, 1792.)

The necessity of engaging foreign correspondents in these conditions rendered the service one of the most expensive of the editorial items. The postage of a single letter from any part of Holland, France or Flanders to Printing House Square was 10d. ; from Spain 18d. Foreign correspondence, with its " immense cost," was in large measure an answer to the activities of Walter's rival, John Bell, denounced by *The Times* as a " vagabond Jacobin," who made a special journey abroad in the spring of 1794 for the express purpose of establishing a regular chain of Continental agents to continue his own series of dispatches. *The Times* referred to the competition of the *Oracle* in alluding to the unreliability of the foreign intelligence of all other newspapers :

Not one of which contained an article of news respecting the events now passing in West Flanders, to which it could speak as a positive fact. . . . It is not, however, to be wondered that such contradictory and false rumours should be circulated, when those who write them from the Continent are for the most part vagabond Jacobins, who report as a fact every thing they hear ; which is farther aggravated on this side the water by all the virulence of disappointment and malignity.

We have offered these remarks, because we feel it impossible to keep pace with the intelligence of the many expresses which these communicative purveyors of news receive, according to their own account, every hour. Of the Correspondence of this Paper the public are to judge for themselves. We shall merely state, that on Monday night, though it was at a late hour, we received all the Newspapers printed at Brussels on *Saturday last* ; and we had a letter from Ostend, dated on *Sunday afternoon*. We do not contend for any greater expedition ! (June 18, 1794.)

The " immense " expenses of these, and, indeed, of the whole of the editorial services, were met by revenue first from advertisements, secondly from puffs, and thirdly from contradiction fees. Revenue from advertising in the eighteenth century is difficult to calculate. The rates were vague ; a charge was made for notices of " moderate length " and increased for those of " greater length." The minimum of the *Daily Advertiser* in 1730 was two shillings—and " to be pasted up at the several Publick Parts of the Town in the usual Manner." The *Public Ledger* (No. 1, 1767) prescribes that " the charge for every Advertisement of a moderate length shall not exceed Three Shillings." The minute book of the *London Packet*, January 6, 1770, authorizes the printer to accept advertisements " from any Proprietor whose name is therein marked and signed by himself " at " half a crown each until ordered to the contrary at a General Meeting ; and the said advertisement not to exceed thirty lines." Though no precise information is available, it is likely that eighteen lines was the " moderate length " of the period. Dr. Trusler reports that in 1786 an advertisement of eighteen lines was inserted for 3s. 6d. A front page position cost an additional 2s. The minimum was 3s. 6d. The tax payable to the Government was 2s. 6d. on each advertisement whatever its length. This was reduced, but not repealed until 1853.

The charges of John Walter did not greatly vary from those of his competitors. An announcement of November 24, 1792, yields a few details, including an early reference to " agents " :

In answer to "A Friend to The Times," we beg to reply, that . . . for long advertisements we charge a small matter more than our Contemporaries, short ones only the same price, and the good sense of those who advertise will readily admit a small advance, when *The Times*, we are well assured, is higher in number than any other Morning Print, and that there are not above three others which sell near half, and many not one-third of the number. We know that some agents will resort to Papers low in sale, to get them inserted cheaper, but their Principals will best judge whether their interests are consulted, as the more their intentions are circulated the better their end is obtained.

The small advance seems, indeed, not to have been grudged. Advertisements came from all the usual sources. On July 1, 1795, the following announcement appears :

Cricket. A grand match will be played on Thursday, the 2nd of July, 1795, in Lords Cricket Ground, Mary-le-bonne, between 11

Gentlemen of the University of Oxford, against 11 Noblemen and Gentlemen of the Mary-le-bonne Club, for 1000 Guineas a side. The Wickets to be pitched at 11 o'Clock. (A list of the players follows.)

The Times was sufficiently established in 1792, at least in the view of loyal anti-Jacobins, to be named by the Vestry of Isleworth as a proper medium, together with the *Public Advertiser*, for the insertion of their resolution of attachment to the British Constitution ; such political manifestos were printed on the front page.

The top half of the first column and, very frequently, of the second column of the first page of the paper, was given to various forms of entertainment : announcements of performances at the King's Theatre and at the Theatre Royal, Haymarket ; of the Royal Circus at St. George's Fields and Handy's Circus at the Lyceum ; boxing bouts ; masquerades, fireworks, galas, and other amusements at Vauxhall and Ranelagh ; Messrs. Harrison & Knyvett's instrumental concerts at Willis's Rooms ; operas, ballets, oratorios and art exhibitions. During the winter the announcements of Drury Lane and Covent Garden Theatres are printed immediately below the sub-title " The Times " at the head of the news. Performances in which J. P. Kemble and Mrs. Siddons are the " stars " appear regularly. (There is a notice of a performance of *Macbeth*, in which they both appear in the principal parts, on November 9, 1795.) Copper bronze medals of Kemble are advertised for sale during January, 1799, and at the same period is recorded the popularity enjoyed at Covent Garden by Mrs. Inchbald's *Lovers' Vows*—the play, it will be remembered, that was rehearsed, but never performed, by the young Bertrams and Crawfords in Jane Austen's *Mansfield Park*. The series of concerts which Haydn gave on his first visit to England in May, 1791, under the auspices of Salomon, the concert-director, in the Hanover Square rooms, were announced ; and on May 20 Mr. Haydn publicly thanked his audiences for their reception. On his second visit in May, 1795, he announced his own concerts at the Opera House. Another outstanding series of concerts, in 1791, was given by Mr. Dibdin at Sans Souci, in the Strand. An announcement of the opening of the Royal Academy, Somerset Place, was printed on April 30, 1799. (Admission 1/-, Catalogues 6d.)

The booksellers Boydell, Cadell, G. G. and J. G. Robinson, Longman, Kearsley, Dilly, Lane of the Minerva, and Hookham regularly used the advertising columns. The Book Trade provided one of the most prominent features of the advertising pages during this period. The usual place is the first column of the second page or the fourth of the first page. Occasionally these announcements covered as much as 2½ columns. Perhaps the largest amount of advertising was done by Robinson, of Paternoster Row, and T. Cadell, jnr., and W. Davies, in the Strand. Three times in September, 1798, the last had a column and a half devoted entirely to his publications (fifty in all). On May 16, 1791 (the actual date of publication), the first edition, in two volumes quarto, of the *Life of Samuel Johnson, LL.D.*, by James Boswell, was announced. On October 4, 1798, the following short notice advertised that :

This day is published, in small 8vo, price 5s. in boards, LYRICAL BALLADS, with a few other poems. Printed for John and Arthur Arch, No. 23 Gracechurch-street.

Other books advertised are a new and enlarged edition of Burns's poems (July 1, 1795) ; Mary Wollstonecraft's *Vindication of the Rights of Women*, Ann Radcliffe's *Mysteries of Udolpho*, Southey's Poems (*Joan of Arc*, December 30, 1795), a translation from Schiller under the title *Cabal and Love* (February 11, 1795), various works by Isaac D'Israeli, Godwin's *Political Justice*, Bentham's *Supply without Burthen*, Mungo Park's *Travels in the Interior Part of Africa*, and in the early months of 1791 new editions of Burke's *Reflections* and Paine's *Rights of Man*. Cooke's announcement on December 2, 1795, of his cheap editions of select novels is an interesting guide to contemporary taste in fiction. It may be also noted that Leigh and Sotheby frequently advertised their book sales (see February 2, 1795, and elsewhere), and that books, usually those printed by F. and C. Rivington, were advertised for sale at Hatchard's and Son, 173, Piccadilly (November 13, 1799).

Short " wants " and " offers " were printed on the front page. Hosiery (ancle socks, night caps, muff linings, under-waistcoats, feet-baskets, mittens, &c.), furs, calicoes, stout dimities, cambricks and bombazeens were advertised by Cheapside houses. Lottery prospectuses are frequent. Medicines by Mr Newbery, Dr Steers, Dr Watson and others are a constant temptation. To readers " curious in Fish Sauce, Essence of Anchovies." Mr T. Young, the inventor, also offers Dutch Hyacinths and Double Roman Narcissus. Mr Burgess offers to the Curious in Sallad Oil a range of Vinegars. Reeves's Colours for the Polite Art of Drawing were made known in the first and second columns of the page. The rest of the space was given to Ward Notices of the City of

London and to announcements of the forthcoming meetings of
genteel associations, such as the London Library Society (Dinner
on the table at Four o'clock). At the back of the paper in the
small spaces the thorough servant (who can also send plain victuals
to table well dressed) was advertised for. The large spaces were
occupied by Mr Christie and other capital estate agents. The conventional position for the domestic notices under the heading,
" Births, Married, Died," was at the end of the news, above mails,
ship news, price of stocks and high water at London Bridge. It is
doubtful whether the announcements of Marriages, &c., were
paid for. Care was necessary in the collection of the particulars.
A notice of April 7, 1792, reads :

It has become a very frequent practice of late, to send an account
of Marriages and Deaths to the different papers, which prove untrue.
Two marriages were sent to this paper on Friday, and were inserted in
all the other morning prints, which have been since contradicted. We
rejected their insertion. It now becomes us now to declare again,
that in future, no Marriages or Deaths will be inserted in this Paper
unless properly authenticated.

In addition to the notices properly displayed in the advertising
spaces, *The Times* printed, increasingly after 1789, " puffs " set out
in the style of the news paragraphs. Notices of Dancing Lessons
(Louvre, Cotillions, Hornpipe, Devonshire Minuet), Beauty treat-
ments and Lotteries constantly appeared towards the end of the
editorial portion.

Longer and more numerous articles of dramatic criticism began
to be accommodated in the daily journals of the twenty years
preceding the foundation of the *Daily Universal Register*. The
dramatic reviews were balanced by periodically recurring advertisements. There is no doubt that the criticisms may be properly
regarded as of commercial inspiration, designed to support the
advertisements. Green Room paragraphs were concocted for the
express purpose of puffing actors in the plays in which they
appeared. On the other hand, details of casts were competed for by
the more enterprising journals and copied by their inferiors with
less exigent readers. The *Gazetteer* of 1767 secured a priority
of theatrical intelligence by payment, and the *Public Advertiser*
followed its example ; both these were profitable journals, in a
position by themselves. Henry Woodfall on behalf of the *Public
Advertiser* paid Drury Lane £64 8s. 6d., Covent Garden £66 11s.,
and the other play-houses £100 during one year for early copies of

the casts. The *Public Advertiser* specialized in dramatic intelligence, the Woodfalls having a family interest in the theatre. The *London Packet*, founded in 1770, was directed by a Board of Proprietors which included David Garrick and George Colman. It was freely alleged that by so closely identifying themselves with the newspapers the managers were able to prevent the appearance of any word of criticism. Quarrels occurred now and then, and led to open condemnation of the managers ; on the whole, however, the entertainment industry was too fruitful a source of advertising revenue and dramatic news to be alienated.

Theatrical dictation took on a political side when Sheridan entered the House of Commons. An idea of his strongly personal power over the Press may be gleaned from a paragraph in Cobbett's *The Political Proteus, A View of the Public Character and Conduct of R. B. Sheridan Esquire* (London 1804).

There is [he writes in an open letter to Sheridan] and always has been in this country a natural alliance, a sort of family compact between the press and the theatre ; and therefore when the chief of the latter happens to deal in politics as well as plays, his political adversaries, unless they have the good luck to deal in plays, combat him at a fearful disadvantage. But you, Sir, from some quality I suppose, more than commonly amiable, have long had the press, in all its branches, completely at your command.

Cobbett (p. 206) gives as an instance the incident of the well-known Delpini, who took action for alleged plagiarism of a pantomime trick against Sheridan.

It was tried in open court, and was precisely that sort of ridiculous thing which newspaper writers thirst for, as the panting pilgrim thirsts for the brook ; your influence was sufficient effectually to prevent its appearance in print, and it has never appeared, from that day to this, in any one of the London prints.

Although Sheridan's position was singular, it was singular in its strength and not peculiar in itself. The old custom was so strong during the last quarter of the eighteenth century that the *Daily Universal Register* inevitably respected its terms. The probability is that the puffs supplied by the managers were paid for at profitable rates. On the other hand, the advertisements giving the casts which were displayed on the front page were inserted against payment only of the stamp duty. John Walter's respect for theatrical puffs, as a source of revenue, was one of the causes which led him partially to disinherit his son, John, who

48

determined to relax the influence, political or other, which the manager had acquired by 1803.[1]

While responsibility for the contents of the paper fell upon the Conductor, it was prudent, proprietors found, to employ an " ostensible editor," one who, as the phrase went, would " officiate in the capacity of editor " to a journal. Such an editor gave general oversight to the columns, wrote paragraphs and took as much responsibility as was delegated to him by the Conductor. The Printer-Conductor, or the Printer only, was bound by law to take ultimate responsibility, for he was sued by aggrieved parties. The editor, however, was an important functionary in journals which subsisted, to any extent, upon personal gossip. From the beginning readers of daily newspapers had enjoyed scandalous paragraphs. Topham and Bell in the *World* set a new standard in personal detraction which *The Times* exerted itself to surpass. There was money as well as entertainment in the system of paragraphing practised at this time. The subject was often informed previously by the journal's agent that a paragraph was in type, and it was hinted to him that the paragraph need not appear if a sum, known as the suppression fee, were paid. If the subject of the paragraph had not been reached before publication, a cutting was sent him with a hint that room could be found for any " statement." Inclusion of the second paragraph was delayed until a payment, known as the " contradiction fee," was forth-coming. The person who officiated in the capacity of an editor managed these important business matters on behalf of his paper. Hence the personal paragraph was regarded by journalists as an essential concomitant of the liberty of the Press.

The ill-repute in which journalists were held until *The Times* had established its independence derives in great measure from the suppression and contradiction system. *The Times* on February 6, 1789, reports an incident in which the Proprietor was himself visited and challenged by the aggrieved subject of one of his paragraphs. On February 4, Charles Smith, brother of Mrs. Fitzherbert, after vainly seeking John Walter at Printing House Square, proceeded to Piccadilly, where he demanded of him whether he was the editor of *The Times*. " The question seeming to *command*, rather than *solicit* an answer," Mr. Walter replied that " it was not usual to satisfy such interrogatories." Upon this, Mr. Smith announced that if he saw any more

[1] See the letter of Sheridan to John Walter junior, pp. 92-3.

49

scurrilous notices of his sister he would punish the editor. Mr. Walter, in reply, observed " that it was not the habit of *The Times* to treat any Lady with disrespect," &c., &c. The paper's notice of the visit concluded :

Whether this kind of *bravado* conduct in Mr. Smith, will have any influence upon the spirited truths sent to *The Times* for publication, either respecting Mrs. Fitzherbert, or any other public character, its future conduct will shew.—At present we shall only say that we are not to be TERRIFIED.

The incident was reported in a conspicuous position. It will have been noticed that Mr. Walter declined to answer the question whether or not he was the editor of *The Times*. Incidents of this sort encouraged the conductors of a certain type of newspaper to employ an " ostensible " editor.

Mrs. Wells who, as Topham's mistress and from time to time herself conductor of the *World*, was acquainted with many of the personalities in contemporary journalism, reports the payment of a suppression fee to the editor of *The Times*. After her desertion by Topham, Mrs. Wells married one Sumbel. Her own notoriety and the singularity of this union gave the Press much entertainment. The paragraphers of *The Times* particularly occupied themselves with the matter, indulging in a style intolerable by present-day standards. Mrs. Wells affirms that Mr. Finey officiated in the capacity of editor of *The Times* at the period of her marriage to Sumbel in 1797. Paragraphs in the paper pressed so heavily upon Mr. Sumbel's feelings that he desired Mr. Finey to call upon him. Mr. Sumbel then requested that he would not annoy him any more, and, " pulling out from his escritoire a large parcel of notes, he handed him over a few saying to him, ' Will that be enough ? ' " According to Mrs. Wells, Mr. Finey replied, " Give me a few more and by St Patrick I will knock out the brains of anyone in our office who dare even *whisper* your name."[1] Mrs. Wells adds that Finey died suddenly soon afterwards.

It can hardly be doubted that in the period of John Walter and William Walter, *i.e.*, 1785-1802, contradiction and suppression fees, or some part of them, assisted the revenues of *The Times*, at least when the income from advertisements, puffs and sales of copies was found insufficient. When William Walter became managing editor on John Walter's retirement to Teddington in

[1] *Memoirs of the Life of Mrs. Sumbel, late Wells* (London, 1811, Vol. II., pp. 218-219).

1795, the system of accepting fees may have been dropped, but the little evidence available tells rather in the opposite direction. And the contradiction fee was by no means relinquished by other London journals of the early nineteenth century.

There was another source of revenue from 1789 to 1799. John Walter I received during these years an allowance from the Treasury of £300 a year in " reward for the politics " of *The Times*. Of this, and of its relation to the common practice of the age, more is said in the next chapter.

IV

THE TIMES IN POLITICS

THE younger Pitt became Prime Minister in the year and month that John Walter first wrote from Queen Square to Benjamin Franklin about his syllabic printing, before the decision to set up a press had been taken. At a general election in 1784 Pitt, whose Parliamentary position had hitherto been precarious, obtained an overwhelming majority. Such large open constituencies as existed in those days of pocket boroughs voted almost unanimously against any return of the unnatural coalition between North and Fox, and in favour of the courageous and incorruptible young Minister in whom the King had placed his confidence. A newspaper, started in the following year, and claiming, as the *Daily Universal Register* and after it *The Times* claimed, to be a better interpreter of public opinion than all its rivals, might be expected to rally to his support. Pitt's friends saw in the new journal, as yet unattached, an opportunity of which advantage should be taken when the moment came. The newcomer to journalism himself sought the favours of the King and the Administration. John Walter failed to become Printer to the Stationery Office, but in 1787 secured the appointment of Printer to H.M. Customs. In November, 1788, Pitt's position was menaced by the King's insanity. It was understood that, should a Regency become necessary, the Prince of Wales, as Regent, would dismiss the Prime Minister in favour of Fox. This situation gave the Press particular importance, and John Walter received additional favours in return for general support and the insertion of supplied paragraphs written against the Prince's claims.

Pitt's campaign was managed from the Treasury, and the arrangement bound Walter to the insertion of paragraphs marked with a distinguishing sign. Unexpected and, for him, most unfortunate consequences followed. As the only serious political principle entertained by John Walter was support of the Ministry, there was nothing to prevent his giving himself enthusiastically to a cause which supported him and to which he looked for further advantage. During the winter of 1788-9 *The Times* was conspicuous among the London dailies for devotion to the King's Government and for opposition to giving unlimited powers to a Regency. When, in February, 1789, it was announced and certified that the King's mind was as sane as it had ever been, there was an outburst of national jubilation, and *The Times* printed article after article attacking the partisans of the Prince. Its rejoicings were shown in lines of capitals, in italic epigrams and in displayed verses. The reader was asked " to determine to which Paper he ought to give credit—to The TIMES which, through the whole of this important and melancholy state of the Kingdom, had preserved its fidelity to its Sovereign, and its character for AUTHENTIC INFORMATION to the Public—or to those low, scurrilous, misinformed Opposition Prints. . . ." Clearly the Proprietor was well satisfied at this period, and considered his place firmly established. During the same spring he completed plans for the establishment of the *Evening Mail*, to be issued on Monday, Wednesday and Friday evenings in each week from March 2. But, despite his confidence, he was nearing the incident in his journalistic career of which he never ceased—and with justice—to complain.

On February 21, 1789, *The Times* contained the following paragraph :

The Royal Dukes, and the leaders of opposition in general, affect to join with the friends of our amiable Sovereign, in rejoicing on account of His Majesty's recovery. But the insincerity of their joy is visible. Their late unfeeling conduct will forever tell against them ; and contradict the artful professions they may think it prudent to make.

It argues infinite wisdom in certain persons, to have prevented the Duke of York from rushing into the King's apartment on Wednesday. The rashness, the Germanick severity, and the insensibility of this young man, might have proved ruinous to the hopes and joys of a whole nation.

The story about the Duke of York may or may not have been true ; but the general effect of the paragraph was fully justified. The conduct of the Prince and the Duke, of the Opposition leaders and the Whig ladies, during the King's illness, had scandalized the nation ; and the recollection of their proceedings heightened the enthusiasm with which the King's return to reason was hailed.

This popular effervescence reached its height on April 23, when the King went to St Paul's Cathedral to return thanks for his recovery. Not until it had died down, and, in fact, four months after the publication of the paragraph, did Walter receive a Bill of Indictment directed at the instance of H.R.H. the Duke of York. Then, on June 16, *The Times* printed a column or more of justification, charging the party and not the Duke with attacking the liberty of the Press :

Temptation often held out its golden prospects to make us desert the King, and support his Opponents ; and when Bribes were found ineffectual, Threats were used as Compulsory Arguments. . . .

These " golden prospects " had been offered by the Whigs, and John Walter had reason for crediting himself with resistance to temptation. The chances during the King's illness were so much in favour of Fox becoming Prime Minister that Pitt was prepared to return to the Bar for a livelihood. Between the publication of this vindicatory article and the trial of the action, *The Times* warned the public that the Opposition Party were buying newspapers directly, appointing purchasers of shares in newspapers in order to secure indirect control, and watching for opportunities to prosecute newspapers they could influence neither directly nor indirectly. On June 23 was printed a new indictment filed by the Prince of Wales for a paragraph in the issue of February 26 expressing sentiments similar to those in the earlier passage on the Duke of York. The Duke's action duly came to trial on July 11. Mr. Kelly, clerk of King's Bench, proved that he had purchased a copy of *The Times* on February 21 at Mr. Walter's in Piccadilly, in a public shop with the name " Walter " written over the door. Answering a question, Kelly said he had seen Mr. Walter in his shop before and since the time he had bought the paper, behind the counter, with his hat off. Walter then was prosecuted as the Bookseller of 169 Piccadilly.

He defended himself as the representative of *The Times*, not as author, printer or publisher of it or the offending paragraphs. In a written statement he pleaded guilty in the eye of the law to publishing a libel, but submitted himself to consideration as well as to sentence. The difficulties which a newspaper encountered, and the hurry inseparable from its composition and make-up, induced unwitting error. Also a proprietor, under the necessity of employing assistance, was unable to control every detail. These paragraphs " were inserted at a time of dreadful tumult and confusion," at " a period in which moderation was considered as a contemptible virtue." Walter stated that he received *no* reward whatever for giving insertion to such paragraphs. They were such as the temper of the day required. Unless newspapers contained what the temper of the day required, they would be read by none but the printer, and the trade would therefore become useless.

Sir Thomas Erskine, who conducted the prosecution, replied that he was in a state of extreme astonishment and wonder at this defence ; to reflect upon what John Walter had said was " enough to confound the reason of man." The imputation of profligacy to the Duke of York was monstrous ; the giving him a character below the rank of brute unpardonable. Moreover, why, when the defendant entered his statement, did he not swear to it ? Against Walter's statement that he had not been rewarded for the insertion of these paragraphs, counsel implied that it was known the paragraphs were supplied under an arrangement with political persons. Erskine added : " If he had sworn that he was misled to insert this unprincipled and infamous calumny, the Court must have sent him to Bedlam instead of a prison."

Mr. Justice Ashhurst, giving sentence, regretted that some things had fallen from the defendant which were very imprudent. " He had attempted to justify his conduct upon the principle of the necessity of the times ; there never could exist any necessity for such calumny ; nor could courts of justice ever admit of the defendant's conduct, and allow him to pick up a destructive weapon, and use a libel by way of set off to the offence of others ; nor could the defendant be allowed to write libels upon those whom he thinks wrong in their political opinions, and whom he chuses to call the other party. The Court could hear nothing of parties, but must punish those who write scandalous and defamatory libels." The sentence of the Court therefore was

That John Walter do pay a fine of fifty pounds.

That he be imprisoned in Newgate one year.

That he do stand in and upon the pillory, at Charing Cross, for one hour, between twelve and three o'clock in the day time.

That he do give security for his good behaviour for seven years, himself in five hundred pounds, and two securities in one hundred pounds each.

Walter was conducted to Newgate. The sentence took effect from November 23, 1789. On November 24, 1790, *The Times* chronicled the expiration of the year's imprisonment for the first libel :

Yesterday the term of imprisonment expired, to which the Court of King's Bench sentenced MR WALTER, for what the Court construed to be a libel against the Duke of York.—The Pillory, which was part of the sentence was graciously remitted by his Majesty. At the same period, however, another year's imprisonment commenced, to which he was also sentenced for what the Court construed to be a libel against His Royal Highness the Prince of Wales.

Thus John Walter was due for release from his second term in November, 1791. It will be admitted that he behaved stoutly, in the most trying circumstances, towards those who in Erskine's phrase had " misled " him into inserting the paragraphs. It cannot be further admitted, in spite of the victim's claim, that he was a martyr to the cause. " Expecting remuneration," he wrote to Lord Kenyon (July 6, 1799), " I gave up no author." For years, as he told the same nobleman, he hoped to be given an appointment to print for Government. Why he came to publish the offending lines, and how he worked out his sentence, are explicitly described in several letters sent to Ministers and others seeking for a reduction in his sentence or an improvement in his conditions. He wrote at length to Bland Burges, whom he knew as Under-Secretary for Foreign Affairs :

Newgate February 1, 1790
Sir,
Little did I ever expect ever to be an inhabitant of this vile receptacle or that any political sin would doom me to so severe a sentence. I am the more astonished when I daily read in the Opposition prints the most atrocious libels and treasonable paragraphs against those who gave birth to my prosecutors and yet without notice. Even Almon, convicted before my time for a most atrocious paragraph against the whole family and the throne, escaped without being brought to judgment. I am ordered up again on Wednesday to receive sentence on the informations on the Prince of Wales and the Duke of Clarence—the measure of my sufferings may be full. Had I not listened to Mr Bearcroft's advice who made a defence on trial versus the Duke of York, and not permitted judgment to go by default—I could doubtless have been at this moment at liberty and not been trapped in my present situation. I was one of the jury who tried Junius's letters to the king

56

twenty years since, and under a similar evidence the printer of the *St James's Evening* was acquitted as the jury did not choose to vest a power in the Court to give a sentence which might have incriminated him of having wilfully, maliciously and seditiously published the papers when only the mere sale in the common course of his business was proved.

I cannot help complaining of the little attention shewn me where I have the greatest right to expect it, both before and since my cruel imprisonment. I am now going into the twelfth week of my martyrdom, without the least dawn of flattering expectation. I should not have troubled you with these remarks had it not been at the same time to suggest a hardship experienced in this prison and which, as I observe in my paper you intend to introduce a Bill for the regulation of jails, may be worth observation.

Newgate was undoubtedly a receptacle for felons, though it is the fashion of the Court at present to extend it to misdemeanours by which means we are subject to more solitary confinement than felons guilty of murder. Though I am confined to what is called the State side, and, paying for a room, have one to myself, the same entrance leads likewise to the felons and whenever any are brought into the jail, the outward door is shut and they are fettered in the common passage, so that it discourages my friends from access—such is the audacity of the turn-keys that they will frequently keep them and those who bring my provisions an hour at the door, even when they are lolling in their chairs in an adjoining room, because several people shall collect together; and what is still worse at 8 o'clock I am locked up every evening in common with the felons after which time no soul is permitted to have a person with them. At the King's Bench the doors are opened till 10 o'clock with liberty to have servants to attend them of night, but here were a person ever so ill they might call their hearts out before any assistance could be procured. Judge, then, what a man must feel who has only lately enjoyed even the luxuries of life. If any remarks here made are of use, though they will hardly avail me, yet I have so much philanthropy they may be serviceable to others hereafter; as such I submit them to your consideration, and am, with the greatest regard,

Your obliged and grateful servant

JOHN WALTER.

Bland Burges sent this letter to Sir Thomas Erskine, who had conducted Walter's prosecution, and who was Attorney-General to that " exalted character " the Prince of Wales. Mrs. Knox, a daughter of John Walter, appealed to the Prince of Wales, drawing attention to her father's ill-heath and desiring the Prince's intervention. According to Erskine, the Prince was afraid of seeming officially to interfere with the exercise of the King's prerogative. At any rate, it was some time before intercession from his side became effective. In the interval Walter addressed himself to Lord Hawkesbury in a letter of great importance in the history of Governmental dealings with the Press. It narrates the precise circumstances in which Walter came to accept the paragraphs for publication :

Newgate, March 2, 1790.

My Lord,

I write your Lordship as a Cabinet Minister, whose long Experience in the affairs of State makes you competent to judge of the Services of others, & who I am sensible are ever open to render Justice to their Complaints.

It has been my Misfortune from the steady Support I have several years past render'd my Sovereign & his Administration through the Channel of the *Times* daily paper, to feel the Weight of an opprobrious Sentence, from the Resentment of an Opposition, who have sheilded themselves under the names of the Princes, & I have incurr'd the penalties of £250—to be imprison'd 2 years in this vile Receptacle, to be set in the Pillory, & at the End of the Term to find security myself in £500, & 2 Sureties of £100 each to keep the Peace 7 years.

This severe Judgment of the Court arises from my Fidelity to Government, & Regard to my Honour, in not betraying those by whose Directions those Paragraphs were inserted for which I suffer, & as I have been cruelly neglected, I consider it highly necessary that some of the Members of the Privy Council should be acquainted with my Case, that I may feel that speedy Relief which Humanity will dictate, the Equity of the Case demands from those, in whose cause I have so long lost my Liberty, & the Justice of that Remuneration I naturally expect for my Sufferings.

Happening to be at the Treasury the beginning of last year, Mr. Steele call'd Me into his Room, & after paying Me some Compliments on the Stability of my Conduct, at a Time when other Papers were veering round to the rising Sun[1] ; made Me an offer of £300 a year, to support the Measures of Government, which I acquiesc'd in, as the *Times* was entirely under my control, & the Paper will bear Testimony of my Zeal & Duty to the Sovereign & his Ministers ; though it is well known I was offer'd £4000 for ½ the Paper, and could have been appointed Printer to the Regent.

[1] Allusion is made to the Prince Regent.

Though £300 a year was to be my Reward for the politics of the Paper, when it is consider'd that I lost all the Advertisements & Civilities of Opposition, I doubt any real Profit arose from it ; but what will your Lordship say, when I relate, that as by Mr. Steele's Directions I was to insert such Paragraphs &c as were sent Me under the Signature &, & that 2 of them are those I now suffer 2 years Imprisonment, & the sentence of the Pillory for, & that neither pending the Prosecutions or since, have I receiv'd the least Advice or Assistance except £30 & £50 towards defraying the Law Proceedings, by the Person who actually was employ'd in writing the Paragraphs.

After Judgment was pronounc'd at the Suit of the Duke of York, & having let it go by Default on the Informations of the Prince of Wales & Duke of Clarence, I thought it respectful, as the Princes had taken offence to send each of them a petition to remit Punishment, & stop Proceedings, it had not, however, the desir'd Effect in one instance, as the Duke of York did not pardon, or the Prince of Wales & Duke of Clarence remit prosecution.

As soon as the last Sentences were pronounc'd, I sent a petition to the King, through Mr. Grenville's office, for his Majesty's Pardon, but though it is over a Month ago, & 15 Weeks I have been confin'd in this horrible Bastile (fit only for Murderers & Felons) I have receiv'd no Tidings to relieve my anxious Moments, nor the least Comfort of any other Nature, but am abandon'd to ruin, disgrace, & infamy as far as the Sentence of the Law can convey the Idea, torn from my Family, my business left to mercenaries, my Health suffering from Confinement in a noxious Prison, where I am lock'd in every Night at 8 o'Clock. A Wife & 6 children left expos'd to the World & its Calumny, the con-nexions my two eldest Daughters were forming in Life blasted, & Anxiety of being exhibited to the Scoff of Mankind from the oppro-brious Sentence of the *Pillory*, which has degraded a character superiour to the Adversity of a Fortune I lost in the American War, & am levell'd among the most abandon'd of Mankind for my Fidelity & attachment —without a Sixpence for the extraordinary Expences I am at. The Assistance necessary to cheque my several Undertakings as a Printer & Bookseller, to oversee my Morng & Evening Papers, & the want of Controul which has sensibly hurt my Business already ; nor have I the least Promise of Remuneration to console my solitary Hours, and a Debt accumulating at Stamp Office, from the slow Proceedings of those I employ to lessen it, by whom I am press'd to discharge it.

This shameful Neglect has induc'd Me to open this matter to the Duke of Richmond, The Duke of Leeds, Mr. Grenville & yourself, as likewise to Lord Kenyon soon after I receiv'd the last Sentence, as from Motives of Delicacy I did not chuse it sooner, & I flatter myself your

Lordship will see the propriety of not extending my Case to the Knowledge of Individuals, who might with my Liberation have a handle to do some Mischief. I cannot have a Doubt, my Lord, that the Members of the Cabinet, who are in possession of these Facts will speedily effect my Pardon, & administer to my Relief, to suppose otherwise would be the strongest Satire on their Justice.

I am, with the greatest Respect
Your Lordship's most faithful,
and Devoted Servant,
JOHN WALTER.

Rt. Hon. Lord Hawkesbury.

Release came at last. Through the intervention of the Prince of Wales, the prisoner was set free before the completion of the second sentence. The *European Magazine* thus notes the fact :

March 7, 1791. This morning Mr Walter was liberated from his confinement in Newgate, in consequence of receiving His Majesty's most generous pardon at the instance of H.R.H. the Prince of Wales after an imprisonment of near sixteen months, of which period one year was the sentence of the Court in the prosecution by the Duke of York. The full term of his sentence was two years with fine and securities.

So ended John Walter's unfortunate experience with the Treasury Press managers. He had been badly treated, but, of course, had nothing to gain by quarrelling with the Government. Pitt's position had improved with the King's health. The Prince did not now seem likely to grasp the reins. Walter could reasonably expect privileges from the Treasury officials responsible for his imprisonment. The buying of journals had by no means ceased during the eighteen months he had spent in Newgate ; and the conductors of other London dailies received in some instances considerably larger subventions than he took as a reward for the politics of *The Times*. The sums paid to writers from Pitt's secret service account include the following[1] :

April 30, 1790	Mr Sayres and Mr Cook writing in the papers	£235
May 1, 1790	Mr Hewardine for same service - -	£100
	Mr Bathie in advance for writing in the papers	£100
Mar. 8, 1791	Mr Field for the papers - - - -	£90
May 17, 1791	Mr Taylor who writes in the papers - -	£100
June 18, 1791	Mr Heriot for writing in the papers - -	£50

[1] The Chatham Papers provide an accurate statement of payments to the Press authorized in 1789, 1790 and 1791. (P.R.O., G.D., 8/229.) The system of paying editors from the Civil List secret service money was continued by Lord Melbourne ; *cf.* Ellice on the *Observer* to Melbourne, September 16, 1840, in Chapter X of the present volume.

John Bell, conductor, proprietor and printer of the *Oracle*, received £200 " for printing and other services." Colonel Topham, who had now given up the Prince, and Mrs. Wells, received £600 for the *World*. The journals in receipt of regular sums from the same source during the years 1790 and 1792[1] were :

The Diary - - - -	£400
St. James's Evening Chronicle - -	£200
London Evening Post - - -	£200
Whitehall Evening Post - - -	£200
The Public Ledger - - -	£100
The World - - - -	£600
The Morning Herald - - -	£600
The Oracle - - - -	£200
The Times - - - -	£300

The secret service accounts for 1792, the year following Walter's release, record the item, " June 1st Mr Walter as a Gift, £250," and Walter's receipt is attached. The " gift " was doubtless intended as a compensation for his imprisonment, beyond the £300 a year first arranged with Thomas Steele in January, 1789. This was paid during his term in Newgate, receipts being then given by William Walter, John's eldest son, who was conducting the paper. A typical receipt in 1792 is thus worded :

Received 29th of August 1792 of Charles Long Esqr Two hundred pounds for the *Times* & *Evening Mail* to the 5 July last.
£200   JOHN WALTER.

The yearly £300 was withdrawn without notice in 1799. It was alleged that *The Times* had printed libels against the House of Commons. The remonstrances of William Walter at the Treasury were in vain. Inquiry elsewhere in Administration circles pointed to the Secretary for War, William Windham, as the instigator of the move against *The Times*. William Walter wrote to him :

Chatham Place, June 1st, 1800.

Sir,

A Gentleman in a very high Department of Government informed me some Time since, that in consequence of a Complaint made by you against a Paragraph inserted in the *Times* a few days previous to the last Prorogation of Parliament, it had been determined to take away a Pension which was granted to my father during the Regency, and which has been continued to him till last midsummer.

1 In some instances paid in advance, in other instances in arrears.

It does not become me, Sir, to make any Observation on the Subject of Complaint ; but I am persuaded you are ignorant of the Manner in which the Pension was granted. It was unasked for ; & it may be in your Recollection that soon after the King's Recovery, my father was imprisoned 15 Months in Newgate on the Prosecution of the Prince of Wales & Duke of York, for two Paragraphs written by Persons employed by Mr. Steele, then Secretary of the Treasury, signed with his private Mark, & still in my father's Possession. I have long known that there were certain Persons, who hold confidential Situations, who think that a fulsome adulation of Ministers is the best Criterion of attachment ; & that no Man has a right to maintain Independence, who enjoys the smallest Degree of emolument from the Government. It is on this account that I suspect your Name has been used in this Business without your knowledge, & I should feel myself much honored either by a personal Interview, or by an Answer to this Letter. It would certainly occasion some Degree of Surprise, Sir, if you had by any Means, much more for a supposed personal Motive, attempted to withdraw a Pension which had been granted to my father as a Reward for Fidelity, & as compensation for actual Sufferings. It is not the value of the Pension, but the Manner in which it has been withdrawn, & the causes assigned, about which I am solicitous.

> I have the Honour to be
>
> Sir
>
> Your obedient humble Servt
>
> W. WALTER.

For answer, the conductor of *The Times* received the following :

To W. Walter.   Park Street, Weston.   June 19th, 1800.

Sir,

I have delayed from time to time to acknowledge the receipt of your letter, doubting whether I ought to reply at all to a letter, containing a question which you were so little authorized to put ; and fearing still more that in giving an answer to that question, I should rather be consulting my own inclinations than conforming to that line which duty and propriety would in strictness prescribe. The answer, however, is so easy that I cannot help giving it.

I never knew of any transactions of yours with the Treasury, nor was apprized of any allowance having been made to you, till I was told it was taken away. It was of consequence not taken away by my desire, nor was it in virtue of any desire of mine, that it is now withheld.

I had read the paragraphs in question, as I took at the time your paper, and continue to take it on account of the manner in which in general French politics are treated. I read it with no great attention, but with enough to satisfy me that it was a gross and indecent breach of the privileges of the House of Commons, and such as in former times would have been made a subject of complaint and punishment, but as that is not the fashion of the present day, and should at any rate have been the act of some one else than myself ; I took no further thought about it, and should have had no wish, as I have not at present, that it should be punished in any way, which, though it might be felt in some degree by you, could not, from the nature of the case, be made to answer any purpose of example.

I am Sir
Your obedient
humble servant
W. WINDHAM.

Windham's letter explains nothing, declares no motives. It seems that the Government suspected the stability of the political professions of *The Times*. On December 16, 1800, Lord Grenville wrote to the Earl of Carysfort, British Ambassador in Berlin :

I have not seen the paragraph in *The Times* of which you speak, but you may say, whenever it can be useful, that *The Times* is a paper which, under cover of a pretended support of Government, is in decided hostility to it.

Before the withdrawal of Government favour and the cancellation of the pension *The Times* received many favours from the Administration. During 1791 and 1792, the period immediately following John Walter's release from Newgate, the paper was in high esteem, and through the Admiralty was enabled to secure news in advance of its competitors.

The French Revolution produced a deep and abiding impression upon London journalism. News from France created a new appetite and a new audience. The flippancy which the *World* had made fashionable and transmitted to the *Morning Herald*, the *Oracle* and *The Times*, was ended by the great upheaval. Tidings of what *The Times* described as the " Rebellion in France " arrived when John Walter was engaged on his defence against the Duke of York. *The Times* was, of course, strongly anti-Jacobin. It exerted itself to the utmost to secure its position, and, rightly divining that news was now essential to a newspaper, procured messages from

Paris, some of which, at least, could justly claim priority over other journals. The messages were given sensational headlines. The heading in *The Times* of October 12, 1789, was unprecedented :

FRANCE.

CONFINEMENT

of the

KING, QUEEN,

and

ROYAL FAMILY,

and

The Attempt to Murder the Queen.

The social implications of the Revolution on this side of the Channel presented a fresh problem to the Government. For the first time, the managers of the Government Press were faced with a growing mass of discontent, much of which was inflamed by ideas imported from France. Correspondence at the Record Office shows that after 1789 the Press activities of Henry Dundas[1] and Evan Nepean were actuated by a new motive, in addition to that of supporting Pitt's personal position. The French Revolution created fears of " sedition," which drove Dundas to make diligent inquiry into the writers, printers and publishers of pamphlets and newspapers. They were genuine fears, and the concern of Ministers descended to the Addingtons, who took office upon Pitt's resignation in 1801. The importance of the Press was growing, that is, the number of papers and the total of their issues were growing ; and the influence of the increased volume of printed matter upon the public was very serious. A closer relation with commercial advertising required political suasion to be less direct. The proprietors were noticeably more independent towards Government. Moreover, the steady growth of the printing industry, resulting in the establishment of new presses in various parts of the country, helped into print the ideas of the new Radical pamphleteers. It is difficult to believe that English journals would accept subsidies from French sources at this date, but the assertion of William

[1] Henry Dundas, first Viscount Melville.

Augustus Miles, a careful writer, is hardly without foundation. Miles, writing to Charles Long, one of the Treasury officials engaged in Press management, says on September 24, 1792 :

I have had several hints at different times from Frenchmen in constant relation and intimacy with M. de Chauvelin and his family, that the editors of the *Morning Chronicle* and of the *Argus* have received considerable sums of money, and that they have each of them a large monthly allowance. I have no doubt of the fact, and wish it could be proved in Westminster Hall, and the purpose for which the money is paid. This I know, that the personal attendance of the parties in Portman Square is constant. All this perfidy and meanness in men who might serve the cause of liberty and of letters disgust me more and more with political literature.[1]

Official counter-propaganda was difficult with an impoverished exchequer ; but even if the Government were disposed to inaction, certain Ministers insisted that money would need to be spent on printers, and always there were writers begging for Government employment. Accordingly the anti-Jacobin cause was driven to employ pamphleteers and newspaper men. *The Times* was among the newspapers directly associated with the Administration, and Walter also placed the columns of his thrice-weekly publication, the *Evening Mail*, at Government disposal. His imprisonment strengthened Walter's claim, and he was able to secure for *The Times* valuable privileges in money and in priority of news. For some time the arrangement worked satisfactorily to both sides.

The practice of conveying news items to a favourite journal was bound to antagonize the other Administration papers. Sensible advice on this point was tendered to the authorities by Charles Stuart, playwright and brother of Daniel Stuart, owner of the *Morning Post* and the *Courier*. At the end of 1793 Charles Stuart communicated his opinions (marked " secret " and now first printed) to his official employer, unnamed, but obviously Henry Dundas. Stuart, in pay as a disseminator of ideas, to the tune of £200 a year, objected to the prevailing custom of favouring *The Times* :

I am afraid [he says] that Government are proceeding on a wrong plan. They do not consider that by *monopolising* Intelligence to a Morning and an Evening Paper, they render the other papers hostile

---

[1] *Correspondence of William Augustus Miles*, 2 vols., I, 333-4 (Longmans, 1890). Lewis Goldsmith, not then such a respectable authority, made a similar charge against the unnamed English journals. " Portman Square " is a reference to the French Embassy then at that address. Chauvelin was the Ambassador.

F

to them—papers, too, that are really devoted to them. . . . They do not consider that while Government is pleased and most highly flattered by an article of intelligence which is in no other of the Morning Papers but one—that at the same time there are thousands of pamphlets circulated on that day primed with lasting materials that totally destroy that ephemera of the day.

Stuart proceeds to insist upon a point which may or may not have been acted upon in England, but which Dundas certainly realized in Scotland :

They do not consider that while they circulate *news*, the others circulate *sentiments*. While Government circulates an evanescent cloud, the others circulate a shower that falls and nourishes and brings forth fruit.

To a Government struggling to achieve stabilization in the aftermath of the French Revolution this was an apt hint. Upon Pitt's resignation in 1801, the Addingtons did endeavour to circulate sentiments rather than news. Stuart urges that :

The truth is, everything is to be managed, by managing the press. The artillery of the French could be not managed a month without they managed the artillery of the press. I look upon the press as flint to a gun, or potfire to a cannon. Whenever I hear of a French victory, I in general ascribe it to their artful circulation of journals and bulletins throughout every municipality in every department. . . . When I hear of the French casting *cannon*, I think nothing of that at all, provided you can only prevent them from casting types. . . .

Stuart's memorandum concluded, as might be expected, with a wholehearted recommendation of his own services :

I firmly believe, without any vanity, that I know as much in the engineering of the press, as any press engineer in Britain.

An excellent specimen of the propaganda of ideas is furnished in *The Times* of December 6, 1794. A notice under the sub-title gave readers the following explanation of the curiosity within their hands :

At a period when Revolutions are so much the general topic of conversation, it may not be unentertaining to the reader of the *Old Times*, to take a peep into what would, most probably, be the diurnal news of a *New Times*, should such a misfortune as a *Change of Constitution* take place in this country.

The New Times.

FIRST YEAR *of the* REPUBLIC, ONE AND INDIVISIBLE. | SATURDAY, JUNE 10, 1800. | PRICE ONE SHILLING *in* SPECIE; *or*, FIVE SHILLINGS *in* PAPER.

OPERA.

THEATRE OF EQUALITY.

THIS EVENING will be presented, for the first time, a new Opera, called,

The MITRE in JEOPARDY;

Or, *The Triumph of* CIVISM *over* RELIGION.

Under the direction of *Citizen* PRIESTLEY.

The Music by the celebrated Authors of *Ca Ira*; and the *Marseillois Hymn*.

After the Opera will be performed the favourite Ballet, which had such a popular run at Paris, called,

THE MARCH OF THE CLERGY TO BEDLAM.

ARCHBISHOP OF CANTERBURY, Citizen *Paine* (being his first public appearance in this nation since the year 1792); ARCHBISHOP OF YORK, Citizen *Skirving* (being his first public appearance since his return from Botany Bay); BISHOP OF DURHAM, Citizen *Winterbottom*; and BISHOP OF LONDON, Citizen *Fysche Palmer* (being his first public appearance since his return from transportation.)

A *Pas Deux* will be introduced between the first and second Act, called *Sedition on Foot*, by Citizen *Hamilton Rowan* and the Female Citizen *Desfon*.

The Characters will be all dressed in the modern *Sans Culotte* fashion, and the whole will conclude with the enthusiastic Song and Chorus of *Ca Ira*.

Pit, 5s. in Money, or 1l. in Paper Currency; First Gallery, 4s. in Money, or 16s. in Paper. Second Gallery, 2s. 6d. in Money, or 10s. in Paper.

*** It is expected that Ladies and Gentlemen will come full dressed to the Pit in red Caps and Bonnets; and that the Patriotic *Sans Culottes* will scrape their shoes at the door, and wear clean shirts. A Woman attends at the door to take care of the Female Citizens pattens. Those of the first requisition, who come in chaise carts, are desired to order the carter to set down with the horses heads towards the *Permanent Guillotine* at Charing-Cross.

Good Small Beer, Gin, and Water, and other elegant refreshments, will be prepared in the Anti room.

Vivant Equality and Republicanism.

THEATRE OF THE SANS CULOTTES, *ci-devant* ROYALTY THEATRE, *Saltpetre-bank, Wapping.*

THIS EVENING the Theatre will open for the first time, with an entire new Entertainment, called,

THE CHIMNEY SWEEPER'S APOTHEOSIS

The Music and Scenery entirely new.

The whole to conclude with a *Solo* on the Salt-box; and the favourite *Marseillois Hymn*, with Marrowbones and Cleavers.

MEETING OF BANKERS.

A GENERAL MEETING of all the BANKERS of the City of London, will be held this day, the 11th of June, at One o'Clock precisely, at the London Tavern. The Dividend to be made to the Creditors will be then finally determined upon. The Head Clerks of all the Bankers killed in the late massacre will be allowed to present the accounts of their *ci-devant Principals*.

SECURITY.

CITIZEN MENDOZA, the TWO SONS of the late BIG BEN, and Five other Citizens of equal reputation, propose to all persons who may wish to visit their friends or acquaintance within the Bills of Mortality, to escort them through the streets. Their prices during the day are, for a single guard, One Guinea per mile; by night, 1l. 16s. They also attend *in mass*, at the rate of 20 Guineas for the 24 hours.

N. B. The Advertisers will not be answerable for accidents by fire-arms, or brick-bats from the tops of houses.

To BUILDERS.

ANY CITIZEN wishing to purchase that Spot of Ground on which stood the Houses lately demolished in Home Tooke Square, (*ci-devant* Grosvenor Square) are desired to send in their Proposals to Citizen HARDY, President of the Committee for the sale of the Effects of the Nobility.

CITIZEN HOPPING, of Aldgate, Shoemaker, informs the Public, that in order to supply the deficiency of leather, which at the present moment is become very scarce, he offers to their notice, his new invented Shoes, made of wood, in which he has endeavoured to combine, as much as possible, elegance with convenience. He is just arrived from Paris, where he worked for several Members of the Convention, and means to remain but a short time in this Capital.

To PROPRIETORS.

To-morrow will be published, by Order of the Executive Power,

A Very accurate EXPLANATION of the PRINCIPLES upon which the FORCED LOAN is to be established.

It may be agreeable, in the mean time, to many Proprietors, to know, that by the most exact arithmetical calculations, the FORCED LOAN will not, in the first instance, absorb more than 13-20ths of their capital; and that, if it should be found necessary afterwards to make some trifling addition, by way of a voluntary Loan, it can never exceed 16-20ths of their whole property.

This interesting Publication is to be found at Citizen Eaton's.

CHEAP ORDINARY.

CITIZEN WELTJIE, *ci-devant* Purveyor at CARLTON HOUSE, now *Barrere-Place*, and who is just arrived from Paris, informs all Republican Citizens that he has just taken and fitted up in the *Sans Culotte* style, that large House, formerly called WHITE'S, in HORNE TOOKE Street, *ci-devant* ST. JAMES'S Street, where there will be an Ordinary every day on the cheapest scale, from 12 at Noon until 11 at Night. *Soup Maigre, Frogs fricassé, Garlic Broth*, and other Carmagnol Soups at all hours. *Skins of Beef* and *Ox Cheeks* baked at 1 o'Clock, with Leek and Parsley Pies, in the Cornish style. *Buttock of Beef* boiled, *a la mode de Paris*, and roast Mutton at 2 o'Clock, with hard Dumplings and Peas Pudding. Excellent small French Wines, which are much wholesomer than heavy Porter. The Bread is made with leaven, in order to give it a fine French acidity.

To PARENTS and GUARDIANS.

THE Female Citizen HONORA GOODWILL informs the Public, that she has taken a house in a healthy situation, near Hounslow, which she has fitted up for the reception of a few young Ladies, and educating them in the truest principles of pure Republicanism. Parents who choose to trust their children to her care, may be persuaded great attention will be paid to prevent their minds from being tinctured with any foolish religious superstition; Nature's laws alone will be their guide, and Reason and Philosophy the sole object of their daily worship. Such being the outlines of the plan, she hopes she may promise that the young persons entrusted to her care, will in a very short time acquire that Republican energy, so preferable to the silly timidity, which was one of the female characteristics during the reign of despotism.

BRITISH NATIONAL CONVENTION.

SITTING OF THE 9th OF JUNE.

PRESIDENT CITIZEN TELWELL.

President.—" It is my duty, Citizen Legislators, to lay before you some letters of importance, which I have received this day; you will there see to what a height the public spirit has arrived, and the astonishing progress which our regeneration has made in every part of Great-Britain."

The Secretary then read:

" CITIZEN PRESIDENT,

Nottingham, June 8.

" I am this moment arrived from a patriotic expedition, the success of which has filled the minds of all the friends of the people with joy and exultation.

" Too long has the soil of Nottinghamshire groaned under the oppressive weight of four immense edifices, and its humble inhabitants been insulted by their disgusting magnificence. *Welbeck, Thoresby, Clumber*, and *Worksop*, could no longer be permitted to exist in the land of equality. A band of chosen *Sans Culottes* proceeded from Nottingham, and, with an energy worthy of the confidence placed in them, passed the plane of the revolution over these ostentatious and useless mansions. The flames did the rest.

" I send to the Convention, as a patriotic gift, all the plate of the *ci devant* proprietors, that could be preserved in the general confusion.

" D*NN**N,

" Mayor of Nottingham."

LIST OF PLATE:

Three silver spoons, two soup ditto, and one shoe-buckle.

The reading of this letter was frequently interrupted by applauses from the galleries; and the Assembly ordered honourable mention to be made of it in the minutes.

Read the following letter from Sheffield, dated June 9.

Liberty! Equality! Sans-culotism for ever!

" Citizen President,

" Treason surrounds us, and *terror must be the order of the day*. In pursuance of the orders of the Secret Committee, we have let loose the instruments of national vengeance, and they are now executing their high commission throughout this neighbourhood. Nineteen proud dwellings, and forty-two farm houses have already been destroyed by the flames of patriotism, and one hundred and sixteen fathers of families have received the just punishment of their atrocious crimes. We should have carried still further the glory and terror of the national arms, if the approach of an insolent and desperate individual had not caused us a sudden alarm. The *ci devant* Earl of WINCHELSEA has marched from Rutlandshire, at the head of a considerable number of banditti, known formerly by the name of yeomen. These dangerous men, animated by their fanatical attachment to property, act in concert with the Royalists in Devonshire, and create a great alarm in the minds of our Republican troops. If we do not receive considerable reinforcements, we shall be obliged to evacuate Sheffield, which place, by the bye, swarms with suspicious persons. (Signed)

" YORKE,

" *General of the Armed Citizens of Sheffield.*"

Citizen *Gamage*.—" I have not been able to attend to the reading of this letter before you, without shuddering. How long is it, Citizens, since I first warned you of the danger attending your criminal moderation. You affect to say you are desirous of shewing some respect to virtuous principles, but are you still to learn, that what was virtue under the yoke of despotism, becomes vice under the reign of Equality.—Beware of these men who were formerly the object of public esteem; if you lend an ear to their speeches, their hypocrisy will soon triumph over your civism. They talk of respect for property; obedience to the laws, and the duties of religion, merely to stop the progress of reason, and suspend in its course the torrent of the Revolution. What miseries has not your moderation already heaped upon the patriots! Awake from your lethargy, Citizens, and decree, for once and all, as a principal, that the establishment of the Revolution is incompatible with the respect for property; that it is not by an absurd obedience to the laws, that you can succeed in sapping their foundations; and that the destruction of all superstition is not to be effected by a scrupulous observance of the duties of religion.—(Reiterated applauses.) I propose that ten thousand men shall be chosen from the French auxiliary *Sans Culottes*, and be immediately sent to garrison the town of Sheffield."

Citizen *Martin*.—" I participate heartily in the admiration of the speech of brother *Gamage*; but by what fatality does it always happen, that the best patriot can never join the boldness of conception to the vigour of execution? Who could suppose, that the animated speech of brother *Gamage* would have ended in the feeble proposition of sending a garrison to Sheffield? I shall therefore endeavour to supply his want of energy, and propose, as a decree of urgency, that all persons known before the Revolution, under the denomination of country gentlemen, yeomen, or housekeepers, be put in a state of arrestation."—(The hall resounded with applauses.) " Equality for ever; housekeepers to the guillotine, huzza!"

The President rings his bell violently—the bell breaks—another bell brought by one of the Secretaries—rings—rings. The President puts on his hat.

Citizen *Mendoza* holds up his fist in a threatening posture. The President knocks down Citizen *Mendoza*. (A calm ensues.)

The Assembly decree unanimously, and by acclamation, " that all persons of the denomination of country gentlemen and yeomen, are in a state of arrestation."—Adjourned.

THE NEW TIMES.

BRITISH NATIONAL CONVENTION.

Business in the House

TO-MORROW

Debate upon the *Maximum* of Provisions.

MONDAY

A new System for the more regular Operation of the Holy *Guillotine*.

LONDON.

☞ *The* PROCEEDINGS *of the* REVOLUTIONARY TRIBUNAL *are obliged to be omitted for want of room. Thirty two persons were yesterday convicted of a conspiracy against the Republic, and are to be* guillotined *this evening.*

This day, June 10, at twelve o'clock, the Rev. Citizen JOYS, Minister of the NATIONAL CHURCH, will celebrate in the *Temple of Reason* (*ci-devant* ST. PAUL'S CHURCH) a festival, for the happy destruction of the Parliament.

On Sunday last, in consequence of orders from the Committee of Public Safety, the MAYOR, at the head of a body of armed Citizens, repaired to Hyde Park, where he seized on all the horses, and declared them to be in a *state of requisition*, for the use of the Republic. The grooms were conducted to the Town-house, and from thence immediately sent, under a strong escort, to join the Southern Army as volunteers.

It now appears certain that the COLONIES refuse to send their SUGARS to England; the constant pillages of the shops having alarmed the Colonists for the safety of their property; and in consequence the price of sugar is raised sixpence per pound. We have now no other chance of drawing to ourselves the commerce of the Colonies, than the establishment of good laws. The late fire amongst the shipping and in the several dock-yards precludes us from any hopes of forcing the Colonies to send us their commodities, unless they choose to do so.

We have reason to believe, that the Ambassador from the French Republic, Citizen *Santerre*, has entered into an arrangement with the Committee, for the sale of the effects of the *ci-devant* NOBILITY, and is to take, for himself and suite, CARLETON-HOUSE, with all the furniture.

The ROYALISTS in DEVONSHIRE have completely defeated the brave Republicans, and killed 4000 of them. General SEMPLE was taken prisoner, and is closely confined. Want of discipline and proper officers, it is feared, will be in the end the ruin of our new forces. The Convention, it is said, mean to decree it death to all the surviving officers of any part of their forces who run from, or submit to the Aristocrats.

There is reason to hope, that the CITIZENS of LONDON will soon be relieved from their suspence in regard to the articles of subsistences; the Committee for the Department has, by perseverance, discovered the method of making bread of *decayed bones*. This resource will unquestionably be as agreeable as it is unexpected; as the *oaten bread* begins already to be very scarce.

Citizen BARRINGTON, Representative from Botany Bay, was yesterday detected picking the pocket of the President of the National Convention, of a gold snuff box. He was reprimanded but defended what he had done, on principles of *Equality*.

Yesterday the following Proclamation was stuck up in various parts of the Metropolis:

" MARGAROT, MAYOR of LONDON"

" In order to arrive at some precise knowledge of the resources of the Republic, and to form a basis for a more just distribution of the public burthens, the National Convention has decreed, in compliance with the request of the Committee of Finances, that every Citizen shall be obliged to give in a true and circumstantial statement of his property and that such statement shall be verified by Commissaries established for that purpose in every Section.

" This is therefore to give notice to all Proprietors, of every denomination, whether Landholders, Bankers, Merchants, Shopkeepers, or others, that they do give in, without delay, a true account of all their property, whether it consist in land, bills, or merchandize of any sort whatsoever; and they are desired to take notice, that any prevarication or false declaration, is, by the decree of the Convention, to be punished with death and confiscation; half of the property of the convicted to go to the informer.

" *Dated at the Town-House, June 9.*

" BONNY, Secretary."

BY ORDER OF THE MAYOR.

In order to stop the foul breath of slander, the MUNICIPALITY has resolved to publish a true and exact account of all the houses which, during the last week, have either been burnt or pillaged. These documents will prove more forcibly than all reasoning upon the subject, the humanity and moderation of the Patriots.

Bond Street, 19 shops pillaged and 3 burnt.

Horne Tooke Square (*ci devant* Grosvenor-Square), twenty-two houses burnt.

In the whole extent of *Oxford Road*, only 168 houses pillaged, and 81 burnt.

Cheapside has been rather more severely handled. The right side has been almost entirely consumed, but the left was only pillaged.

The fire near the *Bank*, in a quarter of the town where the streets are much narrower, raged of course with greater violence; but the public may be assured, that the plan of the Patriots did not extend to so general a conflagration.

The Municipality with satisfaction informs the Public, that, upon the minutest enquiry, no more than 8000 citizens have suffered on his occasion.

BONNY, Secretary.

THEATRE *of the* SANS CULOTTES.

A new piece of considerable merit entitled, the

CHIMNEY SWEEPER'S APOTHEOSIS.

OR

DRESS NO ORNAMENT TO REPUBLICANS.

was performed yesterday evening.

We have not room for the characters of the drama, nor would the story be at all entertaining to our readers—this is a kind of anticipation we detest—The CHIMNEY SWEEPER must be seen, and, when seen, *Ca Ira*.

The author of this piece sufficiently shews, that titles and rank are not in the least obligated companions to genius.

Baring a few coarse expressions, and now and then a want of grammatical precision, we cannot help recommending the CHIMNEY SWEEPER to the notice of real Republicans. The satire on the heads of the Church, in making a *ci-devant* Bishop, Chimney Sweeper to Old Nick, is at once a laughable and admirable hint at those who formerly pretended to bind our reason in fetters.

The characters were all admirably cast, though we do not think the piece was got up with all that professional excellence appertaining to the *ci-devant* THEATRES ROYAL;—but we cannot eat our cake, and have it too. Those Actors and Actresses of both houses, wete convicted of singing " God Save the King" with " heart and voice," almost every night of performance, They were of course, delivered over to the Revolutionary Tribunal, and when they went to the scaffold, such was the obstinacy of the loyal wretches, that the guillotine alone, prevented a repetition of their favourite tune;—in short

Those sung now, who never sung before,
And those who always sang, now sang the more.

The Prologue and Epilogue, in a happy view of ridicule glancing at former times, compared them with the present.—One couplet in the Epilogue was particularly appropriate,

" Citizens male and female, since here so long you've tarried;
" Go home, break lamps and order, let the constable be married."

The Scenery did great credit to the Manager.

The view of Tyburn, Billingsgate, Mendoza's Theatre, and a revived display of Hockley in the Hole, may be deemed the *chef d'œuvre* of the art.

During the performance, the civism of the audience was sufficiently evinced by a call for Citizen *Morris's* songs. A Lady in the stage-box was particularly happy in the fashionable air of " Jenny Sutton."

SHIPPING INTELLIGENCE.

PORTSMOUTH, AUG. 9.

The Grand Fleet, commanded by Citizen SMUGGLER, in the REPUBLIC, *ci-devant Royal Charlotte*, with Commissioner GRAY on board, weighed anchor this morning with a fair wind, to join the French fleet, and proceeded with them to Cadiz, in order to assist in the reduction of Spain, and plant an everlasting Republic there.

Came into harbour *Le Couteau*, a French brig, laden with *guillotines*, for the use of the fleet.

COURSE OF EXCHANGE

Amsterdam - -	0	Hamburgh . .	0
Leghorn . .	0	Lisbon . .	0
Cadiz . .	0		

English Bank Notes and French Assignats at par.

PRICE OF SPECIE

Silver, 22s. per ounce, in Paper.
Guineas, 5l. 2s

PRICE OF STOCKS.

Bank Stock 44 3-8ths
3 per Cent. Reduced 11 a 10 1 half 2 9
3 per Cent. Consols 12
4 per Cent Consols 16
5 per Cent Ann. 26
Bank Long Ann. 1
Short Ann. 0 1-half
India Stock 0

Letters, Advertisements, and Articles of Intelligence will be received at the Office of the NEW TIMES, *Printing House Square, Blackfriars, and meet with every possible attention and impartiality. At the same time we think it necessary to observe, that nothing but what accords with the true patriotic principles of this Paper, can be admitted.*

Anti-Jacobin propaganda in *The Times* (page 3 of *The Times*, December 6, 1794)

There appeared, as the third page of the issue, under a fine wood-cut title embodying a guillotine, a cup of blood and the motto " Liberty & Equality." *The New Times* was dated the " First Year of the Republic, one and indivisible, Saturday, June 10, 1800. Price One Shilling in specie or Five Shillings in paper." The text comprised news of executions, fires, fines, sequestrations, requisitions and famines. Citizens Priestley, Horne Tooke, Hardy, Mendoza, Paine are mentioned in the advertisements. The imprint of this page reads :

Letters, Advertisements, & Articles of Intelligence will be received at the Office of the *New Times*, Printing House Square, Blackfriars, & meet with every possible attention & *impartiality*. At the same time we think it necessary to observe, that nothing but what accords with the true patriotic principles of this Paper, can be admitted.

It can hardly be doubted that Printing House Square sponsored this production at the initiative of Dundas. Perhaps it was a piece of Stuart's Press-engineering. Doubtless the Home Office purchased a number of copies for " artful " circulation in districts known to be influenced by seditious pamphlets.

The sums paid to writers, journalists, printers and publishers during the closing decades of the eighteenth century appear to have been hardly less liberal than those paid by Walpole, although the scale of operations was smaller. Direct payments were, in accordance with custom, made through the Secretary of the Treasury ; indirect payments on account of advertising of public contracts, as, for example, the Navy and the Army victualling, were generally made through the respective officials. It is not clear from the fragmentary records which survive, when the Administration began the practice of exerting economic pressure upon newspapers by granting or withholding, for services rendered, or refusing the advertisements in question. The inventor of the method of bringing editors to heel by the offer or withdrawal of the advertisements of the Theatres Royal is unknown. The opposition used similar methods. There is evidence that Sheridan, Fox's supporter, managed the Press as well as the Theatres Royal.

Dundas, whose propagandist activities were mainly exercised in Scotland, yet found time to attend to similar business in London. Indeed, it was necessary. The Press is an entity ; paragraphs in the London papers were habitually reproduced in provincial sheets ; hence it was essential to a campaign of any pretensions to completeness, that the London journals should be supplied with such paragraphs as would be automatically and freely copied throughout the country. Dundas's tendencies are well known ; Pitt and he had perfect confidence in each other, and, as David Williams[1] pointed out, it was " palpable affectation " for Pitt to affect to despise the Press. The instructions to the Joint Secretaries of the Treasury, Charles Long, Thomas Steele and George Rose, doubtless proceeded from Dundas, who, through his own staff at the Home Office (where he was Secretary of State from 1791 to 1794), bore responsibility. The control was definite.

Have you heard [wrote Bland Burges to Lord Auckland (Feb. 2, 1793)] that we have got two papers perfectly attached to us and considered as the authentic vehicles of such matters as Government choose to make them ? Their titles are *The Sun* and the *True Briton* and I really think they are much superior to any we have seen. It was indeed high time to look a little seriously upon our daily vehicles of intelligence for almost all of them were in the pay of the Jacobins and contained the most extraordinary libels upon Government, the King and all those who were not known to be attached to the French interest. A very good man at this moment volunteered as a friend to Government, and in return Government has taken him by " the hand " and his paper flourishes accordingly.

The " very good man " whose " volunteering " was so convenient to Government was John Heriot.[2] He was an active journalist and quickly rendered the *Sun* and the *True Briton* of some political importance, at the expense of the circulation of the existing journals. *The Times* protested :

I have just had a visit [wrote Bland Burges to Charles Long, October 15, 1792] from young Walter, who is furious about the success of character of the *Sun* and came to me, as to an impartial person, to complain of the partiality shewn by Government and especially by Mr. Rose to that paper, which he said was very unjust considering his long services and the many advantages which Government, and especially Rose, had derived from the *Times*. He told me it was well known that Rose recommended the *Sun* and patronised its publisher ; and he threw out sundry strong hints of Mr Aust giving early accounts of Foreign Transactions, which he also stated to be very ill-usage. . . . On the whole he was very sulky and impudent ; and said if he found things went on as they were now doing, and if he did not

---

1 Founder of the Royal Literary Fund and a highly expert Press engineer.
2 See page 60, where " Mr. Heriot for writing in the papers " is paid £50 from Pitt's Secret Service account.

find some support from me, who he knew by experience never interfered in the newspaper business, he certainly should not suffer himself to be ruined by the success the *Sun* must certainly meet with from a priority of intelligence which he had undoubted information came from the Treasury and our office.

The preference given to Heriot's two papers was regular and extensive. Some idea of the harm caused by their competition may be gained from a letter written by William Walter to Dundas, in the course of which he says :

Right Honble Sir

It is with very great solicitude that I presume to intrude on your time ; but the difficulties under which I in particular labour, and the prospect before me of having my property, the fruit of many years labour and anxiety, diminished, so as to be scarcely worth holding, compel me to address you. I shall confine myself to as short a compass as possible.

The complaint I make may possibly not concern you, Sir, personally, though it certainly does concern you in common with other members of his Majesty's government. As Proprietor of the *Times* I humbly address you, complaining of the unbounded and unprecedented influence given to the *True Briton* & *Sun* Newspapers, by persons in high official situations, which I am sure would never be dared to be given but with the acquiescence of the Cabinet Ministers.

It is notorious, & I could prove the fact, that scarce a Dispatch comes from the Armies, or is there a Paris Journal forwarded to any of the Public Offices, but what is immediately transmitted to the *Sun* office. This system is now become so general, that I foresee my property in particular must suffer, if it continues. Probably I may feel the more vexed at this circumstance, because I know my conduct deserves a different treatment from Government. My father was imprisoned sixteen months in Newgate for Paragraphs written by the Conductor of the two Papers in question, & another person employed by Mr. Steele. I submit it to you, Sir, whether such treatment would not abate the attachment of any person to any sett of men ; the more so, when he sees daily attempts made to injure his property. State Papers are published, Paris Gazettes are forwarded to the office, and in short, the Columns of these Newspapers are filled with writings from persons either paid by Government or Gentlemen in office. How far the Papers in question answer the purposes intended, I leave to other persons to determine ; but I have no doubt that even you, Sir, have much fault to find with the numberless indiscretions and absurdities daily published in them ; which attach themselves to Government as it is known that the Conductors have a very intimate Correspondence with Persons high in Office.

I address this letter to you Sir, from no motives of jealousy. I complain only of the system of sending every foreign Newspaper from the Public Offices to the *Sun* Office. I am sincerely well disposed to the present Government, not only from private opinion, but also from long intercourse with it ; and I am convinced that the Public have a greater confidence in the *Times* than any other print that is published. My father, Sir, has been tried ; and his honourable conduct to Government during his confinement in Newgate is a severe instance of his honour : & sorry, very sorry should I be, were he ever *forced* through ill-treatment to be lukewarm in any cause to which he has ever been strongly attached, since he became a Proprietor of a public Print.

I am

With great Respect,

Right Honble Sir

Yr Most obed^t humble Servt.

WILLIAM WALTER.

No. 5, Ludgate Street, Septr 5th 1793.

I have the honour to enclose you a Letter which I had intended for the Press immediately after the capture of Valenciennes, addressed to Mr. Burgess, but which by the advice of Mr. Long was not published. R^{t.} Honble Henry Dundas.

When it is realized what losses and punishment John Walter had borne, it will be agreed that he had a genuine grievance. Dundas was impressed by William Walter's argument, and Heriot soon found himself at a disadvantage. He had been for several years accustomed to forward to the Home Office any intelligence, which his situation procured for him, of seditious lectures, meetings or similar activities. Being ignored after Walter's protest, he expostulated to Evan Nepean, Under-Secretary of State. His letter deserves reproduction for the light it throws upon the Press system of the period :

Sir,

When you told me you had received directions from Mr. Dundas to exclude me from your office, I readily submitted to such high authority, because I felt convinced it must be proper, and that it would likewise be general.

That it has not been so however the *Times* has lately full proof—it having lately frequently contained the most important official details which could only be procured from your office. As I cannot suppose that Mr. Dundas would condescend to make any distinction between Papers supporting Government, or if he did so that such distinction would [? not] be in favour of a Paper supporting Government upon more disinterested principles than any other, you will pardon me if, in justice to myself, I make an appeal from your partial exclusion to the liberality and justice of Mr. Dundas.

I am not conscious, Sir, of having at any time given you any cause of offence. I therefore feel peculiarly mortified that you should mark me as the particular object of your displeasure. You know, Sir, and it is daily proved in the *Times*, that there are points of information which it is advantageous to Government to give and to have stated in a proper manner. In any intercourse which I have or may ever have with any member of the Government, I can only have one object in view, to serve Government by every means in my power, without a wish to obtain what it may be proper and prudent to withhold.

With these sentiments and principles, I feel much hurt that by you so decided a preference should be given to a man whom all who know him view with contempt and distrust.

I have the honour to be, Sir, your most obedt. servt.

JOHN HERIOT.

Catherine Street, Strand, No. 5. December 10, '93.

John Walter's refusal to give up the name of the author of the paragraphs responsible for his imprisonment so clearly entitled him to special consideration, that Heriot's services were forgotten and his grievances overruled. In 1795 he wrote to the Duke of Portland entreating his intercession, as his French newspapers had been taken by a Government agent from his own courier. Heriot was still responsible for the *Sun*, Pitt's evening paper, but the Government seems at that time to have reduced its direct interest in the Press and to have confined its support to a narrower selection of journals. The French Revolution threw into English political thought new ideas of social order, and these new ideas, in so far as they found expression in the newspapers, could not be officially ignored. Dundas was forced to take account in his propaganda not only of party rivalry (his earlier preoccupation) but of " sedition " ; and the problem of " sedition " increasingly occupied the attention of the Government and its agents after 1789.

Nor did the resignation of Pitt in 1801, although it interrupted, materially change the essentials of the Government Press policy. During the year 1802, David Williams was employed to issue in pamphlet form, with a view to ultimate binding in a book, a series of short essays in political philosophy written for the purpose of inducing other writers to forsake pure partisanship for the more elevated work of championing the time-honoured virtues of the English Constitution. Williams's *Egeria, or Elementary Studies on the Progress of Nations in Political Economy, Legislation and Government* was an attempt by Government to add literary to journalistic propaganda.

A memorandum not before published provides a valuable though slight retrospect of the Press policies of Shelburne and Fox, and distinctly outlines the condition of journalism in the very year when John Walter Junior took sole responsibility for the conduct of *The Times*. It is a Government " Private Paper— *Requiring Immediate Perusal* " ; it is headed " *On the Press* " ; and it was circulated to the Addington Cabinet in 1803. The writer may have been one of the Joint Secretaries to the Treasury, either Long or Steele, who remained at the Treasury and served the Addingtons as they had served Pitt. The endorsement of the memorandum, " Pray read this," is in the handwriting of Hiley Addington, the Prime Minister's brother, who secured and retained for the Administration the support of *The Times* until John Walter II, in his own words, " set the Addingtons adrift."[1] The paper on the press demands the discontinuance of *Egeria* because its object was not fulfilled. That object had been " to circulate the numbers among those who might render it a text-book for discussion, and for the production of new topics for writers in the newspapers." By way of insisting on the importance of using the lower kinds of journalism, the writer points out that Lord Shelburne

a statesman of numerous accomplishments, attained the Helm in circumstances similar to those of the present Ministry. He rose in consequence of the forced circulation of publications ; some of abstruse circulation, and some of metaphysical reasoning ; all securing numerous partizans by fixing principles in their minds. If Lord Shelburne had comprehended in one system every species of political literature, abominable as some of it appeared, he might have been Minister to this day. . . .

[1] See Chapter IX *Pitt and the Addingtons* and *The Times* June 19, 1819.

Lord Shelburne was soon shaken ; principally by the press ; which had certainly decided the American War ; but he resumed his situation in conjunction with Mr. Fox, in whose power the inferior and those which Lord Shelburne deemed the exceptionable provinces of literature were left.

Shelburne, thinking himself secure, attended conscientiously to his public duties—

but being a little tainted with Puritanism, or solicited by the Dissenters, he wished the Government to have a moral as well as a political character.

This solicitude led him to wish Fox " to consider the incompatibility of the direction of a pharo table and the office of Secretary of State." While Fox himself accepted the suggestion with good humour it was otherwise with " the literary hounds," who

well packed and well fed opened on the Premier, and worried him out of his place, his reputation, and even his private character.

The consequences, direct and indirect, were extremely disadvantageous to the country. The mistake was in the

separation made between the Philosophical and Satirical writers ;—the latter of which would have submitted to the former *under proper direction*,—but separated, they confounded good and evil, and misled friends and foes into that perpetual species of warfare which has ever since infested the country.

Thankful that the " present Ministry . . . have improved on the error of Lord Shelburne," the writer insists that

the Ministry are placed at a point where they receive the full effect of a Cross Fire ; to which they oppose virtues which no doubt will stand them in good stead as Christians, but which have nearly ruined them as statesmen. Whether the present negotiations terminate in war or in a temporary and *pretended* peace, it is known there are Phalanxes to attack the Ministers instantly on the determination ; not only by the fleeting arrows of paragraphs, but by publications of another kind, and by solicitations to the country to petition and remonstrate. . . . Europe is at this time in a tremendous state ; and every mutilated division of it looks to England for *opinion* as well as *courage*.

This opinion, this rational and fixed system " which might influence men of good sense as well as fools," was a paramount need, and

literary talents, the instruments of incalculable Good or Evil, are left to the disposal of the vilest factions, or to avoid starvation by hiring themselves to the enemy and abusing the Government of their country.[1]

In consequence the Government had not a moment to lose if they were to protect themselves against the unceasing " cavils and calumnies of interested or disaffect opponents."

So things stood in 1802, and so John Walter II found them at the beginning of the next year, when his term of responsibility in Printing House Square began.

[1] The complete text is given in the Appendix.

V

JOHN WALTER II

I T had become clear by the end of the century that William
Walter, who in 1795 succeeded his father in the conduct of *The
Times*, would never make the editor or business manager whom
the paper needed at that time. Perhaps he was too bookish ;
certainly his journalistic outlook was conventional and old-
fashioned. Combe told Crabb Robinson that the daily sale of
The Times was "sunk to not more than 1700 copies" when John
Walter II, who came into the office in 1797, took up the sole
management in 1803. The printing bills tell the same story. In
1799 the compositors' weekly wages remained constant at
£14 19s. 10d., with extras for occasional overtime ; and at the
end of the year the cost of the presswork was £13 5s. 2d. At the
end of 1802, when William Walter retired, the compositors were
drawing £17 6s. 6d. owing to higher wages granted in 1801,
while the pressmen were paid only £6 9s., though their rates also
had been increased. The inescapable deduction is that, as the
presses were the same, the edition was so small as to be worked
off in half the time previously required. The accounts show a
regular and increasingly rapid diminution of charges for presswork
from 1800. Cobbett, a good witness, assured Windham in 1802
that all the daily papers were declining in sale. The *Morning Post*
sold 1,250 ; the *Chronicle* 900 ; the *True Briton* 350. Cobbett
does not give figures for *The Times*, but asserts that its championship of the Peace of Amiens cut its sales to half those of the *Post*.
Further corroborative evidence of the weakness of *The Times* at
this period is given by Crabb Robinson, who was convinced in
1812 that John Walter II alone had saved the paper.

The reconditioning of a moribund journal was a congenial task
for John Walter II. He interposed when the founder of *The
Times* seriously contemplated its discontinuance, and secured for
it one more chance. Within ten years the paper was firmly re-
established ; and its saviour's reward was his father's displeasure.

75

The will of John Walter I, who died in 1812, imposed conditions which handicapped the son, prejudiced his relations with the other proprietors, and jeopardized his journalistic success. The reasons for the disagreement cannot be explicitly given. A memorandum handed to young John by the executors explained his father's attitude, but it is lost and no copy survives. There can be little doubt, however, in view of an entry in Crabb Robinson's diary, that John Walter I resented his son's concentration upon the risky newspaper business to the exclusion of the comparatively safe book-printing and book-selling business for which the office had originally been furnished ; he disagreed generally with an independent attitude towards Government, and particularly with John Walter Junior's refusal to join him in petitioning for reversal of the action by which the printing for His Majesty's Board of Customs was lost. This contract, secured by John Walter I in 1788, was suddenly cancelled by Lord Melville on account of criticisms in *The Times*.[1] Young John Walter, as good a man of business as his father, but of prouder bearing towards politicians, officials and press agents, changed a dying news-sheet into a flourishing newspaper.

John Walter I had six children by his marriage in 1759 with Frances Landen, who predeceased him in 1798. John Walter II, born in 1776, was sent to Merchant Taylors' School. At the age of 14 he was bound apprentice to Thomas Longman, the publisher and bookseller of Paternoster Row. Very quickly, with the consent of the Stationers' Company (of which he was to become Master in 1830), young John was turned over as apprentice to " John Walter of Printing House Square, Blackfriars, Printer, Citizen and Mason." At the age of 19 he matriculated at Trinity College, Oxford, but remained a year only. On coming of age in 1797, he took up a managerial appointment in his father's office and entered into an agreement with his father for the carrying on " in partnership together in Printing House Square aforesaid the Trade, Art, Mystery or Business of Printers for their mutual and equal benefit." Thus, immediately on becoming a master-printer, John Walter Junior was advanced to one-half partnership with his father in the business of " buying and selling all such articles, merchandizes and commodities as were usually used and employed in the said trade or business." It should be observed that this partnership was between printers for the purpose of carrying on business as printers, and that the agreement

1 For details see Chapter IX.

JOHN WALTER II
A miniature portrait on ivory in the possession
of John Walter, Esq.

in no way touched the property known as *The Times*, the *Evening Mail* or any other publication, to whomsoever belonging, composed and printed in Printing House Square. The agreement of 1797, having run for the covenanted period of four years, was renewed in 1801 for a period of twenty-one years " if both the partners should so long live." William Walter possessed no share in the business. His retirement was doubtless already agreed upon.

In the spring of the same year, 1801, John Walter gave his son a sixteenth share in the profits of the property known as *The Times* and *Evening Mail*, similar shares having already been settled on his daughters Fanny and Mary at their respective marriages. John Walter Junior therefore became for the first time a partner, or " proprietor," in *The Times* from March 28, 1801, holding a sixteenth share, and a half-share in the printing press or business. In other words, he was by trade a printer first, and incidentally a newspaper publisher. No rights, other than a share in the profits of *The Times*, were annexed to this gift of father to son and to the two daughters. The direction of the policy and the ordering of financial principles remained absolutely in the hands of John Walter I. The editorial details were carried out by William.

It was in January, 1803, after William's retirement, that John Walter Junior was made sole manager of all activities in Printing House Square, with responsibility also for the policy of *The Times* and the details of financial and every other sort of administration. His holding of shares was small, but both father and son were now convinced that the whole responsibility must be one man's. John Walter Junior, then, became sole general manager as a salaried officer, irrespective of his shares, irremovable except by the Chief Proprietor and owner of the printing business. On May 28, 1806, he acquired his second sixteenth share in *The Times*, and on March 28, 1810, he acquired his third sixteenth. Hence in 1810 the sole general manager's property in the newspaper was three-sixteenths ; in the printing business it was one-half.

Two years later father and son entered into a new agreement dissolving partnership in the printing business ; in future, John Walter the younger was alone to carry on the business of printing in consideration of an annuity to John Walter the elder of £666 13s. 4d. This agreement of May 14, 1812, also conveyed the freehold of the buildings and " all that capital Messuage or Tenement or Premises formerly called or known by the name of the King's Printing House & all the rooms warehouses yards outhouses gardens premises & appurtenances whatsoever belonging thereto . . . which said premises were heretofore in the tenure or occupation of the Printers of Her late Majesty Queen Anne." It was taken for granted that the main business of the office was the printing " of a daily morning newspaper called *The Times* and of an evening newspaper called the *Evening Mail*." From this date John Walter Junior became sole owner of two properties : first, the freehold and the premises ; secondly, the business of printing *The Times* ; but it must be understood that of the newspaper itself he was " sole manager," and, because manager, " Chief " or managing Proprietor, although owning three-sixteenths shares only. In respect of *The Times* the young Walter's title had hitherto been " Joint Proprietor."

The division of a literary property into shares, in which the printer participated, was a normal arrangement in the eighteenth century publishing trade, whether of books or newspapers. Indeed, newspapers were owned on a copyright basis, exactly as books, *e.g.*, the bookseller John Bell owned one-sixteenth share in Francis's *Horace*. The matter must be made clear, or the litigation of fourscore years later will be misunderstood. The proprietors of a newspaper, who generally included men of business able to influence advertising, found it important to effect such an arrangement with their printer as would effectively give him a motive, in the form of a share in the profits, for keeping down the cost of production. Naturally, in an arrangement of this sort, the printer yielded up his share when the paper was transferred to another house, as happened if the printer's charges or services were found unsatisfactory to the chief proprietors.

In the case of *The Times* the normal arrangement was abnormally complicated by the printer being the owner and operator of a printing business as well as the controller of the newspaper. Normally, the owner of the greatest share controlled the paper and the printer. John Walter Junior was the printer of the paper because his father established it and also the press that printed it. The accounts of the two ventures, the printing business and the newspaper business, were kept separately. There was one manager, but two distinct businesses. And, under John Walter Senior's will, the hereditary owner of the printing business controlled the finances of the newspaper, whether his share in it was large or small. This responsibility could not be delegated.

Particulars of the division and distribution, according to the will, of the property in *The Times* must now be noted ; the reader will appreciate them when he comes to consider the crisis of 1908. The indenture of 1812, already mentioned, made John Walter Junior the absolute owner of the printing business ; it left untouched the share which the printer enjoyed in the newspaper printed by him. But on June 20, 1810, John Walter Senior had made a last will and testament which disposed the eleven-sixteenths remaining in the hands of the founder of *The Times* to various members of his family. He had given his daughters Fànny and Mary *one*-sixteenth share each on their marriage to Knox and Robert Carden respectively ; and John Walter Junior had been assigned three shares (each of one-sixteenth) in 1801, 1806 and 1810 (March 28), the last of which was assigned a few weeks before the making of his father's will in June. That the relations between father and son were pleasant before this last assignment is probable ; that they afterwards changed is certain from the conditions of the will made in June, which did not come to John Walter II's knowledge until his father's death two years later and then occasioned him grief and disappointment, and later brought upon his successors disastrous litigation.

In the period during which William Walter had been responsible *The Times* had yielded hardly any profit ; John Walter Senior's speculations of the Logographic Press, and particularly the huge three-volume quarto edition of Anderson on *Commerce*, had been costly failures ; the branch book-shop in Piccadilly had also involved loss. Only after the appointment of John Walter Junior in 1803 were the shares in *The Times* a source of profit or credit. Putting forth a great effort, young Walter raised *The Times* to a high place in public estimation. If it lacked the political distinction of the *Morning Chronicle*, there was by 1810 little doubt that the paper with the brilliant staff [1] picked by the new manager must before long take the leading position. Circulation was mounting, the advertising revenue was considerable and increasing. The situation of the paper, therefore, had completely changed by the year John Walter I made his malevolent will.

On the day John Walter Senior died at Teddington, John Walter Junior was at his post. It was November 16, 1812. There was a not very cheerful dinner in Printing House Square ; Kenney the actor was there, William Combe and Peter Fraser, besides Crabb

[1] See Chapter X.

Robinson, who noted in his diary : " Walter, I perceived, was absent & in trouble. And soon after dinner he left us abruptly. I then learnt that his father was most probably dead. And it was in fact." Robinson goes on to say that in young Walter's absence the remaining company " talked pretty freely about the old man." Robinson's private judgment had been expressed in 1808[1] : " Old Mr. W. accord^g to all accounts is what there is no need to put down in words—in his time." But on this November evening of 1812 the company felt free to speak their minds. It will be remembered that the speakers were the younger Walter's special friends ; they had helped him to raise *The Times*, which the elder Walter had left moribund, to prosperity and power. Combe spoke from a long personal experience. Robinson's information was drawn from the confidences of Walter II. Robinson testified that he believed the founder of *The Times* " from all accounts to be as dishonest—worthless a man as I have ever known, at least among those who preserved appearances." Combe's judgment was sweeping : he " never did an honest act in his life " and made his money " by the vilest arts—extortion of money through calumny, &c." How different was Walter Junior, reflected Robinson ; under his management " without ever doing one dishonourable act [he] brought [the paper] to the heighth at which it now is." Combe, virtually the Editor of *The Times* before Fraser's and Robinson's time,[2] related an early incident of his connexion with Walter Junior :

J. W. in the first instance applied to him for assistance which he unwillingly gave him, supposing him to be no better than his kinsmen. After he had been with him for a few weeks An article was written against Traverse—[upon which] he sent an Answer with £20.

W. asked C. whether the Answer should appear—I suppose, said C., the £20 is a sufficient answer to the Question. However the Answer should appear. W. then sent T. back the money saying as his letter was in defence of himself it was but just that it should appear unpaid for.

I was so astonished at this, said C., that I could not help saying to him " Who got you ? " I added then—" Until you can get someone more useful to you than myself I will stay with you. So have no anxiety on that head." C. had not consented to stay with him before.[3]

Later, Crabb Robinson, before committing the story to his diary, asked himself whether it was true, or all true, and gave judgment

[1] *Cf.* Crabb Robinson to Thomas Robinson, dated " Printing House Square, past one o'clock, a.m., 12th Feb., 1808."
[2] For further particulars of Combe see Chapter X.
[3] Diary II, 155-6.

that " the part that respects C. in this anecdote is more likely a lye—the rest is probably true." For his part Robinson added a note in his diary :

W. is on such a footing with his brother and four sisters, and there is such a spirit of litigation in the family that there will probably arise very vexatious quarrels among the family—And he has much vexation to undergo.

This last note was soon to be verified by fact. A fortnight later Robinson was again at Printing House Square. An entry in the diary records the visit :

Sunday 29 Nov. 1812. Called on Walter. The old man has made a Will as unfriendly towards him as he well could. He has given him no part of his property, but has left him the power of purchasing 2/16ths of the paper at 4 years' purchase, but estimating that 4 years' purchase at thrice it's real value. He has left 1/16th between Bell & Lawson. And the rest to the 4 daughters in different proportions. My friend W. however has the full power of carrying on the paper as he pleases. And his salary is fixed. This is the only circumstance that is favourable to W., who has 3/16ths of the paper & One half of *the Englishman*[1] already belonging to him. The old man left a written paper stating the reasons why he had left J.W. so small a share of the property. He assigns as reasons his refusing to put in his father's Commerce[2] his having lost the Custom house printing. And the decline of some hundreds in the sale of the paper though the sale has since risen thousands—And the power given to J.W. of managing the paper as he pleases implies a good opinion of him. It seems the old man's malignancy did not leave him in this important act of his life. He had been for years on apparent good terms with his Son but with revenge perhaps in his heart.[3]

One of the conditions in the will favourable to John Walter II was, indeed, that which made " my son John to continue to have the sole management." The words of the testator are strict : " The conduct and interest of a newspaper concern require the most absolute power in the persons carrying on the same in making allowance and payment at their discretion." And it fixed that " my said son John shall be paid by the proprietors of the said newspaper called *The Times* for his conduct and management of the said newspaper at the rate following that is to say the salary of £1000 per annum for every year in which the said newspaper shall

---

[1] John Walter II retained his interest in this Sunday paper until after 1820.
[2] The reference is perhaps to Anderson's *Commerce*, edited by Combe (*cf.* p. 13), but the MS. has no comma following this word and preceding " his."
[3] Diary II, 160.

G

produce over the said £1000 a net profit of £5000 per annum and upwards." It was directed, however, that the salary should be reduced by £20 for every £100 when the profits were less than £5,000.

The will, estimating the value of the two floating shares at four years' purchase, had, of course, to be complied with. John Walter II felt the situation very keenly and said so to his friends. Edward Sterling advised him that a threat to withdraw support from the paper might, in the circumstances, bring round the rest of the family to a juster appreciation of his own position—" With you go your connexions into any other undertaking which it may suit you to embark—and I should be glad to know where then would be *The Times* newspaper."[1] Fortunately, John Walter applied himself to the difficult and ungrateful task of conciliating family differences and of persuading the owners of the floating shares to consider a reduction of the purchase price from four to three years. He declared that " the evident unfairness of the will resulted from causes the most frivolous and unfounded." The family discussions absorbed more than a year's energies before Sir John Hall, an arbitrator, was able to announce a settlement. The general principles could not be modified. Moreover, the power of sole management given to John Walter II was too welcome to be jeopardized, even if an entirely new settlement could have been negotiated. The fundamental ideas governing the undertaking were thus perpetuated. First, John Walter II was, independently of the will, sole and absolute owner of the freehold of Printing House Square, of the premises and the printing equipment. and of three-sixteenths of the property in *The Times* newspaper. Secondly, John Walter II was, also independently, the absolute and sole printer of *The Times*. Thirdly, *by the will*, John Walter II was offered, at a price, the two floating shares which, when acquired, provided him with a total holding of five-sixteenths of the paper. Fourthly, *by the will*, John Walter II was sole conductor, with a permanent sliding-scale salary. Lastly, *by the will*, he or his estate looked forward to the reversion of Walter Wilson's sixteenth.

So, after the arbitration, Walter found himself most securely possessed of the freehold of Printing House Square, the premises and the printing business ; in these he enjoyed unrestricted sole ownership. In the newspaper business he had sole jurisdiction,

[1] Sterling to Walter, November 30, 1812.

JOHN WALTER II

After an oil painting in the possession of
John Walter, Esq.

with a salary and five-sixteenths of the profits, if and when they were made. He had power, with the other proprietors, to deal in the shares, to assign them to whomsoever he would, absolutely or with power of redemption. At no place in the will, and at no time during the discussions which took place during the first years of its operation, was the power of the printer to print *The Times* challenged ; in no way was the printer subjected to control. No echoes were heard of the agreement of 1810, by which Walter II agreed with Walter I to continue the existing formula of charging *The Times* with 50 per cent. on the compositors' and pressmen's bills. The co-proprietors did not challenge the price charged for printing the paper. The will in no way touched the cost of printing the paper ; it was, and remained, an item belonging to the jurisdiction of the Chief Proprietor ; Walter's terms as Printer of *The Times* were accepted by Walter as Chief Proprietor of *The Times*.

The completeness of the freedom and ownership which John Walter II enjoyed as a printer inevitably stimulated his interest in that department. Much of the subsequent history of Printing House Square, as a whole, becomes comprehensible when the financial implications of his situation are fully realized. First, even with the expenditure of an enormous amount of money it was doubtful whether he could ever acquire half as much revenue from *The Times* journal as he already received from the business of John Walter, Printer. Secondly, the management of a printing business, while more profitable, was less exacting than that of a newspaper. Naturally, therefore, having taken the risk, after much preliminary experiment and attendant anxiety, of installing steam apparatus for the printing of *The Times*, he allowed mechanical matters to take precedence over the literary and journalistic side, which could be handled first by Fraser and Robinson, then by Stoddart and afterwards by Barnes.

The difference between John Walter II's economic expectations before and after the will accounts for a change in his attitude towards *The Times* itself. Before his father's death his whole energies were given to re-establishing the journal ; afterwards they went to the development of the press which returned him not three-sixteenths but the whole of the profits of printing. The period of the revolutionary economic change from hand-press to power-press was precisely the period of Dr. Stoddart's editorship during which the paper was most criticized, and for the best of reasons. John Walter, never a good party politician, was then preoccupied with the Koenig press.[1] Preoccupations of this order were permanent because the economic justification was continuous. The application of mechanical power to the printing press was a vital factor in the expansion of the newspaper and book trade in the early nineteenth century, and bears close relation to the size, circulation and distribution, even to the soul, of *The Times*. John Walter's interest in steam, then, succeeded his interest in journalism ; the press became a more urgent concern to him than the paper after 1814. From the invention to the elaboration by Cowper and Applegath, it was the equipment of the office with progressive machinery that called for fresh capital expenditure. The journal once firmly established required less supervision. Moreover, Walter II, as a newspaper proprietor, was not interested in journalism for its own sake ; nor as a member of Parliament was he interested in politics for politics' sake. He looked at his newspaper and his office with the eye, not of an agitator or a speculator, but of an honest trader, a far-sighted business-man.

Yet the second Walter's work as a journalist is of the first importance. It was accomplished between the years 1803 and 1814. Walter II maintained full control until 1819, but the strictly newspaper work for which his name needs to be remembered was effected after 1806 when he threw off the influence of the Addingtons which he had inherited from his predecessors.[2] Thereafter he ceased to interest himself in the detail of home politics, or in the welfare of parties, or in the ambitions of political persons. His championship of the independence of newspapers from party or Government subsidy deserves the utmost credit ; he was the only daily newspaper proprietor who shared the views of the few earnest men (Leigh Hunt being the best known example) looking to the periodical Press for honest and acute criticism of contemporary tendencies in politics, in commerce, and in the arts.[2] He identified himself at once with the first manifestations of the movement which, half a century later, earned general respect for journalism. He was more practical than Daniel Stuart, who is to be credited with the initiative of employing Lamb, Southey, and Coleridge.

The practical abilities, high principles and good nature of John Walter II are consistently remarked by Crabb Robinson, the hypercritical authority and keen judge of scruples, who knew him

[1] See Chapter VIII.
[2] See Chapter IX.

most intimately throughout his long life, and who blamed him not for the unfriendly relations so long separating him from his brothers and sisters. In spite of the injustice of his father's will, Walter succeeded in coming to agreement with Sir Robert Carden, husband of his sister Mary, a lawyer by profession and highly litigious by nature, on the vexed question of the floating shares. Robinson held strongly that John was never responsible for the estrangement with William which had endured since his taking charge of *The Times*. The two brothers at length made it up. Robinson relates a meeting :

1817. 1st Jan. My new year's dinner I took at Mr. Walter's—a very large family party was there—W's brother too was there whom I had never seen before and with whom he has been at variance many years. His countenance would lead one to take for granted that he was the more sinning man in any quarrel between the brothers. There were very few but the family present—nephews & nieces of W : of course a more dull cram cannot well be conceived. I was relieved during the hours of digestion by a rubber of whist and again by chess with W. Collier—I could not read much when I came home.[1]

Crabb Robinson had the highest regard both for the professional and the moral character of John Walter II. In a letter to his brother Thomas, he once said—and never unsaid :

I read to Mr. W. what you wrote on the paper and he was gratified by it. He is very susceptible of praise and he merits it by the liberality of his intentions rather than by the strength of his character or the decision of his judgem't. I have never heard from him a dishonourable or dishonest suggestion but I have often witnessed an hesitation & timidity which arise from modesty & distrust of himself. His disposition & will are always good, but they require to be strengthened and fixed.[2]

A man without personal vanity, Walter was hard with himself ; strict with others ; he was typical, indeed, of English mercantilism in the early nineteenth century. He never tolerated "combinations" of workmen, and, in 1810, successfully broke a strike in which twenty-eight of his printers walked out. An individualist, he was utterly unable to understand trade unions. He denounced the Printers' Pension Fund and refused to support the Fund for unfortunate journalists on the ground that both printers and journalists should, because they were able, themselves assume the responsibilities which were plainly theirs, and not look for

[1] Diary II, 119.
[2] H. C. Robinson to Thomas Robinson dated December 7, 1807 (postmark Feb. 8, 1808).

extraneous support. " I see no claim that gentlemen connected with the Newspaper Press have upon the Public." Printing House Square, he pointed out, had established mutual aid societies for these very objects ; a rule was laid down that every artisan in the establishment should place a tenth of his income in the Savings Bank." He was full of that instinctive and rigid morality which acclaimed the virtues of consistent hard work, of habitual personal thrift and self-reliance. Prosperity was to him the fit reward of intelligent self-help, and property ennobled those who had earned it by their own industry. But he did not consider it necessary to go on toiling when he had so securely based his fortune that he could prudently retire to the country. Then his sense of duty drove him to national, political and local ameliorative work. This was duty, for he had no liking for society as such, still less for politicians, and possessed few intimates. Only with John Wilson Croker, among politicians, was he friendly. The *Quarterly* editor was frequently at Bear Wood, and Walter often visited Molesey Grove.

Crabb Robinson, who reports John Walter II as slow at conversation, caring only for " real things," a man great in reserve, relates in the *Reminiscences* that he once gave a party to which he invited Wordsworth, Cookson, Quillinan and Gooden. There were also Alsager and Fraser, both of whom had for many years worked for *The Times* and yet had never seen each other—" an illustration," remarks Robinson, " of the habits of reserve on the part of Walter." Later at Bear Wood he entertained few besides local friends and political acquaintances from Newbury, Windsor and Abingdon. Dr. and Miss Mitford were occasional visitors. That lady found him the most bashful of men. He followed no organized pastimes or team sports, but he seems, Evangelical though he was, to have tolerated Dr. Mitford's patronage of village games on Sunday. An upholder of the Established Church of England, he built and endowed a church on his estate. He owned the advowson of Bromley-by-Bow and presented Fraser to the living in 1824. Walter's one relaxation was fishing, and to indulge it he set ornamental waters in his grounds, which bore witness to his fondness also for landscape gardening on a large scale. He enjoyed the country. He rode well. He wrote a supremely good letter ; he had a remarkably good head for figures. In the opinion of his lifelong friend and keen analyst of character Crabb Robinson, John Walter II was, above all, a rare business man and a true gentleman. There were few indeed of either in the London newspaper trade of that day.

VI

A NEW SPIRIT IN JOURNALISM

A NEW spirit animated periodical criticism in the first decade of the nineteenth century, owing something to the thirty-four numbers of the *Anti-Jacobin* (1797), edited by William Gifford, on behalf of a group of politicians with Canning as the most active. It came but slowly into the possession of the daily newspapers. Cobbett returned to England and started the *Porcupine* in November, 1800, which he parted with to John Heriot of the *True Briton* within a year. As a matter of course the innovators had to experiment in the least risky form of bookselling. Cobbett started his *Weekly Political Register* in January, 1802. *The Edinburgh Review and Critical Quarterly*, first published in October, 1802, had, as its editor said, " two legs to stand on : Literature is one of them, but its right leg is Politics." Its politics were Whig. Its Tory rival, the *Quarterly Review*, was brought out in 1809. More journalistic, because they were weeklies, Cobbett's *Register* and John Hunt's *The News* (1805) and Leigh Hunt's *Examiner* (1809) pointed out the direction from which were to come the formative influences that would in a few years sharply distinguish the contemporary newspapers from those of the late eighteenth century. The insufficient study given by historians to the literature, journalistic and other, of this period makes positive statement presumptuous ; it cannot be denied, however, that the greatest measure of credit for the revolution in periodical journalism, outside the quarterlies, belongs to members of the *News* and *Examiner* group, who were Radical in their politics, particularly to John and Leigh Hunt, Barron Field and Thomas Barnes.

Hazlitt, who also wrote independent dramatic criticism, was not connected with the *Morning Chronicle* until 1814, and though he served *The Times*[1] for eight months of 1817, John Walter Junior

---

[1] See Chapter X.

had been already ordering himself for ten years by the new tendencies. It is just to insist that the new criticism was supported by *The Times* before the accession of either Barnes or Hazlitt. It was not at first a matter of politics, never politics in the narrow sense ; but politics in every sense were bound to be involved later. The new spirit was not cramped by bookishness ; those critical writers who collected round the Hunts were competent to deal with life in general, politics as well as the arts. Their emergence, together with the *Edinburgh* reviewers, was a necessary preliminary to the enactment of Catholic Emancipation and the Reform Bill, measures of social justice rather than of mere politics. The public mind had first to be freed from the contaminating influences of graft, propaganda and puffery. The Hunts fought against repressive legislation, against political and journalistic corruption in high places, against puffing in all its forms. They championed free speech for its own sake and as an instrument of liberty. This group, young men of an average age of 21, made perhaps a greater difference to the quality than to the direction of English political thinking ; for they were revisionists, neither visionaries nor revolutionaries, but Liberals or Radicals, and honest because they represented no " interest." The effect of this new body of writers upon daily journalism though slow was sure. Editors and proprietors of daily papers were by no means ready to risk loss of patronage by printing the unrepresentative opinions of men so young and pecuniarily unsubstantial. There was, however, one exception. John Walter not only supported but anticipated in some respects the Liberal and independent ideas of the Hunt group. It could hardly have been otherwise. He and Leigh Hunt had a common object. Walter began to strive for the independence of *The Times* in the very year of his appointment as sole manager ; his struggle with the Post Office followed immediately ; and next came the fight with the theatres.

In 1805 Walter appointed as theatre critic a prominent member of Leigh Hunt's circle, Barron Field. This was the first direct contact *The Times* seems to have made with the circle. It is known from Field's letters that Leigh Hunt himself occasionally did duty for him, and to Field Barnes owed his later introduction to Walter. There is no sign that Leigh Hunt contributed political articles to *The Times*, although it is clear from observations by Field that Hunt and Walter Junior were acquainted. The appointment of Stoddart as Editor of *The Times* was a serious setback to the hopes of the *Examiner* group, and a challenge to their respect for the paper. In the *Examiner* for September 25, 1808, Leigh Hunt writes :

> There is one daily paper, *The Times*, which for some time past appeared anxious to do away its former character [the reference is to the conduct of the paper by John Walter I] and has particularly distinguished itself on the present [Portuguese] question. The editor not only throws light on every view of the subject, but he throws lightning ; his pen literally flashes conviction, and wherever it strikes we discover some new chasm, some new appearance of the alarm or the mystery, which warns us how we trust the darkness that is purposely thrown over enquiry. I have the utmost satisfaction in recommending to my readers the excellent articles of this Gentleman, of whom I know nothing but that he writes with an honesty that few other Editors would practise if they could, and with a classical vigour that hardly one of them could practise if he would.[1]

Apart from the error of Stoddart's appointment, *The Times* of the years after 1803 manifested a tendency in accord with the conception of journalism adopted by the *Examiner*. Its growth in independence and candour is well illustrated by its treatment of the theatres. The printing of candid theatrical criticism in daily newspapers appears to date from 1805. At that time it was common, as Leigh Hunt confirms in his autobiography, for news writers and editors to be intimate with dramatists and actors, who received them gladly in the green room. Editors were flattered into the acceptance of ready-written paragraphs and reviews, and if they wanted remuneration they received it. Such notices, says Leigh Hunt, invariably praised the piece and the cast.

> Upon new performers, and upon writers not yet introduced, a journalist was more impartial ; and some times, where the proprietor . . . for some personal reason grew offended with an actor, or a set of actors, a criticism would occasionally be hostile and even severe. . . . Puffing and plenty of tickets were, however, the system of the day. It was an interchange of amenities over the dining table ; a flattery of power on the one side, and puns on the other ; and what the public took for a criticism of a play was a draft upon the box-office or reminiscences of last Thursday's salmon and lobster sauce.

When John Hunt founded his Sunday paper, the *News*, in May, 1805, his brother wrote the theatrical notices.

---

[1] This tribute to the writing of Peter Fraser is important as witnessing to the recognition of another independent writer. Fraser was never associated with any literary or political group. He was appointed to *The Times* in 1807 [*cf.* Chapter X].

We saw that independence in theatrical criticism would be a great novelty. We announced it, and nobody believed it ; we stuck to it and the town believed everything we said. . . . I was then in my twentieth year, an early age at that time for a writer.

Leigh Hunt scrupulously abstained from knowing any actor personally and " would as lief have taken poison as accepted a ticket from the theatres." His precocious enthusiasm worked a gradual and healthy change which ultimately extended to daily journalism. If so much is well known, it is less understood that without the support given by Walter Junior in the columns of *The Times* the change might for long have been limited to the intellectual weeklies. For seven or eight years before the *Morning Chronicle* took up Hazlitt, Walter consistently managed the theatrical criticism of *The Times* and the advertising of the managers, in consonance with the principles of Leigh Hunt and his disciple, Barron Field.

The Times began to print candid notices immediately after Leigh Hunt had set the example in the *News* of 1805. Barron Field can hardly have come to Printing House Square later than 1806, and may have arrived the previous year, at barely 20 years of age. He was a Christ's Hospital boy, son of Henry Field, the school's apothecary, and intimate with Charles Lamb. Like many of Walter's young men, he was studying for the Bar when he came to *The Times* in order to take a share in the Law and Parliamentary reports, and to look after the dramatic criticism. The fresh note sounded by Field in *The Times*, and Leigh Hunt in the *News*, was unwelcome to actors and managers alike. There were many protests. In its Review of the Past Season (of Covent Garden), printed June 24, 1807, *The Times* reported that " Mr. Reynolds' *Arbitration* [was] utterly contemptible ; and Mr. Lambe's *Mr. H—* utterly damned. The musical pieces of the season bear an air of mediocrity in their language and of prettiness in their music. . . . Mr. Reynolds' senseless pageant *The Deserts of Arabia*, a wretched pantomime called *The Enchanters*." *Peter the Great, or Wooden Walls* (Covent Garden, May 8, 1807) by " that ceaseless scribbler Mr. Cherry," with its " insipid songs and nauseous courtesies," was denounced. " Mr. Cherry is undoubtedly the lowest dramatist of this wretched day : Mr. Reynolds can make a laugh sometimes, and Mr. Thomas Dibdin can write a song ; but Mr. Cherry can do neither."

This, indeed, was plain speaking. For the first time the theatres found their productions criticized by reviewers who could not be frightened, flattered or bought, and at last, in John Walter Junior, a proprietor who refused their free tickets. Nor, in young Walter's regard, did the advertising offer the box-office an opportunity to exert pressure on *The Times*. The managers' only course was to attack the new writers in their own press. They wrote against the " damned boys " and " supercilious lads " of *The Times* in the magazines. The line taken is well exemplified in John Browne Bell's magazine of fashion, *Le Beau Monde* ; his number of January, 1808, printed the following paragraph as part of a two-page attack on the new school of criticism :

The writer who furnishes *The Times* with theatrical criticisms, (if that which is exhibited in utter contempt of critical principles can properly be termed criticism at all) is evidently a gentleman of much light reading. And, indeed, he attacks every individual who comes within his reach, with so sharp a superfluity of quotation that his writings make us snift as furiously as a schoolboy does who has been cheated with mustard on his bread.

The writer found, too, that the style of *The Times* critic " is very often extremely inaccurate " ; he alleged that " if this critic knows little of acting, he knows as little of the audience ; he is equally mistaken before and behind the curtain." The attitude of the partisans of the old system of puffing is again expressed in the *Satirist* (not to be confused with the weekly of a later period), which in the same January, 1808, felt itself " obliged to notice the severities and animadversions which have lately appeared in a daily newspaper, and which are uniformly directed against the authors and actors of Covent Garden Theatre." But Covent Garden was not really singled out. Pieces put on at the Haymarket or any other theatre were given the same drastic treatment when that seemed to be called for by the nature of the performance. The *Satirist*, however, went on :

Persons who judge impartially themselves, are apt to imagine, that the critiques they read in *The Times* are the result of great erudition, deep research and profound critical sagacity ; it is therefore, our duty to undeceive them ; for the critic, who disgraces his profession so completely as to oppose indiscriminately performers and writers only because they happen to be attached to a particular theatre, deserves to be exposed, and, we trust, the circumstances that we are about to state, will sufficiently elucidate the secret motives of its *poignant* satire and its *piquant* remarks.

There follows a statement that " it has been customary, time out of mind, for theatres to pay only the stamp duty for the insertion of their daily advertisements in all the newspapers," and publication was considered, " as it really is," a sort of " mutual service." Proceeding, the writer reveals that " the Editor of *The Times*, at the commencement of the present season, refused to admit them without *full payment*, which Mr. Harris very properly refused." The rule of *The Times* was strict. On September 16, 1807, Richard Peake, manager of Drury Lane Theatre, requested the Editor to acquaint him " with the names of the persons, who you think ought to be put upon the free list of that theatre on account of your paper for the present season." The unequivocal reply was that the reporters would pay for their seats. It can hardly have missed the ear of the manager of the Covent Garden Theatre, who, nevertheless, secured the insertion of paragraphs in the *Satirist* alleging that advertising " is the cause of all the spleen and spite which a prejudiced boy chooses to vent against *authors and players*, in revenge for a supposed injury upon his master by a *manager*." The critic of *The Times* is described as a " lad," who does not know pantomime from tragedy, an opera from a play, or a farce from an oratorio, but " takes upon himself to give the world directions what to like, and what to reject, and without any other reason than the one we have mentioned." *Le Beau Monde* for the following March echoed these statements in its review of Leigh Hunt's critical essays just reprinted in book form from the *News*. The author's ignorance of his whole business was insisted upon ; he also was too young for perception.

A letter from Sheridan indicates that the new criticism menaced the relations which the most famous of all the managers had long maintained with *The Times* :

John Walter, Esquire, Junior.

Dear Sir

I confess my surprise at being shown on my return to day to Town a letter in your liberal Paper, containing a gross attack on me personally, and a very foul attempt to obstruct our endeavours to rebuild Drury Lane Theatre— The whole is a string of most impudent falsehoods— and addressing you, not as an Editor, but, on the footing of the fair and friendly intercourse, wh^h, as a private man, I have always met you and your Father, I must regret, that you could have permitted the publications of such Libels— A proper answer will be sent—tho' not from me— And, I hope, I shall have the pleasure of finding you at home between three and four to morrow—

Dʳ Sir   Yours truly

R. B. SHERIDAN

A famous actor-manager with whom John Walter was friendly was J. P. Kemble. During the O.P. riots *The Times* supported Kemble's new prices, and was denounced as having been bought by him. That Kemble and Walter remained on friendly terms in spite of candid notices is suggested in a surviving letter (undated) of this period :

Dear Sir,

I am very sorry that I shall not have the pleasure of seeing you this evening. I was in hopes to have shown you a very gay sight—upon my soul ! You have given us a trimming to-day. As thou art strong be merciful.

Yours truly,

J. P. KEMBLE.

The tickets shall be made out as you desire and sent you tomorrow.

The kernel of truth in the charge that *The Times* was bought by Kemble's gold is doubtless that he was prepared to pay Walter's revised advertising charges, on the principle that new prices in the theatre being economically justified and supported by the paper, new prices in advertising were probably justified too. But they were greatly resented by Drury Lane. The trustees of that theatre wrote on June 22, 1807, to the effect that *The Times* was charging at double the rate of any other newspaper, in spite of the " larger proportion of indulgences that have been granted to the gentlemen of *The Times* than to the gentlemen of any other newspaper." Walter Junior's answer was to insist upon full payment : " The gentlemen trustees must not expect any diminution will be made in it." He said further that the acting manager of the theatre, while agreeing to the charge before it had been sent in, freely offered the indulgences. " The Editor of *The Times* made no demand of that nature, nor ever will." As for the advertising, the paper for some years had been charging at this rate and would accept no less. The trustees, on their part, admitted that the rate " had been so long submitted to from *The Times*, originating as is supposed in a

93

political as well as a theatrical agreement." This brought from the Editor a retort containing two emphatic paragraphs :

[Undated but probably June 26, 1807]

The Editor of *The Times* presents his compliments to the gentlemen trustees of the Drury Lane Theatre and begs leave to inform them that he is not disposed to relax in his demand. It is clearly in his remembrance that Mr. Graham, whose conference on the subject in question was not with Mr. Bell,[1] but with the Editor himself, did assent to the charge, which has been made for advertising representations of Drury Lane Theatre.

Mr. Graham certainly expressed a hope that the price would be lowered to three shillings but on the refusal of the Editor, who stated that he would rather insert them for nothing, Mr. Graham acquiesced in the original demand.

As to the former agreement being considered as of a political as well as a theatrical nature that is a notion which the trustees of the theatre must be intreated to explain, as the Editor has no knowledge of any such transaction.

For his own part he thinks it would be for the interest of the papers in general to render themselves entirely independent of the theatres, and to do their duty to the Public by ceasing to make favourable misrepresentations of their performances.

Evidently Walter thought that, with the help of Barron Field and Leigh Hunt, he had so raised the intrinsic worth of his notices that he could afford to defy the strongest of all theatres. In the following month the trustees wrote to inquire the rate at which, having obliged them by reconsidering the matter, he would insert the advertisements. The theatre was then straightly informed that the proprietors would not " recede from their customary charge of six shillings." In the result there was no advertising of Drury Lane Theatre in *The Times*. Meanwhile the notices of plays remained in the care of Barron Field. In his absence during August they were written by Leigh Hunt.[2] These notices are good examples of the new spirit in criticism. The second notice is excellent ; its subject is Charles Dibdin's *Errors Excepted*, which opened at the Haymarket on August 13. That Hunt was only a substitute for Field the following letter proves :

Hastings, 11th August 1807

My Dearest Friend, I am in ecstasies with your very attentive criticism in *The Times*, which I have only this moment seen ; and cannot help sending you my best thanks for it. The latter part of it, on Mathews, I

1 Charles Bell, the Printer of *The Times*.
2 August 7, 14, 1807.

94

saw copied into the *Courier* a day or two ago, and knew from whence it came directly. Your simile of the clock and dial at the conclusion, however, I think imperfect, for there never was a clock without a dial, or that did not show its meaning after it had struck it. The allusion to waterworks is a masterpiece. Pray let Mr Walter have an article on the new piece of " Errors Excepted " on *Thursday evening*. Call on him after the play, and he will accommodate you.

I find myself compelled to make you the same request from Hastings that you did me from Margate, for money. I suppose it is something in the sea or air that gives rise to it. Will you have the goodness to call upon Mr. Walter before you go home to dinner the day you receive this and make him my request for a £5 note, apologizing as per politeness ; and will you then send it to me at " Miss Frewin's, Northiam, Sussex " where I shall go on Thursday morning to spend the last week of my absence.

Yours, in sure and certain hope of an answer by Thursday,

BARRON FIELD.[1]

Field was also responsible for other important departments of *The Times*, beside reading for the Bar. His professional legal progress seems to have been distracted, for he was not called to the Bar until 1814. His work for the paper was necessarily reduced when he entered the Inner Temple. Thus he wrote to Walter, resigning a portion of his duty :

Temple, Tuesday Novr. 7th 1809

Dear Sir

I dined yesterday in the Temple Hall for the first time, and picked up there, that any *visible connection with newspapers will operate as a preventative to a man's being called to the Bar*. Debate reporting is the only thing that can not be hid (for a student has a right to his note-book in a law court) and I write to request you will dispense with the very poor services in that way, wh^h I can render you next Session, and let me be looked to only for the King's Bench and Theatres. In consideration of this I am willing to submit to any deduction of salary you please ; and let me add that the Court of King's Bench would be better attended of a morning by one, who has not been late at the House of Commons overnight, and that this was the cause of those lapses in my Law Reports, of wh^h you justly complained at the end of last Session—

I beg to acknowledge the sense I have of your constant politeness to

Sir

Your very obedient Servant

BARRON FIELD.

[1] *Correspondence of Leigh Hunt* (Vol. I, pp. 28-29 ; second paragraph from original in the Hunt papers, B.M.).

VII

A BATTLE WITH THE POST OFFICE

JOHN WALTER'S self-reliance, resolution and political probity, his powers of organization and financial ability, were all tested, before the death of his father, by a long struggle with the Post Office. In the early days of his management he found the foreign postal service, and therefore the news service, in an intolerable state. His plans for the expansion of the paper were founded upon a conception, fresh to his generation, of the value of news. Seeing in priority the essence of news, he exerted himself to the utmost to anticipate rivals. But the business required more than mere pugnacity. There were vested interests to be conciliated as well as trade competitors to be outdone. The proprietor was forced to make arrangements " of a magnitude to create no ordinary anxiety in his mind respecting the result," as he himself remarked ; they involved a large monetary risk.

The need for a restrained and tactful approach to the high officials of the Post Office arose from the persistence of abuses, incredible by the standard of our day, in the handling of the foreign mails. Young John Walter was never " diplomatic " in the usual trade sense, nor did he ever rely upon occult political manoeuvres. He was " indebted for his success only to professional exertions and the private friendship of persons unconnected with politics," he wrote. The success was certainly a matter for congratulation, for the objective had been important and the obstacles serious. A special foreign news service, maintained by a corps of correspondents responsible to Printing House Square, was not exactly a new device ; but for some years no other paper had maintained such correspondents, and never on the scale organized by *The Times.* Interference by Government agents, of which Walter complained, extended to foreign newspapers and foreign letters. It must be borne in mind that the London journals were dependent for their foreign paragraphs upon French, German and

Dutch journals ; and while the development of an efficient country post was difficult, it was a small task compared with the establishment of trustworthy mail services abroad. The expense of postage was heavy, yet the communication was uncertain. To pay writers for dispatches which never reached their destination was a constant risk. In the disturbed first decade of the nineteenth century commanders of packets had orders to run while they could, fight when they could no longer run, and throw the mails overboard when fighting was no longer possible. The amount of mail lost was not only large but frequently disproportionate : by corrupt " surrender " commanders conspired to enrich themselves at the expense of the underwriters. Even when, in spite of all perils, the mails did arrive, they were subject to various delays.

There was, for example, a standing courtesy, zealously maintained by Canning, which secured to Cabinet Ministers and foreign Ambassadors the delivery of their correspondence before either newspapers or translations of articles in them could be secured by journalists. But at one time the newspapers were often officially sorted and even translated within the Post Office before the diplomatic correspondence had been left at the Embassies. Thence had arisen among some proprietors a practice of bribing postal officials to go through the foreign papers in their interest and give them a note of important transactions before the diplomats got their bags or competitors received their translations. The *Courier* at one time paid the Comptroller of the newspapers £200 in one year for this priority. Clerks competed and paid for places to which a share in such handsome incidentals was attached. The organized collection of foreign papers and preparation of summary translations for London journals followed ; and in the general interest of the clerks no single journal was allowed any advantage. " Guinea-men," as they were known, became part and parcel of the Foreign Newspaper Post. It was a system costing each proprietor at least 100 guineas a year, being a guinea for every summary of the twice-weekly foreign arrivals.

When attacked, the arrangement was defended as a benefit to the newspaper proprietors. A letter which Francis Freeling[1] wrote to " Their Lordships[2] the Postmaster General " (November 30, 1802) justifies the guinea demand for an abstract translation from the Hamburg papers on the ground that the proprietors had agreed

[1] (Afterwards Sir) Francis Freeling, Secretary to the Post Office 1798-1836.
[2] The office was held jointly by William Lord Auckland and Lord Charles Spencer from March 31, 1801, to July 19, 1804.

97

H

to it, and that, having agreed, " none of them employed Dutch or German translators " of their own. Moreover, Freeling insisted that

the Clerks paid very considerable sums per year to agents abroad to procure the foreign papers, and to translators conversant in the German and Dutch languages, and to clerks to multiply immediate copies for the proprietors, and that so inadequate was the casual Recompence to the permanent charge incurred by the Clerks, that they had more than once come to a determination to decline furnishing the proprietors with translations.

Their Lordships the Postmaster-General, " having every possible reason to believe that the Purity of Mr Freeling's conduct is as indisputable as his peculiar and acknowledged Efficiency in all the important Duties of his department," accepted his explanation, and the system continued.

John Walter I., like the other proprietors, obeyed the conditions imposed by the Post Office. His son determined to devise an alternative. He saw that, though forced to pay the imposed charges, he could not be forced to print the summaries, and he used them only for checking or in emergency. Gradually he secured not only his own newspapers but his own translators and correspondents. The plan brought upon him the increasing hostility of the postal officials and he found it advisable to draw the attention of Addington's Administration to his partiality for their cause. Discrimination against *The Times*, clear enough to John Walter, was not easy to prove. On January 14, 1805, Mr. T. M. Musgrave, secretary to Addington, wrote that he had mentioned to his chief John Walter's " suspicions that directions had been given by the Home Office to intercept " his " correspondence from the North of Europe." Addington expressed the " utmost astonishment and surprise." Not only so, but he authorized Musgrave to give his assurance that the " suspicion is utterly destitute of every foundation " ; Mr. Walter could feel " perfectly confident that no step so base and so unjust has ever been or ever will be taken under the direction of the Home department for the purpose either of obtaining any priority of intelligence or of exposing him to any the slightest injury." Whether the letters were detained by Home Office instructions could not and cannot be established. It is clear, however, that subordinate officials of one Government department or another were interested in delaying correspondence for *The Times*. The copy of a letter, unaddressed, undated, on paper watermarked 1805, survives. It was probably sent to George Hamilton of the Foreign Office during 1807 :

The Post Office are at their old tricks again. My material letter was again kept back last night. I was in hopes that your interposition wd. have put an end to such an iniquitous practice ; but as that seems to be of no avail and my letters are consequently at the mercy of the clerks of the P.O., to be withheld for the purpose no doubt of being examined, as soon as my correspondents can possibly be apprized of a less known and secure channel, I shall beg leave to decline troubling you any farther and shall at the same time save myself from the mortification of bearing these repeated insults from the P.O. I am very much obliged to you for all your civilities and have the honour to be, &c.

Not long afterwards Walter arranged with R. Buller and Co., of Crosby Square, Bishopsgate Street, to permit letters for *The Times* to come under cover to their office. The plan succeeded for a time. Later on Walter found that dispatches from Newman, his Correspondent at Emden, addressed to the mercantile house in the City, were either arriving with strange irregularity or not arriving at all.

The foreign correspondence of City houses was not, in those days, delivered by agents of the Foreign Post Office ; it was called for by the merchants' clerks at an hour announced beforehand by the Post Office as the time of delivery. The clerks received their packets at a window, at the same time paying the postage. Buller's letters had so arrived and been collected for twenty years. In spite of this long-standing arrangement, many of Walter's letters addressed to Buller were brought direct to the merchant's counting-house later, with the excuse that they had been over-looked. Walter could not resist the suspicion that postal officials had opened the covers and removed or retarded the enclosures. A direct remonstrance drew from Freeling the official explanation that, as Newman wrote an almost illegible hand, it was not surprising that letters addressed by him should have occasionally miscarried.

The Prussian Post Offices are very vigilant, Mr. Newman's correspondence relating solely to Intelligence may have caused suspicion of his character and some of his letters may have been intercepted and sent to Berlin.[1]

[1] Statement of the Senior Clerks in the Foreign Post Office in Answer to the Accusations of *The Times* (P.O. MSS. 1807).

Thereupon Walter redoubled his efforts. By a complicated method letters intended for *The Times* were addressed by the respective correspondents to a number of mercantile houses, whose clerks recognized them by distinguishing tokens affixed according to a constantly varying schedule of which the correspondents possessed a copy; a duplicate was strictly reserved to the hands of the Editor " that he might know where to send for his letters, and how to distinguish them from the private correspondence of the gentlemen to whom they were ostensibly addressed." The method was cumbrous although comparatively secure for correspondence. But foreign newspapers by their bulk presented a greater difficulty. Several letters remain to testify to the persistence with which Walter urged the correction of the abused power by which the Post Office deprived *The Times* of its journals. During war years the Post Office clerks themselves failed to obtain Continental newspapers. Nevertheless *The Times*, in common with other London journals, continued payment of sixty guineas a year to the Post Office, receiving, during one interval of two years and a half, deliveries on not more than ten or a dozen occasions. At last, in October, 1805, *The Times* declined to pay any further instalments, and there followed a series of significant incidents.

As a first consequence of its refusal *The Times* was subjected to departmental interference. Postal officials boarded vessels arriving at Gravesend with papers, and proceeded to inquire for and seize any packets addressed to *The Times*. Upon complaint being made through a friendly intercessor of some position in the Government, Freeling stated that no individuals had any right to receive foreign papers except through the medium of the Post Office; difficulties would arise if *The Times* received papers otherwise, as the newspaper deliveries were a private income of the Post Office clerks, who, if they lost it, would require compensation by Parliament. This, he added, would mean an all-round increase of salary and the Post Office would become an expense instead of a revenue to the Exchequer.

These arguments seeming good to his adviser, Walter agreed, while complaining of the inconvenience of the system, to continue the annual sum to the Post Office, " though he should get nothing in return, provided he was not interrupted in receiving papers through his own channels." At a later personal interview, following more interference, Freeling accepted Walter's statement that other papers were allowed to come through Gravesend without molestation, and said that this was a peculiar favour granted only to those which wrote in support of the Administration.[1] He promised that the officer at Gravesend should not be instructed to delay papers for *The Times*, but should forward them with the rest, if the Editor would consider it " as a favour conferred upon him by Government." Walter declined the offer. In these circumstances it is not surprising that, in spite of his efforts and their general success, Walter was occasionally anticipated by a rival. An unaddressed letter, dated November 13, 1806, reproduced here from a copy in Walter's own hand, describes a flagrant instance of victimization :

My dear Sir :

It is not necessary for me to inform you of the dispositions I have entertained to the present Government ; and if there should appear to you to have been any relaxation in my zeal to serve it I think it right to communicate, for your particular information, the circumstances which have affected my conduct.

I will not occupy time so precious as yours, in repeating at length the strange proposition transmitted to me by Mr. Dardis last February, who certainly seemed to be actuated by an attention to his personal interest in preference to any other. The little attention which it was natural for me to pay to a person who seemed so ill calculated to justify my confidence, may be supposed to have induced him, with his views, to obtain the interference of his patron in favour of the most inefficient and unserviceable of all the morning papers. But that circumstance was not made an object of serious consideration with me, while no unfair means were employed to afford the paper alluded to an occasional priority of intelligence.

No sooner, however, did hostilities commence on the Continent, than *unfair* means, to say no worse, were actually practised. Papers which it was known were intended for me, as I had obtained permission from Government to receive them through the Harwich channel, were seized. The next day their contents appeared in the *Oracle*,[2] which immediately disseminated its boasts of having deprived us of our

1 Freeling, considering it his duty to support the Government by every means in his power, maintained a secret censorship of correspondence and newspapers. He had a chain of correspondents throughout the country, who reported to him the use of the press or the post for purposes of " sedition." These instances he reported to the Home Secretary. Cobbett complained that Freeling substituted the *True Briton* for his *Porcupine* in packets addressed to his subscribers. Cobbett also alleged that Freeling was " the most dangerous, because by far, very far indeed, the most powerful " of the " Pitt faction " and that he possessed " the appointment of an active and powerful political partizan in *every town* of the kingdom." (Cobbett to Auckland, June 15, 1801 ; Cobbett to Windham, February 10, 1806.)

2 The *Oracle* incorporated the Treasury paper the *True Briton* in 1804. On the accession to power of the Addingtons, Treasury support was withdrawn and the *Oracle* employed ; hence the amalgamation.

accustomed priority. The interruption has been since continued, though fortunately previous arrangements in other quarters counteracted in the first instance the mischief which was planned against us. Though I am not in possession of all the minutiae relative to this transaction from the very proper reserve exercised by those who had an insight into every particular, yet enough has appeared from the *Chronicle* and *Oracle* to convince me that there have been exertions officially made to advance the interests of those papers at the expense of ours.

What impression such an unprovoked attack upon my fair advantage will make on my mind, I shall leave you to judge ; and you will equally decide upon the impressions the conduct of *The Times* ought to make upon Governm^t. when I assure you, that its daily sale amounts to at least 500 more than the combined circulation of the *Chronicle* and the *Oracle*, the daily delivery of the latter not amounting to 800 papers. Nor is the *Evening Mail*, which may be considered as the handmaid of *The Times*, to be passed by without its recommendation. Its publication is equal to that of the *Chronicle*.

The proceedings in this business are perfectly unaccountable. We are certainly not engaged in a system of petty praise or fulsome eulogism : but we have given that support to the Governm^t. which the understanding of the country to which it has been addressed appears to have approved.

When I have the pleasure of seeing you, I will explain myself further on the subject. In the mean time I am conscious that the purport of this letter is so correctly stated, that I can have no objection to any communication you may think proper to make of it.—

I remain,
My dear Sir,
Your faithful & obliged humble Serv.
JOHN WALTER, jun^r.

The recipient of this letter was probably Hiley Addington. By the exercise of high authority, special arrangements were made with George Hammond (Under-Secretary for Foreign Affairs 1795 to 1809). The nature of these arrangements appears from a surviving note dated Downing Street, April 1, 1807. Mr. Walter Junior is informed that the letters addressed under cover to Lord Howick and Sir Francis Vincent shall continue to be delivered to him, but that he is at liberty in future, if he thinks proper, to direct his correspondence from abroad to be forwarded under cover to Mr. Hammond. These letters contained newspapers and were opened at the Post Office. The following copy letter without date is in the writing of John Walter Junior and was probably addressed to Hammond in June, 1807 :

I feel myself really concerned in being again obliged to trouble you respecting the detention of my letters in the foreign Post Office ; but it is in vain to look for any accommodation from your obliging permission to have my letters enclosed to you, if their delivery continues to be purposely retarded at the Post Office. Mr. Darlot the Deputy Controller I have reason to believe is the person, who takes upon himself the care of occasioning this delay ; he invariably takes away my letter from your first packet.

This fact is capable of proof and I will be ready to substantiate it if you shd think proper to communicate the circumstance to the Post-master Genl. In the hope of receiving a favourable answer, &c.

Hammond took action through his chief. On July 1, 1807, Canning signified to the Postmaster-General that it was his Majesty's pleasure that in no circumstances should letters to the department be delayed. But without any hint from Hammond Canning also took the opportunity to complain " that it frequently happens that the Contents of the Mails appear in the publick prints previous to the delivery of the official Packets."[1] The question of priority was exactly the point at issue.

Meanwhile the Post Office was defending itself. *The Times* had published articles criticizing the Post Office administration and charging it with extortion and the sacrifice of the public interest to individual gain. My Lords the Postmaster-General had been succeeded by two new appointees, Lord Sandwich and Lord Chichester,[2] who were equally ready to maintain the purity of Freeling's conduct. An article in the issue of May 9, 1807, must be quoted :

Every corner of the Royal Exchange re-echoes, in its turn, with the abuses, the delays, the negligence and the extortions of that depart-ment . . . The administration of the Post Office must be considered as disgraceful to our Government. A base, pettifogging spirit seems to pervade every branch of it, and makes a continual sacrifice of public convenience to the avarice of individuals. . . . We certainly have a right to remonstrate, for ourselves at least, against the contributions which are continually levied upon us, under pretence of communicating the obsolete contents of Foreign Papers ; and though we have in general anticipated any intelligence which the Clerks in the Post Office, by the

[1] George Canning to My Lords the Postmaster-General, July 1, 1807. (P.O. MSS.)

[2] John, Earl of Sandwich, and Thomas, Earl of Chichester, May 5, 1807, to June 6, 1814.

connivance, or rather the participation of their superiors, have conveyed to the newspapers, we have regularly paid their unjust demands till last Sunday, when the Clerks were suffered to obtrude on us, as a guinea's worth of information, a parcel of paragraphs which had already, with the exception of a few lines of no consequence, appeared in another paper.

A second article, on May 12, returned to the subject :

We do not hesitate to say that Mr. Freeling and Mr. Stanhope have countenanced these unwarrantable proceedings (of delays etc.). We shall prove that the latter participates in the profits resulting from them. As for the petty pickings of Mr. Freeling, they will be the object of future consideration. Within these two years we made a complaint to Mr. Freeling on a subject connected with that which we have now presented to the attention of the public, when he peremptorily contended, that it was absolutely illegal for any private person to receive Foreign Journals, and that the Post Office was appointed by Act of Parliament to be the sole distributor of them ! ! !

My Lords the Postmaster-General acted quickly ; they adjudged the article of May 9 to be a libel. On May 14 *The Times* wrote :

A morning paper of yesterday threatens us, indeed, with a prosecution on the part of the Post Office. We do not, however, feel the least alarm at such a threat.

John Walter Junior prepared his case during June and the action was tried in the Sheriff's Court on July 3. The affidavit of John Walter the elder and John Walter the younger is too long to quote in full, but a portion, defining and defending their use of the words " Post Office extortions," which illustrates the general conditions, requires to be summarized. The two chief proprietors of *The Times* pleaded that from January 1, 1800, Mr. Darlot and others of the Foreign Branch extorted and took sixty guineas from every London newspaper proprietor (William Cobbett, Daniel Stuart and eight others are named) by colour and pretence of having supplied certain French newspapers when in truth they had not ; that such extortions had been practised upon the named proprietors every year from 1800. Also, they pleaded that each proprietor had paid 5s. a quarter during this time for having letters delivered to them at " early proper and reasonable times after the receipt thereof, when the same might, could and ought to have been delivered to them without their paying [the ' early ' fee] " ; and that Mr. Darlot and others did keep back a hundred foreign mails in order to make a sale of, and did then and there make a sale of their contents, to wit, of very many articles of foreign intelligence. Mr. Abbott thus addressed the special jury of merchants :

The Defendants, conscious, as I may now say, that they could not prove the truth of the matters alledged in this publication (*The Times* May 12 last) submitted that judgment should go by default. . . . The Defendants have consented to an arrangement. We shall, therefore, give you, Gentlemen, no trouble. . . . The terms are that upon payment by the Defendants of the full costs, and upon £200 and an apology being made, the proceedings shall be at an end.

An apology was duly read :

We having inserted several observations in our Paper reflecting on the character of Mr. Freeling as Secretary to the Postmaster General, and Mr. Stanhope, as Comptroller of the Foreign Department of the General Post Office acknowledge such observations *to be totally groundless and unfounded*, and are extremely sorry we were betrayed into any such publications.

Mr. Jekyll, acknowledging for his clients, the prosecutors, that the apology was satisfactory and " that Mr. Walter and his son have acted with as much honour as the nature of their situation admits," &c., testified that he was prepared to say " on the part of my clients, that, looking at their Paper as most of us are in the habit of doing daily, we can hardly see a Paper less prostituted either to party or to individual calumny."[1]

The charges it had brought against the Post Office were, it may be admitted, unprovable ; indeed, investigation of the clerks' statements on oath to their superiors and the replies of Henry Darlot, Arthur Stanhope and Francis Freeling indicate that a number of John Walter's charges were unfounded. Yet *The Times* had won a moral victory. When Canning drew the attention of the Postmaster-General to the fact that news appeared in " the public prints previous to the delivery of the official packets," he was objecting to the privilege by which Walter secured the inclusion of his newspapers in Hammond's correspondence. Darlot, the Deputy Chief of the Foreign Post Office, was able to say that

packets had for some time past arrived by the Tonningen Mails and that they have generally detained them for the second States[2] well knowing that they contained nothing but newspapers for Mr. Walter,

[1] Quoted from official shorthand writer's notes circulated on a broadside issued to the newspaper trade by Freeling and Stanhope with the imprint of H. Teape, Tower-hill. (Post Office Archives.)

[2] A contemporary term for correspondence directed to Government officials below the rank of Ministers.

Proprietor of *The Times*, which it has always been suspected he obtained clandestinely through the connivance of the Messenger or some subordinate person at the office in Downing Street. I must also inform you that Packets of a similar description notoriously known to be for Mr. Walter come by the Gothenburgh Mails which have also been detained till the dispatching of the second States upon the same ground.

Darlot pointed out " that the postage on the packets for Mr. Walter under cover to Mr. Hammond by the mails delivered this morning (July 11, 1807) would have amounted to £1 8s. 6d."[1] It is clear, therefore, that John Walter was engaged in a struggle against the principle arising from the constitution of the Post Office rather than from individual discrimination. As long as Canning was determined to prevent the issuing of newspapers to the London journals before the delivery of the official packets, and as long as Post Office officials were permitted to engage in the business of translation, Walter Junior would inevitably find himself opposed in his plan. In the following year he addressed a petition directly to the Postmaster-General. His position was that, as a newspaper manager, he was as much entitled to the immediate delivery of his correspondence as any other business man.

Three weeks after the publication of its apology *The Times* gave a whole editorial page to a "naked account" of the transactions to which it objected. The Post Office authorities planned a second prosecution, but the Attorney-General, on receiving the requisite particulars, marked them " No action."

A more formidable agency than official discrimination at home was soon to prevent foreign newspapers reaching England. The blockades of the " continental system " gradually became effective and by 1809 the Harwich packet ships found themselves unable to reach the ports of Holland ruled by Louis Napoleon. The last ports open to English vessels were on the north-west coast of Germany. Napoleon annexed these at the end of 1810. Henceforth no Continental newspapers were available either to the Post Office departments or the London editors. Smugglers then became the only agents for foreign intelligence. With the sanction of the Postmaster-General, Stanhope's Foreign Post Office staff secured, at intervals, the Paris papers. From 1811 increased difficulties were experienced. On April 28, 1811, a boat from France was seized by the Admiralty. On the 30th the Comptroller of the Foreign Post Office besought the Commissioners of the Admiralty to remember

[1] Freeling to P.M.G., July 11, 1807. (P.O. Archives.)

Mr John Walter, Editor of The
Times, presents his Compts to Mr Croker; and
returns the French Papers with which Mr
Croker has been so good as to favour
him. Mr Walter's private house is
attached to the Office wherein the Journal
is conducted; and at present he sees no
other mode of addressing himself personally
than by directing to him in Printing House
Square. As such direction will, however
still be liable to the objection which Mr
Croker is so kind as to suggest, Mr Walter
will in the course of a day or two endea-
-vour to form some arrangement which
may do away the existing difficulties; and
should a personal communication on this
or any other subject be deemed more con-
-venient, Mr Walter will have great
pleasure in waiting on Mr Croker.

Printing House Sqr April 7. 1811

JOHN WALTER II TO JOHN WILSON CROKER
From the original in the William L. Clements Library,
Ann Arbor, Mich., U.S.A.

that "it is of material consequence to Government, to have a channel by which Intelligence may occasionally be obtained" and to release the crew. Their Lordships replied on May 1 that they could not "interfere in the case of smugglers."[1] If the use by the Post Office of ships engaged in the business of evading excise could not be sanctioned by the very authority responsible for chasing and arresting smugglers, there remained the employment of private blockade runners not carrying contraband. With this in view Walter Junior wrote to John Wilson Croker, Secretary to the Admiralty, long on friendly terms with John Walter I.[2]

I take the liberty of addressing you on a subject which has been suggested to me in relation to the procurement of French papers. The difficulty of obtaining these has increased lately to an extraordinary degree—to overcome which a plan has been proposed to the following effect. It is pretty certain that no French journals whatever can be procured but by the means of smugglers—a person of this description, who is in collusion with a French officer near a certain port is willing to exchange this contraband traffic in which he has been hitherto engaged, for one, which is perfectly innocent with respect to its operation on the public revenue, namely the conveyance of French papers only to England. He feels disposed to engage in this traffic if he could be well assured of certain facilities, which seem to be necessary to the execution of the scheme. Government will I apprehend be no less desirous than myself of obtaining the information contained in these papers— I do not mean to ask the permission in this instance directly, but only to learn in the way of information (if you would have the goodness to satisfy me) whether there would be any impropriety in requesting the Admiralty to grant this man's vessel a protection for the purpose above specified upon the sole condition that no smuggled goods whatsoever should be transported by him. With this understanding I should of course transmit you the papers received with all possible expedition. As I before specified I only wish now to enquire whether there is any impropriety in making the application, engaging so far as I can possibly be answerable for the conduct of the person employed, that the object of his voyages shall be totally remote from anything connected with contraband trade—

There is no note of Croker's reply, but there is reason to believe that no objection was raised to any attempt to secure papers by vessels not engaged in smuggling, and that John Walter engaged with the man mentioned in the letter to bring the French journals

1 Stanhope of the Foreign Post Office to J. Barrow, 2nd Sec. of the Admiralty. (P.R.O., Admiralty 1/4073.)
2 *Croker Papers*, I, 21.

to *The Times* agent at Deal. This special packet, though strictly watched by Government agents and sometimes interfered with, was reliable enough to satisfy Walter, who made similar arrangements with the owner of a packet at the port of Harwich. There remain at Printing House Square several letters from foreign diplomats in London thanking John Walter II. for news which they could learn only much later from their official channels. Baron Nicolay, Secretary to the Russian Legation, wrote in 1812 :

Dear Sir,

H.E. the Russian Ambassador is desirous to read occasionally the French Papers—as the *Moniteur* & *Journal de l'Empire*—and has consulted me upon the subject. Seeing no possibility of getting them in a direct way I take the liberty to trouble you with these lines to know whether it would be in your power (since nobody here has better Correspondents than you) to get along with your own french papers an additional Copy for Count Lieven,—or whether your own Copy, after perusal, might be sent to the Count and H.E. wishes it to be understood that in the latter case he would bear one part of the charges.—

I should be much obliged to you if you would favour me upon the subject with an answer which I might communicate to the Count.

I have enclosed hereby 2 of my last Russian newspapers in which you may find some articles worth insertion and particularly those I have marked with ink on the margin.—

Believe me, Dear Sir, Your's

NICOLAY.

A similar request in 1813 from an even more eminent source may conclude this account of John Walter's struggle to ensure priority of news for *The Times*.

Foreign Office, Sep. 18, 1813.

Mr. Hamilton[1] presents his compliments to Mr. Walter, & is directed by Lord Castlereagh to request he will have the goodness to tell him if he has received any Intelligence of the reported defeat of the French near Dresden which is now in Circulation.

Mr. Walter, *Times* Office.

Hamilton's question was prompted by the natural anxiety of British Ministers aware that Napoleon's lieutenants had been beaten in the north although he himself was victorious at Dresden. This was the situation in August. The " reported defeat " became an accomplished fact in October, when Napoleon, unable to prevent a junction of allied forces at Leipzig, was decisively beaten.

---

[1] William Richard Hamilton, Under-Secretary Foreign Affairs, 1809-1822.

VIII

THE FIRST STEAM PRESS

WHEN, in his twenty-seventh year, John Walter Junior became sole manager of the establishment in Printing House Square, logography had been tacitly abandoned. Nevertheless the term " Walter the Printer " was still more or less accurate by reason of the book and pamphlet work he conducted besides the composition and presswork of *The Times* every day, and the *Evening Mail* thrice a week. Indeed, the jobbing department enjoyed until 1806 the patent of printers to his Majesty's Office of Customs, over the imprint " I. & I. Walter, Printing House Yard." Work was done for the Admiralty and many small commercial concerns, and there was an increased number of reprints from the columns of the paper. In 1805 the jobbing department earned £1,000 profit.

John Walter Junior became interested in the mechanical side of the press early in his career. In advancing money for new presses he was following his father's logographic example. But his chief concern was for the printing of the newspapers, which in 1805 represented a yearly cost of £3,500. Acting then, as may be assumed, under the influence of his father's example, which itself conformed to a general industrial tendency, young Walter made an agreement on May 9, 1804, with Thomas Martyn, printer, of Golden Lane in the City, to subsidize a printing press " by which manual labour in printing will be rendered nearly unnecessary." He was to advance Martyn sufficient money to perfect the invention. About £600 had already been advanced in 1803 towards the construction of four presses and " the machine now erecting which is to contain and work the four printing presses." Martyn was not to make any other machine or press upon the same principle without Walter's consent. If, after the issue of letters patent, Walter should elect that no other machine or press be made for sale, an extra £500 was to be paid. The agreement, therefore, provided for the acquisition of the machine and for an option on all rights in the invention. The Martyn " self-acting printing press " involved the office in an expense of £1,482 before Walter Junior was satisfied that it was a failure.

The first successful application of power to the printing press, rightly described by *The Times* as an invention only second in importance to that of Gutenberg himself, was the result of co-operation between Thomas Bensley, printer, of Bolt Court, Fleet Street ; Frederick Koenig, printer, of Castle Street, Finsbury Square ; George Woodfall, printer, of Sea Coal Lane, Ludgate Circus ; Richard Taylor, printer, of Shoe Lane, Fleet Street ; and finally John Walter, printer, of Printing House Square. Koenig came to London in 1804, when John Walter was placing his hope in Martyn for the mechanical improvement of printing. Besides Martyn and Koenig, one William Nicholson had taken out a patent for printing by machinery. Nicholson's was granted as early as 1790, but in 1806 he was still endeavouring to accomplish the object to which Koenig also was giving his energy. Needing money, Koenig turned first to Thomas Bensley, well known through and beyond the trade.

The demonstration of the invention had been sufficiently protracted to try the patience. On March 31, 1807, the first agreement between Bensley and Koenig had been signed. The text of the important paragraph was as follows :

Mr. Koenig, having discovered an entire new Method of Printing by Machinery, agrees to communicate the same to Mr. Bensley under the following conditions :—That if Mr. Bensley shall be satisfied the invention will answer all the purposes Mr. Koenig has stated in the Particulars he has delivered to Mr. Bensley, signed with his name, he shall enter into a legal Engagement to purchase the Secret from Mr. Koenig ; or enter into such agreement as may be deemed mutually beneficial to both parties ; or should Mr. Bensley wish to decline having any concern in the said invention, then he engages not to make any use of any part of the Machinery, or communicate the Secret to any person whatsoever, until it is proved that the Invention is made use of by anyone without the restriction of Patent, or other particular engagement on the part of Mr. Koenig, under the penalty of £6000.

John Walter Junior was approached after the construction of the first mechanical parts, which occupied all the year 1808. A letter from Bensley to Koenig, dated August 9, 1809, tells the inventor, amongst other things, that he has seen the Printer of *The Times* :

Having occasion to leave town for the remainder of this week, I made a point of calling upon Mr. Walter yesterday, who I am sorry to say declines our proposition altogether, having (as he says) so many engagements as prevent him entering into more . . . Not without serious concern for the disappointments you have experienced, and with hearty good wishes for your eventual success, I remain sincerely yours, &c.

The refusal of John Walter to take any interest in Koenig's invention at this time led the partners to seek assistance from George Woodfall and Richard Taylor, with whom they concluded an agreement on September 29, 1809. Walter's action was reasonable enough, since the object of Koenig and Bensley was to secure not merely a vague promise to consider the utility of the machine in the office of *The Times*, but immediate financial assistance. As yet no patent had been obtained. Koenig himself had spent a sum estimated at £1,060, and Bensley had advanced £500. The two new members of the syndicate each contributed £250. The 1809 agreement associates with the inventor Andrew Frederick Bauer, a scientifically-minded German, skilled in optics. The press was patented in March, 1810, and was first tried in actual work during April, 1811, printing, for the purpose of trial, a sheet of the *Annual Register* in a run of 3,000. This was the first sheet of a book ever printed on a mechanical press. Koenig's initial trial-press operated by power, but, although involving no other new principle of construction, it was also remarkable for Koenig's discovery of a method of the distribution of ink by rollers, and the invention of the movement of the formes in the bed of the machine, worked in accordance with an automatic tympan and frisket.[1]

The first machine, however, was only a step towards the approved machine, whose speed was to be much greater, inasmuch as it was to incorporate the vital principle of the cylinder. Koenig's first press produced 400 sheets an hour. The second, i.e., the cylinder machine, finished in December, 1812, worked for its successful first trial two sheets of Clarkson's *Life of Penn*. It was patented on October 30, 1812, and July 20, 1813. On the successful demonstration of the press at Koenig's workshop in Whitecross

[1] The *frisket* is a thin iron frame covered with paper. It turns down upon the sheet to be printed and which has been laid on another iron frame known as the *tympan*, holds it flat in its position, keeps the margin clean and raises it from the forme after impression.

Street, the inventor, determining to interest the newspaper trade, invited Perry of the *Morning Chronicle* and Walter of *The Times* to see the machine. Mr. Perry " did not consider a newspaper worth so many years' purchase as would equal the cost of the machine and declined to disturb himself with a visit to Whitecross Street." John Walter II., urged by Peter Fraser, who overcame his objections, saw the machine, and realized at once that its rapid action constituted an economic gain of the first importance. He agreed to purchase two machines from Koenig and his syndicate.

The construction of these machines for *The Times* was proceeded with at the workshop in Whitecross Street. Bauer, as Koenig's manager and chief mechanic, had each of his men bound by a stamped fidelity-bond of £100 sterling not to divulge any description of the machines, their parts, or the names of the persons to whom deliveries were made or to be made. The first agreement between Koenig, Bensley, Woodfall and Taylor and John Walter is dated March 30, 1813. It speaks of Koenig's " invention of a manner of printing by means of machinery," and provides for the sale to Walter of

two double machines of sufficient dimensions and capable of printing sheets 35½ inches in length by 22 inches in breadth, the letter press occupying to within one inch of the length and breadth thereof.

The sum of £1,100 each was to be paid for these double machines. Further, " two Steams (*sic*) Engines of Two Horse Power each to work the said [double] machines " were to cost £250 each. Finally, " to connect by sufficient machinery the said two steams engines with the said two double machines so as to render the said machines capable of effectually and perfectly performing the work of letter press printing " was to cost £100. Walter was to have the use of this equipment " for 14 years and also for the term of 14 years from the date of such further letters patent as may be obtained " by Bensley and Koenig. It was agreed to deliver the machines within twelve months ; also that the proprietors of the patent should not, during the term of fourteen years or any patented extension,

lend, sell or in any manner dispose of any of the said machines . . . to any person or persons whomsoever for the purposes of newspaper printing to be used within ten miles of the City of London, nor work, use or employ or permit or suffer to be worked, used or employed any machine or machines that any or either of them may now hereafter have in use or operation in the printing of any newspapers or newspaper . . . on more beneficial or advantageous terms . . . than they have hereby contracted and agreed to sell . . . to the said John Walter.

It was, however, covenanted by the parties that Bensley, Koenig and Co. " may dispose of any number of the said machines on any terms and conditions whatsoever for the use of the Clarendon Bible and Printing Office." And further

that if it shall happen that either of the said two printing machines shall upon sufficient trial being thereupon respectively had, be found incapable of printing or working off 1100 sheets of the size and dimensions aforesaid and the letter press occupying as aforesaid, within the space of one hour, but then and in such case it shall and may be lawful for the said John Walter, his executors, his administrators or assigns to redeliver and yield up unto the said Thomas Bensley, Frederick Koenig, George Woodfall and Richard Taylor, their executors, administrators or assigns the said two printing machines . . . and recover from the said Thomas Bensley etc. . . . . such sums of money as shall have been paid for the purchase thereof.

To the foregoing provisions for construction, delivery, installation, output and payment for the two " steams engines," &c., there are annexed four highly interesting recitals which reveal the precise and immediate economic gain of the new engine to John Walter. It was, surprisingly, a gain in the composing room.

Whereas the said John Walter hath been accustomed to pay for the working off the copies of the said newspapers after the rate of 4s. 9d. for every 250 copies of *The Times* when the number of copies worked off for one number thereof has amounted to 4,000, and 3s. 2d. for the working off every 250 copies thereof when the number of copies in one number thereof has not amounted to 4,000 (exclusively of the wages of Fly boys amounting weekly to the sum of £3 12s. 0d.) and 2s. 2d. for every 250 copies of the *Evening Mail* exclusively of the wages of a Fly boy and

Whereas the working off 250 copies of the same or any other newspapers can be performed by the use of the said printing machines at a considerably less expence and

Whereas also in order to hasten and expedite the publication of the said newspaper called *The Times* in cases when the number of copies printed and any one number thereof has exceeded 4,500 the said John Walter hath been accustomed to pay over and above the sums herein

I

before particularly mentioned to have been paid by the said John Walter for working off copies thereof for the composition of a duplicate page of the said newspaper the sum of 260 guineas by the year and

Whereas by the use of the said printing machines in working off the said newspapers the composition of the said duplicate page will be rendered and become wholly unnecessary, the expence thereof wholly and entirely saved and avoided and the said sum of 260 guineas by the year will be wholly and entirely avoided and saved by the use of the said machines as aforesaid :

For these reasons it was provided that in consideration of Walter's adoption of the improvements he should pay

a moiety or half part of all the actual savings which shall arise by the reduction of the price in working off and also pay . . . the sum of 130 guineas by the year being one moiety or half part of the sum paid for the composition of the said duplicate page as aforesaid.

The insurance of the machines " from damage or destruction by fire or otherwise either in part or in whole " was provided for at the expense of John Walter, who also undertook their repair " in a good and workmanlike manner and with good and proper materials." For the protection of Bensley and other book printers the agreement provided that if John Walter

should use or employ or willingly or knowingly permit or suffer to be used or employed the said machines with the improvements (if any) thereon in working off or printing of any book, volume, publication, printed work or paper of any description whatsoever other than and except newspapers without the license and consent in writing of the said etc. . . . he shall pay . . . all and every the savings which shall arise by the use of the said machines . . . in working off . . . any such book . . . or paper of any description, whatsoever other than and except newspapers.

A sufficient and proper book or books of account were ordered to be kept. There were to be entered a true, distinct account and description of the names, sizes, quality and number of impressions of all newspapers, books, volumes, publications, printed works and papers of every description or denomination whatsoever printed by the new machines and improvements (if any).

This book was to be open for the perusal and inspection of the patentees. John Walter was not allowed to make any models or drawings or willingly or knowingly to permit others to make any models or drawings.

THE FIRST STEAM PRINTING MACHINE
built by Frederic Koenig and Andrew Bauer
for *The Times* in 1814

It was provided, too, should the inventors make any machines capable of working off any greater number of sheets, that Walter be allowed to acquire them. The full sum of £2,800 was paid, as to £500 on the date of the signature of the deed, another £500 at the expiration of two calendar months from the same date, a further £500 within four months, and the balance of £700 on the erection of the machines ; also £500, being the price of the steam engines, in two instalments, and £100 for connecting apparatus on delivery.

During 1812 and 1813 Koenig, with Bauer's assistance, conveyed the several parts, as they were completed, from their workshop to Walter's private shop, set apart for the purpose in Printing House Square. The transfer was carried out in complete secrecy for fear of an anti-machinery combination within Printing House Square with consequent destruction of the press. There occurred, in fact, a demonstration of compositors, who saw their labour at less demand as a result of the abolition of the hitherto necessary practice of composing duplicate pages. The combination was defeated by Walter, who himself organized the printing on the steam presses and had provided against sudden withdrawal of labour, or attempt at sabotage. Those who had threatened harm to the machine or its inventors were directed to wait for expected news from the Continent. Before six o'clock in the morning John Walter went into the press room and astonished its occupants by saying to them : " *The Times* is already printed—by steam." He promised a continuance of wages to every compositor until suitable employment could be found, but pointed out that if any violence was attempted there was a force ready to suppress it.[1]

The first public announcement was made in the first leading article of *The Times* for November 29, 1814 :

Our Journal of this day presents to the public the practical result of the greatest improvement connected with printing, since the discovery of the art itself. The reader of this paragraph now holds in his hand one of the many thousand impressions of *The Times* newspaper, which were taken off last night by a mechanical apparatus. A system of

[1] *The Times* office ignored the workers' societies. In 1810, four years before the employment of steam, the compositors and pressmen of the *Day* persuaded the men of *The Times* to ask for the advance being sought in the trade generally. The compositors and pressmen gave notice to leave Walter's service if the increase was not given. Twenty-eight men left Printing House Square in May, 1810. When Walter prosecuted for combination nineteen were sentenced, of whom one died in prison. A petition for release, accompanied by an undertaking and an apology, was supported by Walter, who forwarded to the Prince Regent his own petition for the exercise, in their behalf, of the royal clemency. Walter, therefore, had reason to fear a demonstration against the new machine.

machinery almost organic has been devised and arranged, which, while it relieves the human frame of its most laborious efforts in printing far exceeds all human powers in rapidity and despatch.

Then comes a description of the machine and a statement that " no less than 1100 sheets are impressed in one hour " ; added to which is a declaration that

our share in this event has, indeed, only been the application of the discovery under an agreement with the Patentees, to our own particular business ; yet few can conceive,—even with this limited interest,—the various disappointments and deep anxiety to which we have for a long course of time been subjected. Of the person who made this discovery we have but little to add. Sir Christopher Wren's noblest monument is to be found in the building which he erected ; so is the best tribute of praise, which we are capable of offering to the inventor of the Printing Machine, comprised in the preceding description, which we have feebly sketched, of the powers and utility of his invention. It must suffice to say farther, that he is a Saxon by birth ; that his name is Koenig ; and that the invention has been executed under the direction of his friend and countryman Bauer.

The immediate economic gain in saving the composition of the duplicate of *The Times* has already been pointed out. Another, implicit, gain is mentioned in a leading article of December 3, 1814. After a statement that the new machine had not only been working regularly but was now doing so with " improving order, regularity and even speed " the article says that its advantages to the public were particularly manifested on a recent day when Parliament was adjourned :

On such an occasion, the operation of composing and printing the last page must commence among all the journals at the last moment ; and starting from that moment, we, with our infinitely superior circulation, were enabled to throw off our whole impression many hours before the other respectable rival prints. The accuracy and clearness of the impression will likewise excite attention.

A supplementary agreement, made in 1815, and signed by Bensley, Koenig and Taylor (George Woodfall having retired from the syndicate), provided for the alteration of the moiety of savings agreed in the 1813 agreement. For the future, payment was to be made by John Walter " at the rate of 1s. 8d. for every 250 of the said newspaper called *The Times* which shall be printed and published etc. . . . on condition that the copies reached a total of 30,000." Yet a further (undated) supplementary agreement cancels that of March 30, 1813, and that of May 1, 1815 ;

all accounts between them having been settled to this day and the within named having in cash and by his acceptances of bills of exchange paid to the within named Thomas Bensley, Frederick Koenig and Richard Taylor, they having accepted the sum of £2800 in full for the absolute unlimited and unrestricted right of using the said machines within mentioned and of their claims and demands on account of the savings and profits arising from the use thereof or otherwise from henceforth for ever.

Thus John Walter had the satisfaction of seeing in regular work the machines now fully paid for and free from harassing restrictions. A final document, dated November 19, 1816, recites the receipt of full payment, and grants liberty to Walter to employ whomsoever he may choose for the purpose of repair and replacement. The patentees agreed not to sell to the proprietors of any morning paper a double machine similar to Walter's, printing 1,100 an hour, for less than £1,100 each ; nor to accept a less annual premium than £200 for a licence to use each machine ; " these being the terms on which Mr. Walter has had his machines."

Difficulties not rare in such affairs arose in connexion with the patent rights, and harassed Koenig. A letter, the only one remaining in the archives of Printing House Square, tells of the many difficulties encountered by Koenig and the consequent disappointments at Printing House Square :

Closter Oberzell bey Würzburg, 20 D'cebr 1818.

Dear Sir,

Your letter of Novbr 6 would have been answered sooner, if I had not been unwell since 3 weeks.

In Spite of our exertions it has been impossible to complete your work in the time agreed upon with Bauer, and if you knew all the difficulties, we have to struggle with, you would not be severe upon us. The principal reason is, that this is not a manufacturing country, good workmen are extremely scarce, and even inferior ones are not to be had in sufficient number. Now, if you insist to have a thing well done by indifferent workmen, it goes very slow.

It will be, however, a consolation to you, to have it proved, that it would have been altogether impossible to use the machines in their improved state for the present session of Parliament, for suppose the things had been in London by the 1st of December, it would have been impossible, to apply in so short a time. Mr. Edwards[1] has still a laborious task even when we have done our part in the most complete manner. It would certainly have been imprudent in you, to begin such a thing during the session—to have one machine in pieces and only one to go on with.

At present *all* our hands are employed for you, though we have other work equally urgent. I will not commit myself to a day or a week, but I give my promise, that all the things shall be in your hands a good while before the Session ends. Then will be the time for you to begin such an alteration. In the mean while we shall send drawings and instructions to Mr. Edwards, to prepare all such things he can do without taking the machines to pieces. After this explanation, though you may grumble still, you cannot be angry with us.

I thank you for your kind enquiry after my health and prosperity. My health is entirely restored, and as to my circumstances, my way goes still up hill, owing principally to Bensley,[2] who has bilked me completely. Yet, I am gaining ground, and, perhaps, I may still have the sad satisfaction of *dying* rich, after having *lived* poor. I remain

Dear Sir   Yours very truly

FR. KOENIG.

I knew already by Mr. H that you had the goodness to pay the £90 to him, and I am very thankfull for the accomodation. Mr. Bauers best respects to you !

John Walter Esqr
Printing House Square
London.

For his own protection Walter turned for assistance in redesigning the presses to English engineers. William Nicholson had already taken out a patent for a cylindrical press in 1790 ; also there were other inventors at work on the problem. In 1815 William Cowper obtained a patent for a method " of printing paper for paper hanging and other purposes." The salient feature of Cowper's cylindrical invention consisted in his use of curved plates obtained by stereotyping. But the stereotype process, being at that time dependent upon a plaster-of-paris mould, which needed time for settlement of subsequent lead moulding, was still out of the question for newspapers, though the principle could be applied to book-typography. In

---

[1] One of Walter's staff.

[2] Koenig's complaints against Bensley's handling of the finances of the patent do not seem to be without foundation.

Rec.d 20.th Nov.r 1816, of John Walter, Esq.re in
Cash & by his acceptances of our several Drafts or
Bills of Exchange the sum of Two Thousand Eight
Hundred Pounds, in full of all our demands
from this day for ever on account of the profits,
and savings to arise from the use of ^certain printing
Machines heretofore sold by us and George
Woodfall (whose interest therein was afterwards
assigned to the undersigned Thomas Bensley) to the said
John Walter, & in full for the absolute unlimited
& unrestricted right of using the said Machines for
all such purposes as the said John Walter may
think proper.

T. Bensley.

Fr. Koenig.

Richard Taylor

Discharge of final payment to Frederic Koenig on
account of the steam printing machine, 1816

1818, in partnership with Ambrose Applegath, his brother-in-law, Cowper perfected a new printing machine which, among many other benefits, gave a new and better inking by distributing the ink on the forme crosswise as well as lengthwise. The obstacles in dealing with Koenig abroad determined Walter to invite Cowper and Applegath to enter Printing House Square and reconstruct the Koenig machine, as his agreement with Koenig and Bauer allowed him to choose his own repairers. Not only was reconstruction accomplished, but, by a very ingenious combination of the cylinder principle of Nicholson with the plans of Koenig, Cowper was able to pass the paper from one cylinder over the other, thereby printing both sides of the sheet before it left the machine. Cowper's machine was not the first machine to print both sides of the sheet at one operation, that is, a perfecter, but was more practical than the experimental machine made by Koenig for Bensley in 1815, which must rank as the first; and it was the first used for the printing of a newspaper.

From this time Printing House Square took an increased interest in the problems of printing engineering and the commercial result of their solution. In 1827, under Cowper and Applegath, the printing office of John Walter brought out a new " multiple " machine with four cylinders which delivered 4,000 sheets an hour, the most rapid of all machines working flat formes. The forme passed under four cylinders fed by four boys with sheets of paper, which, after printing, passed through the hands of another four for perfecting, *i.e.*, impressing on the other side. The comparative hourly output of the several types of mechanical presses was :

Stanhope hand press	250 sheets.
Koenig	1100, raised to 1800, *i.e.*, 900 on both sides.
Cowper Stereotype	2400 or 1200 on both sides.
Applegath and Cowper	4000 on both sides.[1]

The invention of the rotary press depended upon the process of rapid stereotyping and of curved, not flat, plates; made from *papier mâché*, not from the plaster-of-paris moulds. The stereotyped plates came with sufficient speed; they produced a final effect no whit inferior to impressions from the original composition, and the machines were used throughout the period of John Walter II.

[1] The *Chronicle* used one of these machines producing 2,000, and the *Herald* one giving 2,900.

IX

PITT AND THE ADDINGTONS

THE allowance made to John Walter I by the Treasury ceased at Midsummer, 1799, when Pitt was still in power and was carrying through the legislative union between Great Britain and Ireland. He desired to complete his Irish policy by a measure of Catholic emancipation, but was so strongly opposed by George III that he resigned, and in March, 1801, the King sent for Henry Addington. With his successor, Pitt maintained the formalities of friendship in view of threatened dangers from the Continent. On the change of Ministry Henry Addington and his younger brother, John Hiley Addington, made overtures to *The Times*. The long connexion between Pitt and *The Times* then concluded. The nature of the bargain struck by John Walter I or William Walter does not appear in any of the available memoirs and correspondence. As John Walter's pension had been discontinued, some financial recompense may have been given in addition to the regular provision of advance information. The favours extended by *The Times* to the Addingtons were singularly generous even during the time of John Walter II. Articles by, or supplied by, Hiley Addington were printed in spite of their tone of personal hostility to Pitt and his friends. The " right of rejection," later claimed by John Walter, in respect of articles in favour of Addington, was not exercised in favour of Pitt. The first John Walter's single political principle was to support the King and his Ministers. Convinced that he could always, if necessary, drive a better bargain with the Opposition, he felt that in preferring to serve the Government he sacrificed to some extent his own interests.

The Times, as the Addington organ, supported the peace of Amiens (1801), which was opposed as disgraceful by Lord Grenville and other adherents of Pitt. Windham led the opposition in the Commons and, if Cobbett is to be believed, *The Times* lost many subscribers through its defence of the Treaty. " It is boldly asserted this morning," wrote Cobbett to Windham, " by the *Morning Post*, that it now publishes more papers than *The Times*, which assertion is offered to be proved upon oath." Cobbett considered the statement authentic. " *The Times* certainly published nearly twice as many as the *Morning Post* before the former began to defend the Peace, and the latter has constantly condemned the Peace as disgraceful and dangerous."

William, the eldest son of John Walter I, on leaving the management to his younger brother John at the end of 1802, secured a place worth £600 a year in the Audit Department. The previous connexion between the Walters and the Addingtons is likely, therefore, to have been intimate. Hiley Addington's articles in *The Times* were often a column or more in length ; and, in spite of the assistance Pitt rendered the Administration by abstaining from giving or provoking overt opposition, the tone of these articles was at first unfriendly to him, then strongly critical, and at last personally offensive. Pretyman Tomline, Bishop of Lincoln and Pitt's tutor, wrote to George Rose, a former manager of the Press, who had left the Treasury at the change of Administration, instructing him that he " above all, do not fail to show the last paragraph in the enclosed *Times*," probably of November 17, 1801, " to Mr. Pitt and tell him of the communication between Mr. Hiley Addington and Mr. Walter." In his opinion, " the spirit of Jacobinism is surely visible." During the following year Pitt and his friends noted further evidence in the columns of growing enmity of the Administration. Under date December 3, 1802, Rose penned in his diary a statement of his feelings :

In *The Times* yesterday is a most virulent and elaborate attack on Mr. Pitt and his friends, and a most fulsome panegyric of the present Ministers ; but done with ability. The editor of this paper is in habits of constant intercourse with the Minister's brother. This essay is detestable in all its parts ; but more particularly so for the language in which Mr Pitt is censured for his skulking from office in a disgraceful manner in the hour of danger and abandoning his sovereign.

Rose resolved to speak to Pitt about *The Times*. On December 5 his diary records that

on talking to Mr Pitt this evening about the long article of abuse against him and the late Ministers, he grew to feel the utmost resentment and indignation at it ; and said, if not apologised for in the same paper, or commented upon in the *True Briton*[1] in the next paper, he should

---

[1] A newspaper known to be subsidized and controlled by the Administration.

consider it countenanced by the Administration ; and that he would write to Mr. Steele to desire he would say to Mr Addington that unless it was disavowed in some shape in the same manner the calumny was published, he must consider it sanctioned by him.

But Pitt held back for fear of " embarrassing and equivocal explanations " from Addington, and of Addington's availing himself of the " opening of intercourse of any sort " to introduce " other subjects." In the paper of December 14 Pitt found a libel on himself and the late Government " more gross and offensive than the former one." But he preserved his neutral attitude towards the Government until late in 1803, in spite of the signs of extreme weakness after the outbreak of war with France. When at last Pitt went into open opposition, *The Times* still upheld the Addingtons. By then, however, John Walter II, after ten years' subordination to his father and elder brother, had taken the leading place, and the policy of the paper, though left unchanged, was clarified. It was natural for the young man to maintain the political connexions he had inherited with the paper. A leading article of February 10, 1810, seven years afterwards, explains the position :

The joint proprietor and exclusive manager of this Paper became so in the beginning of the year 1803, and from that date it is that he undertakes to justify the independent spirit with which it has been conducted. On his commencing the business, he gave his conscientious and disinterested support to the existing Administration—that of Lord Sidmouth [*i.e.*, Henry Addington].

Distinguishing his own practice from that of the previous conductor, John Walter proceeded :

The paper continued that support of the men in power, but without suffering them to repay its partiality by contributions calculated to produce any reduction whatsoever in the expense of managing the concern ; because, by such admission, the editor was conscious he should have sacrificed the right of condemning any act which he might esteem detrimental to the public welfare. That Administration, therefore, had, as he before states, his disinterested support, because he believed it then, as he believes it now, to have been a virtuous, and an upright Administration ; but not knowing how long it might continue so, he did not chuse to surrender his right of free-judgment, by accepting of obligations, though offered in the most unexceptionable manner.

Nevertheless, it is certain that the influence of the Addingtons upon John Walter the younger was as direct as it had been upon his predecessor. In the last weeks of April, 1804, Henry Addington found himself in such difficulty that he could not go on, and his resignation was announced to the Cabinet on the 29th, but he remained at his post while the King was in communication with Pitt. In a letter from Hiley Addington dated May 9, half-past ten, John Walter received the following intelligence :

I feel it due to you to inform you, that the Chancellor of the Exchequer will probably resign the Seals to-morrow.

Lord Hawkesbury, Harrowby, Castlereagh & Melville, will hold high situation : Lord Melville, I believe, as first Lord of the Admiralty. Lord Hawkesbury had a message to-day from Mr. Pitt convey'd by Mr. Long.

Lord Stafford, L'd. G. Leveson, Sir John Wrottesley, Sir Robert Lawley &c. have declared against Mr. Pitt.

Messrs. Tierney, Maitland, Bragge, Hobhouse, H. Addington, Lord G. Thynne &c. certainly retire.

More to-morrow. In haste.   [Unsigned][1]

Pitt, in power from the 10th of May, was faced with the hostility of the Addingtons. On the 12th *The Times* printed in the position of a leading article a notice that " Mr. Addington has refused the acceptance of any Rank or Emolument on retiring from office. We understand that His Majesty has been graciously pleased to propose an Earldom to him." The article proceeded to discuss the new Ministry : " We cannot help hoping . . . that the Report may be true of Lords Hawkesbury and Castlereagh being likely to form a part of the new Government. We are inclined to discredit the report of the latter going to the Admiralty." The allocation of the Admiralty to Melville, mentioned earlier, was now doubted. *The Times*, that is to say, Hiley Addington, concluded :

It is positively asserted that Mr. Canning takes no situation. Perhaps Mr. Pitt might do quite as well without him. We have heard, and hope it is true, that the King insists on Mr. Addington's retaining the house at Richmond Park. Sir T. M. Sutton is talked of as the new Chief Justice of Chester. This appointment, we believe, would give universal satisfaction.

Earl St. Vincent has sent in his resignation. Where is the country to find an adequate successor ?[2]

1 Hiley Addington to Walter, P.H.S. Papers.
2 H. Addington to Walter, undated and unsigned ; printed in *The Times*, May 12, 1804.

The adequacy of Lord St. Vincent's successor, thus questioned by Hiley Addington in behalf of *The Times*, was persistently argued after Melville's appointment was announced. Henry Addington and St. Vincent were friends as well as colleagues.

When Pitt and Addington were reconciled in January, 1805, the latter accepted a peerage, and, as Lord Sidmouth, succeeded the Duke of Portland as Lord President. *The Times* was again useful. In the previous year Hiley Addington had acknowledged the handsome manner in which *The Times* had so obligingly persevered in speaking of the former Administration, " to which you gave so independent and honourable support during its existence." The letter ends with an expression of Addington's pleasure " to keep up a friendly intercourse " with one who " in consistency and liberality exhibits a distinguished exception of the conduct of the general mass of journalists." The intercourse probably accounts for the insertion of a letter signed " Mictor," in which Hiley Addington championed the merits of Master Betty, the young Roscius. Relations continued to be intimate for years after the dissolution of the Ministry in 1804. There were controversial exchanges between the *Sun* and *The Times* at the end of 1804 and in the January of 1805, when the Pittites were indulging in sharp criticism of the Addingtons : " I am confident Mr Pitt himself would be offended by the language of *The Sun*," wrote Hiley Addington. After the reconciliation *The Times*, on January 28, 1805, spoke out boldly against " the base and crooked course of endeavouring to depreciate the person at the head of the late Administration, & holding a high situation in the present." But the public were to notice that

we shall never suffer ourselves to be betrayed by our partialities, whatever they may be, into any expression calculated to weaken the confidence that we wish to see reposed in the present Administration. . . . We think highly of Mr. Pitt's splendid talents, and shall feel no small pleasure in being enabled to give an independent support to the measures of that Government.

Immediately the new Cabinet got to work there were divergences on account of Melville, who, in the spring, was charged with misuse of public money while treasurer of the Navy in Pitt's former Ministry. Although he was innocent of fraud it was evident that the commission's charges of misapplication were just. The Addingtons anticipated this, for they had appointed the commission. Indeed, Hiley Addington wrote for *The Times* of May 19, 1804, an article printed as the second leader which said :

We shall be the last to approve the violent and unconstitutional conduct of those public men, whose object seems to be to force His Majesty to admit into his Cabinet an individual, whom he had been advised to erase from his List of Privy Counsellors, however strongly Mr Pitt may have thought it proper to recommend him.

Now, however, that Sidmouth was in the Cabinet, he supported Pitt's unsuccessful motion to move for a Select Committee. Censure in the Commons was followed by an impeachment before the Lords. In the following year (1806) Melville was acquitted, but he had been dropped from the Cabinet and from the Privy Council in the interval. His resignation was offered on April 9, but his successor, Charles Middleton, ennobled as Lord Barham, did not take office for a month. The causes of the delay and perturbation of these weeks were that Hiley Addington had angered Pitt by voting against him on the Melville question and that Sidmouth claimed the Admiralty for one of his friends, doubtless St. Vincent. In these intrigues *The Times* and John Walter II were involved. On April 26, 1805, the Secretary of the Custom House sent a formal notification that by order of the Treasury the printing for the department would henceforth be executed by the Stationery Office. At the same time the departmental advertisements for tenders were cancelled. Walter the younger protested unavailingly. He had no friend in the Ministry when Sidmouth resigned on July 4, 1805, but he continued to be friendly to it. Three letters from Sidmouth to Walter Junior are preserved. One of November 3, 1805, acknowledges receipt of the " first authentic intelligence which Lord Sidmouth had received of the late fatal disaster of the Austrian Army." Another of November 30 thanks Mr. Walter for " the important and most afflicting intelligence received this day from the Continent," and at the same time the writer makes an earnest request that " Mr Walter will have the goodness to send him any further information which may reach Town in the course of tomorrow." A letter from Hiley Addington deserves quotation in full for its reference to Admiral Collingwood and Nelson after Trafalgar :

Langford Court. Novr. 10th 1805

Dear Sir,
    Tho' I don't mean to trouble you with a letter whenever you favour me with any important Intelligence, I cannot refrain from thanking you

for your last very valuable & cheering Communication. If the Disasters on the Danube were occasioned by the violation of the Prussian Territory, and the latter circumstance really occasioned or has even accelerated the Decision of the Court of Berlin, of such Disasters we need have no cause to complain. So often does good come out of apparent Evil ; so foolish, not to say wicked is it ever to despair.—

We are on the tiptoe for further Accounts, particularly from Collingwood. His letter was the most affecting and the most intelligible that I ever read from a Naval Commander. I have a perfect Notion of the disposition of the two Fleets.—Most nobly he seems to have succeeded our departed Hero.—Perhaps today's Post may bring us something. There is abundant reason to believe that Bonaparte's successes may have been exaggerated.

> I am always, Dear Sir,
> Your faithful Friend
>
> J. H. A.

On January 23, 1806, Pitt's health sank under the blows of continual disasters, and the Government passed into the hands of a coalition. Lord Grenville became First Lord of the Treasury ; Fox was Foreign Minister ; Windham (no friend to *The Times*) Minister for War and the Colonies ; Sidmouth was Lord Privy Seal. This " Ministry of All the Talents " received the independent support of *The Times*, and immediately the conductor applied for reinstatement in his position as printer to the Customs. To Hiley Addington Walter II wrote on February 24, 1806, that the " hostility on the part of the then Government arose, and arose solely, from the manner in which *The Times* supported the measures of a former board of Admiralty, whose system, it is to be presumed, will be readjusted in consequence of the late changes in that department."[1] To this demand he received no answer. He wrote to Sidmouth, and again receiving no answer, lost patience with a suggestion made by friends of his family that he should petition for restoration of the contract. It was put to him that he should write " a memorial to be presented to the Treasury." In his own words :

Believing for certain reasons, that this bare reparation of an injury was likely to be considered as a favour entitling those who granted it to a certain degree of influence over the politics of the Journal, the editor refused to sign or to have any concern in presenting the memorial. But he did even more than this : for, finding that a memorial was still likely to be presented, he wrote to those from whom the restoration of the

[1] Draft in Walter II's hand, P.H.S. Papers.

employment was to spring, disavowing on his part (with whom the sole conduct of the paper remained) all share in an application which he conceived was meant to fetter the freedom of that Paper. The printing business to the Customs has, as may perhaps be anticipated, never been restored.

His experiences with the Addingtons, the loss of the Custom House contract, taught him that there were dangers as well as disappointments in giving hospitality to tendentious articles and paragraphs in exchange for prior home intelligence. The true progress of the paper was best served by developing the policy of securing a priority of foreign intelligence transmitted by his own correspondents. Walter Junior was content with modest receipts, and conservative trader that he was, the gains he might have made by speculating with *The Times* and permitting its exploitation in the interest of commercial or political intriguers did not tempt him. A director much more astute politically than young Walter would be required if *The Times* were to seek national political consequence without risking libel actions and loss of independence. Wisely the Managing Proprietor avoided, after 1806, any close association with Ministers, and concentrated upon the task of providing the political audience he had already secured with the earliest news from the Continent. The years 1806-7 represented, in some sort, the coming-of-age of John Walter Junior as a newspaper proprietor. In 1806 he celebrated his thirtieth birthday.

The political conditions favoured a change of policy. *The Times*, which for fifteen years under John Walter I had been absolutely identified with the cause of Pitt, and later was similarly identified with the cause of the Addingtons, chronicled the death of Pitt in January, 1806. The final exclusion of the Addingtons from the Portland Ministry came in 1807.

The refusal of John Walter II to connect himself in any way with a memorial to the Treasury had two consequences for him. The first was a quarrel with his father, which went deeper than he thought, for it ultimately resulted in partial disinheritance ; and the second, the antipathy of the new Portland Government. In Walter's words :

Since the war of 1805 between Austria and France, his arrangements to obtain foreign intelligence were of a magnitude to create no ordinary anxiety in his mind respecting their result ; yet from the period of the Sidmouth Administration, Government from time to time employed every means in its power to counteract his designs, and he is indebted for his success only to professional exertions, and the private friendship of persons unconnected with politics.

Complaints[1] by young Walter to the Portland Government were always met with an offer to redress his grievances " provided it could be known what party in politics he meant to support."

During the following years *The Times* was independent towards home politics, even colourless. The Castlereagh-Canning duel was chronicled, but neither approved nor disapproved. Foreign news was of urgent interest, yet although much space in the paper was given to the war in Spain, hardly less was devoted to the strife in the London theatres. Covent Garden competed for the reader's attention with Talavera and the Scheldt.[2] The political department of *The Times* was reinforced by new and able writers chosen by Walter during the years 1807-12 with a view, in his own words, " to permanent connexion and who supported the growing independence of the paper."[3] In 1812 Walter declared himself unable to support the new Liverpool Government in *The Times*.[4] Two years later *The Times* exerted itself to strengthen the hand of those who believed in a vigorous prosecution of the Peninsular War. Lord Liverpool, particularly, was drastically handled. The national cause occupied the columns throughout 1813-15. *The Times*, though a newspaper of increasing influence, made no specially intimate arrangements with statesmen, but John Walter came into touch with the agents of Lord Wellesley and received through Sydenham and Arbuthnot early news of Lord Wellington's campaigns.

The old association with the Addingtons did not survive the entry of new men into the office. John Walter himself seems not to have forgiven the Addingtons' failure to secure the restoration of the Custom House contract in spite of his demands during the following six or seven years. The denunciation of the Addingtons by *The Times* arose out of the misreporting of a speech in the House of Commons by Joseph Hume, who was made to have said that Canning, by habitually turning into ridicule the sufferings of his fellow-creatures, had been able to place himself far above their

[1] How the Post Office interfered with the news service of *The Times* is described in Chapter VII.

[2] For the theatrical controversy see Chapter VI.

[3] For the staff of *The Times* under John Walter II see Chapter X.

[4] Walter to J. W. Croker, May 20, 1812 (Croker Papers I, 38): " I must hesitate at engaging by implication to support a body of men so critically situated, and so doubtful of national support, as those to whom public affairs are now likely to be entrusted. . . ." *The Times* later disclaimed personal hostility towards Lord Liverpool.

unhappy condition. The editor of *The Times*, being informed by letter from Hume, wrote in the strongest terms of regret and expressed a wish to wait upon him with an explanation. Hume refused to receive the editor, and the paper of June 7 apologized for the error " attributable to the imperfections common to our human nature." When Canning raised the question of a breach of privilege on June 14, Hume admitted that he had deprived the editor of the opportunity of making the apology which might have been satisfactory to Canning. Brougham pointed to the danger of noticing offences of this description, seeing that omission to protest would be taken as an admission of correctness of what might in fact be misrepresentation. But the House ordered that Charles Bell, publisher of *The Times*, attend at the Bar on the following day. He stated that although the reporters had the strictest injunctions from the proprietor to report impartially, the haste with which it was necessary for these gentlemen to write their accounts necessarily resulted in occasional error. After Bell's withdrawal, John Payne Collier communicated a signed letter to the Speaker in which he explained that, seated as he was in the back row, and not having heard Mr. Hume's words, he was obliged to inquire from " a person what the Honourable Member had said, and had been misinformed ; he had been a reporter for ten years, and this was the first complaint." A Member testified to the " great respectability " of the family of the reporter and, as the House considered the committal of Collier to Newgate was too severe, he was taken into custody by the Serjeant-at-Arms, whence he was released on payment of a fine.[1]

Following references to the Canning incident in the *Courier*, there appeared in a leading article of *The Times* (June 19, 1819) an emphatic statement that there are limits to political warfare ; in fact, attempts to ruin the character of public men were " execrably wicked." The *Courier*, with hearty agreement, replied

[1] It has been said that following this step of Canning's, " *The Times* never forgot the insult." It may be admitted that it was the " Catholic," liberal, Canning of a later period that *The Times* admired. " Let but Mr. Canning keep his character up to the mark of his genius, and he cannot fail in being either one of the greatest Ministers, or the most popular ex-minister ever known in England," wrote the paper of April 4, 1827, on the eve of the formation of his Ministry. *The Times*, it may be admitted also, had learnt to dislike Canning from the Addingtons. But criticism after 1821 did not mean antagonism. Brougham's remark to Sir R. Wilson (March 26, 1827) that Canning " supposes himself to be unfavourably thought of by some of our people " probably accounts for Canning's statement to Grenville in 1826 that " it must never be forgotten that *The Times* though borne away . . . by the tide of public opinion, is at bottom as inimical to me personally as ever." A feeling of distrust did exist among Reformers, but, in Brougham's words, " late events I know have put an end to all such ideas, and I can answer for the most cordial dispositions towards him. . . ."

K

that certain writers had made up their minds to destroy the influence of Lord Castlereagh, Mr. Canning and Lord Sidmouth, and to do so " by calumny." It pointed to *The Times*, which found it well to reply. With respect to Sidmouth, the paper said :

Here is a subject upon which, as the Addingtons were for a long time our daily scribes, we are excellently well informed. The Addingtons may have since gone round, and united with Mr Canning ; but if we still find ourselves in our pristine opinions, in which we were along with them (with the Addingtons) and in which they (the Addingtons) placed us, they surely will not be the people to impute blame to us. We took our opinion of Mr Canning from them, at a time when we possessed no great means of judging for ourselves. But we appeal to Mr Canning himself, or to any of his friends, whether, from the period at which we cast off the Addington family, this journal has not ceased to peck at him personally.

The article claims that *The Times* was never tainted by such ribaldry as then appeared against Lord Sidmouth and other members of his family.

No, neither *could* the Addingtons have written, nor *would* we have published, anything so degrading to the persons attacked, as those writings, in which their characters, their talents, their connexions, and even their most innocent peculiarities and family habits, were every day exposed in the *Oracle* newspaper.

By way of further testimony to the absence of personal detraction in *The Times* it was stated that " since we sent the Addingtons adrift," though " opposed to Canning's measures," the paper at great inconvenience had inserted speeches by Canning outside Parliament, notably his famous electioneering speeches at Liverpool. This article aroused much comment. The claim that "we" had sent the Addingtons " adrift " so scandalized Crabb Robinson that he entered in his diary a conviction that he had never known John Walter or any other editor publish so damaging a criticism of his own powers of discretion. The *Morning Chronicle* of June 21, 1819, charged *The Times* with the gravest breach of confidence, and was duly answered. A promise was given " that of the various confidential communications with which we have been favoured, none will, either during our lives or after our deaths, be produced to the detriment of any fair and honourable public man." The editor of the *Examiner* excepted the editor of *The Times* from the range of the severe rebuke he gave to the Proprietor :

We say the Proprietor, because it is clearly he, and he alone, who can be responsible for the publication of circumstances connected with the management of his paper so far back. The change of Editorship is too frequent, and in that particular journal too well known, to render the case otherwise ; and we confess we have more reasons than one, why we are glad to know this fact.[1]

The Moderate Radical weekly and the Ministerial *Courier* agree in finding fault with *The Times*. There were two causes, arising from one simple fact. *The Times* and its concerns had grown too big to be managed in detail by one man. In consequence the paper was not internally united. Again, the supremely difficult years which followed the peace after Waterloo insisted upon greater attention being given to home affairs. As a business man Walter saw that the time had at last come for an important change.

---

[1] The *Examiner* article (June 27, 1819), signed by Leigh Hunt, is significant also for its concluding paragraphs, which discuss the relations between politicians and pressmen. The reference to the change of editorship in *The Times* and Leigh Hunt's friendship for Barron Field, a member of the staff at Printing House Square, has been mentioned in Chapter VI. For Leigh Hunt's connexions with other writers on *The Times* see Chapter X.

X

CHOOSING AN EDITOR

PROGRESS depended upon enterprising management and editorial initiative. Unlike other newspaper proprietors John Walter II as his own printer was charged with a dual responsibility, which increased with the expansion of the paper. Manifestly the Chief Proprietor would, sooner or later, need to reorganize the staff, or rather staffs, and free himself for other work by delegating this or that portion of his duties to chosen subordinates. The conduct of the office and the conduct of the paper demanded the exercise of two kinds of ability which became more difficult to combine as competition increased. The Koenig steam engine precipitated a new set of problems, and John Walter's attention was turned, as it had been turned before by the abortive Martyn experiment, to the rearrangement of the literary staff and the choice of one of his writers upon whom he could devolve more and more responsibility for the contents of *The Times*. Since his first years as sole director at Printing House Square he had been discriminating in the selection of his writers, and when the time came to confer full editorial authority, it went into the hands of one of his earliest acquisitions.

It was young John Walter's habit to pay considerably higher than the usual salary to the best of his literary staff ; for most reporters a somewhat less generous scale prevailed, and for the printing staff less than the union rates, without power to strike, though with favours not obtainable by men on other newspapers. Writers, at any rate, realized that conditions were better in Printing House Square than in any other office, and thus John Walter II was able to gather round him by degrees a body of remarkable men. The diary and reminiscences of Henry Crabb Robinson,[1] who early assisted John Walter II to secure for *The Times* a reputation it had not before approached, reveal a few details of the life at Printing House Square of this picked staff of writers.

[1] The MS. has been used by the kind permission of the Librarian, Dr. Williams's Library, London, to which the diarist bequeathed his papers. Sadler's three-volume edition printed only a small portion of the whole.

The sole personal link between the Logographic Press, the *Daily Universal Register* and *The Times* as it prospered under the hand of John Walter II was William Combe, author of innumerable minor works and the famous *Tour of Dr. Syntax*. He has been mentioned in connexion with early logographica, but he was also an important member of the staff from 1803 to 1810. He began to write for the paper long before ; indeed, during its earliest days. From 1787 or so he was engaged as a member of the corps of Writers maintained by the Treasury, his terms being

to obey such instructions as were given me, and when I had no instructions, to act from myself and my judgement as occasion offered. £200 a year was the stipulated salary.

This arrangement made by Charles Long, Secretary of the Treasury, continued in force until the coming into power of the Addington Ministry. Combe then became more closely identified with Printing House Square. He wrote during 1803 a series of " Letters," in the " Junius " style, signed " Valerius,"[1] which supported the Addingtons against Pitt.

When Crabb Robinson made his earliest acquaintance with Printing House Square he used to notice in John Walter's parlour the tall, stately and handsome Combe. Then " he did not appear to work much with the pen, but was chiefly a consulting man. When Walter was away he used to be more at the office and to decide in the *dernier ressort*." Combe was, in fact, the acting editor ; probably he had so acted in direct succession to William Finey.[2] His services to the paper were subject to unforeseen interruptions. One of these is revealed in the following undated letter addressed to " J. Walter, Esq., Junior " :

King's Bench, Wednesday morn.

My dear Sir

It will astonish you for I am sure it has astonished myself that I am at this moment an Inhabitant of this place and that instead of the pleasure of attending you last night, I had the very great displeasure of being conducted here. I was liable to it, but having escaped for five years I thought myself safe from any inconvenience. Nor can I well devise the malice wh^h has operated on the occasion for malice it must have been.—But so it is—I need not add that it will be necessary for us to meet. It was a most fortunate circumstance however that I had

---

[1] Reprinted (by I. & I. Walter, Printing-house-yard) under the title *The Letters of Valerius on the State of the Parties, The War, etc.* (London, Hatchard, 1804.)

[2] For William Finey, acting editor of *The Times*, 1788-1797, *cf.* p. 32.

obtained some knowledge of Colonel Dennis or I should not have had a place to lay my head upon ; and at his Apartment in the *State House* of this Building I am at present to be found—God bless us all I say—that it should happen at the present moment is abominably vexatious. But who can controul his fate—

Your most obliged humble Serv[t].

W. C.

Combe was destined to spend many nights in the King's Bench Prison.

I believe [says Crabb Robinson] that Walter offered to release him from prison by paying his debts. This he would not permit as he did not acknowledge the equity of the claim for which he suffered imprisonment. He preferred living on an allowance from Walter and was, he said, perfectly happy.

Bohemian as Combe was, he was a highly attractive dinner companion, and was a frequent guest at Walter's table in Printing House Square. He was always " very amusing " ; in Crabb Robinson's opinion " a gentleman in his manners," he abounded in reminiscence acceptable as truth with some qualification. He liked parties and knew he was liked ; witness one of his *Letters to Marianne*[1] dated April 10, 1807 :

I am languor itself,—in fact I am sufficiently indisposed to justify my sending an excuse to W[alter] to decline the party of tomorrow. I would not willingly do it . . . from the peculiar circumstances of the persons who will compose it, my presence is rather essential to the comforts of it.

Robinson at first believed all the details of Combe's stories, but records later that, although " old Combe " came to dinner and was very talkative, " he did not lye so much as usual." The explanation is that Robinson had discovered that Combe's one failing in these reminiscences was to intrude himself either as a witness or the hero of actual incidents reported to him by others. Notwithstanding, he never ceased to like him. Combe has left a testimony to the generosity of Walter the Second :

Tuesday Evening

My dear Sir.

You have conferred too many favours on me not to make a return when it is in my power,—and Christmas Day gives me an opportunity of doing it by giving you an opportunity of doing me a kindness.—

[1] Combe, W., *Letters to Marianne* (London, 1823).

WILLIAM COMBE
From a drawing by George Dance in the
National Portrait Gallery

So that if you have a mind to indulge yourself, as you gave me half my Christmas dinner last year, you may give the whole of it this year,—and as I know when you do a thing you prefer doing it handsomely,—you may gratify your honourable pride, as well as your benevolent friendship, by sending me a small Turkey, a dried Tongue, some Minced pies & a bottle of Wine.—

I ever remain

Your most obliged & faithful

hble. Servt.

W^M. COMBE.

Lambeth Road

[Addressed to " John Walter Esqr. Printing House Square, Black Friars.   very, very Private."]

Combe maintained his connexion with Printing House Square until he was past 75 years of age. Robinson met him at dinner there on February 3, 1817, when Combe told the story of Lord Mansfield saying he should sit on Good Friday, there being a great press of business ; on the proposal being made to the Bar, Serjeant Davy said to Lord Mansfield : " There has been no precedent since Pontius Pilate." On his death six years later the obituary notice in *The Times* made no reference to his work on the paper, to which he must have contributed hundreds of columns. Always to be relied upon to fire off at short notice a long letter or a squib to fill up, Combe was an excellent example of the able and venal journalist of the eighteenth century.

Combe was the only writer of reputation from the period of John Walter I who was continued in office by John Walter II. The other members of the staff chosen by the new manager represented the newer type of journalist, whose relative independence has been already pointed out.   Something was risked by engaging such men ; it was breaking the old tradition that the best journalists had the fewest scruples.   But the younger Walter followed in daily journalism the revolution which weekly journalism owed to Leigh Hunt and Barron Field.   All his men were educated and competent, and superior to the school of hireling writers, as befitted the chosen of a straightforward business man with common sense.   They were men of great and scrupulous ability ; they testified by their long association with the paper to the chief's own soundness of character.

Among the early assistants to John Walter the name of Collier is prominent.   John Dyer Collier, editor of the *Monthly*

Register in 1802, seems never to have possessed any serious practice as a barrister. In 1804, when he was living at Westminster, close to the School, and became known to Robinson, he was a contributor to the *Oracle*, then the property of Peter Stuart. He was able, however, to accept Walter's offer of " something over £200 a year " for reporting the proceedings in the Court of King's Bench. Collier performed this duty for *The Times* from 1804 to 1808, but his chief importance in its history comes of his having introduced Henry Crabb Robinson to John Walter in 1805. When in 1808 Collier left to go to the *Morning Chronicle* under Perry, he had secured places on *The Times* for his sons, William Collier and John Payne Collier. John, though a good, was an unreliable worker. He asked as salary five guineas a week, all the year, on the ground that the versatile Walter Henry Watts (an excellent miniature painter) received that sum as Parliamentary reporter of the *Morning Chronicle*. " But Walter says he allows no man such a salary and that he cannot accede to John Collier's proposal without offending the other reporters—several of whom are at least as good as himself—[James] Murray, the two [John and Charles] Ross's etc." Walter offered Collier seven guineas a week during the sitting of Parliament if the Session began before Christmas, and seven and a half guineas if it did not sit until after that date. If Parliament sat for thirty weeks, John Collier's income would amount to 210 guineas a year. William Collier had three guineas a week as a reporter, but, noted Robinson, "Walter does not think highly of William's talents and does not think he will ever become a first rate reporter." Fortunately it was otherwise ; William Collier gradually rose in his chief's estimation.

John Payne Collier served *The Times* for twelve years or more. In spite of the chequered nature of his career, he never lost his sense of gratitude to the Chief Proprietor of *The Times*.

John Walter [he writes in *An Old Man's Diary*] was the first person who discovered any ability in me, who employed it and rewarded it. How liberal he was may be judged from the fact that he gave me £50 for a few communications and £100 for getting the newspaper out of a scrape in which I myself had accidentally involved it.

The circumstances of the scrape were those of 1819, when Collier erroneously reported that Joseph Hume had stated that Canning owed his progress to a sinister capacity for laughing at the miseries of the poor.[1] Barnes and Walter had to go down and

1 The incident is fully described at pp. 128-9.

effect his release ; and Walter gave the delinquent the handsome present mentioned. " I was useful to him for at least a dozen years," proceeds John Collier, " and I should never have quitted him but for a disagreement with a leading person of his establishment." Barnes is the " person " indicated. According to the story Collier tells in a private letter to John Walter, his father frequently, in friendly fashion, lent Barnes wine out of his own cellar when his friend was too poor to buy his own entertainment ; Payne Collier himself had also once lent Barnes money, which was never repaid. Not liking to be reminded by Payne Collier's presence of these early circumstances, Barnes took occasion to dismiss him.

Mr. W. himself endeavoured subsequently to arrange the affair but failed, as far as both parties were concerned ; though he ever afterwards kept up acquaintance and correspondence with me, and to the last visited me in Kensington just before I determined to retire into the country more than 20 years ago.

Our knowledge of Barnes's character does not make Collier's story too credible. It was in large part due to Crabb Robinson's persuasive powers that Collier was retained on the staff for so long. Robinson's diary manifests on many occasions an increasing anxiety for Collier's future in the office ; tells of the concern given Walter by Collier's indiscretions ; expresses a fear that Barnes dislikes Collier and allows that the laziness imputed to Collier is justly charged. Idleness, more probably than Barnes's spite, brought about his summary dismissal in 1821, and he went over to the *Morning Chronicle*. Between 1825 and 1827 he brought out his volumes on the Old Dramatists, and from 1830 was engaged on the vast series of forged ballads and forged Shakespeariana, the extent of which was not discovered until 1859. On Barnes's death Collier made unsuccessful efforts to rejoin *The Times*. He left the *Morning Chronicle* in 1847, and was Secretary to the British Museum Commission until 1850, when he received a Civil List Pension.

Henry Crabb Robinson was introduced to John Walter Junior in 1805, and then began an intimate companionship that endured for more than forty years. The younger Walter's dissatisfaction with the extortions and delays of the Post Office led him to invent alternative means of transmission, and in January, 1807, he sent Robinson to Altona to act as correspondent for " the North," *i.e.*, Northern Europe. The salary is not noted in Robinson's diary, but there is evidence enough that the correspondent considered himself handsomely treated. The work was interesting to one who already knew Germany and German literature well. He had matriculated at Jena and knew Goethe and Schiller. Robinson was also intimate with Hazlitt, Lamb, Leigh Hunt and Barnes ; he was full of curiosity, though literary rather than political. The cities of Altona and Hamburg were at that time journalistic centres of the first importance ; correspondents and news-men gathered there for the purpose of exchanging intelligence from Northern and Central Europe. Altona, in Crabb Robinson's words, was " an important channel of information, but no source in itself." A long memorandum, written from his post in answer to a request from John Walter, is preserved with the Crabb Robinson MSS. The writer pointed out that, in all likelihood, some years of peace would make it necessary for the Chief Proprietor to reorganize his foreign department following up " the acknowledged pre-eminence which you have attained over your rivals through your activity in securing *priority* of intelligence . . . by a like zeal in providing for *superiority* in the mode of stating, as well as in the selection of information from abroad."

The high and paramount interest which all classes feel in foreign news during a state of war or revolution will give way to a more cool and judicious attention, when all that the foreign mails will bring, will be the domestic occurrences of foreign states.

It was urged that, with Europe on a peace establishment, the foreign department of *The Times* " will not admit of those extraordinary exertions you have been making, but it will still be certainly important, I should think, to merit that kind of attention and management which I mean to suggest now." There followed the suggestion that, by a judicious examination of the English, French, Italian and German periodical works of every description the existing low state of home knowledge of foreign affairs would be improved. At present, according to Robinson, " three-fourths who take up a daily paper read only the leading article and what besides is printed in a larger character." His own idea was to collect " under a catching title " into " one long running article " a summary of the whole body of foreign intelligence. What was new about Robinson's proposal was his insistence that the summary should be written intelligently. " You will perceive that this suggestion amounts in substance to this, that foreign intelligence should be put into the hands of a *rédacteur* (*celui qui rédige*) and not merely a *traducteur*." Robinson was right. The existing summaries were but a perfunctory string of paragraphs.

One sort of writers merely transmits news. Robinson described these as " matters of fact men." " You have had repeated specimens of this kind of correspondence in the French letters from Vienna which our friend has occasionally sent you. . . . I would not buy very dear letters like those I have seen." A second sort of writers specialized in *intelligence raisonnée*.

It would be an incomparable advantage to have as a correspondent a man of letters, possibly the editor of some journal or other, who would every week write on the topick of the week, and though he may not tell you anything new would give you the *tone* and *spirit* of his time and place ; he having a style of his own would document the authenticity of his letters. A correspondent of this description at Paris, Vienna, Berlin and St. Petersburg would be inestimable.

Robinson reminded John Walter that as literary centres Paris and St. Petersburg " are of the very first importance. Vienna and Berlin are of second-rate value. Dresden and Munich are of third-rate only and certainly need not enter into your calculation." This memorandum, dated " Altona, 19th July, 1807," convinced Walter that the writer, possessing analytical and constructive powers, would be even more useful in Printing House Square than in foreign service. John Dyer Collier, interrogated, confirmed that Crabb Robinson would be willing to accept a position in the office.

In the spring and summer of 1807 Walter Junior was busy ; he was disputing with the theatre managers the terms on which *The Times* would insert their announcements, and simultaneously working to preserve the independence of his dramatic critic ; he was still active in his struggle against the impositions and discriminations of the Post Office ; above all, he was occupied in reorganizing his writing staff. As the paper flourished, young Walter had discovered that the combined task of organizing, managing and editing was beyond the capacity of one man, and that he needed at home the services of other writers besides a foreign specialist. *The Times* had at last achieved some definite position ; at any rate, the preservation of its existence was no longer the Chief Proprietor's first thought ; but for further development two disparate talents, attention to commercial detail and intelligent editing, were necessary. Walter Junior had re-established the paper during the four years since 1803 that he had been sole Editor and Manager. The time had come for him to act upon his desire to devolve the detail of his editorial duties upon a suitable colleague, so *The Times* of May 21, 1807, printed among the notices on its front page an advertisement :

Literary Employment.—To superintend a long-established and respectable LITERARY CONCERN, a GENTLEMAN is WANTED who combines with liberal education a general knowledge of the world, and intimate acquaintance with the occurrences of the present times. As the situation is confidential, the qualities necessary to invite and justify confidence must not be wanting. An active mind and the habits of attention, are also essentially necessary. Some acquaintance with the mechanical arrangements of the Press would be desirable, though it is not essential. On the other hand, the liberality both of remuneration and sentiment will be ready to meet in the most satisfactory manner a Gentleman qualified according to the foregoing description. Address post-paid to S.T. at Mr. Vale's, No. 62, Fleet Street.

The advertiser received, among other applications, a letter over the signature of " J. Routh," as follows :

May 22nd 1807.

Sir, The person who now takes the liberty of offering himself to the consideration of the advertisers in the *Times* of May 21st thinks it more adviseable merely to state what he is as a matter of fact than to draw any description of his qualifications, pursuits, or acquirements.

He is in possession of one of those fellowships in the University of Cambridge, which are under no restriction of County, age, or profession and are therefore open to candidates of every description. At the time of his election there were twenty seven competitors. He has long been a contributor to the several periodical works of the day ; & his name is mentioned as supplying matter to others of a more permanent nature. If the employment is political, he has had a very intimate connection in one of the principal Secretaries of State's Office under the recent administration, but of this he declines saying any more till a longer intimacy may justify confidence ; neither would he make any use of this circumstance but such as might become a gentleman & a man of honor—If the employment is merely literary all his studies have been directed to the acquisition of the antient classics, and to the cultivation of what is generally termed polite learning or the " Belles lettres "—

If such a man may suit and the employment is strictly honourable, a letter stating the terms and nature of the engagement will produce a personal interview between the Advertiser and his

humble servant

J. ROUTH

Ware, Herts. May 22nd, 1807.

Correspondence with the writer followed the Chief Proprietor's preference for this application. The details of the situation and of the salary were given to Mr. Routh ; a meeting was suggested in the applicant's reply :

Sir The nature of the employment in wh^h I am to engage & the terms of remuneration being such as to satisfy me, I think probably all other circumstances might be best explained and the agreement expedited most readily at a personal interview. I shall therefore call at Mr. Vale's on Wednesday next hopeing to meet there with your address ; or shd this plan be subject to any difficulties, of wh^h I am not aware, there is still time enough for you to write again to Ware.

I should in my last have informed you that I am unacquainted with the mechanical arrangement of a Press ; but trust that to a man of common adroitness, that circumstance need not form any permanent objection. On another subject I have some delicacy in speaking, lest it shd seem as if I thought myself above the employment in wh^h I am engaging ; I confess I have some dread of the personal invective with wh^h the Editors of Newspapers load each other and therefore as there must now be some ostensible conductor perhaps it may not be necessary for my name to appear ; I will state to you, what I conceive to be a very strong reason for this wish to avoid publicity, when I see you—To that time I shall defer making any other observations and rem^n Sir for the present

Yr ob^dt. Sert
J. ROUTH

Sunday Evening [June 15 1807]

It will be noticed that Walter Junior offered the " superintendence " of the concern ; and that the applicant's desire was to avoid publicity, leaving that to the " ostensible conductor." The position was discussed in detail at Vale's, when the identities of the parties were revealed to each other. Mr. " Routh " acknowledged himself to be the Rev. Peter Lovett Fraser, M.A., Fellow of Christ's College, Cambridge, aged 34. Walter liked him very much, but Fraser, whose health was indifferent, could only close with the offer towards the end of August, when it was settled he should come to Printing House Square. This is the first record in the history of journalism of a Fellow of a College attaching himself to a newspaper office. But while Fraser had overcome his own scruples, his relation to the Master of Christ's College and to public opinion presented more difficulty. Academic opinion would be decidedly opposed to the intimate connexion of a Fellow with a newspaper. In a letter of August 19, 1807, Fraser repeated his objections to the position of " ostensible " conductor and pleaded that the present state of his sight and general health rendered doubtful his success as managing editor ; " rather than be known to manage a business but *moderately* I would retire to College and never put pen to paper again." Although he refused to accept the position of editor, he offered to take charge in the Chief Proprietor's necessary absence in the winter. The arrangement was accepted, and in this manner began a lifelong friendship which closed forty years later when, as confidant and clergyman, Fraser prepared John Walter II for his death. He and Crabb Robinson were made sole executors, and John Walter III named his own second son (principal proprietor of *The Times* from 1894 to 1908) Arthur *Fraser* Walter.

The unwillingness of the Rev. Peter Fraser to assume responsibility for the " superintendence " of the literary department necessitated the appointment of another as " ostensible " editor. Crabb Robinson was still at Altona in the first half of 1807. His dispatches thence relate the fall of Danzig, the French victory over the Russians at Friedland, and the Peace of Tilsit. On being called to take a position in Printing House Square, he returned to London through Stockholm, when the British Fleet faced Copenhagen and Cathcart landed in Zeeland with 20,000 men. After a holiday, he was made, on December 29, 1807, " a sort of foreign editor." But early in 1808 Walter considered it advisable not only to define Robinson's position more precisely, but to appoint him editor. The new arrangements are described in Crabb's letter to his brother, Thomas, postmarked Jan. 25, 1808 :

Some 10 days ago he [Mr. Walter] intimated a wish that I would take a more responsible part in the conduct of the paper. His health was then & is now very uncertain and he loves his pleasures & wants to shake off the necessity of giving the daily attention to business which he now does. He said that he wanted in case his health should be worse, to prevent his father or brothers interfeering by telling them I managed the whole. He then asked me whether I sho^d have any objection to ans^r letters, occasionally make calls upon persons of respectability etc etc. I observed that in case I did anything of that kind I must appear in a certain character—He answered very quickly " certainly you can^t appear otherwise than as a principal you might be known expressly as the Editor." Then, I replied, I saw no objection to it. . . .

Since then, nothing has passed—but I have gone regularly before dinner—Mr. W is every day more confidential—he has told me family secrets—the history of the paper etc I am also on very easy terms as to

PETER FRASER
From a lithograph by Charles Baugniet,
in the Library of Christ's College, Cambridge

the admission or rejection of what I write—Mr. W knows that I am not displeased at his throwing what I have been composing into the fire and I on my part am very free in my strictures on the writings of my colleague. . . . I asked him to say what he most disapproved in my writing—and he said it was my playfulness—Now the fact is that W. has no fancy And tho' he likes wordy pomp he has no perception of sportive allusions—I have written 2 or 3 decent things in this way which he has rejected—With this I have no right to complain—He has once or twice bro^t me F[raser]'s Leaders to look over & if I pleased, correct —And I have done it latterly.

I sho^d add that W. has once or twice intimated the probability that [Fraser] will soon leave him And that I shall have all the Leaders to do. . . . We often gossip. He said to-night—I think we shall agree in Politicks I think you will have no reason to disapprove of the tendency of the paper—I ans^{wd} & laughed at the same time I wont answer for any longer than the war—I hate France and hold that to be the only one thing needful—To oppose Buonaparte is the sum & substance of all our public duties—Should we ever get free from our danger from him—you and I might then disagree for you know I am an old Jacobin—a Whig I sho^d say — " Well said he, And I sho^d have been one had I not *come out* dureing the time of the alarmists "—I replied—however as long as you continue your strictures on the necess^y of economy you will always be in favour with reformers.

A sudden emergency caused Robinson's appointment to Corunna, whence he wrote a series of special articles. He was present with the Fleet in October when Sir David Baird and his detachment arrived and proceeded to join Sir John Moore's forces. In letters Robinson comments on the delay in sending out the troops, but he did not learn of the disaster until later, as he had in the meantime gone to Madrid. He came back to London in a transport in January, 1809, and rejoined the staff at Printing House Square.

The internal situation there in January, 1809, is not easily described. The respective functions of the Chief Proprietor, his Literary Adviser and the ostensible Editor were, even to one another, anything but distinct. Fraser's literary superintendence, though not " ostensible," was always felt by the literary assistants. Another letter of Crabb Robinson's to his brother shows more fully the circumstances in which he found himself :

I do not go to the office (except now and then voluntarily and to no purpose) till past 5 in the Evening, then the Evening papers are published and it is time to prepare for the morrow. My stay there is very uncertain I sometimes come away at 9 & I have staid till between 11 and

12 frequently. As there is a possibility that important news may arrive at night, I generally say where I am going, and once I was sent for to the Athenaeum & was employed in translating (it was the French reply to the Manifesto concerning the Siege of Copenhagen) till 1/2 past two. But having my Mornings to myself generally is so great a comfort that I think nothing of the occasional nightly Labour.

The *quantity* of my employm^t therefore is small, & exceedingly easy & I enjoy it much. Besides this unless Mr. W. is very insincere indeed, he is not less pleased with me than I am with him—We are upon the most friendly footing possible. He seems always satisfied with what I do & has expressed to C[ollier] too his satisfaction in strong terms. . . .

Mr. W. has not given me the more difficult & of course more honourable Tasks to perform. So much of the Leading Article as consists in the compiling of the little articles of information, which is always the beginning, is done uniformly by me, but the elaborate strictures which have occured, as those on the russian manifesto, Mr. Jefferson's speech etc. are done by another person.

I believe that in general Mr. W. has done wisely in making this arrangement and that the articles have been better than I could have made them. My Colleague has a much more flowing style, a certain wordy emphasis which readers like, & also more knowledge in general than I have. . . . I have written one long letter to the Editor & various paragraphs which I dare say you never thought to be mine. One of my duties is a troublesome and ungracious one, it is that of looking over and correcting the Law reports. I have also to break open & read a number of letters to the Editor and I make charming bonfires of them. . .

Crabb Robinson's talents, it is obvious, were in the main what we should nowadays term sub-editorial, while Peter Fraser's were political. Robinson knew the literary world better than Fraser, but was much less " worldly." It is small wonder that, although Walter himself " calls me the Editor and I pass for such in the office," many revisions and decisions were made over Robinson's head. The relations of the Press with the Administration were always delicate, and an ambitious and independent Proprietor necessarily pursued a line which called for the frequent trimming of articles and, on occasion, the trimming of Robinson's convictions. A conscientious Unitarian, possessing no genuine interest in Parliament, Robinson had little sense of opportunism and consequently little aptitude for day-to-day political writing. In contrast to the Rev. Peter Fraser, he brought a theological rather than a political mind to his articles. His position even as " ostensible " Editor must have lacked authority. When, even for long intervals,

Robinson's contributions to the paper exceeded those of Fraser, his colleague's enforced absence in Cambridge was the cause. There was not in 1808 any serious sign of that indolence which later developed to the great reduction of the powerful influence which Fraser possessed during 1807-1819.

The relations of the " principals " at Printing House Square were uniformly friendly. Walter never stinted that natural " liberality of sentiment " which he mentioned in his advertisement. The table in the dining-room of the private house adjoining the press was generous. Even to the sophisticated palate of so inveterate a diner-out as Robinson, Walter's venison, beef and chicken were exceptional. The quality of the turbot was still more noteworthy. John Walter, in no sense a literary man (Robinson says he was interested only in " real " things), was a good listener as well as a good host. The friendship between Robinson, Walter and Fraser was personal, independent of business connexions and changes, subsisting throughout their lives. The company at table was generally as good as the viands. These parties were an institution which lasted for many years. To Combe, Fraser, Barnes and Robinson, the oldest members, there were later added Murray (occasionally) and Alsager. Sterling came seldom, but more often to the country place which Walter built and occupied from 1821. There is no sign that Parliamentary reporters were invited.

But Robinson's happiest hours were spent in gossiping with Lamb, Coleridge, Wordsworth, and many other writers, exclusively literary men with the half-exception of Hazlitt. It could only be a matter of time before one of such tastes would find irksome the ostensible or the responsible conduct of a political paper. Walter saw the position very clearly. He had a very high regard for Robinson's character and he knew he could rely completely upon his honour and sympathy. The paper, nevertheless, was his first consideration, and he arrived at the conviction that a change was necessary in the editorial department. He thereupon wrote to Robinson as follows :

[1809]

My dear Sir,

I rely upon your great good sense in not misapplying the motives to the present communication, as I feel that I am acting under the influence of that duty which I have ever considered in the management of the paper since it has been entrusted to me. I therefore make no apology when I inform you that from the great advance in the sale of the paper, the mechanical business has become so principal a feature of it & now binds me so closely and immoveably to the office, that I am no longer in want of that constant attendance for which I have been so much obliged to you. I most willingly assure you that the same personal regard which I have always possessed during our connection will still continue on my part, tho' circumstances render it unnecessary to continue it. I leave it to you to determine the period that will be most suitable to yourself. Give me leave to repeat my hopes that in this arrangement you will not suppose that I am influenced by the least disrespect or disregard for you as I shall always acknowledge myself

My dear Sir

Your faithful friend & obliged Ser^t

J. W.

Robinson accepted the arrangement in these terms :

[1809]

My dear Sir,

Certainly no apology was necessary for your letter. Engagements like that we formed depend of course upon mutual convenience And when either party finds it in his interest to dissolve it, he has a perfect right to do so.

I shall therefore close my attendance with the current quarter.

It is pleasing to me to be informed by you that your determination has not been influenced by any diminution of personal regard. I on my part can assure you that I shall always recollect with pleasure the short period of our connection And shall ever bear testimony to the uniformly polite & attentive conduct you have observed toward me.

I most heartily wish that whoever occupies my seat in future may discharge his obligations with the same scrupulous attention and much greater ability.

I am Dear Sir Yours sincerely and faithfully

H. CRABB ROBINSON.

And Robinson received the following acknowledgment :

My dear Sir,

I am most happy to find that you view the subject of my recent note in its just light & am truly gratified and obliged by your kind expressions. I hope you will equally command at all times the accommodations which the paper is sometimes capable of affording—

Believe me Dear Sir Very sincerely yours

JOHN WALTER JUNR.

Thus *The Times* was again without an ostensible Editor, and John Walter Junior was again responsible for direction and detail. He relied still more upon the two remaining pillars of the paper. Fraser's position was unassailable ; he was also content with its anonymity and elasticity. He needed his frequent absences, and

HENRY CRABB ROBINSON
From a Water-colour in the possession of
John Walter, Esq.

he had no ambition to enter upon the detail of journalism—he was satisfied to give it a tendency. Barnes, on the other hand,[1] had been induced to stay only by the promise of the editorship whenever the Chief should quit, and it may be assumed that, though second in eminence to Fraser, he was entitled with Fraser's agreement to look forward in the near future to enjoying control. Robinson leaving at the end of 1809, Walter himself edited the paper throughout 1810.

A new and eminent helper offered himself next year. Coleridge, quarrelling in 1811 with the *Courier*, decided forthwith to apply for a position on *The Times*. Through Robinson he put before Walter an offer to attend the office for six hours a day and write a covenanted number of articles each week.

All on the understanding [wrote Coleridge in his memorandum] that the paper be truly independent, first of the Administration, secondly of Palace Yard, and that its fundamental principle is the due proportion of political power to property, joined with the removal of all obstacles to the free circulation and transfer of property and all artificial facilities for its natural tendency to accumulate in large and growing masses.

Walter did not feel able to take advantage of the offer, doubtless having a shrewd idea of the fast and loose interpretation which Coleridge would place upon an agreement. Coleridge consequently planned a series of lectures on " The Principles of Poetry " in the same year. He wrote to Robinson on November 6, 1811, urging him to do what he could to extend among his friends knowledge of the lectures . . . but

what I more particularly wish you to do is to see put an advertisement in *The Times*—if by *power* it can be done so as to *advertise* only as many lines as will not exceed the price of an ordinary advertisement, and to let the rest appear as a part of the paper itself—I certainly should do my best to repay it by sending occasional articles to *The Times*, prose or verse. Perhaps you may have it in your power to conciliate Mr. Walter's good will towards me in this business.

When Coleridge forwarded the report of his first lecture, *The Times* showed so little interest or inclination to print it that the lecturer thus expostulated with Robinson[2] :

Stuart of the *Courier* seemed to wonder at Walter's making anything of a favour of inserting in the tomorrows *Times* an account of the

---

[1] For Barnes's later position see *infra*, p. 166.
[2] Printed, like the two preceding citations, from the Crabb Robinson papers.

Lecture [on the Principles of Poetry] at this dead time of the year ; & added, that if a Birthday entertainment had permitted him to be present, he would have written a paragraph of 20 or 30 lines, sent it to Walter with his compliments, and should have been surprised as at a mark of unusual Discourtesy, if it had not been inserted—there being nothing political or personal in the subject Much more than to me, who have always thought & written in the same tone of Feeling with the *Times*, and when the chief writer in it has sometimes quoted and very often written in the exact spirit of Wordsworth's Pamphlet—and twice quoted sentences which I myself wrote. —The only prose Essay I have & which I fully determined to send to Mr. Walter when I had polished the style a little merely as a mark of my high esteem for a Paper which I not only think incomparably the best Journal that is or has been in G. Britain, but the only one which without impudence can dare call itself independent or impartial—And this I assuredly shall do still : because the compliment was intended to *The Times* itself and was not personal. But yet I do not quite like the notion of chaffering a work of my most serious Thoughts & of my inmost convictions against a compliment or disguised Advertisement for the sake of *money*—Tho' this is perfect purety in my feeling compared with doing it from *Vanity*. Heaven knows I never feel my poverty so painful as when I see my name & a puff tacked to it, and know that I knew it beforehand.

My Poverty and not my Will consenting I am convinced my dear R. you will do all you can for me—After the Lecture write about 20 lines notice that it was not in etymologic severity a Lecture—for tho' the reasoning, the arrangement, the [illegible] bare the clearest marks of long premeditation, yet the language illustrations etc. so evidently the children of the Moment—in short what strikes yourself A precious Recipe for a Puff ! O Jesus ! Embarrassments like misery, make us bedfellows with strange meannesses but that my Soul will not allow herself to be so reviled I should have said, businesses—This paragraph should be in Tomorrows *Times*, or not at all. Doubtless, it would be of the greatest service to me—I brought the Essay with me & if you wish it will give it you rude as it is, at the Lecture.

Robinson's charity and energy availed to secure a summary of the lecture in thirty-eight lines in the issue of *The Times* for November 19, 1811, under the heading " From a Correspondent." The traces of Coleridge's writings in *The Times* are regrettably slight. His articles expected by Perry and Stuart (both of whom gave him a regular salary) generally arrived late, and often never. Walter was a shrewd judge ; he liked value for money. Stuart never got his money's worth from Coleridge for the *Morning Post*.

While for news *The Times* easily held the first position, it was less strong in the critical treatment of affairs. Yet progress on the political side was steady. Barnes supplied occasional letters as well as the Parliamentary summary and some theatrical notices. Fraser's general direction of policy was valuable. It was necessary, however, to secure articles of such importance as to justify large type. These could not be regular leading articles ; the leading article was still inchoate, and as yet lacked any traditional " authority." As Crabb Robinson said, " much of the leading article consists in the compiling of the little articles and information." The general London newspaper convention required the printing of a selection of home and foreign news, all set out in paragraph form ; comment was slight and often absent. Fraser, when in his best form, contributed arguments and " strictures " the form of which was new ; they were picked out for commendation by Leigh Hunt and Cobbett. But this was exceptional. Most of the journals still under the influence of Topham filled out the leader column with items of gossip which only gave place on occasions of war-crisis to relatively long, reasoned statements of policy picked up from Government officials. Fraser was often absent, and the argued leading article had to appear regularly before it could stand a chance of affecting opinion. Any influence exercised during Robinson's editorship came from letters written on the model of " Junius." This was a useful convention, for the paper could refuse to " give up " the author for the good reason, as in the case of " Junius," that it did not know his identity. *The Times* in 1808 published a series signed " Decius," whose name was unknown to the staff. " Decius " was communicated with by messages printed under " Notices to Correspondents," grouped over the sub-title in the body of the paper. The letters were offered to the Editor as " deliberate, disinterested, and unbiassed opinions " on the causes of late military disasters ; and in stipulating that they should be printed as written the author marked passages which might be omitted if they conflicted with " your recorded opinion."

Sir

Should you reject the whole, please to state as much in your " *Notice to Correspondents* " and I will send to your office for the packet—I should wish them to be inserted successively in the course of a fortnight or three weeks, and that the words " Decius on the causes of our late military " &c &c (as in the title) shd be prefixed to each paper with No I. II. III. &c &c.

> I am Sir Yr humble Sert
>
> DECIUS

His preliminary request to Walter ended with a request which indicates the value placed upon complete anonymity. Reprinted in pamphlet form, the " Letters of Decius " made some slight stir at the time.

A more important series followed in 1812 from a correspondent who became known to Walter as Edward Sterling. In the insertion of these " Vetus " letters the greatest pains were taken on both sides ; secrecy was vital to the author and the author's hero, the Marquess Wellesley. Sterling considered the most insignificant details for the sake of preserving his absolute incognito.

> The Post-Master here (Cowbridge) is a shrewd kind of man and a reader of newspapers—I have therefore not ventured either to take the enclosures containing Vetus to the office myself or to send them by my own servant to pay postage—this requires both the intervention of a third person and perhaps the risque of miscarriage.

The Letters were addressed not to Walter but to Charles Bell, his printer, even to Bell's private address in Brunswick Street. Wellesley had been head of the Foreign Office until March, 1812. " Vetus " supported his policy and hoped to further his ambitions, and he drew the attention, if not the commendation, of political observers, both Whig and Tory. " Vetus " demanded a vigorous prosecution of the war in Spain by the effective support of Lord Wellington, and came to be identified with a certain strident patriotism. The liberal-minded saw in him a tendency to exalt war and to enlarge the theatre in which Britain was engaged. Hence the Letters were denounced by Hazlitt :

> The serpent's hiss, the assassin's yell, the mowing and chattering of apes, drowned the voice of peace ; and Vetus, like the solemn owl, joins in the distance and prolongs the dreary note of death.

The same writer directed six stern articles, one or two of them of considerable length, against " Vetus " in the *Morning Chronicle*. Leigh Hunt in the *Examiner* joined in the attack and found room for other criticisms by Hazlitt after the *Morning Chronicle* had dismissed him. Sterling's style, according to Hazlitt,

is not very different from that of Don Adriano de Armado ; every word is as who should say " I am Sir Oracle." Like the hero of Cervantes, haranguing the shepherds, he assaults the very vault of Heaven with the arrogance of his tone, and the loudness of his pretensions. Nothing can exceed the pompous quaintness, and laborious foolery of many of his letters.

Notwithstanding criticism of the letters, *The Times* gained from the publicity. Relations between Edward Sterling and the Chief Proprietor grew personal during November, 1812, when " Vetus " found it necessary to visit London expressly to confer with Lord Wellesley. Walter was strongly impressed by Sterling's powers and rapidly absorbed his convictions. " The Letters of Vetus " appeared in book form as a result of the conference, and the business arrangements were conducted by John Walter. There was no doubt that Wellesley's Press agent, Sydenham, had discovered a pamphleteer of rare ability, yet a headstrong writer who had nearly involved *The Times* in an action. Letter XVI., printed in the paper of December 8, 1812, was an unmeasured attack on the political character and principles of Lord Liverpool. Though he printed it with misgivings, Walter did not know, what the Home Office papers now accessible reveal,[1] that the Home Secretary was pleased to direct *The Times* newspaper of the 8th inst. " to be laid before the Attorney and Solicitor General for their opinion : How far the letter addressed to the Earl of Liverpool and signed ' Vetus ' is a fit subject for a Criminal Prosecution ? " But hints were given to Walter, who wrote to Sterling about December 10 :

My dear Sir

I have not been able to see our friend[2] during the last 3 days ; but was this morning favoured with a note from him, wherein he says that you have been pleased to express your approbation of certain articles, wh^h have recently appeared in the Journal—This of course gives me new pleasure—You will have observed that I published the last V—s with the same rapidity with which it was transmitted to me. The implicit confidence wh^h I repose in everything that comes from you really overwhelms any scruples that I might otherwise have felt as to the

1 P.R.O., H.O., 48/16.
2 Probably Sydenham is meant.

personal danger likely to result to myself from the warmth of the composition—But I am sure you will not feel offended if I inform you that the hints of some of my friends next morning rather astounded me.

For with the same conviction of the goodness of our cause wh^h Erasmus had for the truth of his religion I still fear as he did whether I have nerve sufficient to become a martyr to it. As I have usually told you candidly the opinion of the public upon your other letters, I must also from the same principle of ingenuousness inform you that certain passages have been thought to savour too much of the zeal of party— Have we not, my dear Sir, been somewhat hasty in this last publication ? If you are still convinced we have not I shall feel the greater confidence in disregarding extraneous criticisms. I am sure you will attribute these suggestions to the best motives as they come from

Your most respectful friend

JOHN WALTER

Sterling's reply, admitting the intemperance of his criticism and his unconsciousness of its excesses, must be read as an example of the defective judgment which prevented his later being seriously considered as an Editor of *The Times*.

When the London post of Tuesday last arrived I was myself surprised at the violence, of which I had at first been unconscious— Still however doubting my own judgments, because *You* (observe how we had depended on each other) had not expressed any scruples, I determined to wait another day before I acted on my apprehension of its impropriety. On Friday morning a letter from our friend confirmed the opinion, which had arisen in my mind from a reconsideration of the original document—and persuaded me that it was due both to my own character, and indeed to the individual whom 16 might appear to have injured, to qualify and soften the expressions of that paper, as much as in Honor and Conscience I could do—I hope you will think 17 has answered every purpose. As for any *fears* of the sort of proceeding hinted at in your letter, I confess, I have not the least notion that any such will be resorted to.[1]

Fortunately for Lord Wellesley, " Vetus," and John Walter, the Law Officers recommended that no action be taken : " This Letter contains a gross libel, but we incline to think it more advisable that it should not be made the subject of a Criminal Prosecution."[2] Sterling was convinced that the " mere discovery of my name

[1] Sterling to Walter, December 13, 1812. (P.H.S. Papers.)
[2] Dated, Lincoln's Inn, January 5, 1813. (P.R.O., H.O., 47/16.)

would be so far injurious to our friends and the public cause, as to prevent my being of any use to either under the same character hereafter." The Government, however, knew already something of his identity. In *The Times* of September 22, 1812, " Vetus " mentioned Lewis Goldsmith, as " associated with some vile attempt to justify the assassination of Buonaparte." Goldsmith was at this time employed by the British Government to conduct the *Anti-Gallican Monitor*. Upon his letter denying the charge being returned unprinted by the Editor of *The Times*, Goldsmith wrote to William Hamilton, of the Foreign Office, asking his opinion " how to act in regard to the attack made on me by the Marquis Wellesley, or by his Agent, respecting the ' horrid doctrine of assassination.' . . . I wrote a reply to Vetus and sent it to the *Times*, but it was returned to me. Vetus can afford to Pay £25 for his articles, I cannot."[1] It cannot be doubted that Goldsmith knew the identity of " Vetus " and that Sterling's name was familiar to the staff of the Foreign Office and others. Canning wrote a frank opinion of the letter to Lord Wellesley on November 19, 1812 :

> You have a long-tailed partizan in *The Times* called Vetus, who amidst a great deal of reasoning and eloquence of the very highest sort introduces a strain of flattery to you and disparagement to every other human being, such as makes the friends of every other human being look about them and exclaim : " What can all this mean ? " I do not attribute to you being party or privy to these letters, but the world does.[2]

So also did Lord Castlereagh, to whom " Vetus," without disclosing his identity, was persuaded to write : " Within these few days it has been stated to me on good authority that a great proportion of the hostile feeling entertained by Ministers against a noble Marquis arises from the letters of Vetus . . ." and there followed, according to the copy (dated August 5, 1813) which Sterling sent to John Walter, a solemn declaration that Wellesley had not been instrumental " to one sentence of the letters of Vetus." Castlereagh was not given any guarantee of the authenticity of " Vetus's " signature to this letter beyond a recommendation that it would be verified by " Mr. Walter of *The Times*, a

[1] Goldsmith to Hamilton (P.R.O., F.O. Gt. Br., 83/23), September 24, 1812. There seems no warrant for Goldsmith's insinuation that " Vetus " paid Walter for the insertions. On the other hand, there is no reason to doubt that Goldsmith's Letter to the Editor would have been inserted had he offered to pay. What Goldsmith did was to attack " Vetus " and *The Times* in his paper (see *Anti-Gallican Monitor*, 1812, pp. 709-10, 713-5, *ff*.). Sterling's payment, if any, would have come through Sydenham. But Wellesley was not rich.

[2] *Wellesley Papers*, II, 125.

man of sense and spirit to whom alone your Lordship is at liberty to show this paper." The object of " Vetus " was then described :

What then has been my purpose in these obnoxious writings ? Briefly—the overthrow of the present administration—In one word (so far as a single individual could promote an extensive undertaking) the destruction of that Ministry of which your Lordship forms a part— Not certainly, for the sake of personal mischief to any one of its Members ;—Not certainly, for their final exclusion from Office since there are some amongst them whom I shall be ever ready to hold up as meritorious public officers, though now somewhat misplaced—but I have sought the downfal of *Lord Liverpool's Ministry*, from the firm hope and confidence of seeing established—partly on its ruins, and in part with its materials another Cabinet more vigorous enlarged and enlightened—more qualified to appreciate the luminous Councils of a man, whom Europe and Asia equally reverence, and to imbibe the Spirit of his superior mind.[1]

John Walter was, at this time, well known to the Foreign Office. Like other contemporaries and predecessors, Castlereagh appreciated the efforts by which Printing House Square so frequently anticipated Government couriers and all other news-carriers.[2]

Moderation, it may be admitted, was not Sterling's strong point, but the articles, being in the form of letters, were not taken as the authoritative expression of *The Times*. He contributed, over other pseudonyms, articles on military affairs. A letter which General Sarrazin wrote to the Editor of *The Times* (December 13, 1813) was answered on the 15th by Sterling as " A British Officer." The same writer contributed (March 31, 1813) a letter on the Sinking Fund signed " Bona Fides." Doubtless there are other contributions not identified, for Sterling was an industrious writer. At the end of 1812 he was anxious to make closer connexion with the paper. In a letter to Walter he says :

It strikes my fancy, that a sort of delicacy restrains you, from speaking ; and yet which your inclination would not be averse to entertain. If I am right, it becomes my province to mention it. I believe, I have formerly told you, that at some future period the course of education which I propose for my children would induce me to move my residence towards London.[3]

And he proceeded to offer his services as a staff writer. His reason was that, as " a public education for my boys " (John and Anthony

---

[1] Sterling to Castlereagh, August 5, 1813. (John Walter's Letter-Book, pp. 86, *ff*.)
[2] See Chapter VII.
[3] P.H.S. Papers. Sterling to Walter, December 14, 1812.

were destined to go to Westminster and Winchester respectively) was likely to increase his expenses, he would like to provide for the increase " in such a manner and to such an extent as the application of my faculties with *moderate* diligence might enable me." But his name is not to be mentioned because " it might injure me in a quarter closely connected with Government—and in the next place, because it would close the door against my obtaining information from sources, otherwise, probably in my power." Walter replied that in the existing conditions of the establishment Sterling's suggestion could not be accepted, but that the possible retirement of Fraser rendered it likely that he would be able to find Sterling a position on the staff. Walter made it clear that he had already promised to an assistant " the expectation of his succeeding to my situation, whenever I may be disposed to quit it " ; a reference to Barnes which should be noted, seeing that Sterling's relations with him were destined never to be cordial. The conclusion of the letter contained an assurance that

it would afford the greatest satisfaction to me, if some such plan as this were to fit in with your view—that you should, once or twice a month (not oftener) favour us, from the country, with your sentiments upon any public subject in any form you may please. Were it not for the experience I have of your goodness, I should always be afraid that the offer of £300 per an. for such communications would appear to you a mean one ; but you will take the whole circumstances of the case into your consideration.[1]

On these terms Edward Sterling began his association with *The Times*, which, after interruptions, ended abruptly as the result of a difference with Barnes in 1840 over French policy. Throughout the period Sterling's relations with Walter were happy, even intimate. In his detached fashion, Walter was always glad to share a colleague's friendship whether or not he felt prepared to accept his judgment. Experience, indeed, proved the need of care in printing the articles written by Sterling after the war fever had been dissipated in 1815. On a Friday in September, 1819, Crabb Robinson, dining at Printing House Square with Walter, Barnes, and Murray,

praised the late articles on the Manchester riots. W. received the praise coolly. He is afraid of the spirit of Sterling & distrusts his judgmᵗ.

[1] Walter to Sterling, December 22, 1812. (P.H.S. Papers.)

[But] these articles are written with more simplicity than Vetus—and with more judgement.

Sterling and Walter met regularly at Printing House Square during the term of Walter's responsible editorship and often at Bear Wood during Barnes's period.

Sterling's independence and interest in political and military detail greatly helped to form John Walter's mind. If much of the anti-Canning tone in *The Times* may be traced to the Addingtons, Sterling was responsible for the decision not to support the Liverpool Ministry. The man himself was an Irish Protestant, born on February 27, 1773, at Waterford, the son of a canon of the Cathedral. He went to Trinity College, Dublin, and was called to the Irish Bar, but with that militancy which characterized him throughout his life he joined the Volunteers, fought in action against the rebels, and later took a commission in the Lancashire Militia. As Captain Edward Sterling he commanded the 8th Battalion of the Reserve in 1803. In the following year he married Hester Conyngham, retired from the Army, and became a gentleman farmer in Scotland ; a few years later he went to Glamorgan, following the same occupation. Farming, however, absorbed by no means enough of his energy to keep him content in the country. He was adjutant of the Glamorgan Militia in 1810, and brought out a pamphlet on military reform, dedicated to the Duke of Kent. When and where he became attached to Lord Wellesley's political views does not appear, but with complete conscientiousness— and so far as records go, only with very few presents from his Lordship—he championed that statesman's policies for many years.

The letters and articles written by Sterling, Fraser and Barnes increased the political reputation of *The Times*, though in this respect the *Morning Chronicle* still held the advantage. In 1812 Sterling sent Walter a confidential account[1] of a " memoir on a variety of subjects " which he had drawn up for Lord Wellesley. Apart from a survey of the character and influence of the London journals, the chief interest of this communication lies in its allusions to *The Times*. The paper was described, primarily for Lord Wellesley's benefit, as possessing " a circulation, altogether unrivalled, amongst the reflecting, and therefore most powerful classes of the community," which it owes to the principles of its direction, " not party but national." Walter was a man " awake to

[1] For the text see Appendix of Documents.

slights, but more so to attentions," and it was added " on the best general information " that he " nets by his paper not less than from 9 to 10 thousand pounds per annum,"[1] which places him " equally above the influence of hope and fear."

But even after the appointment of Sterling as a staff writer, Walter felt the need for a politically minded man on the spot, since Fraser was often absent and much of Barnes's work lay outside the office. He met John Stoddart, a Student of Christ Church, Oxford, a travelled man, a linguist and D.C.L., and was much impressed with his talents. Stoddart was politically minded —and narrow minded, although he possessed extensive literary connexions. Like Robinson, he knew Schiller, some of whose works he had translated ; he was on terms of general intimacy with Sir Walter Scott, Charles Lamb, Wordsworth, Coleridge, and particularly Southey. His sister Sarah married Hazlitt in 1808. After a period of radicalism he had, with Southey, settled down into a peculiarly rigid toryism. It appears that Stoddart's services were first secured by Walter in 1810 ; he was then practising in Doctors' Commons, and such assistance as he rendered the paper was known to none but the Editor and Fraser. During December, 1811, *The Times* published a series of " Letters to the Editor " on American affairs, commenting in detail on President Madison's Message to Congress delivered in the previous month. The trend of the letters was anti-Jacobin ; they aroused discussion. All the public knew of their origin was that they were signed " I.S." The curious Robinson turned into Printing House Square and could only elicit from Fraser that the author was a man of consequence in a public office who was anxious to be concealed. Walter himself affected to be unaware of the writer's identity. On December 15 Robinson, having had tea at Charles Lamb's, spent the evening at cards with Hazlitt, and met John Rickman (Clerk to the Speaker), who revealed to the entire party that he had lately dined with Walter at the house of Hazlitt's brother-in-law, John Stoddart, the " I.S." in *The Times.* " So," wrote Robinson in his diary, " Walter's ignorance who I.S. is, is a mere pretence."

After the death of John Walter I Stoddart's influence on *The Times* steadily increased. A changed tone was noticed by readers with some knowledge of the paper. There was discontent, too, not only with Stoddart's political principles but with his manner of conducting controversy. One of Crabb Robinson's entries,

---

[1] The figure is exaggerated.

that of December 16, 1813, indicates the sort of criticism levelled at *The Times* by " liberal " readers :

In the evening took tea with Lamb and after a rubber called on Walter. I informed him that I knew Stoddart to be his Editor. At the same time I frankly told him my opinion of the manner in which the leading article has been recently executed. I believe my mode softened the impression which the substance of my opinion might have produced.

Actually, it was not until April, 1814, the year of the introduction of steam, that a definite agreement for service as Editor of *The Times* was entered into between Walter and Stoddart. Stoddart covenanted to write the leading article. He agreed to attend, if required, from 5 till 10 or from 6 till 12 every evening, except Saturday, unless prevented by illness, and with the further exception of five weeks in the year to be selected in vacation time to mutual convenience. The very high remuneration of £1,400 a year was paid quarterly, and £100 was added " as premium of an insurance to be effected on the life of John Stoddart for the benefit of himself or of his family." The agreement was to continue for six years from the date of signature " if both parties shall so long live and if John Walter shall so long be the managing partner of *The Times*." In any event, John Walter was to pay the entire premium for the six years or such part as John Stoddart lived. The date of this agreement was April 3, 1814. His power over the policy of *The Times*, though not theoretically final, was, from the first, effective. Doubtless Walter hoped Stoddart would long remain his editor.

But with few exceptions the political and literary writers of London during 1815, whether Tory or not, disliked the intemperate zeal of John Walter's principal writer. The incessant abuse of Bonaparte was regarded as undignified and unbefitting an Englishman. In 1814 Stoddart's style was as violent as it was personal. *The Times* was ridiculed as a magazine of curses. If Walter was allowing Stoddart too free a hand, he could offer three excuses : first, his preoccupation with the steam engine ; secondly, his lack of interest in the detail of politics ; and, last, his domestic circumstances. For at this period John Walter II married. The lady was a daughter of Dr. George Gregory, Vicar of West Ham. Although the marriage settlements with the brothers of Miss Gregory led to so many disputes that at one time it seemed as if the match would be broken off, it was finally carried through ; the lady brought John Walter £4,000, which could not be touched until her mother's death. The disputed matter was Walter's refusal to settle on her more than £500 a year. The wedding took place on May 6, 1815. Peter Fraser and Crabb Robinson, Walter's trustees, shared the Chief Proprietor's distraction when, forthwith, Mrs. Walter fell into a consumption. For such reasons Stoddart's power over *The Times* was unlimited during the whole of that summer. By the autumn Walter had brought himself to recognize the probability of an immediate and melancholy end to his marriage. Although he had made a new agreement with Stoddart in April, he was now worried by the low estimation into which his paper had fallen during recent months. Several intimate friends had expressed grave disapproval of the leading articles.

I found [wrote Robinson after a visit, Nov. 1, 1815] that W. was much incensed against the Doctor. He is now sensible of what I urged him long ago that the Doctor's outrageous Bourbon zeal is disagreeable. But till recently he approved of the Doctor's politics and defended him against my reproaches. W. is now on the other hand too much displeased with Stoddart.

But there was a new reason for Walter's access of resentment. The Doctor had come to exhibit so much independence and indiscipline that he refused to attend to his Chief's repeated urging of moderation. Walter even had to rebuke him for suppressing news tending against his own opinions. Robinson, in confidential session at Printing House Square, learnt that Walter had at last taken the step of giving authority to Thomas Barnes, the critic and Parliamentary reporter, to revise and correct the manuscript of Stoddart's leading articles. Barnes, unlikely to sympathize with ultra-Royalism, was carrying out this duty satisfactorily at the moment, but the friction between these two vigorous minds was great and increasing. Robinson prayed that Stoddart would take the Chief's hint, for " the Doctor has a large family and is not rich."

The situation improved sufficiently for Walter to take a journey to France on the death of his wife. During his absence the new house in Brompton Row was given up ; on his return he reverted to his bachelor quarters at Printing House Square, and to his old habit of directing the paper. In April, 1816, he and Fraser together set off on another journey through France, leaving *The Times* to Stoddart and Barnes. They were back towards the end of May, when Robinson dined with them and learnt, from an aside of Fraser's, that the journey had not been agreeable and that they were never to travel together again.

Walter was pleased with nothing ; could eat nothing ; liked nothing ; and not being able to converse with the people was unable to have any pleasure from anything that he saw or heard.

While they were away there had been trouble at home. Stoddart and Barnes had quarrelled. " The Doctor is with difficulty kept in order even by Walter and Barnes together at the same time." So Robinson reports, but he did not know that Barnes had been keeping out many of Stoddart's leaders, and that one of the Doctor's chief complaints was that his influence in *The Times* during the whole of 1816 was declining almost to nothing. Reflecting that " it is the abuse and censure which Walter hears from others which have opened his eyes and not his perception of the Doctor's faults," Robinson still hoped that, by some means, the trouble would blow over. His optimism was misplaced. Walter begged him to come to the Square on November 4, 1816, incidentally for the purpose of introducing him to a Mr. Crabtree, on whose advice he had " a few days ago " bought an estate near Reading. Robinson's diary continues[1] :

After Mr. Crabtree went we had a long convers^n. about Doctor Stoddart. My friend W. is too apt to complain & be jealous & suspicious. He has heard that the doctor is about to edit a work to be called the " Correspond^t "[2] and he is ready to think this a *breach* of the Doctors *agreement with him* I endeavoured to shew that this idea is not well founded particularly as *Mr* W does not wish the Dr to give his name to the " Times " and frequently *refused* to insert what the Dr. writes.

On the latter subj^t I support^d Walter *in his idea that he ought* to restrain the doctor *and not* suffer him to interfere with the paper otherwise than by writing The Dr is so zealous for the Royal Party in France

[1] Here the italics represent shorthand in the original. Robinson occasionally uses this device in his diary for the noting of matter regarded as highly confidential ; the transcription is due to Dr. Herford's labour and ingenuity.

[2] The *Correspondent* was to be edited by Stoddart in association with Southey, the poet. A prospectus was issued in 1816. The first number, published in the early part of the following year, contained six articles by French, and six articles by English, writers ; amongst the latter are two signed J.S., one signed R.S. (on the Life of Wesley), which was continued in No. 2. As each number consisted of 164 pp. or so, the venture is comparable to the *Edinburgh* or *Quarterly*. The three numbers issued contain no reference to *The Times*. The full title of the periodical is : *The Correspondent* ; consisting of Letters Moral, Political and Literary between Eminent Writers in France and England ; and designed, by presenting to each nation a faithful picture of the other, to enlighten both to their true interests, promote a mutual good understanding between them, and render Peace the source of Common Prosperity. (London, Longmans, 1817.)

that he will sacrifice the paper to *his passions on that subject*. W. *also complains* of the notoriety given by the Dr *himself* to his share in the paper, *and I showed that the new work* of the Doctor will rather counter-act the *idea* that he has so much influence over the paper.

The Doctor and Walter *have also* disputed about additions made to his articles by Walter's desire—I believe I appeased Walter and did good in my conversation with him to day.

Nevertheless, in the following month, Walter told Stoddart that *The Times* would have no further use for his services after the end of the year, and on December 31, 1816, Robinson received the following request :

Mr. Walter and Dr. Stoddart request Mr. Robinson and Mr. Burrell, as Their common friends to take into consideration The Memorandum, which will be communicated to them signed by Mr. Walter and Dr. Stoddart on the 3rd of April 1815, and to give an opinion by which Mr. Walter & Dr. Stoddart are willing to abide, whether under all the circumstances known to them, the payment by Mr. Walter of the Insurance on Dr. Stoddart's life, for the remainder of the six years, is sufficient, according to the letter & spirit of the agree-ment ; or whether he should make any & what further compensation to Dr. Stoddart, for putting an end to their connection from this day.

The arbitration was suddenly interrupted. Stoddart did not confine his energies to the *Correspondent*. The circumstances are described in the Diary of February 16, 1817 :

Walter had called on me & after dining at the Colliers I went to him at 7 & talked about the conduct of Dr. Stoddart who on Saturday appeared as the Editor of *The Day & New Times*. In an introductory article he announced himself as the person who had been for some time the writer of the leading article in *The Times* & who having left that paper now purposes to conduct the *Day* alone & without any restraint or hindrance whatsoever. His article was grossly unbecoming & indecent. Treacherous towards Mr. W. and quackishly puffing about himself. I was indignant at it and share Mr. W's feelings of resentment. He had resolved to write nothing. It appeared to me necessary briefly to notice the article and the tone and spirit of the answer which I suggested were adopted.

The result is to be seen in the paper of the following day, February 17 :

It is with the greatest astonishment that we have seen in a Journal, comparatively but little known, and now starting with fresh auspices

161

M

under a new title, pretensions put forth in which we are considerably interested. An individual, who, it seems, is to write the leading article in the *Day* newspaper, endeavours to prove his competence for the task, by describing himself as the person " who conducted the political department, and wrote the leading article " in *The Times*. The Chief Proprietor of *The Times* begs leave to state, that he does not think it is in the power of any-one singly thus to identify himself with the management of his journal : least of all is it in the power of the individual who here assumes that honour. He knows full well, that his articles were rejected from our columns on account of the virulence and indiscretion with which they were written and that for more than the last twelve months, whatever writings have attracted notice by their merit, were exclusively the productions of other Gentlemen. The Proprietor has a letter from that person himself, stating and acknowledging " his influence in the journal during the *whole of the last year* to be LESS THAN NOTHING." What can he then mean by now asserting, that he was in the general management of the political department ? We have also other documents from people of more consequence, pointing out the injury which the journal sustained in character and reputation, at a time when that Person's power to do it injury was less circum-scribed. There are in the office sacks full of his rejected writings, which, if they were published, would exhibit a much more accurate criterion of his abilities than his own puffing advertisement. The Proprietor, therefore, cannot help marking with his strongest reprobation, the treachery of that person, who availing himself of the credit which his employment here conferred upon him, has basely endeavoured, by affixing as nearly as he dared the name of *The Times* to another journal, to plunder our extensive circulation and established fame. . . . We have only to add at present, that throwing out of our computation the great events of the Continent, the sale of our journal increased the more the less he wrote ; and since he has ceased from writing altogether, has extended with a rapidity of which we have known no example since we have had the management of it.

Attempts at compromise proved ineffectual. Stoddart had gone too far to retreat. The Address to the Public by the Conductors of the *New Times*, formerly the *Day*, had gone out broadcast on January 1, 1817. In successive issues of his new paper he repeated his claims and his grievances. The " manager of *The Times* had most shamefully violated his contract with the man to whom he was indebted for thousands and tens of thousands of his present fortune." An accusation that the circulation of *The Times* was recently much diminished in consequence of the change of Editor

drew a reply in *The Times* of February 24, where the question
was put :

> If he does not expect to draw benefit from the adoption of our title,
> why does he assume it ? Why has he not, boldly and like a man, taken
> for his publication an independent name of his own, and left it to the
> world to find out what talents he brought to the work ?

Stoddart's authorship of specified articles was denied. His claim
to have given " a political turn to the journal " was rejected. And
the opportunity was taken to print a certificate of the daily sale of
The Times—the one useful consequence of Stoddart's polemic :

> I, William Watkins, deputy and acting publisher of *The Times*
> Journal, hereby make oath and certify, that the regular daily sale of
> *The Times*, during the five weeks last past, has been as follows :

Jan.	20	6,300	Feb.	6	6,813
,,	21	6,444	,,	7	6,867
,,	22	6,336	,,	8	6,936
,,	23	6,363	,,	10	6,831
,,	24	6,354	,,	11	7,018
,,	25	6,375	,,	12	6,966
,,	27	6,345	,,	13	7,020
,,	28	6,417	,,	14	6,957
,,	29	7,794	,,	15	6,939
,,	30	7,016	,,	17	6,867
,,	31	6,768	,,	18	7,029
Feb.	1	6,903	,,	19	7,074
,,	3	6,678	,,	20	7,011
,,	4	6,804	,,	21	6,921
,,	5	6,840	,,	22	7,002

> And I do further certify, that the above number of papers were bona
> fide disposed of by me at the window to the news-venders, or casual
> purchasers.
>
> WILLIAM WATKINS.

Sworn at Guildhall, London, the 22d. of
February, 1817, before me, M. Bloxam.

So the *New Times* made no difference to the progress of *The Times*.
On the other hand, Stoddart and his paper found it impossible to
subsist without regular doles of money, first from the French and
afterwards from Carlton House,[1] which they drew for years.

[1] See the confidential report of Osmond to Richelieu, 1817, printed in the Appendix of
Documents.

Brushes between the two journals were only occasional after 1817 ; an illustration may be quoted from 1820. In *The Times* of January 17 will be found a letter from the secretary of a certain society on an unauthorized alteration in an advertisement making it read " The New or Mock Times." The following explanation is appended :

The Editor of *The Times* presents his respects to the gentlemen of the Committee . . . and acknowledges most readily that the words " or Mock " . . . were inserted without the knowledge or sanction of the Committee. . . .

In cases where the mention of the spurious paper calling itself the *New Times* is unavoidable the Printer has received a general direction from the Editor to affix a mark in his own way to any act performed by the print so describing itself ; which was on the present occasion erroneously placed in the text instead of being inserted in the note. . . .

It was after Stoddart's dismissal that his brother-in-law William Hazlitt came to Printing House Square for a very short stay. His arrival followed so closely the other's departure that there may be a connexion between the two events. As early as April, 1812, Hazlitt had been brought to Walter's notice either by or through the instrumentality of Crabb Robinson, " the first person," said Hazlitt, " who ever found out that there was anything in me." Hazlitt seems to have juggled with his chances, playing off Walter and Perry against each other, and eventually he went to the *Morning Chronicle* as Parliamentary reporter at four guineas a week. In 1813, when writing theatrical notices for that paper, his Republican spirit revolted against the French policy of his brother-in-law, and, forsaking the drama for the field of controversy, he attacked *The Times* in the series of articles earlier referred to. But Hazlitt went too far for Perry, and was asked to look out for another situation. " How different a man is Walter ! " is Robinson's comment on motives attributed to Perry. Towards the end of 1816 Hazlitt started in the *Examiner* his " Illustrations of *The Times* Newspaper," in which Dr. Slop, an " upstart," was described as " raving like a Bedlamite." On April 25, 1817, soon after Stoddart's dismissal, Robinson was able to enter in his diary :

I dined with Walter—Fraser was with him—I read Hazlitt's article on Methodists from the Round Table. F[raser] acknowledges its merits. Walter has been recommended by Barnes to take H[azlitt] as Theatrical Reporter—which on the account of both H[azlitt] and the

paper I am glad of—I confirmed W[alter] in the project of retaining
H[azlitt] as a writer, at the same time that I did not encourage him to
form a personal intimacy with him.

The warning no less than the support sprang from Robinson's
knowledge of Hazlitt's weakness and strength. He had resented
" the bitter irony and vehement abuse, the hyaena laugh and
savage joy with which he lacerates the most glorious creatures
God ever made," such glorious creatures as Coleridge and
Wordsworth. Hazlitt's appointment, that very April, is evidence
of Walter's magnanimity, for the *Examiner* articles had assailed
not only Stoddart, who had gone, but Edward Sterling, who
remained. Mrs. Siddons was the subject of the newcomer's first
contribution to *The Times*. During the summer he wrote of Kean,
Kemble, and others, in October on *The Beggar's Opera*, and
resigned in November after a notice of Miss Brunton's Beatrice.
Why he resigned is obscure. In his preface to " A View of the
English Stage " (1818) he goes so far as to say :

The volume here offered to the public is a collection of theatrical
criticisms which have appeared with little interruption, during the last
four years, in different newspapers—the *Morning Chronicle*, the
Champion, the *Examiner* and lastly *The Times*. How I came to be
regularly transferred from one of these papers to the other, sometimes
formally and sometimes without ceremony, till I was forced to quit the
last-named by want of health and leisure, would make rather an
amusing story, but that I do not choose to tell. The secret of the prison
house ! I would, however, advise anyone who has an ambition to write
and write his *best*, in the periodical press, to get, if possible, " a
situation " in *The Times* newspaper, the editor of which is a man of
business and not of letters. He may write there as long and as good
articles as he can, without being turned out for it.

Five years later, in the *Edinburgh Review* for May, 1823, Hazlitt
used different language in his observations on " The Periodical
Press." Though Barnes remained his friend—he had dined with
him and Keats at Haydon's in the spring of 1818—he bore heavily
upon the paper.

The Times is, we suppose, entitled to the character it gives itself, of
being the " leading journal of Europe," and is perhaps the greatest
engine of temporary opinion in the world. Still it is not to our taste,
either in matter or manner. . . . It might be imagined to be composed
as well as printed with a steam engine . . . it is not even a patriotic

paper but it is *civic*. It is the witness of the British metropolis ; the mouthpiece, oracle and echo of the Stock Exchange, the origin of the mercantile interest. One would think so much gravity of style might be accompanied with some steadiness and weight of opinion. But *The Times* conforms to the changes of the time, it bears down upon a question like a first-rate man-of-war, with streamers flying and all hands on deck ; but if the first broadside does not answer, turns round upon it, like a triremed galley, firing off a few paltry squibs to cover its retreat. It takes up no falling cause ; fights no uphill battle ; advocates no great principle ; holds out a helping hand to no oppressed or obscure individual. It is " ever strong upon the stronger side." Its style is magniloquent ; its spirit is not magnanimous. It is valiant, swaggering, insolent, with 100,000 readers at its heels ; but the instant the rascal rout turns round with the " whiff and whim " of some fell circumstance, *The Times*, the renegade, not constant *Times*, turns with them.

In a notice of the article *The Times* spoke of the author as a " discarded servant of Printing House Square." A rejoinder in the *Examiner* contained this concluding paragraph :

The Times Editor speaks of Mr. Hazlitt as " a discarded servant " of that paper. We beg leave to state distinctly that this is not true. He was *not* dismissed from *The Times* newspaper, *but gave up an engagement in it, in spite of repeated and pressing remonstrances to the contrary.*

Faced with the necessity of finding a successor to Stoddart, Walter first thought of appointing a man whose position would occasion the least general rearrangement of the staff. Search was made outside for a man of considerable acquaintance with the world of affairs, and on such terms of intimacy with influential persons as to be able to secure early news of political and other developments. That John Walter should have determined to seek a new writer is perhaps curious—hardly, in fact, to be understood except on the hypothesis that no present member of the staff could be appointed. Barnes, the man who had the greatest claim, was, apparently not yet to be promoted, doubtless on account of his radical associations.[1] Peter Fraser remained a most important member of the literary staff, retaining his influence with the Proprietor, although he had for some years attended the office with lessening regularity. He was not a candidate, but his advice was so highly regarded by John Walter that the policy of *The Times* was never free from the possibility of his intervention. Crabb

[1] John Payne Collier's diary tells a story, lacking any sort of confirmation and unlikely on the face of it to be true, that his father (John Dyer Collier) " declined the post of ostensible editor of *The Times*."

Robinson was making a career at the Bar and had no ambition to rejoin the paper. While Sterling held a high place in the Proprietor's esteem, especially for his qualities as a political observer with high official connexions, he was defective in caution ; but Sterling saw himself as an essential member of the staff, and as being more than a political writer. He had, in fact, for some time been useful to the paper in a general way, and at the time of Stoddart's withdrawal he was acting as the theatre critic. Not unnaturally, Sterling considered that he had a definite claim on the editorial succession. In considering him the Proprietor had to face a point made by the man himself—that he was only prepared to " take the principal part in the conduct of the paper if Fraser were to leave it," as Crabb Robinson reports. But a more serious obstacle was the Proprietor's conviction that Sterling, though most valuable as a special writer under direction, was too partisan, lacking in foresight, deficient in sagacity. There were some temperamental similarities between Sterling and Stoddart. And in any case Walter desired to retain Peter Fraser's services as a colleague.

For the time being Walter determined to act as his own ostensible Editor, although he knew he would ultimately need not only an additional writer but even a responsible editor. In his difficulty he took private counsel with Crabb Robinson. On March 2, 1817, they dined at Printing House Square, and, after a long conversation, Robinson agreed to the plan of approaching Southey, " the poet." Southey, like Robinson, was a Unitarian ; but his nomination then for a situation on *The Times* is highly curious, for Southey was well known to Walter and Robinson as a very close friend of Stoddart's ; he had contributed letters and odes to *The Times* during the Doctor's editorship, and the *Correspondent*, to whose announcement Walter objected, was put forth as being edited jointly by Stoddart and Southey. Both of them wrote articles in the first number, which appeared in January, 1817. The policy of the *Correspondent* was ultra-Royalist. Nevertheless, Southey, the poet, was to be approached. He had been Poet Laureate for four years, and was 43 years of age when John Walter set Crabb Robinson to seek his services for *The Times*. First of all, Robinson was to offer the Laureate " £300 a year to write him (Walter) a couple of leading articles a week," a modest proposal which proves that the Proprietor was himself prepared to continue the responsibility for the rest of the paper. If this seems a meagre offer, unlikely to tempt a Laureate, it must be recollected that Southey was obviously not the sort to make an exclusive arrangement with *The Times* or any other journal, for he already possessed other connexions doubtless known to Robinson and Walter. At this time Southey was a sheet-anchor of the *Quarterly Review*; he had joined that militant ultra-Tory organ in 1808, and it was notorious that he enjoyed the rich sum of £100 in payment for each and every article that he wrote for its pages. His interest in daily journalism depended mainly on a few articles supplied to the *Morning Post* in fulfilment of a contract which Coleridge had entered into. Notwithstanding a definite undertaking, Coleridge, in the words of Daniel Stuart, proprietor of the *Post*, " attended not at all to his engagement with me, but went up the country on other pursuits." And Southey wrote the articles.

An incident in Coleridge's career probably occurred to Southey's memory when the question of journalism was mentioned to him by Crabb Robinson. In the year 1800 Coleridge, already settled at Keswick, was offered a regular and lucrative position on the *Morning Post*; he grandly replied that he " could not give up the lazy reading of old folios for two thousand times £2,000." Now £300 a year for two leading articles a week, which Crabb Robinson was authorized by John Walter to put forward, could hardly have seemed complimentary to the vanity of Southey, who, unlike Coleridge, was an industrious and reliable writer, able to appreciate the degree of discipline required to fulfil a regular engagement of the kind suggested. But the story, as told by Southey's son, indicates the offer of a more spectacular emolument. The young and Reverend Mr. Southey, who wrote his father's " Life," says that when Crabb Robinson approached the Poet Laureate, he asked darkly, in full accord with the anonymity of the paper, and with a certain gratuitous but penetrable mystification characteristic of the time, " whether if an offer were made him to superintend a lucrative literary establishment, in which he would have—if he desired it—a property, of which the emolument would be very considerable, and would give him extensive influence over the whole Kingdom, he were in a position to accept it "; rather, as Robinson, afraid to appear indelicate, corrected himself, " whether he was willing to listen to the details of such a proposal." The reply was as curiously worded as the proposal. " My father," says Southey's son, " who knew from whom the proposal came and to what it referred, being aware of his friend's intimacy with Mr. Walter, the Proprietor of *The Times*, was so completely wedded to his present mode of life . . . he did not even request to be informed of the details." Thus, in the son's account, Southey himself does not seem to have mentioned any private feeling for Stoddart or any other motive but that of attachment to things of the spirit.

Notwithstanding this edifying picture of a poet's detachment from material considerations, Southey's biographer would extract the maximum credit for his father's self-denial. He claims that the poet knew that " the situation alluded to was that of writing the chief leading article in *The Times* together with some general authority over the whole paper," and tells his readers that " the remuneration which it was intended to offer was £2,000 a year, with such a share in the profits as would have enabled him to realise an independence in a comparatively short time." It is not easy to imagine even a literary man ignoring an offer calculated to make him independent in a comparatively short time, not only, as in Southey's case, from private subsidies and public pensions, but from dreary hackwork for the Press. But in this instance it is prudent to doubt whether any such offer as £2,000 a year, plus a share in the profits, was ever under contemplation, at least by John Walter. Stoddart, who attended the office daily, and wrote the leading article as a rule, received £1,500 a year. Generous John Walter was, but hardly the man to offer even a Poet Laureate such royal terms without a closer acquaintance with his personality. Moreover, the details of this offer, and the Laureate's reply, as reported by Southey's biographer, so strikingly resemble the story of Daniel Stuart's abortive attempt to secure Coleridge's services in a similar capacity for the *Morning Post* that the figures in both stories may very reasonably be suspected of exaggeration.

It is known, too, from a note in Crabb Robinson's diary, that one of the circumstances which turned John Walter's mind towards Southey was a rumour that the poet was disposed to extend his activities in the field of daily journalism ; " and," noted the diarist, " he [John Walter] makes this proposal more to keep him from any other paper than because he wants him for himself." We may surely conclude that John Walter was not likely to offer £2,000 a year and a share in the paper to an untried and unfamiliar though eminent man, and that he would have shown himself a bad manager had he done so. Also, the work of carrying on *The Times* for the next years of the peace was alone likely to test any man's staying powers. and, most of all, those of a poet sickening all the time for the Lakes.

Thomas Barnes, meanwhile, had concentrated upon Parliament, yielding the theatre to an Irish Protestant clergyman, the Rev. George Croly, who had come to London in 1810. Robinson pictures him as a " fierce-looking Irishman, very lively in conversation," talented and eloquent, but wanting the delicacy and discrimination of judgment which are the finest qualities in a critic. Walter dispatched him in 1814 to Hamburg in the capacity of German correspondent, and there he stayed some years. He left *The Times* for the *New Times*, and remained with Stoddart for a little while. Then he accepted the living of St. Stephen's, Walbrook. Between 1829 and 1834 he published a number of novels and some romantic poems. He stepped aside from literature to add a quota to the national output of anti-papist diatribes. Sterling went to the theatres on Croly's secession.

The failure of the mission to Southey convinced Walter that the policy of the paper must remain in the hands of a man on the spot, whose heart was in his work ; and in the autumn of 1817 he took the step of appointing not merely a leader writer with some authority over part of the paper, but an editor charged with the oversight of *The Times* as a whole. It was an appointment which circumstances had rendered overdue, but the reason for the delay was probably that the most satisfactory candidate professed the least satisfactory politics. When Walter placed Thomas Barnes in the editorial chair he was aware that he had put the paper into the hands of a man unlike Southey, Stoddart or Fraser, of independent Liberal sympathies. Walter might well hesitate before giving such a man even limited editorial control. But his own personal circumstances, as well as those of the paper, finally determined him, by stages, to transfer to Barnes complete editorial authority.

XI

A TRANSFER OF AUTHORITY

THE completeness of the authority given to the new editor was largely the consequence of John Walter's second marriage and his preference for the life of a country gentleman. The idea of a country seat was in John Walter's ambitious mind as early as 1816. The place chosen was the suggestion of an old friend, Edward Jesse, later famous as a naturalist and writer on angling—Walter's favourite diversion. It was a large and, according to Jesse's daughter, " most desolate looking tract of land which had once been within the precincts of Windsor forest." Building began promptly, but difficulties were encountered. Crabb Robinson first heard of the plans when introduced to Mr. Crabtree, the agent through whom " the estate near Reading " was acquired. The house was disappointingly long in building, and the date of its completion is not certain. Robinson's visit there was postponed, but he was finally brought down by a night coach, and, with Walter, found Edward Sterling and David Stewart, who was one of the designers of Bear Wood's grounds and lakes. An enjoyable evening was passed. " Sterling was the talker to-day—on politics he talks well." In the morning (December 15, 1822) Robinson inspected Bear Wood. He criticized the place.

On my first looking at W : house [he says] I was struck with the deformity of its structure. The back front is beautiful—It has three handsome rooms communicating—But on one side is a noble grapery and nothing on the other—the Kitchen & Offices, which might have formed a corresponding wing, being behind the grapery and looking a manufactory on coming up to the house in front. This I could not help noticing, but I soon found that W : far from being insensible to this fault was painfully impressed by the mismanagement of the building—I learned afterwards that he had from good nature employed a young architect out of Wyat's office (Saunderson) who had in every respect blundered in the building. Another prominent deformity is a porch under which the carriage can be driven, out of all proportion with the house. I found that in laying out the grounds he had been equally unfortunate—he employed people to enlarge some water. They actually dug a pond in upper grounds & dammed it up to keep it from below. After vast sums had been spent Stewart was called in—he instantly knocked down the dam And there will be a picturesque piece of water of 30 acres lying where Nature meant it to be, in the lowest ground. The whole gro^d. some 300 & more acres was mere heath & wood when W : purch^d. it—It was Marsh till Stewart drained it. Now walks are laid all abo^t. it—The views are agreea[ble]—The ground is dry—The wood presents fine objects but the house does not stand where it ought—W : says had he had S[tewart]'s assistance at the first he should have saved £10,000 & three years of anxiety & regrets for his whole life, And as it is perhaps the house will ultimately be pulled down.[1]

Nevertheless, Robinson was sufficiently impressed to feel able to assure himself that the house was " a fine place after all." Much money and time were spent in perfecting the estate. Peter Fraser, given an account of the operations, warned his old chief against making too much of a splash. Bear Wood was also costly to maintain ; Walter paid unusually high wages and encouraged his large staff with agricultural fêtes, and was known throughout the county as the Poor Man's Friend. The estate and election expenses were responsible for making John Walter somewhat short of money in later years, particularly in 1847.

With the Chief Proprietor as deeply and deliberately engaged in establishing his family as he had formerly been in establishing *The Times*, the new Editor, Barnes, inevitably succeeded to a far greater command over the paper than had hitherto fallen to any " political conductor," " literary superintendent," or " ostensible editor " preceding him. Fraser remained in the office, influential but irregular in attendance.[2]

Barnes, as acting editor, first took increasing responsibility from the time of the Proprietor's second marriage[3] in January, 1818, to the " rather pretty and chatty " Miss Smithe. The marriage settlement required a certain adjustment of his affairs—John Walter settled upon his lady the sum of £6,000 in the 4 per cents.—and he may have realized certain holdings. Their first home was at

[1] *Diary of Henry Crabb Robinson*, Vol. IX, p. 135.
[2] *Cf.* Chapter XIV. for Fraser's powers 1817-1820.
[3] The first Mrs. Walter, who died of consumption in the year of the marriage, 1815, was the daughter of Dr. George Gregory, Vicar of West Ham. The second was the daughter of Henry Smithe, of Eastling, Kent.

BEAR WOOD

The seat of John Walter II
From a lithograph

Printing House Square, where they entertained somewhat lavishly —Crabb Robinson came to a " sumptious (*sic*) entertainment " in June—but Walter was fitting up a town house in Brompton Row (he later moved to Charing Cross) as well as planning his seat in the country. Robinson, as a trustee of the marriage settlement, was more than once consulted, in the course of 1818, about the condition of affairs at Printing House Square. It is unfortunate, but understandable, for Robinson was not a commercial man, that the diary is vague on the motives which finally determined the Proprietor to dispose of shares in *The Times*. Some reasons are sufficiently clear : John Walter III was born in 1818, and his farsighted father desired to lay the foundations of a family securely seated in the country, with himself holding a position in Berkshire and going on to membership of the House of Commons. As public opinion had not learnt to tolerate gentlemen of the Press because it could not consider them gentlemen, the Chief Proprietor had necessarily to withdraw from the " ostensible " management ; it could be known that he had been connected with the journalistic world, and that he owned a printing business, but a Parliamentary career would be out of the reach of the active manager of a newspaper. John Walter as a debater would find it convenient to be free from responsibility for the opinions of *The Times*. Indeed, whether it was in his mind or not in 1819, the political situation of thirteen years later proved the wisdom of John Walter's determination to transfer authority to the Editor. It may also have been desirable to increase the number of proprietors loyal to himself, upon whom he could rely in any dispute with the other beneficiaries of his father's will. At any rate, when he determined to become a private gentleman, he began to dispose of some of his shares in the paper. There was another and distinct advantage. He could henceforth refer office disagreements to his managers on the ground that he was no longer responsible.

In September, 1819, John Walter told Robinson[1] of his intention to assign shares to members of his staff. " I wished but wanted courage to ask for a share for myself. Yet perhaps he wished me to do it," writes Robinson in a dubious phrase, almost indicating that he thought Walter was presenting, instead of selling, the shares. As the maintenance of Bear Wood, a town house and the private dwelling house in Printing House Square must have cost a considerable sum, Walter may have bargained keenly over his shares. We know from Crabb Robinson that in money affairs

[1] *Diary*, VII, 122 (September 3, 1819).

173

Walter could drive a hard bargain but that he was " liberal when not opposed."

At the time of the sale *The Times* does not seem to have been notably prosperous. When Barnes assumed editorial responsibility the paper was only covering expenses.[1] At any rate, all the shares were sold for cash ; Barnes borrowed the money from one Ward ; Alsager, as the former City Correspondent, no doubt had access to money or moneyed friends ; James Murray, the chief reporter and former assistant Parliamentary reporter under Barnes from 1813, was a Scotsman ; Edward Sterling, the leader-writer with powerful connexions, would have no difficulty in securing funds. The only evidence of the sale price of the shares occurs in the case of Murray. On November 6, 1819, an Indenture of Assignment of one-half of one-sixteenth share was signed. The consideration was £1,400. On this basis a whole share would have been valued at £2,800 and the whole business of *The Times* some £44,800.

The share register shows that at the settlement after the death of John Walter I the relative position of the proprietors was as follows :

SHARES IN *THE TIMES* 1816[2]

Fanny Walter	afterwards	Knox, afterwards				
Wraight		-	-	-	-	2 sixteenths
Mary Walter	,,	Carden	-	-	3	,,
Catherine Walter	,,	Winsloe	-	-	2	,,
Anna Walter	,,	Brodie	-	-	2	,,
Walter Wilson	-	-	-	-	-	1	,,
Charles Bell ⎱						
James Lawson ⎰	-	-	-	-	-	1	,,
John Walter II (with two shares purchased according						
to the terms of the will) -	-	-	-	-	5	,,
					Total 16	,,

Thus, when Crabb Robinson had his conversation with John Walter in September, 1819, the Chief Proprietor owned five sixteenth shares. He owned also the reversion of the share held for life by Walter Wilson, who died in 1847, and which returned to him shortly before his own death in the same year. The share

[1] But the half-yearly dividends for 1837 and 1838 were £150 14s. 6d. and £166 15s. respectively on a half share (*cf.* copies of Mrs. Murray's receipts in Murray *v.* Walter, 1838).

[2] That is to say, after the winding-up of the estate of Walter I, and acceptance of the arbitration on the price of the floating shares. See Appendix for the holdings of the Walter family and an extract from the will of John Walter I.

originally given by the will to Charles Bell and James Lawson for their lives had, subject to an annuity to Bell, been transferred absolutely to Lawson in 1817. Lawson died in the same year, and the whole share did not come into the possession of the Lawson family until Bell died in 1821. Set out in a table, the transactions of 1819 comprised the following assignments of portions of John Walter's holding of five-sixteenths :

JOHN WALTER'S ASSIGNMENTS OF SHARES IN *THE TIMES* 1819

To Thomas M. Alsager - - - -	$\frac{1}{2}$ of one-sixteenth	
,, Thomas Barnes - - - -	$\frac{1}{2}$	,,
(with power of redemption by J. W., subsequently released in 1827)		
,, James Murray (d. 1835) - - -	$\frac{1}{2}$	,,
(with power of redemption)		
,, Thomas Platt[1] (d. 1842) - - -	$\frac{1}{2}$	,,
(with power of redemption)		
,, Edward Sterling - - - -	1	,,
(with power of redemption, subsequently released)		

[Leaving John Walter with two one-sixteenth shares]

The assignments of shares to Barnes and Barnes's colleagues on the paper, whether or not due to Walter's political ambitions, was consistent with a need of money for use in elections, or in connexion with Bear Wood. Money was dear in 1819, five per cent. being the return of Government Navy Loan quoted at 107-8. During the years following, John Walter still further reduced his interest in *The Times*. The position in 1827 was :

THE TIMES 1827

1813	Fanny Walter, afterwards Knox, afterwards Wraight	- - -	2 sixteenths	
1813	Mary Walter	,, Carden -	3	,,
1813	Catherine Walter	,, Winsloe -	2	.,
1813	Anna Walter	,, Brodie -	2	,,
1813	Walter Wilson	- - - -	1	,,
1813	Charles Bell }	- - - -	1	,,
1813	James Lawson }			
1819	Thomas Barnes -	- - - -	$\frac{1}{2}$ of one-sixteenth	
1827	Thomas Barnes -	- - - -	$\frac{1}{2}$	,,
	(with power of redemption)			

[1] Thomas Platt, solicitor to *The Times*.

175

1819	Thomas M. Alsager	-	-	-	-	$\frac{1}{2}$ of one-sixteenth
1819	James Murray (d. 1835)	-	-	-		$\frac{1}{2}$	,,
	(with power of redemption)						
1819	Thomas Platt (d. 1842)	-	-	-		$\frac{1}{2}$	,,
	(with power of redemption)						
1819	Edward Sterling	-	-	-	-	1	,,
1823	George Hicks[1] (d. 1834)	-	-	-		$\frac{1}{2}$	,,
1827	George Hicks	-	-	-	-	$\frac{1}{2}$	,,
1827	John Walter	-	-	-	-	$\frac{1}{2}$	,,
					Total	16	

In 1827 assignments of shares in the separate " business of printing *The Times* " were made to George Hicks, T. M. Alsager, and in 1835 to Thomas Barnes and W. F. A. Delane (the father of John Thadeus Delane, afterwards Editor) upon Hicks's death at that time. The situation was one with which John Walter was well content. Robinson, at Bear Wood, heard of the arrangements :

1829 6 June. Rose early. Walter drove me in his gig to meet the Reading stage ; talked about his affairs. I suppose that he has only one 32^d of the paper remaining in his own hands but retains the right of buying back the shares of Barnes etc. Alsager has also a share of the printing concern. He speaks with satisfaction of his connection with Barnes and Alsager, he speaks well of Thornton but I see no prospect of his coming into a share.

It follows that Barnes enjoyed from 1827 one sixteenth share in *The Times*, and Walter himself one thirty-second. The position of the Chief Proprietor, however, remained exactly as hitherto in respect to final responsibility for the site and fabric of Printing House Square, for the printing machinery and the plant, and consequently for the production of the paper. In accordance with his father's will, he shared the profits with the other proprietors. Barnes's understanding with John Walter gave him control over the policy and responsibility for all that went into the paper. He was strengthened, by his ownership of a full share, in any dispute with the other proprietors. The will, it should be repeated, imposed upon John Walter the duty of financial control, exercised through Alsager (and W. F. A. Delane after 1831), irrespective of shares in

[1] George Hicks, Chief Accountant of *The Times*, brother-in-law of T. M. Alsager, and predecessor of W. F. A. Delane, his assistant in that office.

THOMAS MASSA ALSAGER
From an oil painting in the possession of
the Worshipful Company of Clothworkers

The Times. In spite of his statements to his neighbours and friends that he ceased to be Chief Proprietor in 1819, he yet bore the final responsibility for the carrying out of the terms of the will. It contained no mention of policy, and made no dispositions for the purpose of securing the political independence of the paper, in fact refrained from hampering John Walter II in these respects. He was therefore free to delegate editorial (*i.e.*, political) but not final managerial (*i.e.*, financial) responsibility. He could resign all exercise of power over the views expressed in *The Times*, but he could not divest himself of powers over allowances and payments without risking the interference of other proprietors. Even when he succeeded in withdrawing from Printing House Square he was responsible for certain salary increases, though not, it seems, for the selection of subordinate individuals.

The Times itself, though the central, was by no means the only enterprise of Printing House Square ; it was, as direct income, the least important to the Chief Proprietor, his one thirty-second share representing no more than £650 a year in the most prosperous period. Walter, as the preceding pages have shown, cut down his share in the copyright of *The Times* journal to the smallest figure, beginning with the 1819 reduction. That year marked the beginning of his withdrawal from the sole management and conduct. He then ceased to take the salary of £1,000 a year which his father's will appointed to him as sole manager, considering it henceforth the reward of the Managing Editor. Thus the " ostensible " editorial control, given to Barnes in 1817, was enlarged in November, 1819 ; from this date he received the salary of £1,000 a year appointed to the Manager by the will. The financial department was accepted by Thomas M. Alsager at the salary of £700 ; but Walter exercised important powers of supervision over him and over the Editor until 1820. After a further reduction of his holding in 1827, John Walter fulfilled in 1831 his intention wholly to retire from responsibility for *The Times* journal. Doubtless his approaching election governed the completeness of this year's decision. The fighting articles in *The Times* were not agreeable to some of Walter's friends, who naturally considered him at least partly responsible. When one of his Tory neighbours expressed his disgust for the " vulgar, malignant and most dangerous doctrines of *The Times* " and attacked his own fitness as a candidate on the ground of his connexion with the paper, Walter replied that he had " disclaimed being the chief proprietor of *The Times* for the last thirteen years " and was not therefore

N

" entitled to either the merit or the odium of the articles."[1] He was elected M.P. for Berkshire in 1832 and sat until 1837, when he fought other constituencies.

The relations between Walter, Barnes and *The Times* are indicated with some precision in a document pertaining to the actions which Mrs. Murray brought against Walter in the years 1838 and 1842. In the 1838 case John Walter. answering Clarissa Murray, denied

that he was at the time (1819) mentioned in her bill of complaint or that he did continue until lately the principal proprietor of the undertaking in the said Bill mentioned ; or the principal manager of the same, or that there is any other Manager than Thomas Barnes the Editor thereof.[2]

In the 1842 case Walter deposed :

this defendant says that as well before as upon and after the decease of the said Testator [John Walter I, d. 1812] this defendant had and did take upon himself the sole management and conduct of the said [*Times*] Newspaper up to the year 1819 when Thomas Barnes, since deceased, became the Editor of the said Newspaper.

And this Defendant says that from the time when the said Thomas Barnes became such Editor as aforesaid this Defendant committed to the said Thomas Barnes the care and management of the details of the said Newspaper, and, among other things, the engagement and employment of the several persons who wrote articles in the said Newspaper and who supplied information thereto.

And that although the said Thomas Barnes upon some occasions consulted this defendant as to the employment of such persons yet that on other occasions and more frequently the said Thomas Barnes engaged such persons of his own authority and without consulting this Defendant.

Nevertheless, this Defendant admits that before the said Thomas Barnes became such Editor as aforesaid this Defendant did engage and employ the various Gentlemen who wrote articles and supplied information to the said Newspaper, and that he continued also to engage and employ some but not all of such persons after the said Thomas Barnes became such Editor as aforesaid up to the year 1819 and up to which last mentioned period this Defendant, in addition to the general

[1] Walter II to Merry, August 22, 1832 (Walter Papers).
[2] Chancery Proceedings, September 25, 1838 (P.R.O., 13, 1907).

management of the said Newspaper, did perform the duties of principal Editor and Superintendent of the said Newspaper.

But this Defendant says that at the time last mentioned he withdrew in a great degree from the management and superintendence of the said Newspaper and at the same time this Defendant relinquished and gave up the salary of £1000 per annum to which he was entitled as such Manager as aforesaid.[1]

It is clear that Barnes's position in the office was paramount after 1819. The later position of Barnes as sole executive head of the office is confirmed in Walter's answer to another of Mrs. Murray's interrogatories :

And this Defendant further says that in the year 1831 this Defendant withdrew from and relinquished the management and superintendence of the said Newspaper and did not afterwards assume or act in the management or Editing thereof but such management and Editing was wholly left to the said Thomas Barnes until his death, which took place in the month of May 1841.[2]

So Barnes was the only Editor of a contemporary daily paper independent in his management and editing. He was completely free from influence or interference. John Walter, uninterested in politics for the sake of party, had the mind of a social reformer of the cautious sort. He knew nothing of the theories of the political economists ; his politics began at home. His zeal made him an admirable county member whose detachment from the political machine confirmed the policy of non-interference with the responsible head which his father's will had insisted upon. Constitutionally, John Walter II allowed Barnes the same freedom that he had himself been given by John Walter I from 1802 to 1812. In Walter's words to Croker in 1830 : " You are of course aware that I can interfere very little now in the management of the journal."[3] Walter, therefore, was solely responsible for the choice and retention of Barnes ; Barnes was solely responsible for the paper. The arrangement worked for a time without objection from any quarter.

But the constitution of Printing House Square as created by the will of Walter I and modified by the practice of Walter II depended for its working upon the profitable conduct of *The Times*

---

[1] From the answer of John Walter to Clarissa Murray, May 21, 1842. (Public Record Office, C.13, 1962, fol. 14.)

[2] *Ibid.*, fol. 14.

[3] Walter to Croker, October 6, 1830 (Michigan University Papers) : " . . . Mr. Barnes is not in England . . . you will have the goodness to transmit your communication to James Murray, Esq., at *The Times* office and it will immediately be attended to."

and the absence of friction among the proprietors. As the paper made increasing profits under Barnes, Walter had no motive to change the arrangement. The death of Murray, however, introduced an unexpected dissentient. His widow asserted that the revenue of *The Times* had been used to pay for wages and materials of the printing business and that the printing charges were excessive. The root of the trouble, she contended, lay in John Walter's dual position as Proprietor and Printer. The dispute led John Walter to consider retiring completely from *The Times* by giving up his remaining one thirty-second share. Against Mrs. Murray, John Walter contended that the interest of the proprietors was confined solely to the copyright of *The Times*, to the right of publishing and selling it. He claimed power to refuse to print *The Times*, or to allow any of the types, materials, presses, &c., to be used for printing it ; and alleged, also, that he was entitled to refuse the premises at Printing House Square to be employed for that purpose unless upon his own terms. Finally, John Walter announced himself at liberty to use all the presses, machinery, implements, materials and stock-in-trade for the printing of another daily newspaper differing in nothing from *The Times* but in the name or title. The dispute reached dangerous lengths. Walter was all but forced to decide to take more responsibility, or even less. Crabb Robinson enters a mysterious shorthand note in his diary (February 10, 1836) which indicates that a complete severance between Walter and *The Times* was nearly effected.

Called on Barnes he having sent me a letter about Scargill. He was not at home, but I met with Walter in the Square whom I accompanied to his lodgings. I expressed my gladness that he had given up his interest in the *Times*. This touched him. He has not given up. The declaration was forced from him. He wrote in a hurry late at night. Instruments were executed for form but never carried into effect ! ! ! I shall soon go down to Bearwood.[1]

The documents " never carried into effect " doubtless maintained John Walter's paramount position in the printing business.[2]

[1] *Diary*, XVI, 153.

[2] That John Walter was prepared in certain circumstances to sell outright his entire property in the goodwill and plant of the business of printing *The Times* and *Evening Mail* is definitely stated in the indenture of 1827 between Alsager and Hicks, of the one part, and Walter of the other. Had he predeceased Alsager and Hicks, his son, John Walter III, would have succeeded to the freehold of the premises of Printing House Square and his father's shares in *The Times*. The *Evening Mail*, published thrice weekly, summarized the news and leading articles of *The Times*. It was an additional item in the printing business and a separate publication with a separate board of proprietors, of whom John Walter was chief.

But the action of Mrs. Murray revealed the danger to *The Times* of continuing the arrangements in accordance with custom, of permitting the assignment of shares without power of redemption, of splitting shares and thus of multiplying the number of proprietors. W. F. A. Delane, successor to Hicks as Treasurer of *The Times* from 1831 and a barrister of some eminence, wrote to the Chief Proprietor on these subjects immediately after Mrs. Murray's action had failed. The letter has a prophetic note :

My dear Sir,

The difficulties which have arisen induce me to suggest the necessity of a new arrangement with the Proprietors.

The dangers arising from such litigation should be stated to them. They should each be requested to vest their separate shares in Trustees to prevent their distribution into improper hands by Marriages, Bankruptcies etc and on the condition (with certain other regulations) you could engage to continue to print on the terms mentioned in your father's will etc etc.

Unless something of the kind is done I fear that at some future time your property will be exposed to great risk and the Paper to destruction. If you are agreed to the principle of this, I think that without adding in any way to the annoyance of Mrs M[urray] business, I could manage to obtain the assent of all parties.

The benefit that all parties would derive from the increased security afforded to their property would be a sufficient inducement for their acquiescence, and at any rate you could command three-fourths of the present Proprietors.

Pray think of this and recollect that some very simple rules may preserve the whole in peace for many years.

I remain, Dear Sir,
Yours faithfully,
W. F. A. DELANE.

9 March 1839

Counsel's opinion was taken, but no other action—probably for the reason that it seemed better not to arouse the concern of all the proprietors. In spite of Mrs. Murray the custom was maintained and John Walter himself, or his agents, fixed the amounts to be charged for printing. Delane, at this time, kept the books of *The Times*, and fixed the amounts of the profits. It is possible that the accounts were not well kept, at least by modern standards, for there was a very serious dispute in 1846-47. It does not appear that there was any reserve for emergencies. A provincial observer visiting Printing House Square in 1841 was impressed by the cramped conditions of the composing room staff. The office had outgrown premises which had not been enlarged in spite of the increased volume of the paper. It is difficult to resist the belief that Printing House Square, prosperous from 1831-1841 as it undoubtedly was beyond any previous period of its existence, was, in fact, less prosperous than it thought. It was considered sufficient that John Walter should see and approve the accounts.[1]

In summary, it would appear from his agreements with George Hicks and T. M. Alsager and W. F. A. Delane that, in Walter's mind, " Printing House Square " was subject to three main distinctions. First, there was the copyright of *The Times* ; secondly, there was the business of printing *The Times* and the materials and mechanical means by which the work was performed ; thirdly, there was the ownership of the premises in which the printing business was carried on and the freehold of the site. Accordingly the printing business paid a separate rent of £1,360 a year to John Walter for the premises, while Walter paid the printing business £100 a year for the right to occupy the dwelling house. He was absolute owner of the freehold of Printing House Square and of the premises with their equipment, having acquired them in 1810 before the will was made. The will, as such, could not give the beneficiaries known as the proprietors any power to interfere with the site, the premises, or the presses. On the other hand, the will empowered John Walter II to print *The Times*, taking it for granted that the reduction in salary suffered by decrease of the paper's profit below £5,000 would act as a sufficient check upon extravagant composition or press charges. John Walter II, therefore, as possessor of the plant, regarded himself as empowered to fix the cost of printing *The Times* and to print it without formal approval or independent scrutiny by the vote of the proprietors. Mrs. Murray alleged that the charges of the printing business exceeded the market price of printing.

The separate character of the printing business, its complete distinction from the business of publishing *The Times*, is confirmed in the surviving indentures of partnership. In 1827

---

[1] Mrs. Murray took another action at the death of Barnes and succeeded in bringing into Court certain account books. The schedule lists the Publishing Books, 1821-1841 ; Cash Books, 1837-1841 ; Ledgers, 1831-1841 ; Bundles of Weekly Accounts, 1837-1842 ; Bankers' Pass Books, 1838-1841 ; Receipts for Dividends, 1830-1841. The plaintiff being advised against further action, the suit was dismissed. The books in this schedule were destroyed—probably in 1842.

WILLIAM FREDERICK AUGUSTUS DELANE

George Hicks, engaged on the mechanical side of Printing House Square, with Thomas M. Alsager his brother-in-law, joint manager of *The Times*, both agreed with John Walter " for the purchase of ⅛th part of share of the said business of printing the said newspapers,"[1] and the profit or percentage " upon a certain part of the expense incurred by such printing."[2] Hicks and Alsager paid John Walter £1,875 each for their partnerships, which equally endured for a period of twenty-one years. The money was probably required for expenses in connexion with the steam press which Messrs. Applegath and Cowper had constructed for printing *The Times*. The new machine, of great economic gain to the printing business, was used from 1828.

To John Walter remained six-eighths of the " business of printing *The Times* and *Evening Mail* newspapers," and the agreement stipulated, moreover, that the " joint business should be carried on in premises belonging to the said John Walter where it was then carried on, and the said John Walter should have and receive for the same a clear rent of £340 per annum payable quarterly out of the said profits." John Walter was permitted by the agreement to reside or permit others to reside in the dwelling-house attached to the printing office, on condition that he, or the other occupier, paid £100 a year rent to the co-partnership. A clause requires purchase of materials to be made in the name of " John Walter " ; nevertheless " he should not be bound or obliged to take any more active part in the management of the business than he should of his own free will and pleasure determine, it being the meaning and intention that the said George Hicks and T. M. Alsager should engage to be the active though not ostensible managers and conductors of the business," but Walter reserved the right to dispose of his interest at any time to any person. In the case of the death of John Walter before the expiration of the partnership, the surviving partners were empowered to purchase all, or as many shares as they were able. In 1836 Thomas Barnes and William Frederick Augustus Delane were admitted into partnership " in the business and printing of *The Times* and *Evening Mail* newspapers etc " in the room of George Hicks, died 1834. Accordingly,

---

[1] *i.e.*, *The Times* and *Evening Mail*.

[2] *i.e.*, A percentage upon the cost of printing *The Times* as rendered to the Proprietors. The partnership was dissolved in 1848, when John Walter III reduced the charge for presswork from ten to eight shillings per token in conformity with his father's instructions to be carried out when the Alsager-Delane interest should lapse (a token = 250 backed-up sheets). It seems that the financial benefits of the Applegath machine of 1827 were reserved to the printing business until 1848 ; in other words, *The Times* paid the old rates for twenty-one years—to the discontent of Mrs. Murray. There is no proof, however, that the printing profits were huge during the period.

in 1836, " the business of printing *The Times* and *Evening Mail* newspapers " was divided into the following shares :

SHARES IN THE PRINTING BUSINESS 1836

John Walter - - - -	6/8
Thomas M. Alsager - - -	1/8
Thomas Barnes - - - -	1/16
William F. A. Delane - - -	1/16
	8-8ths

Barnes and W. F. A. Delane each paid £310 to John Walter as their consideration. The partnership ended in 1848, the term of the original indenture of 1827, Barnes's share being purchased and divided at his death among the other proprietors.

John Walter's income from Printing House Square after 1827 comprised (1) one thirty-second share in *The Times*, the whole dividend upon which journal was, according to a memorandum by John Walter III, some £20,000 at the end of the Barnes period, yielding a share to the Chief Proprietor of £625 ; (2) six-eighths of the printing business, the value of the business and plant being fixed by the 1827 agreement at £15,000 ; and (3) freehold of Printing House Square, the annual rent to the printing business being charged at £1,360, less £100 charged against the occupier of the private house in Printing House Square when in the occupation of John Walter.[1] With these and other more remunerative properties to sustain him, John Walter, as a Whig, "nothing more or less," entered Parliament in 1832. His self-reliant nature and habits of independence made him a better representative of the people than of the party. When elected a member for Berkshire he was 56 years of age, not readily adaptable to the machinery of Parliament. He spoke plainly but with a slight harshness, without gesture, and, though slow and infrequent in debate, took a leading part in the agitation against the new Poor Law Bill of 1834. He felt more deeply upon this than upon any other issue, but natural shyness prevented his being a very effective opponent. He enjoyed, however, the respect of the House, having only a single personal antagonist—Daniel O'Connell, who unsparingly attacked the member for Berkshire on account of his supposed responsibility

[1] John Walter rented lodgings at No. 8, Charing Cross, when Parliamentary duties increased the frequency of his London visits. He did not return to live, except on rare occasions, in his old quarters until after the death of Barnes. Letters addressed to John Walter, Esq., at *The Times* were, by his instructions, refused.

for the columns of *The Times*. Though without special distinction as a politician, Walter was uncommonly well entrenched in the affections of his constituency. His conscientiousness made him instantly available to all his constituents. From the beginning of his apprenticeship to public life as a magistrate he was open to stories of misfortune, to complaints of mistreatment or injustice ; he was always to the front in work for relief of the poor in detail as well as in principle.

The dissolution of Parliament upon the accession of Queen Victoria forced John Walter to reconsider his position with regard to the county. The national and party situation was very different from what it had been at the outset of his Parliamentary career, when the idealism of Reform was still strong. Although in power in 1837, the Whigs were sustained only by the " tail " headed by Daniel O'Connell. The Reform party had lost much ground to the party which had been developed by adversity into a chastened and wiser Toryism willing to be led by the enlightened Peel. Even when Peel was supported by *The Times*, Walter preferred to attach himself to a " neutral " group in the House of Commons. This independent group subsequently split, the fragments departing to one or other parties, with Walter, as O'Connell said in a phrase which delighted the House, like " the last rose of summer left blooming alone." After this sally, Walter joined Peel's party and faced criticism from his constituency. Rashly, in the opinion of observers, he stood down from Berkshire in 1837. He unsuccessfully contested Southwark at the election of January, 1840, but was, after a difficult contest, triumphantly elected for Nottingham in April, 1841, a month before the death of Barnes rendered it imperative for the Chief Proprietor to return to Printing House Square and make new arrangements for the conduct of *The Times* journal.

To this man, proud but shy, strict but generous, self-reliant but modest, enterprising but slow, *The Times* owes its character. John Walter I all but failed to sustain the journal he had founded. No separate memorial of the paper as he left it would be required. John Walter II could have declined joining his father in 1795 ; he could have acquiesced in selling the paper in 1803 instead of staying to save it. But by his insight, industry and confidence that he could render *The Times* commercially successful without compromising its independence with either the political or the commercial communities, he formed for it a character no daily journal had succeeded before in retaining. Yet, eager as he was to maintain the paper at the highest possible point of honesty and efficiency, he set aside the vanity of trying to do everything himself. *The Times*, as he handed it to the care of Barnes in 1817, compared with its condition in 1802, was an independent creation deserving a conspicuous place in the history of English journalism. John Walter II placed *The Times* in the forefront of periodical literature in his early recognition of the importance and value of the new school of journalists typified by Leigh Hunt and by his selection for *The Times* of a thoroughly dependable corps of writers ; by his successful struggle with the Post Office for the freedom of communication he secured a reputation for the earliest news at a time when Britain was on tip-toe for foreign intelligence. By sponsoring the steam press in 1814, and by rare commercial management all round, he strengthened the economic position of Printing House Square. Finally, by appointing and maintaining Thomas Barnes as responsible editor, and delegating to him absolute power over the contents of *The Times*, he enabled that greatest of all editors in the first half of the nineteenth century to make the newspaper into " The Thunderer."

XII

THOMAS BARNES

THOMAS BARNES was born on September 11, 1785—the year which saw the foundation of the *Daily Universal Register*—the son of John Barnes, an attorney of some means from Tenterden, in Kent. His mother seems to have died early, and the future editor of *The Times* was committed, first, to the domestic care of a grandmother, and then, with his younger brother, John, to the scholastic care of Christ's Hospital, where his father also had been educated. As a Blue Coat Boy, taught by L. P. Stephens and A. W. Trollope, he developed a taste for letters that was stimulated by the companionship of two contemporaries ; one who later employed him on the *Examiner*, Leigh Hunt, and the other, Thomas Mitchell, afterwards a classical scholar of distinction, whose *Aristophanes* Barnes was destined to review in the columns of *The Times*. He was not precocious, like Leigh Hunt, but he was studious without being priggish. Leigh Hunt writes :

What pleasant days have I not passed with him [Barnes] and other schoolfellows, bathing in the New River and boating on the Thames. He and I began to learn Italian together, and anybody not within the pale of the enthusiastic might have thought us mad as we went shouting the beginning of Metastasio's *Ode to Venus*, as loud as we could bawl, over the Hornsey fields. I can repeat it to this day, from those first lessons.

With Leigh Hunt also Barnes laid the foundation of his knowledge of Ariosto, Tasso and Boccaccio. Though he schooled himself equally well in French, Latin was an earlier and longer enthusiasm, but his Greek was good and he had some Hebrew. When he went boating at Richmond and fell overboard, a more melancholy souvenir than the wet trousers was his sodden Seneca ; and a full generation later he lovingly accepted a Lucan from Armand Bertin, editor of the *Journal des Débats*. In Leigh Hunt's estimation Barnes was as good a scholar as the admired Mitchell ; his erudition, even at seventeen, was reported by Charles Lamb to Coleridge.

187

In 1804 Barnes went up to Pembroke College, Cambridge, as an exhibitioner. In studies he excelled in Latin; in athletics, in boxing. He was admired as a cricketer; he was a notably strong and bold swimmer. He exercised himself as a wit, always hitting hard, but without malice; always enjoying a trial of strength, but prepared for correction from better men. He related once to Crabb Robinson that " when he was at Cambridge, having had lessons from a boxer, he gave himself airs, and, meeting a fellow in a field who did not make way for him, as he expected and thought due to a gownsman, he challenged the man; accompanied by a smile and a tap on the shoulder, he received for answer—' I am Cribb, my lad.' " Barnes took him back to his rooms and gave him a wine supper. It was fortunate for the future editor of *The Times* that he encountered so scrupulous a sparrer as the champion of the ring. Barnes never allowed athletics to interfere with his proper business at the University, but, says John Richardson, " he was not distinguished by the closest adherence to the regulations of the place." He took his degree in 1808. The only way to Honours in Cambridge at that time was through the Mathematical Tripos. He just failed to be a Wrangler, being placed first among the Senior Optimes. This was a very creditable performance, as an essentially classical scholar like Barnes was to some extent handicapped in an examination which was almost entirely mathematical with a slight admixture of logic and philosophy. Yet Barnes had some skill in mathematics. When Mitchell wrote to Leigh Hunt (October 10, 1814) inquiring for a rule to find a number which can be so divided that the square of one of its parts shall equal the whole multiplied by the other part, he added: " Perhaps Barnes can give a solution ? How is he ? Ask him if he has any authority for advancing what I have heard him say, that Cumberland was indebted to his maternal uncle, Bentley's, papers for his translations in the *Observer*." Barnes's year was a good year. A future Master of the Rolls (Lord Langdale) was Senior Wrangler; Bishop Blomfield, third; Sedgwick, the geologist, fifth. Barnes's was the best degree taken by a Pembroke man between the years 1806 and 1810. Mitchell, who was with him at school and college and who became Fellow of Sidney Sussex, graduated in 1806 halfway down the Senior Optimes.

On coming down, Barnes hesitated at first between the ideas of a legal career in London and of an academic career, with a possible Fellowship, at Cambridge. He had some patrimony and an appetite for a free life, and was therefore naturally drawn by the lure of London. Failure in an attempt to secure the post of tutor to Canning's son may have turned the scale ; at any rate, he set aside the project of a life of scholarship and made up his mind to read for the Bar. He was more than disputatious. He possessed a competitive mind which would have stood him in good stead as an advocate, and he had a capacity for spells of hard work. Clearly the law was a sensible choice. And it was a family profession, followed by his father as a solicitor, and his brother as a barrister. Barnes entered the Inner Temple in 1809, and for the best part of two years worked seriously as a pupil of the famous elder Joseph Chitty, " Pleader under the Bar," as the phrase went then. In Chitty's chambers at the time were Rumball, Blackburne, Shepherd, son of the Attorney-General, Sir Samuel Shepherd, and Sir Fortunatus Dwarris. Barnes undoubtedly read with the intention of being called, but a curiosity about politics tempted him away from what seemed, in comparison, to be a life of drudgery.

For so long as his father's legacy lasted he enjoyed his freedom, attending a good deal to the West End and its entertainments. His good looks were remarked by contemporaries ; his wit was respected. Leigh Hunt says : " He was very handsome when young, with a profile of Grecian regularity." The temptation increased for Barnes to slacken in his legal reading. As the future was to prove, he was a born Bohemian, working hardest when freest to do whatsoever he would. In spite of his athletic youth, Barnes in maturity neglected exercise. Nevertheless, for a trifling wager he once proved his prowess by swimming from the steps of the Apothecaries' garden at Chelsea to Westminster Bridge. He was a lover of town pastimes, and, as time went on, his health ceased to be good ; he suffered much from asthma and chronic rheumatism. In later years his good looks disappeared, but, as a contemporary reports, his frank placid countenance never lost its benevolence. He was not conspicuous in height, and, as he grew older, his figure became excessively corpulent ; but his fine forehead, magnificent brow, clear blue eyes and square shoulders impressed his fellow-journalists of the 1830's when the Editor was past 45. A period of poverty and illness followed early years of careless enjoyment of town life, and Barnes bore it cheerfully in his chambers. " A Christ Hospital boy's school friends are his friends for ever," said Charles Lamb, who, with Leigh Hunt, Talfourd, Mitchell and others, helped him.

During all these years the prospect of another career, neither legal nor academic, nor even strictly literary, was opening before Barnes. He had become intimate with Barron Field, then theatrical critic of *The Times*. In 1809 Field introduced him to John Walter as a likely recruit for journalism. Walter was attracted and later gave him an opportunity to try his hand. It was not difficult to combine occasional reporting of law cases, theatres and political meetings with his legal studies and his West End amusements. As the legal studies waned, the reporting work increased, and, on Field's retirement, owing to increase of legal work, from *The Times*, Barnes succeeded him as the regular theatrical critic and quickly took high place in the esteem of the Chief Proprietor. In January, 1811, he was appointed to the Parliamentary staff. If Barnes enjoyed journalism, above all he enjoyed Parliamentary work. Nevertheless, he still wrote much literary and dramatic criticism. Between sessions he assisted John Scott with the *Champion* and Leigh Hunt with his weekly *Examiner*. In the *Reflector* during 1810 and 1811 Barnes proved his scholarship by tracing Herrick's *Night-Piece to Julia* to its source in Propertius and then translating it very prettily into Latin elegiacs (but " silvery feet " beat him ; he could do no better than *pedes albi*). He wrote also a charming set of Sapphics —at once gallant and virtuous—on sending a bouquet to a lady ; and a paper on Theophrastus, in which he argues for the superiority of the Greek writer over La Bruyère, is both learned and wise. Another contribution by " T.B." was a savagely ironical suggestion—in imitation of Swift at his most brutal— for making use of *beaux* and *belles*, creatures of whom the satirist betrays hatred as well as disapproval.

In the *Examiner* in 1813 and 1814 Barnes reached his full stature. His dramatic criticism, written in the florid manner of his time, keeps to the point, dramatic or histrionic, yet brings a great deal of various thought and learning to help make it. Amid much else that is still lively are his remarks on Shakespeare and Dryden in a review of *Antony and Cleopatra*, and on the difference between Shakespeare's Falstaff and Stephen Kemble's Falstaff, and a glorious outburst on the " miseries of critics " and on imbecility, when amusing and when disgusting, aroused by Lawler's farce, *Sharp and Flat*. Everywhere he shows himself a man knowing literature and life as well as drama and the theatre. His weakest spot is a queer dislike of the Restoration dramatists, especially of Wycherley, whom he wholly misread.

Not even the best of his " Theatrical Examiner " papers comes up to the studies of statesmen called " Parliamentary Criticism." They show a powerful mind, well bitted but in full career. They are " character-drawing " of the wisest, the shrewdest, the most fearless ; and the man who wrote them had greatness in literature within his grasp. The *Examiner* and the *Reflector* were run in the Radical interest, and in 1812 the *Examiner's* attacks on the Prince Regent brought about a Government prosecution. Crabb Robinson, turning into Charles Lamb's rooms on March 16, 1812, found Leigh Hunt, Barnes and Field conferring ; ten days afterwards he called late at night at Field's chambers and found Barnes and John Collier talking about the indiscretion of Hunt's articles and the risks of the future. As the group of their friends feared, the defendants, in spite of Brougham's brilliant defence, were convicted and sentenced ; and, one day in February, 1813, Leigh Hunt drove to Horsemonger Lane accompanied by Barron Field, with Barnes following.

The *Examiner* lived through the year 1813, largely by the personal loyalty of Barnes and Lamb. Barnes accepted responsibility for the theatre, and from February, 1813, he wrote notices averaging two columns of each issue. In that for August 15 he began, over the signature " Criticus," the series of articles headed " Parliamentary Criticism."

Of one addition to the value of our Publication [wrote Leigh Hunt in the annual postscript] we can boast with safety. It is the Parliamentary Criticism. In the present unreformed state of things, the chief value of Parliament itself consists in the record of its speeches by the public Press. It is of importance to the readers of these speeches to know at what rate to estimate those who deliver them, either from the extent of their views or the soundness of their principles. This is the Writer's object ; and after the attention his criticisms have excited, both on Senators and Actors, for the extent of their views, the soundness of their principles, and that keen insight into the causes of character and manners, for which they are more particularly remarkable, the addition of our praise can be of little worth to him, except to show how sensible we are of his help.

A " Criticus " series of notices of members of the House of Commons concluded on August 14, 1814, with a postscript addressed to the Editor, still in the Surrey Gaol : " And now, my dear Hunt, having finished one part of my career I must be allowed to return you my most grateful acknowledgments for the candour and liberality with which you have frequently, in the course of these articles, given publicity to opinions which were at variance with your own." Barnes resumed with notices of the Lords on September 25, 1814.

Meanwhile he had not altogether deserted literature for politics. During 1814, as " Strada," he contributed to the *Champion* fifteen *Portraits of Authors*—robust, humorous and perceptive criticism. " Flabby " Moore [1] and " puerile " Byron offend him with their affectations and their slack morals ; Peter Pindar, with his coarseness, does not. He rates Coleridge soundly for his indolence ; the indolence of Thomson only makes him think of an old porter showing a picture gallery, or of that " invitation to sleep ; the spiritual application at the end of a tabernacle sermon." In Montgomery, as in Southey or Campbell, he can find the good to praise, as well as the bad to blame. In a final paragraph he deprives Gifford of existence by looking serenely over the top of his venomous head ; and in a first paragraph on Wordsworth (which deserves to be rescued and made widely known) he writes great prose about a great subject.

Barnes by no means agreed with the whole of Leigh Hunt's policy, but he felt he must give his friend all the assistance he could ; and friends they remained until Barnes's death. He was not blind to Leigh Hunt's faults. Crabb Robinson was edified one night in December, 1814, to hear him admit that he had noticed Hunt to be " so exceedingly sensitive and impatient of censure or reproach." " His wife," Barnes revealed, " is in the habit of opening all his letters and burning whatever she thinks will give him pain." Barnes pleaded guilty to having frequently abstained from giving him advice for fear that it might put an end to their friendship ; and, to the astonishment of Crabb Robinson, who thought him cold and unresponsive, he added : " And I cannot bear to lose Hunt's friendship, for there is hardly a man I love so much." Barnes's judgment was that Leigh Hunt was a person of very strong affections but no general humanity. And Crabb Robinson, always given to scruples, had his reservations in respect to Barnes. Barnes must have thought Crabb Robinson tedious ; Crabb Robinson found Barnes sometimes fierce, though he knew he could be otherwise from his first meeting with him at one of Alsager's parties towards the end of 1812. Crabb

[1] Moore complained of " Strada " to Leigh Hunt at the time, and years later Moore involved Barnes and Hunt in correspondence on the subject. " I have no personal ground of offence with Moore, and even this letter [enclosed] does not seem to me to be unreasonable as far as I am concerned, for I remember I had been somewhat rough in my handling of him." (Barnes to Leigh Hunt, January 11, 1831 ; B.M., MSS. Addl. 38523, 198.)

Robinson then picked out Barnes as " alone of the party a very interesting man. He knows the tone of good company ; never presses but takes the subject from others and throws in a pleasantry as a make-light to an otherwise heavy argument, and he makes you think that he knows more than he says." Talfourd, confirming Robinson, defines young Barnes's temperament as cold.

Tom Moore, who met Barnes later (March 26, 1824), found him not only agreeable but modest—he was not aware that Barnes was " Strada " who had handled him so roughly in the *Champion* ten years before. Samuel Rogers, the banker poet of *The Pleasures of Memory*, gave a party including Lord Lansdowne, Lord Holland, Henry Luttrell, George Tierney, and others. He invited Moore and the others expressly to meet Barnes. The company marked him as being " very quiet and unproductive ; neither in his look nor manner giving any idea of the strong powers he unquestionably possesses."[1] A couple of days later, when Barnes entertained Moore " in Great Surrey Street, beyond Blackfriars Bridge," he was found to be " more forthcoming a good deal than he was at Rogers's." Barnes was evidently more himself at home than at the gatherings of aristocratic Whigs. On another occasion, in 1825, Moore accepted an invitation to dine with Barnes, and listened with pleasure to his discourse on Dryden and Cicero. Greville, brought in as a guest to meet Barnes, also noted that he was not a talker.

Generally, Barnes, who in Leigh Hunt's judgment had it in him to excel as scholar, wit or critic, took, after he became Editor, no notice of literary affairs, attending only parties of friends of some standing, or political meetings. He had a taste in wines and kept a liberal table at his house in Nelson Square, where he encouraged and entertained visitors, mainly political. " We fared sumptuously on venison, turtle, and the richest wines," wrote Le Marchant[2] in his journal, " Rogers and Edward Ellice, secretary for war, were there—but some of the company were not of the first water." Barnes enjoyed the good things of the table. " Permit me to thank you," he wrote to Lord Durham, " for your very handsome present of a quartett of the finest pheasants I ever saw."[3] Whenever

1 Diary of Moore, IV, 171.

2 Journal of Sir Denis Le Marchant, principal secretary to Lord Brougham, 1830-1834. Denis Le Marchant, son of John Gaspard Le Marchant, was educated at Eton and Trinity Coll., Camb. ; Barrister, Lincoln's Inn, 1823 ; secretary to Lord Chancellor Brougham, 1830-1834 ; secretary to the Board of Trade, 1836-1841 ; Baronet, 1841 ; Liberal M.P., 1846-1847. He wrote a Memoir of Lord Althorp and edited Walpole's *Memoirs of the Reign of George III*, 1845. An extract from his unpublished journal, dealing with his relations with journalists, will be found as an Appendix.

3 Barnes to Durham, November 12, 1833. (Lambton Papers.)

O

Moore went to dine he found Barnes with lawyers, embassy secretaries, foreign editors ; seldom with poets or writers of *belles-lettres*. His avoidance, when in the chair at Printing House Square, of purely literary connexions was seemingly deliberate. It could so easily have been different, since his earlier circumstances had brought him into contact with poets. Leigh Hunt, when he was in gaol, wrote to Mrs. Hunt that [at a party in the Horse-monger] " there will be Mr. Brougham, Dr. Gooch, Lord Byron, Mitchell and Barnes," and there are other indications in the memoirs of this period that Barnes interested himself in literary men. A letter to Leigh Hunt demonstrates Barnes's solicitude for the susceptibilities of such friends :

I met Wordsworth last Sunday, & was a good deal pleased with his unaffected sense. I took an opportunity of introducing Lord Byron's poetry in order to sound him on that subject, & certainly from the opinion which he appears to entertain of Lord B.'s mind as displayed in his poems, I do not think that he would feel a very high gratification in his company. At any rate, I think it would be a risk to bring together in a small party two persons who I fear would have no points of sympathy about them. If Lord B. is half as amiable as Wordsworth appears to be, this is a great pity, for the good of the intelligent ought to amalgamate to be a match for the conspiracy of fools and knaves.[1]

That Barnes's preference for politics was a loss to literature rests not only upon the assertion of Leigh Hunt, but also upon the judgment of Sir Thomas Talfourd. The second of Talfourd's conscientious volumes on Lamb and his circle, published in 1848, fourteen years after Elia's death and seven after Barnes's, describes a party of all three late one evening in the year 1816, when only two or three friends remained with Lamb and his sister :

We had heard the chimes at midnight, holding inveterate but delighted controversy with Lamb, respecting the tragic power of Dante as compared with that of Shakespeare. Dante was scarcely known to Lamb ; for he was unable to read the original, and Cary's noble trans-lation was not then known to him ; and Barnes aspired to the glory of according him a glimpse of a kindred greatness in the mighty Italian with that which he had conceived incapable of human rivalry. The face of the advocate of Dante, heavy when in repose, grew bright with earnest admiration as he quoted images, sentiments, dialogues, against

[1] Barnes to Leigh Hunt, B.M., MSS. Addl. 38523, 19.

Lamb who had taken his stand on Lear, and urged the supremacy of the child-changed father against all the possible Ugolinos of the world. . . .

Mention of Charles Lamb's article in the *Reflector* brought from Barnes

a burst of affectionate admiration for his friend, then scarcely known to the world, which was the more striking for its contrast with his usually sedate demeanour. I think I see him now, leaning forward upon the little table upon which the candles were just expiring in their sockets, his fists clenched, his eyes flashing and his face bathed in perspiration, exclaiming to Lamb " And do I not know, my boy, that you have written about Shakespeare, and Shakespeare's own Lear, finer than anyone ever did in this world, and won't I let the world know it ?

He was right ; there is nothing in the world more worthy of the genius it estimates than that little passage referred to on *Lear* ; few felt it then like Barnes ; thousands have read it since, here, and tens of thousands in America ; and have felt as he did, and will answer for the truth of that excited hour.

Le Marchant mentions in his journal that he was present at an encounter of Barnes with Macaulay :

[Barnes] was one of the best masters of the English language and literature I ever knew. I recollect witnessing a discussion between him and Macaulay on the comparative merits of the early English dramatists that lasted above an hour, and I was not the only one of a large company who thought he had the best of the argument.

Barnes, affirms Leigh Hunt, " was famous among us for a certain dispassionate humour." There are complaints in Crabb Robinson's diary that this humour was not always acceptable. Some were offended by his tendency to a peculiar intensity of expression, to him meaning nothing but the excuse to play with words, or rather to pattern with words, words which were like himself, very short, stoutly English, and rare. He often used an outlandish word, though seldom an archaism ; generally his vocabulary, singularly wide, was confined to words which could be called " homely." There was nothing of the pedant in Barnes's character, in his politics, or in his editorship. His delight in the variety of words and his pleasure in watching the diversity of consequences he could produce with them remained all his life, a pleasure that waxed rather than waned with the passing of time. As a young man he would first completely mystify a victim by indulging in a realistic tirade, and next set about performing a service in order to soothe offended feelings. Extracts from his leaders and letters to be quoted in later chapters will prove that his prose grew more and more vigorous as his convictions became more resolute and the political moment more exigent. Barnes's political experience brought him complete self-confidence, and in many of his leaders and letters there is to be found a note of jocularity sometimes amiable, sometimes not. Here are specimens of his more amiable levity in two (hitherto unpublished) letters addressed to Leigh Hunt, the first dated April 3, 1815 :

Had I known you were so near me yesterday I should certainly have paid you a visit, and I am sorry that your forbearance towards Walter deprived me of the pleasure of seeing you. I the more regret missing you yesterday as I am quite unable to fix any probable time for coming down to Paddington. Since that restless fellow Buonaparte put his foot on his " fine France " as he calls it, he has broken my rest as much as his own ; indeed more ; for the dog appears to have slept three or four times on his way from the coast to Paris, whereas he has scarcely allowed me a single wink. I confess I never had much relish for him ; he was always too noisy and pretending to suit my taste ; but now I believe I should hate him if he had every virtue under heaven. What is it to me that he establishes the liberty of the Press, if I must keep the press open till four o'clock in the morning to tell the public of it ? What do I care for his abolition of the slave trade, if I am to be roused out of the first sound sleep I have had for a month by a legion of printers' devils bawling " French papers to translate, Sir " ? Nor is this all : for even the foggy Belgians and the credulous romancers of Germany send over in shoals their stupid diatribes, and tear me out of bed at any hour they please. Such being the case and Saturday being my only day (for thro' that fellow Buonaparte, who I am credibly informed is an atheist, Sunday shines no Sabbath day to me) I am so thoroughly exhausted when that day comes that instead of moving abroad I give myself up to a kind of indolent repose.

I should, however, have roused myself to come to you, but for the last fortnight my father has been lying in a most precarious state, owing to an apoplectic fit, and what time I have had to spare I have dedicated to him. " Quae cum ita sint," as Cicero says—what is to be done ? I can only say that I will come and see you the very first opportunity ; meantime you and I appreciate each other too well to fear that any temporary absence can in the smallest degree diminish that mutual regard which I feel (at least as far as concerns you) arises from qualities which take the stronger hold of me the more I have leisure to reflect upon them. But I must not take advantage of your absence to say what perhaps I might feel some hesitation in saying to your face. . . .

Yours very truly,

T. BARNES.

A second letter to the same friend still in gaol, in which Barnes announces his inability to brave a spell of bad weather, is a little more droll :

Dear Hunt,

There are three things which end in smoke, yea four things, which if a man do, he shall be disappointed :—he that layeth out his all & purchaseth a lottery-ticket with the certainty of its coming up the chief prize,—he that planteth a garden on the sea-shore,—he that buildeth a castle in the air, and he that maketh a certain promise on a contingent event. In one of these foolish predicaments behold me stand—I said I would be with you today & lo! I am unable to stir. My knees which were once movable have ceased to have any joint in them. You recollect how poor Barrymore moves on the stage (I take shame to myself for having laughed at him)[1] you recollect that he has no pivot of action except that which separates his upper from his lower half. So it is with me, if I move at all ; but in general I am too stiff even for this motion. I begin to have very clear conceptions of a petrification, & am firmly of the opinion that the two stories of Niobe & Lot's wife are merely allegorical descriptions of rheumatism. The only difficulty seems this, that the change into rocks and pillars implies rest and quiet, whereas your whoreson rheumatism never allows the least respite. I promised too to sleep at Alsager's : ah—bootless boast— as if I could sleep at all, & as if in such cases it is not better to twist one's limbs about on the familiar mattress which knows all one's ways than to astonish the Genius of an unknown Bed by distortions of which it may not be able to discover the object.

All this absurdity is intended to express nothing more than that I do not feel myself in a fit condition to venture out during this hideous weather : as I cannot see you, you must take compassion on me & write to me, & I hope you will be able to give a more satisfactory account of your health than I can of mine. Send me if you can the *Bride of Abydos*.

Yours sincerely,

T. BARNES.

Tuesday—Temple.

[1] In a notice published in the *Examiner*, April 18, 1813, p. 250. " Mr. Barrymore . . . has long been celebrated for his stately port and solemn pomp of utterance, but his great characteristic has, we believe, been hitherto unmarked. It is this : there is but one pivot of motion, but one joint of action in his whole body : he is a sort of straight lever, whose fulcrum, to speak with mathematical correctness, is about one-fifth from the lower extremity of his back. . . . We feel anxious to know whether it be the effort of nature or art," &c.

Barnes's humour was so much a part of his intense character that it was bound to be unwelcome to some, and, as his acquaintance widened and he pursued his individual line with increased confidence, he was disliked and feared. It was a defect in him that in his self-sufficient, detached frame of mind he underestimated the effect upon others of his strong language, however humorous it might be. In the 1830's he was denounced as a tyrant. Political opponents—and they were of both sides—did not relish the wit with which *The Times* so frequently salted its denunciations of weakness and error. Fellow-journalists on the *Chronicle* (Barnes habitually called it the " Grunticle ") hated him for using his dry humour as a cat-o'-nine-tails on their backs. Members of the Lords and Commons testified to the effect of Barnes's caustic criticism by their frequent invocations of " privilege " and summonses of the printer of *The Times* to the Bar of the House. Barnes was not unaware of the imperfections among his qualities. He was capable, before he became an editor, of committing one of the greatest sins of which an editor has to complain. Redding, the acting-editor of the *Champion*, to whose columns he contributed in 1812 the series of papers signed " Strada," has left a note of his difficulty in securing punctual delivery of copy from his author. Barnes himself suggested a scheme by which the *Champion* might be guaranteed against further disappointment. Writing materials were placed upon a table by his bedside, together with some volumes of the author he was to review, for the purposes of quotation. At his customary hour he retired to rest, sober or not, says Redding, leaving orders to be called at 4 o'clock in the morning, when he arose with a bright, clear and vigorous intellect and immediately applying himself to his task achieved it with a completeness and rapidity that few could equal and which none could have surpassed.

The editor of the *Champion* testifies that, successful as was Barnes's scheme, he did not in later life need to resort to any such expedient. Daniel O'Connell's description of him as " the gin drinking-est editor in London " may be an exaggeration, but he certainly loved wine. Nevertheless, as Crabb Robinson notes in chronicling Barnes's death, he " lived a free life." Le Marchant avers that he was a complete voluptuary, but adds that " he had paid however no less attention to his mind than his body."

For a host of reasons it was impossible that Thomas Barnes should ever have been presented at Court. The editor always

avoided the public he served and had no desire to be
" presentable." His name was seldom mentioned in any newspaper, and never in *The Times* until his death. In the report of
the case of Moscati *versus* Lawson, in which an adventurer alleged
he had dined with the editor, no name was given. The " Mr. B "
mentioned in the evidence was not called, and in *The Times* a
footnote explained that it was against his wishes that " Mr. B "
and his affairs were intruded upon the attention of readers. None
of the " frank self-display " that, in a letter to Leigh Hunt, he
said he was afraid of, ever seduced him from his native love of
anonymity—not even at the very peak of his power in the 1830's.
No doubt the motive was, in part, prideful disdain ; it was not
pious renunciation, for Barnes was no ascetic, but an egoist content
solely with the approval of his own critical intelligence. Yet he
could accept with pleasure a confirmation of his ability by a
competent judge. On the publication of *Lord Byron and Some
of his Contemporaries*, Leigh Hunt caused a copy to be sent to
Printing House Square. Barnes acknowledged Hunt's estimate
with evident satisfaction :

The Times Office. Monday, January 21, 1828.

Dear Hunt,
    I have not yet had time to read your book, but a passage has been
pointed out to me, where you speak of me in very high terms of praise.
I will not affect to say that your panegyric is altogether undeserved :
but I feel that it is abundantly handsome and generous, and above all
I entertain the most cordially grateful sense of the kindness which has
dictated it.

Yours very truly,

T. BARNES.

The motive underlying such frank acceptance of a tribute is
elucidated in another, earlier, letter. In one of his periodical
sicknesses Barnes wrote from Brighton (14, Ship Street) to Leigh
Hunt in 1815 :

Dear Hunt,
    I feel when I look at your last letter as you felt when you saw mine
ten days after you had received it without returning an answer. We
are two miserable fellows to labour under the same fault & to
encourage each other in it instead of resolutely amending it. You
tell me to talk about myself & pay me a sort of compliment as if I
were not an Egotist. I thought you were more sagacious ; in other
words, I am sure that it cannot have escaped you that there is frequently

as much egotism lurking under a proud reserve as is displayed by the most communicative good-nature. The fact is that I am conscious of too many faults perhaps but half cured to venture on any of that frank self-display which I find so charming in others, but which might subject me to many an unpleasant rebuff. I am afraid that this is very obscure, but my object is to convince you that if I am wanting in egotism, I hope I am not wanting in candour : I wish also to deprecate that most unpleasant of all humiliations, to be praised where praise is not due—But enough of this sublime obscurity : & now let me ask you, why have you not sent me your Masque : [1] It must be out by this time. I am wretchedly unprovided with entertainment, & altho' my limbs are acquiring strength, yet I am half afraid that my mind from disuse is becoming feeble. I never in my life wrote with such painful effort as when I worked out the article on Lord Liverpool for Sunday.[2] I am out of the way of my books, & it is impossible to think in this vortex of dissipation. I do nothing but play at back-gammon with an old Annuitant who has but one idea, & who thinks it an insult if I attempt to give him a glimpse of a second. I made at first some feeble efforts towards disputation with him, but he silenced me by misunderstanding half that I said, & calling the rest immoral. Under such circumstances, what can I do ? Pray write to me, that I may at least get some pleasant associations even from the hand-writing : & though it is no joke to make such a request, insert at least one joke in your letter, for I have not heard nor uttered one since I have been here, my aforesaid companion having an utter aversion to wit because as he says it is frivolous. This letter is half querulous & half nonsensical, but receive it kindly, & believe me to be,

Yours sincerely,

T. BARNES.

Leigh Hunt, Esq.[3]

Barnes's self-sufficiency was, in a strange way, impersonal, due to an intense individual sensitiveness of the intellect. Cold he might be generally, but he was often the reverse and in later life a mellowed temperament rendered him instantly available to the unfortunate. Talfourd, who worked with him, says that Barnes " though skilful in finding out those who duped others made amends to the world of sharpers by allowing himself to be abundantly duped." That sympathy·with the individual which was one of the virtues of his character and which led him to attack the new, and to him heartless, provisions of the Poor Law

[1] *Descent of Liberty.* A Mask dedicated to Thomas Barnes published in 1815.
[2] *The Examiner*, September 25, 1815 : " Lord Liverpool is one of the best debaters among the Lords," &c., pp. 619-620.
[3] B.M., MSS. Addl. 38523.

Bill of 1834, was responsible for keeping his door ever open to refugees, pretenders, theatrical wrecks, and impoverished persons of every description. Needy journalists frequent all newspaper offices. Few who had the slightest acquaintance with the Editor of *The Times* were refused an interview. " The inexorable Editor," says Talfourd, " excluded their lucubrations from the precious space of its columns but rarely omitted to make them large contributions from his purse." It was a matter of surprise to his colleague that the " intimate acquaintance with all the varieties of life forced on him by his position in the midst of the morning epitome of the world failed to teach him distrust or discretion." There was in Barnes's character a strain of scepticism, even of cynicism, whence originated a reputation for misanthropy. Creevey told Le Marchant that Barnes was " a thorough misanthropist " and at war with all the human race except Brougham. Barnes was nothing of the kind, but Le Marchant was accurate enough in his statement that " he seemed to regard all public men with equal indifference," for Barnes considered the Editor of *The Times* equal in dignity to any statesman. There was, however, nothing unkind about him even when, as it frequently seemed, he was not only strict, but intemperate, or even savage in his castigation of political sins and sinners. That his heart was quickly touched by the pain of others, the leading articles directed against workhouse masters, cruel magistrates, and the practice of infant labour bear witness.

The single mention of Barnes in *The Times* was printed a year after his death. A disreputable Pole sued the paper for additional remuneration in respect of extracts from a pamphlet of his on Central European affairs. Barnes had already sent the author, one Sawaszkiewicz, the sum of £10, and had been relieving his necessities for years. The paragraph had been published in October, 1840 ; the case was tried on February 21, 1842 ; and a leading article appeared on the following day. It said that this was " simply one among the various attempts made upon this journal, in consequence of its position, to extort money " ; and, referring to Barnes by name, it described him as

a gentleman connected with us who died last year and whose valuable services we must ever most highly appreciate. Among the many excellent qualities which commanded the good will of his friends, he was characterized by one which, though peculiarly amiable in private life, yet occasionally exposed him to some little inconveniences in the particular circumstances of his position—extreme good nature and kindness of disposition. He was quite unable to withstand a tale of distress ; and in a very public situation in London this inability, when once found out, exposes a man not only to expense, but no small amount of imposition.

Barnes was humble before the unfortunate, and apt to recognize himself in the person of down-and-out callers. He reserved his impersonal pride to repel, in the words of his already quoted colleague, " the slightest interference with his function from the greatest quarters, but he was open to every tale from the lowest."

Barnes's detachment from conventional political opinions and the foibles of literary groups on the one hand, and inherited relationships and social customs on the other, left him free to concentrate upon his editorial duties. His health was poor, he was near-sighted ; he continually had to absent himself from this or that political conference on account of his rheumatism ; but his attention was never distracted by the concerns of a family. Barnes's domestic arrangements were loose and from time to time the subject of anxious comment by the Chief Proprietor. There does not seem to have been any very serious irregularity, certainly none of a kind which would have been regarded by his generation as in itself exceptional. If doubts were entertained about his marriage, they were not indulged in public. Crabb Robinson occasionally makes dark references to " Barnes's lady " ; as though she were not quite presentable. It was in 1820 or thereabouts that Barnes met Dina Maria Mondet, who, in the phrase of the 1858 share register of *The Times*, " lived with him." An entry in shorthand under the date October 28, 1823, in Crabb Robinson's Diary, commemorates a visit he had paid to Alsager. " We spoke about Barnes. Mrs. B. is now married to Barnes and he means to let Mrs. A. visit Mrs. B. but they are not to be intimate." Another note in the following month (November 15) mentions a visit of Crabb Robinson's to John Walter, who " talked to me about Alsager and Thomas Barnes, to have my opinion of their marriages. I told him what I thought of Thomas Barnes's wife. It is evident that Walter does not think well of her. He wishes to meet Mrs. Alsager but is afraid of seeing Mrs. Barnes there." The explanation seems to be that Mrs. Barnes, *née* Dunn, was first married to one Kelly, that later, when Barnes met her, she was married to one Mondet, and that Mondet could not make up his mind to take the steps which might regularize a situation which Barnes's friends rather than himself considered inconvenient. Disraeli, in a letter to his sister in the early months of 1838, describes a dinner party at which he met Barnes and the lady :

> We had a queer but amusing party at the Twisses. It was really given to Mr. and Mrs. Barnes ; the W[yndham] L[ewis]'s were got to meet them, and the rest were men—Lord Darlington, Lowther, G. Somerset, Lord Reay, H. Hardinge, Henry Baring, &c., &c. The dinner was good for Twiss, and everything went off well ; Mrs. Barnes, who looked, as H.B. said, like a lady in a pantomime, very funny, surrounded by sons of dukes and privy councillors.[1]

Mary Barnes, to give her the name by which she was generally known, sometimes went with Barnes to Lady Blessington's parties at Gore House. A letter of hers to Robert Owen is preserved by the Manchester Cooperative Society. She was six years junior to Barnes and survived him eleven years. There was neither marriage nor issue. She died on December 26, 1852.

Barnes's unusual abilities prepared his friends for unconventional solutions of common problems. It was enough for John Walter that the Editor was the man for *The Times*, and that he was willing to give himself prodigally to the most exacting task in journalism ; ready to forgo making himself a name in the history of Letters in order to place *The Times* at the head of the Press. His achievement equals in merit much of the literature of that distinguished generation, but no memoir of him was published, in a day which showed much memorializing kindness to hack writers like Alaric Watts. Yet as a literary man alone Barnes deserves to be remembered. " Rarely," says Talfourd, " as he was seen in his later years in Lamb's circle, he was indestructibly associated with it in the recollections of its early days." And while these present pages commemorate, as far as the sparse remaining documents will allow, Thomas Barnes the Editor, Talfourd's words may well stand. Lamb's circle, he writes, will " lament with me that the influences for good which he shed largely on all the departments of life, should have necessarily left behind them such slender memorials of one of the kindest, wisest and the best of those who have enjoyed signal opportunities of moulding public opinion, and who have turned them to the noblest and purest uses."

[1] Monypenny and Buckle, *Life of Disraeli*, I, 418 (two vol. edition).

For a man of Barnes's constitution to accept the position of Editor of *The Times* as it was in 1817 was a sacrifice. His friends, as Talfourd reports, learnt of the appointment with surprise and misgiving. Although the connexions he had made in literary, theatrical and Parliamentary circles gave promise of success as an independent writer, he elected to carry a weight of responsibility from which a literary man is free, and to work at all hours for comparatively moderate compensation. The loss to literature was gain to *The Times*. The *Morning Post*, and, still more, the *Morning Chronicle*, were able competitors. Circumstances called for a man of courage, capacity and determination, a man with a policy. Barnes, having accepted the offered post, put his whole heart and soul into the kind of journalism which he believed to be most needed by the England of his time. As *The Times* Parliamentary Correspondent he had made the acquaintance of the men who were to be the principal actors in that revolution by legislation, the Reform Bill; and he had come to know, as few could have known, the weakness of individuals and of parties. He possessed unrivalled opportunities for advancing his own career at a time when venality amongst journalists was proverbial. Westmacott and Maginn were only types of the dozens of characterless men of education out of Scotland and Ireland who championed and attacked as they were bought. Barnes could have filled a Government place quite as well as William Coulson of the *Globe*, but he had no such ambition. Nor did he regard a seat in Parliament, like Praed of the *Morning Post*, Harvey of the *True Sun*, Shiel of the *Morning Chronicle*. He was well content to see any name but his own on a party " bill," and ignored the prospect of a title as a " benefit " at the end of the run. Without ambition except to lift high the reputation of his paper, he made no concessions to politicians or to party. In Le Marchant's words, " the interest of the paper was all he looked to."

An almost extravagant insistence on the right of anonymity is seen in Barnes's only contribution to the bookshelf, his *Parliamentary Portraits*, the republication in 1815 of the " Criticus " articles. The volume was dedicated to " Leigh Hunt Esq.," and the title-page, avoiding all " self-display," gave no indication of the author's name. His preface spoke a belief that " it will be better for me not to draw aside the mysterious veil which has given an importance to the assumed name of ' Criticus.' " Later, he fought with all his might against an attempt by the Whig-Radical element to force a system of compulsory registration and publication of names and addresses of all journalists. The proposal was fathered by Thomas Spring Rice, Chancellor of the Exchequer in Lord Melbourne's second Government, in revenge for the withdrawal of support by *The Times* from the Whig Party. Then and always Barnes preached, as he practised, the principle that anonymous journalism is the only journalism that will be seriously read. In his very letters he did not easily " draw aside the veil." For long he corresponded with John Cam Hobhouse, Byron's friend, a Cambridge man of Barnes's own year, whom he esteemed for qualities he denoted by the term " manly." During nearly ten years their epistolary relations were kept rigidly formal. Letters from 1820 onward begin : " The Editor of *The Times* presents his compliments to Mr. Hobhouse and regrets that he cannot publish the enclosed letter, etc." Not until 1828 does the Editor mention his own name :

Monday June 30, [1828]   Times Office

The Editor presents his compliments to Mr. Hobhouse : he returns Colonel Wildman's letter for the communication of which he is much obliged to Mr. Hobhouse. The Editor will take care not to rely upon any statement furnished by the person referred to in that letter. The Editor would feel great pleasure in seeing Mr. Hobhouse at his own time, but he will not trouble him to make any further explanations on the subject of the letter signed " Byronicus."

As it is fit that Mr. Hobhouse should know his correspondent to be not merely that abstract personage an Editor, Mr. Barnes begs to add that all future communications may be addressed to him by name ;— that is—if Mr. Hobhouse thinks it necessary. Mr. Barnes is always at the office from 8 to 12 in the evening.[1]

Barnes made *The Times* the most obstinately anonymous newspaper in the world. Power he loved, but it was sweeter to him for its secrecy. It amused him that O'Connell, Roebuck, Cobbett and a host of others thought Henry Brougham, Edward Sterling, Francis Bacon or some other directed the paper. He realized that such secrecy was not merely of great advantage to him in dealing with political leaders, but of advantage also to them. This " Great Unknown " was never a gadabout. Though Barnes was to be seen at political gatherings, his own house from 1821 to 1834[2] at No. 49, Nelson Square, Great Surrey Street, five

1 Barnes to Hobhouse, B.M., MSS. Addl. 36464, 374.
2 Barnes lived at Farrer's Building, Temple, from 1811 to 1817 ; at Manchester Buildings, Canon Row, Westminster, until 1821.

minutes over Blackfriars Bridge from Printing House Square, and from 1834 to 1841 at 25, Soho Square, was the scene of those consultations upon which depended political decisions of the first importance. Once when Le Marchant called late at night at Barnes's another visitor arrived whom he did not see, but who was shown into another room. Greville, who was told the story by Le Marchant, says that Barnes " went to him and after a quarter of an hour returned when Le Marchant said ' Shall I tell you who your visitor is ? ' Barnes said Yes if he knew. ' Well, then, I know his step and his voice ; it is Lord Durham.' Barnes answered it was, when Le Marchant said ' What does he come for ? ' Barnes said he came on behalf of King Leopold, who had been much annoyed by some article in *The Times*, to entreat they would put in one of a contrary and healing description. As Le Marchant said, here was the proudest man in England come to solicit the editor of a newspaper for a crowned head." Murray went to the Continent, Sterling into the Clubs, Alsager to the City. Barnes remained where he was accessible on the shortest notice. Ministers were brought to visit him at his house, their object being largely to ask his views of the mind of the country, though they must also have hoped for a favourable consideration of their policy. A tireless interest in the political and economic thoughts and expectations of every class in the kingdom gave Barnes a sure foundation for his singular position. None of the other notable journalists of the time—not Black of the *Chronicle*, Peter Stuart or Gibbons Merle of the *Courier*, Young of the *Sun*, Taylor of the *Herald*, or Giffard of the *Standard*—approached him for industry, intelligence, practicality, sagacity or learning, or—it must be emphasized—discretion. Barnes gave no publicity to his meetings with public persons. If he boasted of his sources of information, he boasted also of their secrecy.

Occasionally Barnes went to France, to Italy and to Germany, but his interests were predominantly English, and European affairs at the time of his induction to the editorial chair justified this preference. England, the most powerful nation in the world after the settlement of 1815, was face to face with unprecedented domestic problems. The post-war discontent and disillusion were without parallel. The greatest industrial Power needed to reorganize its system of political representation. It was one of the critical periods of English history, that of the transfer of power from a small aristocratic territorial oligarchy, which had ruled since the Revolution, to a large, growing class drawing its money from manufactures. The moment had come to do for England what John Walter had done for the Continent : secure reports from trusted agents in the rural and agricultural, the mining and the manufacturing communities at home, to maintain critical observation of the conditions, and of the increasing number of companies financed on the joint stock principle by those who were both saving and speculative. As a basis for his judgment Barnes surrounded himself with a network of correspondents all over the country, who kept him in touch with the views of shopkeepers, landlords, paupers, squires, bishops, and industrialists. The secret of those changes in policy which drew upon *The Times* the nickname of " The Turnabout " lay precisely in the fact that Barnes consulted, first, public interest, and, secondly, public opinion.

The Times, not being tied to a party, could afford to vary its expressions in accordance with the ebb and flow of public sentiment. It could direct and it could indicate public opinion. Under Barnes it gradually became as conspicuous for the authenticity of its home intelligence and the critical value of its commentary as it had been under John Walter II for its early information on foreign affairs and for its inclusiveness. While the public realized the paper's critical importance, few were aware that the leadership was due to a fundamental revision of accepted notions of editorial responsibility. As Walter II had fought for freedom of communication, Barnes had a struggle for freedom of comment forced upon him. The mass of readers did not know that a struggle for their instruction rather than their deception was proceeding between one man and a host of political and professional corrupters.

His personal position in the matter of salary appears from a letter written to the Chief Proprietor at a time when Walter's share in the paper (1/32) was half that of Barnes (1/16).

March 14, 1834

My dear Sir,

I have seldom if ever made any application to you for any personal advantage to myself ; indeed you have generally anticipated my wishes ; but I really think that circumstances will now fairly excuse an application which perhaps you would also have anticipated, were not your mind occupied by many and various matters more important.

You will I am sure on the slightest consideration feel that the degree of influence which I have now for no short time been able to obtain in certain great quarters, and of which you individually or the

Paper have reaped all the advantage (for myself I have never asked or received the most trifling favour) cannot have been maintained without that personal intercourse which necessarily leads to some expenses. I have heard you say that when the management of the Paper was in your hands you had three hundred pounds a year extra allotted for the purpose of these, to a certain degree, requisite expenses. When you gave me a portion of the printing profits you probably thought that they would supply the means of these social disbursements; but in point of fact the income from that source was, after the first month or two, diminished nearly one half. My last share in the paper, which, like the former, I bought with borrowed money, is not yet free, for an instalment of £300 is still owing to Ward upon it. If that were quite free, my income would be very good; but then it is only within the last year or two that I have had much more than half of it unencumbered, having been forced to borrow and repay with interest the money for each half-share.

I do not think, if you look at the responsibility which I have so long incurred, and still bear—the expense necessary to a prominent situation —that situation which somebody must fill—and my many years of service—23 years this last January—that you will consider £2000 a year unencumbered too large a sum for me to ask or for the Paper to pay.

As I do not wish to take you by surprise and hurry you to a decision, I will not expect an immediate answer: indeed I would rather that what you do should be done deliberately than on the spur of the moment.

Whatever you may decide, believe me,

Ever yours most sincerely,

T. BARNES.

P.S. I wrote this a week ago and have kept it back for a week's consideration; and have seen no reason to alter any passage in it.

Yours ever,

J. Walter Esq.   T. B.

It has been already pointed out that when Walter reduced his share to 1/32nd as against Barnes's 1/16th and appointed Barnes responsible editor, he did so largely in order to be able to declare with truth that he had no responsibility for what *The Times* said, or for its manner of saying it. He was only the business man who printed and published the paper. Barnes was no financier, no business man, and nothing could better have suited his mind than to enjoy the utmost personal independence in his convictions without the necessity to deal with costs and payments. His salary was moderate, but was materially augmented by his share in *The Times* in the years immediately preceding his death. He was thus enabled to take the fine house No. 25, Soho Square.

THOMAS BARNES
After a detail from the oil painting by Sir George Hayter of
the trial of Queen Caroline in the House of Lords, 1820

Those least friendly to him bore witness that he never asked but one favour from a Minister—namely, the promotion of his brother John to a more desirable place in the Bankruptcy Office. He lived simply. Though in personal relations with Lord Durham, Lord Lansdowne, Lord Holland, Lord Aberdeen, as well as Poulett Thomson, Bear Ellice, Creevey and Greville, he remained outside all political groups. He was intimate with Sir John Hobhouse, Lord Lyndhurst and Lord Abinger, and for seventeen years was on the closest terms with Lord Brougham, but was never identified with either the Whig or the Tory party.

Barnes's editorship falls into two main periods. In the early years from 1817 to 1834, he fought first for the maintenance of a healthy opinion, at that time only a nascent element in politics : secondly, for leadership of the public opinion created largely by his own efforts. He fought Cobbett for this leadership, championing the measures of Brougham, whom he had known in *Examiner* days, rather than Whig policy. After the breach first with Brougham and then with all the official Whigs, Barnes fought the party machine which, with men and money, kept up the *Morning Chronicle* in the effort to wrest the leadership of public opinion from *The Times*. No mere question of trade precedence, of superiority in circulation, was at stake in the " war " upon *The Times* which Brougham and Althorp declared in 1834 ; the struggle was that of individual responsible journalism against gross manipulation by Government. Barnes won the battle on behalf of a healthy Press and a healthy public opinion. His quarrel with Brougham was one of the major sensations of the curiously involved series of political transactions which followed the resignation of Grey and Althorp in July, 1834, and the summons to Melbourne to form a new Ministry. This was more than the beginning of a new political shuffle or even the overture to a new Government. It meant a profound change in the relations of the parties. Barnes's line after November, 1834, was described by the Whig Press as " ratting." Policies were dependent upon personalities. Barnes realized that, while the politico-economic situation was developing rapidly, official Whiggery lacked the man-power and character to push through necessary and urgent measures. He determined to take a new course. To the astonishment of the public, to the mystification and rage of the Whigs, *The Times* supported the Duke of Wellington, supported Lyndhurst, and, in doing so, made it possible for Peel to create modern Conservatism in the place of out-of-date Toryism.

P

Having entered in 1817 upon his responsibilities in the chair at Printing House Square, Barnes the Editor so successfully dominated Barnes the Man that, although he enjoyed meeting persons useful to him in the exercise of his vocation, he had no interest whatever in extending his circle of acquaintance; nothing but what was required for the furtherance of the influence of *The Times* was important. Only the extravagant romance of politics interested him, he said. Even his religious ideas were political, depending on his conception of the British Empire, to whose unity he was devoted. Though the behaviour of George IV and William IV sometimes tested his loyalty, he was no Republican. He was denounced as a desperate Radical, but he was never other than a sound middle-class constitutionalist. For long he was friendly towards the English and Irish Catholics, and he supported Emancipation; nevertheless, *The Times* thundered a "No Popery" cry upon the formation in 1835 of the Whig-Irish alliance between Melbourne's Government and Daniel O'Connell. The seventh Earl of Shaftesbury took credit for drawing the attention of Printing House Square to the encroachments of Popery; and these were a subject made for the destructive pen of Peter Fraser, who, after Barnes's death, wrote to John Walter urging a holy war upon Pusey. In Barnes's own view it was intolerable that non-Protestants should interfere with the Established Church, yet he never, even with the O'Connell provocation, entertained anything like the old-fashioned Church-and-King sentiments of the High Tories. Forced to choose—and he thought O'Connell did force him—between the complete toleration of Catholicism in Ireland, inevitably ending in separation, and the maintenance of the Protestant ascendancy for the purpose of supporting the unity of the British Islands, he felt that the only course was to champion Protestantism.

During the late 1830's *The Times* was constantly charged by politicians and their "hireling scribes" with being violent, offensive, and tyrannous. Its style was certainly forcible, and it was always deliberate. The energy and offensiveness were calculated, the nice use of strong language belonging to the essence of Barnes's notion of journalism. To a correspondent who sent him some articles, he wrote that they were "good as far as they went, but they wanted a little devil in them."

Newspaper writing [Barnes explained] is a thing *sui generis*; it is in literature what brandy is in beverages. John Bull, whose understanding is rather sluggish—I speak of the majority of readers—, requires a strong stimulus. He consumes his beef and cannot digest it without a dram ; he dozes composedly over his prejudices which his conceit calls opinions ; and you must fire ten-pounders at his densely compacted intellect before you can make it comprehend your meaning or care one farthing for your efforts.

He himself was excellent at putting " a little devil " into the material which came to him. Le Marchant, who admired the Editor's " elegance," considered him " slow " as a writer. One of Barnes's supreme gifts was the power of adapting to the public taste articles in themselves of inferior merit ; he had the art of infusing into them a spirit and force which gave them an effect they could not have produced in their original form. For, unlike many writers on the Treasury Press, he was a journalist. The leading articles in the *Globe*, written for Palmerston by Charles Buller, and those in the *Chronicle* by Senior, were essays, too often contradictory of the rest of the paper. *The Times*, on the contrary, was perfectly coordinated. Earliness and accuracy of news, authenticity of commercial intelligence, correctness of market information, distinguished it above all other journals ; it gave scrupulous attention to its law reporting, and, above all, to Parliamentary proceedings. As for the leading articles, they had plenty of " devil " in them at that critical period of Parliament : " ten-pounders " of *The Times* earned the paper the nickname of " The Thunderer."

Barnes's consistency was often in dispute. Correspondents searched the files and drew up for publication in the *Morning Chronicle* statements in parallel columns of what *The Times* had said yesterday and what it had said earlier, and still earlier. " Our labours," commented *The Times* of August 29, 1834, " are attacked with their foolish cry of ' You said so-and-so.' " The editorial policy reposed upon ascertained facts. Barnes, like Lord Acton, knew that theory is so far dangerous as it makes for insensibility to the actual. For him public opinion was a fact. Le Marchant says that Barnes was singular in " the quickness with which he caught the earliest sight of public opinion." Regarding it as his only competent authority, he put forth every exertion to train public opinion to inform itself from the columns of his scrupulously faithful commercial and Parliamentary reports. Thus *The Times* answered the *Morning Chronicle* by saying that the important question is not what we said then, but " whether what we say *now* is true and just, and to the purpose *now*." In other words, the indispensable element in journalistic comment for Barnes was not consistent inerrancy but consistent aptness ; and, since infallibility does not and cannot exist either for the editor or for the readers of the day's paper—is, indeed, beyond the reach even of the historian a generation later—an acute and experienced editor must inevitably modify and revise tendencies and opinions. Thus, Barnes strove consistently to give readers of *The Times* an accurate presentation and analysis of the political situation in the light of every scrap of relevant information available to his highly trained staff at the latest moment before press time. Leading articles were designed and written in the circumstances that called for them, in the circumstances in which they would be read. Any action recommended by *The Times* was action within the sphere of practical politics, *i.e.*, within the sanction of public opinion, and therefore within the capacity of public men.

Manifestly, in so far as public opinion changes as a result of new information or other cause, and public men shift their ground, the political situation must be regarded as altered—in greater or less degree. Such changes in the situation must, under Barnes's principles, affect the expression of *The Times* ; hence the paper was repeatedly charged with truckling to public opinion. The *Morning Chronicle*, a newspaper affecting the " holier than thou " attitude, took every opportunity to censure *The Times* ; but the *Chronicle*, more jealously critical than any other of *The Times*, was also the least experienced. The principal writers were not journalists or even literary men ; they were—in Barnes's eye— the much more dangerous political intellectuals, political economists and political scientists. Barnes's classical education, with the literary interests of his formative years, predisposed him to look sceptically on the Benthamite Radicals and their harsh scientific theories. For such men doctrinal consistency was the only virtue : for him, the practicability of a measure, or step to it, was the prime matter. He was consistent in his vocation to the apostolate of Politics in the Concrete.

XIII

THE GOAL OF INDEPENDENCE

THE relations of the Government and public men with the Press in the first quarter of the nineteenth century were more secret though not less cynical than during the previous century. The hiring of hacks to write up persons and policies was older even than the eighteenth century. The practice had been conspicuous during the administrations of Queen Anne and was continued, though less frankly, under George III. The newspapers received regular subsidies from both Tories and Whigs ; partisans of the King and the Prince of Wales, respectively, possessed themselves by purchase of the influence of the morning and evening journals. As has been recorded already, *The Times* received for years a subsidy of £300 a year from the Treasury as compensation for its championship of Ministerial policy and its opposition to the party of the Prince of Wales. Three hundred a year " as a reward for the politics of the Paper," in the words of John Walter I., was a fair sum for a newly founded journal. When the party in office was known to use public money, directly or indirectly, to secure support in the Press, the Opposition necessarily followed suit, and the dependence of certain journals upon party funds became inevitable.

As the restrictions upon Parliamentary reporting by the newspapers were successfully defied, members gradually came to find it desirable that their speeches should be widely read. Hence, during the first quarter of the nineteenth century the relations between them and the Gallery began to develop in a friendly fashion. Members of the Cabinet often found it convenient to supply journalists with early details of measures introduced into the House. They also supplied editors with arguments likely to impress members before going to a division. Yet the Press of the 1820's and 1830's received no social consideration. Persons with a reputation were ashamed of any connexion with a newspaper and never owned to relations with journalists, who were generally regarded with suspicion as intruding upon the privacy of life, as lessening the influence properly belonging to other men, and, above all, as usurping the functions of representative institutions. Few were prepared to give any credit for honesty of purpose to editors and news-writers. They were shunned as rascals and profligates whose pens were at the service of any hirer. The best sort of writers, such as Edward Sterling, were most careful of their anonymity.

It was the prerogative of the Lords and Commons to discuss legislation ; it was the province of journalists merely to prepare, under supervision, reports of occurrences, domestic and foreign, to add the market reports, and, on the right days, to summarize the *London Gazette*. Having disputed the freedom of the Press since the enactments of 1662, Parliament realized at the opening of the nineteenth century that comment could not be prevented. Freedom of reporting had been won by the journals, and the next step taken by ambitious statesmen was the purchase of leading articles. Subsidies grew less direct as the newspapers became more dependent upon commercial advertising. The Government at last discovered in the Ordnance and Admiralty requirements a convenient method of influencing the policy of journals by advertising for tenders. The Duke of Wellington, who in 1810 accused the London editors of " stultifying England," attacked the Press as an institution after the Napoleonic Wars, exaggerating its weaknesses, hoping to restrain its powers. In 1829 he saw that *The Times* could be trusted, and finally in 1834 he was obliged to acknowledge the soundness of Barnes's political judgment and to accept his stipulations.

Comment upon foreign affairs requires a peculiar discretion. Consultation between writers and the Foreign Office or the ambassador of a Power is not only reasonable in itself, but from the public point of view desirable. Castlereagh, during the negotiations at Paris in 1815, found it necessary to point out to Lord Liverpool, at the request of Talleyrand, that means should be adopted of keeping some, at least, of the English papers a little more correctly informed and of moderating the habitual defamation of France. Liverpool's answer was that " no paper that has any character, and consequently an established sale, will accept money from the Government ; and, indeed, their profits are so enormous in all critical times, when their support is most necessary, that no pecuniary assistance the Government could offer would really be worth their acceptance." Newspaper profits were certainly not enormous in 1815 ; many could certainly have been, and undoubtedly were, influenced. There were important develop-ments in the years immediately following Waterloo. Not only the relations between the London Press and statesmen in or out of office, but also the relations of newspapers with foreign statesmen entered upon a new and not more honourable phase.

The official papers of Castlereagh, Richelieu and Metternich testify to the efforts of statesmen, English and French, to move public opinion in both countries towards the acceptance of ideas and policies. The reputation enjoyed by *The Times*, even in its youth, was due in a very large part to its exceptional foreign intelli-gence. The Peninsular War and Waterloo had concentrated public interest on the exploits of the British fighting services ; and although the people had to await the *London Gazette* for details, the earliest news of many victories was given by *The Times*. Canning, as well as his predecessors and successors at the Foreign Office, was indebted to John Walter II for earlier messages than those brought by Government couriers. Inevitably the enterprise of the paper in this respect was known not only at home but also abroad, and its influence was recognized by foreign statesmen. But it was not the only journal with influence. The *Morning Chronicle* still led the London Press in political ability ; James Perry, the editor, was conspicuously independent—as journalistic independence went in those years. The *Courier*, under Street, was a power in the evenings. After Waterloo, Englishmen continued to take an interest in French affairs. Many whose Radicalism ran to Republicanism sympathized with a France now free from militarism, and these hated the restored Bourbons. There were many in France of the same cast of opinion. There was a large body also there of moderate and Liberal Royalists. They were in office from 1816 to 1819, and the leading rôle in the Ministry was played by M. Decazes. In addition, there were Ultra-Royalists opposed to Louis XVIII. *The Times* under Stoddart favoured the Ultras. John Walter did not object to *The Times* being governed by Stoddart's Bourbonism until it was made plain to him by Barnes, Crabb Robinson and Hazlitt that the policy was alienating. support from the paper.[1] " Dr. Slop's " opposition paper, *The New Times*, founded after his dismissal from Printing House Square, naturally continued to support the Ultra-Royalists. The European prestige of English journals was

[1] See Chapter X.

high. The prevalence of censorship on the Continent gave the London dailies an advantage ; diplomats in conference at Paris, Vienna, St. Petersburg and elsewhere were eager students of *The Times*, the *Morning Chronicle*, the *Courier*, and other sheets.

Some foothold in the foreign Press was of manifest advantage to the leaders of a defeated country dependent upon the mercies of the victorious allies. Accordingly, in 1816 Richelieu, the French Foreign Minister, dispatched an agent to Switzerland, Holland, Belgium and Germany with instructions to make a report on the condition of the Press of those countries, with a view to making connexions. In 1816 *The Times* consistently favoured the Ultra-Royalists against Richelieu and Decazes, but early in 1817 its comments became fewer and less outspoken. The change is explained in part by the dismissal of Stoddart from Printing House Square at the end of the year 1816. The line taken by *The Times* during Stoddart's editorship is not unfairly described in the following paragraph from his paper for March 23, 1818 :

> . . . *The New Times* has steadily maintained the cause of the Royalist party in France. . . . Up to the end of the year 1816 the cause of the same party was as strenuously maintained by *the Old Times* not only in its leading articles, but in the valuable communications of a private correspondent at Paris, who always spoke of the Royalists with the respect which their integrity and virtue so richly merited.
>
> The case is now most lamentably altered. The same spirit which has of late marked the leading articles of *the Old Times* now distinguishes still more openly its *private correspondence*. The writer begins his last letter by calling the Royalist Deputies " the faction of Ultras in the Chamber of Deputies." The word *Ultra*, or Ultra Royalist, is a nickname which the infamous Fouché first applied to the Royalists because they went *beyond* himself in their attachment to their King and Country. . . .

It seems possible that Stoddart's dismissal may have been connected with the change in the treatment of French politics, though the next step which Walter took was to invite the collaboration of Southey, who notoriously approved of Stoddart's line. Certainly no approach from the French Liberals could be made while the Doctor was in office. J. B. Salgues, author of a work[1] on the relations of Decazes, Minister, first of Police and afterwards of the Interior, with the English Press, finds traces of his influence upon *The Times* from August 17, 1816. After May, 1817, an

[1] See *infra*, p. 222.

impartial and even tepid feeling is clearly noticeable, such tendency as there was being Liberal. The new tendency gradually became more pronounced. On December 6, 1817, *The Times* printed below a heading consisting of a date only, instead of the customary line " French Papers," the following introduction to a dispatch of 15 inches, leaded :

PARIS, NOV. 27.

[We insert the following letter from Paris, because we know it to be an authentic communication from that city ; but as it is not from our own regular Correspondent, we do not pledge ourselves to the correctness of its opinion—avowed or implied.]

On December 29, 1817, *The Times* gave much space to French affairs. Following a *précis* of the contents of French journals there appeared two long dispatches on the contemporary political situation. These were headed in small capitals :

NEITHER OF THE TWO FOLLOWING LETTERS COMES FROM OUR REGULAR CORRESPONDENT.

The column was signed E. T.

During the whole of 1818 and 1819 definite support was given to the French Administration against Radicals and Ultras alike. The Ultras came in for the heaviest condemnation ; they were in the meantime organizing the expression of their views in the *New Times* and the *Morning Post*. On June 27, 1818, Chateaubriand announced in the *Quotidienne* and in *Le Journal de Paris* that he intended to prosecute the Editor of *The Times* for libel, and to conduct the action in the English Courts. He did not name in his announcement either the libels or the letters in which they had appeared :

" M. de Chateaubriand fait poursuivre en calomnie, devant les tribunaux d'Angleterre, l'éditeur du *Times*, pour les inculpations de la nature la plus grave, comme la plus odieuse, dirigées contre lui et insérées dans ce journal à l'article *Correspondance Privée*."

After a week *The Times* replied that it had not yet heard from Chateaubriand's lawyers and was undisturbed by his threats. No action followed, and *The Times* came out more definitely on the side of Decazes, whom it championed a little later at the height of his struggle for supremacy with Richelieu.

The crop of reports, letters and leading articles in the London papers was so heavy as to excite the curiosity of Castlereagh. He desired Stuart, the British Ambassador in Paris, to ascertain their source. In his reply of June 23, 1818, the Ambassador informed Castlereagh that he had made inquiries from well-informed persons, learning,

as indeed I had previously understood, that the Paris correspondence in the *Sun*, as well as that in the *Star* and *The Times*, proceeds chiefly from the French police. The whole of this correspondence is dictated by M. de Cazes, the principal persons employed in writing it are M. Sanguet, his private secretary, and M. Mirbel, the secretary general of his department. . . . It would seem that most of our public prints are now in the pay of M. de Cazes. *The Times*, indeed, receives with both hands, from the Duc de St. Carlos with one, and from M. de Cazes with the other. There can be little doubt also of the latter having influenced by the same means a principal writer in the *Courier*, Mr. Street.

Some years later Lewis Goldsmith, the conductor of the *Anti-Gallican*, while established in Paris as a confidential agent of Canning, informed Joseph Planta of the British Treasury that Corbière, Minister of the Interior, had stated that Decazes had paid 10,000f. a month to *The Times* to secure insertion of articles against the Ultra-Royalists. Corbière is quoted by Goldsmith as having said that "this stipend was regularly paid during two years."

The statements of Stuart and Goldsmith are given a measure of support by the fluctuations of policy in the paper which extended from the spring of 1817 to July, 1819. No arrangement had presumably been made on April 8, 1817, when Tromelin, a French agent in London, writing to the Baron de Barante[1] on the Press as a public and political influence, remarked that in his judgment " On a par trop négligé de ménager le *Times*." He knew, he says, one of the proprietors to whom articles could be sent showing the spirit of the French Administration " sous un jour plus avantageux." No memorandum survives to indicate any connexion between Printing House Square and the French agents ; the transactions, whatever they may have been, were not of a nature to require detailed record for the benefit of posterity. There was public criticism of the correspondence in Paris and the charges were echoed in London.

The *New Times* of March 11, 1819, accused *The Times* of having given for months " daily circulation to the traitorous ·Private

[1] *Souvenirs* II, 272.

Correspondence which has issued from the bureaux of the French Police. He (the Editor) has become the accomplice and willing tool of De Caze in deceiving the people of England." Stoddart, at this time in the pay of the Ultras, proceeds to hint at the Decazes system : " A full exposition of the means pursued to blind and delude the British Public would lead us into too wide a field at the present moment. We shall therefore pass by the regular system of defamation against every man of distinguished loyalty in France, and the base prostituted adulation of De Caze." In spite of the considerable space given to French affairs in the journals the attitude of most responsible English observers was detached. Elysée Decazes, the nephew of the Minister, wrote to Monseigneur (presumably Maubourg, Minister of War) March 31, 1819, a long report informing him that the English Ministers were too preoccupied with their own troubles to bother much about what was going on in France, except Arbuthnot and Croker.

M. Crocker surtout est très actif et on en a tous les jours des preuves dans les articles du *New Times* où j'ai souvent retrouvé les mêmes expressions dont il avait fait usage dans les conversations que j'avais eues avec lui. C'est un homme de beaucoup d'esprit, d'une impertinence rare et dont les opinions sont si exagérées que les Ministres dans le dernier parlement ont été souvent obligés de lui défendre de prendre part aux discussions qui ne regardent pas directement le Ministère auquel il est attaché.

Elysée Decazes concludes with saying that the Regent is much more interested in the " petites anecdotes et aventures galantes " from Paris than in the political situation.[1]

The Times did not answer for some months. On July 12, 1819, a leading article was given to the matter.

It has been asserted that our private correspondence proceeded from the French Ministry. The suspicion is a proof of the importance attached to it : but if the French Ministers were at the pains to transmit their opinions, to defend their own conduct, and expose that of their adversaries, through the medium of an English journal, would they not at least protect their work to its completion, by securing a free circulation for that which they had themselves consigned to the press ?

The writer misunderstood the object of the campaign. Decazes desired to influence, not Paris, but Europe ; and he obstructed the

[1] Aff. Etr., Corr. Dipl. 611.

circulation of *The Times* in Paris in the summer of 1819 because the public knowledge of the origin of the letters made the reading of them mischievous in France. *The Times* correctly pointed out that it had distinguished between the messages of its regular correspondents and those of the private correspondent. Though dropped in the paper, the matter was still discussed in Paris. One Lagarde being charged by a correspondent in the *Conservateur* with responsibility for the private correspondence in *The Times*, two writers[1] of the name forwarded denials on the 4th and 7th September, 1819.

Decazes's moderate policy, at once Monarchist and Liberal, only exasperated both sets of extremists, the Ultras and the Republicans ; and he was forced to resign in 1819. Revelations by his enemies gave confirmation and some details of what had hitherto only been rumours. A Lyons deputy, Clausel de Coussergues, impeached him for treason on grounds stated in his *Projet de la Proposition contre M. le duc Decazes*,[2] four editions of which were published in successive reply to the arguments of the other side. J. M. B. Robert,[3] another enemy of Decazes, published his *La Police sous M. le Duc de Cazes* in 1821. M. Decazes's nephew, Elysée Decazes, was attached to the Minister's service for secret business. Robert says, at page 30,

M. de Cazes tenait encore dans Londres M. Elysée de Cazes, son neveu, aujourd'hui baron, et attaché à son ambassade pour plusieurs missions secrètes, et même pour recevoir et porter sa correspondance privée au *Times*.

M. Elysée de Cazes transmettait directement au *Times* la correspondance privée qui arrivait quelquefois directement à son adresse, et souvent par l'intermédiaire de M. Descalonne, commissaire spécial de police à Calais.

In 1822 there appeared two volumes of the Private Correspondence translated from the English newspapers, to which Clausel de Coussergues had alluded in general terms as being supplied by Decazes. The two volumes entitled *Les Mille et Une Calomnies extraits des colonnes de la Presse anglaise* are collected

---

[1] One of these was P. Lagarde, colleague of Darby, confidential agent of Stuart, the Ambassador, from 1816 to 1825. " My Colleague, M. Lagarde " is mentioned in Darby's letter to Planta, 27 Jan., 1825 (F.O. France, 97/168). Lagarde and Darby had a working arrangement known to Canning and sanctioned by him.

[2] Paris, Dentu, 1820.

[3] Robert was a journalist whose Ultra *Le Fidèle Ami du Roi* was suppressed by Decazes and he himself imprisoned. Robert says that M. de Brivazac was responsible for the transmission of the *correspondance privée* to the *Courier* (" Car chaque journal avait son paquet ") and that he was intimate with Lewis Goldsmith.

from the *British Monitor, Star, Sun, True Sun, Statesman, Morning Chronicle*, and *The Times*. The editor, J. B. Salgues, himself a journalist, charges Decazes with having paid *The Times* for the insertion of the messages at advertising rates; he asserts, confirming Goldsmith, that the messages were known to be written by men in the French police and says their insertion in *The Times* cost between twenty and twenty-five guineas a letter. The matter does not seem to have been cleared up in the London Press—perhaps because the editors were not anxious to draw attention to it. Only vague and unsupported references to the acceptance of French money by *The Times* appear in the Sunday papers, the least reputable London sheets.

Salgues himself gives no details of the arrangements made with *The Times*. John Walter, as has been mentioned, was in Paris in May, 1816, for reasons not given to Crabb Robinson, to whose diary we owe the available particulars, and Fraser was with him, but there is no record of any meeting or transaction between Walter and Decazes or any agent of his. Street of the *Courier* came later in the same year and arranged for the sale of his columns. Salgues's remark on the details of the presumed understanding between Decazes and *The Times* is that " le traité entre les correspondants et M. Waters fut toujours enveloppé d'un profond mystère. Les deux personnes qui allèrent le signer à Londres en ont probablement seules le secret."[1]

On one occasion, however, an echo of a secret arrangement alleged, with no foundation it would seem, to have been made between John Walter II and a French agent reached the outside world. The incident, it was understood, occurred before the Decazes correspondence, but no charges against *The Times* were made until later, and then only indirectly. In 1822 was published a book by Barry Edward O'Meara. O'Meara had been assistant surgeon with the 62nd Foot in Italy and Egypt, had been dismissed for duelling at Messina in 1807, and later was naval surgeon of the Bellerophon. Napoleon took a fancy to him and made him his medical adviser, a position O'Meara lost on account of some suspicion as to his movements. He came back to England and wrote *Napoleon in Exile, or A Voice from St. Helena*, in which he reports a conversation of March 4, 1816. Writers were certainly employed by the authorities both sides of the channel. Britain employed Lewis Goldsmith during 1813 and 1814 at a

---

1 [Salgues, J. B.] *Les Mille et Une Calomnies* (Paris, 1822, II, 329). Salgues is at times careless with his proper names. Walter is " Waters " ; Street is " Stritz."

salary of £1,200 a year to make attacks on Bonaparte ; and Goldsmith, docked of a portion of his salary by Arbuthnot, complained to Lord Liverpool. His grievances are set out in a letter now in the British Museum.[1] O'Meara's story is certainly not inconsistent with the revelations in State papers of the use which statesmen made of international journalists like Goldsmith. O'Meara said that he :

saw Napoleon in the billiard room. He was in extreme good spirits. Returned me the *Ambigu* for 1816 and desired me to endeavour to obtain the numbers for 1815. In answer to a question of mine about P. . ., he said " P. is a polisson who would work for anybody that paid him. He made offers to me to change his style and write for me in such a manner that the British Government would not be aware that he was employed by me. One time in particular, he sent to the police a manuscript copy of a book written against me, with an offer that it should not be printed provided he were paid a suitable sum of money. I ordered the police to answer that if he paid the expense of printing the work should be published for him in Paris. He was not the only one who made offers of the kind to me when I was in power. Some of the editors of the English newspapers made similar advances, and declared they could render me the most essential services, but I did not then attach sufficient importance to it and refused them. Not so the Bourbons. In 1814 the editor of The * * * * * newspaper was paid about £3,000 of your money, besides having a great number of copies taken. I told you before that I found his receipt among Blacas' papers, on my return from Elba. I do not know if he is in their pay now."[2]

On July 15, 1822, not long after the publication of O'Meara's book, *The Times*, considering its title indicated by O'Meara's five asterisks, stated that " the enormity of the *lie* is very cautiously compensated by the obscurity," and asked whether anybody would put any confidence in O'Meara's account of Bonaparte.

We have had dealings with most of them [the politicians of this country] ; and they must know, from their own experience, that he *lies* if he charges us with venality. They must know the above story to be an invention, if we are meant ; and who can be meant but us ? And if a man invents one lie, of course he will invent a thousand.

O'Meara, having seen the paragraph and considering an apology due to himself, wrote to Walter in that sense. As he received no

[1] B.M., MSS. Addl. 38326.
[2] O'Meara, B.E., *Napoleon in Exile* (1822, 2 vols.), I, pp. 407-8.

satisfaction, he placed himself outside the Stratford Club, having first asked one of the club servants to point out the member he sought. He had started a thrashing with a horsewhip before he learnt that his chastisement was falling upon the person, not of John, but of William Walter, the elder brother, who had left *The Times* in 1802 for a place under Government.[1] The *Morning Chronicle* reported the incident, doubtless with some satisfaction. It received on the following day a communication from Mr. William Walter, of Devonshire Place, in these words :

We have authority to state, that the Gentleman alluded to in the *Morning Chronicle* of yesterday, as having been assaulted by Mr. O'Meara, near Stratford Place, has no connexion with *The Times* newspaper directly or indirectly. As the matter will be the subject of a legal investigation, it is not thought necessary to make any further observation.

The Times informed its readers that the statement that Mr. Walter, of Printing House Square, had been assaulted on Monday afternoon by Mr. Barry O'Meara

is utterly false as regards Mr. Walter, though Mr. Barry O'Meara may enjoy all the glory of having broken the King's peace, and will doubtless attain the unenvied satisfaction of bearing the consequences. The fact is, that Mr. Walter, at the time the outrage happened, was forty miles from London, where he had been for some weeks ; and that the Duke of Wellington, or Mr. Wilberforce, might have been assaulted with equal propriety as the Gentleman who was the object of the outrage.

William Walter summoned O'Meara to attend at Marylebone, where, on its being made plain that William had been mistaken for his brother, he withdrew proceedings. O'Meara apologized. The magistrate, however, thought it desirable that he should enter into a recognizance of £500 to keep the peace towards John Walter.

But the incident did not drop. On November 12 of the same year (1822) *The Times* reopened the subject of O'Meara's allegation :

It is with considerable aversion that we recur to a subject connected with the character of *The Times* journal, from which subject public attention has been for a long time withdrawn ; but it is only now that

[1] See p. 75.

we are able to give an official contradiction to the foul calumny that imputed to us the baseness of accepting money from the Bourbons for the support which we gave their cause at the latter end of Buonaparte's career. When that calumny first appeared, the most flat contradiction was given to it by those who were engaged in the conducting of the journal ; and a letter was immediately addressed to M. le Duc de Blacas, the Minister who was asserted to have paid and taken a receipt for the bribe from a former editor. M. de Blacas, it appears, being continually expected at Paris, the letter was not transmitted to him at Rome, and was consequently only found by him on his recent return to his own country.

This introduction was followed by the text of the Chief Proprietor's letter to Blacas :

M. le Duc.—It is with much regret that I find myself obliged to trouble you. I am induced, however, to think that you will have the goodness to excuse the liberty which I take.

A peculiar circumstance has just occurred—Mr. Barry O'Meara, late surgeon to Buonaparte at St. Helena—(removed from St. Helena, and dismissed the British service)—has lately published a work entitled " A Voice from St. Helena," which contains the following passage :

" In 1814, the Editor of The * * * * * newspaper was paid about three thousand pounds of your money, besides having a great number of copies taken. I told you before that I found his receipt among Blacas' papers. on my return from Elba. I do not know if he is in their pay now."

It is everywhere thought that it is *The Times* which the author has wished to stain by this calumnious accusation. May I also be permitted to add, that such an imputation not only goes the length of compromising the character and integrity of that journal ; but—which ought to weigh much more with you—that it affects th honour of the Government of your august Sovereign, in supposing that his Royal cause stands in need of support by means of corruption so base and revolting ?

It is proper that you should know, M. le Duc, that at the period alluded to, *The Times* was under my direction. Your name is quoted in the article ; and you alone are able to satisfy the public that such a proof or acquittance as Mr. O'Meara pretends, has never had any existence. You alone can testify that I have never received either money or presents of any kind for defending in the above journal the cause of his Most Christian Majesty. Is it, therefore, too much, M. le Duc, to hope from your goodness and justice, that you will support with the authority of your name and word, that the two-fold calumny to which I allude, has never had the least foundation ?

So powerful a motive can alone excuse the liberty which I take, of begging that you will have the goodness to favour me with an early answer.—I have the honour to be, with the most profound respect, M. le Duc,

Your most humble and most obedient servant,

London, July 24, 1822.   JOHN WALTER,
                                        Responsible Editor till 1820, and one of
                                              the Proprietors of *The Times*.

M. the Duke de Blacas, &c., &c., &c.

The answer received was translated and printed in *The Times* thus :

Paris, Nov. 7, 1822.

Sir,—I have only just now received, on my arrival in Paris, the letter which you have done me the honour of writing to me, dated the 24th of July last. It imposes upon me the duty of attesting the falsehood of the allegation got together (*recueillie*) and published by Mr. Barry O'Meara, according to which it might be supposed that you have received from me a sum of three thousand pounds sterling, as the price of those opinions which you professed in 1814, in the journal of which you were at that time the Editor. It is impossible that any acquittance of that or any other sum should have been found signed by you among my papers ; inasmuch as nothing was ever given or offered to you by my intervention. This is a testimony which I have a pleasure in bearing to the truth, begging you also, Sir, at the same time, to receive that of my distinguished consideration.

BLACAS D'AULPS.

To Mr. John Walter, ancient[1] Editor of *The Times*.

At this point, O'Meara wrote to the *Morning Chronicle* of November 15, pointing out that without any word from himself, alone of the " crowd of editors in London, John Walter had felt himself indicated," although no clue to the name of the journal was given except the five asterisks. He emphasized that a briber never gives away the bribed, and further that Blacas does not say that *The Times* was never paid any money by the Bourbons to his knowledge, only that he never gave John Walter any. This, perhaps, may have been a hit at Stoddart. But Walter had the better of this controversy, O'Meara's character inspiring little confidence in his testimony.[2]

[1] *Sic.* *Cf. The Times*, November 12, 1822.
[2] O'Meara and his book were submitted to a searching examination by Croker in the *Quarterly Review*, October, 1822. *Cf.* Sources, Chapter XIII, in the Appendix to this volume.

Q

In the manufacture of public opinion, British statesmen, it has been shown, had little to learn from foreigners. Some sort of regular department seems to have been entrusted with this task during the Liverpool Administration. Influence was exerted through the Treasury ; the Home Office, though also concerned, playing a minor part. The Secretary to the Admiralty was a valuable auxiliary to the Press managers in the service of Ministers. The responsibility for the mail packet service was transferred from the Post Office to the Admiralty in 1815. One consequence was that the larger power of censorship, as well as the minor capacity of obstruction and deprivation, rested with the Secretary of the Admiralty, who thus came into touch with the distributors of news and of newspapers. The Duke of Wellington had the usual low opinion of the general character of newsmen, reporters and editors. He naturally objected to criticism of himself from newspapers known to be unnaturally cordial towards Ministers in office, and on May 2, 1827, complained in the House of Lords of " the manner I have been treated by the corrupt Press in the pay of the Government." When himself in power in the following year, he had to deal on several occasions with advisers recommending adequate newspaper presentation of the Government's point of view. The Duke disliked such suggestions, even from Croker. On September 13, 1828, Croker wrote that " something should be done to set the Press right on the subject of our policy towards Portugal. See *The Times* of to-day. When the newspapers are allowed to go all the same way, and repeat the same story without contradiction, the best and wisest course of policy cannot fail to be damaged in public opinion." An uncompromising reply was written on the following day :

My dear Croker . . . I hate meddling with the Press. The perpetual interference with the Press was one of the rocks on which my predecessors struck. But I am afraid we do meddle, that is to say the Secretary of the Treasury does ; but he does not attend to it ; nor does he meddle with that degree of intelligence which might be expected from him. I must put this to rights. Ever yours, etc.

WELLINGTON.

Unwillingly, but directly and openly, the Duke availed himself of the support of *The Times* for the purpose of passing the measure of Catholic Emancipation.[1] He was more sympathetic to a policy

[1] The circumstances are sketched in Chapter XV.

of " meddling " abroad. Lord Stuart, Ambassador in Paris, reported on August 29, 1828, to Lord Aberdeen that he had prepared a plan " which would allow us to have in our hands the power of publishing in France what it may be interesting to us to communicate to the French public." Wellington expressed a wish for further details, and at the same time noted that the mischievous paragraphs in the French journals were drawn from a common source and " Lord Stuart might be desired to let us know what *Galignani's Messenger* would cost."

In 1829 the partisans of the Duke thought a new daily paper essential, and Joseph Planta was engaged to investigate the possibilities of success. The Tories had previously refused any close connexions with journalism ; indeed, ten years earlier no responsible statesman, Tory or other, could have contemplated so direct an association with the daily Press as was now proposed by Planta. Brougham stood alone, and at that time as a private person, in maintaining connexions of this kind. The Tory scheme sent Planta to Croker, who wrote him a memorandum (August 21, 1829) containing one or two paragraphs that merit quotation by their straightforward indication of the conclusions of an acute and experienced observer of the growth of journalistic power.

It is not everybody [he says] that can write for the newspapers ; the latter is an art, perhaps I should say a *knack*, which one man has in a greater degree than another . . . A short, terse, epigrammatic style, both of thought and expression, is what produces most effect in a newspaper, where people do not expect didactic or dialectic essays, and where indeed they will not read them. The style which I have heard called *coup de marteau* (not the hammering style) is, I think, the best. I suppose you to have a good paper open to you and a capital hand to work ; how is he to be supplied with materials ? He cannot make bricks without straw. How is he to know the line to be taken ? You yourself will often not know. For instance, if *I*, an old, and as some of the gentlemen of the Press used to think a good hand, pretty high in office, not inattentive to the state of Europe, had been obliged to answer the article in the morning journal which you sent me, I should not have known what to say. As to England and France, I could perhaps have spoken pretty safely, but I have, upon my honour, not the most distant guess of what turn it might suit the position of our affairs to give to the observations on Spain, Portugal, Russia, Turkey or Prussia.

Giving his opinion that none but a member of the Cabinet could undertake this work safely, Croker added that in the past he had himself " conveyed to the public articles written by Prime and Cabinet Ministers and sometimes have composed such articles under their eye—they supplied the *fact*, and I supplied the *tact*, and between us we used to produce a considerable effect." His suggestion to Planta was that one person should be appointed for the work with the understanding that " it ought to be done in the most profound secrecy, and every possible precaution against even a *suspicion* should be taken, and the Minister who should undertake it, and you his *conveyancer*, as Junius calls it, should throw in, here and there, such a slight mixture of error or apparent ignorance, as should obviate suspicion of its coming from so high a source." Croker thought so well of this memorandum that he brought it to Peel's attention five years later, when the Conservatives came into power on the dismissal of Melbourne's first Cabinet and needed advice on the Press.

Apparently Croker was unaware that his predecessor, Sir Evan Nepean, Secretary to the Admiralty, had in 1794 conducted arrangements with the Press similar to those recommended to Planta. But his view that " the times are gone by when statesmen might safely despise the journals or only treat them as inferior engines which might be left to themselves or be committed to the guidance of persons wholly unacquainted with the views of the Ministry," was new. Moreover, Croker saw that " the example of France will soon be contagious, and we shall see men of high hopes and attainments conducting journals, and obtaining, at last, through their literary character, seats in the House of Commons " —a prophecy fulfilled, at least in part, by the allotment of safe seats to deserving newspaper hacks attached to the Whig party machine. " Depend upon it," added Croker, " all this is coming ; and the day is not far distant when you will (not *see* nor *hear*) but *know* that there is someone in the Cabinet entrusted with what will be thought one of the most important duties of the State, the regulation of public opinion." Evidently Croker was a close observer of the methods of Henry Brougham, the first modern politician, who had attached the Press to his service twenty-five years previously.

At the end of its life the Wellington Administration seriously considered buying Press support. Ellenborough, the Lord Privy Seal, notes in his Diary[1] that at a Cabinet on October 31, 1830, there was a discussion about the Press. It was necessary to decide whether to prosecute or buy it.

[1] Diary, II, 408. The Government was defeated on November 15.

Scarlett (Attorney-General) appears to be quite cowed by opposition and the Press.

This Press may be bought, but we have no money. Five-sixths of the Foreign Secret Service money are preoccupied by permanent old charges—the Secret Service money of the Treasury is preoccupied in the same way.

There is a small sum of droits which may be turned over to the Privy Purse, and then by the King to the Government, but it is not more than 3,000*l.* It is thought that perhaps some of the pensions on the Secret Service money of the Treasury may be turned over to the Foreign Office. The Treasury money is the only money applicable to the purchase of newspapers.

Personal and Ministerial propaganda increased after the rotten boroughs were swept away. The Whig Ministry appointed James Silk Buckingham as their Press agent, paying him £500 a year to arrange for a supply of Government articles to three London newspapers, whose editors undertook to insert them "as editorial articles and without alteration or delay ; to adopt also a generally friendly tone to the Administration." No money was offered to the journals, but in return for their complaisance early information of intended changes was promised. Buckingham's function was to write, or procure the writing of, these articles for submission to Lord Durham before publication. Very soon Buckingham appealed for a place in one of the Government departments or the British Museum, with a salary of £1,000 a year, promising that he would be responsible for the management of an evening paper, provided he also received the £500 a year he was already enjoying. It does not appear that this appeal was listened to, but the Whigs continued to maintain a Press Bureau, paid for in all probability from the Secret Service vote. Slight as the direct evidence is, owing to the disappearance of official papers, there can be no doubt that the adoption of the French methods, together with the personal activities of Henry Brougham, formed one of the Whig machine's most valuable secret assets. The Tory party, it would appear, relied until 1835 upon the direct bribery of the electorate from the resources of a central fund for which Lord Lyndhurst had considerable responsibility.

The function Croker describes as one of the most important duties of the State, namely, " the regulation of public opinion," was precisely the function which *The Times* wished to exercise freely. The success of its struggle against Croker's doctrine was

Barnes's greatest contribution to journalism and to England. While the Whigs and Radicals were agitating for the " freedom " of the Press, meaning relief from taxation, Barnes was concentrating upon the vital point of the " credit " of the Press, meaning relief from propaganda. The " regulation " of public opinion by a Government bureau was a thousand times more degrading to the Press than the imposition of a fourpenny orange stamp. The self-respect of a journal depended on exemption from venality. When Barnes came down from Cambridge, daily journalism was notoriously venal ; nothing but the most determined opposition could have reversed this age-old newspaper tradition. After the Reform Bill, some Whigs tried to make a scientific affair of it. There could be no peace between *The Times* and such Whigs. *The Times* made the point quite clearly in a leading article published on December 22, 1834 :

For some time before the dissolution of the Ministry a kind of inquisition was instituted to take secret cognizance of the political heresies of the newspaper press, and to persecute the authors by damaging their publications by various contrivances. Our power enabled us to defy such arts, but we fear that a portion of the independent press must have felt the workings of an untraced and unseen enmity. An " obstinate, impracticable journalist " saw unfair advantages heaped upon his rivals, and calumny and detraction were busy upon his reputation. The direct operation was to reward the subservient ; but necessarily this was attended with a proportionate depression of the independent and unbending, where there was not great power to bear up against the hostile machinations.

The management of the press was one of the arms of the late Government, and if the attempt had been carried on to success, it would have ended in a rotten representation of public opinion, similar to the rotten representation of the people before Parliamentary Reform. There were Gatton and Sarum newspapers—nomination journals. The editorship of one paper was as much a Government appointment as a seat at the India Board or the Admiralty. A committee regularly organized, an inquisition, a secret tribunal, used to hold daily sittings in a Government office, and contrive things for the reward of the servile and the damage of the untractable. The effect of this, where it had effect, was infinitely worse than a censorship.

This revelation of a regularly organized committee sitting in a Government office, engaged in the work of " managing " the Press, is, from its very nature, difficult to document from State papers.

The effect of this " management " was, indeed, infinitely worse than censorship, being at once subtle and secret. Croker, it will be remembered, advised Planta to insert calculated errors in Government *communiqués* for the better deception of the people. The mischievous activities of the Secretaries of the Admiralty, above all of Croker, were known. When, in 1829, the talk of establishing a Tory journal led to the correspondence between Croker and Planta, the former put forward John Gibson Lockhart as a possible editor. Lockhart in due course received his invitation. It impressed him so badly that he made up his mind to consult Sir Walter Scott. " I will not," he said, " even to serve the Duke, mix myself up with newspapers. That work it is which has damned Croker. I do not admire, after all that has come and gone, being applied to through the medium of friend Crokey." Sir Walter's reply supported Lockhart in his determination to have nothing to do with the business.

Your connexion with any newspaper would be disgrace and degradation. I would rather sell gin to poor people and poison them that way. Besides no gentleman can ever do that sort of thing by halves. He must, while he retains a rag of a shirt to cover his nakedness, be inferior to the bronzed, mother-naked, thorough-going gentleman of the press.

It became the endeavour of Barnes to remove all justification for such strictures as Scott's upon the profession of his choice. Sir Walter, though at the time rather old-fashioned in his views, had unfortunately more than sufficient grounds for his scorn of " gentlemen of the press," and he accurately estimated the consequences of Croker's secret " regulation of public opinion."

The leading article in *The Times* of December, 1834, from which two paragraphs have been quoted on the previous page, proceeded to affirm that :

These remarks proceed upon more solid grounds than common reports and suspicions. The chief manager of the press (the description is a disgrace to the Ministry) under the late Government can be named, and remarkable it is that his post was nearest to the noble person whose plain-dealing and straightforward ways have been the theme of the loudest praise.

The plain-dealing nobleman was doubtless " Honest John," Lord Althorp ; the " chief manager " must have been Thomas

Drummond, his private secretary from April, 1833. Drummond was a friend of Bellenden Ker, and intimate with the group responsible for the new Poor Law Bill. It is plain from Drummond's biography that he was occupied almost daily in pushing out hints for leading articles in the *Scotsman*, and was busy writing for the *Globe* and the *Morning Chronicle*. At the same time his letters abound in criticism of *The Times*. " I question," says Mr. Maclennan, who wrote his life in 1867, " whether *The Times* was ever so cordially detested as it was by the Melbourne Whigs." Drummond was assisted by his brother John, also a Whig operator, in circulating Whig newspapers, large numbers of which were purchased, sometimes from the party funds, sometimes, it is to be feared, from the funds of the Treasury. Thus Drummond wrote to his brother John on November 21, 1834, a month before the appearance of the leading article quoted :

If there are any district committee-rooms to which you would wish the *Chronicle* or *Globe* to be sent, let me have the names and it will be done. The *Chronicle* advances rapidly, so does the *Globe; The Times* quails and wavers as such a miserable deserves to do.

The objection to these manoeuvres is primarily that the articles in the *Chronicle* and in the *Globe* were in no sense the independent expression of a journalist regarding himself as responsible to the public opinion of the country ; room was found for them, certainly in the *Globe*, and most probably in the *Chronicle*, as the result of a financial bargain.

In a final paragraph of its article, *The Times* made a first reference to the Brougham-Althorp correspondence of June, 1834, and to a " war " of which more will be heard later :

For ourselves we have the evidence that the system was to be worked against us. The question was proposed by one noble Lord to another noble and learned Lord, whether open war should be declared with *The Times*, or peace attempted ? How is a Ministry to wage war with a newspaper ? What ostensible powers has it for such an undertaking ? Prosecutions were out of the question : what then could be the form and manner of the hostilities meditated ?—what the arms with which we were to be combatted ? There can be but one answer—the sap and mine, the underhand practice, the undermining process of the engineer of the secret tribunal or committee for the management of the press. And what had we done to bring this warfare upon us ? We had maintained our independence, and exercised an unbiassed and impartial judgment upon the measures and the conduct of the Ministry.   When these things are borne in mind, surely it will be acknowledged that our provocation has only been exceeded by our forbearance.   Holding, as we do, a mighty instrument in our hands, we struck no blow at the Administration whose powers were unscrupulously exercised against us.

We must add, that we acquit the majority of the late Ministry of any share in the malpractices adverted to, which were confined to a section ; but the sound part had not energy enough to throw off the tainted, and suffered as men must always suffer by such connexions.

Thomas Drummond, at the time of the appearance of this article, was still fixed in his position, but fortunately for the credit of the Whig section to which the final paragraph refers, his health compelled him to retire to Brighton for a time—on a pension of £300 a year given by Lord Melbourne.

XIV

THE STRUGGLE FOR PUBLIC OPINION

THE Liverpool Administration, in dealing sternly with agitation, was, it must be allowed, engaged in self-defence. The Government, however illiberal, was supported by moderate Progressives when advocacy of political murder found expression in Radical prints. When Spencer Perceval fell, even Cobbett rejoiced. There were attempts to murder the Cabinet; arms were discovered in the possession of secret societies. The strict enforcement of the laws against seditious libel was obviously necessary in the interest of the maintenance of order as the Government understood it. Extreme nervousness on the part of printers, whether of books, pamphlets, periodicals or newspapers, followed; Printing House Square was nervous also. *The Times* had a moderate Reformer, of Radical associations, in the position of ostensible editor. The necessity for caution temporarily increased the influence of Fraser at Printing House Square. A letter from Barnes to Walter dated March 31, 1819, assents to the Chief Proprietor's " doctrine of mutual control," and Barnes promises to " endeavour to avoid the necessity of any exercise of it on myself by checking, of my own accord, my scribbling propensity, which, after all, is not very strong." Events, notwithstanding, carried *The Times* forward in the direction of Reform.

That the national reputation of *The Times* rapidly developed, as it did, during the summer and autumn of 1819, was due principally to the pressure of politics. For long the paper, while denouncing agitators, stigmatised as " incendiaries " those who talked " only of putting down by force every culpable, however pitiable, expression of popular suffering." But as the Government programme seemed to consist of repression without relief, the attitude of *The Times* so stiffened that in June and July the *Courier* could charge the paper with " championing sedition." In

234

fact, *The Times* was never weary of denouncing the activities of Sherwin, Wooler and Orator Hunt, and the Radical reformers generally. It denounced the intention of holding the assembly at Manchester; though, since the Radical reformers persisted in that intention, *The Times* expressed its hope that " nothing will occur to divide the blame of any tumult with the parties who *prima facie* have provoked it." (August 17, 1819.) Seven out of the twelve columns of reading matter in the issue for August 19 were given to the completest of all press accounts of the massacre of Peterloo. The reports were written by one of the best of the paper's reporters. He was on Hunt's platform at the time of the charge and was arrested in the course of his duties.

Our readers [wrote *The Times*] will find amongst the names of the prisoners, that of a gentleman of the name of Tyas. Mr. Tyas went down from London to take notes of whatever he should see and hear, and report it for *The Times*. He is a gentleman of talent and education; nephew to an individual of great respectability in the town of Manchester, and, so far as we can judge from his preceding conduct towards this journal, about as much a Jacobin, or friend of Jacobins, as is Lord Liverpool himself. Mr. Tyas had been very seriously indisposed from the day of his arrival at Manchester. Anxious, however, to discharge in the most satisfactory manner, his duty to us and to the public, he determined to procure, if possible, a place near Hunt on the day of the meeting, for the sake of sparing his own infirm health, and for the greater facility of sending us a complete report.

The reports of *The Times*, in spite of this set-back, were remarkably full; they were reproduced all over the country. The Ministerialists took note of the circumstances. *The Times* was broadcasting its comments as well as its reports. The paper called all its readers to acknowledge " the dreadful fact, that nearly a hundred of the King's unarmed subjects have been sabred by a body of cavalry in the streets of a town of which most of them were inhabitants, and in the presence of those Magistrates whose sworn duty it is to protect and preserve the life of the meanest Englishman."

During the spring and summer of 1819 action against the periodical Press proceeded all over the country. The Home Secretary, Lord Sidmouth, favoured prosecution, in some instances, for high treason, but the Cabinet decided generally to prosecute for seditious libel and for conspiracy. Immediately after the publication of reports of Peterloo, Lord Sidmouth's activities grew busier. Provincial and London printers and news-vendors bore the brunt ; it was difficult for the Home Office men to trace the authors of seditious libels.

On August 25, 1819, an opportunity presented itself for a spectacular prosecution. Sir Francis Burdett, Member for West-minster, a moderate Reformer, regarded by reactionaries as a Radical, was so moved to indignation by the newspaper reports of the Manchester Massacre that he published an open letter addressed " To the electors of Westminster." *The Times* gave the letter with a short leader directing attention to it.

Will the gentlemen of England support or wink at such proceedings ?
. . . I propose that a meeting should be called in Westminster which the gentlemen of the committee will arrange, and whose summons I will hold myself in readiness to attend. Whether the penalty of our meeting will be death by military execution I know not ; but this I know, a man can die but once, and never better than in vindicating the Laws and Liberties of his country.

Excuse this hasty address. I can scarcely tell what I have written. It may be a libel, or the Attorney-General may call it so, just as he pleases. . . .

Lord Sidmouth upon reading this immediately consulted the Attorney-General, who advised prompt action.

The sequel is described in a letter from Barnes to Walter dated six o'clock p.m. of Wednesday, August 25, 1819 :

Wednesday 6 °clock P.M.
Dear Sir,

I have this moment returned from an examination at the Home office before a very full Cabinet Council consisting, as well as I could distinguish with my nearsightedness, of Lord Liverpool, Lord Sidmouth, Lord Castlereagh, the Duke of Wellington, Lord Harrowby, the Chancellor of the Exchequer,[1] Lord Bathurst, & another, I believe, Mr Robinson.[2] The Attorney-General was in attendance. I went at 4 °clock to the Smithfield meeting[3] & on my return at 5 °clock, found a letter from Mr Hobhouse requesting on behalf of Lord Sidmouth the Editor's immediate attendance at the Home office. Conceiving that it was my business to attend, I took a Hackney-coach instantly & pro-ceeded to White-hall, & on sending in my address, was introduced

[1] Vansittart.
[2] F. J. Robinson.
[3] The speeches of Watson, Thistlewood, Preston and others at Smithfield, August 25, 1819, are reported in *The Times* of the day following.

before the " great divan." After the mutual ceremony of bowing, I was desired to sit down : the Ministers formed a semi-circle, in the midst of which & facing them all, my chair was placed, I suppose, purposely. Being conscious that they could have no matter against me, which I need be alarmed at, I was, notwithstanding a slight hurry of spirits, perfectly firm. Lord Sidmouth began the business by asking where Mr Walter was—I said that you were out of town—but for shortness I will put the conversation into question & answer—

Lord Sidmouth.—What is your name, Sir ?

B.—Barnes.

Lord Sid.—In the absence of Mr Walter you have the management of the Paper ?

B.—I certainly consider myself responsible.

Lord Sid.—Well, Sir—that being the case, I will now inform you why we have troubled you to attend. A letter bearing the signature of Sir Francis Burdett appeared in *The Times* of this morning, as well as in two other papers. His Majesty's Cabinet Council, now present, have after consulting with their legal advisers determined to proceed by criminal information ag^t the author *or* publishers of that letter, but I hope you will fully understand that there is no wish to molest you—*The Times* personally, if you can put us into any mode of ascertaining that the letter really proceeds from Sir Francis Burdett.

B.—I can have no hesitation in telling your Lordship the exact mode in which I procured that letter. Last night the *Statesman*[1] (a paper which we do not take in) was brought to the office by a person who said that it contained something worthy of being inquired into. I read it & saw that Sir Francis Burdett was represented as having written a letter to his constituents & that the letter was in town. I immediately dispatched one of the persons employed for such purposes to Mr Place, a man well—publicly known as a partisan of Sir Francis, thinking that he might be able to give some information as to the letter in question. Mr Place referred the messenger to Mr Brookes, who is also well-known as the Chairman of Sir Francis Burdett's Committee, & our messenger on his arrival found the Clerk of Mr Brookes in the act of making 3 copies of the original for the purpose of sending them to 3 newspapers. One of the copies was given to our agent who brought it to me, & having no doubt of its authenticity I then inserted it as a piece of public intelligence.

Lord Sid.—Your account is perfectly satisfactory.

[1] Evening paper founded by Cobbett and identified with Radical views.

Lord Castlereagh nodded assent & Lord Liverpool repeated Lord Sidmouth's words, adding " You, of course, consider that you received the letter from the agent of Sir Francis Burdett." I replied in the affirmative. Lord Sidmouth then in the most marked manner deprecated any idea of personal hostility to the paper,[1] saying that the only object was to proceed regularly ag^t the Author of the letter. I replied that I felt that such was the object of their Lordships, & was glad that the unconditional & public way in which I had received the letter in question had enabled me to be explicit without hesitation or regret. The Ministers then rose, saying they need not trouble me any further & I took my leave. Nothing could exceed the courtesy of their behavior I have not time for any more.

Yours faithfully
T. BARNES.

Burdett's agent, Brookes, was in due time called to account by the Attorney-General, but the meeting was held by a large gathering of between 20,000 and 50,000. Prosecution followed, and on February 8, 1821, the Member for Westminster was fined £2,000 and given three months' imprisonment. In the meantime, *The Times* sustained its position.

The inquests on those killed at Peterloo were held elsewhere than in Manchester. *The Times* determined to obtain the fullest reports and to print them. John Ross was dispatched to Oldham to report the inquest on Robert Lees. In spite of official obstruction against *The Times* reporter as such, he succeeded in sending full accounts to Printing House Square. *The Times* for October, 1819, is largely given up to reports of these inquests. The Ministerial Press protested and alleged that *The Times* was desperately Radical. The paper answered that :

There is scarcely any falsehood, however glaring, that has not been uttered, and would not almost have been sworn against us, by the servile adherents of Ministers during the late commotions ; because there is nothing which they so much dread as a free journal, unattached to any other cause than that of truth, and given to speak boldly of all parties. (October 22, 1819.)

The treatment meted out to *The Times* and its staff by sympathisers with the Administration naturally increased the paper's sympathy with the popular appeals for relief. As it became more outspoken, the ministerialists increased their attacks upon the Press.

---

[1] A welcome assurance in view of the leading article in *The Times* two months previously, which asserted that the paper had " sent the Addingtons adrift." *Cf.* p. 130.

The Times laid down its own doctrine on September 25, 1819 :

. . . many taunts have been thrown out against the press, as a vehicle of mischief to the best interests of society ; and often have we been assured within this twelve-month, that if the penal law be left no stronger than it now is, there will be a speedy end of our Government, as well as of our morals. We beg leave to say, that it is not the question whether or not the freedom of the press be productive of unmixed benefit to mankind. The question is, whether its advantages do not overbalance its evils. The question is, whether. if it be destroyed, or its actual freedom sensibly curtailed, we may not exchange occasional turbulence and conflict for the calm of despotism and the repose of death. The writers of the Treasury are prompt to persuade us, that when a case of oppression or hardship occurs from the mal-administration of power, our constitution upon the whole is the best in the world, and we must take its abuses with its blessings.

The alternative was plain : with restrictions on the freedom of the Press, and with the power of the law to closure discussion in the Press, there could be no hope of an educated political society such as Barnes desired England to become, for " public opinion would be modelled, like a soldier's regulation cap, according to the newest patterns from headquarters."

The jury system made difficult the realization of the Administration's plans. The country gave itself over to sympathy with the victims of Peterloo, subscription lists were opened in London and Liverpool, meetings were held in Norwich, Bristol, Nottingham and York, besides Westminster and Smithfield. The Government, nevertheless, resolved upon restricting still further the dwindling legal liberties of speech and publication. The six measures enacted between November and December, 1819, included an Act for the prevention and punishment of blasphemous and seditious libels, and another to subject certain publications to the duties of stamps upon newspapers and to make regulations for restraining the abuses arising from the publication of blasphemous and seditious libels.

The Times argued against these Acts with obstinate patience and knowledge, but to little purpose. A flattering private notice of the paper's persistence has survived :

Lord Holland with his best compliments sends the Editor two protests for insertion in his paper. They were entered against the rejection of the amendments moved by Lord Holland on the report of seditious libel bill last Friday.

Lord Holland in taking this liberty cannot resist the pleasure of thanking the conductors of *The Times* for the spirit, judgement, ability and success with which during these last five months they have continued to expose the principles and designs of two factions who from very opposite quarters are assailing the free constitution of the country. The one by exercising their privileges in a manner useless to every good purpose and disgusting to every rational man, and the other by seizing every pretext for abridging them permanently and assimilating them to the Military Monarchies of the Continent.

The Times spoke plainly during the autumn of 1819. The change in the tone of *The Times* was not unnoticed by the friends of the Government. On November 20 there appeared the first number of a propaganda sheet, the *Anti-Times*, published by J. Ilbery, British and Foreign Library, Cavendish Square.

In designating our paper the *Anti-Times* we are anxious to have it clearly understood that we do not intend to throw down the gauntlet of perpetual contest against the paper we appear to oppose, but we avow, clearly and distinctly, that the versatile conduct of that journal since the lamentable transaction of the 16th August has suggested to us the title.

The *Anti-Times* was doubtless subsidized by the agents of the Administration. The sheet was small ; its short life ended on December 11. The Government machine worked slowly or inefficiently. Number one of *John Bull* was not produced until the following December. It was launched with official support, and thenceforth *The Times* was never without an unscrupulous enemy.

In such circumstances *The Times* moved consistently towards support of the Opposition. In January, 1820, George III died ; the " First Gentleman of Europe " became King and immediately repudiated Queen Caroline. *The Times* hesitated. It was against the King, but slow in championing the Queen. Articles in her favour began to appear in June. They drew protests, but it was evident that popular sympathy was wholly with her. Cobbett, a powerful advocate, was on her side. On July 9 Lord Liverpool introduced an Act to deprive the Queen of her position and to dissolve the marriage, and thereafter *The Times* championed her cause. The Queen, as a non-political personage, possessed a cause which could be safely used as a basis for attacking the King's Government without falling into danger from the Six Acts. Thus Queen Caroline was linked with Reform, and the case powerfully, if accidentally, extended popular education in purely political subjects. Both Denman and Brougham, her counsel, were known to Barnes, and there were frequent consultations. The Press was recognized as of vital importance to the Queen's cause, for she was being libelled in the gutter Treasury papers, *John Bull*, the *British Monitor*, and vilified in the *Morning Post* and *Courier*. Brougham considered prosecutions and sought advice from newspaper men. " It strikes me," he wrote to Leigh Hunt, " that the best way of forming an estimate of the probable risk to which the respectable part of the press might be exposed by such proceedings, is to ask one or two journalists how they feel ; and I think of consulting Messrs. Coulson and Perry as well as yourself and no one else. I have already spoken to Mr. Barnes and to no other, but he knows nothing of this letter. I trust you will excuse this trouble, and write me what occurs to your brother and yourself."[1]

In the event *The Times* became the Queen's most important champion in the Press. When Lord Liverpool's Bill of deprivation was introduced in July, the Queen was advised to make a final protest to the King. The letter, drafted by Cobbett, was sent on August 7 and returned unopened. It was printed exclusively in *The Times* of August 14 and thence copied into every other journal in the country. It may be assumed that the letter came to *The Times* through the Queen's legal advisers rather than from Cobbett. " We, the counsel," wrote Brougham in his memoirs, " had communicated with the paper through Barnes, the chief editor, whom Denman[2] and Williams[3] had known well at Cambridge."

The instinct of Cobbett, which saw in the Queen's case a shocking travesty of justice, saw also that the enormous popular sympathy which she enjoyed made her a national rallying point of all anti-Ministerial sentiment. Petitions became henceforth of vital importance ; in the making and sustaining of public opinion the Queen's cause played an essential part. A further consequence was the increased public demand for reading matter ; above all, for daily newspapers. *The Times*, like Cobbett, was quick to appreciate the numerical importance of the popular manifestations in the Queen's favour. When the excitement had

[1] *Correspondence of Leigh Hunt*, Vol. II, 98. Coulson was Editor of the *Globe* ; Perry of the *Morning Chronicle*.
[2] Thomas (Lord) Denman, 1779-1854, St. John's 1796-8, was Solicitor-General for the Queen.
[3] (Sir) John Williams, 1777-1846, at Trinity College, 1796-8, was Junior Counsel for the Queen.

R

passed away it found that the new and keen interest shown by the country in its Royal governors and their Ministers remained. *The Times* set itself to sustain and vitalize the growing force of public opinion of England.

In the immediately succeeding years Barnes found himself strong enough to acknowledge dependence only on public opinion. He made it his purpose to foster, to guide, and to ally himself with the feeling of the country, slowly becoming too strong to be disregarded by politicians. Writing to Croker, Peel asked : " Do you not think that the tone of England—of that great compound of folly, weakness, prejudice, wrong feeling, right feeling, obstinacy and newspaper paragraphs which is called public opinion—is more liberal—to use an odious but intelligible phrase—than the policy of the Government ? "[1] The letter, dated on the eve of the verdict in the trial of " Orator " Hunt for his connexion with Peterloo, written also in the circumstances created by the arrival of Queen Caroline, is important for the recognition by a then Tory of a " tone " as well as for the manifestation of his dislike of it. Peel, no doubt, was thinking of the middle classes ; but the working people, by their championship of Queen Caroline, asserted a claim to a " tone " of their own. Since their voice could not be heard in the unreformed Parliament, they expressed their feelings by breaking the windows of the Duke of Wellington's carriage and forcing recalcitrant aristocrats to put candles in their windows on the day the Queen landed.

In choosing to support public opinion because it was public opinion *The Times* initiated a definite change of policy. Its older tradition had been to support the party in power. When Peel wrote he must have seen that the paper had struck out a line of its own. In taking the people's view of the Royal dispute it was running counter to the prejudices not only of those who were against the Queen but also of those who were against popular manifestations. Many of the habitual subscribers, especially among the sophisticated, felt uncomfortable when *The Times* began to urge the claims of the Queen. Crabb Robinson's Diary records a visit to Printing House Square on October 13, 1820 :

Called on Walter and dined with him. Fraser and Barnes there. We of course talked of the Queen's trial. I related the anecdotes I had heard without effect. *The Times* has pledged itself by one uniform course of justification of the Queen to go on to the end.

[1] Peel to Croker, March 23, 1820. (*Croker Papers*, Vol. I, p. 170.)

But in allying itself with the feeling of the public, *The Times* acquired a goodwill more valuable than could be secured by association, however intimate, with any exalted person or with either of the historic parties ; more permanent than could be gained by the ablest journalist of the old school—Perry, for instance—or even a genius of the new school like Cobbett. There was no doubt of the practical wisdom of following the popular " tone " in respect to Queen Caroline. A vital consequence was the notable increase in circulation. Crabb Robinson, remarking that " I have no doubt W. really thinks he is doing right and I believe he may be," goes on to say that " he (Walter) is not aware perhaps how much he is influenced in the line he is pursuing by finding that since the trial the sale of the paper has risen from 7,000 to more than 15,000." The effect of the increased sale was to give a fair financial sanction to the adoption, as policy, of the course taken on the trial. *The Times*, with Barnes in the chair, consequently felt strong enough to work for what was called "liberal" government. Hence, by cultivating and serving public opinion, with reasonable respect for the traditions of the Constitution, a condition which prevented its ever being a Radical organ, *The Times* set itself to help forward Reform.

The deliberate cultivation and service of public opinion by a daily newspaper could not but alienate Court and party agents powerful enough to embarrass the news department of any paper, and accustomed by generations of corruption to mislead that very force now championed. But *The Times* grew in strength by the simplest and most effective means : readers liked the paper and its freedom of speech, and made a habit of taking it.

Two years after Peel had remarked on the existence of a public " tone," Canning spoke at Liverpool of public opinion as a " mighty power." Embodied in a free Press, he said, " it pervades the constitution, checks and perhaps, in the last resort, nearly governs the whole." He compared it to the new force, *steam*. Nevertheless, Canning thought it expedient to restrain the journals. Not only did he keep journalists out of the Foreign Office, but, after an encounter with *The Times*,[1] he seems to have kept himself so completely in ignorance of their organization as to allow John Stoddart, of the *New Times*, access to an important State paper. The incident, which occurred in 1825, much annoyed Canning. Writing to the British Ambassador in Paris, he confessed

[1] In June, 1819. See p. 129.

that " the most mortifying thing in the whole is the destruction of my system (hitherto persevered in and with tolerable success) of abstinence from communication with the newspaper writers." In the latter part of his life, though he refused the offer of William Jerdan to act as his personal Press agent, he is credited by the Princess Lieven with a bold claim :

Feb. 27 [1827]. Canning was at Brighton also very ill. When he was convalescent I took him out driving every morning in my carriage, and it was on one of these promenades that he first spoke to me of the perplexities of the ministerial crisis [probably about February 24]. He explained himself at first, so as to make me understand he was the most powerful man in England. He had first inaugurated the power of the Press by making it take an interest in affairs. He governed it.[1]

The conversation occurred when Canning had made up his mind that he wanted to be Prime Minister. If, as Professor Temperley thinks, the Princess Lieven's reporting may be trusted, the position taken is an advance upon that of his earlier career. Canning had been affected by the events of the French Revolution, with their consequence in England of restrictions on the expression of any form of political conviction differing from those of the Government. He had refused to communicate with the *True Briton*, although he must have known that it was in Government pay. He had supported the repressive legislation and contributed to the abrogation of such rights of public assembly as had been secured. These had to be fought for all over again during the first quarter of the nineteenth century ; and Canning, however disdainful of the help of the Press in educating the public mind, became conspicuous for his recognition of the respect due to public opinion and public political discussion. From the fight emerged, as a developed institution, what is known to us as the " platform."

After 1828 there was no Canning claiming to " govern " the expression of public opinion. As time went on it became clear the governing force was *The Times*, which throughout the Reform agitation opposed to the irresolution of Lord Grey the resolution manifest at public meetings and in its private correspondence. William IV. might see in the demonstration of the people only the " promotion of discontent and the disturbance of the public peace," but *The Times* insisted that Reform was the prime

---

[1] *The Unpublished Diary and Political Sketches of Princess Lieven*, edited by H. W. V. Temperley. London, Cape, 1925, p. 116. The phrase " he governed it " may perhaps mean that " he *had* governed it " in the period of the *Anti-Jacobin* and that its influence was still felt, or that his governance automatically resulted from his general popularity.

necessity, " discovered and displayed energetically in speech and writing by intelligent men throughout the Empire."

It is not very long since the people began to entertain hopes of acting successfully on that knowledge, because facility of communication through the Press, and that of cooperation by means of meetings and societies, had not yet been so far matured as to teach the people that they need but unite to be irresistible.

So numerous were the resolutions passed by tradesmen and workmen that the newspapers were inundated with reports. While *The Times* continued to urge the need of petitions from every county, town, and village, it was driven to confess in February, 1831, that " Reform meetings throughout England begin to be almost too numerous for us to notice," and in March that the people

have far outstripped our utmost efforts to keep pace with their still increasing ardour in the cause of Reform . . . at meetings held throughout every county in England, and attended by principals, wealth, intelligence, high reputation, and consequent moral power, such as never before were seen, or imagined, in connexion with any political question at the most animated period of English history.

This new prestige of the platform was not won at the expense of Printing House Square. When the 1831 official return of stamps was published in March, 1832, *The Times* wrote :

It has been asserted again and again that our sale had decreased in consequence of the part we have taken in that great Measure, and thence was inferred the indifference and indisposition of the people to Reform. We want no better criterion of the feelings of the people.   Our sale for the year 1830 was 3,409,986.   For the last year [1831] it was 4,328,025, so that the increase has been nearly 1,000,000 ; 25,000 more than we anticipated in December.   Such is the indifference to Reform ! . . . We observe that the great Conservative paper, the *Morning Post*, sells about 2,000 a day.   So much for the popularity of Anti-Reform doctrines.

In further assistance of the popular cause—and, it may be confessed without reservation, its own sale—*The Times* urged the formation of " political unions."   These organizations were a source of anxiety not only to the King but also to his Ministers, pledged though the latter were to Reform. The Birmingham Political Union, first of its kind, was immensely powerful in itself, and therefore in its example. On the rejection of the first reading of the Reform Bill by the Lords[1] the movement took a powerful impetus. Sir Francis Burdett presided over the Political Union of London, " as becomes a distinguished patriot." Persistent in the advice to " form Unions everywhere," *The Times* called on the people over the heads of Parliament, Ministers, Tories, Whigs and Radicals. It taught the mercantile middle class, jealous of the vote but indifferent to party, to value measures for their essential merits ; if they were sound, it was not because they were in agreement with what was imagined to be a sound theory ; they were sound because they corresponded with the experience of men of business and could be expected to work in the circumstances in which they were designed to work. The paper differed from the Tories in justifying property as the reward of individual initiative ; it differed from the Radicals by making political representation conditional upon property. When, therefore, *The Times* referred to the " people " it had no intention of conferring responsibility upon the artisan without property or the impoverished labourer. It is not the task of a daily newspaper to indulge in prophecy which is impossible of political achievement and verification for half a century or more, but it cannot escape the task, imposed by its nature, of dealing with the events of yesterday in terms of the policy of to-day. In periods of crisis *The Times* undertook a task immeasurably more difficult and responsible than forecasting. There never was anything Utopian in its leading articles. By the "people" *The Times* meant the elements whose material interests were bound up with the commercial system. But if *The Times* pitied the poor for their poverty and consequent unfitness for power, it scorned the aristocrats and their claims to privilege. In the view of *The Times* ability to achieve economic independence was itself a political virtue of the first order. Its conviction that the possession of property was the one sure guarantee of electoral responsibility made it implicitly a conservative influence. Its sympathies were expressed compendiously in an article on January 4, 1836 :

It is a matter of notoriety that Sir Robert Peel has never been very cordially supported by some of the more lordly aristocrats of England, because he is a *novus homo*—because he has sprung more directly from

[1] The Bill passed the House of Commons in March, 1831, and was rejected by the Upper House by 41 votes in October, 1831.

the people than themselves—as immediately, for instance, as the greater number of their ancestors did in the last or the preceding century; and that the sting which vexes them is the more severe by reason of the Right Hon Baronet's possessing in an eminent degree the great feature of that rival aristocracy of which the thing called " birth " is naturally, but meanly and absurdly, jealous—viz., the aristocracy *of wealth.*

For twenty years the " tone " of this rival aristocracy, of its highest supporters and lowest adherents, was reflected in *The Times.* Barnes found the middle classes nervous and irresolute; he taught, urged and thundered their duty to them in his daily articles until they recognized themselves as the largest and most coherent body in the State. Nothing like this service could have been rendered without the enterprise of John Walter. It was of spiritual importance to Printing House Square that it should have been the birthplace of the first steam press. The paper's contribution to the cause of free speech, first by campaigning for public meetings, secondly by the organization of an express service of reports by the best shorthand writers of the day, was an extension of the same enterprise. The tremendous Birmingham meetings were broadcast to the country from Printing House Square. A speaker was enabled to address all Britain from a platform in Manchester, Liverpool, Sheffield, Birmingham, Edinburgh or Glasgow. Public opinion and the responsibility of the electorate were quickened in a double sense by rapid reporting and rapid printing. The dominating political position of *The Times* in the 1830's is partly explained by its superiority in circulation, its printing facilities, its matchless reporting by express; with the fourth basic support of a body of " special," or permanently retained, correspondents in every part of the country. In choosing, therefore, to accept as its sole authority the consensus, checked by its own correspondents, of that section of the inhabitants of the country which was able to deal intelligently with political affairs, *The Times* was following out the implications of its material existence, at the same time taking the best means to extend the power of itself and its constituency. Meanwhile advertisements poured into the office in such numbers that supplements (themselves an enormous advertisement of the paper) became first frequent and finally regular. These supplements, more than anything else in *The Times,* convinced the world of its unique position, which after 1832 was almost that of an estate of the realm.

After 1832 the working classes, having done a lion's share in the Reform struggle, discovered that the fruits of their labour were reserved for a new electorate of fewer than a million voters. They became " deaf with passion," to quote words which Barnes used privately to Henry de Ros when the Whigs were out of power in 1834. The artisan class, lacking the sense of responsibility to be developed later by compulsory education, were not yet entitled, as a class, to dominate by force of numbers. It was necessary to buttress the institutions of the Throne, the Church and the Legislature. In the turmoil of 1835 *The Times* fell back upon the converse of the elder Pitt's theory that " the effective exercise of public opinion is a compensation for defective Parliamentary representation." Effective Parliamentary representation now compensated for defects in public opinion. Incipient Chartism must not be allowed to distract the working classes from their true interests, so closely connected with those of the middle classes that they were sufficiently and effectively, if not directly, represented in Parliament as reformed. The dislike of *The Times* for universal suffrage is traceable to its recognition of the rights of property. Any science of politics was worthless which did not begin with respect for private accumulations earned by personal initiative. Nor was " defence of property " an idle phrase. The provocation involved in the refusal of the Lords to pass the Bill, and the reports of its countrywide network of correspondents, forced the paper to reckon with the imminence of attacks upon the property of anti-Reformers. The Unions composed of the propertied middle classes could be trusted to protect " life and property against the detailed but irregular outrages of the mob, as well as for the maintenance of *other* great interests against the systematic violences of an oligarchy made desperate by opposition." Hence there was no justification for alarm on the part of respectable citizens nor any justification for optimism on the part of noble boroughmongers. When the great meeting of the householders of the Metropolis, held in Lincoln's Inn Fields under the chairmanship of Sir Francis Burdett, announced its sole object to be " good government and social order," the alternative of " Bill or Barricades " was compromised.

Between the trial of Queen Caroline and the passage of the Reform Bill *The Times* had demonstrated to the discontent of professional politicians of every party that " the just criterion of the sentiments of the people," to use the words of William IV, was to be found in its leading articles. Modern England dates from the Reform Bill of 1832, the Tamworth Manifesto of 1834, and the recognition by politicians that their cause cannot be served by the secret manipulation of the means of communication by an occult " press bureau." The struggle for the representation of public opinion between the parties and *The Times* was a struggle for the only freedom of the Press that counts : freedom from cant and corruption.

William Cobbett disputed the claim of *The Times* to speak for the public. Perry, of the *Morning Chronicle*, had died in the year in which Barnes took sole control in Printing House Square. Cobbett was the most formidable of those journalists of independent character who remained. Over a score of years Cobbett's criticisms were direct and unsparing. They present the arguments of Barnes's first able and determined antagonist. Cobbett was neither a conscious nor an unconscious agent of the Treasury or the party machines. His articles, nevertheless, were welcomed by all sorts and descriptions of political wirepullers with whose ambitions he could not have had the slightest sympathy. In the struggle for public opinion he was a clean fighter. Though he sometimes went beyond fair comment, his excesses were of a very different order from those of Roebuck, for instance. Cobbett hated the power of Printing House Square ; Roebuck and the later luminaries of the Radical Party were merely jealous. Cobbett hated the idea that any newspaper should be so powerful ; the Radicals, like the Whigs, wished to have its power for themselves.

Cobbett knew England as few have known it. Barnes also knew England and knew the worth of Cobbett ; knew, too, that there was nothing dishonest in his attempt to undermine the power of *The Times* with a public he himself desired to influence. In 1823 Cobbett's evening paper, the *Statesman*, devoted some of its space to a series of articles on the London daily Press. *The Times* was described as *The* " old " *Times* in order to distinguish it from *The New Times* which " Dr. Slop " established in 1817 when dismissed from Printing House Square. When the Doctor was still editing *The Times* there had been hard words between the two. During the Luddite disturbances Cobbett and *The Times* were at furious loggerheads, for " the vile *Times* " was then for a strong hand with the agitators. Cobbett wrote in his *Political Register* that " to speak of them (the Reformers) as *The Times* has done, as an organized rabble, easily beaten by soldiers ; and to say, that it may be desirable that the spirit should break out in all places at once, so that the trouble of subduing it may be the sooner over . . . is calculated to swell discontent into rage and despair." Nevertheless, " the vile *Times* " next demanded that all rioters should be " put out of the protection of the law," which Cobbett never forgave. Cobbett thought that most of the power of newspaper men was derived from their anonymity.

The mysterious WE that they make use of, gives men an idea that what they are reading proceeds from a little council of wise men, who have been sitting and deliberating upon what they wish to put forth. Each paragraph appears to be a sort of little order-in-council ; a solemn decision of a species of literary conclave.

And Cobbett proceeds to tell his readers that " if they could but know what wretches those are from whom these paragraphs proceed . . . if they could but once *see* all the rebel rout of proprietors, and hear their bickerings and quarrellings about the *profits* . . . the illusion would vanish." In order to expose more completely the " stupid and beastly old *Times*," the *Statesman* published a copy of the affidavit recorded at the Stamp Office in virtue of which " this miserable old paper is permitted to be published." The affidavit was, of course, a declaration by the printer of the paper, whose name was associated with those of a number of the proprietors, accepting responsibility for printing and publication. It was signed by Charles Bell, the printer, James Carden, Mary Carden, Alexander Brodie, D.D., and Anna Brodie, Mary Carden and Anna Brodie being daughters of John Walter I. and sisters of John Walter II. The affidavit is dated 1821 ; it gave Cobbett an admirable opportunity for the display of his literary gift :

Here are the mighty and mysterious WE ! An attorney and his wife and a parson and his wife. The two women you see, the real proprietors, for the shares are secured to them, notwithstanding their *coverture* ; thus, then, the infamous blackguards who have been reporting me as keeping a butcher's shop at Kensington have been fighting under the shelter of the petticoats of these two impudent women. . . . But these women are not to escape in this way. Swift very justly lays it down, that when women quit the behaviour of their sex and behave like bullying men, they are to be treated like bullies and kicked down stairs accordingly. Every word contained in this indecent and atrocious newspaper, must be deemed and taken to be the words of these two women. . . . It was only the other day that these impudent women talked of my "PAUNCH." I do not at present know the persons of the audacious termagants; when I do I shall be by no means sparing in descriptions of their paunches and such other parts belonging to them that I may think worthy of description.

According to Cobbett it was foolish in the extreme for any man to pay attention to the counsels of *The Times* since, in his opinion, they were calculated upon the basis of the profits they would yield to the proprietors in general, and particularly to Anna Brodie and Mary Carden. He saw, as Brougham had seen, that the reading rooms were giving *The Times* a power greater than the King's Ministers, temporal and spiritual. The *Statesman* articles were copied into the *Political Register*, which was issued in two forms : one at a shilling included news, and the other at twopence gave only his writings on politics. The " twopenny trash " was designed to counter the influence of both Barnes and Brougham, whom Cobbett equally disliked. Brougham saw in his own *Penny Magazine*, excellent in its primary educational purpose, an instrument for controlling public opinion ; for he was jealous of *The Times*, though so far more or less friendly. But Cobbett and Brougham alike were beaten by man's greater desire for news than for instruction or even for entertainment. Cobbett, indeed, was well aware of this human appetite. In the *Political Register* for February 8, 1823, he pointed out that

one cause of the faith, which people give to these newspapers, is produced by the reporters. People see them with pencil and book in hand. They afterwards read with astonishment that which they have heard. They think that men capable of taking down with so much accuracy what others say, must be wonderfully clever men. And this is really the case. It is a fact *indisputable*. But like many other indisputable facts is made to lead to most erroneous conclusion. The conclusion generally is : if the reporter, who is employed by the proprietor, be so clever a man, what must the proprietor himself be ! . . . The reporter comes, unless he be a supple knave, and brings his true report. The vile hunks of the proprietor, then garbles, guts, swells out, cuts short, or otherwise manages the report according to his interest . . . so that the report which you see in his paper frequently bears no resemblance to that which has been brought him by the reporter.

After Cobbett's death on June 18, 1835, *The Times* devoted more than half a column of its leading page to a notice of " perhaps in some respects a more extraordinary Englishman than any other of his time " from a hand which was evidently the Editor's.

Birth, station, employment, ignorance, temper, character, in early life were all against him. But he emerged from, and overcame them all. By masculine force of genius and the lever of a proud, confident and determined *will*, he pushed aside a mass of obstacles of which the least and slightest would have repelled the boldest or most ambitious of ordinary men. He ended by bursting that formidable barrier which separates the class of English gentlemen from all beneath them, and as a member of Parliament representing a large constituency which had chosen him twice. . . .

The first general characteristic of his style is, perspicuity unequalled and inimitable. The second is homely, muscular vigour. The third is purity, always simple, and raciness often elegant. His argument is an example of acute, yet apparently natural, nay involuntary, logic, smoothed in its progress and cemented in its parts by a mingled stream of torturing sarcasm, contemptuous jocularity, and fierce and slaughtering invective.

The article inevitably discriminated between Cobbett the writer and Cobbett the political doctrinaire. His claim to consistency was found to be untenable. " The man wrote as if he was wholly unconscious of having ever written anything before." A final paragraph took leave of a valiant foe and suggested a reason for the failure of his fight.

For years this journal was the favourite weekly victim of an animosity which we suspect to have been on his part more affected than real. We never deliberately injured him, as he must have known, and in his grave we should be sorry to offer him any injustice. He was a man whom England alone could have produced and nurtured up to such maturity of unpatronised and self-generated power. . . .

Though a vigilant observer of the age, and a strenuous actor in it, he lay upon the earth as a loose and isolated substance. He was incorporated with no one of our political or social frames. He belonged neither to principles, to parties, nor to classes. He and his writings form a remarkable phenomenon. He was an English episode and nothing more, as greater men have been ; for what is Napoleon, while we write, but an *episode* ? As a portion of history he is extinct. He has struck root nowhere, not in Europe, not even in France, as Cobbett has not, either in America, where his intellect first sprung to life ; or in England where it ripened into almost unexpected vigour.

The *Political Register* of the following week reprinted this testimonial from the journal which Cobbett had for twenty years described as that cunning old trout *The Times*, that ranting, canting, trimming old *Times*, that brazen old slut, the stupid *Times*, and the bloody old *Times*.[1]

The power over the intelligent working classes which Cobbett watched passing slowly into the hands of the Editor of *The Times*, and its power over the commercial classes which had grown steadily for ten years before Barnes's appointment, combined to form an engine of publicity impossible to rival except by a great journalist working in the same diurnal medium. Cobbett, however, was never a good daily journalist, and his evening paper quickly failed. *The Times* had henceforth no fear that Cobbett could reduce its influence over the public. But *The Times* could and did learn from him that the immediately powerful journalistic means of securing urgently needed measures of reform was to push forward the transformation of the newspaper paragraph into the leading article. In order to justify reliance upon public opinion it was necessary to teach it.

The Times gave a degree of care unprecedented in daily journalism to the recording and exposition of relevant political and economic facts ; an unintelligent public was worthless to the Editor. The Parliamentary transactions, the summaries of the debates, the reports of public assemblies, country demonstrations and political meetings of every kind were given completely and candidly, as never before, for the better information of the politically conscious and for the education of the potentially conscious. Thus *The Times* laboured to create a public worthy of political responsibility. The object which Barnes set himself to accomplish at once drew the criticism of those who demanded that *The Times*, like any other journal, should take a definite line and stick to it. *The Times* ought to be known either as an Administration or an Opposition journal. Thus its editorial policy would be appreciated by believers in this or that principle or party. Nevertheless, the most sincere believers in party and in principle claim, as individuals, the privilege of changing their principles and parties. In a predominantly commercial nation the change of political party or of political principle depends upon observation and experience, seldom upon theory or dogma. Barnes's

[1] So, in *Cobbett's Weekly Political Register*, Nov., 1822 : " I will another time when I have my books handy, point out some of the numerous efforts made by the bloody and stupid old *Times* in favour of the Bourbons."

cultivation of public opinion, therefore, necessarily earned for the paper accusations of inconsistency.

Grey, writing to the Princess Lieven in 1828, informed her that *The Times* " which, being conducted without the least regard to principles of any kind, and solely with the view of an extension of its sale, may in its frequent changes be taken in general as no bad barometer of the general sentiment."[1] The truth of the matter is that the consistency to be expected from an individual is a totally different thing from the consistency to be expected from a newspaper edited with the object of expressing the aspirations of a nation. Barnes's conception of journalism, not as pure intellectual exercise, but as an activity concerned with and bounded by fact, has already been noted.[2] A superficial logic was part neither of his temperament nor his policy. But the views of *The Times* were not arbitrary or volatile. They were threaded upon a determination to express consistently the critical reflections of the body of opinion standing equally between the masses and the classes, and between the Whigs and the Tories.

[1] *Correspondence of Princess Lieven and Earl Grey* (London, 1890), I, 167.
[2] See page 212.

XV

CATHOLIC EMANCIPATION

URING the short Goderich Ministry, which came into power
on the death of Canning, *The Times* extended its reputation
for an unmatched, even unaccountable, intimacy of political
knowledge. It was not precisely known then, even by the well-
informed, to whom Barnes was indebted for communications of
this nature. It is certain, however, that he was in communication
with Greville, and it was in that day almost notorious that *The
Times* derived intelligence and forecasts from Brougham.[1]
Moore's diary notes the exasperation felt by Lord Lansdowne
and others at the publication by the paper of what had been
regarded as secrets. Similarly, William Huskisson, a Canningite
member of the Ministry, complained to Lord Granville that while
the moderate and reasonable Whigs were friendly, " they cannot
manage their friends, especially in the junior branches," and that
the Ministry was much criticized on this account by the active
and radical Whigs. " Look at the *Times* of Wednesday (the
day of my first interview with the King)," wrote Huskisson. " He
commanded me to read it to him, paragraph by paragraph,
commenting upon it as I proceeded. How is it possible
to go on with such a Press, supplied from Brooks's with a comment upon everything that is pending in matters of this delicate
nature ? "[2]

There is reason to believe that Brougham was the source
here indicated, as also on a later occasion, when Lord Carlisle,
writing to Huskisson, September 20, 1827, pointed out to him " a
curious article in the *Times* today upon the subject of the
Solicitor Generalship," adding, " one can, I think, guess the
prompter."

[1] The *Standard*, January 10, 1828, stated that Brougham had even " avowed himself the
author of the leading article in *The Times* " of that morning. *The Times* frequently
published statements that its leaders were its own. To a correspondent who offered a
leading article it replied " this we will not suffer," and printed the communication as
a letter. The paper insisted more than once that " we write the leading articles ourselves."
Cf. p. 279.
[2] Huskisson to Granville, August 31, 1827.

Brougham during the years 1825 to 1830 was at his best. He was recognized as insatiably ambitious, and men knew him to be unconscientious, but all listened to him with pleasure. His gaiety was not yet spoilt by ill-humour nor his enormous range of knowledge too deeply compromised with charlatanry. Barnes, deeply impressed with his mental gifts, viewed him also as a man of action, resource and independence, uniquely serviceable to *The Times*. " I never saw any man whose conversation impressed me with such an idea of his superiority over all others," wrote Greville in 1828. Rogers remarked, after Brougham had left him one day about this time, that " this morning Solon, Lycurgus, Demosthenes, Archimedes, Sir Isaac Newton, Lord Chesterfield, and a great many more went away in the same post chaise." This was the statesman to whom *The Times* was indebted for much of its early political intelligence. But that Barnes's admiration for Brougham was tempered, even in these years, by his deeply critical judgment is proved by an entry in Moore's Diary for February 15, 1828, which notes that at a party at Longman the publisher's, Moore heard Barnes " speaking with contempt of Brougham's last speech."

How closely Barnes was in touch with Brougham at this time is proved by letters which, by a rare exception, have survived. They enable the inspiration of Brougham to be illustrated from leading articles in *The Times* on the Test and Emancipation questions, and on the Duke of Wellington's difficulties in forming a Cabinet at the beginning of 1828.

Huskisson had left the Government at the end of 1827, and Goderich, unable to keep his Cabinet together, had resigned. The formation of a new Government was beset with much difficulty. It was understood that the King had directed Wellington to preserve a liberal tone in his Administration. As he was some time getting his Cabinet together there was much speculation in the newspapers. The position of Herries was much canvassed. Herries enjoyed the support of the *Morning Chronicle* and the *Standard* and the active opposition of *The Times*. *The Times* stated that the Rothschilds and the Stock Exchange were bent upon imposing Herries upon Wellington. Finally, it was rumoured that Peel would not accept office without Huskisson. During this interval the parties were naturally impatient. The attitude of the younger Whigs, whose independence of the party's leaders had caused Huskisson to complain, may be appreciated from a letter which Brougham wrote to Barnes on the eve of the completion of the new Government :

Private

Thursday
[18 Jan 1828]

My dear Sir,

The reports are persisted in & I plainly see they are much more settld & gain more belief yesterday & today—that Huskisson is in treaty & will take office, giving up those who stood by him in consideration of Wellington (who is talked of for Prime Minister) & Peel letting him lead in the House of Commons, with other concessions.

It is an incredible & impossible story & cannot be believed. What ? Does anyone suspect Lords Lansdowne & Carlisle & Mr Tierney of joining Herries & Co & leaving out Huskisson ? Why ? Because all know them incapable of such baseness. Then what right has any man to slander Husk^n by imputing to him worse baseness ? For it is worse in him in as much as the quarrel was his, not theirs. Besides his feelings are alive, keenly alive on the insults & persecutions that hunted Canning to his grave. Then can he be more slandered than by being suspected of joining his enemies agt his fast defenders ? The object of these rumours is easy to see & H^n should give authority to contradict them. If Well^n is to be premier, Peel a favoured member & Dawson Secy for Home dept includg Ireland Husk^n is responsible to Ireland for this and we buy free trade at a high price.

Who has a right to say that Husk^n has plotted a dark intrigue in order to turn out the Ministry & get a better place ?

Yrs ever

H.B.[1]

These hints were accurately reflected in an editorial passage in *The Times* next day :

It is astonishing with what eagerness the Tories are spreading the incredible story that Mr Huskisson is in treaty to join that party, to whose insults and persecutions of his friend, Mr Canning, he has always appeared so keenly alive. The inventors of this calumny pretend that he is ready to give up those colleagues who have been fast defenders of his friend's memory, and of his own pretensions, and who have stood by him in the recent quarrel, wh. be it observed was *his*, not *theirs*. . . . The manly character of Mr Huskisson makes the story incredible and impossible. (January 19, 1828.)

Nevertheless, on the following day, the Money Market article, often used for the conveyance of political reports for which *The*

---

[1] P.H.S. Papers.

s

Times was unwilling to accept responsibility, printed a forecast of the new Cabinet with the Duke as Prime Minister and including Peel and Huskisson. A day later, on January 21, *The Times*, hoping that concessions had been made *to* and not *by* the friends of Mr. Canning, assured its readers positively that not one of Mr. Huskisson's essential reforms in finance, in commerce, or in Colonial policy would be abandoned. " Of the Catholic question we have more fear. We would gladly fall into the belief that his Grace's opinions have undergone some modification," wrote the paper in a separate article on the same day. The Cabinet, indeed, was not absolutely united against Emancipation. Huskisson, like some others, was anxious that the Catholic question should remain open. He wished to be free to exercise his own judgment in this respect, taking, for himself, a position of neutrality. But Barnes took a very different, and a very definite, line. *The Times*, indeed, determined to take the field against neutrals and opposition alike. It became the most powerful champion of Catholic Emancipation in the daily Press.

In spite of several relieving Acts passed during the previous generation, Roman Catholics still suffered from penal disabilities, of which the most conspicuous was disqualification from sitting in Parliament, with the result that Ireland, more than three parts Catholic, was represented at Westminster exclusively by Protestants. The way to emancipation was blocked originally by George III, who held that his Coronation Oath bound him to refuse consent ; and George IV had since maintained his father's attitude, supported by the high Tories and the Established Church in England, and by the bulk of the Protestants in Ireland. But the progressive section of the Tories, who wished to carry Pitt's policy out, steadily increased in numbers and in influence, and the Whigs and the Radicals were of the same opinion. The Catholic question was felt to be urgent. Nevertheless after Canning, the leader of the Progressive Tories, had died, and after the feeble Ministry of Goderich had faded out, the Duke of Wellington, who had responded with reluctance to a Royal appeal to his sense of duty, found himself at the head of a Ministry, with Peel as the leader in the Commons, pledged to resistance to the Catholic claims.

If the Wellington Government was received with mixed feelings by the " Catholics," the Radical Reformers would have none of it. Yet *The Times* gave it general support, hoping that the Government, with its programme still unannounced, might yet yield to persuasion and insisting throughout that the unity of the Empire was being risked by delay in the concession of elementary rights to Catholics. The new Cabinet was from the first faced with petitions from Protestant Dissenters praying for repeal of the Test Acts. *The Times*, urging that the Established Church was safest when least dependent upon enactments of this sort, supported the Dissenters, making the single condition that Catholic Emancipation be first passed.

The Government sustained an immediate reverse. Peel was defeated in a debate on Lord John Russell's motion to repeal the tests on February 26. On the 28th, when the House went into Committee, there was an " incident." Peel was understood first to have left the House hurriedly and in anger, and afterwards to have denied that his action possessed any significance. When asked why he went out Peel replied that he needed to eat. The incident was much discussed. On March 2, 1828, Brougham thus wrote to Barnes :

Sunday

My dear Sir,

Pray don't omit these two matters. Rely on it the cant & palaver of some of the ministers about having no desire agt the Repeal of the Test Act is too gross to be borne.

They were literally forced up to town—many of whom voted with *us* tho' reckoned upon by *them*. One came 150 miles at 12 o'clock he voted with Govt. Never question was more made a Govt one—never. The defeat signally shews their general weakness. Again—What can Peel mean by saying he only went out to eat on Thurdy ? Did 95 others who went with him all go to eat a mutton chop too ? It was a manifest secession from mortification, if not in him certainly in his party.

Lastly, Lord Grey & his little knot who have inflicted Well[n] on us speak of the question not having been influenced materially by the Opposition. Indeed ! ! ! Why of the 240 we were between 190 & 200 known party men. So much for ministerial trick & pseudo opposition spite.

Yrs ever
H.B.[1]

Again the confidential promptings found willing editorial expression. In view of the Report stage, to be taken on the following Tuesday, *The Times* published that morning an exhortation to patience. The importance of the question had, it said, been realized on the eve of the debate during the previous week.

[1] P.H.S. Papers.

Something little short of force was in several cases applied. We have heard of one gentleman who had travelled 150 miles in the course of the day, and before midnight. He voted against the repeal. Others that had been called upon, or sent for, by Ministers, to oppose the new measure, supported it. . . . How readily can men in power find obsequious imitators, even in their most indiscreet freaks ! Mr Peel was thought by those around him to have retired in pique from the debate on Thursday night, because he was defeated. Instantly is his indignation communicated to ninety-five of his adherents. . . . Mr Peel, however, returned before the debate closed, and resumed his place, vowing that it was hunger, and not anger, which had put him to flight. His *followers* gave no account of the cause of their movement. . . . (March 4, 1828.)

This comment received immediate contradiction from a correspondent signing himself " C " (not unlikely to be Greville), who explained that Peel left in order to avoid voting one way or the other. Upon this " B " (surely Brougham), as his " next door neighbour in the alphabet," replied on the following day, March 6, 1828, that " Mr. Peel was in a passion, and everybody knows ' that he can afford it ' ; but that there should be any *sympathy* is the wonder ; and this is a good gauge to measure the baseness of his backers—not so much his backers as the backers of the Treasury bench."

In the meantime, however, there was more wavering on the Catholic question inside the Cabinet. A dramatic election contest brought matters to a head. In the course of a reconstruction of his Ministry caused by the Canningite defections, Wellington chose an Irish Protestant to preside over the Board of Trade. Mr. Vesey Fitzgerald sat in the House of Commons as member for County Clare. When he sought re-election on taking office he found himself opposed by, and ultimately rejected for, Daniel O'Connell, who, being a Papist, could not, as the law stood, take his seat in Parliament. This election of O'Connell in the spring of 1828 was an immensely serious incident. The Penal Laws met for the first time the challenge of a Catholic lawyer of great eloquence, vitality and organizing ability. In 1823, O'Connell had founded in Ireland the Catholic Association, which, though suppressed by the Government as an unlawful combination in 1825, was revived with a new constitution. One of the testimonies to O'Connell's influence was the Clare victory in 1828. He was the first professing Papist returned since the " glorious Revolution." Some of the anti-Catholics at Westminster, amongst them Peel, and Wellington even, now realized that to prevent the duly elected of Clare from taking his seat was likely to precipitate a civil war. Peel, however, was personally pledged against Emancipation and was prepared to resign.

More important, the Duke's mind was moving in the direction of Emancipation. In June, 1828, he spoke so moderately against it that some observers thought a change imminent. He had, in fact, been making up his mind that concessions to Catholics were necessary in the interest of peace in Ireland. The delicacy of the situation was extreme. The King, as utterly opposed to Wellington on this point as his father had been to Pitt, headed an irreconcilable Church, Court and High Tory faction. *The Times* argued persistently for concessions. By the autumn of 1828 an Irish outbreak seemed inevitable ; matters could no longer be delayed, and the Government proceeded slowly with the preliminaries to a measure of concession. On December 6, 1828, *The Times* printed a significant notice :

We rejoice to say again, what we made known some months ago —viz. that we have the very strongest reasons for attributing to the Duke of WELLINGTON *a fixed determination to introduce a Bill for the relief of the Catholics in the ensuing Session.* We announce this, and we stand to it as our firm conviction, *founded on intelligence from a quarter alike incapable of being deceived itself, and of deceiving others.*

The Opposition were thrown into consternation by this strong hint that the Duke of Wellington had succeeded in overcoming the King's objections and that the Cabinet was resolved upon Emancipation. For the better recommendation of the forthcoming Bill the Duke authorized recourse to *The Times.*

In exchange for the earliest intimation of the Duke's intentions and any advantages that the Foreign Office could give, such as intelligence from foreign countries, *The Times*, says Sir Denis Le Marchant (in his unpublished journal), stood by the Duke " manfully " in all his difficulties. February, 1829, was a crucial month. The King's Speech had been delivered. *The Times* said on February 7 that the situation was " amazing." Wellington was telling the House of Lords that the majority of Englishmen were in favour of the Catholics' civil rights being granted to them, and Peel, hitherto opposed to every petition of the Catholics, had become their agent in the Commons. " The Reason ? *Necessity.*

He has avowed it—State necessity—stern impossibility of resistance,—*the safety of the Empire*." And the Duke ? " Without settling this question it was impossible to go on."

The dealings between *The Times* and the Government were conducted by Digby Wrangham, a Foreign Office chief, and Barnes, generally at the latter's house in Nelson Square, occasionally at the former's in Wilton Crescent. There was reserve on both sides. Wrangham wrote on February 10, 1829, as follows :

I ought perhaps to apologize for the appearance of reserve towards you indicated in my so frequently accompanying the information I give, with a request that you will not make use of it for the purpose of confirming any statement you make, as if it came from authority. But I hope you will not suspect the existence of any feeling of the kind on my part. Indeed the reason for thus qualifying my information must be obvious to you, as well as the advantage which results from it both to you & the Gov^t.—To You, by avoiding the appearance of too intimate a connection with the Gov^t., and thus preserving your character for independence quite beyond suspicion—And to them, on the other hand, by having the benefit of that independent support, which is of course much more valuable than it could be, if any intercourse & understanding was supposed to exist between the parties.

But I will take the opportunity of saying more upon the subject when we meet. Shall I find you at home tomorrow between 12 & 2 ?[1]

The connexion was known to the Protestant opposition, which alternately described *The Times* as the " Duke's own " and as the " hireling of Popery "—the sort of language employed by Lord Winchilsea, with whom the Duke fought a duel upon an accusation that he was conspiring to bring back the Pope.

On February 13, 1829, *The Times* published some of the important provisions of a Bill projected for introduction on a date not yet settled. Wrangham wrote to Barnes from the Foreign Office on February 18 as follows :

Private

My dear Sir

The day for the introduction of the emancipation bill is not positively fixed, but will probably be immediately subsequent to the present bill receiving the Royal Assent ; this will in all likelihood be given this day week, so that we shall not be long before the details of the bill will

[1] P.H.S. Papers.

come before the publick. In the present however I must beg you to persevere in the system of reserve which you have so religiously maintained respecting them :—excepting always under the circumstances which we then agreed might unloose your pen, viz. to contradict false accounts of the bill proceeding from other sources.

What you say of the Attorney Gen[1].[1] gives *me* individually no surprise. And at all events, if at the time he is disposed to be factious, he will have the satisfaction of indulging his patriotism at his own expence, in a private capacity. Sir Ch. Wetherell[2] may vote as he pleases. The King's Attorney Gen[1]. must support H.M.'s Gov[t].— However you have said quite enough on the score of the Duke's determination to enforce discipline in his camp. And perhaps to press the topick further, might tend to produce the evil, which your previous articles upon it, have, I doubt not, contributed to remedy.

As they have put off the Portuguese question for five weeks I won't trouble you with anything on that score just now ; of other foreign intelligence we have literally " nil " ; though we hope to hear every day from Constantinople that our Ambassadors are expected there with favour.

I may as well mention that the Duke of C.[3] has engaged to be " quite quiet." What will the Brunswickers say, when deserted by their great chief ?—

Yours very truly
D. C. WRANGHAM.

T. Barnes Esq.

The Times on March 6, 1829, reported that " a Measure for the Removal of the Catholic Disabilities " had been presented to the Commons. And after the Clerk had read from the table the full text of the King's Speech, Peel spoke for four hours. " The proceedings gave the *quietus* to the scandalous reports of the vacillation of the King," and a majority of 188 on Peel's motion for going into Committee on the Bill accentuated its favourable position in the world outside. In Committee, a resolution that " it is desirable to repeal the laws imposing civil disabilities on Roman Catholics " was carried without a division. For several days *The Times* spoke as one with the leaders in both Houses, certain that both protagonists alike " had the spirit of the Kingdom with them."

As *The Times* pointed out next day, Peel was driven by necessity to admit that the majority of Englishmen were in favour of

---

1 Sir James Scarlett, later legal adviser to *The Times*.

2 An irreconcilable Tory.

3 Duke of Cumberland.

civil rights being granted to Catholics. "This honest evidence of the improved sagacity of the Nation," said *The Times*, was conducive to the "safety of the Empire."

The enemies of the Bill thought themselves powerful enough to exploit the King. They alleged that his Coronation Oath would prevent his signing the Bill even though passed by Parliament ; that something or other must and would happen to prevent signature. Lord Eldon declared in the Lords that " if ever a Roman Catholic is permitted to form part of the legislature of this country, from that moment the sun of Great Britain is set for ever." A letter from Wrangham reassured Barnes :

Private & Confid[1].   Foreign Office, March 15 : 1829
My dear Sir

I don't know that I can give you any *facts* to assure the publick of H.M.'s unchanged disposition to support his Ministers, but the fact itself is certain : and you may safely contradict any rumours to the contrary.

Sir Henry Halford's visits to the Duke of Wellington have had reference solely, I have reason to believe, to the Duke's own health. At least I know that that cause has existed, and I have never heard a whisper of any other, except in the papers.

Then again the Evg Press are very busy pointing publick attention to a sort of clandestine audience which they represent the King as having given to the D. of Newcastle. Now the fact is that all the circumstances which gave that interview it's mysterious character, such as the " walking from Eton to the castle " seem even the Duke's own " *Getting-up*," and the issue of his conversation I *know* to have been a most complete and personally a most peculiarly *mortifying* failure.

As to old Eldon's speech spiteful and mischievous as it was in an eminent degree, he was so taken to task for it by the Duke of W., Plunkett & the Chancellor, that I think the King was fairly extracted from it. And after all, the passage which has been scored up in capitals, in the *Morning Journal & Standard*,[1] amounts to nothing more than a statement of his fixed conviction that the King will strictly abide by the declaration of his speech, at the beginning of the Session.

Yours very truly
D. C. WRANGHAM.

The Bill had a fairly smooth passage. Eldon's speech had no effect. There was a majority of 320 on the third reading. *The*

---

[1] The ultra-Protestant party papers were, daily, the *Morning Post*, the *Morning Journal*, the *Standard*, and the thrice-weekly *St. James's Chronicle* ; on Sundays *John Bull* exposed the " blasphemous quackery of the Popish party " led by *The Times*.

Times wrote in optimistic strain. " It is a victory of which the beneficial consequences will be felt to the remotest generations, giving peace and happiness to Ireland, dignity and strength to Great Britain. . . . The chains now are struck off, and the Irish and the British may henceforth look each other in the face with equal confidence and mutual good-will." On April 11, 1829, it recorded that " under the happiest auspices of success . . . the important Bill which is to consolidate the British empire " had passed through the House of Lords with a majority of 104. Where Grattan, Irishman and Protestant, failed, O'Connell, Irishman and Catholic, succeeded in extorting elementary civil rights for his co-religionists. Inevitably O'Connell became not only a hero in Ireland but, after the Reform Bill, a political power in England of the first importance.

The High Tory Church-and-King party took their defeat with ill grace, and abused the Government, as well as *The Times*, without stint. They were determined never to forgive Wellington or Peel. *The Times* did its best for the Ministry, now in a very precarious position. Menaced by the High Tory factions and by the extreme Radicals, the Government were thankful indeed for the support *The Times* willingly gave in return for a measure for which it had campaigned. The paper's support was sought in an election at Cambridge which occurred in the summer of 1829. By a mischance the Government had pledged their support to Bankes, a well-known Tory Protestant whom *The Times* had ridiculed years before when he first won the seat. The Government were suddenly embarrassed by the presentation of a strong Opposition candidate in the famous physicist, Cavendish. The Ministerial position is explained in the following letter from R. C. Scarlett to Barnes :

It would be of great importance if you could state in the *Times* of tomorrow the fact that the Government have given to Mr Bankes as little support since it was certain that Mr Cavendish would stand, as is consistent with their honour. The knowledge of this truth may serve to set the question between the two candidates upon the right grounds to some of the clergy who have taken up the notion assiduously urged by Mr Bankes's friends, that this is a contest between the Govt & the liberal party. It would also have the effect of conciliating such of that party who reside at a distance from London & who are ignorant of what we know upon Mr Cavendish's committee.

We know that tho the Chancellor's secretary has withdrawn from Bankes's committee & has stated that he had orders to make no further canvass, we understand Mr Peel & his connections to have canvassed in no sense whatever, that the King's household vote indifferently and that more than one undersecretary of State franked Mr Cavendish's letters. I mention these facts, not that they may be stated publicly but to shew you that we have grounds for our assertion.

Between ourselves the promise to lend the Govt aid to Bankes was rash & impolitic. It was given however when *no other* candidate was in the field. Had Mr Cavendish declared earlier doubtless he would have had the Govt interest & Mr Bankes would not have come forward. As it stands, how could the Govt change sides with honour. It has done all that could be expected viz to exert no influence as a Govt since Mr Cavendish declared. Pray state this matter in the way your discretion points out to you as the proper one. It is particularly important in the last mentioned view viz to conciliate an angry feeling among some of our friends which might have the effect of much confusing the cards.

Heaven send us well out of this scrape. We are very confident & talk of more promises than were ever heard of at Cambridge election. Can you find time to go down ?

I could insure you Commons & a Bed at Trinity Colledge if it were convenient & agreeable to you on any of the nights of the election. You would only have to use my name, if I am not there, with Peacock tutor of Trinity to whom I will speak on the subject.

I go tomorrow and back on Wednesday.

I had something else to say to you from the Atty General if I could have seen you.

Yours very truly,

R. C. SCARLETT[1]

Scarlett's request encountered no difficulty with Barnes, for Bankes was no favourite of *The Times*. During the campaign of June, 1826, when Bankes lost Cambridge to Sir N. Tindal, Moore contributed to *The Times* a ballad, then much quoted, containing the lines :

> Goulburn of the Pope afraid is,
> Bankes, as much afraid as he ;
> Never yet did two old ladies
> On this point so well agree.

Again, when Bankes was a candidate for Cambridge in 1827, he had pledged himself with determination against concessions to Papists in a pompous election address which he distributed

---

[1] P.H.S. Papers. Robert Campbell Scarlett, of the Inner Temple, was the eldest son of Sir Robert Scarlett.

post free. The wide postal circularization of the address inspired Macaulay to a set of verses printed in *The Times*, May 19, 1827, of which one runs :

> A letter ! And free ! Bring it here :
> I have no correspondent who franks
> No !—Yes !—Can it be ?—Why my dear,
>   'Tis our glorious, our Protestant Bankes.
> " Dear Sir, as I know you desire
>   That the church should receive protection,
> I humbly presume to require
>   Your aid at the Cambridge election."

In response to Scarlett's request *The Times* promptly affirmed that :

It is not fair to accuse the Government of a strenuous support of Mr George Bankes for Cambridge. We have reason to think that if Mr Cavendish had come forward at as early a period as his less noble adversary, no individual, ever so slightly connected with the Administration, would have breathed a syllable in favour of Mr Bankes. (June 16, 1829.)

This disclaimer was followed by articles championing Cavendish and ridiculing Bankes, and in the event Bankes was defeated.

The Cambridge episode did nothing to temper the animosity with which the old Tories already had reason to regard *The Times* ; and their indignation was further inflamed with the unceremonious and pointed candour of its references to George IV when he died on June 26, 1830.

The day after the King's death *The Times* published an obituary article. It began with a long political estimate of the reign, which gave it credit for one achievement at least :

One vast measure of wisdom and integrity will distinguish to remote ages the reign of George IV from all that preceded it, & from all by which it can be followed. The single act of Catholic emancipation was, to Catholic and Protestant, an act of political redemption.

The paper then took up the duty of estimating the career and character of the late monarch as " a task to be executed which it were disgraceful and pusillanimous to evade."

The late King had many generations of intimates, with whom he led a course of life, the character of which rose little higher than that of animal indulgence. . . . Never have we seen recorded, among the Prince's *intimates*, the name of one man distinguished in the world for any intellectual attributes (we say nothing of the moral) which it would not have been Charity to forget.

The *St. James's Chronicle* for the evening of June 29, 1830, attacked *The Times* for its obituary, heading a reprint of its leading article as " Libel upon the Late King from *The Times*, the Duke of Wellington's journal."

The Times made no reply to the comments of the Tory papers until after the funeral. On July 16, 1830, it answered a charge of persecution by admitting that it had certainly never feared to censure George IV and that *The Times* had been slandered, if not persecuted, by a certain class of newspapers willing to be the tool of the Court circle. It reminded these " desperadoes " that, instead of joining the " foul-mouthed hue and cry " in 1820 it, *unbought*, stood forth the champion of the destitute, and that although it " fluttered the King and the courtiers in their castle " and used its efforts to " stem the course of profligate extravagance pursued by George IV," it did not persecute. It was true that there was no " new Palace projected, or an old one spoiled, or any fresh half-millionary gewgaw undertaken which did not call forth from us the loudest expressions of dislike and indignation," but it defied " any human being to lay his hand on a solitary allusion employed in this journal not founded in fact." In conclusion, *The Times* delivered the following judgment :

The truth is, however,—and it speaks volumes about the man,—that there never was an individual less regretted by his fellow-creatures than this deceased King. What eye has wept for him ? What heart has heaved one throb of unmercenary sorrow ? Was there at any time a gorgeous pageant on the stage more completely forgotten than he has been, even from the day on which the heralds proclaimed his successor ? Has not that successor gained more upon the English tastes and prepossessions of his subjects, by the blunt and unaffected—even should it be the grotesque—cordiality of his demeanour within a few short weeks, than George IV,—that Leviathan of the *haut ton*—ever did during the 68 years of his existence ? If George IV ever had a friend—a devoted friend—in any rank of life we protest that the name of him or her has not yet reached us. An inveterate voluptuary, especially if he be an artificial person, is of all things the most selfish. . . .

Nothing more remains to be said or done about George IV, but to pay—as pay we must—for his profusion ; and to turn his bad example to some account, by tying up the hands of those who come after him, in what concerns the public money. At all events we shall always to the utmost of our power do our duty, and we think we are not likely to do it flinchingly.

The paper only said one word more on the subject, a day or two later, to the " blockhead editor of a foolish evening paper of haberdasher loyalty," that it could have added worse " compared with which what we have said is not merely forbearance but panegyric."

The immediate importance of the accession of William IV was that it meant a general election. The Reformers put forth all their efforts to secure a majority for Parliamentary reform, and were successful. In the middle of the election a *coup d'état* in Paris overthrew the elder branch of the Bourbons, and placed Louis Philippe, who stood for popular rights, on the throne. It was a middle-class movement and in several ways analogous to that proceeding in England ; the Reformers attached to the French movement the vital importance of a precedent. *The Times* raised a fund for necessitous Parisians, itself contributing £50. Soon, all over England, there were first manifestations, then riots and revolts, for which, in large part, Cobbett was responsible. *The Times*, though deprecating all violence, insisted that these troubles were eloquent of a popular demand which it would be most provocative to refuse. The Wellington Administration met the new Parliament in the late autumn. On November 2 Earl Grey, taking part in the debate on the King's Speech, pointed out the desirability of reform.

To this Wellington answered that he had

never read or heard of any measure up to the present moment which could in any degree satisfy his mind that the state of the representation could be improved. . . . He would go further and say, that the legislature and the system of representation possessed the full and entire confidence of the country. . . . He would go still further and say, that if at the present moment he had imposed upon him the duty of forming a legislature for any country, and particularly for a country like this, in possession of great property of various descriptions, he did not mean to assert that he would form such a legislature as they possessed now, for the nature of man was incapable of reaching it at once ; but his great endeavour would be to form some description of legislature which would produce the same results. . . . He was not prepared to bring forward any measure of the description alluded to by the noble lord . . . but he would at once declare that, as far as he was concerned, as long as he held any station in the government of the country, he should always feel it his duty to resist such measures when proposed by others.

The Times forthwith informed its readers that the Duke must resign, in consequence of the differences between himself and his colleagues on the subject of Parliamentary reform. On November 9 the ceremonial entry into the City of the King and Queen was abandoned for fear of attempts on Wellington's life. There was no Lord Mayor's Show on that occasion. *The Times* urged that it would be more dignified for the Government to retire than to continue under threats.

At last the Wellington Government was defeated on the Civil List. Bidding the Ministers farewell *The Times* said on November 17, 1830 :

If the management of public affairs has been difficult during his Grace's Premiership, the difficulty has resulted more from petty perplexities than great affairs. . . . When the Duke of Wellington made the declaration, to the effect that he was opposed to every species of Parliamentary reform, we saw that his fate was sealed. We do not know that he did not court it. . . . Mr. Canning made a declaration to the same purpose . . . but Mr. Canning was loved by the people. . . . Since the Catholic Emancipation he [the Duke] has been hated by the Tory aristocracy with a bitterness equal to its injustice.

The fact was that, after alienating the Protestants without pleasing the Catholics, the Duke had now infuriated the Reformers without gaining the confidence of the Boroughmongers.

It is noted (in Le Marchant's unpublished journal) that the connexion between the Duke and *The Times* " ceased when the Duke went out of office because it was obviously the interest of both parties that it should cease, and the Duke resorted, I presume, to the Tory papers."[1] For his own part, the Duke recognized the independence of *The Times*. When the King called him to form a Government in 1834 he warned Lyndhurst that he thought *The Times* could not be influenced. The arrangement between the paper and the Duke was honourable to both parties. As Barnes had occasion to remind Le Marchant some years later, *The Times* " never had any engagements with the Duke's Administration which precluded us from uttering our sentiments in the most decided manner on all topics on which we differed from it : as for instance on the Greek question, the Civil List and lastly Reform in Parliament."[2]

[1] The Press activities of the Duke's friends, of Croker particularly, are sketched at the beginning of the chapter on the Struggle for Public Opinion.
[2] Barnes to Le Marchant, June 13, 1834.

XVI

"THE ADVOCATE OF REFORM"

IN the general election of June, 1830, Yorkshire was the centre of political interest. There Henry Brougham, as a Reform candidate, a sponsor of elementary education, a worker in the cause of working-class instruction and the eloquent defender of Queen Caroline, won a great victory. He soon became the most powerful statesman in the Whig party, and with the exception of Lord Grey, and perhaps of Lord Durham, had scarcely an equal in the popular imagination. With unexpected directness he announced, when Parliament met in November, his determination to press for Reform, consenting after remonstrance to wait till " the 25th of this month and no longer ; I will then, at no more distant period, bring forward the question of parliamentary reform, whatever may be the circumstances, and whosoever may be his Majesty's Ministers." Before the month was over he was Lord Chancellor in Lord Grey's Whig Ministry, having among his colleagues Althorp as Chancellor of the Exchequer and Leader in the Commons, Palmerston as Foreign Secretary, Melbourne as Home Secretary, Durham as Privy Seal, and Graham as First Lord of the Admiralty, while other posts were occupied by John Russell and Stanley, afterwards to be Prime Ministers. *The Times* considered " the composition of the Grey Ministry as good as the present state of the parties would admit of. . . . But the first and last subject of solicitude for the new Ministers must be, that they accede to office by cooperation with the people—they must *redress* our grievances or be for ever disowned."

At this critical time of 1830-31 Barnes and Brougham saw a good deal of each other ; they breakfasted together frequently. Brougham was restless against delay ; daily *The Times* urged action. The paper was satisfied that at long last the country had obtained an Administration pledged most solemnly to four great principles of domestic and foreign policy—peace, reform, retrenchment and non-interference in the internal affairs of Europe—as necessary for the salvation of the country. (November 24, 1830.) The peace policy was certainly vital. The King's Speech to the Wellington Parliament on November 2, 1830, had emphasized the endeavour, " in concert with my allies, to devise such means of restoring tranquillity as may be compatible with the welfare and good government of the Netherlands, and with the future security of other states." The Duke, suspected of a policy of urging a Continental excursion as a diversion from the country's preoccupation with Reform, had to live down the same suspicion when he was sent for in 1834. The Whigs meant peace, but they continued the enormous Civil List. Reform, however, was another matter. Lord Grey seemed, not only to the Radical hot-heads, but also to *The Times*, to be only half-hearted. *The Times* feared that the Government, though committed to Reform, might, if left to itself, do no more for Reform than for retrenchment. There was more at stake than the settlement of a few academic political points. Mere disfranchisement of a few boroughs would not content the country. *The Times* said that political levity would be followed by very serious outbreaks. It called upon the public to encourage the Government. " We repeat our earnest counsel to the people, to be strenuous, indefatigable and uncompromising in their demands for reform. Without their *most vigorous* aid the Ministers may be defeated in their national and noble enterprise. The enemy is *in the field*,—we can assure our countrymen of that fact ; and his intrigues are even more to be dreaded by us all than his numbers. If the reforming Government be not encouraged and stimulated from without, we may live long before we see another defeat of the Tory boroughmonger." (January 26, 1831.)

Three days later, in a much quoted passage, *The Times* urged forward still greater efforts :

unless the people—the people every where—come forward and petition, ay, thunder for reform, it is they who abandon an honest Minister,—it is *not* the Minister who betrays the people. But in that case, reform, and Minister, and people too, are lost. (January 29, 1831.)

The agitation throughout the country became prodigious. There were Radical Republican societies and revolutionary groups, as well as middle-class reformist groups, all writing, preaching and petitioning. The Opposition stigmatized *The Times* as a revolutionary journal inciting to violence, although the paper itself (February 1, 1831) had quite clearly said that it was only by Parliamentary reform that a revolutionary overthrow against Church and State could be prevented. But the business was urgent and (February 14, 1831) recognized in august quarters . . . no credence should be placed in rumours that an illustrious personage[1] was insincere in his attachment to the popular cause. (February 28, 1831.) On March 1, when Lord John Russell brought in his Bill, *The Times* wrote that politicians had " now arrived at the grand crisis for which the country has been so long preparing itself," and it even warned its readers that representative government was itself at stake, that if the Commons rejected the measure " they have no kind of connexion or sympathy with us. They cannot be Englishmen." With the Bill under debate, *The Times* pressed the friends of Reform to sustain the cause without delay and without hesitation. (March 6.) " The measure, it is said, is revolution. How ? It meddles but with one branch of the legislature, that of the people ; and it only prevents others who are not of the people, and have rights of their own which we do not want to touch, from interfering with our rights ; and beyond this it merely facilitates our manner of exercising those rights which are acknowledged to be ours. (March 8.) . . . Our advice to the people of England is deal MILDLY but FIRMLY with the rotten Boroughmongers."[2] (March 14.) " It is beyond question a piece of the broadest and coolest effrontery in the world ; for these hired lacquies of public delinquents to stand up as advocates of the disgraceful service they have embarked in. . . . All England calls aloud for the Reform Bill." (March 25, 1831.)

On the 26th *The Times* said, prematurely as it turned out, that

The all-important question of Reform, of full and satisfactory reform is, we have no doubt, now completely settled. The people, the brave English people have won it as decidedly as they ever won battles in the field or on the ocean ; nor can they by any possibility be cheated or robbed of the fruits of their victory. They petitioned,—they addressed,—they resolved. We proposed these courses to them, we urged the prosecution of them with vigour, and our advice prevailed to a degree that even we, used as we are to move the noble feelings of our countrymen in a just cause and on subjects of vast moment—could hardly have conceived, and were almost surprised at our success.

1 The reference is to the King.
2 The full capitals are in the original setting of *The Times* leading article.

The fact was that, in spite of the unprecedented agitation, the Reform Bill passed its second reading by a majority of only one. *The Times* called for a dissolution. Grey called for a dissolution. The King refused it. The Tories, surprised as well as worried by defeat, relied upon the King and the Lords to save them. In Committee the Government sustained a defeat ; again the King refused to permit dissolution. He urged the introduction of a more moderate measure. The position of the King, refusing dissolution while allowing that the Government represented the people, was dangerous in the extreme. *The Times* at this period cried out for " The Bill, the whole Bill and nothing but the Bill." The King changed his mind and Parliament was dissolved in April, 1831. At last *The Times* saw the consummation of its tactics. It had for some time been urging the people to petition for dissolution. The general election of 1831, it was convinced, would effectually secure " The Bill, the whole Bill and nothing but the Bill." While *The Times* " thundered for Reform," the Tory Press accused it of organizing a system of terrorism. The paper did point out the rashness of the Boroughmongers. " Once and again we warn them to desist,—not if they value the lives and happiness of others, for they are too selfish to be moved by such considerations, but if they value their own." According to the *Standard* and the *St. James's Chronicle*—and there was much to be said for their view—these words were an incitement. Nevertheless, *The Times* persisted, prophesying how the populace would receive " any high-born and high-bred young Tory, sent from some Club-house in St. James's Street . . . with the wages of corruption in his pocket, and travelling luxuriously to some comfortable corporation constituency, consisting of some 13 or 16 persons." There would be no doubt about the quality of the reception to be given to such gentlemen. " They will become acquainted with every village pump ; the clear river and the muddy pond will alike receive them ; they will carry away undesired samples of the soil from each county, and will consider themselves fortunate if contumely and contusions be all they meet with." (April 30, 1831.)

The temper of the entire country was excited, suspicious and irascible. It could be guided—but in one direction only. *The Times* was the advocate of the Reform movement as a whole, not merely of the London section. It was an advocacy requiring the greatest self-restraint on the part of Barnes as conductor of *The Times*, the most powerful of all stimulants of public opinion.

274

The Tories often demanded the prosecution of the paper. It may well have been that any prosecution of *The Times* would have led to a serious outbreak. The solidarity of *The Times* and public opinion throughout the country was so close that interference with it would have been provocative. Through the organization of the political unions which *The Times* persistently fostered the Editor was in daily touch with the progress of the campaign. " All of us," once wrote Joseph Parkes, the Birmingham attorney, to George Grote, future Member for the City of London, " were up most of the night and again at six this morning, to get the report composed and fit to go to the printer which at half past seven we accomplished. . . . William Hone happened to be here so we set him to write to Barnes so that it will be printed in London before you get this."[1] Reports, petitions and resolutions poured into Printing House Square during the height of the agitation.

In estimating the importance of *The Times* at this period, it should be borne in mind that although the paper cost 7d. the number of readers was multiplied tenfold by the system of illegal lending. Advertisements from those who were willing to lend their copy of *The Times* were of frequent occurrence in provincial newspapers, and the Tory party sheets (*e.g., St. James's Chronicle*) endeavoured to stop the practice :

> For one copy of *The Times* that is purchased for the usual purposes of a public journal, nine we venture to say are purchased to be lent to the wretched characters who, being miserable, look to political changes for an amelioration of their condition. . . . They hope to find encouragement to persevere in their own vices among the pictures of profligacy by which *The Times* malignantly caricatures whatever is respectable in the country.

In the general election of 1831, which gave the Reformers a great majority, the Editor went up to Cambridge to give his vote. John Cam Hobhouse, also there for the same purpose, " dined with Dr. Davy at Caius College. Mr. Otter, of Jesus College, and Barnes, Editor of *The Times*, were at this most agreeable dinner, when we did not fail to congratulate each other on the news which came pouring into us from all parts of the country of the victories of our friends." Cambridge, however, fought solidly against the reform, and leading spirits of the University expressed their dislike of *The Times*. Tories, while disliking the Press on general princi-- ples, announced their respect for traditional Whig papers like the

---

[1] B.M., MSS. Addl., Place MSS. No. 35149, 77.

Globe and *Morning Chronicle* ; they thought sufficiently well of the *Examiner*, which they classed as a Radical paper. The *St. James's Chronicle* for January 19, 1832, prints a letter from its University correspondent, sent from Cambridge, on the 17th :

Mr. Editor,—I take the trouble of sending you the following little piece of information, which I shall be glad to see noticed in your valuable journal :—*The Times* newspaper was yesterday unanimously ejected by the Fellows at Trinity College from their combination (or common) room and the *Morning Herald* substituted in its place.

You are perhaps aware that Trinity considers itself the most liberal college in the University, the fellows being almost entirely Whigs.

They have of late been much disgusted at the violent and unprincipled language and doctrines of *The Times* ; but what gave the paper the *coup de grâce* was, I understand, the profligacy and perversion of the spirit which actuated it in ascribing the late riots at Derby, Nottingham and Bristol to the Tories.

In this agitation *The Times* had, besides the help of practical workers like Parkes and Hone, the support of Ministers themselves. It was especially Barnes's friend, Henry Brougham, who provided him with information. *The Times*, in return, gave Brougham and the activist section of the Cabinet general support. For years past many letters and articles had been contributed to *The Times* by the Chancellor directly, and through his brother William, and Denis Le Marchant, his principal private secretary. This intimacy of Brougham with *The Times* was naturally unwelcome to Cabinet colleagues less active in the Reform cause than himself. The Chancellor's Press connexions made his colleagues first anxious and then angry.

Lord Grey, in a letter to Brougham dated December 30, 1830, agreed that " All you say about O'Connell, his motives and his conduct, is quite true. His abuse of me, I care little about, though full of falsehood and injustice," and he added that " You have an equal right to complain of him, but I do not think the notice of it which I have seen in to-day's *Times* was worth while." Brougham was indeed not without justification in believing that Lord Grey's progress would depend upon pressure from public opinion. Barnes shared the same view. Unfortunately a purely personal element intruded itself. Lord Grey was embarrassed by certain articles in which *The Times* mentioned the undesirable effect upon public opinion occasioned by the number of the Prime Minister's relations " associated with him in place." The articles were attributed to Brougham's inspiration.[1]

These articles annoyed Grey's relations even more than they annoyed Grey himself. Lord Durham, his son-in-law, indulged in a characteristically temperamental outburst much exaggerating the matter and thereby playing into the hands of Brougham, who addressed himself to his leader in the character of a maligned colleague. Lord Sefton was the hero of an encounter with Brougham on the subject. Brougham having asked him if he had seen *The Times* that morning, Sefton answered : " No, not to-day, but I have read it with great uneasiness the three or four preceding days, and I want of all things to talk to you about it." According to Creevey, " Sefton then described the *deliberate* attack then being made upon Grey," which, being accompanied by

constant panegyrick upon Brougham, made it necessary for Brougham to summon the editor and to insist upon these attacks upon Grey being discontinued. Otherwise, as Brougham's influence over that paper was notorious to all, and his brother William was known to write for it, it could not fail to beget suspicion that he—Brougham—had no objection to these attacks, and that Lord Grey felt them most sensibly. If however he—Brougham—thought he would make a better Prime Minister than Grey, and was preparing the way for that event, that was matter for his own consideration ; but if he really meant the Government to go on in its present form Sefton conjured him to lose no time in imposing his most positive injunction upon *The Times* newspaper to alter its course. Sefton says nothing could equal the artificial rage in which Vaux flung himself. He swore like a trooper that he had no influence over *The Times*, and that he had never once seen Barnes, the Editor, since he had been in office and that William had never written a line for it. He then fell upon Lambton [Durham], said all this came from him—that he had behaved in the most impertinent manner to both his brothers upon this subject—and if he went on as he did he *must* break up the Government and that he, for one, would never submit to his influence.

This storm being over, Sefton collected from him distinctly that he had seen Barnes *perhaps* once or twice, and that brother William might *perhaps*—though quite unknown to him—have written an article or two in the paper. In short, as our Earl observed, never culprit was

[1] Brougham himself, in his *Memoirs* (III, 412), describes Lord Grey as " having a weakness for his family which was grievous and produced the not unfounded charge of nepotism. He once even sounded me on making his nephew, Sir George Grey, *Solicitor-General*, knowing that he scarcely ever held a brief, and that few in or out of the profession knew he belonged to it. Of course I would not hear of it seriously. He complained himself of the attacks of *The Times* on this score of nepotism."

more clearly proved guilty than he was out of his own mouth and it ended by his affecting to doubt which would be the best channel for getting at Barnes—brother William[1] or Vizard[1]—but at all events he pledged himself to Sefton that it should be done.

Brougham next wrote to Lord Grey protesting, not very candidly, that :

I have not the most remote influence in the quarter referred to, as soon as I heard of the thing, I asked my brother to see the person supposed to be concerned and express how annoyed I was at such a way of praising me at the expense of those I most loved and respected. . . . I had intended to reserve this . . . meaning to say nothing till the Reform motion was over. But having seen my brother to-day and knowing Lambton is not apt to be very quiescent when he has got a thing in his head (or rather a ruffle in his temper) I could not tell how far he might be influencing you.

Grey permitted himself only to answer that " You have somewhere a most injudicious friend and I a most unprovoked and malicious enemy."

The support of *The Times* was so valuable that the convinced Reformers needed the publicity which its columns alone could provide. Lord Durham was frequently in relations with Barnes. Barnes's capacity to divine what the country thought was already famous. When the Reform Bill, being finally through the Commons on March 23, 1832, went to the Lords, Lord Durham was in charge of the measure. In the debate on the second reading, Henry Phillpotts, Bishop of Exeter, insinuated that Lord Durham had violated Cabinet secrecy in conveying information to *The Times*. Durham was not a temperate man, and a " scene " followed. The affair happened on April 13, 1832, and Grey and Brougham were dragged into it. Durham angrily denounced Phillpotts for " gross and virulent invective," for " malignant, calumnious and false insinuations, gross perversions of historical facts," and stigmatized his speech as " decked out with all the well-known powers of his pamphleteering slang." The interruption and hubbub were so great that Durham, his speech unfinished, considered it proper · to resume his seat. Phillpotts, on being challenged, referred to a communication that appeared in *The Times* on January 22, " purporting to be a faithful transcript of a correspondence between the Duke of Buckingham

[1] William Brougham, brother of the statesman, had written leaders for *The Times* at intervals since 1822 ; Vizard, one of Brougham's secretaries.

and the King." Grey, who followed, said that he understood the Bishop to charge Durham with being party to some communication to *The Times* involving a violation of official secrecy and honour ; that was the accusation.

Now mark, my Lords, the charge of the Rt. Rev. prelate. He makes a merit of exculpating me individually of all participation in this crime, while in the same breath he most unwarrantably endeavours to sever the dearest ties which can connect a colleague and a relation rudely asunder, by insisting that my noble relative has secretly furnished a newspaper with information which could not be disclosed without a violation of his duty as a Minister and gentleman. (*Cheers.*) Is this religion ? Is this Christian charity ?

On the following day *The Times* wrote :

Few things can be conceived more absurd than the frequent intimation of the enemies of reform, that we are assisted in our daily labours, in those writings, of which we shall not here venture to repeat the extorted praises, by certain members of the Administration, first one and then another, even persons of the Cabinet, being named at successive opportunities. The charge is the more remarkable, inasmuch as those who make it are accustomed to depreciate the talents of Ministers, when openly displayed in defence of their own measure ; while the lucubrations in our journal, admitted to possess great power and influence, are said to be inspired by the genius of the same Ministers, thus underrated and contemned. Now, that we possess various sources of information, both foreign and domestic, is certain, for we cannot be believed to obtain our knowledge of facts by intuition ; but we beg leave to assure both our friends and our enemies, that our mode of treating these facts, our selection of such of them as we deem it advisable to make public, and our reasoning upon them, are all entirely our own : and if we support ministers, it is not that we are bound to undertake such a task, but because we have hitherto generally come to the same conclusions with them upon the necessity of a great and comprehensive measure of Reform ; that we argued for reform before the present men were united into a ministry ; and should they fail of their object through irresolution or weakness, shall continue to argue for it should they unhappily be dissolved.

Our writings, such as they are, are our own. They neither are, nor ever have been, those of Lord or Mr. Anybody connected with this or any other Administration,—with this or any other Opposition. We stand by and observe the passing events and measures proposed or put in execution, and frankly and impartially give our opinions of them, in our own language and with our own powers. (April 14, 1832.)

The Durham incident and Phillpotts's charge were referred to again on April 19, 1832, when *The Times* asked the Bishop :

Will it be believed, *can* it be believed, after the Duke of Buckingham has thus asserted that he had seen extracts from his letter to the King in *The Times* journal, and that " they were copied verbatim " from the original document,—can it, we say, be believed, that no such extracts ever did appear in *The Times* journal—that the editor never either saw or heard one tittle of the letter in question and therefore could have put none of it into the journal and that all that ever did appear in *The Times* was the letter of an anonymous correspondent stating that a letter had been sent to the King by the Duke of Buckingham ?

Following this a quarter of an inch space was left blank :

We leave a space vacant, as the author of Tristram Shandy says, " for the reader to swear in, any oath he is most accustomed to," only hoping it will be an innocent one.

The Bishop's outburst is significant of the contemporary belief that, while the columns of *The Times* reflected the policy of highly placed statesmen, its information was correspondingly early and authentic. As a consequence, the Government being committed to reform, *The Times* became necessary both to the Administration and the Opposition.

The Bishop later made a similar charge in more guarded language, but, finding the Lord Chancellor's name taken as that of the man in his mind, he wrote as follows to remove misconception :

Private   34, St. James's Place, [September, 1833].
My dear Lord,

I have been informed that it has been supposed, or that it has been affected to have been supposed, that I alluded to your Lordship the night before last, when I said something about the offices or officers of State who have been believed to communicate with *The Times*. *I give your Lordship my honour that I had no such purpose.* The party to whom I really alluded was Lord Durham, and the ground of my allusion was, what has been so much the subject of recent talk, the alleged estrangement between his Lordship and Lord Grey, on the notion whether true or not, that *The Times* had been enabled to say what ought not to have been put within its power.

The simple truth behind this supposed violation of Cabinet secrecy is that one of a series of " letters to the Editor " signed

" Radical " did contain an oblique reference to a letter written by the Duke of Buckingham to the King. Much of the power which *The Times* exerted in defence of the principles of Reform was expressed through this long series. They were widely attributed to an aristocratic person, and, although Lord Durham's name was not always mentioned, it was freely alleged that he was their author. Creevey wrote to Miss Ord (July 17, 1832) :

You must know that for months past I have been firing into Ellice, and through him into Durham, for their joint patronage of Barnes, the Editor of *The Times* newspaper ; being convinced that the vindictive articles in that paper were written or directed by Durham.

So much comment was occasioned that *The Times* found it necessary to explain that they in no way differed from any other letters to the Editor. Readers were warned that such correspondents did not necessarily speak on behalf of the paper. A letter from " Radical " published on April 18, 1832, supported the explanation :

Sir,—You are perfectly correct in stating that you have " no more connexion with me than with any other correspondent, and that I am in no way identified with *The Times*." Within the last six months we have never met but once and that accidentally. Indeed, if I coveted interviews with you I should find more difficulty in obtaining entrance into the recesses of Printing-house-square than into those of St. James's. You are more inaccessible than the First Lord of the Treasury.

The author was in fact Colonel Leslie Grove Jones, a middle-class reformer of mildly Radical tendencies. He was in constant touch with Lord Durham, but there is no evidence that on this occasion he acted under Durham's direction.

Tumult in the country was on several occasions laid to the influence of *The Times*. The paper had only to point out to Tories the degree of popular resentment and the possibility of outrage to find itself accused of instigating what it had merely predicted. The Duke of Wellington's safety was the source of some concern. The newspapers for the week-end of Sunday, May 28, 1832, mentioned the matter, and one of them even asserted that *The Times* had been crying out for the assassination of the Duke. Replying, *The Times* pledged itself to go further in the defence of the life or honour of the Duke of Wellington than many of his multitude of flatterers. When the Duke was attacked on Sunday, June 18, 1832, *The Times* spoke out. " Yesterday was the anniversary of the Battle of Waterloo, fought in 1815 ; the greatest event of modern history,—next to the Reform Bill of 1832. . . . Without, then, dipping into party questions, we will venture to reassert what has often and many years ago been insisted on in this journal, that the battle of Waterloo was no less than the salvation of England, France and Europe. . . . To the Duke of Wellington we are indebted for the seventeen years of peace which, with few and partial interruptions, hardly, indeed, deserving to be enumerated, this nation has enjoyed from June 1815 to June 1832." After a reference to the murderous attack on the Duke the paper asked : " Is there on human record a fact more disgraceful than this ? Would the most stupid savage have overlooked the reverence due to the actor of so mighty an achievement ?—and made choice of such an anniversary for the perpetration of so vile an insult as the conqueror of Napoleon suffered yesterday at the hands of a banditti of miserable ruffians ? " These were the sentiments of *The Times*, yet, " after writing the above we received a letter from some anonymous blackguard charging us with having instigated the outrage of yesterday upon the Duke." Later in the week a member of the House of Commons asserted that *The Times* was responsible for the attack on the Duke and the subsequent attack at Ascot upon " his sacred Majesty, William IV."[1]

In a speech to the Lords on May 17, 1832, Lord Lyndhurst spoke of the efforts of *The Times* to reinforce agitation and to stimulate the efforts of those members of the Cabinet who were in agreement with its policy of creating Peers in sufficient number to ensure the passing of the Bill. He said : " I should be ashamed to belong to a Government which permitted the article in *The Times* journal to pass unprosecuted and unpunished ; and if I were the Attorney-General I should consider myself guilty of misprision of treason if I neglected to prosecute such an article as that, which I have no hesitation in pronouncing revolutionary, treasonable and subversive of the monarchy of the State." Lord Carnarvon, speaking later in the same debate, urged that the Bill, if sent down, would not be modified, so great was the power of the extremists. In his view " the determination not to alter one single portion of the Bill was in direct accordance with the demand of *The Times*—a journal which it would seem would not suffer or permit the slightest modification of the Bill."

[1] As *The Times* described the King in its report of the outrage.

The part which *The Times* had played was prominent in the final debates on the Reform Bill. A leading article from the issue of March 7, 1832, was quoted in Croker's famous speech against the Bill. " The people, the people of England, have stuck the spurs deep into the flank of many a shy and shuffling jade, (*laughter*), amongst those who are called their representatives, and forced the dogged animals onwards. It is the nation that has performed the work. The Ministers had only to look on and be borne forward by the mighty current." Croker drew the moral that those who had supported the Bill under the pressure from outside the House could not know what its consequences must be. Lord Althorp rose to say that, despite *The Times*, the supporters of the Bill before the House would meet with gratitude from their constituents. The term " jade " displeased members on both sides of the House. Sir Charles Wetherell, the Tory Recorder of Bristol, responsible in the view of *The Times* for the misuse of the army against the " mob," taunted the Reformers with quotations from *The Times*. Peel's speech, delivered on Thursday, March 22, in urging members to consider and reconsider the consequences of passing such a Bill, adduced the example of French conditions as revealed in the Paris correspondence of the paper. He quoted a message from *The Times* of March 2, and reminded the House of Commons that his extract was taken " from the columns of the great, principal, and powerful advocate of Reform—*The Times* newspaper."

There is no room for any to doubt the " principal " position occupied by *The Times* at the end of the Reform agitation ; or to doubt that this position was achieved by the energy, ability and consistency with which it had urged Reform and the speed and accuracy with which it had reported the proceedings in the country.

The caricatures of the period[1] amply prove that *The Times* enjoyed a dominating position in the Press and that its influence was recognized to be of vital importance upon opinion. Its value to the Reform cause was, as Peel recognized, unique. It brought energy and sagacity to the direction of opinion, it sustained and encouraged every effort to correct abuse. For the first time the country possessed a supremely competent, independent political guide and an up-to-date record of what the believers in the political rights of the people were doing. *The Times*, by restraining violence

[1] See for instance *McLean's Monthly Sheet*, and *The Caricatures of H. B.*, 1831-3.

and organizing disciplined action through the political unions, spurred on the Reform. The aim was the " correcting of abuses existing and the attainment of a future beneficial administration of our national interests and resources through the establishment of a control in the people over the management of their own affairs." Of this aim *The Times* was, in the opinion of the Opposition statesman, the " great, principal and powerful advocate."

XVII

"WAR WITH *THE TIMES*"

THE London daily Press emerged with increased prestige from
the struggle over the Reform Bill. But genuine respect from
statesmen had yet to come. It might be recognized in those
high quarters that the newspaper had given proof of increased
influence upon electors, but the unsatisfactory consequence was
a new resolve to " manage the Press." The obedient were given
preference in the distribution of news. Even papers generally
favourable but not officially trusted as amenable suffered discrimination from the Treasury as late as 1836. The annals of the
Press from Reform until the return of Peel in 1841 are full of
incidents of various kinds discreditable to Parliament and the
Administration.

Freed by its circulation from enforced allegiance, *The Times* was
the only paper which could afford to defy the encroachments of
statesmen. The *Morning Chronicle* had formerly been free of close
party attachments and then, after 1832, had been giving support
to the Whig cause. Few could have imagined that it was to
become a thorn in the side of *The Times*, and from 1834 a powerful
rival—all with Whig money and political support. The story of
the change makes a long and complicated chapter in the dual
history of Printing House Square and of the competition for
public influence.

The Grey Government had alienated many non-political
elements in the country. The Reform Bill had been followed by
an important Factory Act and the great Act for the Abolition of
Slavery. In the name of an impatient country, with all its expectations aroused, the Government were then pressed to undertake
reconstruction at home. But it was urgent that something should
be done about Ireland, and the Cabinet was ground to pieces by
the question of Irish Tithe and Irish Coercion. The country, too,
was sharply divided. On the one hand were those who, in their

anxiety for the unity of the Kingdom, were bent on maintaining the privileges of a definitely loyal ecclesiastical establishment; and on the other hand were the advocates of the claims of a clear majority in Ireland, prepared therefore to grant relief, and looking for freely given friendship in place of sullen rebelliousness. Hobhouse in his " Recollections " describes the first breach in the Cabinet, which was threatened as early as the end of 1832 :

I had a note from Lord Durham asking me to see him on important business. I went and he showed me a correspondence respecting the proposed Irish Measure ; [Edward] Stanley's[1] complaint in print, and his remarks thereon. Stanley stated that if there had been objection to his Measure he ought to have been told so before, and altogether took a very high tone indeed.

Durham consulted Hobhouse on the propriety of resigning, and was advised that such a step was unnecessary, whereupon, still undecided, he begged his colleague to see the Editor of *The Times*. Hobhouse records :

I found Tom Barnes in bed at half past one, the shutters closed, and there talked to him " in cloudy tabernacle shrined." The result was : he thought nobody knew Lord Durham's merits ; and nobody would think about him if he went out ; that except Lord Grey and Lord Brougham no one had such influence as to interest the public and that the Protestant feeling in England was so strong as to make it very doubtful whether the Government would be supported at home in upholding Catholicism in Ireland. It was time for Lord Durham to go out when the Bill came in. (November 21, 1832.)

Hobhouse appends the reflection : " How Tom Barnes must laugh in his sleeve at a Cabinet question being referred to the editor of a newspaper ! Nevertheless I believe there was no better course to take in order to keep my friend straight." On the following day he reported his conversation to Durham. He " was rather piqued at the result of my interview with Tom Barnes but agreed that it would be better for him to acquiesce in the decision of the Cabinet." But Durham's position in the Cabinet was not destined to survive the following spring. His health, like his temper, was always frail ; and, for the time, it took a serious turn for the worse. On March 12, 1833, he wrote a letter of resignation to Lord Grey which was announced in *The Times* of March 14, with the comment that " the country loses one of the

---

1 Stanley was Chief Secretary for Ireland.

soundest and most decisive understandings ever employed in public affairs "—an estimate Barnes revised within the five following years, which included the Canadian troubles.

In May, 1833, the Cabinet lost further prestige, the Government being beaten on a proposal to tax malt. Lord Grey himself proposed to go, but in fact the only resignation came from Hobhouse. This caused consternation, for he resigned not only his Secretaryship for Ireland but his seat in Parliament, and, standing for Westminster, was defeated. In a private letter to Hobhouse, Barnes wrote : " Though I admire the straightforward and manly step which you have taken, yet I regret that Ministers will lose one of their most efficient functionaries and Parliament one of its most upright and eloquent members." More serious than the technical defeat of the Government was the moral drawn by the people, who, with no confidence in those holding power, began, as Greville writes, " to turn their eyes to those who are more capable." Again and again *The Times* complained of the inefficiency of the Cabinet at a time when constructive measures were plainly required by circumstances and by the country ; and Barnes, in the search for men to put those measures through, must often have pondered in his mind the possibility of turning the Tories to useful account.

He would have found cooperation awkward at that time. The Tory attitude to *The Times* at this period is revealed by Tom Moore, who went out to John Walter's place, Bear Wood, on November 16, 1833.

I travelled [writes Moore in his *Journal*] in the Reading Coach leaving at 12 with two inveterate Tories as my companions. One of them said the object of the Ministry was to lay England at the feet of France ; they received their instructions from Paris, or, " perhaps from Rome." The fellows at Brooks's Club and Holland House settled everything. But *The Times* newspaper was the great object of his abhorrence. " If there is one corner in Hell," exclaimed this wiseacre, " hotter than another, it is reserved for the Editor of *The Times*." He stated that it was well known *The Times* people received money from the French Government for their labours, and were under the special direction of Talleyrand. I took but little share in the conversation, being employed, as far as amusement would let me, in reading the *Quarterly Review*. Within a few miles of Reading the coach stopped and the coachman, opening the door, asked if there was a Mr. Moore inside as a gentleman wanted him. Guessing what this meant I got out and found Barnes by the roadside waiting for me, not in the corner of Hell, but in a Reading post-chaise which he had brought to take me the short way to Walter's. I left my friends in their ignorance as to who I was and proceeded with the condemned Editor to Walter's.

Old-fashioned Church-and-King folk, who hated to think of the sovereignty of the people, would have shared the feelings of the Tory wiseacre. He spoke, indeed, only as Tory and Anglican newspapers had written for years.

The year 1834 was crucial in politics and in journalism, and the relations of *The Times* to both were to undergo a vital change. The incompetence of the Government, obvious during the second half of 1833, became notorious in the spring of 1834. On April 21 observers of all parties were disquieted by the great procession of trade unions in London. The Government, in a panic, filled London with troops, artillery and police, but the 25,000 or more processionists marched without noise or tumult. At a moment when the English and Scots were in danger of losing their faith in the representative Parliament they had fought to secure two years earlier, and the Irish in danger of rebellion against continued delay in the question of tithe, the Government brought in a new Poor Law Bill. Legislation of this kind, even were it proceeding from an unembarrassed Government, could only be highly contentious and difficult.

Yet, on May 27, 1834, the Ministry was further weakened by the secession of Stanley, Graham and the Duke of Richmond over the appropriation of surplus Irish tithes to non-ecclesiastical uses. Moreover, for some time Barnes had felt uneasy about the Chancellor. Like all men, he had learnt that Brougham did not enjoy for nothing the nickname of " Wicked Shifts." In the spring and summer of 1834 Brougham's vagaries went to the verge of dishonesty ; and his egoism and quarrelsomeness were increasing. Nevertheless, *The Times* had championed Brougham for so long that the bond was not to be broken in these, of all circumstances, by mere personal antipathy between him and Cabinet colleagues. It was of the first importance to organize a strong Government. *The Times*, fearing that the Cabinet might be merely botched instead of reconstructed, gave a hint to the Lord Chancellor :

Lord Brougham would be the first to reprobate a peddling or manoeuvring process in the regeneration of the existing Ministry, and that in such case, but in such case only, he would feel compelled to withdraw himself from the side of Lord Grey. Were the noble and

MACKEREL!

A day or two before the announcement in the *Gazette* of the elevation to the peerage of Sir Thomas Denman, Lord Chief Justice of the Court of King's Bench, *The Times*, aware of rumours, wrote: "A more honest, upright, honourable man than Sir Thomas Denman does not exist; but God knows there are plenty of Law-Lords. Even the dignity of the profession requires that law peerages should not be as cheap as stinking mackerel." The drawing shows Barnes, Denman, Grey and Brougham. (From H.B.'s Sketches, April 8, 1834.)

learned Lord himself to advise or undertake the formation of a Ministry, there cannot be a shadow of doubt that it would be one at which the cordial and enlightened friends of constitutional reform would have no just cause to murmur.

But to everybody's surprise, and Barnes's in particular, no decisive move was made. The new appointments were not such as would restore confidence. The paper dealt in some detail with the situation on May 31, 1834 :

Our fear was, and we call to witness our leading articles for three or four days past, that the paddings, linings, waddlings, the staytape and buckram, the scrapings and sweepings of the ministerial shop would be resorted to, and strong and serviceable materials excluded— that old clothes would be turned—old holes darned—rags new dyed— and ancient calf-skin covers fresh gilt and lettered—and all this nick- named a reformed or amended Cabinet, by which not even the infant pupils of our Sunday-schools would be imposed upon. . . . Why was a man of such decided ability and such manly and open bearing left out as Lord Durham, for example, to make room for one like Lord Auckland ? Lord Durham in his own person, and by his mere acceptance of the seals of Colonial or (we wish it might have been so) Foreign Secretary—nay, or any other office of the Government— would have been received with open arms by the country as a *pledge* of the liberal and straightforward measures which could not fail to be pursued. Lord Durham would have brought with him as allies to the Government the whole weight of the numerous intelligent and well- organised, and we are now afraid alienated and embittered, Dissenting body. . . . This miserable " lath-and-plaster Cabinet."

Manifestly the Editor had lost all patience with the Government, and one of its most important Bills—the New Poor Law— antagonized his deepest feelings. Moreover, he was compelled to realize that Brougham had now become a grave danger to public life, and incidentally to the Press.

When it came to Barnes's ears that Durham's exclusion was due to Brougham he chose publicly to regard the fact as " an atrocious and incredible calumny." Consulting with Brougham and Le Marchant, however, he found Lansdowne and Palmerston preferred to Durham and Abercromby. In a letter to Le Marchant written on June 3, 1834, Barnes complained with great heat that when they had discussed the prospects of a " more liberal and decided course being pursued and when the names of

u

Lord Durham, Abercromby and others were mentioned you never hinted the possibility of dislike to any of them " ; and he asked :

How could I imagine that I was not serving the cause of your friend [Brougham] by urging the appointment of such men ? When you talked of the Chancellor standing down rather than a Liberal Government should not be formed, how could I suspect that in the formation of the Cabinet the Chancellor would yield to his enemy, Lord Lansdowne, the appointment of two members and the exclusion of others ? You never gave me a hint about Lord Durham's temper and the insuperable dislike of other Ministers to such a colleague : and yet as I frankly told you I was in communication with Lord Durham, I surely ought to have had some intimation of the sentiments of the Chancellor and his friends.[1]

Further, Barnes proceeded, " whatever your intentions were, you had given me such strong impressions of the certainty of some bold, decided course being adopted, that my astonishment even surpassed my vexation when you announced to me the result of the negotiations : and I confess that the attempt to evade the real merits of a great question by such a course as that adopted by Ministers last night filled me with indignation."

Replying to Le Marchant's complaint of the critical tone of leading articles, Barnes said :

Do not imagine that we turn against the Ministers in any spirit of wanton levity—for myself, at least, I can say that I have never experienced more painful sensations in my life than I have during the last week when I have found myself compelled by a sense of duty to the paper to attack those whom I have always wished to serve.

I must however be allowed to say that Ministers have little personal grounds of complaint. Thro' their well-known organs the *Chronicle* & the *Globe* they began the attack upon us in the most unqualified personal abuse—for the charge four times uttered in those Papers of " base and wilful misrepresentations " I, for one, consider as infamous a charge as if I had been accused of picking pockets. Even in the article to which you refer—in the *Globe* last night—your champion has been instructed to pour out against us a similar charge of personal motives.

Let the Ministers deal frankly : let them not try to keep us in a good humour by civil communications while at the same time they are

[1] Chobham Papers ; Barnes to Le Marchant, June 3, 1834.

employing agents, or are themselves taking the trouble, to abuse us through some of their public organs. Of their private abuse (tho' I am pretty sure to hear of it) I say nothing : but the other mode of proceeding is a gross insult.

In Barnes's opinion *The Times* was being used badly because it was independent. Ministers were genuinely afraid of criticism. They handed out pieces of information to his paper when they were already well known elsewhere, and when they were not known elsewhere they were only of " trumpery importance." In all the circumstances Barnes believed that Ministers were less interested in carrying measures beneficial to the country than in maintaining themselves and their friends in office. To his greater regret Brougham was behaving more and more oddly. After affecting to put forth every endeavour to save the Government—after going the extraordinary length of usurping the Prime Minister's functions by himself personally acquainting the King with the state of affairs and assuring him of his own determination to see that the Government was maintained—Brougham was now playing fast and loose with everybody, with his own chief and colleagues in the Cabinet, and with *The Times*. Barnes concluded a long expostulation to Le Marchant by saying :

I have no personal complaint to prefer against you. I feel and appreciate the delicacy of your position and have admired the tact with which you have discharged your sometimes very embarrassing functions. But I must say that I do not think I have always been treated by your *friend* with that frankness to which his long knowledge of my character ought to have ensured me. I have been ready always to comply with every request and even anticipate his requests : but it is not on that account—it is because *he* must know that I am incapable of betraying or injuring him, that I have been mortified by partial explanations and half confidences when I ought to have been altogether and unreservedly trusted.

The cleavage was rapidly enlarged by the Chancellor's own actions. He was compromised by his part in a correspondence highly improper in itself and treacherous to the Prime Minister, Lord Grey. On June 11, 1834, the Duke of Wellington's elder brother, the Marquess Wellesley, sent to the Cabinet his final dispatch as Lord Lieutenant of Ireland. It affirmed that none of the extraordinary powers conferred by the Coercion Bill could be safely omitted. Yet Littleton, who had succeeded Hobhouse as Irish Secretary, shared with Brougham a determination that concessions should be made ; and he was not only in communication with O'Connell, but together with Brougham was urging Wellesley to give up his demand. Not a word was said to the Prime Minister of these manoeuvres.[1]

The open breach between *The Times* and Brougham had still to come. Up to the present no outward sign had been given of the increasing tension between them. When the editorial tone left no shadow of doubt that there had been a decisive rupture between the two, it seemed to many statesmen and politicians, to the journalists and to the general public of that day, a startling and unaccountable revolution.

Before June 19, 1834, Brougham the man, as well as Brougham the statesman, was afforded, at the very least, the benefit of every doubt ; in return for what he had already accomplished *The Times* was willing to forgive or to gloze over vagaries and eccentricities. With dramatic suddenness the same paper, under the same editor, attacked the same man equally as man and statesman. That was the contemporary view.

It must be repeated that throughout his editorship, and particularly after the Reform Bill, Barnes's principle was to support measures, not men. Yet he had not merely affection, but deep affection, for Brougham as a man and as a genius, energetic as none else in progressive legislation. Brougham and Barnes were alike in their hatred of caste. But though Barnes's whole political ideology and hereditary instincts were middle-class and anti-aristocratic, he respected the owners of hereditary titles. Similarly, he could hate landlordism without hating property ; and he could hate the new race of scientific experts without including Brougham among them. He was determined to work for amelioration in the conditions of the working-class ; but, unlike the Radicals, whose policy he was wrongly accused of forwarding, he was not prepared to see Parliament superseded by national unions of operatives. All things considered, he believed that Brougham, with his energy wisely guided, was a most valuable asset to the country. Thus Brougham, as leader of the attack on the privileged classes, received the support of *The Times*, with which, in Barnes's editorship, his relations were so intimate that

[1] When Grey and Althorp resigned on July 8, 1834, *The Times* found " that the proximate cause of this catastrophe was the conduct of Mr. Littleton in communicating confidentially with Mr. O'Connell, wholly unauthorized, as it turns out, by Lord Grey, and disapproved by the noble Earl as soon as the fact was made known to him ; unauthorized likewise by Lord Althorp in the extent to which Mr. Littleton had carried his unfortunate frankness towards the member for Dublin."

he was implicitly believed in certain quarters when he professed to do what he liked with the paper. Barnes breakfasted with him continually, and until the very day of the rupture was in the society of Le Marchant, the Lord Chancellor's principal private secretary. Henry Brougham, whatever his faults, was a man to get things done. Such was the old judgment.

The confusion over Irish Coercion was succeeded by what appeared to Barnes to be the inhuman provisions of a new Poor Law introduced by Althorp in the Commons and by Brougham in the Lords. It was destined, said Barnes, to " sow seeds of perpetual enmity between the Poor and the Rich." The persons chiefly responsible for the scheme were not likely to be agreeable in his eyes. There was Blomfield, Bishop of London, a Trinity man of Barnes's year, whom he greatly disliked, and there were Nassau Senior and Edwin Chadwick, both Benthamites, lovers of statistics, professors of the new-fangled science of " political economy," heartless theorists—so Barnes thought. Senior returned Barnes's dislike, and attacked *The Times* in the *Globe* and the *Chronicle*. Brougham seemed to be getting hopelessly out of touch with the principles of individual liberty, as Barnes understood them, and out of touch with real life and its virtues, its " manliness," to use the favourite editorial word. The Poor Law Commission, at Brougham's suggestion, was organized into a Central Board with a number of itinerant and well-paid " Commissioners " to supersede the authority of the resident magistrates, who knew to some extent the individuals they were relieving. *The Times* heartily disliked these Commissioners on the suspicion that they must be somebody's relations ; it saw the job-seekers being given unlimited powers to pauperize, and the abolition of outdoor relief except to disabled persons it considered most odious. But it was a foregone conclusion that the Bill would pass, for it had the support of Wellington on the Right and of Grote and Hume on the Left. A typically Whiggish measure, it was the sort, so Barnes told Le Marchant, for which the Government showed " no want of courage when the Tories stand forward to support them." *The Times* was against it ; and *The Times* believed the country was against it.

Yet, whatever the country thought, the opposition of *The Times* was largely due to Barnes's lifelong compassion for the poor and his distrust of a centralized scientific bureaucracy ; with Tories and Whigs in association, Barnes realized that he would do well for the poor if he could even mitigate some of the more objectionable features. Little or no support could be relied on. Peel and Wellington were on the side of Brougham. But for once Cobbett fought on the same side as Barnes. Seven years later John Walter won Nottingham from the Liberals on his anti-Poor Law record, for this Whig Bill played into the hands of Conservatives and Chartists, so grievous was the resulting distress in the country. Early in 1837 a commission was appointed to inquire into the alleged hardships created by the New Poor Law, and in 1838 Disraeli supported a Radical motion for repeal. The attitude of *The Times* was so far vindicated ; and before then the paper had been able to take some credit for such improvements in the detail of the Bill as the curtailing of the Commissioners' powers.

Brougham, Althorp, Senior, and others responsible for the Poor Law Bill were extremely anxious for the support of *The Times* ; they knew that the volume of opposition would be immense. Harriet Martineau (not invariably a trustworthy authority) relates in her Autobiography that " one of the editors " sent " a message declaratory of interested support " to " some of the managers " of the measure. She proceeds :

How the other newspapers would go there was no saying, because the reform was not a party measure : but with *The Times* on our side we felt pretty safe. . . . It was no small vexation to me, on opening *The Times* at breakfast on the 18th, to find a vehement and total condemnation of the New Poor Law. Everybody in London was asking how it happened. I do not know, except in so far as I was told by some people who knew more of the management of the paper than the world in general. Their account was that the intention had really been up to the preceding day to support the measure ; but that such reports arrived of the hostility of the country-justices—a most important class of customer—that a meeting of the proprietors was held in the evening when the question of supporting or opposing the measure was put to the vote. The policy of humouring the country-justices was carried by the vote—So went the story.

It is a story needing examination and correction. The opposition of *The Times* was decidedly gradual in development. It was never Barnes's practice totally to condemn in one leader any new measure. A letter from him to Brougham's secretary proves that he was not supplied with the promised print of the measure as introduced into the Commons by the Chancellor of the Exchequer :

I waited till a late hour for the summary of Lord Althorp's measure which Mr. Drummond was to send : it has not come. The report furnished by our reporters was not finished until so late an hour that I have not time to read it tonight, but in any discussion tomorrow you may be assured that the utmost temper and moderation shall be employed. In fact our principal objection is to one branch of the measure—a very important branch certainly—the refusal of relief except in workhouses : a system in my opinion enormously expensive, degrading to the honest pauper and ruinous to fathers of families who will not any more receive that temporary relief which might set them on their feet again without being torn from their wives and children who will all be pauperised and imprisoned under the new system because the parent requires 20 or 30 shillings to set his loom or stocking frame a-going.

Besides what is the work which is to be performed in workhouses ? I see none which will not either interfere with the regular operations of independent trader and manufacturers, or which will not by being utterly useless degrade the workhouse labourer into a mere tread mill walker.

The first article after the introduction of the Bill, in the issue of April 19, was critical but not wholly unfriendly ; and on the publication of the complete text there followed a hostile but moderately worded comment. On receiving expostulations Barnes wrote to Le Marchant :

I have treated the subject as gently as I could consistently with the opinion which I cannot help entertaining. Having never myself been impressed with the idea of that enormous power of the *Times* to which you refer I never for a moment supposed that we could prevent a measure from being carried which Parliament had thro a thousand channels been prepared to support. Besides the present state of the Poor Laws is such a flagrant nuisance that, as in the case of a frightful epidemic, every body eagerly seizes the first remedy offered whether by a quack or a man of sense and science.

The same was the case at the time of the Irish Coercion Bill. People were frightened out of their wits and would have consented to any measure however monstrous which was presented as a cure for an alarming evil. In such cases all that the Press can do is to calmly state its own judgment and let the event decide. In the Irish case, we were clearly right. You never will be able to repeal that cursed bill, or if you do, the riots will begin again with ten-fold exasperation. The Poor Law Bill you will I suppose carry : but you will never execute it.

What necessity was there for encumbering the bill with that odious scheme of the workhouses : A scheme which will begin by degrading the honest pauper into a convict, and end, after a general degradation of the humbler classes, in converting, as in Amsterdam, half the population of your towns into tenants of the poor-house.

Surely it was sufficient to alter the law of settlement of bastardy and to annihilate the practice of the allowance system without clogging the measure with a provision which is founded on the monstrous assumption that a man must stand in need of *all* assistance or none : in other words that there is no such thing as temporary distress which temporary aid may relieve, but that the mere fact of wanting 30 or 40 shillings to pay an apothecary's bill after or during a fit of illness shall at once be taken as a sufficient cause for tearing the applicant from his family or dragging his family with him and consigning them all to irremediable ruin. There are thousands of cases in London and in other great towns where a gift of even 10 or 20 shillings will set the casual and honest pauper on his legs again : and yet these precious Commissioners would instead of giving this scanty but beneficial aid consign the applicant to unmitigated and perpetual pauperism : for who ever became an independent labourer who had once been immured in a workhouse ?

I do not think that I have exchanged a score of words at any one time with [John] Walter on the subject, tho' I know he feels a very natural surprise that the authority of his neighbour Russell should be so frequently and emphatically quoted, knowing as he does that Russell lives in a parish of an extent of about 5 or 600 acres and in which the average number of paupers has not exceeded a dozen. Certainly such a man, however shrewd and able, is not a very competent judge of the general condition and management of the Poor.

I shall be very happy to receive the statement which you promise but will be obliged to you to send it before 12 on Sunday, as I may have to go out of town that day in which case I should return rather late.

Pray make no excuse for your long letters.

I assure you very sincerely that I am greatly obliged to you for the trouble you take in detailing facts and opinions. You cannot do me a greater kindness than in pointing out any errors which you perceive in my statements or comments. Unless I very much deceive myself, my chief object is truth and one of the best modes of avoiding error is to listen to the suggestions of able and honest friends.

The objections of *The Times* gradually increased in number and in strength ; the subsequent offensive was spread over many weeks, and the campaign grew bitter as the Bill progressed through both Houses. Criticism was relentless in leading articles and letters. By April 30 the powers of the Commissioners were denounced as being inconsistent with the spirit of the British Constitution and the framework of the new system condemned as " an invention " ; it " leaps forth *de novo* like Pallas out of the head of Jupiter, complete and perfect, from the plotting pericrania of Mr. Senior and other political economists." Hence it followed that not only Althorp and Brougham, but a number of other influential persons joined in opposition to *The Times*. Nothing could be more natural than the determination of Althorp, the responsible Minister, to retaliate against *The Times* for its opposition to the Poor Law Bill and the personalities with which it was fighting the measure, and, as far as he could, to close the sources of information against it. After the decisive point was reached, the style was not only vehement but often vitriolic. Althorp was the victim upon whom the attack was first concentrated ; Brougham's turn came later. Barnes, knowing Althorp personally, struck at weak points like a tiresome " habit of ' aggravating his voice ' to so gentle a pitch that none could follow him " in his addresses to the House. Althorp was the soul of honour and a most popular leader of the House, but he possessed little ability to master the details of an intricate measure. On the occasion of his replying in the debate on a clause in the Bill to which *The Times* attributed great importance Althorp replied at length. " But, as usual," he spoke " in a voice not audible in the gallery. One sentence of his speech, and one only,—we are very grateful to the noble Lord for that,—relieved his pantomime, and the dumb show was broken by the sound of his Lordship's voice proclaiming that ' it was not the intention to give the Commissioners powers either to make new, or to alter existing laws ' " ; and the leading article proceeded to state that such was his Lordship's mind that he did not understand his own Bill.[1] The contempt for Althorp's professional unskilfulness which *The Times* constantly exhibited from the beginning of May grew into daily persecution during June.

A leading article on June 9, 1834, asked a question—it appeared afterwards, a dramatic question—on workhouses :

Now we put it to any rational being,—we put it even to Lord Althorp,—whether we have not made good our proposition, and whether it is not quite true that the Central Board may establish work-

[1] May 28, 1834.

houses throughout England and Wales *without the consent of the ratepayers* ?

It was a new experience for a Chancellor of the Exchequer, and Leader of the House, to be so addressed in a newspaper. The audience of *The Times* comprised the voters whom Althorp and Brougham would have to reckon with at elections, it might be, in the immediate future. A politician's faults need not come to the knowledge of any serious proportion of his constituency if only recorded in the Parliamentary reports, even when published in the small type of the Parliamentary report of *The Times* ; but when that journal, with its unparalleled circulation, castigated a politician's conduct in a leading article, the most pungent extracts from which were circulated from mouth to mouth wherever the perpetrator possessed reputation, it was different. The leading articles were read aloud from borrowed copies of the paper ; they were re-read in the news-rooms of working men's clubs ; they were reprinted in many country newspapers and summarized in the monthly magazines. Lord Althorp's attention would be drawn by officious persons to many of these printed notices.

The creation by *The Times* of a hostile public opinion, informed as to the details of a politician's speaking and teaching and determined to vote against him at the next election, could not fail vastly to increase that jealousy between Parliament and Press which had existed ever since journals first struggled to report debates and to publish proceedings—as *The Times* did—in the interest, not of politicians or of parties, but of readers of all classes, master and artisan, rich and poor ; those who could not read had the paper read to them. The monopoly of Parliament in information of its proceedings failed ; it was inevitable that the privileges which were lost by the House as a whole should be fought for by individual members. With the knowledge that the power of Printing House Square was within measurable distance of achieving a decisive influence over the opinion of the country, politicians were in search of a countervailing means. Moreover, the political circumstances of the time made acutely desirable some attempt to challenge the power over public opinion which the ability of Barnes and the superiority of its printing facilities had conferred upon the paper.

To compete with *The Times*, to wrest from it the virtual control over the middle classes which it enjoyed, was an ambition which no

Whig would have entertained so long as his party was benefiting from its freely given support. The opposition to the paper in the years before 1834 came from the Tory and from the Radical quarter. In June, 1834, however, the Editor's warnings and threatenings, coupled with the personal nature of his attacks, roused the determination of the more active Whigs to attempt an enterprise of which Tories and Radicals had been incapable, the humiliation of *The Times*.

In the summer of 1834, disillusioned in Brougham as a progressive Minister and angry at the direction taken by the Cabinet, Barnes had employed a vehemence which was calculated, if not designed, to exasperate a Minister like Lord Althorp (" a damned conceited man " in the opinion of Creevey) into indiscretion. In the event the indiscretion involved Brougham ; and although not of its nature public, the story made its way round the clubs pretty rapidly. Althorp, smarting under references to himself which he had just read in the leading article of *The Times*, made up his mind to go for the paper. It seemed necessary for their very political existence that Ministers should hit back. Hence, for reasons of self-preservation, Althorp determined to talk over a certain plan with the Chancellor. He wrote to Brougham :

My dear Brougham,

As I am not quite right today, I shall not come down to the House. I wish therefore you would give me a call. Believe me, my dear Brougham, etc.

ALTHORP.

The Lord Chancellor, much pressed by his affairs, sent back a note asking if the matter were urgent. Althorp replied by the same messenger. The Lord Chancellor was sitting in the Court of Chancery when Althorp's second note arrived. He read it, tore it up and threw the pieces into his waste-paper basket ; finishing his sitting, he left the Court. Upon his departure the fragments were rescued and assembled on a sheet of paper, which was folded and directed " To the Editor of *The Times*, Printing House Square, Blackfriars," marked " Immediate." It was delivered to the Editor, who read the following message pencilled on the margin of the sheet :

Picked up by a Friend and sent thinking it may be of service as a private principle of action.

Turning to the message, Barnes read in Althorp's handwriting these words :

Private

My dear Brougham,

The subject I want to talk to you about is the State of the Press, & whether we should declare open war with the *Times* or attempt to make peace.

Yours most truly,
ALTHORP.

Downing Street,
June 11.

Within two hours Le Marchant received the following letter from the Editor :

Show this to the Lord Chancellor.

June 11th, 1834.

My dear Sir,

I told you I would always treat you frankly : and in that spirit I think it right to say that I am aware of Lord Althorp's application to the Chancellor for his opinion whether " the Govt. should declare open war with the *Times* or attempt to make peace."   What does the Gaby mean ?

Yours ever,
T. BARNES.

Le Marchant's acknowledgment is lost, but its nature appears from the long and important letter to him from Barnes on June 13 :

June 13, 1834, 49 Nelson Square.

My dear Sir :

I have read your letter again with attention, & will answer it with the same frankness with which it is written.

In the first place I find it difficult to understand what is meant by our " entering into the same engagements with you which we contracted with the Duke of Wellington." We never had any engagements with the Duke's Administration which precluded us from uttering our sentiments in the most decided manner on all topics on which we differed from it : as for instance on the Greek question, the Belgian question, the Civil list & lastly Reform in Parliament.

If you mean merely to stipulate that there should be no *personal* attacks, there can be no objection to such a stipulation in principle :

300

still there may be occasions where the want of energy or striking deficiency of a particular Minister on some important subject may make an individual allusion necessary. Suggestions of this sort have, as you know, been sometimes recommended by one Department towards another. In the case of Lord Grey, tho' we are not under the most distant obligation to that nobleman (who I had been led to think always has disclaimed in a very haughty manner any communication with the Press) yet he has on various & repeated occasions been spoken of by us in the highest & warmest terms of panegyric : (you yourself lately mentioned an instance of his great pleasure on this account) & it was only within these few days when he seemed to cling to office at the risk (as we thought) of forfeiting his character for high-mindedness and straight-forward bearing, that our surprise, mixed with indignation found vent in *language* probably too severe but in *sentiments* I am sure perfectly just. I don't know what you allude to in your complaint of a misreported passage in Lord Grey's speech : our comment referred not to any particular speech but generally to his conduct since the breaking up of the Cabinet.

As you yourself allow that the Cabinet might have been better formed, I need say nothing on that point except to express my astonishment at the very strong language of depreciation which you now use respecting Lord Durham whom, on all former occasions in all the communications which I have had with you or Mr. Ellice, I had considered as the man whom all the more liberal part of the Cabinet were anxious to have as a colleague. I care nothing about Lord Durham personally beyond that regard which his personal kindness entitles him to, & should probably never have thought of him in connection with the Administration, had I not repeatedly heard from Mr. Ellice professions of the greatest admiration and esteem for him.

I have already pointed out to you more than once the gross personal attacks in the *Globe* sanctioned by Lord Palmerston and written indeed by Sir G. Shea[1] under his direction. They were, as I proved to your satisfaction at the time, infamous calumnies.

After all, our support is in a great measure indeed I may say altogether a matter depending on yourselves.

If you bring forward beneficial measures and urge them on with the same persevering firmness with which you passed such unpopular measures as the Coercion Bill last Session and the Poor Bill now, we *must* support you.

If you postpone all your good measures, or mutilate them to please your enemies, or abandon them rather than your offices, then as

[1] Secretary to Palmerston.

independent men we cannot be expected to be wholly silent or even to abstain from occasional expressions of, at least, regret.

Yours sincerely,

T. BARNES.

P.S.   Since this was written I have recd. your note of this morning, which certainly is satisfactory as regards the feelings ascribed to Lord Grey & as to the general statement of the disposition of your friends towards us : but I must be allowed to say that you should be a little more explicit as to those measures which Govt. intends to introduce or carry in furtherance of those principles which they have always professed and on which we have founded such support as we have hitherto afforded.

I repeat that I give up the point as to the general impropriety of *personal* attacks.

I ought to mention that your friends should be cautious about their letters.   Fragments are picked up by a set of hangers on of the Press. Luckily they have fallen into safe hands : but they might have been taken to some of the slanderous Sunday Papers.

Once more yours,

T. B.

I rec'd the mem. about Ferguson.
D. Le Marchant, Esq.

None can doubt the wisdom of Barnes's advice or his magnanimity in the matter of Althorp's communication. He said nothing about the letter. Brougham did. Greville heard of it and entered an account in his diary. The affair was bruited abroad, for the Radical Thomas Wakley, under the signature "Veritas," sent a communication on June 19 to *The Times*, which, under the heading "Answers to Correspondents," acknowledged receipt thus : " We are obliged to ' Veritas ' for his information. We have in our possession the originals of the two letters to which he refers." On June 27 the same Wakley, being candidate for the Finsbury constituency, delivered a nomination speech, which was condensed in *The Times* but fully reported in the *Morning Chronicle*. The candidate was the medical reformer who founded the *Lancet*, a partisan of Cobbett, something of a fanatic, and hence radical enough to be outside the favour of *The Times*. Wakley's speech comprised an attack on the Government's relations with the Press and he quoted the letters. In the second letter the words " open war with the *Times* " were ingeniously misprinted in the *Morning Chronicle* as " open war with the

June 11. 1834

My dear Sir, I told
you I would always
treat you frankly;
& in that spirit I
think it right to
say that I am aware
of Lord Althorp's
application to
the Chancellor for
his opinion whether
"the fort should
declare open war
with the Times or
attempt to make
peace". What does
the Galaxy mean?

Yours ever
J. Marshall Esq.   W. Adam

Tories." The report in *The Times* included Wakley's statement that he had sent the copies, under the signature of " Veritas," but the texts were not reproduced. A note was added : " Supposing Mr. Wakley's story to be true, we do not see what it has to do with him or the Finsbury election, or the contest at that election." The *Morning Chronicle* considered the whole matter " passing strange " and demanded " How came the originals of Lord Althorp's letters to Lord Brougham into the possession of *The Times* ? " Brougham's efforts to make an example by dismissing the offender came to naught because the offender could not be found. The only clue was in Barnes's hand : the pencil note on the margin of the sheet to which the pieces were affixed. The handwriting, " Picked up by a Friend," is that of an educated man, but is not now identifiable.

Although by no means so momentous as open hostilities by a Government, the declaration of " War with *The Times* " by even a small group of Ministers was a serious thing. When the Ministers were the Lord Chancellor and the Leader of the House of Commons, the resulting discrimination against the offending journal could never have been less than vexatious. No doubt the idea of direct competition, by the starting of a rival morning journal, did not at first occur to Althorp. The opportunity was made by the group of politicians and economists with whom he and Brougham were associated in the Poor Law measure. The two Ministers must indeed have congratulated themselves on the opportunity of acquiring a dominating interest in the *Morning Chronicle*. Joseph Parkes, the Birmingham solicitor who had advocated armed rebellion if the Reform Bill was rejected, was reported to have carried through the negotiations for the transfer of the moribund *Chronicle*. The enmity of Brougham and Althorp and the Whig-Radical economists cost *The Times* enormous sums, and Barnes and his successor Delane, unremitting effort for nearly twenty years.

The future of *The Times* seemed secure and prosperous enough in the spring of 1834. In circulation, revenue, and influence upon opinion the paper was not only unequalled but unapproached. It was ubiquitous, and for a decade had been much more than the " lungs of the British Metropolis " of Hazlitt's description.

The first house we set our feet in [wrote an inimical correspondent of *Tait's Magazine*], on arriving in Mexico in 1825—a time of war, trouble and yellow fever, and before speculators and travellers had ventured their lives and fortunes to work mines, or write a book—there sat the Vice-Consul's clerk, blowing swift clouds of smoke from a much excited cigar, behind a copy of the incorrigible, omni-present *Times* newspaper.

The power and prestige of *The Times* in June, 1834, when " War with *The Times* " was proposed by the Chancellor of the Exchequer to the Lord Chancellor of England, were, at the most modest estimate, immense. Barnes could deny that he shared Le Marchant's idea of " that enormous power of *The Times*," but the public did share it. In truth there had never been anything in journalism like *The Times* at this period. The attempt to set up a rival involved, therefore, a very serious expense. Indeed, the successful management of a paper of the size and importance of *The Times* was so considerable as to exceed the resources of booksellers, printers, papermakers and others in the typographical trades among whom newspaper proprietors had, in the past, taken their origin. The Stamp Tax, excessive as it was, operated in accordance with its original intention to the restraint of all newspaper enterprise, old-established or new. With all the money found, a new paper could not for years hope to succeed in taking the position of *The Times* with the singular position which it owed to dominating circulation and unique news service. Before June, 1834, political interests had on several occasions been desperately embarrassed by doubt as to the line which *The Times* would take. This element of incalculability, this refusal to conduct the paper according to party, became more irritating as party alignments became increasingly definite. The point is made in a leading article which the *Globe* printed on June 27, written according to instructions :

How happens it that *The Times* has now so little influence on public opinion ? The fact is in these days of general intelligence, when the minds of men of all classes are, according to their several opportunities of cultivation, so highly informed, no newspaper can maintain its standing unless it is written with ability, judgment and tact. Newspapers cannot now twaddle with impunity. . . . Newspapers, moreover, are nowadays expected to be conducted upon some intelligible public principle, and not to be the mere organ of individual feelings, or the blind instruments of personal objects ;—not to make it their aim to write up one man, and to write down another.

This was pure cant, for the writer knew well enough that he had been instructed to write down *The Times*, knew that the Cabinet, or at least one section of it, had been warned by Barnes that the support of *The Times* would be withdrawn if nothing was done to fulfil pledges. Charges and countercharges of lying, quibbling, inconsistency are common enough in controversy on all subjects. In the first forty years of the nineteenth century such accusations were sharpened by the peculiar degree of freedom of speech permitted to Members of Parliament and journalists.

The *Globe* as an evening paper had no chance of stepping into the position of *The Times* however much money was made available. The Whigs therefore acted wisely in deciding to purchase the dying *Morning Chronicle* and to reorganize and revitalize it. It was an astute move, but even so, the Whigs paid a large sum for the property, and they assumed the additional handicap of the dourest of editors in John Black, dull successor of the great James Perry, who had followed the illustrious William Woodfall, founder of the journal in 1769. Barnes had heard rumours of changes in the *Chronicle*, and in May, 1834, he asked Le Marchant in the following letter if he knew anything about it :

I did not believe the rumour [he wrote] but it was told me with such an air of confidence by a man acquainted with many " eminent " lawyers as the phrase is, that I thought it right to ask you the question.

If Parkes has advised Easthope to give £30,000 for a property certainly not worth £5,000, he is a most ruinous friend, and can be injurious only to his friends. Easthope I suppose thinks of making it useful as a medium of Stock-Exchange speculation. He will find himself wofully mistaken. No attempt of that kind could succeed beyond a week—and the baffled speculator would ruin his paper without forwarding his money-bargains. *The Times* as you know has been accused of speculating in the funds. No charge was ever more unfounded. Any person connected with it would immediately be driven from the partnership or from the direction, if he engaged in even the most trifling speculation : and this not because we affect any extraordinary purity or virtue, but because we know that such conduct would in a very short time totally ruin the influence and with it the property of the paper.

Parkes probably carried through the preliminary arrangements a few weeks before the foregoing letter was written to Le Marchant in May. Although Brougham and Althorp knew Black the editor, a group headed by John Easthope were the only ostensible purchasers. They appear to have paid £16,500 to Clement for his property, but enjoyed the control of large sums of money. All were Whigs, and all were chairmen of various banking

x

or merchandising companies. Easthope had been member of Parliament for St. Albans, and later for Banbury. None had previously been connected with newspapers.

The paper immediately made sure of its position as an Administration journal by championing the Poor Law Bill. While John Black remained in the editorial chair, a new staff was engaged and the paper rapidly progressed. Michael Quin was foreign editor, Eyre Evans Crowe Paris correspondent, and John Payne Collier (formerly of *The Times*) headed the Parliamentary reporters. A young reporter and special writer then unknown, Mr. Charles Dickens, supplied also an occasional feature in his " Sketches " (by Boz). Young Mr. W. M. Thackeray, a candidate for a sub-editorship, contributed to the columns, although he did not succeed in getting on the staff and was better pleased later to write for *The Times*.

The date of the transfer of the *Morning Chronicle* to the new proprietors is not known. An announcement of " extensive improvements " in every department was deferred until June 11, the day of Althorp's warlike communication to Brougham. But examination of the file proves that the tone of the paper towards *The Times* changed in the early part of May. A reference to John Walter in the issue of the 10th was disliked at Printing House Square, and *The Times* gave the authors a few lines on the 13th :

We have no unkind feeling either to the stockbroker or to the provincial attorney who are said to have purchased the property, we conjure them for their own sakes to get rid of the scribbler, whether a coxcomb professor or a meddling tailor, who for the first time disgraces its pages with virulent personal attacks and calumnious imputations of base motives.

Thus warned, neither John Easthope the stockbroker, nor Joseph Parkes the provincial attorney, not to speak of the unidentified scribbler of a coxcomb professor (probably Nassau Senior was meant) or the meddling tailor (Francis Place), indulged in other immediate provocation, and for the rest of May there was little sign of the new management. At the beginning of July, however, Barnes had to complain to Le Marchant of bustling intervention in Parliament by the rejuvenated rival :

One of our Reporters (Tyas) sent a letter as is usual on such occasions to Lord Grey for copies of the documents read by his Lordship in the course of his speech last night.

Shortly afterwards his Lordship came down to the bar with the intention of giving them (as our Reporter thinks) to him : but was suddenly intercepted by your new ally—the " Brumagem Attorney " Joseph Parkes : who took them to the *Chronicle*. The consequence is that Lord Grey's speech is very imperfectly reported. I think his Lordship ought to be informed of the conduct of your worthy supporter.

The Poor Law Bill, passed by the Commons at the beginning of July, was introduced in the Lords by Brougham in a speech delivered on July 6. On the following morning *The Times* rebuked his manoeuvre of frightening the Peers into immediate decision by " holding up to their startled imaginations the probable, indeed, certain loss of their estates. . . . What injudicious flattery calls profound policy his best friends (and we are happy to enrol ourselves among the number) will denominate a mere indiscretion—a hasty effusion of temper, to which even the highest minds are sometimes subject." This insistence on its regard for Lord Brougham, and the date, July 7, are worthy of note. The occasion was nearly a month after the incident of the Althorp letter, a fortnight after the changes at the *Chronicle* office.

There is no doubt that the Chancellor held aloof from personal contact with the *Morning Chronicle* during these weeks. He was, nevertheless, working in a subtle way to undermine the influence of *The Times*. Most unwillingly Barnes was driven to the conclusion that the Chancellor was playing a double game. The Editor's conviction is embodied in a letter addressed by him to Le Marchant. It is headed " Monday night," but is otherwise undated.

Monday night.

My dear Sir :

I thought it impossible as indeed I stated in my letter that the Chancellor could have uttered any personal abuse against me or Mr. W[alter]. He might wish to disguise the connection existing between us, (& I fully admit the policy of not bruiting it abroad) but I could never for a moment believe that he would have recourse to so shallow an artifice as abuse in order to disclaim his knowledge of us. I therefore (tho' I should have thought myself wanting in frankness if I had not mentioned the rumour to you) paid little or any attention to my informant. I ought to tell you that the evidence which my informant supplied would have staggered a weaker faith than mine. He showed to me that those blackguard *personal* attacks and imputations of corrupt motives which have appeared agt. *The Times* in the *Chronicle* were written by Senior : that the articles in the *Globe* in which a gross calumny was twice launched agt. *The Times*—viz. that we had wilfully suppressed a passage which we had quoted at length—were also written by Senior. Now Senior and Senior's friends are constantly talking of his acting under the immediate sanction of the Chancellor. All this was puzzling, but as I have stated did not convince me.

The Chancellor's expressions of personal regard to me are very gratifying to my feelings : I say it without the slightest exaggeration that I shall ever consider the personal esteem of so eminent a man to be a very distinguished honour : & the greatest pain which I can contemplate would be that which I should suffer if I were ever called upon to admit one word in the Paper which (I will not say could do him injury but which) could occasion him a moment's personal annoyance.

I trust to you to acquaint the Chancellor with these my sentiments.

Yours ever,

T. BARNES.

In the course of a postscript to this letter Barnes complains of attacks in the *Globe* by Sir George Shea upon O'Brien, *The Times* Correspondent in Lisbon. Shea " in mere wantonness (the man must be an idiot) absolutely volunteered the shameful attack."

You state (I think for the first time) that the *Globe* is a Govt. Paper.[1] . . . Really if the *Globe* is a Govt. Paper, this calumny ought to be contradicted : Shea should be called upon to make the amende in the *Globe*. O'Brien is every way as respectable a man as Shea and must not be called a tool & a spy by way of sport. I could give you decisive proofs that every word about the English Secretaries sent by O'Brien has been furnished by Lord William Russell and by Lord Howard de Walden. . . .

Without any doubt, Brougham encouraged the *Morning Chronicle* and its writers, for it was his Poor Law Bill the paper was destined to defend ; yet the Chancellor had not come out into the open against *The Times*. Indeed, until the middle of July there had hardly been sufficient interval to allow either of the combatants to come to blows. It was known to political personages, however, that the Althorp letter had come into the possession of Barnes, and there was speculation as to the attitude of the paper when days went by without any reference to them. Could it be that matters had been adjusted ? That there would be no " war " because peace had been patched up ? The situation was dark, since, for what it was worth, Lord Brougham still talked to his friends as if he could influence *The Times*.

[1] Barnes knew quite well that it identified itself with Palmerston's policy.

But by the middle of July—*The Times* not backward with invective—the two papers were attacking each other daily, semi-polite exchanges developing into downright charges of hypocrisy, mendacity, tergiversation, and worse. On July 14, 15 and 16 the *Chronicle* printed letters signed "Vindex" in which the policy of the Chancellor was supported. On the 17th a correspondent, perhaps in Printing House Square, asked of *The Times* if it were true, " as generally reported, that those slipshod rigmarole letters are written by Lord Chancellor Brougham?" Two days later *The Times* inserted a paragraph :

In answer to Publius, who, however, we think has scarcely any right to ask the question, we must say that we do not believe that the letters of " Vindex," published in the *Chronicle* can have proceeded from the Lord Chancellor. We cannot for a moment believe that such tawdry attempts at fine writing, such bull-frog efforts at energy of diction, can proceed from a man whose taste has been formed on the best models, and who has always shewn himself a master of language. The maudlin affectation of some passages, and the fussy splutterings of others, indicate rather the manner of a waiting gentlewoman who has quarrelled with her master's valet.

The *Standard*, among other journals, took it for granted that " Vindex " was the Chancellor, and it may be presumed from the acid tone of its paragraph that *The Times* felt equally sure. Issue was now joined between the paper and Brougham, who complained to his friends and wrote to his leader of Barnes's caustic language. Grey replied in a chilly message that

the only way with newspaper attacks is, as the Irish say, " to keep never minding." This has been my practice throughout life. There is nothing that better answers the purpose of those who attack than to answer them. . . . Time and conduct set these things right.[1]

Indications of a deepening divergence from contemporary official Whiggery appear in a leading article of July 19. Grave dissatisfaction with Lord Brougham's contradictory utterances on the Coercion Bill was thus expressed in terms which the Chancellor's friends considered " diabolical " :

It is not often that we feel justified in any strong concurrence of opinion with Conservatives in either House of Parliament, but really neither conscience as regards ourselves, nor justice or sound policy towards other persons, will permit us to withhold our full acquiescence

[1] Brougham, *Memoirs*, Vol. II, p. 278, August 28, 1834.

from the expressions of astonishment and more than astonishment, which proceeded from some of the Tory Lords on Thursday evening, at the contrast between Lord Brougham's vehement speech on the 4th instant in defence of those clauses of the Coercion Bill which aimed at the suppression of seditious meetings, and his contemptuous allusion on Thursday to those very clauses, which he declared he would always have got rid of if he could ! We will venture to say that an inconsistency so palpable—that a levity of political principle so all but preternatural—that a forgetfulness of everything like public decency so wonderful, has never before been exhibited by any man conscious of being exposed to the observation of his fellows, and to the moral and social consequences of his own actions. . . . We see that even the greatest talents are not exempt from that liability which is proverbially said to be the concomitant of a certain offence ; and that in all cases the cause of Truth is finally protected by the providential want of memory in those who would assail her. One fact at least has been clearly established in the midst of all these inconsistencies and indiscretions : it is evident that but for these disclosures Ministers would have passed the Coercion Bill with all those tyrannical clauses which now, both by their speeches and acts, they admit to be unnecessary.

This was tantamount to the greater excommunication, and was so interpreted by the Chancellor's friends. But there is no sign in the available papers of Brougham himself having had any realization that those July days were critical for him and that the excommunication of *The Times* was to be upheld by all the successive Governments of his long life.

Brougham's dealings with the Poor Law brought further occasion for fierce attack and sometimes embarrassed defence. The feeling of Barnes may be detected in a reference to the frailties of ability : " So do great men slip—to fall where they might stand firm and fast for ever, when they once surrender their minds to fanciful theories, and run after will-o'-the-wisps, from a love of novelty, or wish to surprise instead of serving mankind." And the handicaps of championship are similarly evident when the *Chronicle*, in the middle of its defiance of *The Times* and support of the Ministry, must declare that " . . . we have unsparingly pointed out his inconsistencies and are not unaware of the source of most of them ; if Lord Brougham has a weakness it is that he thinks himself more cunning than he really is."

XVIII

THE WHIG OFFENSIVE

YEARS before the Whigs made up their minds for " war," Radicals had followed the example of Cobbett and denounced *The Times* as an enemy. The war with *The Times* declared by Brougham and Althorp, and maintained by other Whigs, was supported by Radical and Irish members of the House of Commons. In 1832 O'Connell began his accusations of wilful misreporting, which provoked the animosity of the London reporters in general. He threw rash allegations at the *Morning Chronicle* as well as *The Times*. The first reporter to suffer from his recklessness was an Irishman named Nugent, educated at Trinity College, Dublin, a collaborator with Sir James Mackintosh the political philosopher and judge, and a member of the Gallery staff of *The Times*. Before making a protest in the House O'Connell sent a remonstrance to Printing House Square :

4, Parliament-street, June 21, 1832.

Mr. O'Connell feels that he owes it as a duty to himself, and perhaps to others, to remonstrate with the editor of *The Times* upon the circumstance, which has now occurred for the second time, of assailing him in that paper through the medium of pretended reports.

Mr. O'Connell assures the editor of *The Times*, and is ready to confirm his assertion by the most solemn sanction, that the report of the speech attributed to him is, with the exception of a few unimportant ideas, a total and most unfounded misstatement.

He also is authorized by Mr. Hunt to contradict in the same manner the speech attributed to him. Mr. O'Connell has underlined part of the speech attributed to Mr. Hunt, of which not one word, nor any idea bordering on such sentiments, was uttered by Mr. Hunt.

The allusion is too plain to be mistaken. Mr. O'Connell thinks he could treat the foolish story to which it alludes with silent contempt, as he has hitherto treated it ; but had that allusion been made in the House of Commons, he would certainly have found it his duty to give it a quiet but most emphatic contradiction.

He cannot bring himself to believe that the editor of *The Times*, as a man of integrity and a gentleman, could possibly countenance a proceeding of this description,—the circulation of calumnies not

311

uttered but put into the mouth of a man quite innocent on *this occasion* of any sort of connexion with them.

There is a very strong reason why Mr. Hunt should not be the person to make any allusion to *that* calumny—he certainly did not do so.

Mr. O'Connell is also authorized by Mr. Callaghan to assert in the most positive manner that, short as is the speech attributed to him, it contains matter totally different from anything he said.

Under these circumstances, Mr. O'Connell having no claim on the editor of *The Times*, but on the score of mere justice, thinks himself entitled to this redress,—namely, that sufficient care should be taken to prevent the recurrence of *similar* attacks on him.

Mr. O'Connell demands no retractation—he requires no apology—he solicits no dismissal of any reporter. He would feel unhappy if any being were to suffer for an injury which he forgives. He is quite convinced that this occasion will not be taken to aggravate the injustice done him *by the shape* of anything purporting to be an apology.

Mr. O'Connell, however, does not shrink from any mode of warfare that may be adopted against him, and without deprecating hostility, and looking only for *justice* in future in the mere matter of reporting, he feels that he thus has discharged a duty, and rests content.

He duly made his speech and subsequently saw Mr. Nugent, upon which he wrote another letter to the Editor, which he addressed, on this occasion, to Edward Sterling, erroneously supposing him, as the Radicals did, to be Editor of *The Times* :

4, Parliament-street, June 21, 1832.

Sir,—I venture to address you *in your proper person*, because I have to ask a favour.

Let me say by way of preface, that if the house had continued to sit another half-hour, I should have exonerated the " management " of *The Times* from all blame. I intend to do so *in my best manner* to-morrow.

I have seen Mr. Nugent, the reporter, and am quite satisfied on the subject of the report. The favour I venture, therefore, to ask, is that you will overlook his error. I should feel unhappy if I were the means of doing him any injury.

It is quite true that I can have no means of compensating you in any mode for granting me this favour, but I will not be the less sensible of it.

Will you, then, allow me to say that if, on the whole, you think I have any claim to have my feelings consulted, you will comply with my request and grant me this favour ?

I have the honour to be, Sir, your very obedient servant,

DANIEL O'CONNELL.

The second letter from Daniel O'Connell brought the following reply in the typical style, and from the hand, of Thomas Barnes :

Thursday, June 21, 1832.

Sir,—I have the honour to acknowledge the receipt of two letters with your signature, which have been delivered to-day at *The Times* office ; one addressed to the editor of the paper the other to Mr.—— [1]. You will, I have no doubt, at once recognise the propriety of the answer to your letters being written in the name of the editor : in that character, therefore, I state most unequivocally, that my indignation even exceeds yours at the gross misrepresentation which you have imputed to our reporter. There are certainly many points on which you and the conductors of *The Times* hold very different opinions, but this very circumstance makes me peculiarly and sensitively anxious that every word which falls from you should be reported with the most scrupulous precision, and I should treat any attempt to distort the expression of your opinions as an act of intolerable baseness.

If our reporter, Mr. E. Nugent, can satisfy you that his error was unintentional, I shall be most happy for his sake ; if you will further extend your kindness to him, and declare your satisfaction as publicly as your charge, I shall feel that the journal is also exonerated from all blame ; but unless this public declaration (which, however, I have no right to require) shall be made, it will be impossible for Mr. Nugent's connexion with *The Times* to continue for another day.

Permit me to thank you for the very courteous terms in which you have expressed yourself in both your letters.

I have the honour to be, Sir, your obedient servant,

THE EDITOR OF THE TIMES.

Daniel O'Connell's acknowledgment was forwarded by return :

Mr. O'Connell feels gratified by the letter which the editor of *The Times* has favoured him with. He cheerfully and thankfully embraces the offer kindly made to him respecting Mr. E. Nugent, and will, he hopes satisfactorily to the editor of *The Times*, comply with the condition on which Mr. E. Nugent is to remain on the establishment.

4, Parliament-street, June 22 [1832].

O'Connell promised to comply with the condition, and in a statement to the House exonerated the management of the paper from all blame.

[1] The name Sterling is omitted in the text of the letter as printed in *The Times*.

He had also seen the reporter, who had satisfactorily explained to him that there was no intentional misrepresentation in the case, either with respect to himself or any other hon. member; and when he considered that, from the inconvenience with which reporters had to contend in the gallery it must often happen that speakers were only partially heard, and also that one reporter frequently followed another in the middle of a speech, he could easily see how misrepresentation might occur without any intention of attributing to an hon. member sentiments which he did not express.

O'Connell, however, forgot what he had previously acknow-ledged, and persisted in intemperate criticism of the Press. On July 25, 1833, he drew attention to breaches of privilege by news-papers engaged in publishing the debates of the House, and a debate followed in which several members, including Lord Althorp and Sir Robert Inglis, bore testimony to the general accuracy of the reports.

The repercussions of the July debate were more serious than was foreseen. On July 26 *The Times* contained, besides a report of the proceedings, the following letter from its reporting staff:

TO THE EDITOR OF THE TIMES

Sir,—We, the undersigned Parliamentary Reporters of your paper, beg to inform you, that without any wish to prejudice the interests of the establishment, with which many of us have been long connected, and to which all of us are sincerely attached, we have deliberately resolved not to report any speech of Mr. O'Connell until he shall have retracted, as publicly as he made, the calumnious assertion that our reports are " designedly false." We are ready and willing to take upon ourselves personally all the consequences with which the House of Commons may think fit to visit this our determination.

Respect for our own characters has dictated this resolution, and be the consequences to us what they may, we will abide by it.

We beg, as an act of justice to us, that you will publish this our declaration.

We are yours obediently,

J. D. WOODS.	E. NUGENT.
JOHN TYAS.	MICHAEL NUGENT.
GEORGE FISHER.	JOHN ROSS.
JAMES SHERIDAN.	THOMAS THORNTON.
RICHARD M. BOUSFIELD.	FRANCIS ROSS.
	CHARLES ROSS.

The Times-office, July 25 [1833].

The sympathy of *The Times* with its own corps was thus expressed :

The gentlemen, many of whom have acted long and meritoriously for this journal, and have powerful claims on the gratitude of members of Parliament, received at the hands of Mr. O'Connell, when president of some pot-house club or mob meeting, the grossest insult that man can endure from man. He called them nothing less than a pack of deliberate liars. . . . They declare they will not report the speeches of their slanderer, and some wiseacres there are who exclaim : " Why this is a conspiracy."[1]

A year later O'Connell's complaint found eager Whig support. The word " conspiracy " was often in the mouths of the Irish and Radical enemies of *The Times*, and the Whig supporters of Brougham's schemes for the diffusion of useful knowledge always talked of the paper's " monopoly " ; all were equally jealous of its growing power. The scheme to reduce the influence of *The Times* by reviving the *Chronicle* in 1834 and lowering the stamp tax found in O'Connell a welcome accession of strength. Like the Radicals, O'Connell was persuaded that *The Times* had some sort of financial advantage and that the reduction of the stamp would materially alter its position. That the Whigs and Radicals meant to press their own " war with *The Times* " to a decision became evident in the autumn of 1834, and the paper chronicled Brougham's speeches with increasing derision. It should be borne in mind that the Chancellor was still widely popular and that his position in the Ministry remained a very strong one. While Brougham's general untrustworthiness was known, the general view of the quarrel between the Chancellor and *The Times* was that Barnes was suffering from pique. Crabb Robinson, for instance, took the view that *The Times* was indulging in an inexcusably coarse personal attack. The most generous of its critics did not hesitate to condemn *The Times* as being " the mere organ of individual feelings." Polemic of unaccustomed violence resulted, new even to the hardened writers and readers of that day. The *Globe*'s pages before June, 1834, contained no reference to *The Times* ; it was a little nervous of attacking it, but gave greater obedience to its

---

[1] The opposition paper, the *Morning Chronicle*, gave hearty support :
" We, the Parliamentary reporters of the *Morning Chronicle*, feel it due to our honour and character thus publicly to repel, as far as we are concerned, with the utmost scorn and indignation, the false and calumnious charges which have been brought by Mr. O'Connell against the reporters of the proceedings in Parliament.
WALTER HENRY WATTS, THOMAS HODGSKIN, C. CLARK, CHARLES R. DODD, JOHN HILL POWELL, EDWARD FITZ-GIBBON, JOHN WHEELER, WILLIAM HAZLITT, T. FRASER, J. PROVAN."

Whitehall masters as the summer advanced. By September the *Globe*, like the *Morning Chronicle*, progressed from charges of inconsistency to charges of profligacy, coarseness and apostasy. The business of answering *The Times* and championing Brougham's personal interest was, for the *Chronicle*, not always easy. The backers of the *Chronicle*, although they wanted to attack *The Times*, hesitated to champion the Chancellor. But Joseph Parkes wrote to Lord Durham on August 23, 1834, that he was greatly annoyed at Barnes's attack on Brougham. " It is breaking a man essential to the popular cause." Yet within six months the astute Parkes saw that Barnes was correct in his estimate of Brougham's position.

The Times of August 26, quoting a remark by the Chancellor on the presumption of ignorance, observed :

We have never seen a remark so strongly supported by example as in the speech before us. The speaker has hit himself off with singular truth. Perhaps the portrait may be a little strengthened in likeness, by substituting *quackery* for ignorance, though persons acquainted with the furniture of Lord Brougham's mind, know that it is like the specimens of an upholsterer's show-room—some piece of every set, but nothing in completeness and arrangement—a lumber of fineries, odds and ends, at once more and less than necessary to the fitting of any one mansion of the understanding.

Parkes at this time was ready enough to use the Chancellor could he but control him. *The Times* campaign forced the *Morning Chronicle* to swallow him whole. By August 26, 1834, the *Chronicle* warned its readers that the object of Printing House Square had been for some time " to break the present ministry," and it " picks upon Lord Brougham as it knows him to be an important member of the Cabinet. We are not blind to the faults of Henry Brougham —we have never been his flatterer." If the Government did not overcome *The Times* the paper would overcome the Government— that was now the view of Brougham. The Chancellor himself threatened *The Times* in one of the series of public addresses, delivered in the North during September, the nature of which infuriated Parkes and many more active Whigs.

At Aberdeen he had stigmatized as " absurd and stupid and indefensible " the charge that he had intrigued against Grey, and had promised in impassioned tones that " a day of retribution

THE CELEBRATED
VAUX-HALL PERFORMER

H.B.'s cartoon of the activities of Lord Brougham in the summer of 1834. (H.B.'s Sketches, September 16, 1834.)

Published by Tho⁵ MᶜLean, 26 Haymarket Sep.ʳ 16.ᵗʰ 1834.

THE CELEBRATED

ON T

HALL PERFORMER

Ducôte & Stephens, Lithographers, 70 St Martins Lane

is at hand—it approaches for those who had circulated such charges " ; and he alluded, as everybody realized,[1] to *The Times* :

I have allowed certain persons to go on—they have gone on—the net is enclosed around them, and they shall soon be held up to ridicule and to scorn—ay, and to punishment. . . . The falsehood of these attacks all shall be made to believe in a very short time, except perhaps one or two contemptible individuals, but although they may not be made to believe, they may be made to feel, and their conduct held up to the view of a discerning country.

The Chancellor's references to " certain persons " he had " allowed to go on " were noted by journalists, daily and weekly. *The Times* naturally would not allow them to pass without acknowledgment. The first leading article on September 17, 1834, was a long one ; it was wholly dedicated to Brougham and his several speeches. It began :

The public sees that *The Times* yet exists. Lord Brougham has *allowed* us *to go on* for another day, as he has *allowed* us *to go on* for some weeks past, and it is possible that we may appear to-morrow, but if not, let us be looked for in the Lord Chancellor's pocket. The thought is almost too affecting for men in our unhappy circumstances, but we must endeavour to bear it with fortitude, and to say what we have to say before we are extinguished. It is hard to be so cut off in the flower of one's days, and the full tide of prosperity, but relentless Brougham wills it so, and as he has *allowed* us to go on, so he must have the power to stop us.

The retort in *The Times* concluded with a comparison of Brougham to Alexander in Dryden's poem :

The listening crowd admire the lofty sound,
A present deity ! they shout around ;
A present deity ! the vaulted roofs rebound :
 With ravished ears
 The Brougham hears,
 Assumes the god,
 Affects to nod,
And seems to shake the spheres.

[1] The *Spectator*, edited by the Durhamite Left-Whig Rintoul, contained the following paragraph, perhaps written by Parkes after he had broken with Brougham and the *Chronicle* : " Who does not remember his repeated denunciations of the press during his Scottish tour ; and his famous speech at Aberdeen, when in allusion to certain persons, he said : ' The net is enclosed around them, and they shall soon be held up to ridicule and to scorn, ay, and to punishment.' The meaning of this enigma was explained subsequently at Edinburgh where the Chancellor made no secret of his intention to prosecute *The Times*. This threat he has refrained from executing but we do not believe it is love of the press that has kept him back." (October 25, 1834.)

Decidedly the " war " must be fought to a finish. The weapon of stamp-duty reduction was to be employed without delay. The " monopoly " of Printing House Square would be broken by the new competition thus stimulated. To patronize the Radical opposition to the stamp tax seemed to Brougham and Althorp a certain means of embarrassing the enemy. The blow might be driven home, first by the refounded *Morning Chronicle*, and then by the *Penny Magazine*. Brougham had the idea of using against *The Times* his Society for the Diffusion of Useful Knowledge, founded in 1826 under his own chairmanship ostensibly for the purpose of " imparting useful information to all classes of the community, particularly to such as are unable to avail themselves of experienced teachers, or may prefer learning by themselves." The Society engaged only to publish low-priced volumes of specifically non-political character.[1]

On March 31, 1832, there had appeared, with the cordial support of the Chancellor, the first number of the *Penny Magazine of the Society for the Diffusion of Useful Knowledge*. It was issued tax free with the agreement of the Stamp Office. At the end of the year the *Penny Magazine* had averaged a weekly sale of 200,000. Such a figure was unprecedented ; it intoxicated Brougham as much as it disquieted the newspapers. When several of them complained of the rivalry, Brougham believed that now he had in reserve an alternative power to the newspapers. The dailies were certainly uneasy, less on account of the circulation than because the *Penny Magazine* might accept advertisements. For what, thought some of them, if the *Penny Magazine* should be made into a Penny Newspaper ? Brougham did not think in terms of advertising, but in terms of circulation, calculating that, if judiciously " managed," this low-priced Press might in time grow in importance to himself until first the power and finally the influence of Printing House Square should be exceeded.

The obstacle to turning a popular educator which did not print advertisements into a newspaper that did was the stamp tax. As the law stood, the taxes consisted of, first, a duty of 3d. a pound weight on the paper, or about ¼d. a sheet ; next, a stamp duty, nominally 4d., but subject to a discount of 20 per cent. ; and, thirdly, a tax of 3s. 6d. upon each advertisement. The whole duties, with the price of printing and trade discounts for distribution, amounted to 5½d. out of each 7d. charged for a London morning newspaper. It was calculated by Bulwer, who spoke against these

1 Knight, *Passages*, II, 46.

taxes in the Commons on June 14, 1832, that an advertisement of twenty lines in a London paper would, if published every day for a year, amount to £202 16s., whereas in New York the cost for the same piece and same frequency would be £6 18s. 8d. If the taxes restricted advertising they equally restricted sales. The number of readers able to afford a tax of fourpence a day could not be large, but the circulation of the paper was infinitely wider than its sale. Regular borrowers had the papers for an hour a day. Issues were read and re-read all over the country by all classes in newsrooms. The existence of the tax required the enforcement of the law against illegal cheap publications. *The Times* benefited no more from this protection than did rival journals. To make the *Penny Magazine* into a penny or twopenny newspaper was impossible as long as the Stamp Act existed. But what would be the situation if the stamp were abolished? As for competition of the genuine trade kind, Printing House Square considered itself equal to any of its demands. A leading article of May 24, 1834, may be quoted :

It is not the stamp duty that forms the grand outlay of a newspaper. If it deserve the name of what the British public now understand by the term " newspaper," the same capital, and that is no doubt a large one, which the business at this moment requires, must *still* be wanted, notwithstanding the repeal of the duty, for the search after and transmission of intelligence from every quarter of the world—for political correspondence, at home and abroad—for reports, Parliamentary and forensic—for writers capable of attracting public attention and conducting public discussion in all departments of knowledge bearing upon the general interests and immediate movements of the various classes of society, or of society itself as a whole. What has the repeal of the stamp duty to do with this ? . . . Compare one number of an unstamped penny publication in reference to quantity of matter only, (we set aside the consideration of priority of intelligence, domestic and foreign and refer only to the mere amount of letter press) with a single number of *The Times*, which sells for 3d. exclusive of the duty, and see on which side even in point of quantity, relative to cost, the best of the bargain lies. . . . If, therefore, Mr. Bulwer and the cheap knowledge advocates imagine that men without capital would obtain one particle of *relative* advantage through the repeal of the duties, we believe they are mistaken ; but, as we said before, let them try—on selfish ground we *can* have no objection.

Nevertheless, that the tax helped *The Times* was a fallacy prevalent in political circles, and the reduction of the stamp tax upon newspapers was an essential part of the " war with *The Times* " directed by the Brougham-Althorp-Spring Rice faction of the Whig Ministry. Bulwer was not a party to the conspiracy.

The *Penny Magazine* and other publications of the Society for the Diffusion of Useful Knowledge were small beginnings, so Brougham thought, of a Press to embrace ultimately the whole country. With the removal of the tax a Press more powerful, because much cheaper, would reach the people in their own homes, where copies would be owned, not borrowed ; re-read, not merely scanned. Brougham would supply the political direction, his friends would write the articles. An independent property of Charles Knight's, called the *Companion to the Newspaper*, was taken over in August, 1834, by a new organization, the Society for the Diffusion of *Political* Knowledge. The chairman was, again, the Lord Chancellor, and the committee counted such names as Denis Le Marchant, Brougham's Press " manager," Henry Bellenden Ker and Nassau W. Senior, all fervent supporters of the Poor Law Bill.

" The Society," affirmed a notice, " have made arrangements for the future publication, under their superintendence, of the *Companion to the Newspaper*." The same August, this paper printed a significant article on the " Influence of Newspapers on Public Opinion," which wrote up the Chancellor's side of the quarrel and gave clear indications of the policy and inspiration of the *Companion*.

On the 16th July *The Times* began to abuse the Chancellor about his ugly bantling (Poor Law Bill) and from that day to the present hour these attacks have never ceased. . . . The offence which the Lord Chancellor had given to *The Times* was mortal. He had dared to think that a *Poor man's magistrate*, a maker of orders for relief on overseers was, in these respects, a mischievous member of society, although he might represent a county[1] and have some remote influence upon *The Times* newspaper ; moreover the Lord Chancellor had dared to praise a gentleman[2] connected with the Poor Law Commission who had acquired the honour of having *The Times* for his enemy. These were offences not to be forgiven. (pp. 151-3.)

It was easier to make Mr. Walter the centre of controversy than to answer the arguments of *The Times*. The paper found it necessary to remind the new friends of the Chancellor that their

[1] A reference to John Walter II.
[2] Nassau Senior.

objection to his late behaviour went deeper than the details of any one measure, important as it was. It was not true that the Chancellor had the best interests of the Press at heart. As an instance of his extraordinary discrepancy from himself, *The Times* referred on July 25, 1834

to Sir John Campbell's speech last Wednesday night, where the Attorney-General hints pretty broadly, that the Lord Chancellor was an actively consenting party to that prosecution of the *True Sun*, which before the now sitting committee on libel, he is everywhere reported to have denounced as inexpedient and improper. It is, however, with a sense of suffering infinitely more acute than any which it is in our inclination, were it in our power, to inflict upon him, that we see ourselves compelled to notice those aberrations, which if not soon corrected will involve his reputation in irremediable ruin.

The importance of the incident referred to is that Brougham's mind was alternately for and against actual prosecution of the Press in 1834. He wanted to diminish the power of any organ to criticize himself or his policies, but he was not sure that legal proceedings would help. At this time he wrote to Wellesley and to Grey telling them that he was finding much support " for the war he was waging with the London Press."

Albany Fonblanque, in the *Examiner* (October 19, 1834), pointed out that " in the circulation of the *Penny Magazine* there is a great publishing interest ; and its agencies are determined to carry on the newspaper which is to be started in the Chancellor's service as soon as the duties are repealed." A similar warning was given by the *Quarterly Review* (August, 1834), which had " long ago foreseen " that the Society for the Diffusion of Political Knowledge was—the Lord Chancellor. This Society, it went on,

is of course substantially the same with that for the Diffusion of Useful Knowledge ; the time has now come for dropping the mask and any one who considers Lord Brougham's evidence before the late Committee on the Law of Libel, together with this new prospectus, will perceive that the grand scheme for which all this machinery was originally set on foot and organised, was that of concentrating the whole management of the Newspaper Press throughout the empire in the hands of a snug committee of Bellenden Kers, and Le Marchants, mixed up with Unitarians, etc.—under the tranquil superintendence of the Lord Chancellor Brougham ! The stamp-duty is, of course, to be removed forthwith.

Y

To this account of the objects of Brougham's societies it should be added that he and his friends designed their magazines mainly to undermine the influence over public opinion possessed by *The Times*, and urged on the campaign for stamp duty reduction with the same motive.

The renewed campaign for reconsideration of the duty began with a public meeting at the Crown and Anchor Tavern on July 18, 1835, with Lord Brougham in the chair, supported by Grote, Joseph Hume, O'Connell, Bowring, Roebuck, and many other Whigs and Radicals. The room was crowded in every part, " chiefly by persons of the working class." Brougham, deprecating violence both of language and opinion, opened the meeting ; and it was resolved to petition Parliament for the total repeal of the stamp duties upon newspapers. The matter was further argued in public and in Parliament. Charles Buller, answering a question in the House of Commons, mentioned that the *Penny Magazine* sold some 200,000 copies a week and *The Times* only about 30,000. Later he corrected this inaccuracy ; he " ought to have stated " *The Times* circulation at double the number. *The Times*, answering the argument for cheapness, pronounced the *Penny Magazine* " to be almost incalculably dearer than *The Times*." In spite of the stamp, the sevenpence paid for *The Times* provided the reader with six times as much matter as the " mere scissor-compilation " of the *Penny Magazine*. In spite of the *Penny Magazine* having no Parliamentary reporters, no law reporters, no police reporters to be paid, no writer's original discussion, no correspondence, no expresses, foreign or domestic, *The Times* alleged the *Penny Magazine* to be anything but a cheap magazine. " Such a journal, compared with *The Times*, or any well conducted morning paper, would be dear if sold at the rate of six for a farthing. And yet the Honourable Member for Liskeard, in the plenitude of his ignorance, calls this a cheap publication." The understatement of the circulation of *The Times* was natural. Buller, in company with a great many others in 1835, believed *The Times* to have been severely injured ; the effects of the " war " and the supposed widespread discontent at the paper's political line were exaggerated, while the competition of the *Morning Chronicle* was overvalued.

In the early part of 1836 it became known that the Government projected legislation. The relief from the tax was welcomed by Whig believers in the diffusion of knowledge, and by Radical mystics who would redeem the world from all evils by the unrestricted circulation of the printed word, at a final meeting before the introduction of the Bill. On March 7, 1836, at Guildhall, there were present Messrs. Grote, O'Connell, Roebuck, Hume, Buckingham, Duncombe, Wilks, Wakley, Bowring, Sir Thomas Molesworth, and many aldermen and members of Parliament. Grote spoke first, urging that the tax stopped up the only sources through which the majority of the community could obtain political knowledge. John Travers, who followed, held up the usual American paper, sold at a halfpenny and alleged to be as good in type, in composition and arrangement as any London journal. Benjamin Wood, asserting that where there was no printing there could be no knowledge, proceeded to the assertion that the basis of newspaper prosperity was the advocacy of liberal principles. He informed his audience that

the paper known as *The Times* . . . (great uproar) would not have obtained its overwhelming circulation but by its support of liberal opinion. (loud cheers). It was the people at large who had raised *The Times* to its importance ; and what had it done in return as an acknowledgment to that people ? Why, it had turned its back upon the people. (Uproar). . . . As soon as the parties connected with it had gained their ends, their own purposes, they turned their backs upon those who had elevated their paper to its height ; they forsook them, they deserted the people and supported the Tories. (Hear ! Hear !)

The next speaker, Daniel O'Connell, admitted

that there was a great capital embarked in the newspapers at present in existence. They did not want or desire to take away that capital from them. . . . Did they think that *The Times* would ever have made such an interest but by being the champion of the people ? No, the monopoly alone would not have effected that for it. But see one consequence of the monopoly. *The Times* had no sooner answered its own ends than it sold itself to the Tories (groans). It had no sooner answered its own purposes, than it let itself out to every scoundrel who was rich enough to buy it, and having done that it assailed with literary outscourings and abuse every man who, like himself, had had the courage to brave it.

That *The Times* was the only journal mentioned proves the agitation to have been manipulated, if not originated, by a group of politicians and others jealous of its power. *The Times*, alluding to the Guildhall meeting on March 10, asked Mr. Wood the simple question : how, if *The Times* turned its back upon the people, it could retain the circulation which it only secured by the opposite policy. Having obtained

its overwhelming circulation [*The Times*] turns its back on the people ; and then, of course, deserts our " overwhelming circulation," if there be any force in Benjamin Wood's argument. Now, this is so far from being the fact, Benjamin Wood, that our circulation, even on the day on which we published these your falsehoods, was something which your narrow mind cannot comprehend, and which almost surprised ourselves. But that circulation resulted from well-tried integrity, Benjamin—of which you have no conception,—it was the fruit of talents, from which you are still further removed,—and of industry, which we are sure you do not practise in so good a cause.

The Times article went on to trounce Daniel O'Connell for his assertion that *The Times* had sold itself, and ridiculed his statement that the press, meaning *The Times*, " now almost performed the office of thought." On this point *The Times* reminded O'Connell of its own part in the development of printing. " By what part of the press, Daniel, was this wonderful invention first patronised and introduced into the world ? Whose columns first rolled round the wide cylindrical surface, and were tossed off as it were by magic into the hands of children ? " A month afterwards the Government Bill was brought in by the Chancellor of the Exchequer, Thomas Spring Rice, a committee-man of the Society for the Diffusion of Useful Knowledge. The proposal was to reduce the tax to one penny on condition that the newspaper sheet did not exceed a certain size. For a newspaper printed on a larger sheet the tax was to remain fourpence ; the only way of qualifying for the reduction was to adopt the size specified in the Bill.

Cognizance by law of the size of a journal originated in 1712. By degrees the tax was increased and the size also. By 1804, when the tax became fourpence, the size of the sheet was limited to 32 inches by 22 inches. In 1825 Huskisson removed all restrictions on the size, thus making possible the issue of eight-page papers. The first additional four-page sheet, printed for delivery with a four-page paper, was occasioned on June 13, 1806, by *The Times* report of the impeachment of Henry Dundas, Lord Melville. This issue consisted of three four-page sheets, the extra four-pagers being headed respectively " First Supplement " and " Second Supplement." Similar extra sheets were published in the same year, but afterwards there was no repetition of the enterprise known to the trade as the " double paper " until 1817. The first gratis supplement came out in 1822 (July 22) ; it was composed entirely of advertisements, then an exceptional expedient. The six-column format, 16½ by 22½ inches, first appeared on July 12, 1825. From 1825 onwards, " double," *i.e.*, eight-page papers, became increasingly frequent. By 1831 such issues of *The Times* came out more than once a week, and by January, 1836, they averaged four a week. The *Morning Post* and the *Morning Herald* seldom produced supplements, but they printed on as large a sheet as *The Times*.

The return in the Bill to the principle of size limitation aroused protests. A petition signed by John Joseph Lawson, printer of *The Times*, E. R. Hearn, printer of the *Morning Herald*, Charles Baldwin, printer of the *Standard*, and Thomas Payne, printer of the *Morning Post*, was brought to the House of Commons. It was not signed by the printer of the *Morning Chronicle*, for the new " admeasurement " exactly suited the dimensions of the *Morning Chronicle* and the machinery upon which that paper was printed. Hence the four petitioners appealed with justice to the House of Commons, claiming that

the partiality of the measure will be no less striking when laid before your honourable House than its general oppressive character ; for the admeasurement recommended to be imposed by the law is exactly such as will spare a journal unaccustomed to publish double papers, which is peculiarly attached to the present Administration, and oppress and impoverish all the others which adopt a more independent and impartial line of policy.

Spring Rice, in the debate which followed the presentation of the petition by Goulburn, repudiated any intention to protect the *Morning Chronicle*, telling the House " upon his honour " he personally had not known what papers the dimension would affect and which it would not. *The Times* refused to be solaced. In one article (May 5, 1836) it estimated that " a journal no larger than a child's curl paper would suffice us for making Mr. Rice's quietus at any time," and in another article it said that the Bill was

in perfect keeping with the whole conduct of the Whigs towards the press. For one " breach of privilege " that has been brought before Parliament by Tories or Radicals, there have been half-a-dozen by the Whigs : and when we recollect the question from a Whig Chancellor of the Exchequer to a Whig Lord Chancellor—" shall we make war upon *The Times* ? " we have, perhaps, no reason to be surprised that another Chancellor of the Exchequer of the same pure and liberal school should have answered it with, "Yes, and against the *Herald*, *Post*, and *Standard* too."

The circumstances were turned into verse by a correspondent, whose rhymes were printed in the issue of May 10, 1836:

> Mr. Broad-*sheet* of *The Times*,
> You are punish'd for your crimes.
> Though with talent, toil, and trouble,
> You have beat your rivals *double*,
> In the blackguard brainless " ring,"
> Could you hope to cope with *Spring*?
> Or the claret, in a trice,
> Tap in pudding-headed *Rice*?
> Turn your double number out,
> Span the edges round about,
> 'Tis some sixteen feet or more,
> Wand'ring news and knowledge o'er.
> All offences " weighed " and treasured,
> You're found " wanting " when you're measured:
> Not in wisdom, not in wits,
> Not in caustics, not in skits,
> Not in *Leaders* (Rice don't want 'em),
> Not in quality or quantum:
> But you're wanted, if I guess
> Rightly—to be something *less*.
> So, as *Chrony* with the town
> Can't go up, you must go down.
> With your game fly-leaves no more
> You may o'er the dunghills soar:
> Rice, with cockney sportsman's skill,
> Takes a license out to kill:
> His *single-barrel* loads and primes,
> And bags your *brace* of morning *Times*.
> So 'twas destined, and 'tis meet,
> Rice measures out your winding-*sheet*:
> The *foe*! ('tis there the Whig shoe pinches),
> That *liv'd by yards* must die by inches.

The measure itself had a difficult passage through the House of Commons. "The formidable minority," said *The Times* on June 22,

which resists Mr. Spring Rice's clap-trap scheme for the reduction of the stamp on newspapers will have a wholesome tendency to make that dexterous personage look about him. . . . We have often said that a lowering of the stamp duty from fourpence to a penny could not work the slightest injury to *The Times*, as an established daily journal, or in any way affect our interests, unless the Chancellor of the Exchequer should contrive to mix up with the reduction of duty certain unfair regulations, not properly belonging to a measure of relief, or on the other hand omit or perhaps reject, such precautions as must be rendered necessary for the protection of ourselves and parties circumstanced as we are, from dangers to which the diminution of the scale of tax would of itself have exposed us. Observing these two conditions, we are not aware of any personal ground on which we should be justified in complaining of a reduction of the stamp duty.

The paper in this leading article gave a reasoned answer to the irresponsible agitation and ignorant claims made by those who continually cried out that *The Times* had a "monopoly" and that the stamp would reduce its dominating circulation to some sort of average of the London Press. *The Times* pointed out that a tax equally applied had no sort of connexion with journalistic success, which was all the so-called "monopoly" amounted to. *The Times* owed nothing to the tax but everything to its

large and incessant outlay of capital in the remuneration of editors, the most efficient that we can procure,—of political and other writers, the most efficient that we can procure,—of a corps of accurate, able, and indefatigable reporters,—of correspondents, all over the inhabited world, who have access to the most authentic sources of information in foreign courts and countries, who are capable of inquiring and observing, and of preparing the results of their observations for the public mind of England. What we now state with regard to ourselves is common to us with our contemporary journalists ; the sources of expenditure, and the means of indemnification, let either be what it will in amount, are alike to all. The whole consists of money laid out, not in obedience to any law, but in a spirit of enterprise more or less judicious, and the fruit of it is a return of profit, of reputation, or influence upon the public mind more or less extensive and complete.

Radical sentiment was automatically in favour of unrestricted circulation, and further debate on the measure demonstrated that it was a purely Whig contrivance, lacking the support of the Radical element. Wakley of the *Lancet* joined John Walter as a teller for the Opposition, Walter being against the measure for one reason and Wakley for another. The Radicals objected to the reduction of the stamp duty as a palliative measure blocking the way to abolition. The Government accepted the demand of George Grote that the stamp should comprise the name of the journal, a prescription which the Whigs expected to demonstrate, in the next Parliamentary returns, the claimed superiority of circulation by the *Morning Chronicle*. When the Bill went to the Lords the clause for the registration of newspaper proprietors was rejected. Melbourne, in stating his objections, grew personal at the expense of John Walter, who took the first occasion to retort upon him. *The Times* of August 13 declared that men of good sense and decent taste would have no two opinions about Melbourne's speech. It advised Walter to console himself with the reflection that " if he be insolently treated by Lord Melbourne, the House of Lords has to endure the same nuisance," though " it is, indeed, rather novel for the First Minister of a great commercial country to make it a reproach to a member of the Legislature that he raised himself from a humble station." The Lords' rejection of the clause for the registration of newspaper proprietors was a further bar to Radical support of the Bill. The registration of editors or proprietors was an old crotchet of the Left-wingers. Cobbett in his *Register* had attacked the anonymity of the Press generally and *The Times* particularly. Joseph Parkes wrote to Francis Place (December 3, 1826) urging him to watch the " Bloody old *Times*." "The first thing I shall move in the Reformed Parliament Session will be a Committee of Inquiry : who wrote the leaders in *The Times* of the last 15 years ; and if Slop, Barnes, Sterling and Fraser are dead I shall have their bones placed as a coral necklace round the neck of Billy Pitt's skeleton."[1] Parkes's facetious tone disguises the genuine anxiety of active political agents, particularly Whigs and Radicals, to know the secrets of Printing House Square.

The Times noticed the registration clause in a leading article :

We have often said, and now repeat, that so far as we are ourselves concerned, the novelties of this measure, whether decided on or threatened only, affect us very slightly if at all, save in so far as the general character of the press, and through it the public interest, may thrive or suffer. The chief proposition of Monday evening which bore anything of an unprecedented aspect was one introduced by Mr. C. Buller, that all the proprietors of newspapers or shareholders in them, should be registered, and this on the ground that at present newspapers " could circulate all sorts of slander, and he therefore insisted that every proprietor should be registered. It was not right that anonymous writers should hold up individuals to infamy, by the lucubrations of obscure and worthless persons, whose obscurity and worthlessness shielded them from responsibility. He contended that every individual having an interest in a paper should be registered by name at the Stamp

[1] B.M., Place MSS., 37949, 185.

Office." . . . In answer to this gentleman, who, we suppose, holds himself to be as celebrated as we are obscure, we shall merely say, though with perfect indifference as to the result, that the public have no business with the details of sleeping partnerships in newspapers any more than in magazines, reviews, or other literary speculations. The country indeed has a right to adequate security against the violation of *the law*, and that in the case of *stamped* newspapers is already provided for. (July 13, 1836.)

After the registration clause, the scheme of measurement by superficial inches was struck out of the Bill, which went through with the Lords' amendments ; without Radical support a struggle with the Peers was out of the question. So the Government lost their chance of discriminating against *The Times*. But there still remained one device.

The " distinctive die," *i.e.*, the stamp embodying in the design the name of each paper, was considered a sure method of bringing down *The Times*. The Government were honestly persuaded that *The Times* was losing ground so rapidly that it bought stamps which it knew it would not use, and which it either turned over to the use of the *Evening Mail* or secretly sold to unnamed papers in the country. While it is certain that the practice obtained whereby London journals did buy stamps in order to impress their advertising patrons, who were unaware of the subsequent re-sale to country papers, *The Times* had no need of such an expedient. The penny stamp made its appearance on September 15, 1836. A notice over the leader read : " In consequence of the reduction of the stamp duty on newspapers, the price of *The Times* in future will be 5d." In its issue of the day before, *The Times*, in good humour, as it could afford to be, prepared its readers for the new operation :

[In the] act there was inserted a clause which rendered it imperative upon each paper to publish with what, in the Radical slang, is denominated " a distinctive die." The meaning of this, in plain English, is, that the name of the paper for which each stamp is issued shall be marked upon the stamp. This jocose proposition originated with the *Grunticle*, but, unluckily for our contemporary, Mr. Grote, one of the city members, took it for earnest. . . . Against this proposition of a " distinctive die " we never said a syllable. In truth we were positively in love with it for a moment—for that moment in which we vainly flattered ourselves that we might have the " die " done after our own fashion. We like it still, though the fashion of the " die " is to be fixed by the Government. We confess, however, candidly, that we have been not a little disappointed in learning from the Stamp Office that this said " distinctive die " is not yet ready, nay that it will not be ready till the first of January !

The paper, in these circumstances, suggested that as the design was not yet ready, Mr. Rice, who had (in Lord Palmerston) a " Cupid " for a colleague, should himself take a hint from his namesake Mr. Rice, of the Surrey Theatre, who personated a black Cupid there. " Surely here is an opening for the Government. Why not make a graven image of Mr. Rice, Senior, of the Treasury, in the not unappropriate character of a black Cupid and give him never dying fame on the ' distinctive die.' ? . . . We have three and a half months good yet till the first of January. In this case, it is further recommended that the representation of the *Black-Amour* be displayed, like a cherub on a tombstone, with an exchequer bill at a discount in its mouth." The stamp, however, was ready before the first of January, appearing on the issue of

The first penny stamp,
September 15, 1836

The new " distinctive " die,
December 3, 1836

The Times of Saturday, December 3, 1836. *The Times* took the opportunity to inform its readers accordingly :

We publish to-day with what Mr. Grote, directed by the *Grunticle* and adopting its peculiar slang, is pleased to denominate " a distinctive die." The Whig-Radicals are constantly insinuating, or plainly declaring, that this journal supplied other papers with stamps which it took as for itself. Like Major Longbow, they told this falsehood so often, that at last they believed it ; and, in order to put a stop to the supposed practice, and ascertain, what they could not believe they already knew—the real circulation of *The Times*—they got Mr. Grote to propose that the name of each paper should be put upon its stamps. The stamp so altered was dubbed " a distinctive die." The public will do us the justice to recollect that so far from opposing this ridiculous crotchet, we over and over again expressed our willingness that it should be carried into execution, being well assured that we could not more effectually " show the eyes and grieve the heart " of the envious Whig-Radical curs that bark at and bay us, than by affording the precise evidence they required of the extent of our circulation, and consequently of their falsehood respecting it. The state of the country at this moment furnishes us with an additional ground of satisfaction that our blockheaded enemies hit upon this scheme to injure us. We mean, that the greatly increased and increasing circulation of *The Times* will add another to the thousand proofs already before the world. . . .

That this was not rodomontade soon became certain even to the most unwilling Whigs. After all the agitation, the meetings and the petitions on the one hand, the Treasury doles, party moneys and literary efforts on the other, the preponderance of power over public opinion rested with *The Times* in 1836 as in 1834.

Brougham had boasted to Wellesley," I have succeeded, I believe, in putting an end to the newspaper stamps, which the great papers hold to be one of their securities against competition."[1] Brougham gave little credit to his following. It took two years' hidden work by Althorp, Joseph Parkes, Nassau Senior, Charles Buller, Thomas Drummond, Denis Le Marchant and public agitation by Radicals and Irish members, as well as the Diffusion Societies, to reduce the stamp duty and thus accelerate the supposed losses of *The Times*. There never was a word of truth in the story of the losses of *The Times* which were alleged to follow its having " ratted." The figures of the sales of stamps before the distinctive die were :

LONDON NEWSPAPERS 1835.[2]

Title of Newspaper	January	February	March	April	May	June
The Times & Evening Mail ..	221,997	240,000	240,000	240,000	260,000	205,000
Morning Chronicle & Evening Chronicle	140,000	151,000	150,000	167,500	185,000	160,000

Title of Newspaper	July	August	Sept.	Oct.	Nov.	Dec.
The Times & Evening Mail ..	157,997	236,000	204,000	260,000	250,000	230,000
Morning Chronicle & Evening Chronicle	192,500	150,000	160,000	185,000	132,500	185,000

[1] Brougham to Wellesley, July 19, 1834. (*Wellesley Papers*, II, 244.)
[2] Statistical Department, Somerset House, MSS. *Accounts showing the Number of Stamps issued for Newspapers in Certain Years*, s.a. 1835.

But in a year or two more, the Whigs comforted themselves, *The Times* would take the lowest place in the circulation figures of the London Press. The Parliamentary Return for 1837 was anticipated by all parties with the greatest curiosity, and by the Whigs with the utmost confidence. The figures were at last available. " I well remember," says Charles Mackay, then reporter on the Whig paper, " the consternation excited in the office of the *Morning Chronicle*, of which the daily issue was about 9,000, when it was proved on the authority of the Parliamentary returns that the circulation of *The Times* was 11,000."[1] By the date of Barnes's death in active service *The Times* sold four times as many copies as the *Chronicle*.

[1] Mackay, *Forty Years' Recollections*, 1877, II, 81.

XIX

BARNES'S TERMS TO THE TORIES

BY the summer of 1834 the Whigs had forfeited their credit by clinging to office. Brougham was alone among them in retaining any public reputation as a man of policy and action, but Brougham had now been found intolerable by his own colleagues. He had fought hard to protract the life of the Grey Cabinet, and of its feeble successor, and even now he was battling against any change of Government and against the newspapers which demanded it. " You'll see the London Press furious at me," he had written to Wellesley, " especially *The Times*. . . . The key to it is that they all wanted *dissolution* and *revolution* . . . and some want government at the mercy of the *gentlemen of the Press*, and they accuse me, most unjustly, I am glad to say, of having defeated their prospect by standing firm." But it was *The Times*, and his own colleagues, who had the last word.

When Grey and Althorp resigned on July 8, 1834, Brougham affected to believe that nothing had happened but the resignation of two Ministers. *The Times*, however, called imperatively for a reorganization of the Cabinet :

> The rubbish must be wheeled away to the last barrowfull before any sure foundation can be laid for a new building. Good God ! Are we to have another downright fraud passed upon the rightful expectations of the country ? Are we to have putty and whitewash laid over " lath and plaster " and then told that such an edifice will stand the hurricane of times like these ? (July 11, 1834.)

Any new Cabinet must be more liberal than Lord Grey's ; " it must rid itself effectually of that more than half-Tory section which has for these two Sessions of Parliament paralyzed and disabled the best efforts of its more patriotic and enlightened colleagues." Neither Lord Lansdowne nor Lord Althorp was fit to be Prime Minister ; and, in fact, the new Whig Administration had Lord Melbourne for leader. But the Reform period was over ; behind the scenes old connexions were being revived and new alliances planned ; and the Melbourne Government, a stopgap at the best, lasted only for five months of masterly inactivity. The end came with the death of Lord Spencer, Althorp's father, which sent Althorp to the House of Lords and deprived William IV. of his confidence in the stability of the Government. To Melbourne's surprise the King sent for the Duke of Wellington. *The Times* informed its readers :

We have no authority for the important statement which follows, but we have every reason to believe that it is perfectly true. We give it, without any comment or amplification, in the very words of the communication, which reached us at a late hour last night, or rather at an early hour this morning :—" The KING has taken the opportunity of Lord Spencer's death to turn out the Ministry ; and there is every reason to believe that the Duke of Wellington has been sent for. The Queen has done it all." (November 15, 1834.)

It is astonishing to think that history for long accepted as a fact the story that the informant of *The Times* was Brougham, with whom the paper had broken absolutely since the summer. According to Greville, Melbourne had told only Brougham, and that under a stipulation against saying a word to anybody. " He promised," writes Greville, " and the moment he quitted the house sent to *The Times* office and told them what had occurred, with the well-known addition ' that the Queen had done it all.' " To the same effect Sir Theodore Martin records in his biography of Lord Lyndhurst that the Chancellor " posted down to the office of *The Times* with the intelligence." A third and more reasonable version is given in a letter of Croker's, written on November 24, 1834, and not published until fifty years later :

When Melbourne came from the King on the Friday night about ten, he, in his usual *poco curante* way, did not think it worth while even to send round a box, to tell his colleagues they were out, contenting himself with summoning a Cabinet for twelve next day. He, however, happened to see our friend the *Bear*, who is as watchful as a fox, and the Bear lost no time in sending the news to the *Chronicle* and *Times* with an addition that it was all the Queen's doing. When Lord Holland saw the papers next morning, he said, " Well here's another hoax." Lord Lansdowne equally disbelieved it, and I believe one or two others of the Cabinet also learnt their Dissolution from the newspapers. How like Melbourne all this is !

The "Bear" was Edward Ellice,[1] Secretary at War, and there need be little hesitation in accepting Croker's statement, though it is clear that others in London attributed *The Times* article to Brougham. By November 17 the Editor had been able to ponder over the statement he had published "without examination, and under the first excitement of such extraordinary intelligence." His second article included a paragraph taking the "opportunity of stating that the passage (in the communication sent to us on Saturday morning) relating to the Queen has no foundation in fact. Her Majesty had not the slightest concern with this revolution in the Cabinet." In the correspondence columns of this same Monday's issue there appeared a short letter :

To the Editor of *The Times*.
Sir,
    It has come to the knowledge of the writer of this that *The Times* is in secret correspondence at this moment with Lord Brougham. Is there any objection to the publication of this fact ?
                                                        ACHATES.
Nov. 15.

An editorial footnote was appended : "We publish this letter of ' Achates ' for the sake of declaring that what he calls a fact is a mere falsehood." Indeed, if Greville were correct, it would connect Brougham with the paper some four or five months after the break in the summer, and in that case the tone of leading articles of the following week would be difficult of comprehension. Respecting " one individual (by courtesy called ' learned ') of the late Cabinet "—plainly Brougham—

the King makes no scruple of speaking out, as of an itinerant mountebank, who has not only disgraced the Cabinet of which he formed part, but has dragged the Great Seal of England through the kennel, and degraded, by his unnumbered antics and meannesses, the highest office of the law and state in England.

This was the end of Brougham's political career. *The Times* had written on July 25, 1834, that it had for fifteen years sturdily upheld him, enabling him to achieve the good ambitions which then predominated in him.

We are at this late hour called his " detractors " because with pain and repugnance we strive to rouse him from that dream which, if it

---

[1] Ellice was a brother-in-law of Lord Grey and nicknamed " Bear " from his connexion with the fur trade.

endure much longer, will end in an abrupt and frightful, but fruitless awakening, to the irredeemable loss of all which such a man can or ought to value—the fame and character that were achieved by Henry Brougham.   (July 25, 1834.)

Barnes's warning was in vain. Brougham was not to be roused from his dream.

The abrupt dismissal of Melbourne precipitated a situation which compelled the journal to do more than inveigh against the complacency of Whiggery. The tendency of moderate opinion was in the Conservative direction, but *The Times*, though recording that the Conservatives were being " looked up to," had mainly been exerting itself to demand such a reorganization of the Whig Cabinet as would inspire public confidence. " If, as you have always told me," wrote Madame Lieven to Grey, " *The Times* represents public opinion, all this is not very favourable to the Government. And if the Ministry really does not enjoy the public favour (and seeing they have no great talents in the Cabinet) I am curious to know how they will manage to keep on their legs." Madame Lieven wrote on September 6. The King's unexpected action two months later compelled *The Times* to face the Whig, Conservative, Radical and Irish parties in new circumstances. Long, cool and sagacious articles discussed the political prospect. The King had sent for the Duke of Wellington, but it was known with certainty by *The Times* that the country would not stand an old-fashioned Tory Government. Peel's absence abroad was a dangerous complication, for, while his Toryism had moderated, the Duke was still thought to be uncompromising. In July, when Grey resigned, the King had desired the impossible coalition of Melbourne, Stanley, Peel—and the Duke. Peel then had declared for cautious and well-digested reform. None knew whether the Duke had made any advance towards a Liberalized Toryism. Melbourne told Grey in the middle of November that the King's sending for the Duke was a " fearful expedient."

The Duke advised the King that, as the greatest of the several difficulties before the Tories were those in the Commons, he should call a member of that House—Peel. The King's messenger caught Peel in Rome on November 28.

On November 18, 1834, the attention of readers of *The Times* was drawn to assurances by the Duke's friends that he was meditating " Reform " ; and the comment was that " we must wait for his actions before their sufficiency can be relied upon ; and if they fall short of what the evil requires . . . the result is clear—neither the people nor the press will maintain the alliance with him." There were many who asked what the words signified. Sir James Scarlett, a Cambridge contemporary of Barnes and legal adviser to *The Times*, and deep in the Duke's confidence, was one who thought there might be a chance of securing the support of Printing House Square. Scarlett, after years as a Whig member of the Commons, became Canning's Attorney-General and was continued in the same office by Wellington in the " Emancipation " Government. He had opposed the Reform Bill, had become a Tory, but remained friends with Barnes and kept his position of legal adviser. Greville was one who thought the tone of *The Times* significant. When the King came to town to receive the resignations, and Ministers went to St. James's with their seals, Greville, in attendance that day as Clerk of the Privy Council, took the opportunity of asking the Duke if he had seen *The Times* that morning.

He said " No " ; and I told him there appeared in it a considerable disposition to support the new Government, and I thought it would be very advisable to obtain that support if it could be done. He said he was aware that he had formerly too much neglected the Press, but he did not think *The Times* could be influenced.[1] I urged him to avail himself of any opportunity to try, and he seemed very well disposed to do so.

Lyndhurst, whom I afterwards talked to for a long time, went into the whole business. He said that it was very desirable that the publick should know the truth of what had taken place between the King and Melbourne both in conversation and by letter, because it wd. be seen that the former was in no way to blame.

Nov. 26th. [Added on Verso of 322.] This case, such as Lyndhurst described it to me, was afterwards put hypothetically in the *Times*, to which it was furnished probably by Scarlett—but the Whigs emphatically declare that it is not correct.

A little later on November 18 Greville again saw Lord Lyndhurst, the Lord Chancellor-designate, and asked him if he had seen *The Times*, told him what had passed between the Duke and himself, and told him he would do well to obtain its support. Lyndhurst said he could desire nothing so much as an understanding with the Editor of *The Times*, but in his situation he did not like personally to interfere, or to place himself in its power. On Greville, with pardonable exaggeration, assuring him that he had some acquaintance with Barnes, Lyndhurst entreated him to see what could be

[1] B.M., MSS. Addl. 41105 : Greville Diary, Vol. XI, foll. 322-376, *ff.*

done. Greville's knowledge of Barnes was not more than second-hand, but they had possessed since 1830 a discreet acquaintance in Henry de Ros, who had been of service to the paper with its Paris correspondence. De Ros contrived an interview with Barnes and put it to him whether or not the paper would support the new Government, to be formed on Sir Robert Peel's return from Rome. Taking his chance, Barnes placed on paper conditions which, as he could not help knowing, would be difficult for the Duke, for Lyndhurst, or for any true Tory to swallow. The terms comprised complete abstention from any interference with the Reform Bill, and adoption of those measures of reform already sanctioned by the votes of the House of Commons—*i.e.*, the Tithe Measure and the Corporations Act. There was to be no change in foreign policy. The last was an important point, as Wellington was thought to favour armed intervention against democratic movements in Europe.

" I have sent his [Barnes's] note to Lyndhurst and begged him to talk the matter over," concludes Greville's entry of November 19, 1834.

He noted in his diary later in the day :

6 o'clock. Lyndhurst has just been here—he had seen the Duke, who had already opened a negotiation with Barnes through Scarlett. I offered to get any statement inserted of the causes of the late break up and he will again see the Duke and consider of inserting one. He said " Why Barnes is the most powerful man in the country." The *Standard* has sent to offer its support—The Duke said he should be very happy, but they must understand that the Government was not yet formed, etc.

Barnes asked for immediate acceptance or rejection of his terms, on the ground that the situation had to be dealt with by him daily ; yet, inevitably, the Duke was slow in making up his mind. The Editor grew impatient, and on November 23 sent a letter. Barnes, " evidently much nettled at not having received any specific answer to his notes, stating the terms on which he would support the Duke," demanded an immediate reply.[1] On this reminder, which came through de Ros, Greville hastened to the Exchequer Court and waited to give the note to Lyndhurst as he came out.

[Saturday night 23rd] . . . He took me away with him, and stopt at the Home Office, to see the Duke, and talk to him on the subject, for he was evidently a little alarmed, so great and dangerous a Potentate is the wielder of the thunders of the press. After a long consultation

[1] The words are Greville's, *cf.* MS., Vol. XI, fol. 342 ; (B.M., MSS. Addl. 41105).

He [Lord Lyndhurst] said : " Why Barnes is the most powerful
man in the country."

Photographed from a page in Greville's Diary, the original of which is
in the British Museum

he came out and gave me a note the Duke had written saying he could not pledge himself, nor Sir Robert Peel, before he arrived, who was to be the Minister, and eventually I agreed to draw up a paper explanatory of the position of the Duke and his expectations and news with regard to *The Times* and its support. This I sent to him and he is to return it to me with such corrections as he may think it requires, and it is to be shewn to Barnes to-morrow—in the way Lyndhurst told me.[1]

Within two days the Duke had made up his mind, and wrote a note ; Lyndhurst drew up a memorandum " much better," says Greville, than his own. On November 24, 1834, " The Duke's note and this paper were read to him [Barnes] and he expressed himself quite satisfied—was much gratified by an offer Lyndhurst made to him and proposed a meeting—so I take leave of the affair."

On December 2 Lord Lyndhurst gave a dinner for Thomas Barnes at his mansion in George Street, Hanover Square, to which he invited Sir William Follett, a Cambridge man soon to become Solicitor-General, Sir Henry Hardinge, the Irish Secretary, and Sir William Bolland, another Cambridge man and a Judge. Greville also was there, but Wellington, though engaged to be present, was prevented. This evidence of the value placed upon the paper and of Lyndhurst's personal relations with its editor, and the fact that the dinner took place in Lord Lyndhurst's house, gave rise to much comment.

I could never [writes Greville on December 5] understand the Chancellor's making such a display of this connexion, but whatever he may be as a lawyer, and great so-ever in his Wig, I suspect he is deficient in knowledge of the world and those nice calculations of public taste and opinion which are only to be acquired by intuitive sagacity, exercised in the daily communion of social life.

So unusual was it in those days for a Cabinet Minister to entertain a journalist that Lyndhurst's dinner caused a positive uproar. Here was public recognition of the institutional importance of *The Times* by its most obstinate, hereditary antagonists, and, less immediately, public recognition also of the whole profession of journalism. Such recognition was the more unexpected as coming from the Right rather than the Centre or Left. For years Barnes had been vaguely known as a bohemian ; to the younger generation of Tories his early literary career was a blank ; he was still only a " Cockney " to the young bloods of *Fraser's*. In 1827 Barnes's very position as a pressman prevented him from securing

[1] B.M., MSS. Addl. 41105, fol. 343.

election to the Athenaeum[1] ; he was black-balled when Sir James Scarlett proposed him for the United University Club. Connexion with the Press had been sufficiently compromising in itself to compel Ministers of both parties to deal with newspapers only through intermediaries like Denis Le Marchant, Thomas Drummond, Thomas Young, Charles Greville and John Wilson Croker. Whatever Greville might say, Lyndhurst and his colleagues must have known that their action would be socially reprobated, and that party solidarity was risked in publicly strengthening the ties between Whitehall and Printing House Square. But Lyndhurst did not hesitate to deal directly and constantly with the Editor, in defiance of criticism friendly and unfriendly. The practical quality of Barnes's advice was observed and appreciated by the Lord Chancellor-designate, as Greville's entry on December 6, 1834, proves :

Dec. 6. He [Lyndhurst] is doing all he can to draw closer the connection between *The Times* and the Government and communicates constantly with Barnes. He said they must make a liberal and comprehensive Government, and sketched an outline of such a cabinet as he would like.[2]

Peel landed at Dover towards midnight on December 8, 1834. He spent a quarter of an hour at the Ship Inn and posted to London. He conferred with Wellington and came to the conclusion that he would accept the King's invitation, and that he must form a broad, comprehensive Ministry.

That same day John Walter made a suggestion to Scarlett which had a notable sequel.

No 8, Charing Cross   Dec[r] 10, 1834

Dear Sir James :

A conversation I have recently had with a common friend,[3] leads me to fear that you are not accurately informed respecting the feeling that prevails in the County of Berks.

I have within the last fortnight visited the principal towns of that County ; & although I have experienced nothing that shd alarm the

[1] On January 30, 1830, Walter wrote to Croker asking him to assist a candidate for the " University Club " (presumably the United University Club), " a most particular friend of mine, Mr. Barnes, of Pembroke Hall, Cambridge." *The Times* is not mentioned. " He [Barnes] is proposed by the Attorney General [Scarlett], and therefore I need not say any thing about his claims. I will exert any power I may possess, on any similar occasion, for a friend of yours ; and I know many University Men." Croker replied (February 1, 1830) : " I very readily accept your testimony of Mr. Barnes being what old Johnson called a clubbable man, and shall be glad to have him amongst us at the Athenaeum." But in a postscript Croker observes his error and regrets that, since he is not a member of the club in question, he is unable to help. [Croker MSS., Wm. L. Clements Library, Ann Arbor.] In the same year Barnes was elected, by Croker's influence, to the Athenaeum together with Macaulay and James and John Stuart Mill.

[2] Greville, fol. 376.

[3] Most probably Barnes.

340

friends of the projected Ministry, yet, among what is called the Liberal Party, the change contemplated is not talked of with indifference by any, nor with approbation by more than a very small number : while the half of them, perhaps, so far as I could judge, expressed themselves decidedly opposed to what they call " the Return of the Tories to office." You must recollect that I speak of one party only, among whom, however, the feeling I describe was exceedingly strong—so much so indeed, that some of them actually talked of raising a cry of " Duke, or no Duke " ; & making this a pledge for the Candidates who should solicit their votes. Nor is this all. I believe that the sentiments which I have heard expressed by these parties in private would explode in public meetings and writings, were it not that they persuade themselves of the impossibility of the formation of a Tory Administration. Whether these impressions may be removed by the reasoning or the personal influence of others who think differently—or whether they are more likely to increase than to subside upon the actual formation of the Ministry, I think it would be difficult for any one safely to predict. I however incline to the opinion, that the same hostile feeling will remain at least as strong as it exists at present in a very large portion of the Inhabitants of the towns. In the Villages, & in the Agricultural Districts, where politics are less cared for & party spirit can hardly be said to exist, much undoubtedly may be done in correcting wrong opinions & inculcating right ones ; & nothing would tend more to bring about this desirable result than some frank explanation, some popular declaration, *previous* to a Dissolution of Parliament. Indeed without this, I see no hope of preventing the explosion of that unreasonably angry hostility to the Duke of Wellington which has blinded men even to the great services he has rendered to the State : but with it, & with the fact that Sir R. Peel is by no means looked upon with the same distrust as the Duke, the least violent among the party of which I speak may be induced to give the King's Ministers a fair trial.

As to the strength of this party, if it be not very formidable I am quite sure it is at least so strong that it would be exceedingly unsafe to leave it out of the calculation in the event of a contested election ; especially as there is ground for suspicion that they are looking out for a Candidate who will pledge himself to oppose the Duke of Wellington's Government ; & I think they will find one.

If you will give me the earliest intimation of the determination to dissolve Parliament, I shall know how to shape my Course. I need hardly say that I will make no indiscreet use of the intelligence.[1]

I am,

Dear Sir James,

Yrs most faithfully,

J. WALTER.

1 Peel Papers, MSS. Addl. 40405, 24-5.

The utility of Walter's suggestion that Peel should make some public announcement of his acceptance of Reform principles was clear, and Scarlett hastened to put it before him. A statement of policy, with the names of members of Parliament who, by their signatures, would pledge themselves to its support, was thought of. With the country in a state of acute speculation on the intentions of one who was regarded as an old Tory, it was desirable, election or no election, somehow or other to pacify public opinion. The only way of securing approval was to do what no pre-Reform Tory would have considered for a moment—namely, to ask for it in a " popular declaration," to use Walter's phrase, or in a word since become famous in this connexion, a " manifesto."

The famous Tamworth Manifesto was not issued, however, before various methods had been considered and rejected. The Administration knew it was on dangerous ground. The address was examined by Scarlett and discussed with one Minister and another in the early part of December ; drafts were made for submission to the Cabinet by the middle of the month. A letter from Scarlett to Peel proves that one of these drafts, drawn up for signature by members of Parliament, was communicated to Barnes :

New Street, Tuesday [*endorsed* 16*th December*, 1834].
My dear Sir Robert,

I now send you the proposed address as altered by Mr. B. He will be ready to adopt any other alterations that may be suggested in the language. If you approve I will return it to him saying that I think it will do and that most probably it will meet with a satisfactory answer, if signed by any considerable number of members, but that it will perhaps not be thought of sufficient importance if signed by a few. In [fact] I should doubt whether Walter could procure many signatures and I would not in the first instance commit you to anything.

Ever yours truly,
J. SCARLETT.[1]

The same Tuesday Peel wrote to Scarlett that the plan of issuing the address had been changed : " I think every object will be answered—and in the best mode—by an Address from me to my Constituents and which I can issue on any day—on the ground that my seat is now vacant. My answer to the inclosed therefore would be in substance contained in that Address, and I had

[1] Peel Papers, MSS. Addl. 40405, 325.

rather give it in that form." [1] On the following day the Cabinet considered the matter at dinner at Lyndhurst's. According to Greville :

They sat till twelve o'clock upon it, after which it was copied out, a messenger despatched to three great newspapers, *The Times*, the *Morning Herald* and the *Morning Post*, to announce its arrival, and at three in the morning it was inserted.

The address, while committing Peel to the view that the Reform Bill was " a final and irrevocable settlement of a great Constitutional question," denied that the spirit of the Bill meant " that we are to live in a perpetual vortex of agitation." That the spirit of the Bill implied a " careful review of institutions civil and ecclesiastical " was accepted. There was no intention to interfere with the Corporations inquiry. Church revenues here and in Ireland should be examined and redistributed. *The Times* differed from Peel on this point, but " the difference may turn out to be one much more of theory than of fact." What to do with the surplus depended upon its amount and the sittings of the committee of inquiry. The penultimate paragraph summed up Peel's policy :

Our object will be the maintenance of peace, the scrupulous and honourable fulfilment, without reference to their original policy, of all existing engagements with Foreign Powers, the support of public credit, the enforcement of strict economy, and the just and impartial consideration of what is due to all interests, agricultural, manufacturing, and commercial.

Doubtless the reason for excluding the *Morning Chronicle* lay in the final refusal of those Whigs who had parted from Grey and Melbourne to cooperate with Peel. Stanley had refused to join the Cabinet, and a purely Conservative Government resulted from this and other abstentions.[2] The *Morning Chronicle*, consequently, was not included on the Press list. It is clear from the aspect of *The Times*, the *Herald* and the *Post* that the address was expected, but none, not even *The Times*, provided readers with any commentary, the *Herald* and the *Post* giving only a few lines of introduction : " Sir Robert Peel's Address to the electors of Tamworth appears in our paper this day "—so the *Herald*. " We will not

[1] MSS. Addl. 40405, 327.
[2] In Peel's Ministry, as finally completed, Lyndhurst was Lord Chancellor, Wellington Foreign Secretary, Aberdeen Colonial Secretary, and Goulburn Home Secretary.

detain our readers for a moment from the perusal of the following important document "—so the *Post*.

The Times, immediately below the date, Thursday December 18, 1834, thus introduced the document :

At an early hour (half-past 3) this morning, and when the article which follows this was in type, we received the address of Sir R. Peel to his constituents at Tamworth. The anxiety of the public for some authentic declaration of the policy of the new Government has induced us to give this document as conspicuous a position as its importance demands. The hour at which it reached us precludes all possibility of comment till we can bestow upon it that calm consideration to which, on every account, it is entitled.

Friday's *Chronicle* reproduced the text of the Manifesto from *The Times* and instructed its readers what to make of it in a two-column leading article :

Sir Robert Peel having ruined his Cabinet by the selection of its members, and the dubious appearance of its policy, has published a Manifesto in the form of an " Address to the Electors of the Borough of Tamworth," the Right Hon. Baronet having vacated his seat by the acceptance of the Premiership. This singular document, received by *The Times* at half past three o'clock yesterday morning, before break of day, is the palpable production of a " diplomatist," one " versed in affairs of state." A more despicable or contemptable (*sic*) effusion of party cunning never met the public eye. . . .

Greville again is responsible for the statement that it " made a prodigious sensation, and nobody talks of anything else." Barnes had suggested alterations in the address ; it is reasonable to believe that some of them were adopted in the published text—the phrase " vortex of perpetual agitation " is suggestive of Barnes's style. In the prodigious sensation *The Times* shared to its momentary cost. While the country was amazed that the Duke, Peel and Lyndhurst should have gone back on the hallowed traditions of Toryism, the paper suffered torrents of abuse from the followers of Althorp and Melbourne, and with the abuse hundreds of withdrawn subscriptions. People, said Barnes, were " deaf with passion." But *The Times* was in a very strong position with regard to the Government, its support being indispensable. A rumour that it had " changed hands " and been sold to the Carlton Club appears to have arisen from Croker's confabulations with John

Walter during the election. So much is to be gathered from the following letter, dated from West Molesey, February 5, 1835 :

My dear Peel,

I think it as well to let you see the inclosed from my old Walter.[1]

He is as you will see stout in his advice—I hope he may be so in his vote—You know that they placarded London with a notice that I had been at Walter's house in the country & bought him & *The Times* for only 2 millions—I only wish I had kept £100,000 for myself ; for really, on consideration, I do think that £1,900,000 would have been quite enough for my friend.

Let me have my letter again & you need say nothing about *us*.

Yours affectionately
J. W. CROKER.

The Prime Minister was at first apprehensive that *The Times* might transfer its sympathy elsewhere. There were many changes of allegiance. John Walter stood as a Peelite for Berkshire, and Peel wrote to Sir Herbert Taylor, the King's Secretary, in his behalf :

Whitehall, Jan. 1. 1835.

My dear Taylor,

I need say nothing as to the importance of keeping the *Times* & Mr. Walter in good humour.

Walter is Candidate for Berkshire, as you probably well know. It is said that the *Windsor Clergy* have considerable influence.

Can you through any private channel, so far propitiate them, or any of them, as to make them favourably disposed towards Palmer, Pusey & then Walter, in preference to Dundas.

Ever Yrs.
ROBERT PEEL.[2]

The Tamworth Manifesto resulted in a great increase in the number of Conservative M.P.s at the General Election of 1835, but they were still a minority, and the Government was left dependent upon the support of moderate and friendly Whigs. Peel and Barnes had tried and failed to persuade one or two of them to become Ministers. Barnes complained of the " bad composition " of the Government. Opposition journals made a dead set against *The Times*, the more cynical prophesying a return to Whiggism as soon as the Conservatives fell into difficulties. Early setbacks were a defeat on the choice of the Speaker and

[1] The letter from John Walter cannot now be traced.
[2] B.M., MSS. Addl. 40302, 131.

a forced withdrawal of the appointment of Lord Londonderry, brother of Lord Castlereagh, as Ambassador at St. Petersburg. Ministerialists anxiously speculated whether *The Times* would be tempted into another course. The Government knew no more than could be gathered from highly-coloured reports of meetings at which *The Times* was burnt and resolutions passed exiling the paper from hotels and coffee-houses. A confidential agent wrote from Paris towards the end of January, 1835, to inform Wellington that it was likely *The Times* would turn round. The Duke forwarded his correspondent's letter to Peel and received a reply in these terms :

Private   Whitehall Jan. 7, 1835.
My dear Duke,

    I return the inclosed. I think there is some confirmation of the probability of the statement it contains respecting the *Times* in the *Times* Newspaper of this day.

    First there is a lamentable falling off from the usual number of advertisements—and secondly the tone taken in the Paper, quite shews I think that it is at single anchor.

    But look at the *Herald* also of today—and you will see in its article respecting Lord Stanley that it is much in the same position.

Ever yours &c

ROBERT PEEL.[1]

    P.S. I well know the writer of the inclosed. *Mr. John Wilks,*[2] late member for Sudbury, son of Wilks the Dissenter, Member for Boston, and I believe author of the letters published some time since in the *M. Chronicle* signed OPQ.

Peel's nervousness was not altogether unjustified. " Why not inquire," *The Times* had suggested in the " single anchor " leader of January 7, " into the feasibility of an alliance with Sir Robert Peel, and on the principles of constitutional reform ? There might possibly, on the Irish Church question, be less difference between Lord Melbourne and Sir Robert Peel than between Lord Melbourne and Lord Stanley. We hazard the opinion that if ever the ultra-Radical pressure is to be effectually resisted it will—it must—be by such a union as that which we have now suggested— between the rational and moderate portions of the Conservatives and the Whigs." Such a phrase as " We hazard the opinion "

---

[1] MSS. Addl. 40310, 24 [*copy*]. The advertisements for January 7 were indeed thin, but they were deliberately reduced in order to assist the make-up of the issue for January 8, which was an 8-page paper.

[2] Wilks was also the Paris correspondent of the *Standard* and was later convicted as a forger and swindler. The Duke's covering letter to Peel (40310, 22) misdescribes Wilks as correspondent of the *Morning Herald.*

was certainly not characteristic of *The Times* in confident mood ; nor was the suggestion itself much to Peel's taste. Barnes reminded Lyndhurst, through Winslow, his secretary, that he was very anxious to serve Ministers " as long as the Government is conducted on Liberal principles."[1] Nevertheless, John Wilks was able to inform the Duke that no change was known to have taken place in the policy of Printing House Square, so far as foreign correspondents were aware :

Private and Confidential.
My Lord Duke,

I have heard from Mr. Turnbull[2] that, " *The Times* people think it possible, that the Government of Sir Robert Peel, may have a majority for it on the question of the Speaker, and the Address ;—and that consequently all the matters are to remain between it and its correspondents as during the last six weeks."

As this intelligence is satisfactory for more than one reason I hasten to communicate it to you—and authorize you to shew this letter to Sir Robert Peel—I have only learn't this result this morning, and do not delay an hour. The circulation of *The Times* is " a little improving ! " —and that of the *Chronicle* " a little falling off ! ! "

I am,
My Lord Duke
Your mo. obedt. hble servt.
JOHN WILKS.[3]

20 Rue du Helder, January 26 : 1835.

It is clear that the relations between the paper and the working officials of the Government were distant. In fact, *The Times* was finding it hard to get into contact, when notice was short, with a responsible Government spokesman. Croker, an old hand at the Press business, advised Peel on this matter, " always important, now vital."[4]

Nothing, however, seems to have been done for weeks. *The Times* complained again and again of the lack of cooperation of

---

[1] MSS. Addl. 40411, 205.

[2] A well-known staff correspondent of *The Times* at this time in Paris for the paper.

[3] MSS. Addl. 40310, 41-3.

[4] " Things seem on the whole to look better than I ever expected to see them. Who is to manage your press—*managed it must be* & by a Cabinet Minister too : I think Herries your best man. I once wrote Planta at his own request a long letter on the subject of such management—if he has kept it, it might be worth looking at. You, I believe, have no adequate idea of what the Whigs & especially Brougham did in that way, & how much literary good feeling they conciliated by their patronage of Galt, Gleig, Kelly & other Tory writers to say nothing of their own penmen. Pray think—soon & long & deeply on this subject, always important now vital." (Croker to Peel, December 17, 1834 ; MSS. Addl. 40321, 26.) John Galt, author of *Annals of the Parish*, was editor of the *Courier* in 1830 ; the Rev. G. R. Gleig was a contributor to *Fraser's*.

Government officials. In February Barnes had to write a protest in strong terms, upon which Lyndhurst wrote to Peel as follows :

Wed. [*endorsed Feb. 26, 1835*].

My dear Peel,

I am very much afraid we may lose the *Times* unless we make some arrangem^t respecting it. It is worth *all* the other papers put together. In the City in particular it is the only paper that is read.

The paper was offended at not having received a hint about the K.'s Speech while it appeared in full detail in the *M. Post*. Will you appoint some *confident^l person* to be in regular communication with the *Times* and that may set all right? You will perceive by the accompanying letter what they feel and what they wish. I think you will agree with me that this ought not to be neglected.

Ever sncy. D^r. Peel,

Y^r LYNDHST.[1]

If you *name* a *person* will you have the kindness to let me know who it is.

The letter drew a practical reply from Peel on the same day (February 26) :

My dear Chancellor,—No one's surprise could be greater than mine at the insertion of the headings of the Kings Speech in the *Morning Post*, with an accuracy (which in spite of all assurances to the contrary) seems to preclude the possibility of their having been given by anyone who had not seen—in fact was not in possession of the speech. The *Morning Post* applied to me for the heads of the speech and received a positive refusal from me. Sir George Clerk will most readily communicate with any confidential person who may be sent for the purpose by *The Times*.

Ever etc.

ROBERT PEEL.[2]

Sir George Clerk's appointment was welcome though late. That no foundation ever existed for Ministerial suspicions of the paper is shown by its subsequent policy, which was one of consistent support for the Government. But a Government in a minority in the Commons is beset by threats and rumours. Peel's was no exception, and in April, 1835, the end arrived from the direction of Ireland. Beaten on Lord John Russell's resolution to appropriate for educational purposes the surplus revenue of the Irish Church, Peel resigned.

[1] MSS. Addl. 40316, 164.
[2] 40316, 165.

O'Connell now held the balance of power. *The Times* was accused of raising religious passions in expressing such a sentiment as this :

We shall soon see whether the people of this country, who have hitherto considered the Protestant reformed faith as the richest inheritance they have received from their ancestry, will allow that faith to be sacrificed at the shrine of the graven images of Popery in any part of these realms.

The editorial answer to criticism was that No Popery was not a religious but a political cry, and being an element in the Irish question affected vital British political interests. So began a new phase of policy the development of which remains to be traced.

Delay between the resignation of Peel and the announcement of the new Ministry was due in great measure to the Protestant King's desire to protect the Protestant Church. At length Lord Melbourne completed a new Cabinet. On April 18 Peel gave back the seals. During the day he wrote a letter[1] to the Editor of *The Times*, as follows :

Private.   Whitehall, April 18. 1835.

Sir—Having this day delivered into the hands of the King the Seals of office, I can without any imputation of an interested motive, or any impediment from scrupulous feelings of delicacy, express my due sense of the powerful support which that Government over which I had the Honour to preside received from the *Times* newspaper.

If I do not offer the expressions of personal Gratitude, it is because I feel such expressions would do injustice to the character of a support which was given exclusively upon the highest and most independent grounds of public principle.

I can say this with perfect truth, as I am addressing one whose person even is unknown to me, and who during my tenure of Power steadily avoided any species of intercourse which could throw a suspicion upon the motives by which he was actuated.

I should however be doing an injustice to my own feelings, if I were to retire from office without one word of acknowledgment, without at least assuring you of the Admiration with which I witnessed, during the

[1] MSS. Addl. 40310, 41-3. This letter, printed from the copy made by Peel's Secretary to be seen in the Peel Papers in the British Museum, is also printed in Carlyle's *Life of John Sterling*, where the part played by Edward Sterling at Printing House Square is exaggerated, Sterling being given a position which he himself publicly disclaimed more than once. For Sterling's actual position see Chapter XXIV.

arduous contest in which I was engaged, the daily exhibitions of that extraordinary ability to which I was indebted for a support the more valuable because it was an impartial and discriminating support.

I have &c.
ROBERT PEEL.

The Editor of *The Times*.

The acknowledgment, in Barnes's hand, sent to Peel reads thus :

The Times Office, April 19, 1835.

Sir,

Your letter has given me great pleasure. I am not surprised that a gentleman distinguished alike by the extent of his talents and the delicacy of his honor should appreciate the motives of the support which *The Times* Paper has under circumstances of no ordinary difficulty afforded to his Government : but tho' not surprized I am not the less gratified that you have taken the first fitting opportunity of delivering your sentiments in a manner at once cordial and liberal. Such an acknowledgment is the only one which an Independent Journalist should expect from any Minister. Such reciprocities are, in my humble opinion, creditable alike to the Govt., and to the Press of this Country : because they demonstrate that each is actuated by motives which, whether of good or evil tendency, are at least personally pure.

I have the honour to be Sir with much respect
Your very obedt. servt.
THE EDITOR.[1]

The Right Honble. Sir R. Peel, Bart, &c &c &c

---

[1] MSS. Addl. 40420, 29. It would be natural for Barnes to send such a letter as Peel's for Sterling to see, with perhaps a request for a draft reply. Carlyle says that the letter, " after meandering through I know not what intricate conduits, and consultations of the Mysterious *Entity* whose address it bore, came to Edward Sterling, as the real flesh and blood proprietor," and he adds that " with due loftiness and diplomatic gravity and brevity, there is Answer, Draught of Answer in Edward Sterling's hand, from the Mysterious Entity so honoured." The draft as printed by Carlyle (*Life of Sterling*) materially differs from Barnes's letter.

XX

THE TIMES "CONSERVATIVE"

THE defeat of Peel was the deliberate work of Lord John Russell. He had realized that the Whigs could not oust the Minister except upon an issue which would unite them with the Radicals and, if possible, the Irish. Unanimity was reached at meetings between Russell and O'Connell which took place at Lord Lichfield's towards the end of March, 1835, and Peel was defeated in April. An understanding was arranged, though Melbourne, the Whig leader, had refused any communication with the Irish leader. The Whigs and the rest of the Opposition, in accordance with the Lichfield House understanding, united against Peel. Not only so, but Lord John's scheme comprised a formula upon which the O'Connellites and the Radicals would unite against Conservatism after Peel's defeat had been accomplished.

On the day of Peel's defeat, according to plan, on the Irish question, *The Times*, discussing the situation which would result if in consequence of the majority against him the Prime Minister thought it his duty to resign, supported the idea of appealing to Lord Grey, who " conveys to the general mind the idea of a Conservative and constitutional Whig." If the hand of Parliament were vigorously set to the work of law, church and corporation reform, *The Times* was unable to perceive " wherein consists any practical or prospective difference between the policy of Sir Robert Peel and that of the official parent of the Reform Bill. For some of Sir Robert Peel's colleagues we cannot safely affirm that, if left to themselves, they would approximate, as he does, to the liberality of Lord Grey." *The Times* could not undertake to be confident of the liberality of some of the " partners of the noble earl. . . . But, lamenting as we do in our inmost heart, the apparent impossibility of an immediate forgetfulness of all party strife between those two great leaders of the two most estimable parties in Great Britain, the Conservative Whigs and moderate Tories, we feel it to be some compensation that such men do exist, and that they know where and how to find each other, when circumstances admit of their uniting."

It was not then suspected, except by *The Times*, that the Irish situation demanded a united front. When Lord Grey declined to form a Coalition Government *The Times* pointed out that he could hardly be expected " to leave without extreme unwillingness the peaceful dignity of an old age crowned with honour, and trust again the angry ocean of politics." The prospects were indeed dark.

The result of the election of January, 1835, had been the rein-forcement of the Radicals by the addition of more than a third of their former numbers, while the Conservatives were more than doubled ; all gains at the expense of the Whigs. But no single party had a clear majority of the House. Neither the English nor the Irish Radicals were strong enough to contend separately against the Conservatives or the Liberals ; together they were strong enough to dictate policy as the price of their alliance—and Melbourne was ready to pay the price in order to keep out Peel. Therefore it was Melbourne's turn. But the Conservatives were increasing in numbers and they were more compact than the Opposition, and there were some forty " moderate " Whigs who preferred Peel to Melbourne. How long, then, could Melbourne hope to be in office ? Friends as well as enemies of *The Times* were puzzled by the crisis and by the paper's position. *The Times* in fact, was not really changing its line. Five years before, a leading article had laid it down that " the breaking up of the old Tory party, by the separation of those portions of it which were teachable and convertible . . . may prove, if turned to its natural use, the salvation of the British Empire." Thus *The Times* wrote, before the Reform Bill, on February 16, 1830. So well known was it that Barnes never regarded party that it was absurd for the Radicals and agitators to accuse *The Times* of treachery. Yet the volume of criticism was immense. *The Times* had " turned," had " ratted," had " apostatised."

Answering critics on April 18, 1835, the paper noticed first the charge that

in urging the Whigs to cooperate at this moment with the Conservatives, rather than with the Radicals and Repealers, we give advice inconsistent with that on which we recommended the former to act a year ago. Our censure, pretty frequent, and pretty strong, we admit, was directed against the Melbourne Cabinet, and against the later periods of Lord Grey's, not because it was not *Radical* enough, but because it seemed to have no character at all. . . . Its promises, most, though not all, of which we approved, were hardly ever executed, after the accomplishment of the Reform Bill had put almost everything within its power.

The article of April 18, 1835, in a full length answer to friends and enemies, gives a reasoned justification of the line *The Times* had followed during the past three years :

There was scarcely a measure of any large public interest which was not either all but abandoned by the Whig Ministers or egregiously botched. . . . We attacked the *inefficiency* of that Cabinet therefore, and not its illiberality—and we appeal to the frequent articles wherein we attacked it—formed the main staple of our castigations. . . . In the last Parliament, the old Whig party constituting the Government was numerous and powerful ; the Conservatives few, and nearly passive ; the Reform Bill, then in all its freshness, or rather crudity, having operated characteristically upon both ; but the Radicals, though impetuous and active, had no power to work mischief but such as might be lent to them through the manifest impolicies of the Whigs. Then with the ball at the foot of the latter party, which supplied functionaries to all the departments of the State, what was the effect of their full enjoyment of office, and of its attributes, down to the day of their dismissal ? It was this— that the Whig Government and the Whig party became every hour more unpopular throughout the entire kingdom, being almost universally regarded as the most incapable, *or* the most insincere, but at all events the most vacillating and least to be relied upon of any that the oldest man in England had remembered. The sentiment prevailed from north to south of the United Kingdom.

That sentiment deepened with the prospect of a Melbourne Cabinet disdaining Conservative aid, and therefore placing itself at the dictation of a concert of determined irreconcilables. Yet the opponents of *The Times*, criticizing its recommendation that the Whigs should form, if they could, a " Conjoint Cabinet " with the Conservatives of Peel and his allies, accused it of making a suggestion obviously likely to lead to insincerity. *The Times*, answering, urged " the old Whigs " to take this prudent and advantageous course because

we know that in combining with the Radicals they will have to make far more pernicious compromises of political opinion—because we

AA

know that to form a junction with ultra-Radicals they must throw up all their known principles and tenets—because the coalition to which they are blindly rushing will be the most corrupt, dishonest and desperate that ever was recorded of English gentlemen, exacting from them a total sacrifice of all our fundamental institutions, the Church, the Peerage, the Crown, and the union of the Monarchy.

In so writing *The Times* was convinced—and the near future confirmed its judgment—that it truly spoke the country's thoughts.

The paper made few predictions, but it had prophesied that the Irish Coercion Bill would make for everlasting hatred between the two countries ; that the Poor Law Bill would set class against class in England ; and it now prophesied that if an alliance were struck between Melbourne and the Radicals it must make for the impairment of British prestige abroad and tranquillity at home. Britain had become the greatest trading country in the world, and *The Times* its oracle. The paper was conscious that it represented that vast interest in the country whose future depended upon relief from present agitation and from the prospect of convulsion. It urged its readers to be content with the incorporation of the middle classes into representative government. It was determined upon the consolidation of Reform and would tolerate no going behind it or any other progressive measure. But the very necessity for the country to earn its living imposed a limit upon professional political commotion. After the Tamworth Manifesto the City, hitherto Whiggish and even Radical, turned to Peel, and the mercantile middle classes more completely trusted *The Times* and distrusted patrons of short cuts to absolute democracy.

The Times, aware that these were no superficial tendencies, reminded Lord Melbourne more than once that the Conservatives were his " natural allies." In so saying *The Times* meant that the Whigs could coalesce with the Conservatives with the least compromise of constitutional principle :

Ay, and eventually, should interests more sordid cross his mind's eye, at a less expense of the share and patronage of office. . . . The Conservatives, we acknowledge, have proved that they cannot govern England *against* a coalition of Whigs with English, Scotch and Irish revolutionists.—and the Whigs must be already convinced in their own hearts that they cannot govern *without* such a coalition—an expedient at once terrible and disgraceful.

This leading article of April 18, 1835, from which some paragraphs have been extracted, possesses all the signs of having been written by the Editor. It appeared on the eve of the formation of the new Government. That Government, according to *The Times* of Monday, April 20, consisted of names

which even amongst the Whig party themselves would present to the nation either the recollection or the hope of talents or services above the flattest mediocrity. Lord Grey is not there,—nor Lord Brougham (who, whatever be asserted of him, is unquestionably not of the noble family of the Humdrums),—nor Lord Althorp, the keystone of the Grey and Melbourne Administrations—nor Lord Stanley, beyond all comparison the ablest and most resolute of the living generation of active Whigs—nor Sir James Graham, as incontrovertibly the best administrator that has belonged to them for the past forty years.

The only figures of public importance in the new Ministry were Lord Melbourne himself, Lord Palmerston, the Foreign Secretary, and Lord John Russell, the leader of the House of Commons ; and its exclusive Whiggery naturally aroused the anger of *The Times*. The paper was angry with the arrogance and snobbery of a party claiming to be peculiarly representative of the people, yet willing to put up a Cabinet of twelve, seven of whom were peers, one the son of a duke and only four commoners. " This was Whiggery." It was angry, too, because " three-fourths of the intelligence of the United Kingdom, nine-tenths of the property, and at least a considerable majority of the representatives of Great Britain are strenuous defenders of a Conservative Government." Thirdly, *The Times* was furious that Englishmen should be treated as pawns in a game.

Rather than approve Whiggery, *The Times* wrote on April 21 :

We have no doubt that the public voice will re-echo our declaration, that the time has at length arrived when the fittest men must be selected for office, without reference to conventional, or party, or factious distinctions. The country is sick and tired of furnishing the stakes for which political adventurers play ; and of all substantial reforms this is perhaps the most desirable reformation, both for the interests of the nation and the character of public men.

It was little use Melbourne hoping that the influence of *The Times* might be given to his Government. The Editor had made up his mind ; he wrote thus to Winslow,[1] Lyndhurst's secretary :

Saturday [April 18, 1835.]

My dear Sir,

Now that the Ministry is formed, I take the first opportunity of stating that I hope our connection with you & your friends will continue the same as before. I have refused in the most decided terms to have any political connection with the new Ministers. Shew this to Lord Lyndhurst.

Yours ever,

T. BARNES.

Lyndhurst himself was glad to send Barnes's letter to Peel.[2]

Daniel O'Connell's terms to the Whigs were at last clear. The question of repeal was to be held in abeyance ; Melbourne was to undertake, first, the appropriation of the surplus revenues of the Irish Church to national purposes ; secondly, an extension of the Irish suffrage ; thirdly, reform of the Irish corporations. It was also perfectly clear to the Government that O'Connell's next demand would be for repeal of the Act of Union. *The Times* insisted that the O'Connell-Melbourne understanding made the Whigs, in spite of themselves, a party to a campaign for the break-up of the unity of the kingdom.

Meanwhile the Whig party was itself in confusion. " There is nothing more remarkable," wrote Disraeli in *Endymion,* " than the sudden break-up of the Whig party after the successful revolution of 1832." The first sign of that break-up was the resignation of Durham in March, 1833. Stanley and Graham left in May, 1834 ; Lord Grey resigned soon afterwards, and Lord Althorp succeeded to the peerage in November. Not enough Whigs remained to give the Government any character.

Barnes's refusal to support the new Government was, therefore, definite. He was convinced that the disintegration of the Whig party had gone much too far to be mended in time to prevent graver consequences, and that as the evidence was overwhelming that the Conservatives had gained most where the Whigs had lost most, he must support them. Some thought the Radicals were in the same position as the Whigs. Macaulay returned from India to

1 Edward Winslow (1801-1876), whose brother Forbes Benignus Winslow (1810-1874) presently secured a position on the staff of *The Times.* Forbes became famous as a mental specialist. The family was a branch of the Winslows of Massachusetts.

2 Lyndhurst to Peel enclosing Barnes's letter, April 19, 1835. B.M., MSS. Addl. 40316, 194.

TEMPORA MUTANTUR

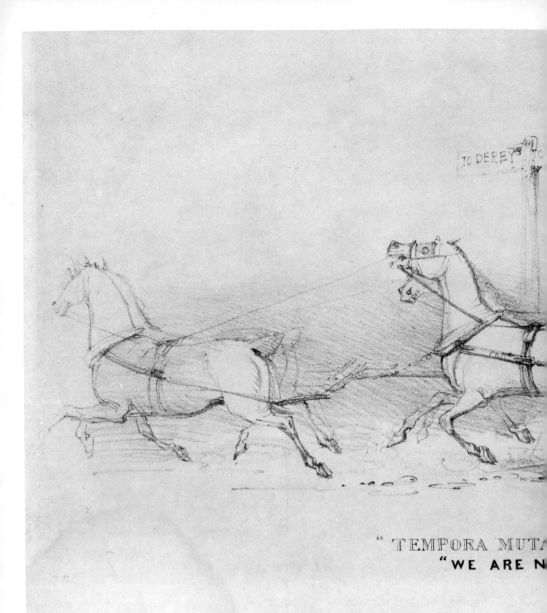

TO DERBY

" TEMPORA MUTA

"WE ARE N

Pub. by

TEMPO
" We are not
Lord Stanley, the Duke, Sir James Graham, Sir Robert

"ET NOS MUTAMUR IN ILLIS"

NGED, NO, NOT WE!"

iccadilly.

T A N T U R

o, not we!"

ir Francis Burdett are represented on *The Times* coach

find that the party as a party consisted only of Mr. and Mrs. Grote. Joseph Parkes had worked hard but vainly to construct a party under the leadership of Durham. The mind of the country, Barnes knew beyond a shadow of doubt, was steadily consolidating in a Conservative sense.

Hence Barnes's declaration to Lyndhurst meant that *The Times* would give its free and critical support to the Conservatives; and that it would fight a Government maintained by Irish and Radical Destructives, principally on the Unionist issue raised by O'Connell's suspended threat of Repeal.

357

XXI

O'CONNELL THE ENEMY

BARNES knew where the new Conservatism was strong and where it was weak. While, as he was aware, the support of *The Times* would do much to commend it to a country still distrustful of the late enemies of Reform, the paper was never in danger of becoming a " Conservative " journal in the party sense. Peel's friends never felt able to rely upon *The Times* to champion the party as a party. Barnes's intention now, as formerly, was to give a lead to public opinion, which at this time he knew was fast turning in favour of Peel, though it was still far from convinced that Melbourne's Government was as dangerous as Barnes contended. The Conservative party officials were in touch with Sterling, whose articles on Irish intimidation were commended by Hardinge to Peel in November, 1835.[1] Graham, however, still considered the course taken by *The Times* to be " devious."[2] Devious as it may have been by the party tests, it was in truth consistent and direct. *The Times* stood for Free Trade and for a united British Empire under a Monarchy. It had its differences with Peel, but it believed that none but Peel was able to withstand the disruptive forces of the Whigs, the Radicals and the Irish, upon whom it bestowed the title of " Destructives."

In coming to terms with Wellington, Lyndhurst and Peel, the paper had insisted that there must be no war abroad, and that domestic peace must not be jeopardized by unfaithfulness to the Reform Bill. In 1835 it was equally insistent that there should be no tampering with the Act of Union between Great Britain and Ireland. Melbourne and John Russell, in accepting O'Connell's terms, well knowing that he would a little later agitate for Repeal, risked the unity of the kingdom in order to keep power. Barnes was determined to fight with all his strength for the Union. There was nothing " devious " about the conduct of *The Times* in this paramount respect.

1 Peel Papers, MSS. Addl. 40314, 108.
2 MSS. Addl. 40429, 199.

Barnes as a Unionist also objected to the Whig action in accepting support from the Radicals, several of whom were doctrinaire Republicans. Thus *The Times* fought, unswervingly, for the maintenance of the Monarchy, the Peerage, and the Church—at a time when many observers thought the fight was as good as lost. Croker wrote his opinion to Peel in January, 1836 : " I look upon the Church and the Peerage as doomed, but we ought to make a parliamentary and literary fight for them."[1] The nervousness in English society was pronounced. *The Times*, though joining in the effort to stem the Radical " Movement," considered that the Irish party as dominated by O'Connell was a more immediate peril to domestic peace. O'Connell, now the greatest of the "Destructives," was the first of the Catholics to enter the House of Commons. It was inevitable that the cause of his Church and of his country should suffer from the peculiar passion and impatience of O'Connell's championship. *The Times*, even before Catholic Emancipation, had seldom agreed with his tactics.

Yet Barnes was never anti-Irish, nor was he possessed by the insular middle-class Englishman's antipathy to Catholicism as such. When, in 1828, Tom Moore introduced Barnes to his friend Philip Crampton, he wrote :

I have ventured to introduce to you by letter our great gun of the press here, Barnes, the Editor of *The Times*, who is about to take a trip to the Lakes of Killarney, and means to stop a day or two in Dublin on his way. The chief service you will have to render him is to keep him out of the hands of the Catholic Association, who are in a state of deadly ire against him, and with justice, on account of his late views on our Irish Question, which I disagree with him on, *toto caelo* or rather *totis inferis* myself. He is, however, a good fellow, as well as a devilish clever one, and has done more for the Catholic cause here than ever O'Connell could undo, let him try ever so hard. . . . Be kind to Barnes, if he gives you the opportunity.

When Barnes returned from Ireland he wrote to Moore : " I have been delighted with my journey." The visit had " removed from my mind a vast deal of prejudice and false impression : it has made me feel an interest for Ireland and its people which will render the support of its cause no longer a task but a cordial service. I did not see the great Dan O'Connell, but I met one of his brothers at Killarney. I do not know whether he was

[1] Croker to Peel, Peel Papers, B.M., MSS. Addl. 40321.

aware of his companion, but he certainly showed no instinctive antipathy." As Moore said, he did much for the Catholic cause. O'Connell's haste was responsible for the alienation of a true helper of Ireland. On April 20, 1831, when Lawson, the printer of *The Times*, was haled before the Bar for committing to print the qualification of Lord Limerick as a " thing with human pretensions," *The Times* protested its friendship :

We call ourselves the friends of Ireland, and know that we have been her benefactors to a degree to which no individual Irish Lord could serve her, even if he spent all the revenues of his estates in the country, and for its benefit. We do not now speak of the aid which we rendered on the question of the Catholic Emancipation, for the merits of that measure may still be contested by blindness and infatuation. None, we presume, will dispute the duties of humanity, or deny the obligation of relieving the distressed ; and a few years ago, when no small portion of the Irish population was exposed to perish by famine, and many sunk under its pressure daily, we took up their cause. Our columns teemed with articles, into which we breathed all the force we were able, calling upon our countrymen to succour their dying neighbours by liberal subscriptions. We taxed the funds of our journal ; individual members connected with the establishment taxed themselves, for the same benevolent purpose. The project succeeded ; Ireland was relieved, and, what is more, we have been assured that many landlords—some, too, with titles, and absentees,—ultimately received their rents from those funds which were originally raised by our incitement to save the dying peasantry of their estates from absolute starvation ! It was the same principle, and they were the same motives, which at this time prompted that article, however incautiously expressed, which has been made the subject of complaint in the British House of Peers. A certain part of Ireland is again suffering from extreme distress. We do not, as before, move our countrymen to a fresh effort ; but we say, " Tax the land to supply its own poor " ; and knowing, as we do, what the Irish labourer has suffered from being the object of a voluntary and precarious bounty, we felt indignation, and do still feel it, that any opposition should be made to giving him a legal and permanent security against the horrors of famine, and the strong probability of perishing by want.

The tyranny of landlordism in Ireland was attacked by *The Times* as a sin against justice and against law and, incidentally, an act of impolicy against Conservatism and against Protestantism. On another occasion it reproduced an account, abridged from the *Leinster Independent*, of a meeting held at Boherduff, Carlow, protesting against the action of Tory landlords. The landlords, as *The Times* put it in a leading article, having

in the lust of political power, loaded their estates with a population which, at best, the soil was illfitted to support,—but a population, of which the rapid increase frightfully aggravated the original sufferings— and which, again, the abolition of forty shilling freeholds rendered no longer ministerial to the interests of the landlords' ambition, the squirearchy betook themselves to the expedient of ejecting these unprofitable occupants from the land, for no crime, on no plea, but that they had become unprofitable. The impatience, however, of the squirearchs was not to be tranquillised by the usual process of eject- ment. They insisted on establishing more barbarous facilities in aid of a barbarous act. (December 29, 1835.)

The Times castigated the Legislature for not attending to the defence of the poor in Ireland " at a time when the landlord's power was likely to be exercised against them with augmented harshness, but instead passed statutes enabling the landlord to drive his tenantry by speedier and cheaper methods." *The Times* pointed out that English landlords were not afforded such facilities, and that the poor Irish, " when turned off the land which has fed them, have no resources but begging, robbing or perishing in the next ditch . . . the despotism of landlords has been bolstered up to a pitch that leaves the tenant at the mercy of his caprices."

The leading article went on to demonstrate that these practices " must operate as a tremendous power in the hands of priests and demagogues who inflame the miserable people." It concluded with practical suggestions for the establishment of a contributory scheme for the relief of sickness and blameless destitution. " Until a change of this description, or on this principle, is thus made by law in the relations between rich and poor in Ireland, it is a vain delusion to imagine that there can ever be peace."

The turbulence and the poverty of the country had, perhaps, been too easily thought removable by the simple act of liberating religion from certain disabilities. *The Times* then considered (April 21, 1838) that the troubles were not the fault of Catholic Emancipation, which it had championed and sustained :

If the measure of 1829 has not succeeded in removing all the evils against which it was directed, and in conciliating the Popish priesthood, as it has the nobles and gentlemen of the Romish faith, we are willing to trace the partial failure to the omission of every attempt at securing, or even recommending to Parliament, a moderate provision for the Roman Catholic clergy, such as might have drawn them by the strong tie of interest in the service of the State and made it independent of the turbulence and brutality of their own rabble.

Both the Roman Catholic Archbishop Murray and the Protestant Archbishop Whately, in their report as Commissioners on the State of the Irish Poor, ascribed the prevailing evils to the penal laws of the eighteenth century. Religious intolerance then was the ultimate cause. *The Times* made no doubt of the grievances of the Irish people, which it depicted as plagued by the priests, parsons, politicians and landlords.

The Times, indeed, was very frank and vigorous in expressing its dissatisfaction with conditions in the sister-island and in its reprobation of English bigots. On one occasion in 1832 it wrote :

If religious people are anxious that there should exist for another half century in Ireland, any traces of a Protestant Church—we mean a spiritual, not merely endowed, and wealthy, and political Protestantism —they will with heart and hand concur in this effort to rescue it from utter annihilation, by separating the cause of the Reformed Church from that of injustice, animosity, confusion and civil war . . . they will shrink from the madness of withdrawing rent, and debts, and lawful obligations of every kind, with the desperate and revolting cause of making proselytes from Catholicism, by fraud, bribery or compulsion. (March 13, 1832.)

Again, in another leading article, *The Times*, well knowing the strength of anti-Catholic feeling in England and Scotland, spoke severely of Protestant bigotry :

The " Protestant interest," be it remembered, has, in the dialect of the party we speak of, not the most remote relation to the interests of the Protestant religion. . . . The " Protestant interest " means nothing else than that monopoly of all the good things of this world—namely, places, pensions, patronage, power, bishoprics, archbishoprics, pluralities, tithes of every thing,—for doing nothing—which have been enjoyed in Ireland by righteous Protestants since the end of the seventeenth century, and which monopoly of things temporal is regarded by the faithful as but a modest and self-denying indemnification for the monopoly of things eternal claimed by the righteous Catholics as their own peculiar freehold. (July 28, 1832.)

It was therefore with the keenest possible regret that the paper saw that O'Connell in these circumstances was bent upon the supreme mischief of separatism. Nothing, it thought, could now prevent Catholics and Protestants organizing first into Repealers and Unionists and then into Whigs and Tories. In 1836 *The Times* was obliged to confess :

Everything Protestant in Ireland is English—it rests on Great Britain, and clings to her, and constitutes the only bond of union between these islands. Everything Popish is anti-English—it rests on animosity towards Great Britain, clings to the hope of separation from her, and constitutes the only vulnerable spot in the British empire, the sole element of weakness and of ruin. (February 26, 1836.)

Thus the Irish issue overshadowed every other because it was an Imperial issue. The situation was intricate and anxious. Besides Ireland, Canada was known to be disaffected. The Irish, much to the exasperation of the English, were far from pacified by the emancipation of the Catholics in 1829. The Catholic element was strong in Canada. *The Times*, surveying these elements of unrest, and observing the character of Daniel O'Connell's agitation, foresaw a danger that political debate would extend to a vast sectarian wrangle.

O'Connell's error in attacking *The Times* about the reporting of his speeches has already been described[1] ; it was unfortunate, though not more. The serious quarrel between O'Connell and *The Times* came to a head in 1835. It was not a religious matter, but political ; and as to politics, *The Times* and O'Connell differed fundamentally on the very rules of the game. The divergences which began before the passage of the Emancipation Bill widened as the agitator's power increased. The O'Connell " Rent," contributed by O'Connell's following to his campaign fund, eventually drew in the whole of Catholic Ireland and was collected in every Catholic parish. The money raised represented a very large annual sum, of which no less a figure than £15,000 was set aside for use in connexion with newspapers. The chest was, in fact, purely a political fund, and *The Times* had no criticism of it as such. But the collection of funds through parochial organizations brought into active cooperation first the parish officials, and ultimately the parish priest. Numbers of the Irish clergy called for subscriptions from the steps of the altar ; members of the Irish laity who did not subscribe found themselves intimidated.

The Times insisted throughout its campaign against O'Connell that it regarded all religious matters solely from the point of view

[1] See Chapter XVIII.

of the political observer : "We plead no right to condemn the religious doctrines of the Catholic, or any other professedly Christian Church." But *The Times* condemned priestcraft, the power of the priest to occupy a position, "in name alone religious, but political in fact, and the functions assigned to him by the discipline of his nefarious church, which has no serious aim but temporal aggrandisement." It seemed a sort of borough-mongering that a minister of religion should give his powerful religious authority in the field of politics. Whatever Catholicism might be as religion, the association of O'Connell with the priests was held dangerous to true political representation. How could a man vote independently with a quiet conscience if told by his *parochus* that O'Connell's was the party of God ? *The Times* went so far as to lay it down that the peculiar degree of authority enjoyed by the priests so reduced the individual responsibility of laymen that it could only be contemplated with misgiving by progressive statesmen. It gave generous space to leading articles, speeches, letters, and reports of lectures directed against the encroachments of a priesthood that failed to condemn intimidation. During 1835 and 1836 it affirmed repeatedly that the self-sufficiency of Catholicism made the Church politically undesirable. "Popery may be a safe form of church government under a military monarchy, where the sword is everlastingly suspended over it and compels it to a course of abject subordination ; but it is the only system of civil polity which has not the dread of the insatiable encroachments of that meddling and ambitious church." All these considerations rendered *The Times* suspicious of Irish political action. It objected first to the intrusion of the Irish priest into politics, secondly to O'Connell's fraternization with English Republican Radicals, and thirdly to his announcement that Repeal was his object. But the policy of the Irish, to be judged on its political merits, was overshadowed by the personality of the leader. The controversial methods of O'Connell were the immediate cause of a series of incidents which drove *The Times* to declare war on such a man and such methods.

The alliance between O'Connell and the Whigs arranged by Lord John Russell in the spring of 1835 led to a memorable encounter. The battle between O'Connell and *The Times* was not wholly conducted by either side with the weapon of argument. From principles the two champions warmed to personalities in a combat of invective which grew more vigorous with every clash. When the Irish Reform Association was inaugurated in 1835

O'Connell warned his followers against the inveteracy of the " Tory " opposition and " named " Barnes. " I ask you whether you can contemplate anything more horrible to Ireland than the restoration of Peel or Wellington ? " He pointed to the spread of Orangism, the growing truculence of the Protestants, the lack of unity amongst Irish Reformers and their consequent dependence upon Whigs—all at a time when the Tory faction in England was ready to join with Orangism in acts of repression against the Catholic clergy and laity of Ireland.

Look at their great literary organs—the indicators of the intentions of the party. You will find in them a scurrility, a virulence and truculent atrocity of language addressed to the Catholics of Ireland which has not been used in England since the days of Cromwell. . . . The abuse which those authorised miscreants pour upon the Catholic people of Ireland is so virulent as to exceed description and to be calculated as a prelude to massacre. What a patient, what a forbearing people we are ! Is there on the face of the earth any other people who would endure this villification ? Yet we are so patient and forbearing that the prime traducer—Barnes of *The Times*—goes on from day to day expressing the contumely and rancour of his party for the Catholic people of Ireland in the most ferocious language, without the least apprehension of punishment.

In reply *The Times* observed that the " revolutionist threatens those whom he assumes to be conductors of this paper, with the implied punishment of *assassination*—and that he later holds out to the united Empire that the mere return to office of the Duke of Wellington and Sir Robert Peel would be a signal for letting loose all the crimes and cruelties of the savage multitude . . . driven to despair of any legal remedy." To O'Connell's allegation that *The Times* had abused the " Catholic people of Ireland," the paper opposed the reminder that " of their religion we have said not a word." Although " their *Church Government* was a *political* and *social* nuisance," *The Times* was deliberate in aiming its arguments only at a single man : " It is against O'Connell, himself the real grievance of Ireland and the Empire, that we have declared open war ; we would not assassinate him, (as he significantly hints his wish respecting us,) but we would chain him. We deem the peace of Ireland and the public safety in danger by his being at large." (December 12, 1835.)

In Derrynane and in Westminster O'Connell made his own all the Radical stories that *The Times* had been bought by the Carlton

Club, and taunted it with baseness and inconsistency. In the House of Commons on June 14, 1836, O'Connell went to the length of attacking John Walter through *The Times*. The scene in the House was, according to independent report, one of the most uproarious which contemporaries had witnessed. The subject of the debate was the Irish Corporations Bill, and John Walter had spoken. Speaking after Walter, O'Connell said he did not see

why the hon. Member should introduce the Irish Church Question and the Poor Law Question, into this debate ; though the Poor Law, indeed, formed a favourite topic in *The Times* newspaper. *The Times* was the mighty thunderer on the poor laws (Order). Order. Why, had that paper the slightest decency ?

When other members rallied to John Walter's defence and denied his responsibility for what appeared in *The Times*, O'Connell replied to them in a second speech :

Was he not to speak of that vile journal which had falsely, foully, and wickedly calumniated him, every day and on every subject—a journal which exhibited the foulest instance of political tergiversation that had ever disgraced the press of England—a journal whose talent had served only to enhance the price of its prostitution ? If there was any one out of that house who consented to prostitute his talent and the columns of that journal for base hire, he was a creature too low and contemptible to deserve notice. If they held in abhorrence those who should attempt to poison the fountains of a country, what should be the degree of detestation in which to hold those who poisoned the sources of literature, and who turned that which was intended to the good into an instrument of destruction to mankind ? The wretch who earned the wages of the most infamous prostitution in that way deserved to be held up to public scorn, and every man should know him. He hoped that anything which fell from him on this subject would not touch the hon. member for Berkshire. If it did not, all that could be said was, that he (Mr. O'Connell) had attacked that vile instrument that had attacked him. If, however, the hon. member took the observations to himself, he would only say, " qui capit ille facit "—if the cap fitted, he could not help it.

The Times replied to the charges of corruption and desertion in a leading article.

We rejoiced at the [Emancipation] act of 1829, the natural fruit of that great change which had been wrought upon the opinion of the

DANIEL O'CONNELL
From a caricature by R. Seymour, 1833

contesting Taunton, was visited by the whole force of the agitator's unequalled power of invective. On the basis of a faulty newspaper report, for which he had no responsibility, Disraeli was denounced as possessing " the qualities of the impenitent thief on the cross." Disraeli's reply taunted O'Connell with having " forgotten the clank of his fetter " ; the young Tory whom O'Connell " believed " to be the author of " a couple of novels " gave the warning that " I know the tactics of your church ; it clamours for toleration and it labours for supremacy. I see that you are quite prepared to persecute," and ended with a challenge. *The Times* of May 5 printed a letter from Disraeli addressed to Morgan O'Connell, son of the agitator, demanding satisfaction " for the insults which your father has too long lavished with impunity upon his political opponents."

Notwithstanding the constancy of its support to the Protestant cause, *The Times* was distrusted by the militant party. Ernest Augustus, Duke of Cumberland, Earl of Armagh, Chancellor of Trinity College, Dublin, Grand Master of the Orange Lodges, with his Grand Secretary, Colonel Fairman,[1] and Lord Kenyon, hated the paper for its advocacy of Emancipation and Reform. The Protestantism of *The Times* was suspected as mere political opportunism.

The Times, according to the *Morning Post*, was not a good party paper, not a good Church paper, not even to be trusted as a Protestant paper. Watching and stimulating the rapid flow of public sentiment towards Conservatism it took a central position. The truth, perhaps, was that *The Times* would have given a hearty welcome to a different Daniel O'Connell, a cooler, more deliberate, but not less Irish statesman.

But *The Times* drew a clear distinction between the social and the constitutional answer that could rightly be offered to the social evils afflicting the Irish. As the agitation gathered way, the paper held none the less firmly to its criticism of social conditions in Ireland and all the more firmly to its conviction that political Catholicism threatened the highest interests of the State. The political importance of Protestantism to the United Kingdom,

---

[1] Colonel Fairman's language had been fanatical. He wrote in 1831 to Lord Kenyon that " That filthy concern, *The Times*, which spares neither age nor sex, public bodies nor private individuals, which at a less degenerate era would have been burnt by the common hangman, ought to be forthwith checked in its flagitious course of unparalleled infamy. This can only be done by the aid of an uncompromising journal of opposite principles, for the intrepid exposure of its vile fabrications in all their deformity." (*Cf.* R. Barry O'Brien, *Thomas Drummond, Life and Letters*, London, 1889, p. 145.)

369

BB

as *The Times* understood it, is set forth in a leading article which it was moved to publish on January 15, 1836 :

> By the letter and provisions of the British constitution, the united kingdoms constitute a Protestant realm, whose public institutions are required to be of a *Protestant* character, according to the doctrines of the Reformation. But though Christian Protestantism (which of course includes none but such as hold these doctrines in their usually accepted sense) is *uniform in its essence*, it may nevertheless assume, and does in fact assume, various forms of ecclesiastical discipline.
>
> The establishment of *Presbyterian Protestantism* in Scotland has, we confess, always appeared to us to be just as defensible as the steady maintenance of *Episcopal Protestantism* in England, which is so completely interwoven with the convictions, tastes, laws and habits of the people of this section of the empire. To affirm, then, with the revolutionary and logical expounders of Government-sentiment, that because the Protestantism of *the majority* of the Scottish people, whose principles are in harmony with our Protestant constitution, has been established by law, therefore the Popery of the *majority* in Ireland, whose principles *are directly hostile* to that constitution, is also entitled to the same distinction—this, we acknowledge, is a piece of reasoning which we can only admire as an intellectual curiosity. The Protestant Government of the Revolution wisely allowed the Scottish people to select the form of Protestantism which they liked best ; and because no majority could be found in Ireland who would choose any form of Protestantism at all, the measure which this necessity imposed was just as wisely resorted to—namely, the establishment of that form of Protestantism which was most agreeable to the largest portion of the minority.

The bearing of this article is manifest. Its re-formulation of the fundamental purpose of the Royal supremacy in ecclesiastical affairs was a necessary warning to the Irish clergy, who were championing O'Connell in spite of his known determination for Repeal. It was time to oppose a unionist to a separatist clericalism. Thus Graham counselled Peel's Whip that " Protestantism is the only weapon with which we can encounter Republicanism ; we have the staff in our hand and we must lay about us, wielding the Church against O'Connell and tail."[1] The Irish Church indeed had more than an Irish significance. It was in itself a bulwark of the power of the Sovereign and privileged as such.

[1] Graham to Bonham, January 2, 1839. B.M., MSS. Addl. 40416, 45.

XXII

THE LAST YEARS OF BARNES

WHEN Princess Victoria was called to the Throne at the age of 18, *The Times* asserted that Conservatism was the only power which could save the Monarchy from destruction, but it placed its own broad interpretation on the term. " For some of those who affect to number themselves with the Conservative *party* they enjoy just as much of our esteem and consideration as a certain ill-conditioned cur in a certain morning paper, the manual of semstresses, and the housemaid's guide to fashion, that in the two last numbers has been alternately whining and snarling at *The Times* and in the name of *the* Conservatives." The general election, which by law at that period was held automatically at the beginning of a new reign, proved that the Whigs had now determined to follow the Conservative lead in the direction of stability. Lord John Russell himself championed the Church. Most of the Radicals were defeated and revolutionary fervour evaporated from those that remained. On the polling figures England was dominantly Conservative, Scotland Whig, and Ireland for O'Connell. Since Melbourne remained in power, supported by the O'Connell tail and a remnant of Radicals, *The Times* was unconvinced by the new Whig truce. Its Unionist and Imperialist convictions still constrained it to attack with all its power the " mercenary and jobbing clique " responsible for jeopardizing the kingdom by their connexion with O'Connell.

Suddenly, the country and the Government were faced with open rebellion in Canada. It was suppressed with little difficulty, but the Government decided to suspend the Canadian Constitution and to order the investigation of the causes of dissatisfaction by a High Commissioner in the person of Lord Durham.

Lord Durham went out in 1838 on his most important mission as Governor-General of the Canadian Provinces ; he went, apparently, without salary, but with provision for expenses. It was known that he liked magnificence, for when he was in Russia as Ambassador he had been given to display. His expenses in Canada promised to be more than considerable. He took with him much equipment for his many horses, and several ships were required for the transport of his effects. *The Times* looked with no favour upon this " parade." " We would ask Lord Durham, if we thought there was any chance of penetrating his vanity-crusted intellect, for what purpose he seeks all this parade. He is going to enquire into the grievances and allay the heats of a distracted colony : he is not going to assist at the Coronation of M. Papineau,[1] or at the inauguration of an indivisible republic under the presidency of Dr. Mackenzie."[2]

Lord Durham set to work in an unfortunate manner. " Verily," wrote *The Times*, " Lord Durham has much of the Roman Dictator about him." He appointed a new Executive Council ; three out of the four were his own private secretaries. If Melbourne was taken aback, English opinion generally was staggered at the evil results that might follow these and more serious indiscretions. It was impossible for the Government to overlook Durham's action in deporting to Bermuda Canadians convicted of rebellion. It was against the law. Melbourne was forced to disallow Durham's Ordinance proclaiming the amnesty and the deportations. Durham replied by publishing a justification of his measures and censured the conduct of the Imperial Government.[3]

In November he resigned his office and left Canada for England to set about the preparation of his report. This historic document, which was awaited eagerly by the whole Empire and has become a kind of Colonial Charter, was published exclusively in *The Times*. It was known that Lord Durham's report had been printed for the consideration of the Sovereign and her Ministers, but there were unaccountable delays attending its circulation. The copies of the report for which the Cabinet and the country waited had been somewhere in proof since January 31, 1839. On February 8 *The Times* was able to inform its readers that " We have received a printed copy of the Report on the Affairs of British North America, from the Earl of Durham, her Majesty's High Commissioner etc., etc., etc. ; presented by her Majesty's Command.

[1] Leader of the rebellion in Lower Canada.
[2] Rebel leader in Upper Canada.
[3] *The Times*, attacking Durham's Proclamation as inflammatory, dubbed him " Lord High Seditioner," and earned John Wilson Croker's envious applause.

It has not, we believe, been yet delivered to the members of either House of Parliament." Later in this article the paper observed cautiously that : " It would be absurd and presumptuous to attempt to describe or dispute, till we have had more time, the correctness of the statements, or the soundness of the reasoning, in a document occupying 119 closely printed folio pages, and which did not come into our possession till yesterday evening." The conclusion of the report, with Lord Durham's signature, dated London, January 31, was given, the whole making twelve and a half closely-set columns of matter. Another twenty columns were given in the following day's issue. The same issue reported that Durham in the House of Lords had asked " when it will be convenient for me to lay the papers relating to the British possessions in North America before the Council." He had " seen with the deepest regret the publication to-day of a portion only of that address," and he protested it was not fair to him. Durham then urged the Government to publish and to circulate the complete report. As to the partial publication, he himself, he said, " was not in the habit of taking that journal, as it was generally not very complimentary to himself—*The Times*; and it was only in consequence of being informed that it contained the report that he had purchased a copy of it." He knew absolutely nothing of the means by which *The Times* had secured its text. Several members of the House of Lords supported Durham in pressing for the publication of the report.

In the House of Commons also the question was pressed ; Lord John Russell, answering, " could only say that he had seen the publication of part of the report alluded to with great astonishment. (Hear, hear, and laughter.)" *The Times* itself in its next leading article quoted Melbourne's words : " How it has happened that so large a portion of that report should have transpired before it was known to either House of Parliament, almost as early as it is made known to her Majesty's Government—it is impossible for me to say." *The Times* then reminded readers that though it possessed the entire report its significance precluded all immediate comment except

that it will be found to be replete with interest ; and with regard to our exclusive, and as some of our legislators seem to think, premature publication of it, we shall content ourselves with a single observation. It has been rumoured for some days past that it was the intention of Ministers to lay before Parliament parts only and not the whole, of this report of Lord Durham ; or that, upon various pretences, the Ministers would delay the presentation of it, injuriously to the ex-High Commissioner . . . but whether we have been enabled to do this by the favour of her Majesty herself, as some wise people have whispered, or by the favour of Lord Melbourne, or of Lord John Russell (a sly fellow, by the way), or of Lord Durham, or of his friend Sir John Conroy, as others have suggested—or if not from any of these, from what other quarter we derived the document, we must leave the more sagacious of the *quid nuncs* of Brooks's and the Reform Club to decide. (February 9, 1839.)

The medium of communication with *The Times* is still debatable. It is possible, but unlikely, that Gibbon Wakefield, a member of Durham's secretariat, sent it to Barnes. Joseph Parkes, Lord Durham's trusted Press agent, may well have determined, upon his own responsibility, to give it the widest publicity in order to force the unwilling Melbourne into complete and immediate publication. Henry Reeve asserted that R. D. Hanson, of Durham's secretariat, was persuaded by Wakefield to send the report to Barnes, a view towards which the latest biographer of Durham tends.[1]

Publication by authority followed on February 11, 1839, Melbourne having said that since *The Times* possessed a complete copy the whole must now be published. *The Times* then gave it rapid examination, describing it as

a political kind of dissertation, about as long as the *Cyropaedia* of Xenophon, of which it reminds us occasionally by its didactic tone . . . everything in it indicates a well-stored mind, and great industry in the application of its resources, as well as diligence in the attainment of every species of information applicable to the business which he might have in hand. But will it be not thought daring in the extreme, in the present state of his own country at home—the Chartists at the doors of Parliament, and every part of our monarchical institutions threatened—to decide, as if it were a matter of no dispute, that the Sovereign of a realm thus situated must govern one of the largest of her foreign possessions, not as a federative, but as a legislative union ? . . . Whether it was within the letter or spirit of Lord Durham's instructions to carry these hazardous political theories into execution we know not.

1 *Cf.* Chester W. New, *Lord Durham, A Biography of John George Lambton, First Earl of Durham* (Oxford, 1929). Appendix, On the Authorship of Lord Durham's Report, pp. 565-576. Professor New, against Reeve, thinks Durham, not Buller, wrote the Report. Harrop, A. J., *Amazing Career of Edward Gibbon Wakefield* (London, 1928), not seen by New, records a family tradition that Durham, giving his assent to publication, wished to withhold the document at the last moment, only to be answered by Wakefield, " My Lord, it is already gone " (p. 110).

They are well stated and ably argued in the work now before the country; and the question between himself and Ministers will in some degree depend upon that fact. . . . There will be so many opportunities of discussing this very remarkable writing of Lord Durham's, that we shall abstain from further details at present. We have even yet hardly had time to do more than cursorily glance it over once. It is undoubtedly deserving of a more attentive and closer perusal, and will give rise to many minute divisions of opinion.

The Government was grievously embarrassed by Durham, the country in its turn was sick and tired of the Government. *The Times* was using all arguments to convince and to sustain readers in the belief that the Conservatives were numerous, able, and powerful enough to govern. Ashley (the philanthropic Lord Shaftesbury) urged Peel in 1839 to " cast aside all other views, and let us endeavour to get the Government out on a Protestant point. We shall combine the truths of religion (God be praised for it) and the feelings of the Country.[1] . . . I have stirred up *The Times* to warn the country to learn wisdom . . . and prepare itself for resistance or disgraceful and perilous submission to the Progress of Popery." Peel agreed that " he had long thought that there were fearful indications of the approach of a great religious struggle which will probably be co-extensive with Popery and Protestantism in Europe."[2] O'Connell's party was the political " tail " which encouraged *The Times* once more to make political use of the No-Popery cry. When, in the same year, the Parliamentary situation of the Whig-O'Connell party became critical, *The Times* was naturally jubilant. At last, on Wednesday, May 8, 1839, it could write :

Well, the despicable farce is over. The Ministry are out. They are OUT according to their own formal notifications to both Houses of Parliament yesterday evening. The majority of 5, in a House of more than 600 members, pairs included, has at last shewn *them*, that of which they alone, amongst 25,000,000 of people, pretended to be ignorant, namely, that they were utterly incapable of conducting the affairs of the British monarchy.

The issue was the rejection of the Government Bill on the Jamaica Liberties. The Jamaican Assembly had denied the right of the Imperial Parliament to interfere with the status of former

[1] C.S.P. II, 414.
[2] Peel to Ashley, *cf*. Hodder, *Life and Work of the Seventh Earl of Shaftesbury* (London, 1886), I, 241-2.

slaves, though it had agreed to abolish " apprenticeship," itself
not very different from slavery. The Bill of 1839 in consequence
suspended the Jamaican Constitution. Peel was against it as
overhasty, but he was prepared to grant time for reconsideration.
The Bill required more than ordinary support. It met with a
reception which proved that the House had no confidence either
in it or in the Government—which, accordingly, resigned.

Thursday's paper (May 9, 1839) informed readers that the first
result of the Queen's conference with the resigning Prime Minister
was a summons to Wellington. The Duke recommended her to
call Peel. *The Times* pointed out that the truly formidable
power of the Conservative Party lay not in mere numbers but in
the " consistency and harmony of its parts." The party consisted
at that moment of 317, the Radicals numbered 150 and the Whigs
some 130, and, last of all, " a tail of between 60 and 70." But the
non-Conservatives had not one public or constitutional principle
in common. In the view of *The Times* a sound Conservative policy
would be to uphold the monarchical state against the Radical effort
to convert it into a Republican democracy, and against the Whig
plan to keep office and patronage with the Irish tail pushing
forward the encroachments of Popery upon Protestant Church
and State.

On Friday (May 10, 1839) a retrospective leader appeared which
analysed the tactical position of the Conservatives :

The greatest misfortune of the last six years was the premature
conscription of Sir Robert Peel and his friends to serve in office towards
the close of 1834. . . . The mischief was, that the King, who rightly
judged the Ministers, had got before the public estimate of their
demerits. Two or three months more and they would have rotted off,
as they have done lately ; two or three months more and Sir Robert
Peel might have felt justified by party policy, as he then did, by a loyal
sense of duty and deference towards his Sovereign, in accepting the
reins of Government, because they would have been seized by a vigorous
hand, and would have enabled him to *direct* the state, instead of having
it turned from the straight road by a sinister and malignant power. . . .

The State had come to its present pass by the premature exercise
of power by the Conservatives and by the coquetting of the Whigs
with the Radicals. The people, more significant than the parties,
were monarchical, attached to Church and State, to Crown and
Peerage. The country was rather for a parliament of gentlemen

than of turbulent demagogues. Finally, in Barnes's analysis, public opinion allied with the commercial interest was for Sir Robert Peel. *The Times* thus rallied all the forces in favour of the Conservative leader.

But a personal consideration intruded itself into the situation. On Saturday, May 11, 1839, *The Times* wrote in a first leader :

Public rumour, from 12 to 5 o'clock yesterday, must already have informed the whole metropolis that Sir Robert Peel had met with such an extraordinary and unlooked-for obstacle towards the completion of the task which he supposed that Queen Victoria had confided to him, as to feel himself under the necessity of relinquishing the impracticable office.

There followed the explanation that Peel had represented to her Majesty the expediency of removing from their offices certain ladies of Whig and Radical connexion who occupied the chambers of the Palace and performed the duties of Ladies of the Royal Bedchamber, and that the Queen had insisted on supposing that Peel required all her female advisers to be changed. It increased the exasperation of Conservatives and of *The Times* to see the news of the Queen's again sending for Lord Melbourne published in the *Globe* before Sir Robert Peel's resignation was announced. *The Times* was at first mortified beyond words ; but it found words on Monday, May 13, 1839, and printed a long leader. Two-and-a-half columns denounced the " Bedchamber Plot " :

In all our long experience of the frauds and iniquities of faction, it does not occur to us that we have had the evil fortune to witness a course of proceeding so mean and vile, and disgraceful to the name of " gentleman," as that which has originated in the O'Connell Cabinet, and has occupied men's attention during the last week. . . . How came it that one of their evening papers of *Thursday* announced the " finality " of the Queen's resolution against suffering Sir Robert Peel to interfere at all with the O'Connell household, before the right hon. baronet himself was made acquainted with any such peremptory resolution ? Is it, or is it not, a fact that on the preceding Wednesday Lord Normanby declared openly at a certain great dinner table in Berkeley Square that *his wife* should not *resign her office* as a Lady of the Bedchamber ? Was there no intrigue in this ?

The question was put " whether the people of England would adopt and support this war of antechamber petticoats against all the great and serious interests of an endangered Empire," and the article ended by referring to Lady Normanby as " the puppet of such an itinerant showman as her husband." The same issue of May 13 contained an argued letter from Benjamin Disraeli signed " Laelius," addressed to the Queen. As is, of course, now known, the Queen recognized in later life that on this occasion she had made a mistake.

The matter could obviously be carried no farther by a Conservative Opposition which prided itself upon its respect for monarchy. In Barnes's judgment the Imperial reasons for maintaining Royal privileges were not to be denied. The Queen was not mentioned, but *The Times* sharpened its criticism of the Melbourne Cabinet.

The last political issue to require the exercise of Barnes's sagacity was the complicated situation resulting from the Egyptian, Syrian, and Turkish unrest. The so-called "Eastern Question" gathered urgency and importance during the second half of 1840. The course taken by *The Times* shows how little Barnes spared himself in his last illness to control the paper's treatment of highly involved foreign and domestic issues. In particular, Barnes exerted himself to withstand powerful influences working against Lord Palmerston, Foreign Secretary in the Melbourne Administration, though *The Times* was striving to destroy the Administration as a whole, and though in former years it had been consistently hostile to Palmerston.

The primary cause of the incidents of 1840 was the Treaty of Unkiar Skelessi, concluded between Russia and Turkey in 1833, which virtually made Turkey a Russian Protectorate by giving Russia the exclusive right to champion the Christian subject races of Turkey. The concern excited among the other Powers by this treaty, and the subsequent diplomatic exchanges, crystallized the " Eastern Question." It occupied European Chancelleries for several years. The text of the treaty was not officially published until the beginning of 1834, when Palmerston had returned to the Foreign Office after the resignation of Peel's short-lived Government, with the determination to prevent a combination of Russia with France.

For some years the paper had been printing letters and articles from David Urquhart.[1] After 1836, when Urquhart was relieved

---

[1] Urquhart (1805-1877) had, as British Commissioner in Greece and Turkey, been specializing in Eastern affairs since 1831, and succeeded in obtaining the complete confidence of the Turkish Government.

of his post as First Secretary to the Embassy at Constantinople, *The Times* gave all possible prominence to the agitation for the maintenance of an adequate defence against Russia. Increased naval provision was demanded as well as closer treaty connexions with countries in Europe and the Near East. Urquhart contributed letters on these subjects to *The Times* during 1837 and 1838. There were special articles on the Russian influence on the German Press.

In 1840 Barnes was much tempted to attack the Foreign Secretary ; it seemed that the country was being dragged into an unnecessary foreign crisis, if not into war. Yet, disliking what he called Palmerston's dandyism, his flippancy and his habitual refusal of information to the House of Commons, he respected Palmerston's knowledge and powers of application. Lord Aberdeen, an experienced Ambassador, who became Foreign Secretary under Peel, agreed with the main line of Palmerston's policy. In principle it sought to prevent a Franco-Russian rather than create an Anglo-French alliance, to obstruct the further weakening of Turkey, also to counter the ambitions of Mehemet Ali, Pasha of Egypt, whose weakness for French experts had earned him the unofficial protection of France. Aberdeen set himself the task of persuading Barnes to support Palmerston. After a long discussion Barnes agreed, for the time being, to take a passive line.[1]

On July 15, 1840, Palmerston succeeded in superseding the Unkiar Skelessi arrangement by a new treaty between England, Russia, Prussia and Austria, and communicated the *fait accompli* to Guizot, then French Ambassador in London, on July 17. When Thiers, Louis Philippe's Prime Minister, heard of the new Quadruple Treaty, his extreme anger at the exclusion of France seemed to make war imminent.

The treaty astonished those who expected a treaty in which both England and France were partners. Many, probably most, English observers thought that Palmerston had been imprudent ; many, like Barnes, deplored a dangerous element of irresponsibility in the Foreign Secretary, and contrasted his superior knowledge of facts with his unaccountable capacity for getting

[1] Maxwell, *Life of George William Frederick Villiers, 4th Earl Clarendon* (London 1913), I, 208. The Diary of Lady Clarendon (September 15, 1840) records a visit from Charles Greville, who told her that it took Aberdeen two hours to secure Barnes's agreement " to be passive at least." The date of Aberdeen's interview is not recorded. It was probably in the early part of the year.

into scrapes. The Conservatives were anxious. Among those of his Cabinet colleagues who considered Palmerston's line dangerous were Lord Clarendon, Lord John Russell, " Bear " Ellice and, above all, Lord Holland. Charles Greville, Clarendon's intimate, who shared these views, at this point made the discovery of a brilliant and ambitious young man with connexions, decided opinions on foreign affairs, and a desire to express them in print. He favoured the French. Nothing could be more convenient to the enemies of Palmerston than the discovery of Henry Reeve. The Foreign Secretary, however, had his hands so firmly on the Press that it was not easy to find a place for attacks on his policy. Easthope, for example, of the *Morning Chronicle*, waited on Palmerston every day for instructions.

During the summer Melbourne himself had grave fears of war, and the Queen communicated to him her personal anxiety. It was known that the foreigners in London were preparing to leave. Still Palmerston held his ground, only condescending to defend himself in his own anonymous way in the columns of the *Morning Chronicle*. Lord John Russell replied for his side in the columns of the *Globe*. Palmerston even had weeklies in his grip.[1] Ellice wrote to Melbourne on September 16, 1840 :

They may write and lie about me as they will, I feel it still my duty to do all in my power to prevent more mischief than is inevitable from the present crisis ; and I, therefore, again beg your attention to the *Observer* newspaper, received to-day, the 13th. Are some of our madmen really disposed to urge the violence of the old ruffian (as they called him) Mehemet Ali, and seeing no way out of the pass in which they have involved us, to force on a general conflagration and bury themselves in the ruins ? Whether these articles are directly furnished to the *Observer*, or written by the inspiration of such parties, I know not ; but I do know that Mr. Scanlan, the Editor, is paid for them out of the money under your control from the Civil List secret service money, and you have it in your power either to moderate their tone or to stop their supplies.

God knows what this escapade of the Foreign Office is to bring upon us.[2]

[1] Palmerston's hold on the *Morning Chronicle* had embarrassed the Cabinet in 1839 Poulett Thomson assured Melbourne (June 10) that " without a newspaper [of its own] the Government must fall." Melbourne reported in the same month to John Russell that " nobody seems to approve the [Press] undertaking except Lansdowne, and he does so from his very strong sense of the necessity of something being done " (pp. 399, *sqq.* ; *cf.* Sanders, Lloyd C., *Melbourne's Papers*, London, 1890).

[2] Sanders, *op. cit.*, p. 462.

The difficulty of finding a place for the Reeve articles was, then, considerable. Greville finally made up his mind that his exceedingly clever young man might be clever enough to change the course of *The Times* and to turn it against Palmerston. He himself saw Barnes and talked to him with the authority of Lord Mahon, Lord Clarendon, and the anti-Palmerstonians. As a result the Editor resolved to try Henry Reeve with a contribution on the provocative Quadruple Treaty. Henry Reeve's first article in *The Times* discussed the relations between the Powers, severely deprecated the exclusion of France, and justified Thiers's irritation. Reeve was "influenced," says Greville, "by the circumstance of his having a considerable acquaintance among the reigning powers, the Thiers Party in France," and so " exerted himself with all his strength to turn *The Times* against Palmerston." Hence the first of his articles on July 31, 1840, was the first also of a series attacking the Quadruple Treaty. Barnes did not share Reeve's positiveness, but he recognized the ability of his articles. " Barnes, almost *malgré lui*, was dazzled by their brilliancy." When, very soon, Reeve was obliged to go abroad for a time, he urged Greville to do what he could to support the pro-Thiers policy.

I am not disposed to do this, but I have allowed him to tell Guizot that if at any time he has any *fact* which he wishes to be put forward, he may send to me and I will take care to have it inserted in the *Times*. I know very little of Guizot, but yesterday (August 31, 1840) I made Madame de Lieven ask him to dine here and he did. He is very civil and conversible, of course full of information, but rather priggish in his manner and has a sort of falsetto voice which is disagreeable.

Greville adds, " I don't intend however to seek him, or do more than I undertook for Reeve."

But the situation increased in urgency and, for the French, in alarm. Guizot sent for Greville and begged him to listen to a long dispatch from Thiers detailing a French diplomatic reverse at Alexandria. He was successful in persuading Greville to go to *The Times* to see if he could influence Barnes to turn public opinion in favour of France, " all reluctant as she is for war." Greville found Barnes regretting ever having allowed Reeve to use " much stronger language than his own judgment and opinion altogether sanctioned." He countered Greville's suggestion with a letter from *The Times* Correspondent in Constantinople[1] giving

---

[1] William Arden, Colonel Lord Alvanley, the second Baron (*d.* 1849), according to Greville a man of marvellous wit and drollery, the delight and ornament of society.

news of a violent and insolent note which the French Ambassador, de Pontois, had presented to the Porte. Greville went back to Guizot with a suggestion that *The Times* should be enabled to contradict the Correspondent's story ; but, as Greville reported to Reeve on September 10, Guizot did nothing.

In the meantime, while Cabinet intriguers were making plans to supplant Palmerston with Clarendon, Palmerston's tone was moderating. On September 22, 1840, he had instructed Bulwer in Paris to convey to Thiers that if France threw down the gauntlet Britain would not refuse to take it up, but Granville was told on October 8, 1840, that if France made a friendly communication tending towards an amicable discussion it would be received. Then, on October 12, the Thiers Cabinet fell. The Eastern Question was virtually over and Palmerston's prestige rose at a bound. His determination and skill in the face of French threats and of open animosity at home were triumphantly vindicated. Palmerston had said throughout that the French talk of war meant nothing.

The moment Palmerston was isolated in Melbourne's already weak Cabinet, the Egyptian and the French business became for Barnes as much an English as an Eastern question. However difficult as a colleague, Palmerston was the one man of character in Melbourne's Cabinet. Cabals against him naturally aroused the sympathy even of the Conservatives who were nervous of him. Reeve, not knowing the details of the Cabinet situation, was surprised in September and October to find that *The Times* was now printing articles against the interest of his friends. Barnes had knowledge, weeks before others heard of it, that Palmerston was prepared, if the necessity arose, to leave the Whigs. It only came to Reeve's ears in the third week of October. He then wrote to Greville, October 24, 1840 : " I have reason to believe that the plot for Palmerston going over to the Tories is not idle invention. On the contrary it is already in a forward state. This in one word explains the conduct of Barnes." When Greville heard of it does not appear, but he was doubtless correct in replying to Reeve that " I have no doubt that Palmerston is quite capable of joining them on the terms of keeping the F.O.," and he was doubtless equally correct in thinking that Peel " would never stand this." It may have been that Barnes was not only prepared to detach Palmerston from the Whigs, and to support his claims to the Foreign Office, but to do so in open opposition to Peel.

Reeve had now to clear his mind on the line to take about France. He wrote to Greville on October 26, 1840 :

> I saw Barnes on Saturday. He says he had been forced to take a decided tone—? turn—by the remonstrances of the Clubs and all his friends,[1] who declared that the honour of England was assailed by the insolence of the French press. I argued a few points with him, and then said that as retrospection and recrimination were unprofitable and needless, I hoped he would support the new French administration with Guizot in it. He said he certainly would and particularly asked me to write him an article to feel the ground a little. This I did yesterday, but he has not put it in, perhaps from a notion that Thiers will come back after all. . . . I charged Barnes with the intention of keeping Palmerston at the F.O. in the event of the Tories coming in. He did not deny it. He admitted that Lord Aberdeen had always declared that P.'s appointment was the only one which did the Whig Ministry any credit, and that he knew more about foreign politics than anyone else.[2]

Reeve, in spite of his effort to commit *The Times* to the opposite course, was compelled to admit to Greville that " Lord Palmerston has now bowled everybody out."[3]

Guizot succeeded Thiers on October 29, 1840. *The Times*, at the instance of Reeve, pressed Palmerston to give the new Cabinet a chance. " The first great advantage of M. Guizot's accession to the Government was the opportunity it gave to all parties of letting the past alone ; but, instead of availing himself of it, Lord Palmerston hastened to fling the noose over M. Guizot's head." The leader ended with regretting that in this first dispatch to be laid before M. Guizot, now Prime Minister, " Lord Palmerston could put forward no more conciliatory and more straight-forward principles for future agreement, and the publication of this document is certainly rather calculated to strengthen the suspicions we have already expressed of Lord Palmerston's wilful opposition to every species of concession than to encourage those hopes of amicable arrangement, which are so warmly and generally entertained in this country."

[1] Edward Sterling protested with great vigour and sent in his resignation.
[2] A. H. Johnson, *Letters of Charles Greville and Henry Reeve*, 1836-1865 (London, 1924), p. 39.
[3] Letter to Greville, November 24, 1840, *cf.* J. K. Laughton, *Memoir of the Life and Correspondence of Henry Reeve* (London, 1898), p. 141.

How keenly Palmerston watched the Press at this time appears from an entry in Greville's diary. On November 15, 1840, he wrote :

Yesterday, I got a note from Lady Palmerston asking me if I had written (as somebody had told her) a certain article which appeared in Friday's *Times*, the same somebody also asserting that I was in constant communication with the *Times*. I was able with perfect truth to deny both charges, but I told her that to such questions as these I should never hesitate to give a denial. However, she was satisfied and wrote back a very amiable reply. It shows how sore they are.[1]

Notwithstanding the changes in Paris, the Eastern question still furnished matter for debate in London. There were revelations of Government difficulties. Lord Holland, Chancellor of the Duchy of Lancaster, died on October 22. *The Times* reported on December 1, 1840, a sensational speech by Thiers. He had said that " not only the English nation, but even *in the Cabinet*, I am at liberty now to praise a man, for he is dead, who was not afraid to support our cause and to do us justice, the *Honourable Lord Holland*." *The Times* dismissed the statement as " base and malignant and unprincipled gossip."

On Saturday, December 5, 1840, *The Times* printed a letter, it can be presumed, from Lord Aberdeen :

To the Editor of The Times.

Sir.—I am much surprised that you do not believe the late Lord Holland assisted M. Thiers in the English Cabinet upon the Turco-Egyptian Question. M. Thiers was unconditionally supported by Lord Holland at the last Council he ever attended, and I was not aware before that any secret was made of the fact.

A.

A long article in a following issue said that a portion of the British Cabinet had informed Guizot, who had informed Thiers,

[1] *Cf.* Greville's note, January 7, 1841 : " Clarendon said he could not imagine what Palmerston had to complain of in the *Times*, as though there had been some articles attacking him, the far greater number had been in his favour. Melbourne said there had been a great deal the other way, and that he and his Tory friends with whom he had communicated, had been constantly surprised to find that there was an influence stronger than their own in that quarter, and with reference to one article in particular, ' from a Correspondent,' they were convinced that it proceeded from me. Clarendon told him, he was quite sure it did not proceed from me, and gave him several reasons why, but the suspicion is curious, because it shows how little credit was really given to my denial to Lady Palmerston. Duncannon had previously told Clarendon, that Palmerston suspected me of being the author of the articles against him in the *Times*, and that I derived my information from him. Such is the suspicious disposition of this man, who with all his talents has nothing great or generous about him."

that Lord Holland had not so much supported the cause of France as he had stood out against Lord Palmerston. *The Times* concluded : "The expulsion of Lord Palmerston from office, or rather the tormenting the noble Lord into a resignation, that some other noble person should be enabled to succeed him, was a confidently alleged motive for nearly the whole apparatus of opposition got up against his policy." (December 7, 1840.)

At this point Greville again needs quoting :

December 13, 1840. . . . The friends of Lord Holland have been extremely annoyed at certain virulent attacks that have been made upon him in the *Times* and *Courier* newspapers, together with insinuations against others of the Cabinet for their supposed bias towards France, and betrayal of the secrets of the Cabinet to Thiers. Nothing would be so easy as to answer these calumnies, but there is no paper which would insert a reply, for all the Government Journals are Palmerstonian. If he had any generosity he would use his influence with the *Morning Chronicle* (which he has so often abused) and put in a handsome article in defence of Lord Holland, and besides being generous it would be wise, for the glorification of himself at the expense of his colleagues, however gratifying to his pride and vanity, is very prejudicial to the Government generally. There has been a great deal of discussion about the expediency of making the *Chronicle* insert a reply, and Melbourne was applied to, for the purpose of getting him to send for Easthope, and desire what might be done, but of course he would do nothing, and perhaps after all it will be better to let the matter drop.

The Whigs, indeed, were supremely weak at this time ; Palmerston apart, they possessed very little influence except with the most venal Press. Ellice pressed Melbourne to found a new daily when the *Morning Chronicle* passed under Palmerston's domination. The *Morning Post* and the *Morning Herald* were Tory. *The Times*, though objecting to Palmerston's manner, supported the substance of his diplomacy. Indeed, all question of *The Times* supporting Palmerston in principle was settled by an unexpected speech by Guizot, and Barnes sent Reeve an unequivocal instruction as to the line the paper was to take on French affairs :

November 21, 1840.

My dear Sir,

I waited to see M. Guizot's speech on the address before I gave you a decided answer. After reading that speech which, I confess, not a little surprized me, there can be no doubt as to the course to be pursued.

The warmest friend of Palmerston could not have uttered a more emphatic and complete justification of his policy. M. Guizot most distinctly avows that France has not, nor has had, the slightest ground of complaint ag^t. England & the other parties to the Treaty of July.

What an unprincipled scoundrel that Thiers must be to have raised the storm which had nearly threatened the peace of Europe.

I cannot help thinking too that M. Guizot has been amusing himself by mystifying us.

In fact it is never safe to trust a Frenchman on the subject of his Country.

I don't see that anything remains for us to do more than to justify Palmerston.

Yours very truly,
T. BARNES.

Palmerston's success strengthened his position in the Cabinet, while it emphasized the weakness of the Government. Yet dissolution was staved off, although Melbourne himself told Clarendon that " it's impossible that this Government can go on ; Palmerston is in communication with the Tories." This was in January, 1841, but the Government did go on.

Between 1837 and 1841 Barnes's health caused some slackening in his effort. An anonymous observer had written as early as 1834 that Barnes would do well to take more exercise : it was not good for one so fanatically interested in his work to live only a quarter of an hour away from Printing House Square. In 1836 Barnes moved from 49, Nelson Square, to No. 25, Soho Square, the house formerly occupied by Marshal Conway. His health, however, gave increasing anxiety, though he insisted on continuing his work.

In domestic politics after 1839, the dominating figure, made more conspicuous by the political dependence of what *The Times* called the " Bedchamber " Government upon his support, was still Daniel O'Connell. After the crisis the Agitator proclaimed his familiar political objects with a new note of passion. The imminent possibility of a defeat which should end the career of the Whig Government induced him to affirm his determination to rebel rather than accept any " Tory " domination. " I tell Wellington, that if the hateful Tory faction are to be forced upon Ireland we will not have a ' little war ' as he calls it ; that he and they would have to contend against the united population of Ireland." This speech, delivered at the end of the year 1839, was followed by renewed denunciations in which *The Times* duly figured. On January 3, 1840, the paper, taking the responsibility for having printed " a couple of hundred articles that scorched and blasted and consigned him to an age of infamy," affirmed its determination that " if he fails to complete our threatened assassination " it would not fail to visit him with still more such articles. *The Times*, urging that " the end and object of our labours is to our country's good," even doubted or professed to doubt whether it had not wronged England by giving its support to the Bill of 1829.

We—ay, WE it was, *The Times*—and we glory not in it—that after 17 years of long unaided struggle, brought round the repugnant voice of the British nation in favour of a Roman Catholic bill. And well have we and our Protestant countrymen been requited.

But we have years ago told this poor man's robber that we were at war with him—open war—war to the political extinction of one of us —of DANIEL O'CONNELL or of *The Times* newspaper and the Conservative and Protestant cause.

In 1840 Barnes journeyed to Cambridge in order to vote for Lyndhurst at the contested election for High Steward of the University. His visit is recorded by Disraeli, himself present in the Senate : " Fat old Barnes, of *The Times*, waddled up to give his vote ; he was recognised and the undergraduates mightily cheered ' The Thunderer ' to his infinite satisfaction." This was on November 12, 1840. It was fairly certain that Lyndhurst would secure, as he did, a large majority of votes ; so it was generous of Barnes to go to Cambridge in November of all months. It was his last recorded appearance in public. He was ill continually in the early spring of 1841, suffering great pain.

The new year saw the Conservatives not only winning by-elections but making gain after gain. John Walter, as a Conservative candidate, won Nottingham on April 27, 1841, from the Whigs. On April 29 the Whig Government was defeated by ten in a full House voting on the Irish Registration Bill. The resignation of the Government was daily expected. Clarendon wrote to Greville that at a Cabinet on the defeat, when he expected a decision to resign, various expedients were suggested—" but the thought of going out was not entertained."

The expedient chosen came to the ears of the Conservatives on April 30. A Committee on Import Duties had been appointed in 1840, as the result of agitation by Joseph Hume. Twelve months later it published a report exposing the defects of the existing fiscal system. In April, 1841, the Government determined to use the report as a basis for an attack on the duties upon sugar, coffee, tea and other commodities—and corn.

Barnes, though naturally sharing the curiosity and interest of the hour, was too unwell to come to the office. He had expected the Whigs to strive their hardest to retain office, but not that they would raise the question of the Corn Laws. The position of the Conservatives on that point was none too confidently held. Barnes had tried to teach them the necessity of unity, and here was a question which divided them. He now saw that " a tottering, floundering and falling wreck of a Ministry . . . meddles with these questions only for sinister purposes." (May 1, 1841.)

The Times never made any secret of its difference from the Conservatives on the Free Trade question. On a speech by Peel in the previous session, for example, it wrote, after an interval for consideration :

Among the questions on which Sir Robert Peel thought it necessary to declare his sentiments was that of the corn laws ; and on this head his views are opposed to those of *The Times*. But he expresses them manfully . . . distinctly declaring himself in favour not only of a protection, but of a " *liberal* protection to domestic agriculture," and unequivocally deciding for a " graduated duty, variable inversely with the price of corn," as against any fixed duty. . . . It is precisely because food is an essential article that *The Times* regards it as especially unfit to be tampered with by any Government. Any steady principle on subjects of first-rate importance is, however, preferable to that uncertainty, of which the only fruits are the disappointment of hope and the encouragement of agitation. But if it be blameable in us, as independent men, to bestow our general support upon a Government from which we happen to differ on an important question, how great must have been the crime of all that phalanx, the Whig-Radical newspapers not excepted, who have been supporting the present Ministry on every question affecting its retention of office, notwithstanding their difference from it upon the most mortal question of the constitution . . . for instance that greatest of Irish questions, the maintenance of the union, and that greatest of English, or rather of Imperial questions, the maintenance of the established church.

The Melbourne Cabinet itself was again divided. Clarendon reported ten years afterwards to Lord John Russell that the Prime Minister, as his colleagues were leaving the Cabinet, had said, " By the bye, there is one thing we haven't agreed upon, which is, what are we to say. Is it to make our corn dearer or cheaper, or to make the price steady ? I don't care which : but we had better all be in the same story."[1]

The position, then, of *The Times* was clear, even if Peel and the Conservatives hesitated. Was this the occasion to break with the Opposition ? Were the Whigs the men to be allowed to carry through a revision of the Corn Laws ? The answer came in a trenchant leader, which began with a reminder to Lord Melbourne of his judgment, expressed as lately as 1839, that " to leave the whole agricultural interest without protection, I declare before God that I think it the wildest and maddest scheme that ever entered into the imagination of man to conceive." Concluding, the paper said " Lord Melbourne and his colleagues have just now lost the confidence of the country and *must resign*, unless, by stirring society to its foundations, arraying the commercial and agricultural interests in deadly bitterness and animosity against each other, and taking their side with the former, they can contrive, upon a dissolution, to gain such a majority as may enable them to fester on a few years longer in the infamy of salaried contempt." (May 5, 1841.)

But Barnes's own term of years was almost ended, and it fell to others to confront the issues raised by the resignation of Melbourne.

[1] Spencer Walpole, *Life of Lord John Russell* (London, 1889), I, 369.

XXIII

"THE THUNDERER"

THE anonymity of *The Times*, carefully guarded, is seldom mentioned explicitly in its own columns. That Barnes attached importance to the principle of anonymity in journalism is proved in his earlier career on the *Examiner* and the *Champion*.[1] The only pieces he signed, with his initials only, were essays in literary criticism contributed to the *Reflector*. There were additional reasons for an even stricter maintenance of anonymity in *The Times*. The journalistic convention which had preserved it not only in Printing House Square but in the other journals was elaborated into something more by Barnes. Thomas Moore reports the anger of the politicians that *The Times* should have secured information of the break-up of the Goderich Ministry in January, 1828, on the same day that the decision had been taken. When asked for an explanation, Barnes answered that his sources of information were secret and would remain so. Moore enters his reflection that Barnes delighted in mystification, but the Editor's point was that correspondents must know that their letters were safe in his hands. Correspondents to whom Barnes was indebted for immediate news of political changes signed their communications with initials; the information was acknowledged in the paper under the heading "Answers to Correspondents." Among these correspondents was Charles Greville, whose communications were signed " B."[2] A single reference to anonymity has been noted in the columns of the paper during the earlier years.[3] It occurs in the reply to the complaint of a country clergyman whose pamphlet on the New Poor Law had been examined

[1] See also pp. 204-5.
[2] The same correspondent supplied similar news to Delane. On September 2, 1841, " B." wrote to the new editor : " Mr Reeve will have prepared you for the possibility of hearing from me. . . . If at any time you wish to communicate with me, just put in *The Times* that the address of ' B ' is wanted. I use the same signature which I used to my friend Mr. Barnes whose loss I so sincerely regret. I am sir, yr obdt. sert. B."
[3] December 9, 1835.

in two fierce leading articles. The Rev. Mr. Cotes wrote in his letter of " the benefit that your concealment gives you (the Editor)," and the second leading article reminded him that such concealment was advantageous to the public. " The writer in a newspaper sacrifices all the pleasures of literary fame for what— impunity ? no—the impunity is merely nominal ; for though he is obliged by a bond of honourable confidence not to claim even the honour due to his own writings, he is sufficiently known to be subject to all the usual responsibilities and penalties for any violation of social decorum. The public is a gainer because it obtains a free and full discussion without any mixture of that egotism and self-intrusion which are almost inseparable from the compositions of any individual writer in his own personal character." Incidentally, Mr. Cotes was advised that he could verify for himself in its own columns " the conduct of *The Times* during a long series of years for its uniform, unflinching and zealous support of the rights of the poor and unprotected classes of society."

A greater freedom of action and expression than had ever fallen to a strong editor made "The Thunderer" possible. Thomas Barnes's egoism, governed only by his exceptional intelligence and aptitude, gave his work a peculiar political power. He had especial skill in rewriting the articles of others, and his habit, then new, of looking at the paper as a unit led him to coordinate its contents and its policy. Not a few issues of *The Times* may have betrayed political misjudgment, yet the paper was on the whole well organized against self-contradiction, organized also to speak its mind. The old method of grouping paragraphs in the centre and printing them under the sub-title was abandoned ; the old summary chronicle of events was radically transformed into a critical examination of the policy, the motive and the sufficiency of this or that act of whatever Ministry or of the individuals composing it—" not the prying into private life indeed, but the full and fearless investigation of all public acts of public men."[1] Whereas newspaper readers had been accustomed since the days of " Junius " to devote their attention to " Decius " or " Vetus " or some similarly signed communication addressed " To the Editor," Barnes brought them to regard the leading article as the vital part of the paper. He addressed not a governing class but all classes. He was eager to be read by all who could read. He wrote as a teacher ; he accustomed the whole

[1] *The Times*, October 1, 1840, on one of the chief uses of the public Press.

country to ask " What does *The Times* say ? " The change was fundamental ; and there were other changes which assisted the paper to dominate journalism.

" What does *The Times* say ? " was not a question restricted to Parliamentary politics, though politics were a national prepossession in the period 1819-1841. Barnes's doctrine that, in order to affect John Bull's somewhat sluggish mind, leader-writers must fire ten-pounders at him, equally governed the treatment of domestic subjects like the common right of the people to the lawns of Regent's Park (" not for the exclusive use of rank and opulence "), the treatment of the poor by Marylebone magistrates, the charges of the Post Office, the delays of the law, the activities of the commercial and financial world. Wide in his range of comment, the Editor invited, challenged, and, when necessary, shocked the Englishman to the painful duty of reflection and action. To get the Englishman to think, he employed a militant and at times intemperate vehemence new even to a generation accustomed to strong language. The clock device over the leading article became, to the political cartoonist and general reader alike, the insignia of an unique authority. In the words of the *Morning Chronicle*, most bitter of enemies, the readers of *The Times* leading articles received them as the " true and apostolical gospel thundered from the Vatican in Printing House Square."

It was a comment on a domestic incident that gave *The Times* a famous nickname. Rivals had spoken of the " Leading Journal " ten years before the more familiar description was originated. " Leading Journal " was supposed to be Barnes's own term for the paper in an article of 1819.[1] In January, 1829, fashionable and unfashionable London was shocked by a " tragedy in high society." For some time rumour had been busy, first with the estrangement between a Lord and his Lady, and next with an illustrious personage by whom the Lady was consoled. One Sunday afternoon Lord Graves went home as if for dinner. On his not appearing at table, the servants went into his room and found him with his throat cut, dead, with two razors beside the candles. Gossips, in the absence of any letter, were divided ; some regarded the affair as suicide and others as murder. Public curiosity received a severe repulse when a short

[1] It has not proved possible to trace the article.

inquest was held early in the morning in deference to a strong desire on the part of relatives to avoid publicity. *The Times* gave a first leader (written perhaps by Sterling, who would be well acquainted with the feeling in the clubs, where the interest was intense) to a trenchant statement of the unwisdom of such a procedure in such a case, insisting that in any matter of life and death inquiry could never be too careful, frank or open. The tone of the article provoked comment in the following day's *Post*, *Herald* and *Chronicle*. On February 11 *The Times* returned to the subject in another first leader :

Nothing can excuse the brevity of so important an inquest as that upon the body of Lord Graves. . . . Had this inquiry been gone into at length, in how very different a situation would the surviving members of the family have now stood.

Other journals had regarded the tone of the previous leader as unnecessarily sensational, and as giving unnecessary pain, and *The Times* defended itself :

every post, twopenny and general, brought us letters charging us [before the inquest] with . . . desertion of the popular cause. Still we were silent. But when the Coroner's inquest, which should have elicited the truth was curtailed of its fair proportions—then we thundered out that article in Tuesday's paper which caused so great a sensation.

The " sensation," it may be admitted, was chiefly journalistic. Among other newspapers the *Morning Chronicle* immediately rallied *The Times* on the style of its leading articles, and on February 17, 1829, the *Morning Herald* printed at the top of a column of its leader-page the following squib :

" THUNDER FORTH THE ARTICLE "

" Our readers will see the application of the following paragraph," said a " Leading Journal," on publishing a description from Cicero's Orations of the notorious conspirator, Catiline. But the application was far from being as evident as was the intention of the writer. No one, however, who recollects the *thundering* on that occasion, can

393

misunderstand the following extracts, in which a slight change of the *metre* is made for the sake of the meaning :—

> Cœlo tonantem credidimus Jovem
> Regnare : præsens Divus habebitur
> " *Horrendum* "———

For the said " Awful " one day thunders forth the foulest calumnies, and wounds the feelings of the innocent family of a late lamented Nobleman, regardless alike of the " mischief " that " has been produced," and the propriety of its conduct.

> Fertur pudicæ conjugis osculum
> Parvosque natos, ut capitis minor,
> Ab se removisse, et virilem
> Torvus humi posuisse vultum.
> The " *Awful*[1] Monosyllable."

—But on the following day it refutes its own " scandalous falsehoods " ; being by some extraordinary means made fully *sensible* of the injury and disgrace which such an incautious proceeding must bring on the " best possible instructor," which " could find no facts to fix upon."

> Hoc caverat mens provida *reguli**
> Dissentientis conditionibus
> Fœdis, et exemplo trahentis
> Perniciem veniens in *Tempus*.

———

*Not the Roman who would sooner die than counsel his countrymen to do wrong ; but the *little King* of a certain *print*, who says, " WE thunder forth," &c.

—At such tergiversation and " Punic faith " the public may well exclaim—

> O pudor !
> O Magna Carthago probrosis
> Altior Italiæ ruinis !—(*Horace*, Lib. 3, Ode 5.)

Now though this consistent Journal has so ravenously devoured one day what it had put forth on the preceding, still, if an appetite for slander should hereafter bring out a repetition of the falsehood, and other papers pamper that appetite by publishing particulars, there is no doubt but that the " Awful " would feel jealous, and, disputing the originality of the mischief, again sing out " that's my thunder."   X.

[1] " *Times*." The reference would seem to be to the reserve manifested by Walter, Fraser and Barnes who seldom mentioned the paper in speech or writing. Sterling always wrote " T——s " ; Fraser " the journal."

The identity of X is not known, but it is possible that the originator of the nickname " The Thunderer " was William Maginn. The *Morning Herald* gave prominence during the following year to a set of paragraphs headed " The Town Crier " ; they were signed " P.P.P.—Registrar," initials, according to William Jerdan's *Autobiography*, employed by Maginn. It is fair to assign to him[1] a paragraph, signed " P.P.P.," from the *Morning Herald* of February 15, 1830 :

O YES ! O YES ! O YES !—This is to give notice, that *The Great Earwigger of the Nation*, otherwise *The Leading Journal of Europe*, otherwise *The Awful Monosyllable*, otherwise *The Thunderer*—but more commonly called " *The Blunderer* " ; is ready and willing to contract for a regular supply of *anti-Cumberland lightning*, of the reddest and very fiercest quality.—Any person or persons, willing to enter into a contract for a supply of the same, may receive further particulars, and minute instructions, by application to THOMAS TIT TONANS, Esq., at the office of *The Thunderer*, Printing House-square.—The contractors will not be required to produce very strict testimonials of character.

GOD SAVE THE KING !

There was generally an intense and even personal note in the style of its articles when *The Times* was leading an offensive. It has been illustrated in the vigour with which Barnes attacked Althorp's policy and person. Joseph Hume, floater of a Greek loan in curious circumstances, an eminent Radical, bosom friend of Francis Place and tedious Parliamentarian, apt to weary the House with figures and fractions, was consistently assailed in all these capacities from 1831, and his reputation sank accordingly. Barnes treated with habitual irony the honesty of " Joseph the Noodle," or " Joseph the Ass." A set of verses contributed to the *Morning Post* by Praed[2] faithfully testifies to the effectiveness of Barnes's combined ridicule and reasoned exposure of Hume :

The cunning man has scowled on me
Who changes black to white ;
There never came wizard over the sea
More strong to blast and blight ;
He breathes his spell in a dark dark den
The Chancellor[3] well knows where ;
His servants are devils, his wand is a pen,
And his circle is Printing House Square.

[1] Maginn knew Barnes in 1825 and then, it appears from a letter of Disraeli to Lockhart, discussed with him the details of the *Representative*. (*Cf. Letters of Sir Walter Scott*, II, 407.)
[2] Winthrop Mackworth Praed was a contributor of verses to *The Times* from 1828. He took the *Morning Post* in hand from 1832, conducting it with much ability.
[3] The reference is to Brougham.

Many a strange and quaint disguise
The crafty conjuror wears ;
Sometimes he mutters blasphemies,
Sometimes he mumbles prayers ;
And if he rides to burn a town
On a galloping Broom[1] today,
Tomorrow he quakes from the sole to the crown
Like a Friar of Orders Grey.

I once was fair ; not Waithman's[2] face
Was a fairer face than mine
Ere the sorcerer's eye had marred the grace
Of the features so divine ;
On my brow a few black drops he threw,
And a few fierce words he said,
And lo—and lo—wherever I go,
I wear an Ass's head.

There is no need to reproduce the whole poem, but, omitting two more verses, particularly on Hume, Praed's conclusion aptly summarizes " The Thunderer's " general reputation at this time :

A mighty man that juggler is,
So gloomy and so grim ;
You shall not find a task I wis,
Too difficult for him ;
He can make Lord Althorp half a wit,
Lord Morpeth not a bore,
And give Lord Palmerston hope to sit
In the seat where he sat before.

Would you retain for a twelvemonth's space
The selfsame hue and shape ?
Would you shun to change your natural face
For the face of an owl or ape ?
Would you pray, through life's uncertain span,
The fame you win to wear ?
Avoid, if you can, the cunning man
Whose circle is Printing House. Square.

[1] The reference is to Brougham.
[2] Alderman Waithman, city draper, attacked by *The Times*, earned a rebuke in the House from Lord John Russell :
        (Ah, whence was Waithman's sorrow ?)
        " I wish " he sighed, " that eight or nine
        Good liberal customers of mine
        Mayn't see *The Times* tomorrow."
                (W. M. Praed in the *Albion*, February 7, 1832.)

The style of *The Times* was as much detested by public men as it was relished by the general reader. Quotations from its leading articles formed an indispensable feature in the town weeklies and country newspapers of both parties ; the raciness of its comments on the public acts of public men gave proverbial standing to certain phrases—*e.g.*, " Honest Joseph [Hume]," " the Lath-and-plaster Cabinet," " Thunder for Reform," " The Bill, the whole Bill and Nothing but the Bill," and " the Crim-Connell Government." Public men affected to despise its " Billingsgate ruffianism " ; the agnostic puritan Francis Place lamented the blackguarding of his friends—he was, like Parkes, a dupe of the Brougham of 1834. Croker gave one side the cue in 1829 when he lauded the French Press at the expense of the home product, knowing well enough, none better, that the literary qualities of the Paris journals were called into existence by the expenditure of Government money—an arrangement he considered eminently satisfactory. Charles Buller, speaking in 1836 on behalf of the Whig Government's measure of stamp reduction, took occasion to repeat Croker's view, alleging the literary superiority of the French Press to be so well known as to make argument unnecessary. *The Times* did not let Buller's statement pass, but replied in a leading article which presents a comparison of the Press of London and of Paris :

We know not with what purpose Mr. C. Buller took upon himself to pronounce *ex cathedra* the superiority of the daily press of France over that of England. It had little or nothing to do as an argument applicable to the question, and as a fact is not true.

A French article is a smart, dressed up, exhibition, where abstract theories, pretty phrases, and studied circumlocutions, are fitted solely to catch the fancy for an instant, and be forgotten the next. There is no wear and tear in them—they are not for practice. They are as jejune as *soupe maigre*, and are as trivial and light as the gossip of the *salons*. Here everything—speeches, as well as newspaper articles, have an eye to business ; they are designed to be acted upon. They bear the impress of activity and work. It may be true that Chateaubriand flourished in newspapers, but so on our side did Canning and Mackintosh. With the press of the United States we will not descend to a comparison.[1] Mr. C. Buller, indeed, stated " there is not connected with any portion of the daily press any name that occupies a high station in the literature of the country." Mr. Buller might just as well have said that there is no eminent rope-dancer

[1] The American Press was then commonly regarded as purely sensational.

connected with the daily press. The reason of both facts is the same. Men whose time is wholly and incessantly occupied in one pursuit cannot possibly be eminent in any other. We do not, of course, pretend to guess what Mr. Buller may mean by " literature," but let him limit or enlarge the meaning of the word as he will, still we should be very glad to learn what " literature " we have at present which requires one quarter the knowledge and talent that are indispensable in those who conduct a morning newspaper with credit. We are very much mistaken, if we have not seen very many times, in a single number of a London daily newspaper, more valuable information, more sound reasoning, and more original and eloquent writing, than are to be met with in any modern volume of the so-called *littérateurs*.

In conclusion *The Times*, referring to Charles Buller's efforts in Palmerston's *Globe*, asked :

What qualifies Mr. Buller to sit in judgment upon the talents of public writers ? He has leisure, though he belongs to a profession : he is a member of the House of Commons : he tried his hand for some time at newspaper writing in an evening print : and still we defy the whole town to put their hands upon any recorded speech of his, or upon any production of his pen, which is calculated to raise him above the level of a forward fourth-form schoolboy.[1]

Barnes's statement that his leading articles were written with an eye to business, " designed to be acted upon," is the key to his editorial policy. *The Times* spoke out, called out, shouted out, thundered out with the intention of stimulating public opinion towards public action.

As a paper jealous of its right to speak out, *The Times* pressed for tolerance even towards unworthy newspapers. On February 10, 1834, a leading article appeared on the Government prosecution of the *True Sun* for " seditious libel." *The Times* objected because it felt in its own instance the injustice of many actions taken under the existing law, and because it regarded such actions as tending to exaggerate the importance of the journals in which the libels were printed :

Nobody, where the press is free, cares one straw for the mere ebullitions or instigations of factious phrenzy : if laughed at one hour, they are forgotten the next, unless an unnatural gravity and permanency be affixed to them by a notice from the Attorney-General, which has been in all human likelihood the very object of the libeller's ambition.

[1] The punctuation at least must be Barnes's ; he was inordinately fond of the colon—as his manuscript letters demonstrate.

It was argued that Ministers were more powerfully defended by the Press than by themselves ; the responsible part of the Press always corrected the merely factious. Moreover :

What conceivable mischief could have arisen to Lord Grey's Government from even a hundred consecutive columns of " sedition " put forth by that mean and wretched publication which calls itself the " *True Sun* " ? Why, the paper just prosecuted and found guilty wanted nothing but the drag-rope of a sentence to pull it a few inches out of the muddy obscurity in which it has all along been immersed.... The whole ward of Billingsgate has been daily ransacked by its writers for terms of foul and rancorous abuse of *The Times*, which never did aught to offend, save only by never speaking of it. But we cannot bear to see these unhappy persons harassed and oppressed. We abhor these political prosecutions, and so do the people of England.

The situation in respect to the libel laws was at this period more anxious than it is even to-day and was aggravated by threats of Government prosecution and speculative suits by common informers. *The Times* employed very strong language in the same month concerning an action in which a newsman was indicted for selling a copy of a newspaper in which a libel had appeared. The Judge found that any newsman or coffee-house keeper, being a publisher of a sort, was bound to know whether the newspaper contained libel or not, and if he did not ascertain the fact, he was equally liable with the author. " There is a precious law for you ! " —and *The Times* asked in emphatic language, " Why, good God, was such rank nonsense as this ever before sanctioned by any civilised legislature ? " There followed a half-column of argument to show that even the oilman or chandler who furnished light might have reason to be punished for assisting publication. The law officers of the Crown were called upon to bring in a correcting Bill : " It cannot be done too soon."

Common justice was an end for which the paper perpetually contended. Its unafraid attitude to the organization of the working classes is well seen in its treatment of the incident of the Dorset labourers, now celebrated as the " Tolpuddle Martyrs." On April 2, 1834, the agitation in favour of the labourers culminated in a demonstration by the trade unions which was announced to conclude with a procession. *The Times*, taking a strong line against some Ministers and many journals, considered the incident no excuse for panic. But London had never seen such a massing of the workers, and the more nervous property-owners were so gloomy that the Government brought up for their comfort not only the Life Guards and other Household Troops at strength, but also detachments of the 12th and 17th Lancers, two troops of Dragoons, eight battalions of Infantry, 29 pieces of ordnance, and the whole of the Metropolitan Police. A court of the Lord Mayor and Aldermen had the duty of swearing in special constables. The day was still young when it became obvious to the Government that the whole of this parade was unnecessary, and that only a modest force of constables was required for dealing with the regular " omnibus nuisance " and the special direction of traffic. A petition in favour of the Dorset unionists convicted for the administration of unlawful oaths was peacefully presented but firmly refused by a Home Department official, in the deliberate absence of Lord Melbourne. *The Times* praised the peaceable and loyal disposition of the 30,000 men in London that day. " Nothing, we must say, could be more conspicuous than the peaceful and steady behaviour of the whole procession, nor anything more well-tempered or accommodating than the readiness of the files to admit the passage, where required, not only of persons, but of horsemen and carriages." The article ended with a challenge :

We have been called enemies of the working classes ; but by whom ? By miscreants who cheat and prey upon them. We are too upright to be flatterers of the wealthy, and what honest man will dare charge us with having *ever* abandoned or betrayed the poor ? Who has pleaded more strenuously than we have done for that reform which has put power in the hands of so many of the working classes ? Who has pressed so vigorously against the landlords the wickedness of their tax upon the poor man's bread ? Who raised and directed the public spirit of England against the vile massacre of the manufacturing poor at Peterloo in 1819, when every man that dared to open his mouth against the Castlereagh and Sidmouth despotism must have set the Six Acts at defiance ? Who would now open the poor man's eyes to the snares and treacheries which his mock friends are practising against him, who but this *Times* journal ?—the object of every villain's vengeance and of every slanderer's abuse. On such creatures we disdain to waste words —we despise and defy them.

The paper, however, was attacked not by Radicals alone, but by the Right. " As for the attacks on us by the Tory journals and the Tory clubs (the frequenters of White's will know what we mean), their splenetic effusions have amused us ; indeed, we forgive their rage which, it must be confessed, is natural. They expected that there would be a riot yesterday, which might embarrass the Government, and the quiet and orderly result, owing, as they no doubt think, in a great measure to our remonstrances and warnings, has baffled their hopes and covered them with disappointment and confusion."

A similar line was taken on April 16, 1838, when the various trade unions celebrated the release of the Dorset labourers by a mass meeting on Kennington Common. But a facetious turn was given to the theme consistent with the paper's opposition to the Melbourne Government :

With the sufficient notice which the Government have had of it, we consider it their bounden duty to have created a simultaneous diversion, either by a grand review in Hyde Park, or by some other plan ; whereby this procession might have been left to drag itself along amidst the silence and security of streets comparatively deserted. Could not Mr. Spring Rice have undertaken to dance on the tight-rope on top of the Bank ? Or Lord Glenelg to walk through the part of the somnambulist at Greenwich Fair, or Lord Melbourne to play the *gastronome sans argent* at Pimlico ?

The day of the procession was Easter Monday and therefore a general holiday. A report which occupied a couple of columns described the appearance of most of those taking part as " very decent," though " many looked as if they could ill afford to lose a day's work." The improved manners and dress of the working men were attributed to the influence of temperance societies. The five labourers were in the procession and were much cheered ; and the affair passed off without any sort of disorder.

These convictions of *The Times* had, indeed, been proved as early as 1819. Barnes's friend, Robert Owen, conceived a plan for ameliorating the condition of the lower classes ; it was discussed in the House of Commons and the opportunity was taken by Barnes to protest against coldhearted professional economists. A leading article of December 17, 1819, regretted that the question of dealing with the poor had " diverged into discussions of theoretic points connected with the processes of nature and the multiplying of the human race " :

This is very ridiculous. The obvious duty of the legislator is to supply to man all the possible means of comfort, increase, and happiness ; and to leave the result to Providence. It is hardly credible that

DD

philosophizing noodles should have carried their mental wanderings so far, as to have thought and spoken of prohibiting, by law, the grand impulse of nature, under the forms legalized in the gospel dispensation. When this is said of a system, we presume that all is said, which can or need be, to show its ludicrous absurdity.

The cold efficiency of the high priests of political science on the one hand and of the high capitalists of the industrial system on the other was hateful to *The Times*. The abuse of child labour particularly aroused its anger ; it gave facts and figures and vehemently denounced the practice which " confined infants to sedentary labour for 12, 10 or even 8 hours in succession," so that they " can never reach perfect health and vigour, and must soon be worn out and become chargeable as paralytics or aged." About this time the horrors of the Lancashire factory system were becoming more widely known, but Lancashire had partners in its iniquity. The number of persons employed in the flax spinning mills at Dundee under 18 years was 1,073, and of these most were under 14, a considerable number under 12, some under 9, while a few between 6 and 7 were admitted and compelled to labour along with the rest. At some of the mills the children laboured 13 hours 20 minutes a day, or a total of $79\frac{3}{4}$ hours per week, exclusive of meal time. None labour for a shorter period than $12\frac{1}{2}$ hours a day or $74\frac{1}{2}$ per week. In mills situated in solitary or thinly populated parts of the country the hours of labour extend to $14\frac{1}{2}$ and 15 hours a day. This, when allowing 50 minutes for meals and the time spent in going to and from work, leaves between 6 and 7 hours of sleep.

So *The Times* proved its concern to speak for a nation, not for a class merely.

The publication on May 8, 1838, of the demands of the London Working Men's Association in a document subsequently known as the " People's Charter " passed by without notice in *The Times*, but the great space given later made some amends for this apparent lack of realization of the Charter's significance. " Chartist " as a term appears for the first time on January 5, 1839, in a dispatch from Manchester describing a meeting of some 600 persons in support of the principle of Magna Carta, the Carta de Foresta and the Charter. The concern and surprise of *The Times* reflects the mind of the commercial and middle classes on the Chartist disturbances. During 1839 the paper discerned, as a consequence of disputes and tumult, a pronounced public trend away from extreme Radicalism. The Chartist movement was in fact turning the leading spirits of Radicalism and Whiggery into more conservative channels. The older Whigs thus laid themselves open to the charge, not new in the columns of *The Times*, that they never valued principle half as much as they valued office, and office for the sake of patronage. Philosophical Radicals also were a rapidly dwindling force. Both Parkes and Roebuck were destined to help *The Times* under Delane. Although Barnes did not live to see it, Peel's return to power in 1841 was followed five years later by his acceptance of the fundamental issue which had hitherto lain between them—namely, the Corn Law question.[1]

During 1839 the independent judgment of the editorial mind, in a matter of journalistic rather than political significance, was notably vindicated. On the evening of October 22 in that year general excitement was caused by news that Lord Brougham had been killed in a carriage accident. The papers came out next morning with long obituaries ; *The Times* printed a short denial of the report. On the following day, October 24, the paper gave its first leading article to the topic :

The intelligence of Lord Brougham's death, believed so generally, and with so much confidence, throughout the whole of Monday last, and on authority supposed to be so unquestionable, owed no part of its circulation to this journal, the only one among the morning newspapers of Tuesday by which the disastrous incident was not assumed for fact, and made the occasion of some sort of obituary notice.

Giving the true particulars of the occurrence, *The Times* characterized as " shameful " the spirit of " impudence and inhumanity " responsible for the statement which " we found ourselves justified in treating as a fabrication," and deplored the cruelty which had launched the tale with all the risks of its "reaching the learned Lord's wife and daughter separated from him by at least 400 miles." After this introduction, while admitting that " to expatiate would require an exercise of pen or speech almost as cumbersome as his Lordship's own productions," the paper proceeded to correct certain accounts of his Lordship just published. *The Times* reminded its readers that any radiance " bursting " from him was

but a stream of sparkles from a firework—there is neither steady light nor animating warmth. His co-operation is precarious, his spirit of

[1] In 1845 *The Times* was the first to announce Peel's conversion to free trade in corn which had been what the Tory Press described as the " little idol of *The Times* " from 1829 (*cf.* Chapter XXII, The Last Years of Barnes).

intrigue incorrigible, his ambition wild and indefinite, his absence of fixed principle and steadfast purpose as conspicuous as it is terrible, both to followers and to colleagues.

In society, as one of the most agreeable, amusing, witty, kindly and convivial of associates, there is no individual capable of filling the space which would have been left void by Lord Brougham's untimely exit. There are a multitude of friends who loved him for what he was and is, as there are observers who have admired him for what he might have been. . . .

Setting aside all affectionate or private feelings, those members of both parties who are best acquainted with Lord Brougham, and have tried him, would, after a little while, have felt his removal a lightening of many cares and a release from many imminent embarrassments. For it is by impulses of temper or of pique, more of a selfish than even a capricious nature, and abstracted from all broad or distant considerations of national or general good, that the course of this impetuous, and in some respects formidable, adventurer on the scenes of public life has hitherto been shaped and directed.

The authorship of the news, whether it was mere rumour or deliberate hoax, was much discussed at the time.[1] There had, indeed, been only the slightest accident to the frame of a coach to justify the story. Well-known persons wrote to the Press to prove their innocence. Although it was never brought home to him, Greville and others concluded that Brougham had been at his tricks.

The handling of the " news " by *The Times* and the character of its " obituary " were regarded by journalists as proving the superiority of Barnes as a master of the craft.[2]

The freedom of opinion which *The Times* expressed under Barnes was not more conspicuous in political than in other great questions of the hour. It was frequently severe with the University of Oxford. It disagreed with it on the Catholic question and the Nonconformist question. *The Times* was for emancipation, Oxford for monopoly. *The Times* was for giving Dissenters degrees, but no power over the ecclesiastical settlement ; they

[1] See letters to the Editor of the *Morning Post* from the Count D'Orsay (October 23), Lord Methuen (October 24), H. Duncombe Shafto (October 24, 1839).

[2] Two years later the article was attributed by the *Scotsman* to Barnes. Knight Hunt (II, 177) tells a story illustrating the Editor's penetration. Barnes was reading the *Morning Chronicle* while waiting in Brougham's private room, and coming across a denunciation of an article the Chancellor had the day before written for *The Times*, welcomed him with " Well, this is almost too bad to demolish yourself in this way."

should be satisfied to be outside the Establishment without wanting to influence it. Oxford's refusal of Peel because he came to believe in Catholic Emancipation was difficult to forgive. A paragraph which follows was printed in *The Times* as late as June 16, 1834 :

The Conservatives fancy that they can govern England because they have the support of the nonage and dotage of Oxford. That University is the seat of isolated barbarism amidst an ocean of wholesome knowledge and of useful action. It is generations behind the rest of the kingdom, and fitter to sympathize with the monks of the Escurial than with a free and reflecting people. Yet the oligarch faction will take Oxford for their guide. . . .

Yet Oxford's treatment of Dissent was forgiven when it later became clear that the Nonconformists, as a whole, supported Melbourne and therefore O'Connell, and thus brought the Church under the interference of Dissenters and Papists in the manner which a small group in the University of Oxford had foreseen and resented. Before long this group, which was to attach the name of Oxford to one of the most memorable movements of the early nineteenth century, came to enjoy no little attention and sympathy from the paper. The new ecclesiastical doctrine came to be put forward in *The Times* when it was clear that the Royal supremacy was not objected to by the writers of the " tracts." The new tone became manifest at the end of Barnes's period, three months before his death. " Puseyism," as its enemies called it, began hesitatingly, but later became more confident, ultimately created dissension in Printing House Square, and for a time alienated John Walter II from his son, then an adherent of the " Oxford " Movement. John Walter III, in later years, retreated from the new to a more central Anglican position.

On February 5, 1841, was published the first of a series of letters addressed " To the Editor of *The Times* " and criticizing a recent address by Peel at the opening of a reading-room at Tamworth. Peel championed the view that education, the parent of virtue, exalted man to his highest perfection. He described the neutrality of culture, where men of every shade of politics and religion met together, disabusing one another of their prejudices and practising toleration, cooperation, and mutual understanding. The critic stigmatized this as the very theory on which Brougham had expatiated in the University of London : it was secularism. The mystifying signature " Catholicus " concealed a Fellow of Oriel College, Oxford, the Rev. John Henry Newman, then a member of the Established Church. A second letter, printed on February 9, pursued the argument against Brougham and Bentham, and lastly Peel. " If virtue be a mastery over the mind, if its end be action, if its perfection be inward order, harmony and peace, we must seek it in graver and holier places than libraries and reading-rooms." In a third letter, on the following day, the writer adjured the Knowledge Society, the Gower Street College, the Tamworth Reading-room, Lord Brougham and Sir Robert Peel to reverse the order of things. " Put faith first and knowledge second ; let the university minister to the church." On February 12, 1841, a fourth letter drew attention to the insult placed upon faith by the disparagement of doctrine as " controversial divinity." There was some murmuring in political circles at the nature of these articles and the position they were given in the paper. Was *The Times* about to "assassinate" Peel ?[1] The papers hostile to Printing House Square were full of the talk that Puseyism was nothing less than ecclesiastical Toryism. A leading article in *The Times* cautioned the reader to use his own judgment :

We find an idea gradually creeping forth—probably only among very hasty reasoners—that our attachment to Sir Robert Peel is sustaining some diminution. . . . Now the answer . . . is easily found in the letters themselves. Was it fit that such letters should be suppressed or rejected ? Sir Robert Peel himself, we are convinced, as a man of learning and knowledge, would answer that question in the negative. The attention which the letters have excited concurs also in that decision. We know not whether it be our misfortune or not, but certainly the fact is—and we refer to the past history of this journal for the confirmation of it—that we have judged of public men, have adhered to or rejected them, without any reference whatever to their political position ; whether they were in or out of office has made no difference with us. . . . He [Peel] is beyond all doubt a great and able statesman—virtuous and disinterested . . . but still not infallible. . . . The speech at Tamworth we think not a wise one. What man is wise at all times ? Its errors and blemishes are ably exposed in those letters which we have published : Sir Robert Peel, we are convinced, will be the better for them. . . .

The fifth letter of the series (there were seven, but nothing more need be quoted here) reached the crucial point. It opposed the

[1] It was known to Greville that Peel was much vexed by the unknown writer in *The Times*.

dogmatic basis of Christianity to the cult of physical science, proposed by Brougham, and to those who would admit " Pascal and Julian the Apostate, Cromwell, Ovid, Lady Jane Grey and Mme. Roland, human beings who agreed in nothing but in their humanity and their love of knowledge . . . to one beatification."

The leading article of February 12 did not succeed in disposing of criticism other than political. On March 10, 1841, a long letter signed " A Member of Parliament " stated first that the writer could not regret that the communications of " Catholicus " had been concluded. " I do not know that in giving them so prominent a position in your columns you have overrated their literary value or incidental importance, but I think you can hardly have calculated the effect they were likely to produce on your readers." Challenging " Catholicus " to be consistent, he asked why Bibles should be studied " when the saving doctrines of Christianity can be taught in a few sentences " ? *The Times*, aware that endless argumentation was pending, confessed to some doubt of the prudence of reviving the subject, but explained that the letter of the correspondent " whom we know to be what he signs himself " had been printed " upon the principle of *audi alteram partem*." This was expected to dispose of the matter.

But the letters of " Catholicus " brought out diatribes on the subject of Puseyites in the *Globe*, expostulations and remonstrances on political and theological grounds from the *Standard*, and a triumphant intellectual screed in the *Morning Chronicle*, where a picture was drawn of an alliance between effete, plausible, hollow Toryism and Puseyism, described as a principle which for earnestness and strength had no parallel since the Reformers and the Puritans, and was expected to breathe new life into the defunct stronghold of the privileged classes. *The Times* noticeably leaned towards the Puseyites ; its eye was political, for it discerned in the movement one more argument against Melbourne and against O'Connell's eagerness to impair the religious sanction of Imperialism. It might be useful at this crisis to champion the apostolicity of the Church against a House of Commons dominated by Dissenters, Papists and Radicals.

On March 4, 1841, *The Times* referred to a debate upon the Maynooth grant. Lord Morpeth had attacked the University of Oxford on the ground that certain of its graduates were " constantly employed in disclaiming the doctrines of the

Protestant Church to which they belonged." *The Times* answered that the whole aim and object of " the gentlemen at Oxford " was

to recommend certain doctrines as *identical* with those of the Liturgy, Canons and Articles of the Church of England. They prefer indeed to rescue from Popery the appellation of Catholic, which has ever been the inheritance of all Apostolic Churches, and they are not over-zealous for the denomination of Protestant, which occurs nowhere in the Prayer Book, which expresses no positive belief, and which is the common property of all who are separated from Rome, however widely differing among themselves.

A couple of days later a generously leaded editorial article informed readers that

Several journals have laboured very perseveringly for some time past to connect *The Times* with what they are pleased to call Puseyism ; and the fact of our having on Thursday last expressed a feeling of regret that we had formerly spoken in terms of unmerited harshness of the author of the Oxford Tracts, is declared to be " ominous " by a contemporary whose qualifications for deciding upon questions relating to the doctrine of the Church of England are tolerably notorious. . . . With respect to that school of theology in the English Church, of which so much has been said, we take its actual position to be this. It originated in a feeling of alarm at certain legislative measures which were passed, or known to be in contemplation, during the first three years of Lord Grey's ministry ; and more especially at the persecutions and privations of the parochial clergy in Ireland, consequent on the refusal to pay tithes ; the increasing power and pretensions of Popery in Ireland, and Protestant dissent in England and the disposition manifested by many of the clergy and laity ; to call for important alterations in the Prayer Book.

The letters of " Catholicus " were, it became obvious, preliminaries to a campaign. In the paper of March 17, 1841, there appeared on the leader page a news item, " The Oxford Tracts," heading a letter addressed to the Editor of *The Times* and signed " Oxoniensis Catholicus," with the date-line " Oxford, Tuesday morning, March 16." Above it appeared independently a letter addressed to " Mr Vice-Chancellor," signed " Your obedient servant, John Henry Newman, Oriel College," also dated March 16. The Vice-Chancellor had signed a resolution, passed at a meeting of the Heads of Houses and Proctors on March 15, condemning Tract XC. This resolution held that " modes of interpretation evading rather than explaining the sense of the Thirty-nine Articles and reconciling subscription to them with the adoption of errors which they were designed to counteract, defeat the object, and are inconsistent with the due observance of the above-mentioned statutes "—statutes which enjoined that " every student shall be instructed and examined in the Thirty-nine Articles, and shall subscribe to them." In his letter to the Editor " Oxoniensis Catholicus " (evidently a friend of the author of Tract XC or Newman himself) warned his readers " that this board [of Heads of Houses, etc.] consists indeed of individuals who from their age and station are worthy of every deference, but who are in no way authorised by the statutes on such a subject to represent the University." Another correspondent reported that the University was in a state of great agitation ; on both sides the printers were hard at work. Newman's announcement of the discontinuance of *Tracts for the Times* was printed in the issue of April 2, with this editorial comment :

Of Mr Newman's talents and learning, we presume, there never could be any doubt ; and of his submission to his ecclesiastical superior he has now given a striking proof. As the matter will not be carried any further by the chief parties, we shall ourselves be cautious of committing that error by anything we write. We simply copy Mr Newman's announcement of the fact.

The ecclesiastical position of the paper under Barnes, subject indeed to some development, can be summed up in a few editorial sentences :

The essential difference between an established and an unestablished church lies in this—that the one is recognised as the national organ of religion ; and every citizen, whether belonging to it or not, is compelled by the State to contribute to its maintenance ; the other has no rights beyond its own pale, and no man need be a member of it unless he chooses.

The paper of April 24, 1834, contained a polemical article against the Bishop of Exeter,[1] himself a controversialist of the greatest ability, who had horrified the House of Lords by declaring that subscription to the Thirty-nine Articles by undergraduates did

[1] " Twas dead of night when Bigotry came
     With Phillpotts for her guide "
are the first lines of a set of verses by Praed in *The Times* (June 9, 1828) on the Bishop's war on Catholic Emancipation.

not mean that members of the University of Oxford understood and believed these Articles ; " No, it is simply tantamount to a declaration that the subscribers are members of the Church of England."

So [*The Times* wrote] we are to understand from the pious and single-hearted bishop, that when a man signs any given declaration it is by no means incumbent on him to declare *the truth* ;—that when he writes a solemn pledge of his believing certain doctrines, he means no more than to assert that other people (to wit, his parents) believed them. . . . There are some things indeed which we cannot bear gravely to contemplate. The shock to the moral sense would be intolerable. They must be treated with a sort of levity, as one tries to laugh away the approaches of that sea-sickness under which one is ready to sink.

And attention was directed to the verses in which Bishop Phillpotts was made responsible for the proposition that

> " our revered thirty-nine
> Were made, not for men to believe, but to sign."

The Times had never any liking for this Bishop, but he shared the country's fear of Chartism and Socialism. In 1840, when some four thousand inhabitants of Birmingham entrusted Phillpotts with their petition to the House of Lords against Socialistic doctrines, the comment of the paper was sympathetic and spirited :

Of the vile propensities professed by the execrable monsters who style themselves Socialists—for, to dignify their appetites with the name of *doctrines* were a gross perversion of language—we cannot allow ourselves to speak, except in the most vague and general terms. Relieved from the necessity which obliged their right rev. denouncer to be somewhat explicit in his details, arising from his Lordship's anxiety to deprive the Government of the slightest pretext for declining to interfere, we certainly shall balk the gang even of the doubtful gratification of having their poison analysed and circulated by any direct instrumentality of ours. Nevertheless, connected with the nominal condemnation and practical encouragement extended to it by the Government, we must needs submit a few warning words to our countrymen : and the rather, as there are certain prevalent misconceptions entertained by Lord Brougham and others in regard to the original propagator of this pestilence, which we have it in our power to correct. . . . Between the " new views of society " as propounded by Owen when he was proprietor of the Lanark mills, and the " New Moral World," as exhibiting the more matured and infernal atrocities of the Horse bazaar, there is a great and palpable difference. When he contented himself with aiming at what he then called the regeneration of mankind, by employing an intelligent Quakeress to educate the children of his cotton-spinners, inculcating upon them a visionary optimism, and handing them over to the dancing master on Sundays, he had not uttered a syllable *at that period* either in absolute disparagement of marriage, or in opposition to the rights of property.

Such was the attitude of *The Times* at the end of Barnes's period towards a question destined to grow in complexity and seriousness.

XXIV

MEN AND METHODS UNDER BARNES

THE very appearance of *The Times* was majestic after 1820. Not only was the broadsheet enlarged in dimensions, but also the number of pages was increased. The " Free Supplement " was initiated. At first experimental and exceptional, it became frequent and was finally given regular publication. The periodical surprises given to the public by the several enlargements of *The Times* still further impressed readers with the authority of the paper. During the 1830's *The Times* became a thing of wonder. Elaborate calculations were made of the distance covered by the length of the columns multiplied by the number of copies. The issue of February 11, 1839, containing an account of Queen Victoria's betrothal, sold 30,000 copies, and a contemporary elaborately calculated that, the length of the column being 22 inches, the letterpress of the edition would reach from London to Paris. This record was equalled by *The Times* of February 11, 1840, containing the account of her Majesty's marriage. Vast sums were credited as the income of the paper and unprecedented salaries mentioned as the reward of Barnes, Sterling, Alsager and other members of the staff of *The Times*.[1] The " Great Daily Miracle " required, of course, the labour of many expert hands.

Indeed, the organization of the labour and plant for the execution of this unique volume of printing resulted in the arrangement of a printing office on new lines. The office in Printing House Square achieved permanent entry as a spectacle in the guidebooks to London. Crowned heads, foreign nobles and English scientists came to inspect " Barnes's Panopticon," as Tom Moore called it. The office aroused also the curiosity of the general public, who regularly sought permission to view it. The discipline of the staff, as well as the size of the office, impressed visitors. Charles Babbage, a friend of Barnes and Professor of Mathematics in the University of Cambridge, and the inventor of a calculating machine, made an examination of the printing department in 1831, and embodied

[1] For an idea of the salaries of the principal writers of *The Times* see Chapter X.

his reflections upon the mechanical perfection of the office in his publication *On the Economy of Machinery and Manufactures*, London, 1832. His visit was timed to take place during the composition of the report of a very important Commons' debate. He then found " The place was illuminated with gas, and was light as the day ;—there was neither noise nor bustle ;—and the visitors were received with such calm and polite attention, that they did not, until afterwards, become sensible of the inconvenience which such intruders, at a moment of the greatest pressure, must occasion, nor reflect that the tranquillity which they admired, was the result of intense and regulated occupation."

Babbage found that nearly 100 persons were employed on the establishment ; fifty of them were compositors.[1] The presses were of the new type, patented by Applegath and Cowper,[2] which served *The Times* from 1828 until 1848, when Babbage saw Applegath's first rotary machine.

The new mechanical equipment of 1828 was clearly necessitated by the increased advertising, which demanded more space and therefore enlarged papers. The early supplements (as, for instance, the report on the impeachment of Lord Melville[3]) consisted of three sheets at sixpence each, stamped. The *raison d'être* of these supplements was public eagerness for the details of the trial. May 23, 1818, presented the journalistic innovation of a supplement published to give additional space for advertisements. Editorial matter was carried over to the supplementary sheet. The sensation was great when, instead of charging 7d., *The Times* offered the supplement free.

We know how much we owe to our advertising friends ; but they will have the kindness to recollect, that the preference which they show to this journal results from its more diffuse circulation and greater sale ; and that our pre-eminence in these respects can only spring from, or be maintained by superior talent in the political and literary departments of the work. We must not, therefore, sacrifice one class of customers for the sake of another. Whoever views the quantity of reading-matter in these our columns ; whoever contemplates the power and influence of this journal upon all questions of foreign or domestic policy ; whoever travels in other countries, and has heard it cited as authority, and appealed to as evidence, would be sure, if his own reason did not convince him, that there is no scarcity of that matter which is

[1] There were sixty-two in 1841.
[2] See pp. 118-9.
[3] June 13, 1806.

calculated to attract and satisfy intellectual and scientific readers. But in our zeal for supplying this, we have unavoidably fallen into arrear with our advertising friends ; to whose partiality we are unable to do that justice which we could wish in our daily and ordinary circulation ; and whose favours in consequence crowd our bureaux to such an excess, that we have been obliged to adopt the novel, and to us very expensive expedient, of publishing two sheets in one day ; paying, as we find we are obliged to do, the stamp duty upon both, and presenting one of them gratuitously to the public.

There had been five columns to the page since January, 1811. The column was lengthened in 1812, and widened in 1813. In 1816 it was again lengthened. In 1822 the column was further extended to 22 inches, the present measure. In 1841 three machines of the 1828 pattern were used. The first printed the normal issue of *The Times* ; a second printed the Supplement ; the third was retained as a " stand by " for use in case of an accident. These machines of the improved 1828 design printed a double sheet of eight pages, the first of which appeared on January 19, 1829.

The office conducted its business in two storeys and a basement, forming the east side of the Square. There were two main rooms on each floor, the staircase being in the middle. The advertisement office was on the ground floor, off the entrance lobby and over the wetting room, where every third quire or so of the paper was dipped and then piled and pressed. The machine rooms were in the basement. The composing rooms, one for news and a second for advertisements, were on the upper floor. Adjoining the news-composing room was the reporters' room. There was another room, approachable through the reporters' room, with a character of its own. A visitor who inspected the office soon after Barnes's death " which lately happened " describes the Editor's room as " a plain library room or study, with one square table-desk in the centre, the surrounding shelves being filled with Annual Registers and other works chiefly of a historical kind. . . . There are no other accommodations here for intellectual labourers ; but the fact we understand to be, that much of the original matter of *The Times* is produced elsewhere. . . . Less is known of the editorship of *The Times* than of the other departments,"[1] &c.

The business management of such a concern required the attention of a directorate combining prudence and enterprise.

[1] *Cf.* Visit to *The Times* Printing office in *Chambers' Edinburgh Journal*, June 17, 1843.

The manager of the office of *The Times* during Barnes's period was Thomas Massa Alsager, born in 1779 (died 1846). He was versatile and held an eminent position in two arts : finance and music.[1] Though literary, he was not prominent in letters. Alsager was first a bleacher with a factory near Farringdon Street. His house in Suffolk Street, Southwark, was so close to Horsemonger Gaol that he was a frequent visitor to Leigh Hunt during his imprisonment. Hunt had much affection for him and dedicated a sonnet to his name. Crabb Robinson met him in 1812, together with Allingham and Barnes also, who thought it odd that dealing in canvas (Robinson called it " floorcloth ") should make Alsager think he had a right to talk about pictures. Robinson's opinion then was that Alsager was " not very agreeable because of pretension," but he later came to like him and his music and his whist parties. There was an element of mystery in the personality of this financier-artist, unexplained by any papers left after his death from self-inflicted wounds in 1846. Lamb, however, was very fond of him and chronicles his sayings and doings in letters to their friend Wordsworth. All loved the perfect serenity of his mind. Alsager's musical ability was considerable ; he could himself perform on all the instruments in an orchestra, and his private concerts were greatly valued by musicians. Lamb wrote to Leigh Hunt in 1824 that " Alsager is in a flourishing house with wife and children about him in Mecklenburg Square—almost too fine to visit." He was sociable, enthusiastic and generous. On December 24, 1832, Beethoven's Mass in D was given at Alsager's for the first time in England, under the direction of Moscheles. In 1834 Alsager arranged the first performance in England of Cherubini's Requiem. He became Master of the Clothworkers' Company in 1830 and held the position until 1836, being held in such esteem that his portrait was painted for the Company's Hall, where it still hangs.

Alsager worked on *The Times* for twenty-eight years. He joined in 1817 as City Correspondent, founded *The Times* City office in Birchin Lane, and inaugurated the " City " article ; he later came into the office as Money Market expert, and in 1821 was appointed a manager.

After 1827, when Alsager had received a share in the printing business, *The Times* expanded from a regular issue of four pages

[1] Lamb wrote to Barron Field, August 31, 1817 : " Barnes is going to Demerara or Essequibo, I am not certain which. Alsager is turned actor. He came out in genteel comedy at Cheltenham this season and has hopes of a London engagement." The last statement was probably facetious.

to an occasional issue of eight, twelve, and even, on June 25, 1840, sixteen pages. Under him the news service was further improved ; *The Times* " expresses " aroused the admiration of the world of journalism. He was responsible, under Barnes, for the maintenance and extension of the staff of home and foreign Correspondents. Thus ably were Barnes's political successes supported by Alsager's enterprise on the commercial side. Throughout his period, he gave oversight to the Market News —*i.e.*, the Mark Lane Intelligence, Dock and Shipping News, Produce Quotations, &c. As a writer, Alsager was responsible for, and doubtless wrote, many leading articles on City affairs, banking and currency. In addition, occasional obituaries of notable persons in the financial world may be traced to him. Contemporaries reported Alsager's knowledge of monetary questions to be outstanding. " If private report speaks truth, he has, by means of his articles in *The Times*, saved the Directors of the Bank of England from some serious errors," wrote an observer.[1]

The printer of *The Times* during Barnes's period was John Joseph Lawson. He was responsible not only for the technical staff and equipment, but for the contents of the paper. The actions for libel cited the printer as the party responsible for printing and publishing a number of famous libel cases. It is still the law that all concerned in publishing a libel—proprietor, editor, printer and publisher—are equally responsible. They may be sued, separately or together, whether the author be sued or not. Lawson attended at the Bar of the House of Lords in the case in which Lord Limerick complained of being called " a thing with human pretensions,"[2] and parried questioners who demanded the name of the author of the article. Lawson's reply was that he considered himself to be holding a confidential position in *The Times* newspaper office, and that he could not answer the questions without breach of trust to his employers and loss of character to himself. To a noble Lord who " then asked whether a certain gentleman, whose name he mentioned, was not the editor of *The Times* newspaper," Lawson returned a similar answer.

The most famous case in which Lawson was involved cost *The Times* much in time and money. In May, 1840, O'Reilly, one of the correspondents of the paper in Paris, discreetly journeyed to

---

[1] James Grant, *The Great Metropolis*, London, 1837, II, 24.
[2] Lord Limerick had spoken against a tax imposed on land for the benefit of a fund to alleviate the poor of Ireland. *Cf.* p. 360.

JOHN JOSEPH LAWSON
From a mezzotint by David Lucas after a
painting by James Sant

Brussels and forwarded thence a despatch describing in detail the operations of a group of financiers directed by one Alan Bogle, of the firm of Bogle, Kerridge and Co., Bankers, of Florence. Upwards of ten thousand pounds of English money was involved in what *The Times* described as an " Extraordinary and extensive forgery and swindling conspiracy on the Continent." The system of letters of credit had recently been introduced ; a gang had been organized to exploit it by forging the forms of Messrs. Glyn, Halifax and Mills, of London. *The Times* had charged Bogle by name with the responsibility and he decided to sue it. Within a few weeks Lawson was informed that Bogle considered the libel " so utterly destructive of all reputation, that before admitting it to a place in your journal you were bound to satisfy yourself that it did not implicate a perfectly innocent individual." In reply, Alexander Dobie, the solicitor to *The Times*, undertook to appear in the contemplated action, but asked for a little delay.

At the end of June, Bogle was informed that instead of making an apology for the despatch of May 18, 1840, *The Times* had determined to allow the action to proceed, and on August 22 Dobie went to the Continent, visiting bankers who had been robbed at Turin, Genoa, Coblenz, Brussels, Antwerp, and other towns. With the assistance of a letter from Lord Palmerston instructing Lord Granville to render " such countenance and protection " as might be useful to him in procuring evidence for the defence, Dobie succeeded in accumulating materials for a complete justification of the correspondent's allegations. He returned from the Continent in December, 1840. The case was tried on August 16, 1841, and the plaintiff was awarded one farthing damages. Thus the whole cost of the exposure fell upon *The Times*.

The case was of such keen interest to the City that on October 1, 1841, a number of eminent London bankers, headed by representatives of the houses of Rothschild, Barings, Barclays and the firm more immediately benefited by the exposure, Glyns, met for the purpose of presenting to *The Times* a testimony of their gratitude. The sum of £2,700 subscribed was declined by *The Times*, and at a meeting in February, 1842, it was resolved that the money be applied to the foundation of scholarships at Christ's Hospital and the City of London School to be known as " *The Times* Scholarships." A portion was set aside for the provision of memorial tablets to be erected at Lloyd's and in Printing House Square respectively. The circumstances of the unveiling of these tablets are described in the course of a letter from Alsager to John Walter written on the 20th of August, 1846 :

It may not be superfluous to remind you that today at 2 o'clock the Lord Mayor in his private carriage attended by Mr Masterman and some members of *The Times* Testimonial Committee will proceed to Lloyd's to uncover " The Tablet " when the inscription will be read aloud in the presence of the Members of Lloyds & any other persons who may congregate on the occasion, the number of whom is not likely to be great as care has been taken not to spread it abroad which would infallibly collect an inconvenient crowd. When this ceremony at which I intend to be present is over the Lord Mayor will repair to *The Times* Office & do the same thing there. It will be necessary to have some refreshment ready in the drawing room no matter how simple for the occasion but I would suggest as part some first rate Champagne as Johnson is so exceedingly attached to the liquor that I believe he avoids all others and for ought I know to the contrary may wash his face with it in the morning.

After the dinner the Committee are to give *us* on the 2nd September, there must be of course a feed on the part of *The Times* (we shall altogether lose *caste* in the city if there is not) & this I would suggest shd take place at the Albion. To have the return dinner at Bearwood as you have proposed would be very agreeable if practicable but the time it would require would put it quite out of the power of most of the party.

The Lord Mayor, accompanied by a party of distinguished citizens, after visiting and marvelling at the printing office of *The Times*, unveiled the tablet commemorating the " indefatigable industry, perseverance and ability shown by the proprietors of *The Times* Newspaper in the exposure of the most remarkable and extensively fraudulent conspiracy ever brought to light in the Mercantile world."

George Hicks, the son-in-law of Alsager, was treasurer of the paper from 1827. He was also charged with responsibility for the direction of the printing office. In 1831 a new treasurer was appointed in the place of Hicks, whose time was increasingly given to the printing business. A Berkshire neighbour of John Walter's, William Frederick Augustus Delane, had been for some years a contributor to the paper and later had entered Printing House Square as an assistant to Hicks. Delane, a barrister of Gray's Inn, was the author of *A Collection of Decisions in the Courts for Revising the Lists of Electors for the Counties . . . & Boroughs etc.* (1834), which went through several editions, and *The Present*

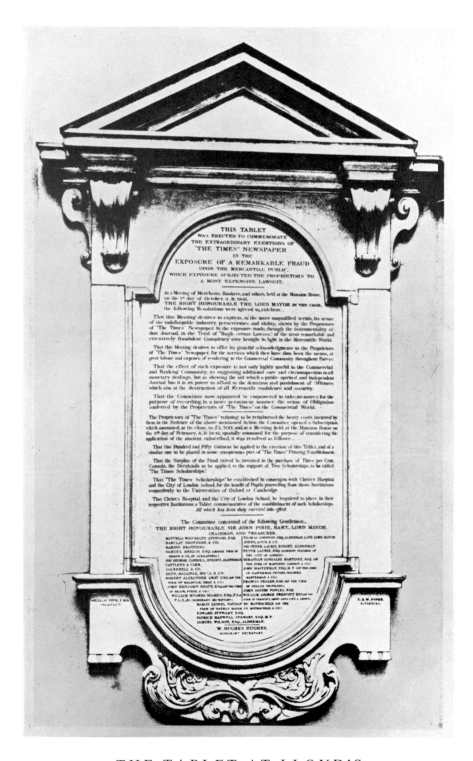

THE TABLET AT LLOYD'S
commemorating the exposure by *The Times* in 1840 of
"A Remarkable Fraud upon the Mercantile Public,"
erected by public subscription

General Laws for Regulating Highways in England (1835). His advice and experience were of great value for John Walter's Parliamentary business and for his interests in Printing House Square. He was responsible to John Walter for the financial management of *The Times* and the other departments in Printing House Square. He was not a proprietor of *The Times*, although, from 1835, he enjoyed a share in the printing business.

Thus Barnes was solely responsible for what was published in *The Times*, while Alsager and Delane between them were responsible for the administration and finance of Printing House Square. All became financially interested in the printing business, Alsager and Barnes also in *The Times* proprietorship.[1] In addition to the printing and production and distribution of *The Times* the management was responsible for the stimulation of the advertisement revenue and for the details of the news service.

During the 1830's the newspapers cooperated only in the system of police court reports. There was no press agency of the modern sort. Newspapers extracted matter from each other, duly acknowledging the source. The examination of the country papers was an important duty ; the paragraphs in *The Times* were considered to be specially well selected. It was necessary to scrutinize the paragraphs with the greatest care, but contradiction was not rare. It was thought sufficient if *The Times* could prove that the offending paragraph was copied from another journal. For the rest, each newspaper had its own Correspondents in the Houses of Parliament and in the principal European countries. *The Times* possessed independent writers at Paris, Madrid, Lisbon, Brussels, Hamburg, The Hague, and Constantinople. It maintained also a Correspondent at New York. Each newspaper also prepared its own reports of Parliamentary speeches, as *The Times* still does. Each paid for its own foreign expresses, each maintained a standing corps of reporters at the principal foreign cities and ports. *The Times* prided itself upon its network of arrangements all over Britain. It was one of the outstanding claims of Printing House Square that it was in ubiquitous touch with the town, the country, and the world.

In the organization of foreign correspondence *The Times* was ably served by James Murray, who joined the Parliamentary staff of *The Times* before 1815. In 1817 he was sent as Special Correspondent to the Congress of Aix-la-Chapelle, where he

[1] See Chapter XI for the distribution of interests in the printing business and in the paper respectively.

brought *The Times* into prominence by obtaining a copy of the secret *mémoire* of Alexander Stourdza, head of the Russian delegation. In 1823 Murray was sent on a special mission to Naples. Three years later he went abroad for *The Times* as Special Correspondent with the British Army in Portugal. This was his last Continental appointment. From 1827 James Murray filled the post of Foreign Director of *The Times*, writing many leading articles. Barnes was willing to leave the paper to him during his summer absence. Murray was a distinguished, but anonymous, contributor to the *British and Foreign Review*, the articles in which were known to be written by specialists in very close touch with foreign Chancelleries. He died in 1835, while in active service.[1]

The best known leader-writer of Barnes's period was Edward Sterling. Secret as his activities were, they were suspected by fellow-members of Brooks's Club, and he was widely regarded as the " great gun " from whom all the " thunder " proceeded. *Tait's Magazine* of January, 1835, stated categorically that the support given by *The Times* to the Duke of Wellington was " entirely attributable " to Sterling.

Roebuck's campaign against the newspaper tax led him to attack Sterling by name.[2] " I am not content with speaking of the mysterious *Times*, I wish to be more particular, I shall speak of Mr. Barnes and Mr. Stirling (*sic*), editors of that journal. I have often read the pages of *The Times*, and great has been the abuse and foul language employed." There followed the usual Radical argument against anonymity. " Yet I have never found attached to any articles the name of either of these worthy personages. How comes this to have happened ? " He tells a story that he had some time ago been in the habit of meeting Edward Sterling in society, and was not a little amused by the charlatan game he played to hide his editorship of *The Times*. " If anyone had assumed the fact, he would have taken it as an affront. Often has it been whispered in my hearing ' That is the Editor of *The Times*, but hush !—he will hear us.' ' Well, and what then ? ' ' What then ?—he will abuse us, to be sure ' ; and the man of the types was allowed to pass unnoticed because people feared him." There is little doubt that Roebuck's view of Sterling's omnipotence was then shared by political agents, though it

[1] Murray's widow brought two actions against John Walter II, in 1838 and 1842 respectively. *Cf.* Chapter XI.
[2] Roebuck, *The Stamped Press of London and its Morality*, 1835.

was also " understood " that the people of *The Times* were good at keeping their own secrets. So Roebuck qualifies his estimate : " The friends of Mr. Stirling (*sic*) are in the habit of saying that the ' blackguard ' parts of *The Times* (such is the phrase they use) are not his." This disclaimer has some confirmation from Harriet Martineau. Though she was not an impeccable authority by any means, she may be accepted as giving the contemporary view in a passage of her *History* :

Mr. Sterling, the Thunderer of *The Times* and at that period editor-in-chief, visited me, alleging that he himself had never written a disrespectful word of me. My reply was that he was responsible, as editor, and that I used the only method possible to a woman under a course of insult like that, of declining his acquaintance. Not long afterwards . . . he declared that it cut him to the heart that I should impute to him the ribaldry and coarse insults of scoundrels and ruffians who treated me as I had been treated in *The Times*. I dare say what he told of his own feelings was true enough ; but it will never do for responsible editors like Sterling and Lockhart to shirk their natural retribution.[1]

Roebuck, similarly, contends that disavowal of the " blackguard " parts will not do as an excuse and that by this very defence Sterling is " allowed to belong to a disgraced and disgraceful company."

Roebuck's estimate of Edward Sterling is not exactly that given circulation through the pages of Thomas Carlyle's *Life of John Sterling*. " The emphatic, big-voiced, always influential and often unreasonable *Times* newspaper," says Carlyle, " was the express emblem of Edward Sterling ; he, more than any other man or character, was the *Times* newspaper, and thundered through it to the shaking of the spheres." But Carlyle's notion of the relative importance of personalities in Printing House Square had been destroyed years before he wrote—even before Roebuck wrote his pamphlet on the London Press. Writing to the editor of *Tait's Magazine*, Sterling himself said :

Knightsbridge, Feb. 14, 1835.

Sir,—My attention has been drawn, within these few days, to an article in the Supplement to *Tait's Magazine*, for 1834, where my name is obtruded upon the public, for no purpose, as it would appear, but to make me the subject of a series of gross misrepresentations.

[1] *History of England during the Thirty Years Peace*, 1849.

It is utterly untrue that I have ever exercised or possessed the influence which you ascribe to me, over the *Times* newspaper—and which, if it existed, would be no less discreditable to the gentlemen who direct that powerful Journal, than invidious as regards myself.

It is equally untrue, that I have ever taken, on certain great public questions, the part which you unscrupulously assert that I have done ; nor is there the shadow of foundation for such a statement. The whole article, so far as concerns the manner in which you exhibit my political opinions and conduct, is, from first to last, a tissue of mere fabrications.

While, therefore, you profess " to tear off masks," I would recommend you to begin by unmasking the impostor who, in this case, has abused your confidence, and converted your Magazine into a vehicle of gratuitous and offensive falsehood. Acquitting you, personally, of all wish to mislead your readers, and satisfying myself with this protest against any further unauthorized and unwarrantable use of my name—

I am, sir, &c. &c.
EDWARD STERLING

It is probable that Roebuck had seen neither this nor the article occasioning it. It is certain that Roebuck did not foresee the action which Sterling would take upon his own statement that he [Sterling] " by a secret and irresponsible power . . . ruined your reputation . . . and sought to make your life a burthen," &c. Roebuck's paper was published on June 27, 1835. Forthwith the following message was sent to Roebuck :

St. James's Street, June 27, half-past 2 p.m.

Sir,—Within these two hours a pamphlet has been sent to me, bearing for its title *The Stamped Press of London and its Morality, &c.,* by J. A. Roebuck, Esq., M.P.

Probably, Sir, I make no mistake in identifying that name with yours.

The pamphlet sets out by an announcement that the author means to " try conclusions " with certain " gentry " whom he charges with endeavouring to " frighten " him, and then, as if he had the slightest reason for insinuating that I was one of " these gentry," he applies to me a long series and extensive variety of the foulest epithets in the English language—such as " cowardice," " baseness," " skulking," in order to escape the punishment due to my acts ; " dishonesty," " selling myself to the Tory party " ; " charlatanism in society, to hide my editorship of *The Times*," and a degree of depravity worse than that of an " assassin."

EDWARD STERLING
From an oil painting in the possession of
John Walter, Esq.

Now, Sir, if the folly of such expressions were not exceeded by their iniquity as directed against myself, I should not have deemed them worthy of the slightest notice.

There is only one word in the English dictionary by which they can be fitly characterized. Wishing, however, to write like a gentleman, I shall just say that, from whatever quarter they proceed, they are gross and shameful misrepresentations of every part of my principles and conduct.

I cannot violate confidences reposed in me by going into specific refutations of charges which no man living has the shadow of right, in truth or justice, to affix to my name or history.

I never have been technically or morally connected in any manner with the editorship of *The Times*, not possessing over the course or choice of its politics any power or influence whatsoever, nor, by consequence, being responsible for its acts.

This, however, I beg you to understand is beside the subject of my application to you as the avowed author of the pamphlet in question.

My first purpose is to contradict in distinct and unequivocal terms, generally and individually, one and all of the assertions which the author of that pamphlet has made with reference to myself.

Your absolute ignorance of every fact which concerns me does not seem to have prevented you from assuming such as are absolutely false in themselves, and of the most discreditable nature, if capable of being supported ; nor has it restrained you from coupling them with language the most personally offensive, and wantonly insulting.

I state this one unvarying absence of truth in each and every one of the accusations in the pamphlet, rather as a warning to your conscience, against the injustice of persisting in them, than as any indulgence of temper or resentment on my part. My friend, Colonel Campbell, who delivers you this letter, will apprise you of my claim to a retractation of those outrageous and scurrilous phrases which the author of the pamphlet has thought proper to apply to me.

I cannot permit myself to doubt that you will see the moral propriety of relieving your own mind from the consciousness of having given them circulation.

I have the honour to be,
Sir, your obedient servant,
EDWARD STERLING.

J. A. Roebuck, Esq., M.P., Gray's Inn.

Roebuck's withdrawal was immediate :

72, Pallmall, June 27. [1835]

Sir William Molesworth, on the part of his friend, Mr. Roebuck, remits to Colonel Campbell a letter from Mr. Roebuck, addressed to Mr. Sterling, the contents of which Sir William considers as perfectly satisfactory to the honour and gratifying to the good feelings of both parties.

Lieutenant-Colonel Campbell.

June 27. [1835]

Sir,—Your letter has been delivered to me by Colonel Campbell. In that letter you express yourself in the following manner :—

" I never have been technically or morally connected in any manner with the editorship of *The Times*, not possessing over the course or choice of its politics any power or influence whatsoever, nor, by consequence, being responsible for its acts. My first purpose is to contradict, in distinct and unequivocal terms, generally and individually, one and all of the assertions which the author of that pamphlet has made with reference to myself."

In reply thereto I am ready to state my belief that I have written the passages bearing upon you personally under erroneous impressions of your character and conduct. I therefore request you to consider the language which you complain of as disavowed by me and withdrawn, and I regret the misapprehension, and the words which I used in consequence thereof, and that I should have thus hurt your feelings.

I remain, Sir, your obedient servant,

J. A. ROEBUCK.

This correspondence was sent to *The Times* by Colonel Campbell and printed on June 29, 1835.

It has been pointed out that Barnes's relations with Edward Sterling were official rather than cordial. There was a dispute in 1838 referred to by Barnes as a " breeze."[1] Sterling resigned. He resigned again two years later. Sterling's relations, however, with John Walter were not only friendly but affectionate. His services as a writer were, without question, of the greatest value, second only to those of Barnes.

---

[1] Sterling told Walter that he had resigned rather than " tolerate, especially from a man for whom I entertain but moderate esteem, such unprovoked impertinence." The misunderstanding was explained and Barnes wrote to Walter (December 20, 1838) that " if he can be extremely violent, he has the generosity to redeem his error."

THOMAS NOON TALFOURD
After an oil painting by H. W. Pickersgill in the
National Portrait Gallery

Thomas Talfourd, an old friend of Crabb Robinson, author of the important though somewhat floridly written tribute to Lamb which contains valuable reminiscences of Barnes, joined *The Times* in 1813. He had already made some connexions with the Press as Dramatic Editor of the *New Monthly Magazine* and as a contributor to the *Retrospective Review*, but was known earlier to Barnes as a great admirer of Wordsworth, and particularly of Lamb, to whom he acted as executor. According to Crabb Robinson, Talfourd came to him in 1813 asking " that I would procure for him employment as a reporter for *The Times*, that he might be enabled to marry. This I did, and no-one could fill the office more honourably, as was acknowledged by his associates on the Oxford Circuit." Talfourd served also with the Parliamentary Staff. He retained his connexion with *The Times* for at least ten years, at the end of which period he was, as a letter of Charles Lamb reveals, engaged in writing the theatrical notices. Talfourd came before the public in 1835 in the two disparate capacities of member of Parliament for Reading and the author of a drama, *Ion*, produced at the Covent Garden Theatre, the principal character being performed by Macready. *The Times* was generous in its notice of the play and of Macready's performance. It was, in fact, one of the few occasions upon which the paper was pleased with the actor, and the actor with the paper. Macready habitually considered the paper unfair.[1] He had, however, confidence in Talfourd, and acted in his second tragedy, *The Athenian Captive*, in 1837, and again in 1840 in his *Glencoe*. Talfourd's liberality to men of letters and artists in distress, particularly to Leigh Hunt and Benjamin Robert Haydon, is well known. He had also a true understanding of Barnes, to whom he gave the longest and most appreciative of the few contemporary references.

The reporter Thomas Thornton (1786-1866) also came to *The Times* in 1824, on the recommendation of Crabb Robinson, whose niece was Thornton's wife. Succeeding Talfourd, he went straight to Parliamentary work. It was a high compliment to Thornton's powers as a reporter, for he had had no previous journalistic experience, his life having been spent in the East India Office

---

[1] " *The Times* was, as usual, insidious and malignant under a seemingly candid and liberal admission. I am not mistaken in that paper—it is my *enemy*." Macready's relations with *The Times* were indeed " tragic," but he declined to answer its criticisms. " How can I wrestle with a scavenger ? Filth is the commodity in which the men like these—Messrs. Westmacott, Nugent, Gregory, Barnes, Bacon, Thompson, Sterling, Kean, etc.—deal. What has a gentleman, a man of honour, to do with such vermin ? " Here is exasperation indeed which could bracket together Westmacott, the blackmailing editor of the *Age*, with Barnes and Sterling.

specializing upon Eastern affairs. He was the author of several books upon Oriental commerce and trade with India, a history of the Punjab, and a history of China. His three-volume edition of Thomas Otway, in 1814, won the blessing of Sir Walter Scott. In the year following his introduction to *The Times* he rejoiced Crabb Robinson with the sight of a note from Barnes offering him further work during the Session. This was a great boon to a Parliamentary reporter. He was to report in Common Pleas and Chancery at four guineas a week, and the Ecclesiastical Courts were added in the next year. His work on *The Times* continued for a quarter of a century, and his powers of application earned him a high position in the office. Thomas Robinson was able to write to his brother Crabb Robinson that

Tom seems to be doing very well indeed and to be in high favour with Walter and next to Barnes is frequently consulted by him—Walter is now *High Sheriff* of Berkshire and takes a great lead among the *Squires* who in these times are greatly put to the non plus and are making sad blunders throughout the Countryside frequently interfering in a mischievous way betwixt master and servants—and have in many cases too much encouraged the dissatisfaction among the Labourers—they have gone the length of advising by public resolutions the disuse of Threshing Machines—a most barbarous policy for which they have received a rebuke from the *Home Secretary*. I have rather digressed from what I was about to tell you that T.T. and Barnes were sent for by Walter to his country house previous to a meeting with the Magistrates in the District.

Thornton claims in his Reminiscences that for several years after 1826 many of the reviews of books published in *The Times* were written by him, besides some leading articles. Occasionally Thornton acted for the Editor :

With the present Emperor of the French, Napoleon III, I had a full quarter of an hour's conversation at *The Times* office, when he was only " Prince Napoleon." He was ushered into the room where I was standing, and coming up to me in a manner at once dignified and courteous, commenced conversation on matters connected with the paper. He spoke English fluently, but with a decidedly French pronunciation. His remarks did not give me a very high opinion of his capacity, which is a proof how easily we may fall into error by forming a too hasty judgment of men. When he was gone the printer (Mr. Lawson) told me that, on his quitting the room, he remarked to him, pointing to it, " Ah, there is great talent there." No doubt he thought it was the room where the able leading articles in the paper were written.[1]

Thornton does not say but implies that Barnes and Sterling wrote their leaders at home, and not in the office.

One of the best of *The Times* reporting staff was John William Tyas, described by Crabb Robinson as a scholar and a gentleman, who came to *The Times* in 1817. He reported the Peterloo incidents for *The Times*, and was interrupted in his duty by being made prisoner.[2] Tyas was intimate with the Chief Proprietor and an occasional visitor to Bear Wood.

Such men took a personal pride in their responsible task. After the close of the Napoleonic wars *The Times* had been the first journal to be quoted by statesmen ; the authenticity of its Parliamentary reports was conceded, and, after the Reform Bill, proverbial. *The Times* was jealous of their accuracy. Frequent leading articles during the course of the 'thirties point out to readers the responsibility of the task and the precautions taken by *The Times*. On July 5, 1832, the Bishop of Exeter, Phillpotts, quoted in the House of Lords a passage in a speech of his from the *Mirror of Parliament*. This was a different version from that in *The Times*. Accordingly the paper found it advisable to point out that

No-one who knows anything about the *Mirror of Parliament* can understand it to be any such thing [as an authentic record of the proceedings of Parliament]. It is an authentic record of the speeches which noble lords or hon. members, after a day's reflection, think they *ought* to have made ; but it is not an authentic record of the speeches which they actually *did* make. The version of a member's speech, given by the reporters for the *Mirror of Parliament* (who have been frequently the reporters for the morning papers and some of them reporters for *The Times*), is sent to the member who made the speech, in order that he may *correct* it—as the operation is delicately termed. If this version contain passages which the noble or honourable orator repents him of, or which may be disagreeable to his constituents, he strikes them out, of course ; and if (which after having heard the speeches of others, is not improbable) any good things occur to him, as things which he might have said with advantage, it is not to be expected that he will resist this temptation of inserting them, though he never thought of uttering them

---

1 Thornton's Diary (unpublished).
2 *Cf.* p. 235.

at the time. Now, it can hardly be necessary to suggest, that no reliance is to be placed upon reports of the proceedings in Parliament which are conducted upon such a system as this.

The Times was emphatic that suspicion would attach to the appointment of reporters under the control of the House. When a proposal was made, two years later, for official support of the *Mirror*, Barnes had another word to say.[1] Horne Tooke had recommended Parliament to make a grant on behalf of the *Mirror of Parliament*. This publication, after running through successive hands, was then owned by Mr. Gye, proprietor of Vauxhall Gardens. *The Times* wrote :

Now, if the choice were left to us, we would, with ten times as much goodwill, vote money to help Mr. Gye out with his rope-dancers, fireworks and illuminated promenades, as pay him out of the taxes for continuing a work so bad that it perishes under free competition—so bad as to poison its readers with every secondhand flippancy of fifth-rate speakers,—a work so swollen up with all the suspirations of the most voluble blockheads in this multitude of 658 rhetoricians, that no man ever dares to meditate a syllable of its contents, beyond the boundary of his own speech, for fear of getting a windy colic.

When its reports were criticized by the *Morning Chronicle*, *The Times* on one occasion allowed the reporter himself to answer. On March 10, 1835, W. C. H. (in all probability the son of Hazlitt)[2] wrote to the *Chronicle* : " Pray do expose the infamous conduct of the old *Times* in garbling the report of Friday night's Parliamentary proceedings." Immediately Charles Ross, one of the Parliamentary reporters of *The Times*, replied :

I reported the speech and as the charge contained in your correspondent's letter imputes to me a breach of trust towards the establishment with which I am connected, and is therefore, unless disproved, calculated to do me serious injury with the proprietors of *The Times*, as well as to expose me to serious punishment by the House of Commons I have to request that you will be good enough to furnish me with the writer's name in order that I may adopt legal proceedings against him. I will only add that in the event of your withholding this information I must commence an action against the *Morning Chronicle*.

[1] The Editor of the *Mirror* replied to *The Times* in the *Morning Chronicle*, May 24, 1834.
[2] Hazlitt died September 18, 1830. Mrs. Leigh Hunt shortly afterwards wrote to Barnes asking an appointment on *The Times* for his son. Barnes replied : " We have no vacancy for giving Hazlitt." MSS. Addl. 38523, 103.

When the Editor, John Black, denied that any injury had been done and refused the writer's name, Ross instructed an attorney, but owing to technical difficulties an action could not be brought. Hence Ross had to rest content with a letter in *The Times* (March 13, 1835), in which he said that the *Chronicle's* accusation " would have gone nigh to cancel the engagement of a young reporter, who had it not in his power, as in my case, to appeal to the character acquired during many years' attendance in the gallery."

On another occasion Charles Dodd, also a Parliamentary reporter of *The Times*, considered himself aspersed by remarks in the *Globe*. On this occasion Alexander Dobie, *The Times* solicitor, secured an apology.

In 1834, in order that *The Times* should maintain the paramount position as a newsgetter that John Walter had secured for it, Alsager and William Delane arranged a new organization for home news. *The Times* had long used the system of simple " expresses." The essential of the new scheme, the extraordinary express, was the provision of special horse carriages at definite stages. The issue of *The Times* for Wednesday, September 17, 1834, contained the following :

EXPRESS FROM EDINBURGH

THE TIMES OFFICE, 6 o'clock a.m.

GRAND DINNER TO EARL GREY.

The dinner had been held at Edinburgh on the evening of the previous Monday, and *The Times* of Wednesday printed the whole of the speeches and toasts. It was regarded as a miraculous feat of reporting and rapid news-collection. The paper itself wrote in a descriptive paragraph :

We have received, by extraordinary express, a full report of the proceedings at the dinner given to Earl Grey, at Edinburgh on Monday. The festivities of the evening appear to have encroached upon the morning of Tuesday ; and the time at which our express reached us, and the length to which the report extends, not only preclude the possibility of all comment upon its contents, but compel us to postpone the publication of many articles of intelligence, which were intended for *The Times* of to-day.

This " exclusive " was also a feat of composition and printing. Although the composition of the report only began at 6.30 a.m., the publication of this issue of *The Times* began at 10.30 and finished at the very late hour of 12.30 noon. In other words, the arrival of the report just before 6 o'clock delayed the complete edition by more than four hours. Publication normally began at 6. The extraordinary express was late. It had been expected to drive in between 2 and 3, and the anxiety of the editorial and managerial staff whether their delaying of the paper might yet prove in vain, owing to an accident on the road, may be imagined. The sensation next day was great; the cost to *The Times* £200. Competitive papers, particularly the *Morning Chronicle*, endeavoured to diminish the credit of the scoop by giving out that the report of the Edinburgh dinner only appeared in the second edition. To this falsehood *The Times* on Friday answered that the report in question appeared in the whole impression of that day's paper. It added that for any newspaper to display its own report of the dinner, as the *Chronicle* had, in its issue of Thursday morning under the heading " By Express," was ridiculous, since the ordinary mails would have brought it in time for such ordinary and normal publication. " Indeed, an express of that sort, must have been run by cart-horses or donkies, and ridden by the heaviest Dutchmen that were ever fattened." The pride of *The Times* may be excused, for success had been won in the face of accidents and handicaps. There had been fifteen hours of night-time in the thirty hours which the whole enterprise involved; in addition, there was the complication that the St. Leger was being run for on the Tuesday, and that there was very great difficulty in procuring post-horses anywhere in the vicinity of Doncaster.

In the following month, on the occasion of Lord Durham's festival dinner at Glasgow, the *Chronicle* also ran an extraordinary express. The rivalry on this occasion was intense. The *Morning Chronicle's* effort was made in association with Palmerston's evening paper, the *Globe*.[1] The weather was very bad. It is described in a letter from *The Times* reporter which his editor printed :

Our lamps were blown out in a storm we encountered on the moors beyond Hamilton, and, proceeding in the dark to the third stage, we ran foul of a post-chaise standing stock-still in the middle of the road, and broke our splinter-bar to pieces. This post-chaise belonged to the rival reporters. We got, however, into the post-house before them, and whilst we were changing they came up, but the man had no horses

[1] In the following year Palmerston made arrangements with Easthope to use the *Morning Chronicle*, upon which Lord John Russell acquired influence over the *Globe*.

beside those we had engaged. They asked us for two of ours—to join in our express, and made various other proposals, all of which we declined, though much abused for our ill nature. We left them unable to get horses and going to supper which they had ordered. We wished them good appetite, and have seen nothing more of them. We got on very badly during the night, owing to the storm and dark. It blew a hurricane on the moors. We could not get the Scots to work. We have done well since we entered England. . . . Our rivals must be two hours at least behind us.

It has to be borne in mind that the reporters did their best to write out their copy for the printer while on the journey. " It is certainly not very agreeable," *The Times* assured a correspondent, " but it is by no means impossible to write in a post-chaise whirled along at the rate of more than 13 miles an hour."

The date of the Durham dinner was Wednesday, October 29, 1834 ; *The Times* express left Glasgow at midnight on Wednesday and arrived in Printing House Square at 7.30 on Friday morning. Publication began at 11 and finished at 1.30 p.m.

The speech of Lord John Russell at Exeter on Friday, May 1, 1835, was the occasion of a race between Mr. Charles Dickens, reporter of the *Chronicle*, and Mr. Denison, reporter of *The Times*. Dickens described the race in a letter to Beard (also of the *Chronicle*), written from Wincanton on Saturday morning :

I arrived here (57 miles from Exeter) at 8 yesterday evening having finished my whack at the previous stage. I arranged with Neilson, whom I occasionally saw in the course of my journey, that I would stop when he did ; and finding him housed here, I ordered dinner, beds and breakfast for two. I am happy to say that our friend Unwin, when on duty, is the most zealous, active and indefatigable little fellow I ever saw. I have now, not the slightest doubt (God willing) of the success of our Express. On our first stages we had very poor horses. At the continuation of the second, *The Times* and I changed horses together ; they had the start two or three minutes, I bribed the post-boys tremendously and we came in literally neck and neck—the most beautiful sight I ever saw.

The next stage, your humble caught them before they had changed ; and the next Denison preceded Unwin about two minutes leaving Neilson here to return to Exeter to-morrow evening, and I to get up by the Telegraph at 11. The roads were *extremely heavy*, and as they had 4, I ordered the same at every stage and empowered Unwin to do the same until he wilt his horses, indorsing on the parcel that the rain rendered it a matter of *absolute necessity*. . . .

On the Continent *The Times* made similar efforts to secure new " exclusives " by the organization of specially rapid services. The rivalry of the *Morning Chronicle* extended to foreign correspondence in the autumn of 1834. *The Times* on September 1, 1834, and the *Morning Chronicle* on September 2, devote much space to claims and counterclaims of priority. The matter at issue was the speech of the Spanish Queen at the opening of the Cortes in July. The *Chronicle* alleged that their correspondent had agreed to take charge of *The Times* dispatch on the understanding that it should not be delivered to Printing House Square until six hours after the *Chronicle* had received it. *The Times* observed silence until it could communicate with its own Correspondent, Daniel Turnbull, an old servant of the paper, formerly Correspondent at The Hague, and at this time posted at Madrid. He was able to prove that the Royal speech was delivered between 12 and 1, and that before 2 o'clock a copy had been dispatched to *The Times*, by the courier not of the *Morning Chronicle* but of the Spanish Government. To the *Chronicle* courier had been handed letters for delivery, but not the report of the speech. The *Chronicle's* effort for priority would, so the paper said, have succeeded but for the fact that " part of the machinery gave way."

Nor were less striking Continental reports forgotten. *The Times* was able to write on November 9, 1840, as follows :

Our Courier with the King's Speech at the opening of the Chambers left Paris on Thursday afternoon, a little after 3 o'clock, and our despatches were delivered at *The Times* office at 7 minutes before 1 p.m. on the following day. The whole journey from Paris to London was thus performed in a few minutes less than 22 hours. The weather was far from favourable for such an undertaking ; a gale of wind . . . rendered it necessary that the Britannia steamer, which was engaged to carry our despatches, should go out of Boulogne harbour on Thursday night, and lie off in the roadstead till she was wanted on Friday morning. On the arrival of the courier at Boulogne the sea ran so high that it was not an easy task to convey our despatches on board the Britannia, but when that was accomplished Captain Bushill soon placed his vessel in a position to receive all the aid that could be derived from both wind and steam.

The Times carried its speeding-up of dispatches still farther abroad. In the summer of 1838 the paper had made a reliable arrangement by which a celebrated express forwarder expedited the arrival of the Indian mail by rushing it through Egypt to

Marseilles, and thence through France to Calais and Dover. *The Times* wrote :

There was an arrival yesterday by the Egyptian route of steam communication with India, and being now the third of the kind, at regular intervals of a month each, . . . the best proof is afforded that the system so far is working well. . . . It may be collected from some of the letters by this arrival, that a despicable sort of intrigue is carrying on for the removal of Mr. Waghorn from his station at Cairo, where he has taken up his residence as agent and superintendent of the steam communications with India. Now, if ever any man was entitled to derive a permanent reward and occupation from the completion of a great measure in which he has personally borne an active part, it is Mr. Waghorn.[1] (July 10, 1838.)

The service was greatly appreciated by readers. When the overland route became the established means of communication *The Times* exerted itself to rush its dispatches by extraordinary express from the French port. The issue of November 11, 1840, contained eight columns expressed from Marseilles. " We have received by extraordinary express," the paper said, " in anticipation of the overland mail, advices from Bombay of the 1st of October, from Singapore of the 13th of August, and from China of the 3rd of July. The lateness of the hour at which our express arrived, unfortunately prevents our inserting more than a portion of the very important intelligence we have received." This " exclusive " express is timed in the date-line as " The Times Office, 3 o'clock." A leading article on the subject appears in the following day's paper, the first paragraph of which reads :

The intelligence given by this paper yesterday, in anticipation of the overland mail from the East, covers a vast space of earth and ocean, and creates anxiety for an immense portion of the national interests of Great Britain. (November 12, 1840.)

In the late 'thirties the express system was applied to the service of readers in another important respect. In 1832 there seems to have been some delay in the delivery of *The Times* to great provincial cities, where the arrival of the paper was impatiently awaited. The issue for February 14 contained the following notice of a new attempt to secure rapid service to the country :

By a special arrangement entered into with the proprietors of *The Times* newspaper, William Lewer, of number 4, Wellington-street,

---

[1] Lieut. Waghorn in 1845 inaugurated a new route *via* Trieste which enabled *The Times* to circumvent the jealousy of the French Government and its delaying of the paper's dispatches through Marseilles.

Strand, wholesale news-vendor, is enabled punctually to forward that paper into the country by morning coaches, so as to ensure its delivery in Birmingham, Manchester and Liverpool etc., quite as early as any contemporary morning journal. In case of political excitement, *The Times* will be forwarded by express from the above establishment, where orders are received for all the London daily and weekly newspapers.

Seven years later the delivery was still speedier. Readers were provided with copies of the paper in advance of other journals. In 1839 *The Times* was able to congratulate one Gaskell upon being the first to bring *The Times* to Liverpool as early as 4 o'clock in the afternoon. Mr. Gaskell was presented by " a numerous and highly respectable party with a magnificent gold snuff-box, bearing a suitable inscription, as an acknowledgment of his valuable services in having supplied *The Times* at an early hour of the afternoon, instead of a late one at night." (December 30, 1839.)

On December 10, 1839, news was brought to *The Times* by one of the most rapid of the extraordinary expresses on record. The Judge's charge in certain high treason trials left Monmouth on that day at 4 o'clock p.m., and arrived in London the same night or early next morning ; the report appeared in *The Times* on December 11. Copies of the paper were in Mr. Gaskell's office, Lord Street, Liverpool, by 3.45 in the afternoon of the same day. No other morning paper contained the charge on that day.

Naturally the circulation of *The Times* in London itself was a simpler matter. Nevertheless, the compositors and pressmen were under continuous pressure to accomplish the printing in time to admit of publication by 6 o'clock in the morning. Punctuality was important in the interests of the newsmen, whose clients were apt to cancel orders if *The Times* arrived later than 8 o'clock. If anything delayed the arrival of an important dispatch, and compositors and pressmen were unable to produce the edition at the usual time, the newsmen were placed in the position of having either to delay their entire distribution, including that of the other journals, or to distribute the other journals and to make a second round for a separate delivery of *The Times*. There was. a further consideration ; even when publication was punctual, there was always the risk that competing papers might persuade newsmen to offer a substitute on the fictitious ground that *The Times* was not yet published. For all these reasons the paper was timed as well as dated. On December 6, 1803, the following notice was printed immediately over the first leader :

LONDON
TUESDAY, DECEMBER 6.

Having received complaints from various quarters of the late delivery of *The Times* ; in order to enable our readers to judge where the fault lies, we shall regularly insert the hour of publication.

The Times was published this morning at a ¼ past 9.

The device, rendered familiar as an ensign of *The Times* by its use over the first leader, and subsequently by its appearance in the work of political cartoonists, first appeared on January 7, 1804.[1]

The clock, it should be noted, is at 6.6 a.m., which was the average time of normal publication. The minutes were important ; the newsmen were always impatient. Uproarious complaints followed the most trifling delay. The wholesaler's part in newspaper distribution was beginning in the 1830's. There were one or two dealers through whom small newsmen, ordering less than a quire, secured their copies. In doing so they lost the odd copy given with the quire of twelve, and the wholesaler received the benefit. After the reduction of the tax in 1836 from 4d. (less 20 per cent.) to 1d. net, the price of the daily newspapers fell from 7d. to 5d. The newsmen were supplied with the 5d. newspaper at 4d., with thirteen as twelve. The first delivery to subscribers having been effected by 8 o'clock, the newsmen turned to a subsidiary but most important branch of their business. An efficient newsman would, between the completion of the delivery to subscribers and the late afternoon, when he had to procure the evening papers, make some seventy or eighty separate lendings of *The Times*. The rate of lending was at 1d. an hour. The read copy was then posted to a country subscriber, who contracted to pay the price of 3d. for the paper in its handled

---

[1] The block did not include the scythe, which was added in 1845.

condition. For handled copies posted any day after publication 2d. a copy was charged. The arrangement was useful to many. Few, even after the reduction to 5d., could afford to subscribe at first hand to a morning newspaper. A letter dated 1830 may be quoted for the period of the 7d. paper :

I hereby impower Matilda Hone to superintend daily the putting into the two penny post, *The Times* newspaper of the day before, directed *Mr. Lamb, Enfield*, which shall be held a full and sufficient direction ; the said directions to commence on Monday next.

And I do engage to pay to William Hone, Coffee and Hotel Man, the quarterly sum of £1, to be paid at the ordinary quarter days, or there-abouts, for the reversion of the said paper, commencing with the 24th inst., on the Feast of John the Baptist ; the intervening days to be held and considered as nothing.

C. LAMB.

Vivant Coffee, Coffee-potque.[1]

Literary criticism was not a conspicuous feature of *The Times* under Barnes. Until there were regular supplements there was little room for *belles lettres*. " We are not in the habit of noticing the novels which are issuing in an almost continued stream from the press—not, certainly, that we undervalue a species of literature adorned by Fielding and Smollett or Scott and Edgeworth, but because we have little time for amusing ourselves with any romance except the extravagant romance of political life."[2] These words were written in a review of Lady Blessington's *Two Friends*. There followed a critical appraisement of the book displeasing to the author, who knew Barnes (and Mrs. Barnes) as a guest at Gore House and expected a salesmanlike notice more gratifying to her pride and pocket. The criticism led to correspondence. Scarlett, Lord Abinger, replied to " My dear Lady Blessington " as follows :

As you place yourself in my hands touching your communication with Barnes, I shall play the part of a loyal, as well as a faithful ambassador, in using the best discretion to advance your object. I shall not, therefore, send your letter, not because I do not concur in the remarks it contains but because it has a tendency to whip up the old quarrel, by putting him in the position of recanting his criticism or of

---

[1] Lucas, *Correspondence of Charles Lamb*. Lamb wrote to Wordsworth, January 22, 1830 : " A newspaper is the single gleam of comfort I receive here, it comes from rich Cathay with tidings of mankind. Yet could I not attend to it read out by the most beloved voice."

[2] February 27, 1835.

vindicating it. Now I think the peace is a good peace, and promises to be lasting unless disturbed by a recurrence to former differences. It is better, therefore, for you to allow me to make your acknowledgments in general terms of civility. He knows already my sentiments on the fallacy of the former critique ; he must also know yours and the recurrence to it looks as if you made it of more importance than it becomes you to do. I will come and see you as soon as I can, at present I hardly dare go out of my beaten track for fear of exciting my eye, which will become more and more inflamed by the sight of *you*. Ever yours etc.

Macaulay, who suffered later much from Barnes's contempt for Whiggery, was once intimate with the Editor. He was once at breakfast with Samuel Rogers, Tom Moore, Lord John Russell, Tom Campbell and Tony Luttrell. " We were all lively," Macaulay told his sister,

and an odd incident took place after breakfast. While we were standing at the window and looking into the Green Park, somebody was talking about diners-out. " Ay," said Campbell, *Ye diners out from whom we guard our spoons.* Tom Moore asked where the line was. " Don't you know ? " said Campbell. " Not I," said Moore. " Surely," said Campbell, " it is your own." " I never saw it in my life," said Moore. " It is in one of your best things in *The Times*," said Campbell. Moore denied it.

Hereupon I put in my claim, and told them it was mine. Do you remember it ? It is in some lines called " The Political Georgics," which I sent to *The Times* about three years ago. They made me repeat the lines, and were vociferous in praise of them. Tom Moore then said, oddly enough, " There is another poem in *The Times* that I should like to know the author of : ' A Parson's Account of his Journey to the Cambridge Election.' " I laid claim to that also.

" That is curious," said Moore. " I begged Barnes to tell me who wrote it. He said that he had received it from Cambridge, and touched it up himself, and pretended that all the best strokes were his. I believed that he was lying, because I never knew him to make a good joke in his life. And now the murder is out."

They asked me whether I had put anything else in *The Times*. " Nothing," I said, " except the ' Sortes Virgilianae,' " which Lord John remembered well. I never mentioned the " Cambridge Journey " or " Georgics " to any but my own family ; and I was, therefore, as you may conceive, not a little flattered to hear, in one day, Moore praising one of them and Campbell the other.[1]

[1] Clayden, P. W. *Rogers and His Contemporaries* (London, 1889), II, p. 65.

Thomas Moore himself contributed to *The Times* during 1827 and 1828 scores of topical verses on the currency question, the Corn Laws, and Catholic Emancipation. Many of these are reprinted in *Odes upon Cash, Corn, Catholics, and other Matters selected from the columns of The Times Journal* (London, 1828). Barnes and Moore were intimate for some years after 1825. Later, when Moore had accepted a Civil List pension and his talents seemed to play a political purpose, *The Times* protested :

We have often expressed, and still express, admiration for Mr. Moore's talents, and we have no personal feeling towards him inconsistent with goodwill ; but, thus bullied into the controversy, we shall not shrink from giving our real opinion as to the impropriety of a public pensionary being a private or party satirist. As to the connexion with Mr. Moore alluded to in such indecorous terms by the writer in the *Globe*, we shall only say, that whatever honour we may have derived from it, we neither solicited its beginning nor importuned its continuance.[1]

Disraeli, who had shown his partiality for *The Times* in 1835 by issuing his challenge to O'Connell in its columns, later gave a temporary preference to another journal. " I have sent you the *Morning Post*," he wrote to Sarah Disraeli in August of the same year, " which is the only paper now read, and in whose columns some great unknown has suddenly arisen." The new writer's articles were the topic of the hour, and according to this account the sale of the *Post* rose by nearly one-third. These, Disraeli's latest efforts in morning journalism, were written as part of Lyndhurst's plan to stop the Radical " Movement." After the autumn of 1835, when Disraeli had published his *Vindication of the English Constitution*, he began, with Lyndhurst's introduction and counsel, to cultivate Barnes. It was agreed that, if they were satisfactory to the Editor's eye, a series of Letters to Statesmen, to be signed " Runnymede," should find place in *The Times*. The letters were to combine political actuality and wit, but Disraeli added a note of reckless animosity which brought him a warning, repeated as the series proceeded, from Barnes :

" I object to the personalities," he wrote to Disraeli on January 17, 1836. " The allusion to Lord Melbourne's Sultana is I suppose metaphysical, but I fear that instead of the old classical abstraction, the "Siren Desidia" you will be thought to refer to a very

[1] *The Times*, June 17, 1836.

438

substantial Siren whose fleshly attractions are supposed to be as agreeable to Lord M. as the last patent-easy-chair. The allusions to Lords
Russell Howick & Holland are also too personal, as well as that to
poor Thomson. That the strictures are just, only makes the sting more
intolerable. Pray modify, however slightly, these passages."[1]

" Runnymede " made an immediate sensation. " Barnes will
worship you," prophesied Lyndhurst to his disciple. " You have
a surprizing disdain for the law of libel," wrote Barnes. The Editor,
however appreciative, was not either slow to criticize or to warn.
On receipt of the manuscript of Letter VI addressed to Thomas
Spring Rice, Chancellor of the Exchequer, Barnes wrote :

Your letter stands over for one day, partly that it might not be
swamped by the deluge of Irish trash which it was necessary to admit,
partly to give you an opportunity of making one or two corrections.

If the first passage marked refers to Croker, is it not at least
injudicious to attack a man who is one of the ablest of the literary
Champions of your party & who may yet have to fight its battle in the
H. of Commons ?

You can easily modify the passage so as to retain the humourous
expression of that agreeable old raff Cumberland & yet omit the
allusion to the person to whom it was applied.

The other passages marked are not important, tho' I wish you could
find a better man for eulogistic reference than that supreme humbug
Coleridge, who babbled transcendental nonsense at which he laughed
in his sleeve while he was mystifying his dupes. I know the man well.
He wrote in early youth 2 or 3 beautiful poems : all afterwards was
" leather & prunello." . . .

Are you careful to preserve your " Incognito " ? Your name never
passes my lips, but I see the Sun mentions you as the author. You
understand perfectly the importance of secrecy in matters of this kind.
Our friend " Vetus " some years ago by disclosing his name found
himself compelled to stop. Mystery gives force by diminishing the
personality of the satire. It is no longer a quarrel between man & man.[2]

Another Letter was twice returned to the author for revision.
The original form brought Disraeli the following rejection from
Barnes :

It is quite impossible to insert your letter to Sir John Hobhouse. It
is so fiercely personal that he will have a right to demand the name of

[1] Hughenden Papers.
[2] Barnes to Disraeli, January 28, 1836. Mention of Croker was dropped, and the
reference to Coleridge revised thus : " Lord John, perhaps, will take down his dusty lyre,
& console us for having starved Coleridge by pouring forth a monody to his memory."

the writer, which tho' of course on individual ground you are ready enough to give would if known destroy all the effect & object originally proposed by yourself as well as by the Paper.

I have another reason for rejecting the letter. Hobhouse is a man with whom I have been on terms of friendly intercourse & I cannot be party to a furious assault on his personal character ; his political conduct you may do what you please with.

Whatever faults Hobhouse labours under, he is not mean nor cowardly ; but his understanding is weak & uncertain.

And Barnes was compelled to return the amended version :

I cannot conquer my objection to the last paragraph.

You are an anonymous writer : it is fit—it is necessary that you should preserve your incognito : & yet you put yourself in personal contrast with a man who has no means of retaliating by any *tu quoque*, as you & your actions must be totally unknown to him. This is unfair on the face of it & there is nothing for which the public has so quick an eye as unfairness in fight—whether physical or intellectual. I think you will not find it difficult to give the passage a different turn. You can assume the allegations agt Hobhouse to be true & then without reference to yourself ask if such a man has a right to complain of rough treatment.

The " Runnymede " series ended with a third and final Letter to Lord Melbourne published on May 15, 1836. " You can yet perform an act which will still command the gratitude of every lover of his country ; you can RESIGN," was its last paragraph. The best of the series, Barnes told Lyndhurst, was the Letter to Lord John Russell.

The identity of " Runnymede " was never authoritatively acknowledged. When appreciative readers besought Barnes to arrange for the re-issue of the Letters in book form, he told Disraeli that " I have no doubt they will bear republication " ; and, when Macrone published the book later in the year, the dedication to Sir Robert Peel was unsigned.[1] Anonymity was also preserved in respect to another contribution of the summer of 1836.[2]

On December 15, 1836, Disraeli attempted, with less success, a series of commentaries entitled " A New Voyage of Sindbad the Sailor, Recently Discovered," in which public personages were concealed in allegory. He wrote a notice of Fonblanque's

[1] Colburn was Disraeli's usual publisher for novels. The Letters of " Runnymede " were reprinted in 1892 and in 1900.

[2] Benjamin to Sarah Disraeli, August 20, 1836 : " I suppose you have recognized four bolts of veritable Olympian thunder in *The Times*. It is considered worthy of Jove & nobody can discover behind what cloud the god is shrouded."

" History " which appeared on March 17, 1837,[1] and a destructive review of Harriet Martineau's *Society in America* on May 17.[2] In the spring of 1837 Disraeli turned his hand to satirical verse. Over the signature " Skelton, junior," he contributed three long pieces during March (9, 13 and 20) which Barnes considered barely satisfactory. Disraeli's efforts at versifying drew from Barnes several letters of rejection, criticism, and one of severe reproof. From the first the Editor objected to his " depreciating all the ' poetry ' of our columns except your own," and on receiving the " Heroic Epistle to Lord Mel——e " the Editor replied with " I send it back at once that you may purge it of some of its personalities. . . . Rich is no more grovelling than any other party writer & is much cleverer than nine out of ten of them." The strong hints which the Editor had conveyed in not a few earlier letters having failed to qualify Disraeli's self-confidence, the Editor was moved to a tactful remonstrance :

I don't know exactly the difference of our ages, but I suppose there must be at least fifteen or sixteen years to be added to my account above your quantum : so that, as you will learn, (should you make inquiry among our common friends) I had the reputation at least of being tolerably well-versed in ancient literature & more than tolerably familiar with modern literature—especially English—at a time when you were probably still studying your primer. Judge then my surprize at receiving a letter from you in which with the didactic & patronizing air of a tutor to a child of ten years old you condescend to inform me who is the author of a well-known line & to give me a sort of elementary lesson on the meaning of the word Irony. I am perfectly convinced that you intend no offence nor am I apt to be offended, but really such a tone is inexpressibly ludicrous : you ought to take it for granted that there is no good author (with whom you or any other literary man may be acquainted) who is not at least as familiar to me as to yourself.

If you chuse to send the first portion of your verses back I will publish them leaving out the notes about that very insignificant Papist at the Chronicle & also the abuse of Rich.

[1] Fonblanque, editor of the *Examiner* and a leader-writer on the *Morning Chronicle*, had republished his articles under the high-sounding title " England under Three Reigns." Barnes's instructions to Disraeli were " Be as severe as you like with the man, but abstain from all personal attacks on the man in his private life & conduct." The review (" From a Correspondent ") concluded : " One of the most over-rated public writers of the day . . . we have thought it worthy of some trouble to expose the astounding disproportion between his pretensions and his powers."

[2] Barnes recommended Disraeli to observe that " Its vanity, its presumption, its ignorance (but this is the most venial part of its delinquency) deserve a smart chastisement : but I must beg (indeed your own good taste & feeling make the request unnecessary) that she may be treated personally with all the courtesy due to her sex. In the midst of her offensive conceit & flippant impertinencies there are sometimes some just & shrewd observations : and where she relates facts she may I dare say be depended upon. But in her case as in that of Mrs Trollope it is curious to find that at least three fourths of the facts supposed to be characteristic of American Society are quite as common in England."

441

Bentley *was* slashing & Theobald was a poor piddling word-catcher with a modicum of scraps of Elizabethan reading : but Fonblanque (who writes a wire-drawn article to illustrate a quotation from Joe Miller or a farce of Durfey) is no slasher : he is merely a scratcher : nor is Rich piddling : his style is free, copious & manly.

Now let this be our last letter of criticism (at least *I* shall write no more) but send as many public contributions as you like, subject of course to my revision.

Thackeray who was an acquaintance of Edward Sterling's began to write for *The Times*, on his friend's introduction in 1837. His first known contribution is a review of Carlyle's *French Revolution* on August 3 of that year. He contributed dramatic criticism. From Paris he also sent articles ; although discontented with the work and its reward, he recognized that

My game, as far as I can see it, is to stick to the *Times*. I have just come from seeing " Marion Delorme," the tragedy of Victor Hugo, and am so sickened and disgusted with the horrid piece that I have hardly heart to write. The last act ends with an execution, and you are kept a long hour listening to the agonies of parting lovers and grim speculations about head-chopping, dead bodies, coffins, and what not —I am as sick as if I had taken an emetic.

I have been writing all day, and finished and despatched an article for the *Times*. My next visit will be to the Spanish pictures, the next to Versailles, and on Monday next, please God, I will be home.

From 1839 to 1840 he wrote reviews of *The Widow Barnaby*, by Mrs. Trollope, Ranke's *History of the Popes*, and *Letters of Horace Walpole*. A bill of his addressed to *The Times* has been preserved :

13, Great Coram Street,
29th November, 1838.

My dear Sir :

I beg to send you my account with the *Times* for November & remain,

Your very faithful Serv.

W. M. THACKERAY.

The Times to W. M. Thackeray

Nov.	2	Annuals -	-	-	-	-	$2\frac{1}{4}$
„	8	Steam in the Pacific	-	-	-		$\frac{3}{4}$
„	12	Henry V. -	-	-	-	-	$3\frac{1}{4}$
„	16	Fraser -	-	-	-	-	$2\frac{1}{4}$
„	27	Krasinski -	-	-	-	-	$1\frac{1}{2}$

10.0
£21.0.0

On September 2, 1840, Fielding's Works were reviewed. In a letter to Mrs. Brookfield Thackeray said of it that " *The Times* gave me five guineas for the article. I recollect I thought it rather shabby pay." The figure seems to have rankled and Thackeray apparently made no further contributions to *The Times* until the 'sixties.

Charles Lamb contributed a sonnet. In 1830 he organized a subscription for Hone " which my friends of *The Times* are most willing to forward for him." The list of receipts was duly published in *The Times*, and included Charles Lamb, Esq., £10. Hone was generously treated by Barnes. His *Table Book* was well reviewed, and several of his articles on archaeological subjects appeared in the paper. Southey contributed a poem on Lamb ; Croker a set of verses on Sydney Smith's alleged refusal of a bishopric. W. L. Bowles wrote some lines in 1834. There was a poem by Béranger, *Le Lion Muselé*, on July 26, 1832. Verse for the most part followed the journalistic custom by being semi-political. Occasionally it emphasized the implication of a foreign dispatch. On Thursday, August 30, 1832, there were lines concluding :

> I dearly love the Frankfurt Diet,
>> Think newspapers the worst of crimes,
>> And would, to give some chance of quiet,
>> Hang all the writers of *The Times*.

Now and then works of erudition were noticed. There was a long review of Mitchell's *The Wasps*. Aristophanes was a lifelong study of Barnes's school-friend. The notice ended with a defence of classical education for the benefit of Isaac Tomkins's School of Journeyman Authors for the Confusion of Useful Knowledge— an obvious hit at Brougham.

The longest review ever given to a book in *The Times*, perhaps in any newspaper, was spread over nearly half-a-dozen issues in March, 1840, each instalment nearly filling a page of small type. The book was *The Oration of Demosthenes upon the Crown, Translated into English, with Notes*, by Henry, Lord Brougham, F.R.S., and Member of the National Institute of France. Before entering upon " the vapulation which we intend to inflict upon Lord Brougham's literary hide for his innumerable acts of mistranslation, interpolation and mutilation upon Demosthenes," the review contained a few general observations on the effrontery of the performance :

With respect to the translation itself, the *magnum opus*, which is to be more durable even than the brass which enters so largely into the noble lord's own composition, the only reason why we do not feel ourselves justified in asserting that it is the very *worst* translation of the very *finest* specimen of oratory that the world ever listened to, is, that we have not consulted any one of the translations by Leland, Francis, Dawson, Millot, or Cesarotti, all of which have been criticised with unsparing severity by Lord Brougham. But having heard, from competent authorities, that each and all of these individuals had a great knowledge of the Greek language, and having ourselves discovered that Lord Brougham has a very limited knowledge of it indeed, we believe that we should not err much in advancing, unhesitatingly, so bold an assertion. With the exception of Xenophon, the language of Demosthenes is more easy to understand than that of any other Greek author with whom we are acquainted ; and yet we wish to have our words understood to the letter, when we say that *there is not one single page in the two hundred and sixteen pages, over which Lord Brougham's version of Demosthenes spreads itself, in which there are not, on an average, three or four blunders, which would be unpardonable even in a stripling of fourteen.*

On nearly every page of this " foul, wallowing, boisterous and unEnglish " translation *The Times* found howlers which it particularized and commented upon for a week. The writer, administering to Brougham what Brougham was " never slow to inflict upon those he found meddling with matters they had either not taken the pains to examine or wanted capacity to comprehend," was allowed every licence of detail, space and expression. Knight Hunt, editor of the *Daily News*, heard that the articles were written by John W. Tyas, an eminent reporter.[1] Thomas Ingoldsby's *Black Mousquetaire* drags in an echo of the discussion of the critic's identity :

> But the fees and delays of " the Courts " are a shame,
> As Lord Brougham says himself—who's a very great name,
> Though the TIMES made it clear he was perfectly lost in his
> Classic attempt at translating Demosthenes,
> And don't know his " particles "—Who wrote the articles,
> Showing his Greek up so, is not known very well ;
> Many thought Barnes, others Mitchell—some Merivale.

[1] *Cf.* Hunt, F. Knight : *The Fourth Estate, Contributions Towards a History of Newspapers* (London, 1850), II, 280. Tyas was well known as a classical scholar.

In fact, the " vapulation " was administered by Joseph W. Blakesley, Fellow of Trinity College, Cambridge, and later Dean of Lincoln, who also reviewed for Delane Newman's *Grammar of Assent*.

The practice of *The Times* in obituary notices was slightly disappointing even as late as 1834. *The Times* was not yet a " National Register " and decidedly no mere " Gentleman's Magazine." The death of George Lamb, a personal friend of Barnes in his Temple days, is recorded in a very honourable position immediately below the thick and thin rules following the final leader :

> We lament to state that Mr. George Lamb, the Under-Secretary of the Home Department, and brother of Lord Melbourne, died yesterday at 2 o'clock. The public lose a sensible, straightforward, upright officer and his relatives and friends a warm-hearted man, who was never more pleased than when he was rendering a service. Few men have lived more beloved or esteemed, or have died more regretted.[1]

In the following day's paper a notice in conventional form, comprising some seven inches of nonpareil type, summarized Lamb's career—but was quoted from the *Globe*. It should be explained that the *Globe*, an evening paper, had more time in which to draft an adequate obituary, but clearly there could not have been any standing obituary prepared beforehand in the manner of to-day. *The Times* gave memorial space—when it could not help it—to the recognition of genius. When Sir Walter Scott passed away on September 21, 1832, " the greatest genius and most popular writer of his nation and his age," there was a leading article as well as half a column of extract from the *Globe*. "Though Sir Walter Scott was an unflinching Tory all his life, his politics never degenerated into faction, nor did they ever interfere with literary candour or his private friendships." This, which sounds like Barnes, was followed by a call for national recognition of Scott's family. *The Times* received from one writer £100, and, in acknowledging receipt, said that it had scarcely any room for the insertion of letters and could not itself accept subscriptions ; the £100 would be handed over " to any organisation as soon as one is organised and authorised to receive it."

In the final years of Barnes's life the office witnessed far-reaching changes. The paper lost many of its valued writers by death or resignation. James Murray, the head of the Foreign Department,

[1] January 3, 1834.

died in 1835. Francis Bacon, who had begun as theatre critic, had later been transferred to the Gallery of the House of Commons, and had been brought into the office as assistant editor in 1835, died suddenly in 1839. Peter Fraser, who had written occasional articles and leaders and letters during 1835, now seldom wrote. Edward Sterling resigned in 1840.

The complete secrecy upon which Peter Fraser insisted when, as a Fellow of Christ's College, Cambridge, he first joined the staff of *The Times*, was no longer necessary, though anonymity was none the less strictly preserved in the columns of the paper. Journalists were at last recognized, and Barnes had even been elected to the Athenaeum Club. Leader-writers and editors of other journals might and did accept jobs ; Barnes was not the man to take a comfortable post on one of the Administration's Commissions, to enter Parliament, or to subject himself in any way to party. Nor were Barnes's assistants encouraged to depart from this policy of detachment. The office as a whole refrained from accepting favours. The fight for independence had been won, but the victory was still jealously guarded.

The old militancy declined to some extent during Barnes's last years. There were new hands at work. William Delane's second son, John Thadeus Delane, had taken his degree at Magdalen Hall, Oxford, in 1839, and in July of the following year he joined *The Times*. Roundell Palmer, later to become Lord Chancellor as the first Earl of Selborne, came to the paper in September, 1840.

The newcomers were young men. They were joining not only an established but also a wealthy journal, nationally and internationally famous. The foreign reputation of the paper had long been made. Louis Philippe, whatever he thought of its politics, read no other paper, French or English—only *The Times*. *The Times* now provided a desirable career for young men of ambition. There was all to gain and nothing to lose in being connected with it. Lyndhurst, Lord Chancellor of England, with *The Times* in mind, assured the ambitious Disraeli a few years earlier that were he himself a young man with his way to make he would choose to be the editor of a London daily newspaper. Lyndhurst, knowing of Barnes's failing health, must have speculated upon the opportunity coming to some young man still unknown.

In the early days of May, 1841, the health of the Editor took a sudden and alarming turn. Too ill to move, but clear in mind and still indomitable, Barnes continued to send instructions to his young men at the office. One of these notes was received and preserved by Henry Reeve. It touches the question of the duties and the manoeuvre of the Whigs in raising the issue of the Corn Laws when their other political resources were plainly exhausted. It is dated " Sunday " and says :

I was extremely unwell yesterday and could not attend to any kind of business. . . . The commercial questions are so mixed up with the Corn Question, that I think it best at present to say nothing more about them. We have always advocated the lowering of the duties on Baltic timber, sugar and French Brandies, but for a paltry object of extending their existence for a short time the Ministers have broached the Corn question under circumstances which we must be the blindest dupes to sanction.[1]

Another instruction, sent to J. T. Delane, also acknowledges his illness :

My dear Sir, If XX[2] will adhere to the opinions expressed by Lord Aberdeen he may write a very useful article. On this as on all occasions the Premier made a fool of himself.

Lord Ripon's was a sharp & clever hit : the point about protection & taxation was cleverly put.

As to Melbourne & his party going out I tell you what I hear : but I certainly shall not believe they are going out till they are actually out.[3]

The inclosed par. is not a bad one.

I am very far from well.

Yours ever,
T. BARNES.

Do what you like with Dubois' letter.

The letter is undated. Lord Ripon's speech demanding to know whether the reduction in imposts was designed to produce increased revenue or to furnish an enfeebled measure of protection was delivered on Monday, May 3.[4] The Editor's letter—the last that has been preserved—was probably written on the Tuesday or Wednesday.

---

[1] P.H.S. MSS. 101. Reeve's endorsement reads : " Memorandum. This note was written on the 2nd May, 1841. On the 7th Barnes died. A man who used the utmost power of the press without arrogance, and without bitterness to any one. I deeply lamented his sudden and premature death."

[2] Possibly Reeve.

[3] Melbourne eventually resigned in August, 1841.

[4] Hansard, 1841, column 1375.

On May 6, 1841, Barnes's condition was so serious that his medical advisers called in as specialists Robert Liston, F.R.S., Professor of Clinical Surgery in University College, London, and (Sir) William Lawrence, President of the College of Surgeons. An operation was performed between seven and eight o'clock on the morning of Friday, May 7. It was technically successful; but the patient did not survive the day. Before he died Alsager was permitted to see him. Thus the unremitting connexion with the paper which had marked Barnes's every year in its service was maintained to the last.

On Saturday *The Times* printed, as its sole reference, an advertisement in the usual position :

On the 7th inst., at his house in Soho-square, Thomas Barnes, Esq., in the 56th year of his age.

Barnes was buried in Kensal Green Cemetery. One side of the simple box grave bears the inscription :

IN MEMORY OF

THOMAS BARNES M.A. of PEMBROKE COLLEGE CAMBRIDGE

and EDITOR of " THE TIMES " JOURNAL

DIED MAY 7th 1841   AGED 55 YEARS

HE WAS A MAN OF EMINENT SERVICE TO HIS COUNTRY AND HIS DEATH TO A NUMEROUS CIRCLE OF FRIENDS WAS A PERSONAL MISFORTUNE. AS A POLITICIAN HE CONDUCTED PUBLIC OPINION WITH GREAT MORAL COURAGE INFLEXIBLE INTEGRITY AND GENUINE PATRIOTISM WHILE HE WAS DISTINGUISHED BY FINE TALENTS AND GRACEFUL ELOCUTION. LEARNING IN HIM WAS UNITED WITH FACILITY CRITICISM WITH TASTE AND ELEGANCE WITH EASE. THE NATION FOUND IN HIM A MIND FAMILIAR WITH OUR NATIVE MANNERS AND INSTITUTIONS AND ACQUAINTED THROUGH EVERY GRADE WITH THE VAST FABRIC OF OUR SOCIAL SYSTEM. HE WAS NOBLE BY BEING BENEFICIAL TO OTHERS AND DISINTERESTED IN HIMSELF. IN MAGNANIMITY ABOVE THE VICISSITUDES OF THE WORLD HE WAS A GENEROUS SPIRIT AMIABLE IN HIS DOMESTIC RELATIONS AND IN HIS SOCIAL QUALITIES WITHOUT AN EQUAL.

APPENDICES

APPENDIX I

The following documents, hitherto unprinted, illustrating the relations of Governments and statesmen with the Press are referred to or quoted from in Chapters IV, XII-XIV, XVII and XVIII. In addition to the authorities in the text and in the footnotes, the reader is referred to Appendix II. : *Sources.*

I. *The Use of the Press by Government*
　　1. C. Stuart to Dundas, 1793.
　　2. [?Addington's] Memorandum on the Press [1802-3].
　　3. Treasury Notice on the Press, 1809.

II. *The Use of the Press by Statesmen*
　　1. Edward Sterling to John Walter II.
　　2. Extract from Le Marchant's Journal, 1834.
　　3. Joseph Parkes to Lord Durham, 1834.

III. *The Use of the English Press by French Statesmen*
　　1. Report forwarded to Paris by the French Ambassador in London, 1817.
　　2. Report forwarded to Lord Castlereagh by the British Ambassador in Paris, 1818.

I. THE USE OF THE PRESS BY GOVERNMENT

1. CHARLES STUART TO DUNDAS, 1793

[P.R.O., H.O. 42/26]

Sir,

I have the honour to transmit you the first Number of The *Parody*.

I am afraid that Government are proceeding upon a wrong plan—
They do not consider that by *monopolizing* Intelligence to a Morning
and an Evening Paper, they render the other papers hostile to them—
papers, too, that are really devoted to them—They do not consider with
Louis XIV that by managing the Literate, which he did I believe, at the
expence of 5000 a year, he in a great degree managed all Europe, &
managed his fame to posterity.—They do not consider, that altho'
every paper were to be annihilated but the *Morning Chronicle* and the
True Briton—the *Sun* and the *Star*—that there is an *under current* of
Jacobin Pamphlets that deluge the land by thousands, and perhaps they
know nothing, or very little about them, or their circulation—

They do not consider that while Government is pleased and most
highly flattered by an article of intelligence which is in no other of the
Morning Papers but one—that at the same time thousands of pamphlets
are circulated on that day, primed with lasting materials that totally
destroy that ephimera of the day. They do not consider that while they
circulate *News*, the others circulate *Sentiments*.—While Government
circulates an evanescent cloud, the others circulate a shower that falls
and nourishes, and brings forth fruit.

The truth is, every thing is to be managed, by managing the press.—
The artillery of the French could not be managed a month, without
they managed the artillery of the Press—I look upon the press as flint
to a gun, or potfire to a cannon—Whenever I hear of a French victory,
I in general ascribe it to their artful circulation of Journals and Bulletin's
throughout every municipality in every department.—What has con-
vulsed the mind, here, of late, but the press ? What can do it away, but
by taking every advantage of destroying, and multiplying the same
engine ? I say to Government, that you must either lead it, or I am
afraid it will destroy you. When I hear of the French casting *cannon*,
I think nothing of them at all, provided you can only prevent them from
casting *types* !—at least, to direct their pressure to your views.

I firmly believe, without any vanity, that I know as much in the
engineering of the press, as any press engineer in Britain—The system,
I am afraid, that Government is proceeding on, is wrong.—If you, or
Mr. Nepean entertained an idea that such a declaration of mine, is not

altogether preposterous or wrong, your commands are enough for me to give in an immediate Plan, which I am now turning in my mind. . .

Your ever devoted Servt.

C. STUART.

[Endorsed] 27 Octo. 1793.   Mr. Stuart.   Secret.

---

2.   ON THE PRESS [1802-3]

Private Paper—requiring immediate perusal.

[B.M., MSS. Addl., 33124, 78-81]

Though now brought to the true and false principles of *Reform*,—a subject I know to be in the contemplation of a party as soon as it is reinforced from abroad,—I think *Egeria* must be discontinued.—I am of this opinion because the considerations, on which I understood it to be undertaken, are not fulfilled, viz—to circulate the numbers among those who might render it a Text book for discussion,—and for the production of new Topics for writers in the Newspapers, who weary their readers and hurt their employers, by ringing changes on hackneyed phrases of censure and panegyric.—

Philosophic disquisitions and enquiries cannot immediately be rendered popular, without peculiar notice from persons of rank and influence both in conversation and in Parliament—if circulated and commented by persons of popular talents, Egeria might be more useful than declamation and satire, which had no reference to a real system, by inducing readers to *think*, on subjects which have furnished only occasions of Irritation and Passion, during the greater part of the present reign.—This method of concentrating the Principles in one work, and diffusing their explanations in numerous ramifications from it, appears to me a certain method of properly informing and directing the public mind,—and this method would, more effectually than any other I know, comprehend the proper instruments of Chastisement for abuses of liberty of every kind—It was in this manner Lord Shelburne, a statesman of numerous accomplishments, obtained the Helm, under circumstances similar to those of the present ministry.— He rose in consequence of the *forced* circulation of publications ; some of abstruse calculation, and some of metaphysical reasoning ; all securing numerous partizans by fixing Principles in their minds—If Lord Shelburne had comprehended in one System every species of political literature, abominable as some of it appeared, he might perhaps have been minister to this day.—

I expressed a similar opinion to Mr. Dunning who treated it as the Idea of a sanguine youth—Lord Shelburne was soon shaken ; principally by the Press ; which had certainly decided the American War ;

452

but he resumed his situation in conjunction with Mr. Fox,—in whose power the inferior, and those which Lord Shelburne deemed the exceptionable, provinces of literature were left.—Thus provided, his Lordship thought himself secure ; and applied with zeal and intelligence to his public Duties,—but being a little tainted with Puritanism, or solicited by the Dissenters,—he wished the government to have a moral as well as a political character,—and he spoke to Fox in a friendly manner, wishing him to consider the incompatibility of the direction of a Pharo table and the office of Secretary of State,—Fox took it, as he does everything, with good humour,—but the signal was given, in that department where Lord Shelburne had no influence, and the Literary hounds, well packed and well fed, opened on the Premier, and worried him out of his Place, his Reputation, and even his private character— I believe that Event, produced by such causes, to have had consequences direct and indirect extremely disadvantageous to the country ;—and it was owing principally to the *separation* made between the Philosophical and Satirical writers ;—the latter of which would have submitted to the former *under proper direction* ;—but separated they confounded good and evil, and misled friends and foes into that perpetual species of warfare which has ever since infested the country.— The present Ministry seem to me to have improved on the Error of Lord Shelburne.—I am old enough *to be able to produce Proofs*, that the Press is a *power* seldom much inferior ;—sometimes *superior* to the Government. Since the accession of the present Ministry, that power, usurped and monopolised by the lower orders of writers, has had more divisions than usual.—

The Funds of the Whig Club are low ; but hope, tho' long deferred, still retains several of its literary adherents.—The new opposition are more active, and though Placemen and Pensioners of Government, they countenance its Assassins.—The Ministry are placed at a point where they receive the full effect of a Cross Fire ; to which they oppose virtues, which no doubt will stand them in good stead as Christians, but which have nearly ruined them as statesmen.—

Whether the present negotiation terminate in War or in a temporary and *pretended* peace,—it is known, there are Phalanxes to attack Ministers instantly on the determination ; not only by the fleeting arrows of paragraphs, but by publications of another kind, and by solicitations to the country to petition and remonstrate—the various dissatisfied Sects, political and religious are sounded, with what effect it would be important to know—In these circumstances the public are to look for the justification and actual system of Ministers, not in any work which may give Gentlemen or Scholars the trouble of thinking, but in occasional and unimpressive paragraphs in two or three papers of no respectability—I do not mean to insinuate that these paragraphs are unnecessary—They would be useful in larger numbers if they made parts of a rational and fixed system, which might influence men of sense as well as fools.—

Europe is at this time in a tremendous state ; and every mutilated division of it looks to England for *Information* as well as *Courage*,— And where is it to be had ?—I see with astonishment and sorrow the only Legitimate Government now remaining, ennabling Fidlers and Singers to invest £40.000 in the funds for their decayed and poor associates, who would play and sing for Bonaparte with as much alacrity as for the King of Great Britain,—while Literary Talents, the instruments of incalculable Good or Evil, are left to the disposal of the vilest Factions, or to avoid starving by hiring themselves to the enemy and abusing the Government of their Country—I will not say as Lord Mansfield said of the Americans, " If you do not destroy such writers they will destroy you,"—though this opinion might be very usefully enforced,—But if Ministers should not favour every effort and take every occasion to separate the Chaff from the Corn ; to apply the one to instant and useful purposes, and give the other to its appropriate uses,—they will not only sink themselves, but aggravate the present difficulties and dangers of their Country.—

In measures of this nature Government has not a moment to loose— Why should Ministers at a Crisis so important, and with the opinion of the best Friends of the Country in their favour, suffer themselves to be degraded in the public opinion, and loose the public confidence, thro' unanswered misrepresentations ?—

Why should the Country be deprived of the benefit of their councils and labours by the unceasing Cavils and Calumnies of interested or disaffected Opponents ?—

[Endorsed] Observations on the Press. D. W. [rangham] ; Pray read this J. H. A. [ddington]

3. TREASURY NOTICE ON THE PRESS, 1809

[F.O. 83/16]   Dec. 11, 1809

If the Treasury is to be responsible for the Newspapers, it ought to have the Assistance of every other Department actively & exclusively. It should seem that priority of Intelligence would more than anything else distinguish the Government Papers from those that are opposed to it, but the contrary is notoriously the case.

The Ministerial Papers, are some of them accidentally & privately connected with one of the Departments from which Intelligence is to be obtained ; but at the Treasury where only they are, or can be under any sort of Controul, & which Department is considered by the Government in general as responsible for them, they seldom or never procure any information beyond that of an immaterial appointment. If the Treasury is still to be considered as the Manager of the Press (& every Department is ready to blame the Treasury if attacked thro' this Medium) it is absolutely necessary that the Department of War, Foreign Affairs, & the Admiralty, should abstain from direct communication with any of the Newspapers, and should furnish the Secretary of the Treasury with the Intelligence or Suggestions which they now give to the favoured Paper.

As long as the Newspapers shall continue to be considered as important as they now are, some Person in each of the three Departments ought to read the principal Newspapers every Morning, & send to the Treasury (of course if necessary after communication with his Principal) either a correct Statement of the Facts, if Facts are to be stated, or a Hint of the Line which it is wished should be taken. And this should be attended to as well when it is desirable that *no* notice should be taken of any Comment in an Opposition Paper, or where an Answer is required. The Treasury will of course be very glad to receive from any other Department, a Communication in the Terms in which it is wished to be inserted, but the Departments must be aware that in some Cases it may not be expedient to conform exactly with the Terms of an Article—Consistency in Tone being an essential advantage to a Newspaper.

Should these general Principles be agreed upon (of which there can scarcely be a doubt) suggestions shall be furnished to the several Departments, as to the Nature of the Communications with which it is desirable that each should furnish the Treasury ; as well as the periods of making them, and other Details.

[Endorsed]
Communication from the Treasury.
D/ Decr. 11 1809.
R/ Decr. 15.
On communicating intelligence to the Editors of Newspapers.

II. THE USE OF THE PRESS BY STATESMEN

1. EDWARD STERLING TO JOHN WALTER II, 1812

[P.H.S. Papers] *Private and confidential.*

My dear Sir Cowbridge, July 7th 1812

My stay in London had been so unexpectedly prolonged—and so many little matters crowded upon me at the conclusion of my visit, that all the efforts I could make did not enable me to see you again.

Having spoken with various members of the Wellesley interest, while in town, on the importance both to the public welfare and to their views as a political body of establishing a common feeling with some leading and highly principled branch of the diurnal press, I, on Saturday morning just before my departure, completed a memoir on a variety of subjects, for the perusal and consideration of Lord W. The above mentioned subject was discussed at some length, and the following topics relative to it were brought forward and enlarged upon to such a degree that I can only touch on the heads of my memoranda in a Letter —I stated—

1st That this country was Governed by the periodical but especially the diurnal press—That there was no party altogether independent of it—and none, which had not in point of history derived more or less of their importance from its exertions.

2ndly That if the interests of Lords Grey and Grenville had not been more successfully promoted by the great ability, wh[h] often displayed itself in the *Morning Chronicle*, it was because the vicious nature of their party was not to be cured by any advocate, because their views were so selfish, exclusive, incroaching, and therefore generally odious as to defy all attempts at palliation or disguise.

3rdly That the weakness and impudence of the *Morning Post* and the *Courier* exposed, rather than excused those qualities in their present employers.

4thly That the principles, wh[h] in my opinion directed the *Times* newspaper, and recommended it to a circulation, altogether unrivalled, amongst the reflecting, and therefore most powerful classes of the Community, were analogous to those, on wh[h] the character and consequence of L[d] Wellesley ought to be founded—namely, that they were not party but *national* principles—the only ones calculated to control the action or to satisfy the ambition of a great mind or to constitute the foundation of permanent power in this country.

5thly That I had now for the first time in my life conversed with Mr. John Walter, proprietor and Editor of the *Times* Newspaper. That he appeared to me to be a man of . . . &c. and spirit—awake to slights, but more so to attentions, and alive to a remembrance of some of the latter, wh[h] he had received from the Foreign Office, whilst L[d] W was in power, and impressed with opinions, as well as inclinations, highly favourable to Lord W.—and that therefore from a regard, whether to circumstances, persons, or principles, I was anxious to instil into his Lordship's mind the strong sense, which animated my own of the immense advantages, that might accrue, both to the public, and to himself, from taking every possible and honourable means to strengthen the highly improvable relations already subsisting, between a scheme of policy, wh[h] comprehended the interests, and a system of discussion, which addressed itself to the feelings not of a party, but of the Nation.

6*thly* That from the best general information that I was able to collect, the proprietor of the *Times* netted by his paper not less than from 9 to 10 thousand pounds per annum—that such a person therefore was equally above the influence of hope and fear, and was unquestionably more qualified to give than necessitated to receive either countenance or assistance—and that finally I saw no other quarter in which his confidence could be so well reposed or by which it could be so powerfully requited—so much for my representations to Lord W—, which let them have what effect they may upon his Lordship, cannot to you at least, I hope, be productive either of disadvantage or discredit—

Tell me what you hear of the last Vetus—but tell me *candidly* the bad, as well as good—it gave me more trouble than any of the others—because the subject is one, wh[h] I detest—The very narrative of an intrigue soils ones fingers—Should any of the other papers—ministerial, opposition, or neutral, take any notice of this last of our performances send me down a spare copy of all such papers—I shall be always happy to hear from you and am my dear Sir

Very faithfully yours
Edw[D] Sterling.

---

2. FROM THE JOURNAL OF DENIS LE MARCHANT, SECRETARY TO LORD BROUGHAM, 1830-1834.

[Chobham Papers]   [Before Autumn, 1834]

One of the most difficult and delicate tasks which the Chancellor imposed upon me, and which we had been some weeks together before I was trusted with, was the management of the public press. He had long been on a more or less intimate footing with the Editors of the principal Newspapers on the Liberal side and he had contrived to make them materially instrumental in extending his influence over the middle classes of society. They were all ready to serve him in preference to any public man of his day ; indeed he was the only one of his party that gave himself much trouble about them. Strange to say the Whigs took less pains than the Tories to guide and regulate public opinion. Lord Grey prided himself on having always kept himself independent of the Press and he had the worst opinion of those who were connected with it. The Duke of Wellington was more sagacious—he spared no pains to propitiate the *Times* whilst he was Minister, giving them on all occasions the earliest intimation of his intentions and any advantages that the Foreign Office could give, such as intelligence from foreign countries. In return that Journal stood by him manfully in all his difficulties. Their connexion ceased when the Duke went out of office because it was obviously the interest of both parties that it should cease and the Duke resorted I presume to the Tory papers. It was understood that he set up the *Albion*[1] as his own paper under the care of Praed, but I have no doubt that he soon gave his confidence to the *Morning Post* which for some years had been supported by Lord Ellenborough.

The Times was at this period without doubt the leading Journal in *Europe*. It owed its success to the skill of its Editor, Mr. Barnes, whose management of its concerns had been consummately able. He found it on his appointment hardly paying its expenses, and he contrived in a few years to make it yield a clear profit of above £20,000 a year. He told me that he was the son of a farmer[2] at Tenterden in Kent and having obtained a nomination to Christ's Hospital he was in due time removed to Pembroke College, Cambridge where the Hospital possesses some scholarships, and soon established his reputation there as an excellent classical scholar. He carried away but few honours, for it was perhaps the most brilliant era of Cambridge scholarship, and he gained only the barren distinction of being usually named as the first of the unsuccessful candidates. He tried his fortune at the Bar, which he was tempted to leave by an offer from *The Times* of £1200 p.a. He was a short and very corpulent man, unpretending in his manners and vulgar in his appearance. He looked what he was, a complete voluptuary. " One of the stye of Epicure." He had paid however no less attention to his mind than his body, for he was one of the best masters of the English language and literature I ever knew. I recollect witnessing a discussion between him and Macaulay on the comparative merits of the Early English dramatists that lasted above an hour, and I was not the only one of a large company who thought he had the best of the argument. His morals had been very loose and I am afraid his sense of public virtue was not more exalted. The interest of his paper was all he looked to and he told me his study had been to identify it with that of the middle classes whose representative he professed to be. He had correspondents in all the populous parts of England from whom he endeavoured to

1 Evening, No. 1 Monday Nov. 15, 1830. " We shall support the Duke of Wellington as Minister." *Cf.* 1st leading article.
2 This is an error of Le Marchant's ; Barnes's father was a solicitor.

learn the state of public opinion and whether he guided or followed it was much the same to him so that his paper enjoyed the credit which he always claimed of being the guardian of it. He was a very elegant writer, but a slow one :—where he excelled was in adapting the articles of inferior merit to the public taste, and he had the art of infusing into them a spirit and force which gave them an effect that certainly they would not have produced in their original form. He was of great service to the Journal by the quickness with which he caught the earliest signs of public opinion, and in his selection of interesting topics he was unrivalled. He entertained the most profound contempt for the vast majority of his readers and often told me that if he only was allowed time he could direct them as he liked. " Tell me " he used to say " what you are going to do in good time and I will prepare the public for it, but there must be no irresolution in carrying your measures into effect—no concession to your opponents, for *I* cannot afford to admit that I was in the wrong tho' you may." He seemed to regard all public men with equal indifference, or as Creevey once told me he is a thorough misanthropist, and at war with all the human race except Brougham whom he loves as warmly as he detests everybody else. He once assured me that his devotion to Brougham was such that he was ready if Brougham chose to change the politics of the paper. The only essential favour he ever received from the Chancellor was the promotion of his Brother to an office of £600 p.a. in the Bankruptcy Court. Now and then some unimportant intelligence was given him, but what gratified him most was a constant correspondence with me in which I freely stated my views on the public questions of the day and commented on the course which his paper was pursuing. I also occasionally asked him to dinner taking care to have some persons of distinction to meet him, and once I dined at his home where I was a little surprised at finding Rogers the poet and Edward Ellice. We fared sumptuously on venison turtle and the richest wines, but some of the company were not of the first water.

The other newspapers were comparatively insignificant. The *Chronicle* was conducted by John Black, the translator of Humboldt and many German works—a man of very extensive reading, but very little knowledge of the world being more fit to be a German metaphysician than the Editor of a paper. He had written the *M. Chronicle* from a large sale down to one that barely paid its expenses, and yet he continued his daily task as complacently as if his labours met with unqualified success. The columns of his paper were filled with long disputations on subjects about which the public was wholly indifferent, but they interested him, and that was sufficient. The only service he rendered to his employers was to preserve the consistency of his paper, for he was a man of exemplary probity, and far above the influence of pecuniary considerations. His was the only unblemished character in the circle to which he belonged. I communicated with him much less than with

Barnes, but he was ready enough to admit anything I sent him, and accordingly published many of the compositions both of the Chancellor and of myself.

The *Courier* was entirely in the Chancellor's hands. The Editor, one [Gibbons] Merle, who had formerly been a printer hoped to obtain a place in one of the public offices thro the Chancellor's interest and was therefore his willing tool. The principal proprietor Mr. Stuart took some part in the Editorship and was equally obsequious. He had supported the last administration, and on our coming into office the first thing he did was to hand over to us the letters he had received from the last administration whilst he had been in connection with them. It taught us how to deal with him—of course I took care to leave him no specimens of my correspondence. Merle was a feeble and diffuse writer and the paper did not prosper under his hands. The *Globe* tho' avowedly the Government paper was less under Brougham's control than the other papers. The principal editor Mr. Coulson was a perfectly independent man, living a retired life and not mixed up with the political intrigues of the day. He merely wrote the leading articles. His assistant Mr. Gorton the Editor of some compilations of merit was an estimable person and a sound Whig, but he was timid and irresolute and under the superintendence of some of the proprietors who were not particularly ambitious of Brougham's protection. Lord Palmerston was the patron of the *Globe* and wrote many articles in it on foreign politics. Some of them are spirited. His support of the paper has given it a circulation on the continent beyond that of any other Journal.

The *Sun* was conducted by its proprietor one Murdo Young, an active shrewd speculating Scotchman. He was always distressed owing to his connection with Mr. Patrick Grant the brother in law of Charles and Robert Grant, both of whom at one time were believed to write in the paper. Young was an adventurer, and whether he considered the Chancellor a congenial spirit or hoped to get something from him, he prided himself on being one of his retainers.

The *Morning Herald* was conducted by a Mr. Sydney Taylor, a barrister of dubious repute who was well disposed to the Chancellor and supported him when he dared. The proprietor of the paper an ignorant man named Tact who had formerly been a plumber and got possession of the paper by marriage interfered a good deal in its management so that the Chancellor only occasionally profited by Taylor's partiality. The paper might have been purchased for £20,000 during the whole of 1830 and Lord Dover pressed the Government to buy it.

The *Standard* was edited by Dr. Giffard, the brother of the late C. Justice of Ceylon, Sir Hardinge Giffard. He was an honest Orange-man and as violent and fanatical as most of his faith. He was however the intimate friend of Phillips the catholic barrister who was a creature of Brougham's and wrote many articles in the paper on law reform full of the warmest admiration of Brougham, much to the scandal of the Tories.

The only papers with which I communicated were *The Times*, *Chronicle*, *Globe*, *Sun* and *Courier*. The rest were managed by the Chancellor himself through other hands.

---

3. JOSEPH PARKES TO LORD DURHAM

[Lambton Papers] *Private*

London, 13 Oct. 1834

Dear Lord Durham.

I got your letter duly to day of the 11th. I entirely agree with you, & you now know sufficient of me to believe that I always frankly state any disagreement. Indeed I hold it to be the greatest abomination to flatter or deceive under the mask of friendship—& still more iniquitous to act such a part towards a *Public Man.* The chief Actors in political life, though from their position naturally acute, are often not the best judges of their public conduct ; that is to say, of the *effect* of their public acts. This does not apply to their *character*, for no *Honest* man, however occasionally wrong in judgment, can long injure himself in reputation. But I repeat, that I greatly admire the whole of your Edinburgh and Dundee progress.

I did intend, as I told you, to have written you a long letter instead of my shabby notes—but I have had an arrear to overcome—I have had to overcome the morbid idleness of " an out at grass " run—& further I really have wanted a little temper & nerve on the subject of the M[orning] C[hronicle]—I had no sooner turned my back, & left town 5 weeks since, than the Dr.[1] began to *dribble* & fall into the Chancellor's snares. Now I fully admit that the *Times* has often been guilty of gross assassinations of public men—that the *Times* who had never had sufficient excuse to worship Brougham as a God had not sufficient justification to colour him as a Devil. Still, making that discrimination— allowing his retrospective merits—& that he had done no *overt* act of treachery to the Reformers (save the Warwick Bill & his Tom fool conduct at the close of the Session) Black was bound as an *honest* public writer to expose & punish his recent departure from the straight course, especially his palpable despicable attempt to *humbug* the King. I wrote Black from Edinburgh, after we met, strongly stating this ; & I enclosed

---

[1] " Dr." John Black, editor, *Morning Chronicle*, 1817-1843.

461

the letter open to Easthope[1] that *he* might also know my opinions. Further, I sent him various letters which reached me—or rather extracts—complaining of the course of the paper on the subject. I told him that in his controversy, apart from the *Times*, he—the Dr.—had failed properly to shew up the Aberdeen and Inverness Speeches of the Chancellor—& that he might rely upon it that in the temper of the Chancellor the paper would be speedily committed by such an absurd ultra defence of a scene-shifting Politician. It had *some* avail, & stopped a little of it. On my return home I found that both Easthope & he differed somewhat from me, & I dropped the subject. On the Dundee affair I wrote the leader—approved by Black—& in the morning Easthope was quite disconcerted at my hit about the Chancellor's words of *doing too much*—especially at the italic letters & stress on that part of the article. In vain I argued with him. His position was the bad judgm^t. of meddling or committing the paper between 2 Public men of the same caste. But I said " you *have* meddled ; you have been cockling up Lord Brougham—tacitly by silence approving his abominations—& the question between him & Lord Durham is one of *principle* not of personal *Cabal*."

On Friday night late I was at the office when after midnight a special messenger came with the Salisbury report. I was writing on the Dissenters in another room when Black came in & said " there is a strange report of another speech of the Chancellor ; he is attacking Durham & is mad." I said " well, pray on Monday do the right thing, & say little so late." Indeed it was after one o'clock.

On Sunday I got a note from Easthope, see it enclosed. I went up to dinner when he shewed me a miserable hash of comment on the subject. I entered my protest against it, & ultimately at Black's last night they two begot a *mule*—somewhat mended it, & shewed it me in type. In type I much still disapproved it—modified some reflection or rather unfair implication on you, & suggested some of the sentiments towards the end of the article on the Peers & difficulties next Session.

In this smothered state you see it—*tolerably* decent under all these circumstances. But is puling stuff ; palpably cowardly & trimming : unjust to you because *you* did *not* set the example. Lord B. began lying about Warwick at preceding opportunities & violating principle in his false pretences of Conservatism. And you did nothing *personal* at Edinburgh ; you only took your ground on *principle* ; nor had the Reformers any " apprehension " ; they approved your course.—

You cant imagine how this matter has annoyed me. You are aware that the original project of the share in the paper is *off* ; that I have been in consequence a little awkwardly placed to extricate Ellice—,[2] & that

---

[1] Sir John Easthope, chief proprietor *Morning Chronicle* from 1834.

[2] A valuable hint of the, at least partial, responsibility of Ellice for the scheme for the revival of the *Morning Chronicle* described in Chapter XVII.

I never dreamt of so much devotion to it but for the opportunity of securing a valuable organ of Public opinion, & to promote thro' its agency the Cause in times of great & coming difficulties. I had & have no idea in my position & future views of being a Journal Editor ; but I did think that my judgment & power of writing would have kept them right.

However, I won't split, because it is only *one* abomination ; and by pocketing the affront I may retain the power of doing much good & preventing much harm. But give me your ideas on the subject as there is a limit outside which I dont choose to commit my political reputation by connection with such a course, disapproved by all I act with.

Easthope is a liberal honest & most active man—but not well backed in opinion or instruction ; & like all men of vulgar origin accessible to the praise of great men. I never knew such an active Devil as the Tight Rope Dancer. In my absence they have been corresponding, & big wig promising him exclusive Colonial, Foreign Office, and Home information ! all this in his own hand writing ; & to carry out his foolery sending him some foreign news 2 *days old* ! When the fly would not take me he seems to have thrown it towards the largest Proprietor.

III. FRENCH STATESMEN AND THE ENGLISH PRESS

1. REPORT MADE TO THE MARQUIS D'OSMOND, FRENCH AMBASSADOR IN LONDON, SEPTEMBER 30TH, 1817, AND FORWARDED BY HIM TO PARIS[1]

[Archives des Affaires Etrangeres, Quai d'Orsay, Paris, Vol. 21 Suppt. Angleterre 1790-1829]

The Examiner, Weekly Dispatch, Bell's Weekly, Observer, Register, Legislator, The News, all Sunday papers and edited with an Ultra-Liberal, or to be more explicit, Jacobin bias, expected to see a victory in France for the faction of which they are the faithful exponents. Because in the Seine constituencies a few Ultra-liberals succeeded in obtaining a temporary majority, which ultimately proved to be factitious, these revolutionary papers vied with each other the day before yesterday in publishing spontaneously long tirades against the French Government and personal criticism of our Ministers.

Such a unity of understanding can only be the effect of Whig or Jacobin designs ; the articles of the *Legislator* and the *Black Dwarf* in particular, are veritable diatribes, worthy of Meliée or of Cobbett. The *Anti-Gallican* alone last Sunday kept up its character and opposed with facts the risky assertions and vague declarations of their colleagues.

Among the numerous daily papers, either morning or evening, four deserve special mention :

(1) *THE COURIER* (Official) is on our side, except for the article of the 23rd . . . but Street no longer edits it—his partner does not share his views—and Mr. Mudford, the present editor, has none of Street's force, character or talent. This newspaper, moreover, is controlled by its Government and the tone of the article of the 23rd was the immediate result of apprehensions aroused.

(2) *THE TIMES* This paper has been written without passion up till now. It would lean towards the Ultra-Royalists but for the rivalry which exists between it and the *New Times.* Mr. Walter takes no part in the editing but it is easy to see that sometimes the *Times* has a fling at us which is all the more dangerous because this paper is anti-oppositionist and unapproachable. With regard to corruption it is independent.

(3) *THE NEW TIMES AND DAY* This paper—which enjoys Government support, is paid by the Treasury and is under the immediate protection of Mr. Arbuthnot, to whose office its editor, Mr. Stoddart, goes three or four times a week,—does us infinite harm. It must be heavily subsidized by the Ultra-Royalist faction, for every day its long columns are full of delirious nonsense against the French Government, the King, and personal criticism of the Ministers, especially of His

[1] Translated.

Grace the Duc de Richelieu, Comte Decazes and Monsieur Lainé. This paper is under the immediate influence of its Paris correspondents : Mr.V. . . . [Vitrolles] and His Grace the V. . . . de C. B. [Chateaubriand] etc. etc. and of the *petite église* Church party. It is becoming a libel to which no one replies. It is supported by the Treasury, where formerly they took 300 copies to distribute gratis, sending them even to the highlands of Scotland. Its subscription list is greatly increasing at the present time because it only warmly espouses a party cause or declaims against the actual state of things in Europe in order to be read eagerly in London.

(4) *THE MORNING CHRONICLE* protected by the English Anti-Ministerial party, likewise attacks the French Government so as to make way for the ultra-liberal ideas which Mr. Perry upholds so strongly. It is possible also that he was the ringleader and designed the plan which all the Sunday papers followed. Mr. Perry, however, is an incorrigible English ultra-liberal and one might add incorruptible also. The policy of uniformity therefore requires that he should be likewise the writer of the French Ultra-liberals, without taking into account his natural leaning towards the ultra-liberal Buonaparte.

The *Mirror of the Times, Morning Post, British Press* are echoes now of one and now of the other chiefs we have just mentioned ; the *Sun* which follows the *Courier* are the Jacobins of the evening press and very pronounced against the English and French Governments.

Amongst this torrent of newspapers, of which I do not mention a third, which we see each morning remaking English opinion and exciting it against us, who is there unreservedly to take our part ? No one ! The *Courier* sometimes, but it is tied up as I said above. It would never print the names of persons along with the statements of the French Government and scarcely dares to hint at them. It would never praise one of our ministers. Did it attempt to contradict the absurd *New Times*, which made out that His Grace the Duc de Richelieu was a mere man of straw, Comte Decazes a Bonapartist and Mr. Lainé a Jacobin ! No, the *Courier* said nothing.

What about the *Anti-Gallican* which has lately started to defend the French Government against its own writings and against all comers ? No, this paper only appears on Sundays, and different silly articles will have appeared in 20 or 30 sundry papers before it is able to refute one of them.

Such is the position of the English press at the present time, even including the reviews, which are all against us to the number of 41. There are scarcely four which would insert an article in our favour, for payment, of course.

While our Parliament is in session this will be a great disadvantage because they will print, as usual, a lot of nonsense against us with regard

HH

to all the anti-ministerial speeches with commentaries; and a few fragments of the ministerial speeches with refutations; that is the adopted plan and the one which will be followed without doubt. To stop them with bribes would cost enormous sums of money and they would begin again soon afterwards. Besides, there are a few which could not be reached by those means. Supposing we did not reply and pretended not to notice? But we know this method is not successful; they become more spiteful than ever, mutually encourage each other and push audacity and insolence to the last degree. Read the last 25 numbers of the *New Times*. Public opinion in England with regard to France is in a hopeless state and it is beyond the power of the English Government to remedy it, even if it positively wished to do so. Who is responsible for this evil? The newspapers. Who must we attack? The leading papers. When one goes to war one must reply to gunfire by gunfire. In the battle of words it is the same. We are always in retreat so it is natural that we should be cut to pieces. The only remedy, the one which seems to be prompt and efficacious, is to launch a newspaper secretly paid for by us together with the cost of printing and bring it out under the patronage of Carlton House (we can do it). It should come out every evening because that reduces expense by one-third at least. It would have to be English Ministerial without receiving the sol.cav. so that it would be in the same category as the *Sun* and the *Courier*. This newspaper would translate and publish all the articles sent from Paris free, consequently it would disprove one by one all the silly things which appear in other English papers.

This experiment should be made during the three months Parliament is sitting, so as not to compromise too large a sum and if the receipts do not cover expenditure, close it down at the end of the session, in the contrary event let it carry on.

It seems to me that this method of operation must have the happiest results. The test which has recently been made proves what we have to fear from the English journalists. The evil is great, without doubt; it is our concern to stop it. I think that the remedy indicated borders on the infallible, because being patronized by very highly placed men and receiving in advance some interesting documents this paper could not fail to hold its own against competitors.

———◆———

[F.O. 97/163; France.]

2. SIR CHARLES STUART TO LORD CASTLEREAGH, 1818

Paris July 23rd 1818

" I have employed a person on whom I rely to ascertain the source of the intelligence from Paris which I have lately observed in several of the English papers, and I enclose a short report which has been addressed to me upon that subject."

[Report referred to in Sir C. Stuart's letter of 23 July 1818.]

Your Excellency has expressed a desire to know who is the author of the Paris correspondence in the *Sun*. I have made some enquiries on the subject, & from well informed persons I learn, as indeed I have previously understood that the Paris correspondence in the *Sun* as well as that in the *Star* & the *Times* proceeds chiefly from the French Police. The whole of this correspondence is dictated by M. de Cazes, & the principal persons employed in editing it are M^r. *Linguet* his private Secretary & M^r. *Mirbel* the Secretary general of his Department. The Letters in question are evidently written originally in French, the translation betrays itself at almost every word. M^r. Mirbel's are known by the metaphors commonly employed in them being drawn from the objects of his habitual pursuits the natural sciences. He was & is still a professor of Botany at the *Collège de France* and was for many years superintendant of some of Bonaparte's botanical gardens.

The author of the letters *sur Paris* in the *Minerva* alluded to his appointment in the Police in speaking of a practice now adopted in France as in Turkey of raising a man from the humble office of Bostangi in the Seraglio to the important offices of Government. It would seem that most of our public prints are now in the pay of M. de Cazes.

The Times indeed receives with both hands, from the Duc de San Carlos with one & from M. de Cazes with the other—there can be little doubt also of the latter having influenced by the same means a principal writer in the *Courier*, M^r. Street. He sometime since made an application to the *Chronicle* for the admission of Articles in favor of liberal opinions & got the following answer which is given verbatim from a letter of M^r. Perry " that M. de Cazes might insert his liberal opinions in the French Journals with more certainty of their being extensively read in France & thus if he did, he might be assured that I (M^r. Perry) would cheerfully & gratuitously copy them." I am unable to say more to your Exc^y. on this subject of your enquiry.

[not signed]

APPENDIX II

SOURCES

The following tables are intended to supplement the references given in the course of the work. The authorities quoted in the text and in the footnotes will, with the documents in Appendices I-III, and the following references, supply the sources of such of the statements made in the chapters as are not verifiable from standard authorities, *e.g.*, *Cambridge Modern History*, *Cambridge History of British Foreign Policy*, *The Political History of England*, &c.

B.M.=British Museum ; B.N.=Bibliothèque Nationale, Paris ; P.R.O.=Public Record Office ; P.H.S.=Printing House Square Archives ; P.O.=Post Office Archives, Record Room, G.P.O. North, London.

I. JOHN WALTER

Manuscript

Memorandum Book kept by Arthur Fraser Walter. (Walter Papers.)

This volume deals exclusively with the genealogy of the Walter family into which A. F. W. made an investigation of some thoroughness. John Walter was the second son of Esther and Richard Walter, Clerk of the Parish of Duke's Place, Queenhithe, and mason, who was b. *circa* 1704, d. 1758. John Walter was admitted to the Freedom of the Masons' Company in 1760, of which he became master in 1788. His father Richard was himself the son of John Walter, citizen and mason, admitted by patrimony into the Freedom of the same Company in 1729. Richard Walter, mason, is mentioned in the Rolls for Parliamentary Elections for the City of London, s.a. January, 1701. The Records of the Chamberlain's Court (Freemen of City of London) note a John Walter baptized December 10, 1701, as the son of William Walter, of Evesham (*sic*), Worcester, currier. John had been apprenticed May 25, 1688, to Thomas Brumhall, citizen and mason, who was admitted to the freedom July, 1698.

John Walter's eldest brother Robert, who became a captain in the Navy, was b. *circa* 1731, d. 1785 ; Richard was b. 1733 and d. 1773 ; John was born in 1738 or 1739.

The family of John and Frances Walter consisted of the following : *William*, b. 1763 ; *Mary*, 1765 ; [*Fanny*, b. and d., 1768] ; *Fanny*, 1770 ; *Catherine*, 1774 ; *John*, 1776 ; *Anna*, 1779. With the exception of *William* and *Anna* the children were baptized at St. Catherine Coleman, Fenchurch Street. Mrs. Frances (Landen)

Walter d. 1798. With the exception of William, who secured from Pitt a place under Government, the children all received shares in *The Times* under the will of John Walter I, d. 1812.

In 1781 was born *Walter*, natural son of John Walter and Catherine Wilson, to whom was left the income for life of one-sixteenth share in *The Times*. Walter Wilson first became a bookseller, with Maxwell, of Bell Yard, Temple Bar, London. Later he entered at the Inner Temple, but does not appear to have practised. He published *The History and Antiquities of Dissenting Churches and Meeting Houses in London, Westminster, and Southwark* ; *including the Lives of their Ministers* (1808, Vols. I and II ; III in 1810 ; IV in 1814). Wilson made a much larger collection of Defoe's works than had previously been brought together, and in 1830 published *Memoirs of the Life and Times of Daniel Defoe*, 3 vols., which won the commendation of Macaulay and Hazlitt. Wilson was a frequent correspondent of Charles Lamb. His signature duly appears on the mutual release to John Walter II signed by all the proprietors of *The Times*, March 22, 1842. He died in 1847. He was twice married, and left a son, Henry Walter Wilson, of the Inner Temple, and a daughter, married to Norman Garstin, Colonial Chaplain at Ceylon.

The nephew John Walter, of Nicholas Lane, Lombard Street, was the son of John Walter I's elder brother Richard Walter, formerly of the Minories, citizen and cordwainer, who d. 1773. He also received a share. Relevant extracts from the will of John Walter I, d. 1812, are given at pp. 475 *ff*.

LETTERS

Holograph

1778 to Chatham. P.R.O. Chatham Papers G.D.8.

1786 to M. Deton, B.N., Français, nouv. acq., 22260.

1789-90 to Lord Hawkesbury ; B.M., MSS. Addl. 38224, 150 ; 38225, 68 ; 38227, 281.

Printed

1783-1789 to Benjamin Franklin, see Eddy, George Simpson : *Correspondence between Dr Benjamin Franklin and John Walter regarding the Logographic Process of Printing* (Worcester, Mass., 1929).
    Reprint from the Proceedings of the American Antiquarian Society,.October, 1928. The originals of John Walter's letters to Franklin (1783-1789) are in the possession of the American Philosophical Society.

1786 to Lord Ailesbury (Hist. MSS. Comm., *Report*, 1898, p. 244).

1790 to John Bland Lamb Burges, *Correspondencr* (London, 1885), p. 187.

1799 to Lord Kenyon, *The Manuscripts of Lord Kenyon* (Hist. MSS. Comm., 1894 Report, p. 551).

Publications

(a) Trade Circulars, &c.

The Case of Mr. John Walter, of London, Merchant, fol., 4 pp.
    Printed after the Bankruptcy of John Walter and reciting his misfortunes in the Coal Trade, as an Underwriter, and announcing the frustration of his endeavours to secure a Government post and expressing the hope that friends will assist him and his family. (*Circa* 1782.) (For the official announcements of the bankruptcy see *London Gazette* March 22, April 15, May 27, July 8, 1783.)

Logographic Office, Blackfriars, April 15, 1784.—By His Majesty's Letters Patent for Printing by Words instead of Single Letters. | Mr WALTER begs leave to inform the Public that he has taken the King's late Printing House near

Apothecaries' Hall, which is now fitting up for carrying on the Printing business in general, under the assignment to him of the said Patent for the " sole privilege of using and casting " or cementing for sale, types of words etc.

He means in a few days to lay before them more fully the very ingenious and simple principles upon which this important improvement will be conducted, both in correctness and in expedition, and he flatters himself that neither assiduity or expense wil' be wanting to render it worthy the countenance and protection of a generous public. The facility of taking up a whole word instead of a letter must be obvious to the most common Understanding.

An arrangement has been formed, after a very laborious study and application, which will be both a useful and valuable acquisition in a branch of the greatest consequence to a mercantile Nation.

Logographic Office, Blackfriars, May 17, 1784. | Mr WALTER begs leave to inform the Public, that he has purchased the Printing-house formerly occupied by Mr Basket, near Apothecaries' Hall, Blackfriars, which will be opened the first day next month for printing by words entire, under his Majesty's patent. The greatest care will be taken of all orders which may be sent either to the printing-house; Mr Searle's, Grocer, No. 55 Oxford-street; Mr Thrale's Pastry-cook, opposite the Admiralty; Mr Taylor, New Lloyd's Coffee-house, over the Royal Exchange; Mr Pratt's, Green Grocer, No. 84 Wapping; Mr Sterney's, Oilman, 156 Borough; where boxes will be fixed for the reception of any letters or messages he may be favoured with.

And in order to prevent any attempt being made either to cast or cement any letters into words to the prejudice of the above patent, for which the sole privilege is granted, Mr Walter hereby offers a Reward of TWENTY POUNDS to any person who will give information, that the party offending may be convicted thereof.

Johnson, Henry: *An Introduction to Logography: Or the Art of Arranging and Composing for Printing with Words Intire, their Radices and Terminations, instead of Single Letters* (London, 1783).

Description of the invention by the original patentee.

Walter, J. : *An Address to the Public on the Origin of the Art of Printing,* with a description of the Logographic Invention; being an Introduction to the Publication of the Works of some of the most eminent authors executed by the New Method of Printing with words instead of Single Letters. (Undated.)

Intended as a Prospectus of an edition of Watts on the Improvement of the Mind, which was published in February, 1785. The surviving copy is at P.H.S.

Miscellanies in Prose and Verse intended as a Specimen of the Types at the Logographic Printing Office. London Printed and sold by J. Walter, Printing-House-Square, Blackfryars, and at No 45 Lombard Street, M,DCC,LXXXV.

" The first publication after this specimen will be an octavo edition of Dr. Watts's *Improvement of the Mind* which will be brought out next month." The types, apparently from the foundries of Caslon and Jackson, range from great primer to nonpareil.

Walter, John : *Letters reprinted from the* Daily Universal Register *in answer to Illiberal Reports* (1785).

A defence in 4pp. folio of the Logographic principle against objectors and trade rivals. John Bell and William Caslon are mentioned. The press-mark on the surviving copy in the British Museum is P B 1418 K 33.

An Address to the Public by J. Walter, shewing the great Improvement he has made in the Art of Printing by Logographic Arrangements (London : Printed at the Logographic Press, Printing-House-Square, Blackfriars, and sold by J. Walter, No 169, facing Bond Street, Piccadilly, 1789).

"I have opened a shop in Piccadilly No 179 . . . a proper person is appointed, to attend and give every information ; and in conjunction with the Proprietor of *The Times*, it is determined to publish that paper there, and to receive all commands and advertisements in Piccadilly, as well as in Printing House Square, Blackfriars, where the paper is printed." pp. xi-xii.

"In a very early state of the business I wrote to that celebrated character *Doctor Franklin*, and took the liberty of troubling him with several observations on the subject of my intended improvement. The Doctor was originally a Printer, whose mind was not narrowed by the prejudices of trade," &c.

Letters are printed from Franklin, Passy, April 17, 1784, August 17, 1784, February 1, 1785, pp. 9-14 (reprinted in Eddy, G. S. noted *supra*) ; Correspondence with Barnard, King's Librarian, and John Walter's request for a share in Government printing. The secretary of the Trustees of the British Museum "the [Logographic] fount cannot be placed in any of the rooms of the Library as you desire ; nor do the Trustees foresee the particular advantage it is likely to be to this Institution" ; William Caslon on Cementing Types and deferred payments ; the Secretary of the Trade Committee of Compositors and Pressmen refusing to allow Apprentices ; List of subscribers to the Logographic editions.

(b) Publications of the Logographic Press.

The most desirable volumes issued by the Press are the quarto editions of Anderson's *Commerce* and Meares's *Voyages* mentioned in the text. In addition the Press published a very handsome quarto in 1785. James Douglas's *Dissertation on the Antiquity of the Earth* (Printed at the Logographic Press, and sold by George Nicol, Bookseller to His Majesty, Strand, MDCCLXXXV) is illustrated with eight aquatint plates.

Amongst octavos the following are characteristic of the craftsmanship of the office :

Watts, I. : *The Improvement of the Mind.* (London, Printed at the Logographic Press, and sold by J. Walter, Printing House Square, Black-Friars, MDCCLXXXV. 8vo., pp. xvi + 464.)

Hurtley, Thomas : *A Concise Account of Some Curiosities in the Environs of Matham, in Craven, Yorkshire.* (Printed at the Logographic Press, by J. Walter, and sold by J. Robson, New Bond Street, and T. Longman, Paternoster Row, MDCCLXXXVI. Three Copperplates by W. Skelton after A. Devis.)

Moffat, John : *Aretaeus*, consisting of eight books on the Causes, Symptoms and Cure of Acute and Chronic Diseases, translated from the original Greek. 8vo, xvi + 502. (London, Printed at the Logographic Press, by J. Walter, Printing House Square, Black-Friars ; for W. Richardson, under the Royal Exchange, n.d.)

The Essays of Francis Bacon, Baron of Verulam . . . together with the Life of that Celebrated Writer. A New Edition in Two Volumes. (London, Printed at the Logographic Press, by J. Walter, Printing House Square, Blackfriars ; and sold by J. Robson, New Bond Street, T. Longman, and R. Baldwin, Paternoster Row ; and W. Richardson, under the Royal Exchange. M,DCC,LXXXVII, 8vo, xxvi + 440.)

Life and Adventures of Robinson, of York, Mariner (Printed at the Logographic Press ; and sold by J. Walter, No. 169, Piccadilly, opposite Old Bond Street. M,DCC,XC).

3 volumes, with copperplates by R. Pollard, after C. Metz and M. Brown.

In addition there were many pamphlets and some novels. Lists may be found in Typographicus' Letters from the *Daily Universal Register* (1787) in the British Museum (1418 k.33) and in Walter's *Address to the Public* (1789).

The King's Printing House, Printing House Square.

Chambers, Edmund : *The Elizabethan Stage* (Oxford, 2 vols.).

Feuillerat, Albert : *Blackfriars Records* (Malone Society, 1913).

Toy, Sidney ; and Martin, William : *The Black Friars in London*, in Transactions of the London and Middlesex Archaeological Association, N.S., Vol. V, §4, 1926.

The name " Blackfriars " originates from the Dominican or Preaching or Black Friars who came into this south-west corner of the City in 1276. After some fifty years in Holborn they were given a spacious site in Castle Baynard Ward of the City by Gregory Rokesley, Mayor ; Edward I, their liberal patron, allowed them to pull down the City wall on the west side and thereby extend their property as far as the Fleet river ; the new wall he ordered to be rebuilt at the City's expense.

The Black Friars' precincts were bounded on the south by the Thames and on the east by Puddle Dock Hill, now St. Andrew's Hill ; to the north they extended beyond Carter Lane towards Ludgate. The monastic buildings were for the most part north of the site now occupied by *The Times* ; but at least one important building stood on ground now belonging to the paper, and under some parts of the office monastic masonry is still visible. Much was cleared away when *The Times* office was rebuilt in 1870. About the same time Queen Victoria Street was opened up and was the culmination of many changes which made a vast difference to the whole quarter. The medieval lay-out of much of old Blackfriars is, however, still traceable in the yards, courts and alleys immediately to the north of Printing House Square. The names of Friar Street, Church Entry and Cloister Court still recall the monastic occupation.

That the Priory was a splendid place is clear from the poetic but close description of it in " Pierce the Ploughmans Crede " (*circa* 1394). The narrator in the poem, desirous of learning the creed, applies to the Dominicans, among other orders, for instruction, and is greatly impressed by their buildings and particularly by their church, which he describes in detail. It stood just south of Carter Lane, and quite recently much of its foundations was unearthed. Adjoining its site is the unused and railed-in churchyard of St. Ann. St. Ann's parish came into being a good many years after the dissolution of the monastery, for the church was consecrated in 1597, though a chapel of that name seems to have been established earlier ; the church was not rebuilt after the Great Fire, and the parish was joined with that of St. Andrew-in-the-Wardrobe hard by on the other side of old Puddle Dock Hill. St. Ann's, Blackfriars, one of the shortest lived of City churches, numbered some famous parishioners, including, among other well-known artists, Van Dyke.

In the Blackfriars' monastery occasional parliaments met down to the time of Henry VIII, in whose reign Charles V of Spain lodged with the Prior, and in a hall at Blackfriars, as Shakespeare knew, Queen Katharine of Aragon was tried.

At the dissolution the whole property passed into the hands of Henry VIII, who refused to assign it to the jurisdiction of the City ; it therefore remained a liberty outside the City for an indeterminate time, but is now part of the Ward of Farringdon Within. Under Edward VI Blackfriars became private property and a fashionable place of residence. It was in consequence of this, and of its extra territoriality, that it soon became also the site of two famous playhouses. Both playhouses apparently occupied the same monastic block, but not precisely the same chambers in it. The block ran from north to south, from what is still Playhouse Yard, as far, perhaps, to the south as across Printing House Lane. It consisted, in its upper part, of the Upper Frater or Parliament House—a long room or hall where Parliaments had met and Queen Katharine had been tried ; below were a monks' parlour and a dining hall.

The first theatre, of boys, was, it seems, in a building adjoining the Upper Frater ; here Thomas Farrant opened his playhouse with the combined boys of Windsor Chapel, the Chapel Royal and St. Paul's in 1577 ; but he died in 1580, and from his vexed and vexatious successors the landlord, Sir William More, got the premises back in 1584 and reconverted them in tenements.

The second theatre was more successful. In 1596 the elder Burbage bought the same block with other premises, and threw together the two chambers under the Frater into a theatre ; his intention was to set up a covered-in and artificially lit playhouse, like Farrant's, in which his company could play in the winter ; he hit on Blackfriars because it was outside the City, where public playhouses were forbidden. But he died in 1597, and his heir Richard was prevented from proceeding with the plan through a successful protest to the Privy Council by the inhabitants of Blackfriars against public performances. He accordingly let the premises to the managers of that private " aerie of children " who, according to Shakespeare, " berattled the common stages " ; but in 1608 he recovered the lease, and the " King's Men," or the company in which he and Shakespeare were partners, began to use the house in winter as an alternative to the open air Globe. Though the neighbourhood protested more than once against the playhouse as a nuisance, it remained open until all theatres were closed in 1642. In 1655 it was pulled down.

In Ireland Yard, at the back of Printing House Square, Shakespeare had a house, as is attested by his will ; another resident in Blackfriars was Ben Jonson. Glasshouse Yard, between Playhouse and Ireland Yards, commemorates a glass factory mentioned in Jacobean literature.

Printing House Square itself acquired its name from its connexion with the King's Printers, who seem to have come to it shortly before the Great Fire and did not leave it until 1770. Here John Bill printed the early numbers of the *London Gazette* ; here Baskett, of the " Vinegar " Bible, made his " Baskett full of misprints " ; here, also, was a disastrous fire in 1737. A new building with a private dwelling house for Mark Baskett was completed in 1740. The private house became the residence of John Walter I in 1784, and is to-day in the occupation of his successors.

II. & III. *THE TIMES* AND THE NEWSPAPER TRADE

The first source of these and the ensuing chapters is the file from Nos. 1-939 the *Daily Universal Register*, January 1, 1785, to Nos. 940-1022 *The Times* or *Daily Universal Register*, January 1, 1788, and No. 1023 *The Times*, March 18, 1788, to No. 17664, May 7, 1841—*i.e.*, the period from the foundation by John Walter I to the death of Thomas Barnes, editor, 1817-1841. Original material documenting this period, now in the archives of Printing House Square, is limited to assignments of the freeholds of the property known as Printing House Square ; assignments of shares in *The Times* ; a small number of letters of domestic importance from members of the staff, Combe, Fraser, Barnes, Sterling, Tyas, addressed to John Walter II ; a small number of official letters from Charles Arbuthnot, Digby Wrangham, Thomas Young ; personal letters to Thomas Barnes from Lord Brougham, Sir James Mackintosh, and others.

As papers of political importance were systematically destroyed, the only means of discovering the point of view from which political articles were written, their authors, the motives for publication in *The Times*, and of estimating the effect of publication, has been by reference to (*a*) the leading matter in contemporary dailies and weeklies, (*b*) the papers of official departments, (*c*) memoirs and diaries of British and foreign statesmen, (*d*) memoranda of Ambassadors and their political agents, (*e*) the reminiscences of journalists, and (*f*) obituaries of pressmen in the newspapers.

473

For the general situation in the newspaper trade during the active life of John Walter I, 1785-1802, the two volumes of Fox-Bourne, H. R. : *English Newspapers, Chapters in the History of Journalism* (1887), are still very useful. A recent work, Morison, Stanley : *The English Newspaper, Some Account of the Physical Development of Journals printed in London*, 1622-1932 (Cambridge, 1932), is wider in scope than the sub-title suggests. The same writer's *John Bell*, 1745-1831 (Cambridge, 1930), a memoir of the founder and part-proprietor of the *Morning Post, the World*, the *Oracle*, and *Bell's Weekly Messenger*, provides new material on late eighteenth-century trade developments. Nichol Smith, D. : *The Newspaper*, pp. 331-367, forms a valuable chapter of *Johnson's England*, vol. II (Oxford, 1933), and although it inevitably breaks off at the death of Johnson, which took place a year before the foundation of the *Daily Universal Register*, it presents details, unavailable elsewhere, of the conditions into which John Walter ventured. There exists no comprehensive modern history of English journalism, London journalism, or even of the London dailies. The best short guide to the subject is [Stewart, Andrew] *Catalogue of an Exhibition illustrating the History of the English Newspaper through three Centuries* (London, The Press Club, 1932). The recent and stimulating von Stutterheim, Kurt : *Die Englische Presse* (Berlin, 1933), is chiefly concerned with the craft during the last thirty years. A recent estimate of the value of newspapers to the historian is given in Woodward, E. L. : *War and Peace in Europe*, 1815-1870, *and other Essays* (London, 1931), Chapter III, *The Classification of Historical Material*, pp. 163-176. " The value of newspapers is perhaps greater than historians have been willing to admit. The exploration of archives and the search for unpublished material have led to a certain exaggeration of the superiority of archival sources, &c." p. 171. For a list of newspapers in London and the provinces established between 1620 and 1920 see [Muddiman, J. G.] *The Tercentenary Hand-List* issued by *The Times*. A Bibliography of printed works on the Press, by Graham Pollard, will appear in the *Bibliography of English Literature* (Cambridge, expected 1935), to the proofs of which reference has been allowed to the present compiler. Manuscript sources—*e.g.*, partnership records, assignments, &c.—are listed in the class catalogue in the B.M., Dept. of MSS.

The principal contemporary newspapers read are :

EIGHTEENTH CENTURY

The *World*, ed. by John Bell and Edward Topham	-	1787-1788
The *World*, ed. by Edward Topham and C. Este	-	1789-1791
The *Oracle or Bell's New World*, ed. by John Bell	-	1789
The *Morning Chronicle*, ed. by Wm. Woodfall -	-	1769-1789
ed. by James Perry -	-	1789-1821
The *Morning Post*, ed. by Peter and Daniel Stuart	-	1788
The *Gazetteer*, ed. by James Perry - -	-	1783-1789
The *Morning Herald*, ed. by Henry Bate -	-	1780
The *True Briton*, ed. by John Heriot - -	-	1793
The *Sun*, ed. by Robert Heriot - -	-	1792

The *Spirit of the Public Journals* (annually from 1797), compiled from the lighter columns in the above and other journals, is of some value.

IV. *THE TIMES* IN POLITICS

Manuscript

Government relations with journalists : John Bell, of the *Oracle*, to Evan Nepean. P.R.O., H.O. 42/29, April 5, 1794.

W. H. Bourne, of the *Observer*, to the same. H.O. 42/31, June 16, 1794.

John Heriot, of the *True Briton*, to the same. H.O. 42/29, April 16, 1794 ; Heriot to Duke of Portland. H.O. 42/35, August 3, 1795.

Charles Stuart, of the *World*, to the same. H.O. 42/26, October 29, 1793.

William Walter to William Windham, June 1, 1800, and answer June 19. B.M., MSS. Addl. 37879.

Publications

Goldsmith, Lewis : *The Secret History of the Cabinet of Bonaparte* (London, 1812).
> Foundation of the *Argus*, p. ii ; *Le Courier de Londres*, p. x ; for a note on Goldsmith see p. 491.

Melville, Lewis : *The Correspondence of William Windham* (London, 1913, 2 vols.).

[Williams, David] *Royal Recollections on a Tour to Cheltenham, Gloucester, Worcester . . . in* 1788 (London, 1788).
> This satire, written as by the Prince Regent, in touching (pp. 42 *ff*) on newspaper management, mentions Topham, Bell, Rose, Steele. " Sheridan is the man for the papers : Steele is too cautious & gentlemanlike," p. 42 ; " the pamphlets under the directions of Rose," p. 50.

V. JOHN WALTER II ; *and* XI. A TRANSFER OF AUTHORITY

Manuscript

(a) Legal.

[1797. Indenture of partnership between John Walter the elder and John Walter the younger.]
> Original missing, but a " recital " in the following mentions this previous agreement which made the younger Walter a partner in the Business of a Printer as from December 31, 1797 ; the partnership to be in equal moieties as from December 31, 1800.

1801. Indenture of Partnership between John Walter the elder and John Walter the younger. November 10, 1801.

1804. John Walter Junior and Thomas Martyn respecting a self-acting Printing Press. May 9, 1804.

1807. Indenture of Lease of premises to Samuel Brown. January 6, 1807.
> Indenture of Release between John Walter the elder, John Walter the younger and Samuel Brown. January 7, 1807.
> Creating an interest on trust of £200 to be paid to John Walter the elder, his executors, administrators and assigns during his natural life.

1810. The Will of John Walter I. Abstract :

AND WHEREAS I am now possessed of eleven undivided sixteenth parts or shares the whole into sixteen equal parts or shares being divided or considered as divided of and in a daily newspaper called *The Times* and in the net profits arising from the publication and sale thereof NOW I DO HEREBY GIVE AND DISPOSE OF the said eleven sixteenth parts or shares whereof I am now possessed of and in the said newspaper called *The Times* and of and in the profits or produce thereof and all my estate and interest in such shares in manner following (that is to say) I GIVE AND BEQUEATH one of such sixteenth parts or shares unto my son John Walter his executors administrators and assigns absolutely UPON and for the several trusts and purposes herinafter mentioned expressed and declared of and concerning the same that is to say UPON TRUST that he the said John Walter his executors or administrators do and shall from time to time as the same shall become payable receive and take the profits gains and emoluments of the said sixteenth part or share and pay the same into the proper hands of my said natural or reputed son Walter Wilson during his life or until the said Walter Wilson shall happen to become bankrupt or be insolvent or make any composition with his creditors or shall sell assign make over or part with his interest in the said share or any part thereof or the profits gains and emoluments thereof or any part thereof or upon the decease of the said Walter Wilson or from and upon his becoming bankrupt or insolvent or making any composition with his creditors or his selling assigning or making over or parting with his interest in the said share or any part thereof or the profits gains and emoluments thereof or any part thereof whichever shall first happen THEN I GIVE AND BEQUEATH the said sixteenth part or share of and in the said newspaper called *The Times* and of and in the profits gains and emoluments thereof to my said son John Walter his executors administrators and assigns absolutely to and for his and their own use and benefit AND I WILL AND DIRECT that the said Walter Wilson shall have no control in respect of the said share in the management or conduct of the said newspaper but that the vote management control and conduct of the same in respect of such share shall be at all times vested in my said son the said John Walter his executors and administrators The Testator bequeathed two other of the one-sixteenth parts unto his nephew John Walter of Nicholas Lane Lombard Street London Cordwainer and John Schubach of Crosby Square Bishopsgate Street London Esquire absolutely UPON TRUST for life for his daughter Mary Carden and after her death UPON TRUST for her children

[Testator bequeathed two other of the one-sixteenth parts or shares unto his nephew the said John Walter and John Schubach UPON TRUST for life for his daughter Catherine the wife of The Revd. Richard Winsloe and after her death for her children Bequest of two other of the one-sixteenth parts or shares to his nephew John Walter and John Schubach Upon similar trusts for his daughter Anna wife of the Revd. Alexander Brodie as those relating to his daughter Catherine Winsloe Bequest of one other one-sixteenth part or share to said John Walter and John Schubach UPON TRUST for his daughter Fanny Wraight widow of William Wraight then late of Blackfriars Road Gentleman and after her decease for her children. Bequest of one other one-sixteenth part or share to the said John Walter and John Schubach for the benefit of his trusty servants Charles Bell of Christchurch Surrey and James Lawson of Saint-Dunstan-in the West in equal moieties share and share alike during their lives and after their death to his son John. Declaration that on account of their share the said Charles Bell and James Lawson should not be entitled to any vote or control in *The Times*]

AND I GIVE and BEQUEATH two other of the said sixteenth parts or shares unto my said nephew the said John Walter and the said John Schubach their executors administrators and assigns UPON and for the trusts ends intents and purposes hereinafter mentioned expressed and declared of and concerning the same (that is to say) UPON TRUST that they my said Trustees and the survivor of them and the executors or administrators of such survivor do and shall as soon as may be after my decease offer the same for sale to my said son John at a sum equal to four years purchase calculated on the net profits made by the same shares in the year ending on the last half yearly day of settlement of accounts of the said newspaper immediately preceding my decease AND in case my said son John shall agree to purchase and take the same two shares at that price then I do direct that they my said Trustees and the survivor of them and the executors or administrators of such survivor do and shall assign and transfer the same two shares and the profits gains and emoluments thereof from the said last half yearly day of settlement immediately preceding my decease to my said son his executors administrators and assigns absolutely for his and their own use and benefit and in the event of my said son John so purchasing the said two shares on the terms aforesaid I GIVE and BEQUEATH to him the sum of £2,000 to assist him in the making good of such purchase and paying for the same

AND I do direct my said Trustees and the survivor of them and the executors and administrators of such survivor to accept and take the bond of my said son John payable by four equal half yearly instalments for the payment of what shall be due for such purchase money after deducting and allowing thereout the said eventual legacy or sum of £2,000 But in case my said son John shall decline neglect or refuse to make such purchase for the space of one month from the time the same two shares shall be offered to him as aforesaid THEN IT IS MY WILL AND I DO DIRECT that my said trustees or the survivor of them or the executors or administrators of such survivor do and shall with all convenient speed thereafter sell and dispose of the same two shares by public auction in one or two lots as they or he shall think proper and the monies arising by such sale or sales and the gains profits and emoluments arising from the same two shares until such sale or sales shall be had shall be deemed considered and taken as part of my residuary personal estate and be paid and applied accordingly

AND MY WILL AND MIND IS AND I DIRECT that the books and accounts of the said newspaper called *The Times and Evening Mail* shall be made up half yearly AND that the several parties interested shall receive their respective dividends and shares of the profits thereof from the last division preceding my decease AND as the said papers were raised under my inspection and I well know that by dissention and difference of opinion between the parties entitled thereto as to the mode of their being conducted the property may be injured and the fabrics I have raised tumble to the ground I do therefore entreat and it is my will and I direct that my said son John may and shall continue to have the sole management of the said papers And it is my wish that my said son John shall be paid by the proprietors of the said newspaper called *The Times* for his conduct and management of the said newspaper at the rate following that is to say the salary of £1000 per annum for every year in which the said newspaper shall produce over and above the said £1000 a net profit of £5000 per annum or upwards And in case in any year the net profits of the said newspaper over and above the said £1000 shall be less than £5000 per annum then that the said annual salary of £1000 shall be reduced at and after the rate of £20 for every £100 the said net profits shall be less than the said £5000 in each year And I direct that the several shares of the said newspaper called *The Times* bequeathed by this my Will shall be liable to pay and shall pay to him my said son John in respect of the same at the rate aforesaid according to the proportion that each share is to the whole of the said newspaper And in as much as the conduct and interest of a newspaper concern require the most absolute power in the persons carrying on the same of making allowance and payments at their discretion I do direct that my said Trustees and the survivor of them and the executors and administrators of such survivor shall have full power not subject to the control of any Court or Authority whatsoever to allow of any payments and make any other allowances they or he may think right in passing and settling the accounts of the said newspaper called *The Times* and to act in the trusts thereof as if they were acting for their own behalves and not on the behalf of femes covert infants and others

1812. Dissolution of Partnership existing by virtue of the Indenture of November 10, 1801, between John Walter the elder and John Walter the younger, who agrees to pay his father an annuity of £666 13s. 3d. May 14, 1812.

1827. Articles of Co-partnership between John Walter, of the first part, and George Hicks, of Wimbledon, and Thomas Massa Alsager, of Mecklenburgh Square, of the second part, taken into the business of printing *The Times* and *Evening Mail*; one-eighth to each—in consideration of the sum of £1,875 paid by Hicks and Alsager. The agreement to exist for 21 years. June 27, 1827.

1831. Endorsed that John Walter and T. M. Alsager acquired the share of George Hicks from his executor H. T. Shaw. January 6, 1831.

1838. Chancery Proceedings: Murray v. Walter, Lawson and Alsager, C 13, 1907 in Public Record Office. Mrs. Murray's demand to see accounts, &c.

477

1842. Murray v. Walter, C 13, 1962 in Public Record Office gives the charges of Mrs. Murray and Walter's answers.

1858. Share Register of *The Times.*

[On flyleaf : My dear Walter I send as promised my history of *The Times* and hope it may on some future occasion prove of use to you when the Writer of it can no longer be referred to. Believe me, Yours most truly, A. DOBIE.

John Walter Esq M.P.]

Alexander Dobie, for many years solicitor to *The Times*, records the several assignments and their dates resulting from family and other causes from 1812 to 1858.

(*b*) Correspondence.

Letters to J. W. Croker 1812-1817, with the Croker Papers in the William L. Clements Library, University of Michigan, Ann Arbor.

A few only of Walter's letters are printed in Jennings, L.J., *Croker Papers* (London, 1884, 3 vols.). The Ann Arbor collection comprises 105 vols. of Croker's correspondence with Brougham, Canning, Huskisson, Spencer, Perceval, Lockhart, and some thirty letters from John Walter II.

Publications

Walter, John : *To the Electors of Berkshire on the New System* (1834).

Pamphlet on the Poor Law Bill. No copy has survived. For extracts see *The Times*, May 9, 1834 ; the *Morning Chronicle*, May 12. The latter observes that Mr. Walter's performance is sincere and that he " roars " much more " gently " than his " thundering " Editor.

Houston, M. C. : *A Woman's Memories of World-known Men* (London, 1883, 2 vols.).

I, 14*ff.*, for John Walter II ; his " fancied allegiance to the Whig party," p. 23 ; visit of her father, Edward Jesse, author of *Gleanings in Natural History* (1832) and other works, with Walter to the site of Bear Wood House and their love of the " gentle art of angling," p. 24.

Grant, James : *Random Recollections of the House of Commons*, 1830-1835 (London, 1836).

Pp. 169-172 for a sketch of Mr. Walter, Member for Berkshire.

VI. A NEW SPIRIT IN JOURNALISM

Publications

Hunt, Leigh : *Dramatic Essays.* Edited by William Archer and R. W. Lowe (London, 1894, 3 vols.).

Archer's essay is the only sketch available of the development of modern dramatic criticism.

Clark, Roy Benjamin : *William Gifford, Tory Satirist. Critic and Editor* (Columbia Studies in English, New York, 1930).

Chapter III, pp. 81-102, " The Anti-Jacobin," presents an account of political journalism at the turn of the century with illustrations also from the *Morning Chronicle*, the *Morning Post*, the *Courier*. Chapter VII, pp. 168-244, " The Quarterly Review," describes the circumstances of the foundation and the policy of the new periodical.

Gray, Charles Harold : *Theatrical Criticism in London to* 1795 (Columbia Studies in English, New York, 1931).

" In 1794 the critiques [in *The Times*] are a little better than the worst type of ' theatrical intelligence.' . . . The next year the reports continued, but in the fall the tone became that of mere puffs—' the indefatigable managers,' ' a reign of sense has begun ' and ' crowded audiences ' always manage to proclaim new performers who never fail to score hits. These are the very things that Leigh Hunt took up the cudgels against in 1805." pp. 287-8.

VII. A BATTLE WITH THE POST OFFICE

Manuscript

Francis Freeling to the P.M.G. on the allegations of Cobbett, November 30, 1802. P.R.O., H.O. 42/64.

Francis Freeling to the Postmaster-General on the complaint of Mr. Secretary Canning that letters addressed to the Principal Secretaries of State were subject to delay and that contents of mails had appeared in newspapers before delivery to the Secretaries. P.R.O., F.O.83/14.

Statement made to Postmaster-General in answer to accusations published in *The Times* of July 27, 1807. P.O. MSS.

Affidavit and Pleas of Walter and another at the suit of Freeling, 1807. P.O.

John Walter's Memorial to the Earl of Sandwich and the Earl of Chichester, Postmaster-General, September 10, 1808. P.O. MSS.

Freeling v. Walter, 1808. *Memorial*, P.O. MSS.

To the Right Honorable The Earl of Sandwich & The Right Honorable The Earl of Chichester His Majesty's Postmaster General The Memorial of John Walter Junr of Printing House Square Black Friars

Sheweth,

That your memorialist is with other persons a joint proprietor of a daily morning newspaper called the Times, and that he is entrusted with the sole conduct and Direction of that paper for their common benefit. That in the late and present State of Europe, it was, and is, an important object to acquire the earliest Intelligence of all transactions and occurrences in the different Countries of the Continent, and that for this purpose he had, at a very great Expence, established a line of foreign Correspondence which, if permitted to proceed in its regular Course and to enjoy the established and legal right of delivery, would have answered the purpose for which he made the arrangement already mentioned.

This Plan, it is humbly conceived, your Memorialist had as great right to adopt in order to forward his views of benefitting the concern in which he is engaged and whose management he directs, as any commercial man whose accompting house in London or in any other part of Great Britain is employed in carrying on a trade with foreign countries. That the post office, which is nothing more than a Channel of Conveyance for the public accommodation, has no discretionary power of transmitting or retaining letters coming in the usual way and by the usual means ; and that if such discretionary power is at any time assumed, it is in direct violation of the Constitution of that office, and the right of every individual to an early and regular delivery of such Letters as are entrusted to the care of it ; It is on this principle that your memorialist begs leave to state to your Lordships, as a duty he owes to himself and the public, that under every arrangement which has been made by him for the acquisition of Intelligence by the Foreign Mails he has been thwarted to his great Injury and Detriment.

In the first instance your Memorialist begs leave to state to your Lordships that the letters from his foreign Correspondents, which were originally addressed to him at the place of his Residence, frequently appearing to have been opened, and as your Memorialist conceived, to have been delayed in their regular delivery, he had recourse to a Foreign House of great respectability in the City to allow them to be sent under cover to it, but this friendly Compliance did not long remedy this and other inconveniences which your Memorialist suffered.

That your Lordships may be satisfied of the Truth of this representation, your Memorialist takes the liberty to state an account of one particular transaction ; about the beginning of September 1805, among other first accounts of important news from the Continent, the State Correspondence between Austria, Russia and France appeared in the Times ; a circumstance which might possibly have excited the Jealousy of every Person in the Post Office who may be allowed the privilege of supplying the newspapers with Intelligence and whose Interests are thus put in competition with their duty. The Letters addressed to your Memorialist under Cover to the Mercantile House already mentioned, were now delivered with irregularity, and letters which your Memorialist expected to have been sent him were not received at all. The custom of the Merchants is to send to the Post Office for all their Letters, at the hour announced for their delivery ; the packets are received from a window where the postage is paid for them ; but now several of the Letters containing an Enclosure for your Memorialist were omitted in the Mercantile packet and brought to the Counting House by a Postman some time afterwards with an excuse they had been overlooked.

In the month of October following, three very essential Letters, which the Foreign Correspondent of your Memorialist informed your Memorialist had been sent to him were never received.

Your Memorialist was now apprehensive that Persons in the post office from some motive kept back his Letters. One morning, therefore, when the delivery of a Mail was announced for half past Eleven o'Clock he went to the Mercantile House already alluded to, an hour before that time, and requested that a Complaint of the Non-delivery of letters addressed to that House from the Continent might be immediately made. A clerk was accordingly despatched to the Foreign Office accompanied by your Memorialist and was requested to make the Complaint before he went to the window for the general packet of letters ; the clerk accordingly made his complaint, and about a quarter of an hour afterwards, when he applied at the Window for his Letters, it appeared that the original charge for postage had been subsequently encreased three shillings (the difference of an additional Letter) while that which contained an Enclosure for your Memorialist had been evidently foisted into the packet.

It would be a waste of your Lordships' time, as it would be an insult to your Lordships' understanding, were your Memorialist to make any remarks of his own on this transaction ; however after various unsuccessful expedients no less expensive than difficult, your Memorialist at length received from a person in high official situation permission to order all Letters from Foreign Correspondents to be sent under cover to him in his official capacity : but here again your Memorialist's endeavours failed, even under such protection and with such sanction, to secure the regular delivery of his Foreign letters.

Such have been the difficulties which have been experienced by your Memorialist, such have been the obstructions he has met with in the legal means he has adopted to procure Foreign Intelligence, thus has he been absolutely compelled by the Proceedings which your Memorialist submits to your Lordships' consideration and Investigation, to limit his Foreign Correspondence and at one time to suspend it altogether ; thus has he been thwarted, by some undiscovered means in obtaining the honest gains which he had a right to expect as a reward for the Industry that was employed and the pecuniary risque that was encountered in order to render the Paper in which he has a considerable interest and for whose right Conduct he is responsible, acceptable to the public.

It cannot be supposed by your Memorialist that the Grievances of which he complains are known to your Lordships ; or at least that when known they will not produce an Enquiry into their Cause. It has been suggested to your Memorialist that a Privilege is allowed to Persons in the foreign Department in your Lordships' office, to be Dealers and Traffickers in Foreign Intelligence, and who derive considerable Emolument from such a trade ; these persons cannot therefore be supposed to be well affected to any arrangements that may be made by the proprietor of a newspaper, to secure original Intelligence for himself, as the failure of such Arrangements compels him to purchase at their Price such Information as they can procure for him in common with every other journalist, and thereby not only deprive him of the fruits of his Exertions but the public of the advantages that may be derived from them.

A monopolising Privilege of this description may be attempted to be justified, on the plea of Inadequacy of Salaries of those who derive considerable Emoluments from it; but your Memorialist confidently trusts that your Lordships will not permit it to be acknowledged that in a department of such importance as the post office, over which Persons of your Lordships' high rank and Character are appointed to preside, and where dispatch, regularity and Punctuality are its declared Characteristics, the Servants in a very leading Branch are suffered to derive the principal part of their Emoluments from Fees and Perquisites, the worst way possible of paying Servants and which mode has so lately in another public office met with its requisite reform.

Your Memorialist therefore most respectfully submits the Circumstances herein recited to your Lordships' Wisdom and Justice in the consolatory Confidence that you will apply the Power you possess to redress the Complaints of your Memorialist.

And your Memorialist, as in duty bound, will ever pray

(Signed) JOHN WALTER JUNR.

September 10, 1808

Francis Freeling to Lord Sandwich, Postmaster-General, on the subject of John Walter's complaint, September 11, 1808. Post Office MSS.

Declaration upon Oath proposed to be made by the Comptrollers and Clerks of the Foreign Post Office in reply to the false assertions contained in Mr. Walter's Memorial to the Postmaster-General. P.O.

Lord Chichester to Francis Freeling on Mr. W.'s " improper " memorial, September 13, 1808. P.O.

The Postmaster-General, October 18, 1808, in answer to Mr. Walter's letter of September 20, declining to re-open inquiry made in the previous year. P.O.

Publications

Hemmeon, J. C.: *The History of the British Post Office* (Harvard Economic Studies, Cambridge, Mass.).

The rates of postage of newspapers and the privileges of the clerks during the eighteenth century are given at pp. 47-9 of Mr. Hemmeon's thorough study.

Joyce, Herbert: *The History of the Post Office from its Establishment down to* 1836 (London, 1893).

This work, compiled from official records, provides an indispensable summary of the postal facilities afforded to newspapers and the practices of the newspaper office. The account of the guinea system is candid, but documents are summarized and not quoted. For Freeling v. *The Times* see pp. 347-350.

Melville, Lewis: *The Life and Letters of William Cobbett* (London, 1913, 2 vols,).

The guinea system, Freeling and Lord Auckland, I, 124-8; Cobbett's attempt to depose Freeling, I, 308-14; the answer to Cobbett's charges is in P.R.O., H.O. 42/64, Freeling to Postmaster-General, November 30, 1802.

VIII. THE FIRST STEAM PRESS

Agreements, &c.

1813. Thomas Bensley, George Taylor, Richard Taylor, Friedrich Koenig with John Walter. P.H.S. Papers.

1816. Supplementary Memorandum by which the same parties agree not to sell machines to other newspaper printers below a stated price. P.H.S.

1816. Receipt for cash paid by Walter and agreement signed by Bensley, Koenig and Taylor that the sum covers unrestricted rights to the use of the machines.

1817. Authority to Bauer signed by Koenig. P.H.S.

1818. Koenig and Bauer with John Walter for supplying apparatus and parts of machinery for delivery December 1, 1818. P.H.S.

1818. Letter (December 20, 1818) from Koenig explaining delay in fulfilling promise for delivery by December 1. P.H.S.

Correspondence

Koenig to Walter. Drafts from the Letter-books, 1817-1823 (Würzburg).

Publications

Abridgments of Specifications relating to Printing . . . printed by order of the Commissioners of Patents (London, 1859).

No. 3321 Frederick Koenig, A Method of printing by means of machinery, March 29, 1810 ; No. 3496 Further Improvements on my method of printing by machinery, October 30, 1811 ; No. 3725 Certain additional improvements in my method of printing by means of machinery, July 23, 1813 ; No. 3868 Certain further improvements on my method of printing by means of machinery, December 24, 1814 (*i.e.*, the month following the successful use of the apparatus for the printing of the edition of *The Times* on and after November 29, 1814).

Koenig, F. : *Beschreibung des Modells der ersten von Friedrich Koenig erfundenen Schnellpresse aus dem Jahre*, 1811 (Würzburg, 1908).

Goebel, T. : *Friedrich Koenig und die Erfindung der Schnellpresse* (Stuttgart, 1883, 2nd edition 1906).

Isaacs, George A. : *The Story of the Newspaper Printing Press* (London, 1931).

A practical man's account of the development of the printing press with illustrations which include, on p. 19, a front view and side view of Koenig's first cylinder press, 1811.

IX. PITT AND THE ADDINGTONS

Manuscript

Letters from Hiley Addington ; Articles from the same during 1804-5. P.H.S.

Hiley Addington to Beckett on offers of literary assistance, February 26, 1818. P.R.O., H.O. 42/174.

Publications

Rose, George : *Diaries and Correspondence* (London, 1859-60, 2 vols.).
I, 437, 439, 509 ; II, 111.

Pellew, George : *Life and Correspondence of Lord Sidmouth* (London, 1847, 3 vols.).
Addington, Heriot (of the *True Briton*), Peltier and the " abuse of the freedom of the press " in 1802-3, II, 148-159.

Periodical

The *Examiner*, edited by Leigh Hunt, 1813, *ff.*

X. CHOOSING AN EDITOR

Manuscript

Lewis Goldsmith to Wm. Hamilton, of the Foreign Office, on Vetus, September 24, 1812. P.R.O., F.O. 83/23.

Culling Charles Smith, of the Treasury, to Wm. Hamilton on Goldsmith, Vetus, the *Courrier d'Angleterre*, &c., September 26, 1812. P.R.O., F.O. 83/23.

Publications

[Palmerston, Lord] The *New Whig Guide* (London, 1819).

The *New Tory Guide* (London, 1819).
Collections of pasquinades originally contributed to the *Courier* (Tory) and the *Morning Chronicle* (Whig) from 1815. They are in the tradition of the *Rolliad* and the *Anti-Jacobin*. The *Whig Guide* prints, pp. 73-89, a Narrative in the style of Pope satirising " Vetus," who is placed in the King's Bench, " in bed, with an Editor of a Newspaper standing on one side of him, and a tall lusty Gentleman in spectacles sitting on the other, whom I afterwards learnt was in the Excise . . . by the fireside there were two-penn'orth of coals in a *Times* newspaper," &c. Here " Vetus " seems to have been confused with Combe. The Exciseman is B. Sydenham, Wellesley's agent, a commissioner in that service. *The Times* was of slight political importance at this period, inferior to the *Courier* and the *Chronicle*.

[Hone, William] *The Political House that Jack Built*. Dedicated to " Doctor Slop."

[Hone, William] *Buonapartephobia, or Cursing made Easy to the Meanest Capacity*.
First printed 1815, reissued in 1820 with a new preface which claims that the exposure of Dr. Slop was so effectual that the Doctor was in a few days dismissed from *The Times*. Stoddart left on December 31, 1816.

[Hone, William] *A Slap at " Slop " and the Bridge Street Gang* (London, 1822).
The Life of " Dr. Slop " traces Stoddart's political career from its ultra-Jacobin beginnings, after a refusal to subscribe to the Thirty-nine Articles had disqualified him from ordination, to its ultra-Tory conclusion.

[Hazlitt, William] (*a*) In the *Morning Chronicle* on " Vetus " and *The Times*.
" Vetus," November 19, 1813 ; *Illustrations of " Vetus,"* December 2, 1813 ; December 10, 16, 18 ; January 3, 5 ; collected in Howe VII, 39-72.
The *Bourbons and Bonaparte* in *Morning Chronicle*, December 6, 1813 ; *On the Courier and Times Newspapers*, January 21, 1814 ; Howe VII, 28-33 ; 34-39.

(*b*) In the *Examiner*. *Illustrations of The Times Newspaper*, December 1, 15, 1816 ; January 12, 1817 ; *i.e.*, three articles : *On Apostates, On Modern Lawyers and Poets, On the connection between Toad-eaters and Tyrants* ; collected in Howe VII, 131-152. The last of these articles indicates that Hazlitt was aware that Stoddart had left *The Times*. There were no more attacks on *The Times*. Crabb Robinson engaged himself to present Hazlitt's claims to a position on the paper.

Howe, P. P. : *The Life of William Hazlitt* (London, 1928).
This thorough biography is based upon original authorities which are also relevant at many points to the history of *The Times*, the careers of its proprietors and its literary staff : John Walter II, Henry Crabb Robinson, John Dyer Collier, John Payne Collier, Barron Field, J. T. Stoddart, T. Barnes, T. M. Alsager, T. N. Talfourd. Mr. Howe has overlooked Crabb Robinson's entry of April 25, 1817 : " Walter has been recommended by Barnes to take H[azlitt] as Theatrical Reporter."

[Sterling, Edward] *The Letters of Vetus* [Part I]. From March 10 to May 10, 1812. London : Printed for T. Cadell & W. Davies, Strand ; and Sherwood, Neeley & Jones, Paternoster Row, By J. Swan, 76 Fleet Street, 1812.
Dedication : TO H.R.H. The Prince Regent. " These letters are written in the purest spirit of affection for his royal person. . . ." Preface states that " the first of these letters was suggested to the Author by that of H.R.H. Prince Regent to the Duke of York, on the expiration of his unrestricted Regency . . . the whole were sent up from the country at irregular intervals between the

10 March and the 10 May ; and inserted, as they arrived, in *The Times News-paper*—the most intelligent and independent as it is perhaps the most widely circulated of our daily journals." The aims of the letters are described as :

 1 The more earnest prosecution of the Spanish war.

 2 The cause of the Catholics.

 3 The reappointment of the only minister capable of conducting the former with success and the latter with safety.

The Letters of Vetus [Part II]. From No. VII to No. XV inclusive, being those which were published between July 1 and November 10, 1812, to which have been added Notes, November, 1812. Imprint as before, but printed by C. Baldwin, New Bridge Street.

The Letters of Vetus, Part III, imprint as before, London, 1814.

[Stoddart's] Prospectus, 1817. *Not Connected with the Paper called The Times. Prospectus of a New Daily Paper, called The Day and New Times published every morning at six o'clock under the direction of a Professional Gentleman, Author of the Leading Articles which appeared for several Years in the " Times," during the great Struggle with Buonaparte, and the Re-establishment of Order in Europe.* (February 1, 1817.)

 " Those who are in the habit of attending to the productions of the daily Press, are well aware, that the *leading articles* in the Paper called the ' TIMES,' (and which, for greater distinction, we may henceforth denominate the *old* Times) had been, for several years, exclusively written by a Professional Gentleman. The Writer was understood, from his situation in life, and from the independence of his character, to be above any slavish control ; and it was clearly seen, by the consistency of his articles, that he was actuated by a steadiness of principle, and capable, from long habit and experience, of applying that principle to daily emergencies, and to the great criterion of public feeling. It was, moreover, evident, that he felt it a duty to place nothing crudely before the Public, but to store his mind with the best information that circumstances would permit, and to discuss the different topics with an earnest desire of eliciting from them new and useful information. Hence he was enabled, during the latter years of the struggle with Buonaparte, not only to maintain the cause of liberty, to combat despotism, and to unmask false glory, but to predict, with more accuracy than any other writer, the results of the great contest, through all its stages. To him, and to him alone, belongs this part of the reputation attached to the Times : and hence his name has become, to a great degree, identified with that of the Journal in which he wrote. The unprecedented increase in the sale of the work, afforded the best criterion of the estimation in which the writer was held by the Public : and the managing Proprietor had testified a similar opinion by the terms of his contract with him. From that contract, however, the Proprietor thought fit to recede ; and the Writer, with regret, perceived himself under the necessity of transferring the *spirit* of the TIMES to a new undertaking."

XI. *See* CHAPTER V.

XII. THOMAS BARNES

Correspondence

With Charles Babbage, B.M., MSS. Addl. 37186, 390, 471 ; 37187, 210, 219, 443 [1832-3].

 John Cam Hobhouse, Lord Broughton, B.M., MSS. Addl. 36458, 286 ; 36464, 374 ; 36465, 160 ; 36467, 2, 89, 123 [1820-1833].

Leigh Hunt, B.M., MSS. Addl. 38108, 81, 92, 38109, 156, 38523, 21, 19, 18, 103, 108 [1813-1836].
John George Lambton, Lord Durham, Lambton Castle Papers [1833-4].
Sir Denis Le Marchant, Chobham Papers [1833-4].
Robert Owen, Manchester Cooperative Society Archives.
John Walter, P.H.S. [1819, 1834].
See also Chapters XXII and XXIV.

Printed Works

(a) Essays contributed to periodicals

I. THE REFLECTOR. A quarterly Magazine on subjects of Philosophy, Politics and the Liberal Arts. Conducted by the Editor of the *Examiner*.

1810. October. *On the Claims of Propertius*, pp. 52-8 ; signed " T.B." Robert Herrick, with a Latin translation of *The Night Piece*, pp. 242-244 ; signed " T.B." On [Antony] Stafford's *Niobe* (2nd edition, London, 1611), pp. 59-62 ; signed " T.B."

1811. January. *On Theophrastus—prefaced with some Remarks on the supposed Inferiority of the Ancients to the Moderns in the Arts of Ridicule*, pp. 409-424 ; signed " T.B."
Dress and Character—a slight Sketch, pp. 477-479 ; signed " T.B."
October. *Project for Making Beaux and Belles useful*, pp. 366-380 ; signed " T.B." Sapphic verses *In Sending a Bouquet to a Lady*, pp. 443-4 ; signed " T.B."

II. THE EXAMINER. A Sunday paper on Politics, Domestic Economy and Theatricals. Edited by Leigh Hunt.

1813. August 15. Introduction on the dearth of oratorical ability in Parliament. Lord Castlereagh, Mr. Ponsonby, Mr. Vansittart and Mr. Fitzgerald, Mr. C. W. Wynne and Mr. Bankes, Mr. Tierney, Mr. W. Smith and Mr. Wilberforce, Sir W. Garrow and Sir S. Romilly, Mr. Canning, Mr. B. Bathurst and Mr. Ryder, Mr. Grattan ; signed " Criticus."

1814. Mr. Wellesley Pole and Mr. Croker, Lord Milton and Lord Morpeth, Mr. Creevey and Mr. Brand, the City Members, Sir William Scott, Dr. Duigenan and General Montagu Mathew, Mr. Robinson and Mr. Peel, Mr. Rose, Mr. Yorke and Mr. Stephen, Sir John Newport and Sir H. Parnell, Sir Francis Burdett, Mr. Huskisson and Mr. Horner, the Speaker of the House of Commons, Mr. Whitbread.

1814. The *Examiner*, August 14. *Note at the conclusion of the portrait of Whitbread.*
" And now, my dear Hunt, having finished one part of my career, I must be allowed to return you my grateful acknowledgments for the candour and liberality with which you have frequently, in the course of these articles, given publicity to opinions which were at variance with your own. This conduct did not surprise me, nor did I ever think it necessary to apologize to you for the expression of my sentiments. I had known your turn of mind too well from the earliest youth to offer you such an insult : but, at the same time, I am glad that I have been partly instrumental in shewing to the public, what I always knew, that the man whom they perhaps considered as merely an ingenious politician, conscientiously supporting his favourite opinions, has yet a regard for the freedom of truth, superior to all considerations of self-love or self-interest.
" Your's, very sincerely, B.
" I would give my name at length, if I thought it would do any credit to your friendship ; but as that might not be the result, I shall decline throwing aside the mysterious veil which gives so much importance to a Critic."

1814. September 25 and after : The Earl of Liverpool, Lord Holland, Viscount Sidmouth ; signed " Criticus."

1813. Theatrical Examiner, No. 126 to No. 159, unsigned.

1814.   do.   No. 160 to No. 185, unsigned.
 The controversy with Hazlitt on Kean's *Iago* was initiated July 24, 1814, in an article which concluded August 7. Barnes criticised these two papers on September 4. Hazlitt replied on September 11, and Barnes had the last word on September 18.

1814. From the *Examiner*, December 25. Editor's note.
 " In the other departments of a Paper of this kind, Theatrical Criticism has, of late years, held the principal place ; and it was in particular a favourite department with the readers of the *Examiner*, the Editor of which, in that as well as in a previous Journal, had done something towards increasing the interest of the subject, and exciting an additional attention to it on the part of other Newspapers. Sickness first, and imprisonment afterwards, prevented him, in this instance, from going on as he wished ; and it has been not a little unfortunate, that the friend who was engaged to supply his place for the last two years, and who was eminently qualified to do the subject justice, has seen his own wishes thwarted by sickness also."

III. 1814. THE CHAMPION. A weekly Political and Literary Journal. Edited by John Scott.
 Introductory Dialogue between a Bookseller and an Author, January 2, 1814. Portraits of Authors : 1, Southey ; 2, Campbell ; 3, Scott ; 4, Moore ; 5, Montgomery ; 6, Coleridge ; 7, Crabbe ; 8, Byron ; 9, Wordsworth ; 10, Rogers ; 11, Gifford ; 12, Wolcott ; 13, Cowper ; 14, Thomson ; 15, Goldsmith ; signed " Strada."

1815. 16, Shakespeare, Spenser and Milton ; 17, Mrs. Opie ; 18, Miss Edgworth. (Papers signed " S." from March 19-December 24 on Kean, Leigh Hunt's poetry, Elgin Marbles, are possibly by the same hand.)

(b) Books.
[" Criticus "] *Parliamentary Portraits, or Sketches of the Public Character of some of the Most Distinguished Speakers of the House of Commons, originally printed in the Examiner* (London, Baldwin, 1815). Does not include Liverpool, Holland, Sidmouth, Members of the House of Lords. Barnes intended to sketch portraits of Peers but did not proceed. See *Examiner* (*supra*), September 25, 1814.

 Biographie Critique des Orateurs les plus distingués et principaux membres du Parlement d'Angleterre. Traduit par Ch. Malo (Paris, 1820).
 Translation of the English publication. Malo was a student of English and American institutions. His *Panorama d'Angleterre, ou Ephémerides anglaises politiques et littéraires* was published in 1818.

Notices by Contemporaries
MEMOIRS, DIARIES, REMINISCENCES, OF.

 (a) MANUSCRIPTS.
Henry Crabb Robinson : Diaries and Reminiscences, with shorthand transcripts by R. T. Herford at Dr. Williams's Library, London. Many references from 1812.

Charles Fulke Greville : Diaries, B.M., MSS. Addl. 41105. Many references after 1830.

 (b) PRINTED.
Autobiography of Leigh Hunt.
 Chapter IV, Schooldays, continued : " Equally good scholar [with Mitchell] but of a less zealous temperament, was Barnes, who stood next me

on the Deputy Grecian form, and who was afterwards identified with the sudden and striking increase of the *Times* newspaper its fame and influence," etc. Chapter XII, Literary Warfare. Barnes's part in the *Examiner*, &c.

Other Works by Leigh Hunt.

Sonnet *To Thomas Barnes, Esq., written from Hampstead* : " Dear Barnes, whose native taste, solid and clear," &c., which originally appeared in the *Examiner*, February 14, 1813, is reprinted in Leigh Hunt's *The Feast of the Poets* (1814), p. 156.

The Descent of Liberty, by Leigh Hunt (1814), dedicated to Barnes as the author's schoolfellow. " How far he was my superior in general knowledge, and the anticipation of a manly judgement I well remember."

Lord Byron and some of his Contemporaries (London, 1828, 2 vols.).
References to Barnes at II, 127 and 261.

Collier, John Payne : *An Old Man's Diary, Forty Years Ago* (London, four parts, 1871-2, II, pp. 14-15).
Barnes's early days in the Temple.

Redding, Cyrus : *Fifty Years' Recollections* (London, 1860, 3 vols.), II, 205 ; III, 22.
Barnes and the *Champion*.

Autobiography of Benjamin Robert Haydon. Edited by E. Blunden (Oxford, 1927).
" The usual companions of my relaxation at this time were Hazlitt, the Hunts, Barnes of *The Times*, Wilkie, Jackson, C. Lamb," p. 210. Keats wrote to Benjamin Bailey, May 28, 1818 : " Yesterday I dined with Hazlitt, Barnes and Wilkie, at Haydon's. The topic was the Duke of Wellington—very amusingly pro-and-con'd."

Memoirs, Journal and Correspondence of Thomas Moore (London, 1854).
Many references, 1822-1830 ; correspondence with Thomas Barnes and Philip Crampton, viii, 268. Leigh Hunt to Moore on " Strada " of the *Champion* : " He is, as you handsomely acknowledge, a very clever fellow, but he is apt, also, to go to extremes both in his censure and his praise. . . ." viii, 172-3.

The Creevey Papers (London, 1905).
Several references after 1831.

Richardson, John : *Recollections, Political, Literary,* &c. (London, 1856, 2 vols.).
Barnes as scholar, cricketer and swimmer at Cambridge, &c., and as journalist. B. " raised journalism in this country to a position of which the most zealous of our forefathers never dreamed. . . . It was in his capacity as editor that I became more intimately connected with him than I previously had been. I aver that I never met with a kinder friend, a more agreeable companion, or a more honourable man." II, 193-200. Richardson was an Etonian, at Trinity Hall, Cambridge in Barnes's time, and went to the Bar, to journalism, and finally into Orders of the Church of England.

Talfourd, T. N. : *Memorials of Charles Lamb* (London, 1848, 2 vols.). " One of the soundest and most elegant scholars whom the School of Christ's Hospital ever produced, Mr Thomas Barnes, was a frequent guest at Lamb's Chambers in the Temple, . . ." Vol. II, pp. 179-186. The best contemporary sketch of Barnes's personality.

Brougham, Lord : *Life and Times* (London, 1871, 3 vols.). One Reference, III.
" At the trial in 1820, we, the counsel, had communicated with the paper through Barnes, the chief editor, whom Denman and Williams had known well at Cambridge. . . . I had occasion many years after to appoint Barnes's brother to a place of emolument, which he had begged me to do. I received a letter saying I had made him my debtor for life. He paid off the debt by instalments of abuse—I won't say daily, but almost weekly. . . ." II, 276.

Jerdan, W. : *Characteristic Letters communicated by Men I have Known.* " Leisure Hour " (June, 1869). Quotes two unimportant letters from Barnes.

Anonymous Notices by Contemporaries

A Shy at the " Great Gun." The Blue-Coat Boy ; or Domestic Reminiscences of Mister Thomas Bounce, Driver of " the Turnabout." By His Friend and Associate, Abel Funnefello. With Illustrations by Andrew Crookedshanks. (London, Effingham Wilson, 1837.)

A satire upon Barnes. The text might be by C. M. Westmacott. One of the four plates depicts " Mrs. B. ' flaring up ' or a Canister for the Great Gun," *i.e.*, Mrs. B. is throwing a breakfast dish at the head of Mr. B., who drops *The Times* and ducks. The publication, announced to be completed in twelve parts, ceased without notice with the second instalment.

An Old Apprentice of the Law : *Editors and Newspapers of the Last Generation*, in " Fraser's Magazine," I and II (February, 1862) : " A man scarcely less known thirty years ago than Cobbett, was Tom Barnes, editor of *The Times. . . ."* 4 pp. ; with mentions of Stoddart, Murray, Sterling.

London Editors and Political Writers III : The *Morning Herald* and the early days of *The Times.* " London Society " (November, 1863).

N.B.—The evidence of the references in the *British Monitor* (Goldsmith), 1820 ; *John Bull* (Potter), 1820 ; the *Age* (Westmacott), 1834 ; the *Satirist* (Barnard Gregory), 1837 ; *Weekly Dispatch* (Harmer and " Publicola " Williams), 1840, needs to be handled with extreme caution. The *Monitor, Satirist, Bull*, &c., confine themselves to sly remarks on Barnes's alleged strong partiality for oysters and for gin (" cold, without "), the *Age* other equally human recreations ; but the attentions of the *Dispatch* (August and September, 1840) extend to the character of Dinah Mary Mondet and that of her mother, Mrs. Dunn. It has to be admitted that Barnes's attacks on Harmer, proprietor of the *Dispatch*, and Williams, his editor, were provocative.

See also works cited under Chapters XXII and XXIV.

XIII. THE GOAL OF INDEPENDENCE

Manuscript Sources

LONDON

Public Record Office.

The bulletins of Thomas Elde Darby from 1815 to 1825 and Lewis Goldsmith after 1825, agents attached to the British Embassy, and correspondents of London newspapers (see for Darby F.O. 97/168 ; for Goldsmith F.O. 97/169), contain many references to English and French journals.

PARIS

(*a*) Archives des Affaires Etrangères at the Quai d'Orsay, Paris,

for the correspondence of the Marquis d'Osmond, Ambassador in London, with the Duc de Richelieu, Foreign Minister of Louis XVIII, which, during the years 1816-1819, include many references to the London journals, including *The Times*. See especially Vol. 609-12 of the *Correspondance Politique* (Angleterre). *Cf.*

(*b*) Bibliothèque Nationale, Paris.

MSS. No. 20280 contains several hundred letters between Richelieu and Decazes, 1817-1821, with references to the Press at nn. 53, 158, 195, 305.

(c) Archives Nationales, Paris.

Vols. F-7 6631 (n. 619), 6633 (n. 1421), 6634 (n. 1666), 6239, May 7, 1818 ; January 9, 1820, in the series Affaires Politiques, Première Restauration, 1814-1830, contain references to the English Press and to Darby, Perry, Stoddart, Street, Goldsmith.

Printed Sources

LONDON

Chabannes, Marquis de : *L'Argus Politique* (Londres, Lewis, 1818). Seven numbers, August 14-September 11 and October 6, with Prospectus.

"Fouché fut le premier qui, par la direction qu'il sut donner à la presse en France et par la venalité des journalistes étrangers qu'il soudoya, organisa un système de correspondance qui trompa si souvent toute l'Europe. Qui aurait pu croire que ses successeurs parviendraient à le surpasser ? Ils n'ont que trop connu l'influence que les journaux ont sur l'opinion publique en général ; ils ne savent que trop que cette opinion influe plus particulièrement en Angleterre sur les démarches de ceux qui sont à la tête de son gouvernement, et comme ils sont persuadés que le Cabinet de St James exerce une influence prépondérente sur les décisions politiques de l'Europe, c'est en Angleterre qu'il leur a paru le plus intéresser de déployer tout leur art ; aussi est-ce à Londres que nous voyons paraître chaque jour les mensonges les plus grossiers et les inventions les plus atroces.

"Il est temps et plus que temps d'opposer une barrière à ce torrent de calomnies. J'en connais la source, j'en dévoilerai le but. Je sais le nom de ces correspondants anonimes, les personnes de qui ils reçoivent leurs instructions et leurs prétendues informations ; les canaux par lesquels leurs lettres arrivent en Angleterre, les agents qui les portent aux journalistes à Londres, et qui n'ont pas toujours été discrets sur les sommes qu'ils répandent. Enfin, je tiens tous les fils de cette trame infernale, et ayant pour but de le démasquer, j'ai cru qu'il était du devoir de tout homme qui accuse de se nommer et je n'ai point hesité à me déclarer l'auteur de cette feuille."

Notwithstanding his mention of a tissue of calumnies which he finds in *The Times*, the author avoids giving names. " Nous pourrions même donner au besoin les noms de ces agents. L'un d'eux, un certain M. D . . . y, est ici en ce moment courant chez les journalistes qui écrivent dans un sens contraire aux désirs de son mandataire, et a inserer, dans leurs feuilles les lettres qui leur seraient adressées de Paris. J'affirme et garantie ce fait." *Argus*, No. 1, p. 6. B.N., Paris, G. 4862.

[Croker, J. W.] " O'Meara's Napoleon in Exile " in *Quarterly Review*, October, 1822.

This thorough inquiry into the allegations of O'Meara makes no reference to his charge against *The Times*, and John Walter urged further exposure of his character. It was proposed that Finlayson, librarian of the Admiralty, with whom O'Meara had been in close correspondence since 1815, should write a second article for the *Quarterly* and that extracts should be published in *The Times*. " I hope," wrote John Walter to Croker on March ——, 1823, " that Mr Murray will not be obliged to delay the publication much. The article will of course be immediately copied into *The Times*, when an opportunity will be afforded of intimating the manner in which I mean to reply to the infamous slanders against the journal." The project came to nothing and the O'Meara-Finlayson correspondence was destroyed in 1824.

One other charge against *The Times* seems to have been brought. In 1830 the *Messager des Chambres* reproduced a rumour that the correspondence of *The Times* was concocted in the office of the *Gazette de France*. The paper replied that as it had, on the contrary, attacked the *Gazette*, logic proved that the *Messager* was in the pay of *The Times*. (*Cf. The Times* July 20, 1832.)

Despatches, Correspondence and Memoranda of F.M. Arthur Duke of Wellington (London, 1867, 8 vols.).

      References to the Press at v, 54 (to Croker) ; vii, 568 (purchase of the *Morning Herald*, 1831) ; vii, 521 (Duke of Cumberland and *The Times*). Vol. IV has important references to the French Press.

Emden, Cecil S. : *The People and the Constitution* (Oxford, 1933), contains valuable chapters (III, pp. 34-72, and IV, pp.73-97) on " Public Opinion and Government," which notices the function of the newspaper as an index of opinion.

Temperley, Harold : *The Foreign Policy of Canning*, 1822-1827 (London, 1925), pp. 297-316. Of the greatest importance for the present section are: Chapter XIII, The Press and Public Opinion ; (1) The British and Foreign Press (1820-7) ; (2) Canning's Personal View of the Power and Use of the Press ; (3) Secret versus Open Diplomacy ; (4) General Attitude towards Press and Public Opinion ; and the notes at pp. 512-3. The writer provides for the first time many valuable references in original documents to the relations between English and French politicians and journalists, and to the use of the Press by politicians. " Even *The Times* and the *New Times* occasionally received articles and inspiration from Ultra sources, and sometimes, apparently, both news and gold from France " (p. 299). Mr. Temperley quotes Goldsmith *pace* Corbière to the effect that the French Government paid *The Times* money for two years under Decazes. French subsidies to the *Courier* and the *Morning Chronicle* during 1823-4 (p. 300). There are numerous references to *The Times* in the course of the work.

Webster, C. K. : *The Foreign Policy of Castlereagh*, 1812-1815 (London, 1931), pp. 41-3. Chapter 3, " Court, Cabinet, Parliament and Public Opinion," provides an account of the periodical Press, principally the *Courier*, the *Morning Chronicle* and *The Times*. Many references to the journals occur in the body of the work ; as also in Webster, *Foreign Policy of Castlereagh*, 1815-1822 (London, 1925, second photolitho edition with additional appendix, 1934), especially pp. 23-8, for the Press and public opinion of this period and the activities of Croker, Arbuthnot and Decazes.

Goldsmith, Lewis (1768-1846), editor of the revolutionary journal, the *Argus* (Paris, 1803—thrice weekly), under an arrangement with Talleyrand, who forced him to insert an article attacking all the London newspaper editors, written by Badini, formerly editor of *Bell's Weekly Messenger*. After four months Goldsmith was dismissed, returned to London, and secured journalistic employment from Lord Liverpool. There is much incidental revelation of journalistic venality in Goldsmith's *British Monitor* (January 4, 1818-April 10, 1825), a continuation of his *Anti-Gallican Monitor and Anti-Corsican Chronicle* (January 27, 1811-December 29, 1817).

      Replying to an attack on Decazes which the *New Times* printed upon his arrival in London as Ambassador of France, Goldsmith, in an article " The Duke de Cazes " in the *British Monitor*, July 23, 1820, says that the Editor of the *New Times* " received a daily douceur for every attack on M De Cazes during his Ministry. Perhaps the same temptations are held out to the editor of The English Drapeau Blanc, to whom, a busy meddling Frenchman, a Marquis of the old régime, is attached as a sort of co-adjutor. This Foreigner is besieging our Newspaper Offices with articles against the newly arrived ambassador. He offered to pay two guineas for the insertion of only 12 lines in our respectable newspapers, and also promised to furnish them with many articles for which he would pay handsomely. . . . The newspaper Editors have, however, all declined the effusions of the Marquis." The Marquis indicated was doubtless Chabannes (*vide supra*). In 1822 Goldsmith published his *Observations on the Appointment of the Rt. Hon. Geo. Canning to the Foreign Department*, in which he championed the personal and political merits of that Minister. He was in communication with Canning in 1823, and in 1824 was sent to Paris as a confidential agent in succession to Darby, whose " notoriety . . . rather than any fault of his own renders it impossible to continue to derive the same advantage from his services " (Stuart to Canning, December 2, 1822, F.O. 97/168 ; and *cf.* Temperley, *op. cit.*, p. 303). Goldsmith was Paris Correspondent of *The Times* from 1831 until his death. His daughter Georgiana married Lord Lyndhurst in 1837.

PARIS

Charléty, S. : *La Restauration*, 1815-30, t. IV in Lavisse, *Histoire de France Contemporaine* (Paris, 1921).
　　　　p. 126 " Decazes defendit sa conduit dans le *Times*."

Dechamps, Jules : *Chateaubriand en Angleterre* (Paris, 1934).
　　　　Chateaubriand's threat to prosecute the editor of *The Times*, the *correspondance privée* of Decazes, the connexions of the ultra-royalists with Stoddart, pp. 11-48.

De Montenon, Jean : *La France et la Presse Étrangère en* 1816 (Paris, Perrin, 1933), describes the mission confided by the Duc de Richelieu, Foreign Minister of Louis XVIII, to Amable de Baudus de Villenôve. Baudus, who had been editor of a French journal, *Le Spectateur du Nord*, published in Hamburg 1796-1802, undertook a confidential journey through Switzerland, Germany and Europe reporting on the conditions of the Press in letters to Richelieu and Hauterive, Director of the Archives des Affaires Étrangères. Colonel de Montenon prints Baudus's reports, his propagandist articles in various journals, correspondence with ambassadors and editors, &c.

[Salgues, Jacques B.] *Les Mille et une calomnies ou Extraits des Correspondances Privées insérés dans les journaux anglais et allemands pendant le Ministère de M. le Duc Decazes* (Paris, 1822, 2 vols.).
　　　　Translations of articles published during 1818 and 1819 under the heading " Private Correspondence " in the *Courier, Morning Chronicle, Sun, Star, British Monitor, The Times.* Salgues, born 1760, was formerly Professor of Rhetoric at Sens, his birthplace, and later adopted journalism as a profession.

XIV. A STRUGGLE FOR PUBLIC OPINION

Manuscript

An example of political discrimination in the placing of Government advertisements may be seen in Admiralty Papers, P.R.O., Ad. 1/3485.

LIST OF PAPERS IN WHICH NAVAL ADVERTISEMENTS ARE TO BE INSERTED

Peel's list, March 16, 1835, was as follows :—	Melbourne's list, May 1, 1835, was as follows :—
Gazette	*Gazette*
Times (always)	*Morning Advertiser*
Morning Herald	*Times* [*always* is crossed out]
Morning Post	*Morning Chronicle* (*always* is inserted)
Standard (always)	*Courier*
Nautical Magazine	*Sun*
Albion (always)	*Globe and Traveller*
	Public Ledger

* " Sir, I take the liberty of offering for your service the *Standard* newspaper " (Stanley Lees Giffard to Robert Peel, December 8, 1834, B.M., MSS. Addl. 40404, 304).
　　It will be observed that the *Morning Chronicle* does not figure on Peel's List and that *The Times* is the only Conservative morning journal on Melbourne's, but that to the *Morning Chronicle* the word *always* is attached, as a supplementary note. The word is at the same time removed from *The Times.*

Publications

Cobbett, William : *The Political Proteus. A View of the Public Character and Conduct of R. B. Sheridan Esq.* (London, 1804).

Sheridan's power of inspiring the press ; his influence able to prevent publication of news inconvenient to him, p. 206.

Cobbett, William : *Weekly Register,* February 8, 1823 ; coll. 356-381 : " The Bourbon War and the London Newspaper Press."

On the " stupid and beastly old *Times* " with the affidavits for stamp purposes, by Charles Bell, James Carden, Mary Carden, Alex Brodie, Anna Brodie.

Babylon the Great, A Dissection and Demonstration of Men and Things in the British Capital (London, 1825, 2 vols.), contains seven chapters (III.-IX. in vol. II.) on the Press generally, and certain specific journals, weekles and magazines. " Among the whole diurnal publications of the British metropolis *The Times* obviously deserves the first place " (pp. 98-111 for a characterization of the paper).

Hazlitt, William : " The Periodical Press " in the *Edinburgh Review,* May, 1824. The article has the appearance of having been delayed in publication. " The *Times* Newspaper is, we suppose, entitled to the character it gives itself, of being the ' Leading Journal of Europe ' and is perhaps the greatest engine of temporary opinion in the world. It is the lungs of the British Metropolis, the mouthpiece, oracle and echo of the Stock Exchange ; the representation of the mercantile interest. . . . It takes up no fallen cause, fights no up-hill battle ; advocates no great principle . . . it is ever strong upon the strong side." Hazlitt gives greater space to the *New Times,* describing Stoddart's venture as " this new Morning Paper." It was " new " in 1817. The paper is reprinted in Howe, P. P. : *The Complete Works of William Hazlitt* (London, 1933), vol. XVI., pp. 211-239, with the editor's notes at pp. 432-4. *The Times* noticed Hazlitt's article on August 28, 1823 : " We are not regular readers of the *Edinburgh Review* ; it has long fallen from that eminence, merited or not, which made it a sort of duty not to be entirely ignorant of its contents. Its present contributors, for the most part, are lads at the two English Universities, or law-students, yet innocent of law, who have now and then occasion for a few guineas beyond their quarter's allowance, and to whose wants Mr Jeffrey generously administers by paying 20 1. a sheet for their crude lucubrations. The main prop and stay of the *Review* for moral, political, critical and metaphysical discussion is poor Wm. Hazlitt, whose malignity even is not sufficient, in our mind, to convert our pity for his infirmities into hatred for his mischievous intentions," &c. " The editor should be cautious how he allows a discarded servant to bespatter and scandalise his employer." As Mr. Walter had retired from the direction of *The Times* the reaction shown in the leading article may be taken as that of Barnes, who had originally been responsible for the introduction of Hazlitt into Printing House Square.

The Periodical Press of Great Britain and Ireland, or an Inquiry into the State of the Public Journals chiefly as regards their moral and political influence (London, 1824).

[The Times] " parliamentary reports have invariably been the best in London . . . it is a pity that . . . it should be so cumbered with advertisements . . . the Cockney oracle." pp. 105-6.

A Student-at-Law : *The Fourth Estate : or The Moral Influence of the Press* (London, 1839).

An enthusiastic address to Thomas Spring Rice urging total repeal of taxes on knowledge as " The Press is now the National Pulpit." At p. 15 the writer reprints in a folding table the totals for three months of penny stamps issued to the newspapers of all England and Scotland, Stamp Office, dated October, 1838. At p. 18 he affirms that each number of *The Times* actually sold, 11,400 daily, is read by 10 persons ; the *Morning Chronicle*, 7 persons ; the *Morning Post*, 2 persons. The list of "Illustrious and other Members of the Press" is inaccurate.

Turner, Ralph E. : *James Silk Buckingham*, 1786-1855 (London, 1934).

Although he misquotes their titles, Professor Turner has diligently read some of the newspapers of the period, and his book supplies material of value. Professor Turner, however, seems not to be interested in Buckingham's ambition to become a paid Whig press-manager. For a note on this the reader should turn to J. R. M. Butler's *The Passing of the Great Reform Bill*, which does not figure in Turner's otherwise inclusive bibliography.

Wickwar, W. H. : *The Struggle for the Freedom of the Press*, 1819-1832 (London, 1928), supersedes, for its period, the work of C. H. Collett, though accepting the early nineteenth-century Radical view that "freedom" of the Press was incompatible with stamping. The book is valuable for its documentation on the libel laws. A poor index is counterbalanced by a list of authorities covering 7 pp.

XV. CATHOLIC EMANCIPATION

Manuscript

Letters from P. C. Scarlett, H. Brougham, D. C. Wrangham to Thomas Barnes. P.H.S. Papers.

Printed

John Bull, the *Standard*, *St. James's Chronicle*, and other journals.

XVI. "THE ADVOCATE OF REFORM"

Jephson, Henry : *The Platform* (London, 1892, 2 vols.)

An invaluable history of political agitation by public meeting, from 1760 to modern times. The section on the (first) Reform Bill contains an excellent account of the action of *The Times* in encouraging public meetings (II, 67-78). The second volume concludes with a summary of the value of public assembly in a democratic society. The Press, Mr. Jephson thinks, only partly fulfils public requirements of discussion. The work is well documented and indexed. There are many references to *The Times*.

Carpenter's Political Magazine. Volume for 1831.

Radical criticisms of *The Times*, pp. 129-134 ; 188-194.

Fraser's Magazine : Article on " The New Parliament," June, 1831.

Tory criticisms. " The retirement of Mr. Ward from the City when he was so fully prepared and resolved to stand the brunt of the contest, was, to our thinking a deep misfortune. It was against him that the brutal bullying of *The Times* newspaper was first directed. His committee absolutely quailed under it. They took fright at the first volley fired from the guns of Printing House Square." p. 640.

Idem : " The Gallery of Literary Characters," December, 1831, pp. 609-10.

A lithographic portrait by Alfred Crowquill of Lord Brougham as " The Editor of *The Times*" illustrated No. XIX of the series. " Our artist has taken him in the act of writing a leading article. The hour is three—just in time for the latest touch for the morning."

Davis, H. W. C. : *The Age of Grey and Peel* (Oxford, 1929).

Penetrating study of political ideas and party developments 1765-1852, but with little attention to Press management.

XVII. "WAR WITH *THE TIMES*"
and
XVIII. THE WHIG OFFENSIVE

Manuscript

Place, Francis : Correspondence B.M., MSS. Addl. 35148, 72.

F. Place to Sir Francis Burdett, July 24, 1830, on the establishment of a new daily newspaper to support Reform. The proposal originally made in 1828 fell through on account of the flight of Rowland Stephenson, a banker whose defalcations upset the City.

F. Place to Joseph Parkes, July 17, 1834, in the *Morning Chronicle*. " An open, impudent rogue like *The Times* is taken for what he really is, and there can neither be any mistake nor doubt about him. He says we watch the public propensities and then endeavour to lead them by an ardent zeal. . . ." The rest of the letter is about Brougham. " I hope and believe that he is now our master, and that he will be the Whigs' master. . . . If, for instance, the Chancellor begin with some measure likely to be popular, e.g. newspaper stamps . . ." 35149, 308.

F. Place to Joseph Hume, September 9, 1834 . . . " the scandalous abuse of the Bloody old *Times*. . . . Few men were better understood by the political and gossiping portions of the people than Brougham, and *The Times*, &c., could do him no actual mischief. One good I hope they will do to the people by stimulating Brougham to . . . promote the repeal of the Newspaper Stamp Duty : Putting all on a level in this respect . ·. . will punish in an exemplary manner the proprietors of the more than rascally *Times*." 35149, 311.

F. Place, Memorandum on the daily Press (1836) : " The Tories found it convenient to make certain arrangements with its (*The Times*) managers to become their base tool." Place describes the other newspapers and adds calculations of the cost of establishing a new daily—the tax having been lowered to a penny. The figures, of great interest and value, were obtained from Stevens of the *Public Ledger* and Black of the *Morning Chronicle*. 35149, 250-311. For the prospectuses of the ill-fated *Constitutional*, London Daily Morning Newspaper, to appear May 23, 1836, and the Metropolitan Newspaper Company, capital £60,000, see 35150.

Publications

Aspinall, A. : *Lord Brougham and the Whig Party* (Manchester, 1927).

An able book, based on original sources. There are numerous references to *The Times*, the *Morning Chronicle*, the *Courier*, &c., but the book does not undertake to investigate Brougham's attitude towards the press.

Buckley, Jessie : *Joseph Parkes of Birmingham* (London, 1926).

While Parkes's connexions with the Press are not fully treated there are several references to the *Morning Chronicle*. Parkes's quarrel with Brougham (in which he sided with Lord Durham) is not described. At p. 144 there is a letter from Parkes to Durham describing the scene in the *Chronicle* office when Parkes objected to Black's allowing Quin to write abuse of *The Times* and succeeded in getting the paragraphs cut. Six months later Parkes left the *Chronicle* and thereafter used the *Spectator* in Durham's interests. " Barnes goes gallantly," he wrote to Durham at the height of the campaign against Brougham. Parkes's letters to Durham from 1833 are full of references to Press activities in London, Birmingham and Manchester, and newspaper matters. Miss Buckley quotes from a number of these.

Campbell [John], Lord : *Lives of the Lord Chancellors* (London, 1869, 8 vols.).
" Meeting Lord Melbourne one day at the King's Levée, I said to him :
' What is the matter with your Chancellor this morning ? He seems very
much disturbed ? ' " Lord M. : " Have you not seen this morning's *Times* ? "
etc. viii, pp. 443-4.

The Sketches of H.B. (1830-1841, 11 vols.) ; *An Illustrative Key to the Political
Sketches of H.B.* (London, 1841, 2 vols.).
H.B. was John Doyle, whose signature was made from two I D's super-
imposed and joined. The political sketches in which *The Times* is referred to
occur after 1832 : No. 123 *Peerless Eloquence*, in which the Marquis of London-
derry vents his indignation at the language of *The Times* towards the House of
Lords ; No. 136 *Varnishing—A Sign of The Times* ; No. 154 " Another Sign of
The Times." Lord John Russell endeavours to support the - Reform
Bill, Lord Brougham and Lord Grey are showing it up by means of *The Times* ;
No. 311 " Mackerel." *The Times* had said that law peerages should not be as
cheap as stinking mackerel, though it agreed that " a more honest, upright,
honourable man than Sir Thomas Denman, Chief Justice, does not exist." The
Editor of *The Times* is seen counselling the Chief Justice not to take the offer ;
No. 341 " The Celebrated Vauxhall Performer." *The Times* leads the orchestra
of dispraise of Brougham ; No. 347 " The Centaur " illustrates the remarks of
The Times upon the Act for the Establishment of the Central Criminal Court ;
No. 346 " Vaux-hunting." Lord Durham as huntsman after Brougham, cheer
on the hounds, the foremost being *The Times*.

McLean's *Monthly Sheet of Caricatures, or The Looking Glass* (London, 1831-5).
Brougham, as schoolmaster swinging that " incorrigible varlet," *The Times*,
July, 1835. Many other cartoons in this series depict the paper, symbolized by
the " clock " device.

Hickson, W. E. : *Taxes on Knowledge. Reduction or Abolition of the Newspaper
Stamp Duty.* (The London Review, January, 1836.)
A characteristic Radical effusion. " When *The Times* was sold to the
Carlton Club, or when the principal shareholders in *The Times* became insane
(we know not which happened) and made over half of their subscribers to the
Morning Chronicle, a new light seemed to break in upon the proprietors of the
latter journal," &c. (p. 5). " The writer wishes to put an end to the anonymous
character which newspapers have hitherto maintained, and which is a principal
cause of their present degraded position. The people of England will have
reason to feel eternally indebted to the Whigs if they have the courage to destroy
the anonymous system." (p. 19.)

Knight, Charles : *Passages of a Working Life during Half a Century* (London, 1864,
3 vols.).
At Vol. I., p. 161, Knight describes how he copied in his *Windsor and Eton
Express* the leading article on Koenig from *The Times* of November 29, 1814,
which had " strongly excited my wonder and curiosity " and the subsequent
extension of the power principle to the printing of books as well as newspapers.
II. 44, account of Brougham's activity in organizing the Society for the Diffusion
of Useful Knowledge. Knight later became Manager (p. 55). 179-185, on the
Penny Magazine and the rise of the cheap press.

Le Strange, Guy : *Correspondence of Princess Lieven and Earl Grey* (London, 1890,
3 vols.).
Lieven to Grey, September 6, 1834 : " What *The Times* says amuses me
greatly ; its strictures on the Chancellor are most biting. If, as you have already
told me, *The Times* represents public opinion, all this is not very favourable
to the Government," etc., III, 15. *Cf.* Lieven to Grey, December 16, 1834,
III, 63.

Mackay, Charles : *Forty Years' Recollections of Life, Literature and Public Affairs from* 1830-1870 (London, 1877, 2 vols.).

The author was on the staff of the *Morning Chronicle*,. 1834-1844, during the period of intense competition with Printing House Square ; New York Correspondent of *The Times* 1862-5. The book is generally useful. There are details of Joseph Parkes and Thomas Barnes at I, 159.

Mackay, Thomas : *History of the English Poor Law*, 1834-1899 (London, 1899).

Pp. 124 *sqq.* for an account of the introduction of the new measure.

Private History of the London Newspaper Press in " [William] Tait's Edinburgh Magazine " (Edinburgh, 1834, pp. 788-792) is a Radical effort to " raise the curtain upon the operators of the morning newspapers, commencing with that monarch of periodical literature—the all-powerful *Times*." The writer attributes all the " thunder " in *The Times* to that " Man in the Iron Mask, Mr. Stirling," as well as control over its policy. The statements were withdrawn in the following year, when Tait printed a second article entitled *The Stamped Press* (1835, pp. 167-175). Both articles are untrustworthy but not wholly inaccurate, but they offer authentic witness to the public estimate of *The Times* in the years immediately following the Reform.

" Powerful in its command of capital ; vast, and regular as vast, in its circulation ; searching and insinuating itself to the remotest creeks and corners, like the hot smoke from a hidden fire ; alarming some, lulling others to a fatal sleep, influencing all ; preceding rumour in the rapidity as in the certainty of its intelligence ; masterly in its arrangements, and maintaining the steadiest judgment to let loose or to withhold the torrent that awaits its nod—the secure old sinner rides triumphant upon the rolling tide ; fattening amidst the war of winds and waves that threaten to overwhelm others—and perhaps the country to boot—with ruin and destruction. There sits the editor, conning over the political leader for to-morrow's paper, written by his Great Unknown—who is *only* known to all the rest of the establishment as ' the Man in the Iron Mask ! ' There he sits, knowing all things fit for his purpose, past, present, and to come. In short, he is like the devil. His knowledge is not the result of elementary powers, like that of the metaphysician, but the consequence of being in possession of all the facts. When the proper season for display arrives, he points to the vast organized pile—the heterogeneous stack ; and at section 40, letter D, No. 9, he finds all the private statements he wants, together with the names and addresses of the actors and eye-witnesses. What can resist this ? Who shall overthrow *The Times* ? It stands impregnable, beyond the touch of man. Nothing but the tide of time, and general march of opinions and things, will ever carry it down. From its ashes another, almost as powerful, will arise.

In speaking of all other papers, we say the principles of such a one are Tory, or Whig, or Radical—the *ultra* this, the *anti* that, or the *ne plus ultra* persuasion ; but, of *The Times*, we say its principles are mercantile only. In its principles, therefore, *The Times* is virtually always the same, a most consistent paper. Considering the mercantile spirit of the English, predominating, as we must confess it does, (certainly *not in theory*), over all other principles, *The Times* is just the paper we ought to have. We are not at present worthy of a better. The proofs are already before us. While everybody admits the audacious ease and perfect self-possession—the result of a consciousness of power—with which the great capitalist veers round to the strongest side, caring no more about what it had so fiercely advocated during the previous session, or the previous month, than if it had been written by another paper—everybody, nevertheless, accords it a portion of his patronage. When any new question of importance is agitated, the universal cry is, ' What does *The Times* say ? Have you seen *The Times* ? ' Mark its circulation beyond all other papers, be its politics what they may at the period ! It has been given as a moderate estimate, that, when *The Times* wrote so violently against the Trades' Unions, and a resolution passed through the different lodges not to read it, or enter a house that took it in, the daily circulation fell 2,000. Let us say that it fell but 1,500, and allow that 100 individuals only among *all* the working classes used to read each copy ; we arrive at the simple conclusion that 150,000 of those poor operatives, whose enemy *The Times* has always been whenever it could gain anything by abusing them, were, notwithstanding, in the daily habit of reading its columns ! The *True Sun* has always been a most constant and uncompromising friend of the working classes—it is their express paper ;— but did these 150,000, when they seceded from *The Times*, adopt the *True Sun* in its place ? Not they ! Or the *Examiner* ? No, nor the *Examiner*. Or the *Weekly Dispatch* ? Nor the *Dispatch*. Or the *New Bell's Weekly Messenger* ? No !—since they could not read *The Times*, they did not care to read any paper —they would ' go by hearsay '—get news anyhow, or do without. The circulation of the *True Sun* was not increased fifty copies per day by the affair ; and so much for fighting the battles of the people, and suffering fines, legal persecution, and imprisonment, in their cause ! "

Roebuck, J. A.: *The Stamped Press of London, and its Morality.* Roebuck's pamphlet [No. 3] undated [June 27, 1835].
" I select first—THE ' TIMES '—but I beg to observe that I am not content with speaking of the mysterious *Times*, I wish to be more particular, I shall speak of Mr Barnes and Mr Stirling (*sic*), editors of that journal," &c., pp. 4-7 ; followed by attacks on Black of the *Morning Chronicle*, Fonblanque of the *Examiner*, pp. 7-12. Roebuck's retractations to Sterling and Fonblanque are given at p. 15 of Roebuck's following pamphlet on the " Dorchester Labourers." Barnes, not being opprobriously mentioned, and Black took no action. Six months later (November 12, 1835) Roebuck's pamphlet on " Mr. Goldsmid and the Editor of the *Morning Chronicle* " described Black's character as base and cowardly. A meeting was arranged, shots were fired and honour satisfied.

Wallas, Graham : *The Life of Francis Place* (London, 1898).
Although essential to an understanding of the development of Radicalism, this work ignores Place's endeavours to found a daily newspaper in that interest and does little justice to his interest in journalism.

XIX. BARNES'S TERMS TO THE TORIES,
XX. *THE TIMES* CONSERVATIVE,
and
XXI. O'CONNELL THE ENEMY

Clark, G. Kitson : *Peel and the Conservative Party, A Study in Party Politics*, 1832-41 (London, 1929).
A first-hand and thorough investigation of the Peel and Bonham Papers in the British Museum. For Peel, the *Standard* and *The Times*, see pp. 215-7, with references to the documents. *The Times* and No Popery, pp. 409-10. A useful bibliography completes this essential work.

Roebuck, J. A.: *History of the Whig Ministry of* 1830 *to the Passing of the Reform Bill* (London, 1892, 2 vols.).
II, pp. 139-44, on the Lords and *The Times* ; II, 304, quotes leader from *The Times* as sample of the real feelings of hatred and bitterness in political quarters on the subject of the Duke of Wellington's anti-reform Government (*cf. The Times* May 14, 1831).

Watts, Alaric : *Life* (London, 1882, 2 vols.).

  Alaric Watts was employed to arrange that a newspaper with the title *Leading Articles and Main Political Contributions* should be set up and printed in an office established by a capitalist in the confidence of the Conservative Party machine and that a local bookseller or printer, titularly the proprietor of the local version, should print in the local intelligence and local political propaganda. This innovation, known as the " party Printed newspaper," was the invention of Watts.

  The Conservative machine established, among other papers, the following provincial journals : *Surrey Standard, Sussex Agricultural Express, Gloucestershire Chronicle, Worcestershire Guardian, Leicester Herald, Dover Telegraph, West Devon Conservative, Bridgewater Alfred, Blackburn Standard, West Kent Guardian.*

Thus the Party followed up an article in *Blackwood* (September, 1834) exhorting Conservatives to organize a Press for the support of order against anarchy. Possessors of education and property were there advised that it was in their own interests to buy up the best writers. *Cf.* Croker to Peel, January 7, 1836 :

  . . . talking of Standards, I am very sorry to find that the whole conservative cause is now in the hands of Doctor Giffard—He is an honest—too honest because over zealous—partizan—but he is obstinate, wrong headed & impracticable ; and I am confident that, trifling a circumstance as the failure of the *Albion* may appear, it is an alarming *sign* & will be in *practice* very inconvenient to the general conservative party. (MSS. Addl. 40321.)

XXII. LAST YEARS OF BARNES

Manuscript

Letters from Thomas Barnes to Benjamin Disraeli, 1836-9 ; from Lord Lyndhurst to Disraeli, 1836. Hughenden Papers.

  Lyndhurst's interest in the " Runnymede " letters was considerable : " My Dr Disraeli I have only read *yr letter*—I put down the paper to say that you have closed the *first act* admirably. Barnes will quite worship you—& Runnymede will not only be a *person* but a *personage*—more ! an immortal. Ever L.

Barnes to John Thadeus Delane, 1841. P.H.S. Papers.

Barnes to Henry Reeve, 1840-1. P.H.S.

Publications

Lord Beaconsfield's Correspondence with His Sister, 1832-1852 (London, 1886).

  References to Barnes and Mrs. Barnes, p. 95 ; " Fat old Barnes . . . The Thunderer," p. 167.

Clarendon (Fourth), Earl of : *Diary* (London, 1913, 2 vols.).

  References to Greville and *The Times*, I, 95, 174.

Johnson, A. H. : *The Letters of Charles Greville and Henry Reeve* (London, 1924).

  Prints important correspondence referring to Barnes's handling of the Eastern question not included in Laughton's *Reeve*.

Laughton, J. K. : *Memoirs of the Life and Correspondence of Henry Reeve* (London, 1898, 2 vols.).

  Reeve's introduction to Barnes on May 15, 1840, I. 120 ; his estimate of Barnes " a man who used the utmost power of the press without arrogance and without bitterness to anyone. I deeply lamented his sudden and premature death." I, 157.

New, Chester W. : *Lord Durham, A Biography of John George Lambton, First Earl Durham* (Oxford, 1929).

A fully documented study based upon original sources, including the Lambton MSS., which comprise letters from Joseph Parkes, Sir John Easthope, Albany Fonblanque and Thomas Barnes. Professor New has read *The Times* and makes numerous references to its leading articles. The leakage of the Durham Report to *The Times* is discussed on pp. 490-4. " Two thousand copies of the Report had been printed by the Government at Lord Durham's suggestion. They had permitted him to distribute some among his friends (' not more than half a dozen ' Durham said) " p. 492. Professor New thinks its publication in *The Times* was a leakage for which Lord Durham had no responsibility. An Appendix (p. 569) deals with Reeve's statement in the notes of his edition of Greville that the Report was sent to *The Times* by R. D. Hanson.

Robinson, G.L. : *The Life of David Urquhart* (Oxford, 1932).

Webster, C. K. : " Lord Palmerston at Work, 1830-41 " in *Politica* No. 2 (August, 1934), pp. 129-144.

    Professor Webster notes that although the *Globe* and the *Morning Chronicle* were most favoured, Palmerston " also paid particular attention to *The Times* " and refers to an instruction of 1833 which lays down " the tone " for *The Times* to take about the acknowledgment of Donna Maria and concludes " let them specially avoid speaking otherwise than in their own Persons and as having any other Lights than their own Reflections."

XXIII. "THE THUNDERER"

XXIV. MEN AND METHODS UNDER BARNES

Hackwood, F. W. : *William Hone, His Life and Times* (London, 1912).
    Several references to *The Times*. Lamb " and my friends of *The Times*," pp. 276-7, 297-8.

Carlyle, Alexander : *Letters of Thomas Carlyle to John Stuart Mill, John Sterling and Robert Browning* (London, 1923).
    Letters to John Sterling sometimes mention his father. " Remember me to Signor Hurricane, the good Father and Thunderer " (T. C. to J. S., August 4, 1841). The letters have useful references to Fonblanque's *Examiner, Fraser's*, the *Westminster* and other reviews, 1831-1841.

Grant, James : *The Great Metropolis*. By the Author of *Random Recollections of the Lords and Commons* (London, 1837, 2 vols.).
    Vol. II : The Newspaper Press, Mornings, Evenings, Weeklies, General Remarks, Parliamentary Reporting, the Quarterlies, Literary journals, pp. 1-360 ; under *The Times*, pp. 4-30, he mentions John Walter, Barnes, Stirling (*sic*), Alsager ; also James Murray, p. 289. The author is a gossip, and his book needs to be read with caution. See *Fraser's Magazine* for a destructive criticism.

Gulliver, H. S. : *Thackeray's Literary Apprenticeship* (Valdosta, Ga., 1934).
    Includes chapters on Thackeray's connexion with the *Constitutional*, the *Globe, Morning Chronicle, Fraser's Magazine* ; and Chapter 7 *The Times*, for which he wrote reviews of books and plays from 1837-1840. Mr. Gulliver identifies a score of books and argues for attributions of reviews of Bulwer's *Ernest Maltravers*, September 30, 1837 ; L. E. Landon's *Ethel Churchill*, October 6, 1837 ; Mrs. Trollope's *Vicar of Wrexhall*, October 25, 1837. These are printed, pp. 201-236, with a Paris letter, probably by Thackeray, and his undoubted reviews of Bulwer, Ranke, Carlyle, Krasinski, Horace Walpole, &c.

Knox, E. A.: *The Tractarian Movement, 1833-1845* (London, 1933).

    To this original study of the Movement Bishop Knox provides an appendix on " Catholicus " and *The Times*. " What was lost to the Tractarians by silencing the Tracts was gained many times over by the adherence of *The Times* to the Oxford Movement. The thunder of Episcopal Charges was answered by still louder thunder of the ' Great Thunderer.' " pp. 256-8.

Mozley, Anne: *Letters and Correspondence of John Henry Newman during his Life in the English Church* (1891, 2 vols.).

    R. W. Church to F. Rogers, March 14, 1841, on " Catholicus " in *The Times*, the reactions of the *Globe*, *Morning Chronicle* and *Standard* and a subsequent *Times* leader. " This led to a second article in *The Times* in which, while carefully guarding against identifying themselves, they gave a very good sketch of the history of things from the meeting at Rose's house . . . and went on to puff the strength and importance of the party . . ." The letter describes the effect produced on Oxford by Tract 90. " *The Times* has confessed that it knows not what to do."

Jennings, L. J.: *Correspondence and Diaries of the late John Wilson Croker* (London, 1884, 3 vols.).

    [Supplemented by the Croker MSS. in the W. L. Clements Library.]

[Newman, J. H.] *The Tamworth Reading Room. Letters on an Address delivered by Sir Robert Peel, Bart., M.P., on the Establishment of a Reading Room at Tamworth.* By Catholicus.

    Originally published in *The Times*, and since revised and corrected by the Author, London, James Mortimer, 21, Wigmore Street, Cavendish Square, 1841.

Sadleir, Michael: *Bulwer and his Wife*, 1803-1836.

    Chapter VI, *Fraser's Magazine*, includes an account of Dr. William Maginn and his literary activities; Chapter X describes the career and character of Charles Molloy Westmacott; Appendix IV, Bibliography, lists the books of Maginn, but does not undertake to trace his work in the *Standard*, the *Morning Herald*. The destructive reviews in *The Times* of Bulwer's novels may possibly have been contributed by Maginn.

Despatches, Correspondence and Memoranda of F.M. Arthur Duke of Wellington (London, 1867, 8 vols.).

The Political and Occasional Poems of Winthrop Mackworth Praed (ed. Sir George Young, London, 1888).

    The introduction is adequate and the collection completed by full notes. Praed's connexions with the *Albion*, *The Times*, *Morning Chronicle* and the *Morning Post* and the magazines are traced. There are references to *The Times* at pp. 100-4 (Praed's verses on Catholic Emancipation published in *The Times* May 22 and June 9, 1828), 131, 134, 148, 167, 174, 175, 195 (" his circle is Printing House Square "), 203, 213 (" Hume has been chid in the fierce old *Times* "), 222, 246, 251, 260 (" If a Tory punishes crimes In Kerry or in Clare, The Wisdom of *The Times* Proclaims it quite unfair "), 264, 267 (" We have got *The Times* adorning Facts with figures every morning ").

Obituaries of Thomas Barnes

The *Examiner*, May 8, 1841 ; the *Standard*, May 10, 1841 ; the *Gentleman's Magazine*, July, 1841, p. 96 ; the *Athenaeum*, May 8, 1841. The Editor of the *Athenaeum*, Charles Wentworth Dilke, who was a frequent visitor with Miss Mitford to 25, Soho Square, wrote :

    " At the last moment, and just as we are about to go to press, we have heard of, and deeply regret to announce, the death of Mr Thomas Barnes, for many years editor of *The Times* newspaper. Whatever differences of opinion may exist, as to the political news and principles advocated in that journal, there can be no question as to the extraordinary ability with which it has been conducted—the existence of that newspaper, its boundless resources and vast power, are, and must ever remain a marking figure of the age, and with it the name of Thomas Barnes is intimately associated. In private life Mr Barnes was a most estimable man, with whom politics never for a moment clouded the intercourse of friendship, and he will be sincerely regretted by many who were politically opposed to him. Mr Barnes was educated at Christ's Hospital, and thence passed to Cambridge, where he took high honours. He must have been in the 55th or 56th year of his age."

Family Tomb

Thomas Barnes was buried at Kensal Green in the tomb made for the mother of Mary Barnes. The inscription reads : In Memory of Mrs. Sarah Dunn, (widow) who departed this life in Soho Square the 10th of March 1838 aged 74 years leaving her only daughter, the last of nine children, to deplore her loss. Fourteen years later there was added the inscription : Also of Mary Barnes Relict of Thomas Barnes and the Daughter of the above, died 26th December 1852 aged 60 years. The inscription for Thomas Barnes is given at p. 448. The position of Barnes's grave at Kensal Green is Square 29, No. 1376.

Will of Thomas Barnes

IN THE NAME OF GOD AMEN

I THOMAS BARNES being of sound and disposing mind and memory though weak in body do hereby make and declare this to be my last will and testament. I hereby give and bequeath all the property I may die possessed of of whatever nature or kind the same may be unto my dear wife or my reputed wife DINAH MARY MONDET and I hereby appoint her to be my whole and sole executrix Dated the sixth day of May 1841—T. Barnes—Anne Pugh—W. F. A. Delane

Will of John, Brother of Thomas, Barnes

The last will and testament of me John Barnes of the Society of the Middle Temple, Barrister at Law, but residing at the Club Chambers, Regent Street as follows : Having some years since invested two thousand pounds three per cent Consolidated annuities in the names of George William Ledger and Edward Chester in trust for my sister Ann Barnes for her life and after her decease for the endowment of a scholarship in the University of Cambridge in memory of our late brother, late a member of the Inner Temple and formerly of the said University, previously of Christ's Hospital where our father and myself had also been educated, I do hereby give unto my said sister the sum of five hundred pounds in the three per cent annuities Consolidated annuities and the sum of one hundred pounds reduced annuities respectively standing in my own name in the books of the Bank of England, and I direct that the same be respectively transferred to her account as soon as may be after my decease. [March 28, 1855.]

The proposal of John Barnes to establish the scholarship was accepted by a grace on February 7, 1844. *The Times* of December 5, 1866, contained the following paragraph :

CAMBRIDGE, DEC. 4.

The Vice-Chancellor has issued a notice with respect to the Thomas Barnes Scholarship, to which the first election will take place next Term. The chief provisions regarding it are,—That the Vice Chancellor, the Regius Professor of Divinity, the Regius Professor of the Civil Law, the Lucasian Professor of Mathematics, and the Public Orator, each for the time being, or their respective deputies to be appointed by grace of the Senate, shall elect the scholars on this foundation, in such manner as they shall determine upon ; but that in all such elections they shall govern themselves conscientiously by the following rule :—" In his eligendis præcipua ratio semper habeatur ingenii, doctrinæ, virtutis, et inopiæ ; ut quo magis quisque ex eligendorum numero his rebus antecellat, eo magis, ut æquum sit, præferatur." That the candidates for the scholarship shall be undergraduates in their first year—that is to say, undergraduates who shall have been admitted between the end of the then last preceding Easter Term and the end of the then last preceding Easter Term but one ; and that this further qualification shall be requisite—viz., that the candidates shall have been educated on the foundation of Christ's Hospital, St. Paul's School, or the Merchant Tailors' School, in the city of London, and shall have come to the University directly from one of those schools ; but that if in any case there be found no candidate so circumstanced who in the opinion of the electors is fit to be elected, then the said scholarship for that turn only shall be thrown open to all the undergraduates of the University who are, according to the terms above specified, in their first year. That every scholar elected on this foundation shall promise in writing to take a degree in the most regular manner, and in case of such promise being broken the scholarship shall be *ipso facto* vacant. That the scholar shall be entitled to the profits of the scholarship for a period of four years. This foundation was accepted by grace, February 7, 1844. Due notice of the examination will be given.

Recent Mention

Blunden, Edmund : *Leigh Hunt, A Biography.* (London, 1930.)
    References to Alsager, Barnes, Barron Field, Talfourd.

Blunden, Edmund : *Leigh Hunt's* Examiner *Examined. Comprising an Account of that celebrated Newspaper's Contents* 1808-1825. (London, 1928.)

" While Hunt was in prison, his old and favourite schoolfellow, Thomas Barnes, devoted himself very eagerly to the *Examiner*, contributing almost all the theatrical notices, and a series of parliamentary criticisms or portraits beginning on August 15, 1813. These various papers, with their wide literary comprehension both ancient and modern, their strength of purpose, and their abundance of incisive phrase and cadence, all point out the author, despite his anonymity, as a remarkable journalist, and were duly fulfilled in his most prosperous industry as Editor of *The Times* from 1816 to 1841. Chance has deprived him of a biographer, but when the history of *The Times* is written it may be hoped that this original and powerful journalist will be brought fully into the light of common knowledge. Barnes was a dramatic critic of deep reading and feeling, and it is worth while noticing here, by way of example, how he received S. T. Coleridge's *Remorse*, etc., p. 36.

" The parliamentary sketches by Barnes continued in all their eloquence and candour throughout the year, and would be a mine for the historian or novelist of the Regency." p. 43.

INDEX

INDEX

PRINTED IN GREAT BRITAIN

BY

JARROLD AND SONS LIMITED NORWICH

BY PHOTO LITHOGRAPHY

1950